Critical acclaim for *Inside Visual C++*

"Kruglinski's book has already become the standard text for VC++. Is Inside Visual C++ *worth the price? Absolutely."*

Visual Basic Programmer's Journal

"This is the book I turned to most often when I was climbing the Visual C++ learning curve. The book remains one of the best programming books I have ever read.... Whenever I turn to this book with a question, I always (well, almost always!) find the answer."

PC Techniques

"This is a solid work that supplements the VC++ reference manuals very well."

Unisys World

"Inside Visual C++ *is especially strong discussing the document–view architecture, which is the basis of MFC and the part new developers have the most trouble with."*

Microsoft Systems Journal

"The book is just plain easy to read, striking a good balance between narrative, source code, screen drawings, and sidebars."

PC Week

"Just as Petzold's Programming Windows *was written for a generation of C-based Windows developers, Kruglinski's* Inside Visual C++ *is written for those who want to exploit MFC. Anyone who uses MFC will find this book useful, but obviously those who also program with Visual C++ benefit from it the most."*

C/C++ User's Journal

"Inside Visual C++ *is the ideal tool for the student of MFC. The meat of the book is in its discussion of MFC, which is the best I've ever seen."*

Software Development

"If you plan to use Visual C++, this book is a must. It helps Visual C++ programmers just as Charles Petzold's Programming Windows *helped programmers clearly understand how to program Windows in C."*

Computer

INSIDE
VISUAL C++™

THE STANDARD REFERENCE FOR PROGRAMMING WITH MICROSOFT® VISUAL C++ VERSION 4

DAVID J. KRUGLINSKI

Microsoft Press

PUBLISHED BY
Microsoft Press
A Division of Microsoft Corporation
One Microsoft Way
Redmond, Washington 98052-6399

Copyright © 1996 by David J. Kruglinski

Library of Congress Cataloging-in-Publication Data
Kruglinski, David.
    Inside Visual C++ / David J. Kruglinski. -- 3rd ed., version 4.0.
        p.   cm.
    Includes index.
    ISBN 1-55615-891-2
    1. C++ (Computer program language)   2. Microsoft Visual C++.
I. Title.
QA76.73.C153K87   1995
005.26'2--dc20   95-39133
                                                                    CIP

Printed and bound in the United States of America.

    3 4 5 6 7 8 9   QMQM   1 0 9 8 7 6

Distributed to the book trade in Canada by Macmillan of Canada, a division of Canada Publishing
Corporation.

A CIP catalogue record for this book is available from the British Library.

Microsoft Press books are available through booksellers and distributors worldwide. For further
information about international editions, contact your local Microsoft Corporation office. Or
contact Microsoft Press International directly at fax (206) 936-7329.

Adobe is a trademark of Adobe Systems, Inc. Apple, LaserWriter, Lisa, Macintosh, and TrueType
are registered trademarks of Apple Computer, Inc. ToolBook is a registered trademark of Asymetrix
Corporation. Borland, dBASE, and Paradox are registered trademarks of Borland International,
Inc. Btrieve is a registered trademark of Btrieve Technologies, Inc. CASE:W is a trademark of
Caseworks, Inc. TETRIS is a trademark of v/o Electronorgtechnica. Forehelp is a registered trade-
mark of Forefront, Inc. ColorPro, Hewlett-Packard, HP, and LaserJet are registered trademarks of
Hewlett-Packard Company. Informix is a registered trademark of Informix Software, Inc. Ingres is
a trademark of Ingres Corporation. Intel and Pentium are registered trademarks of Intel Corpora-
tion. IBM is a registered trademark and Current is a trademark of International Business Machines
Corporation. Lego is a registered trademark of Lego Systems, Inc. FoxPro, Microsoft, Microsoft
QuickBasic, MS-DOS, PowerPoint, QuickC, SourceSafe, Visual Basic, Win32, Win32s, Windows,
and the Windows operating system logo are registered trademarks and Visual C++ and Windows NT
are trademarks of Microsoft Corporation. 3M is a registered trademark and Post-it is a trademark of
Minnesota Mining and Manufacturing Corporation. Nintendo is a registered trademark of Nintendo
of America, Inc. ORACLE is a registered trademark of Oracle Corporation. PowerBuilder is a trademark of Powersoft Corporation. Symantec is a registered trademark of Symantec Corporation. Unicode is a trademark of Unicode, Inc. Visio is a registered trademark of Visio Corporation.

Acquisitions Editor: Eric Stroo
Project Editor: Jack Litewka
Manuscript Editor: Jennifer Harris
Technical Editor: Jim Fuchs

CONTENTS SUMMARY

TABLE OF CONTENTS

CHAPTER FOUR

Basic Event Handling, Mapping Modes, and a Scrolling View **47**

CHAPTER SEVEN

The Modeless Dialog and Windows 95
Common Dialogs   **149**

CHAPTER EIGHT

Using OLE Controls (OCXs) **167**

CHAPTER NINE

Win32 Memory Management **195**

P A R T III: THE DOCUMENT–VIEW
ARCHITECTURE

CHAPTER TWELVE

Menus, Keyboard Accelerators, the
Rich Edit Control, and Property Sheets **263**

CHAPTER FIFTEEN

Separating the Document from Its View   **337**

CHAPTER EIGHTEEN

Printing and Print Preview   **437**

CHAPTER NINETEEN

Splitter Windows and Multiple Views   **457**

CHAPTER TWENTY-ONE

Dynamic Link Libraries (DLLs)   **493**

CHAPTER TWENTY-TWO

MFC Programs Without Document or View Classes   **523**

PART IV: OLE

CHAPTER TWENTY-THREE

The OLE Component Object Model (COM)   **539**

CHAPTER TWENTY-FOUR

OLE Automation   **581**

CHAPTER TWENTY-FIVE

OLE Uniform Data Transfer—
Clipboard Transfer and Drag and Drop **647**

CHAPTER TWENTY-SIX

OLE Structured Storage   **675**

CHAPTER TWENTY-SEVEN

OLE Embedded Servers and Containers   **703**

PART V: DATABASE MANAGEMENT

CHAPTER TWENTY-NINE

Database Management with Microsoft Data Access Objects (DAO)   **785**

PART VI: APPENDIXES

APPENDIX A

A Crash Course in the C++ Language   **813**

ACKNOWLEDGMENTS

A book like this requires more work than you'll ever imagine, and a large portion of that work was done by other people. I was fortunate to have Jack Litewka as project editor and Jim Fuchs as technical editor—the same team that survived the two previous editions. Jack had to decipher my quasi-legible notes, and Jim had to make the sample code actually work through constantly changing versions of the product. Many others worked equally hard behind the scenes, including Jennifer Harris, manuscript editor; Shawn Peck, principal proofreader/copy editor; Barbara Remmele, principal compositor; and David Holter, principal electronic artist. Acquisitions editor Eric Stroo had the important task of releasing my advance checks.

On the technical side there was, of course, Dean McCrory, the font of all knowledge. Other helpful folks in the MFC group were Mike Blaszczak, Adam Denning, John Elsbree, and Jeff Grove. Then there was Walter Sullivan, who supplied me with Visual C++ CD-ROMs. Other Microsoft people who answered dumb questions were Greg Fowler, Bruce Hale, Jon Thomason, Nigel Thompson, and Chris Weight. Jeff Richter, too, was not spared my questioning.

INTRODUCTION

On a snowy evening a few winters ago, I ventured into New York's East Village to visit Charles Petzold, the original Windows guru. After watching Charles shoot a game of pool at the famous Finian's Rainbow, I asked him his thoughts about writing *Programming Windows*. He said he wished he'd known at the start of the project what he knew at the end. I certainly shared the same wish after writing the first two editions of *Inside Visual C++*. My challenge, now that I really do know more about C++, Microsoft Windows, and the Microsoft Foundation Class (MFC) library, is to incorporate my newfound knowledge into this edition.

The software world has changed since the earlier editions were published. Microsoft Visual C++ is now an established mainstream product, and Win32 programming is here to stay. Dozens of C++ and Visual C++ books are available, and the C++ language is being taught at major universities. The subject of programming for Windows is so expansive that no single book can cover it—you now need an entire library plus an update service.

In this edition of *Inside Visual C++*, I'll try to give you enough information so that you can write Windows-based production programs and so that you have sufficient background to make use of the many specialized books about Windows that cover such topics as animation, OLE, thread synchronization, and communications protocols.

Who Can Use This Book

The product name "Visual C++" misleads some people. They think that they've bought a pure visual programming system similar to Microsoft Visual Basic, and for the first few days the illusion persists. Soon, however, people learn that they must actually read and write C++ code. The Visual C++ <u>wizards</u> save time and improve accuracy, but programmers must understand the code that the wizards generate and, ultimately, the structure of the MFC library as well as the inner workings of the Windows operating system.

Visual C++, with its sophisticated application framework, is for professional programmers, and so is this book. I'm going to assume that you're proficient in the C language—that is, you can write an *if* statement without consulting the manual. And I'll assume that you've been exposed to the C++ language—that is, you've at least taken a course or read a book, but maybe you haven't written much code. The C++ crash course in Appendix A might help if you're a little rusty.

I won't assume, however, that you already know Windows programming. From my teaching experience, I've found that proficient C programmers can learn Windows the MFC way. It's more important to know C++ than it is to know the Windows application programming interface (API). You should, however, know how to run Windows and Windows-based applications.

What if you're already experienced with the Windows API or with the MFC library? What if you already own a previous edition of this book? There's something in this book for you too. First you'll get some help making the transition to Win32 programming. Then you'll learn about new features such as Data Access Objects (DAO), OLE Controls (OCX) container support, and Windows 95 controls. If you haven't already figured out OLE, this book presents some important theory that will get you started on understanding OLE Controls.

What's Not Covered

As I said earlier, it's not possible to cover all of Windows-based programming in a single book. I exclude topics that depend on special-purpose hardware and software, such as TCP/IP, MAPI, TAPI, and communications port access. I also exclude Win32s, targeting for the Macintosh, and source code control. I do cover using OLE Controls in an application, but I'll defer the subject of writing OLE Controls to Adam Denning and his *OLE Controls Inside Out* (Microsoft Press, 1995). I get you started with 32-bit memory management, DLL theory, and multithreaded programming techniques, but you need to get Jeffrey Richter's *Advanced Windows* (Microsoft Press, 1995) if you're serious about these subjects. I don't cover animation, but Nigel Thompson's *Animation Techniques in Win32* (Microsoft Press, 1995) does a fine job in that area.

How to Use This Book

When you're starting off with Visual C++, you can use this book as a tutorial by going through it sequentially. Later you can use it as a reference by looking up topics in the table of contents or the index. Because of the tight interrelationships among many application framework elements, it wasn't possible to cleanly isolate each concept in its own chapter, so the book really isn't an encyclopedia. When you use this book, you'll definitely want the *Microsoft Foundation Class Library Reference* at your side.

If you're experienced with the Win16 version of Visual C++, scan Part I for an overview of new features, and then skip the first three chapters of Part II but read Chapters 6 through 11, which cover elements specific to Win32.

The Organization of This Book

As the table of contents shows, this book has six main parts:

Part I: Windows, Visual C++, and Application Framework Fundamentals

In this part, I try to strike a balance between abstract theory and practical application. After a quick review of Win32 and the Visual C++ components, you'll be introduced, in a gentle way, to the MFC application framework and the document–view architecture. You'll look at a simple "Hello, world!" program, built with the MFC library classes, that requires only 30 lines of code.

Part II: The MFC Library View Class

The MFC library documentation presents all the application framework elements in quick succession, with the assumption that you already know the original Windows API. Here you're confined to one major application framework component—the view, which is really a window. It's here that you'll learn what experienced Windows programmers know already, but in the context of C++ and the MFC library classes. You'll use the Visual C++ tools a lot, and that in itself eliminates much of the coding drudgery that early Windows programmers had to endure.

Part II covers a lot of territory, including graphics programming with bitmaps, dialog data exchange, OLE Controls usage, 32-bit memory management, and multithreaded programming. After stepping through the exercises, you'll be able to write reasonably sophisticated Windows-based programs, but those programs won't take advantage of the advanced application framework features.

Part III: The Document–View Architecture

Now the real core of application framework programming is introduced— the document–view architecture. You'll learn what a document is (think of it as something much more general than a word processing document), and you'll see how to connect the document to the view that you learned about in Part II. You'll be amazed, once you have written a document class, at how the MFC library simplifies file I/O and printing.

Along the way, you'll learn about command message processing, toolbars and status bars, splitter frames, and context-sensitive help. You'll also be introduced to the Multiple Document Interface (MDI), which is the current standard for Windows-based applications.

Part III finishes with a discussion of dynamic link libraries (DLLs) written with the MFC library. You'll learn the distinction between an extension DLL (which depends on other MFC DLLs) and a regular DLL (which can be self-contained). If you're used to Win16 DLLs, you'll notice some changes in the move to Win32.

Part IV: OLE

OLE is worth more than a whole book by itself. Part IV will get you started in learning fundamental OLE theory from the MFC point of view. You'll begin with the underlying Component Object Model (COM) and then progress to OLE Automation, which is the link between C++ and Visual Basic for Applications (VBA). You'll also become familiar with uniform data transfer and structured storage. Finally, you'll learn the basics of compound documents and embedded objects.

Part V: Database Management

Windows programs often need efficient access to information in large databases. Visual C++ now supports two separate database management options—Open Database Connectivity (ODBC) and Data Access Objects (DAO). Part V contains a chapter on each option. You'll learn about the extensive MFC and wizard support for both options, and you'll see the differences between and similarities of ODBC and DAO.

Part VI: Appendixes

Appendix A is the C++ crash course. Skip it if you already know the language cold, but go through it if you need a refresher. Use Appendix A in conjunction with a C++ textbook if you're totally new to C++.

Appendix B contains a list of message map macros and their corresponding handler function prototypes. ClassWizard usually generates this code for you, but sometimes you must make manual entries.

Appendix C is a description of the MFC application framework's run-time class information and dynamic creation system. This is independent of the RTTI (runtime type information) feature that is now a part of ANSI C++.

Win32 vs. Win16

Unless you've been living in a cave for the past five years, you probably know that the world is moving from Win16 to Win32. Win16 refers to the 16-bit Windows API as found in Microsoft Windows version 3.1 and Microsoft Windows for Workgroups. Win32 refers to the new 32-bit Windows API supported by Microsoft Windows 95 and Microsoft Windows NT.

Visual C++ version 4.0 is a product for Win32 application development. The Visual C++ 4.0 product comes with two CD-ROMs. One contains the Win32 version, which is described in this book, and the other contains the latest Win16 version, 1.52c. These are two different entities with entirely different user interfaces. There's a provision for porting a Win16 project to a Win32 project, but there's no easy way to maintain one set of source code for Win16 and Win32 targets. Version 4.0 contains many features that are not included in the Win16 version, including the templates, exceptions, and runtime type information (RTTI) at the C++ level and multithreading at the Windows level.

This Win16/Win32 disparity makes life difficult for developers. Microsoft wants end users to convert to Windows 95 or Windows NT as soon as possible, and programmers are aware of the technical superiority of 32-bit programming. A small software company can't stay in business, however, if it offers only Win32 products and its customers are still using a Win16-based version of Windows. Unfortunately, there are lots of old machines around that won't adequately support the new versions of Windows.

I'm taking the extreme approach here of burning the bridges to Win16. This is a Win32 book. By the time you read the book, learn the material, and write and debug an application and get it into distribution, I'm betting that Win16 will be dropping off the end of the earth. All the code and project files are for Visual C++ version 4.0 and Win32; they will not work with Win16 or any earlier version of Visual C++. Because Microsoft has always done a good job of preserving backward compatibility, however, most of the sample code should work with versions after 4.0.

Microsoft does offer a tool for running Win32 code under Win16—the Win32s library. This library is useful if your program can benefit from using

32-bit calculations but doesn't require Win32 features such as multithreading and memory-mapped files. Because Win32s is a short-term solution, I'm not covering it here.

Windows 95 vs. Windows NT

Visual C++ version 4.0 requires either the released version of Windows 95 or version 3.51 or later of Windows NT. All the screen shots in this book are from Windows 95. Some of the sample programs use the new common controls that are supported by both Windows 95 and Windows NT version 3.51. Thus, all the projects build and run under both operating systems, but under Windows NT the screens look like the old Windows version 3.1 screens. The samples were tested only on the Intel platform. Most should work on other platforms, but I'll give no guarantees.

Going Further with Windows: The Purpose of the "For Win32 Programmers" Sidebars

This book can't offer the kind of detail—the tricks and hidden features— found in the newer, specialized books on Win32. Most of those books are written from the point of view of a C-language programmer—in order to use them, you'll have to understand the underlying Win32 API and its relationship to the MFC library. In addition, you'll need to know about the Windows message dispatch mechanism and the role of window classes.

This book's "For Win32 Programmers" sidebars, scattered throughout the text, help you make the connection to low-level Windows-based programming. These specially formatted boxes help experienced Windows C programmers relate new MFC library concepts to principles they're already familiar with. If you're unfamiliar with low-level programming, you should skip these notes the first time through, but you should read them on your second pass through the book. Even though you may never write a low-level Windows-based program with a *WinMain* function, you eventually need to know how the Windows operating system interacts with your program.

For Win32 Programmers: Unicode

Until recently, Windows-based programs have used only the ANSI character set, which consists of 256 single-byte characters. Developers targeting the Asian software market are moving to the Unicode character set, which consists of 65,536 2-byte (wide) characters. There's a third option, the double-byte character set (DBCS), in which some characters are 1 byte and others are 2 bytes, but DBCS is falling out of favor.

The MFC library and the runtime library support Unicode applications. If you define the constant _UNICODE_ and follow some other steps as described in Books Online, all your character variables and constant strings will be wide, and the compiler will generate calls to the wide-character versions of the Win32 functions. This assumes that you use certain macros when you declare character pointers and arrays—for example, *TCHAR* and _T_. The _MBCS_ constant, which is defined by default in your projects, enables the *TCHAR* and _T_ macros.

There's a problem, though, if you try to run your MFC Unicode applications under Windows 95, because Windows 95 does not support Unicode internally. Even though Windows 95 has wide-character versions of Win32 functions, those functions return a failure code. Windows NT, on the other hand, uses Unicode internally and has two versions of the Win32 functions that deal with characters. If you call a single-byte version, Windows NT makes the necessary conversions to and from wide characters.

None of the sample programs in this book are configured for Unicode. They use single-byte types such as *char* and single-byte string constants, and they do not define _UNICODE_. If you run the samples under Windows NT, the operating system will do the necessary single-to-wide conversions; if you run them under Windows 95, the interface is pure single-byte.

One area in which you're forced to deal with wide characters is OLE. All non-MFC OLE functions (except DAO functions) that have string and character parameters require wide (*OLECHAR*) characters. If you write a non-Unicode program, you must do the conversions yourself with the help of the MFC *CString* class and various MFC macros.

If you want to write Unicode applications, you should read the Unicode chapter in Jeffrey Richter's *Advanced Windows*. You should also read the Unicode material in Visual C++ Books Online.

Hardware Requirements

You've probably discovered already that your development machine for Windows needs more horsepower than does a standard target machine. Because 32-bit programs are so much bigger than 16-bit programs and because the Visual C++ development environment has become more complex, you shouldn't consider working with anything less than a 90-MHz Pentium-based computer. Believe me. I had to go out and replace my old 486/33. Plan on 16 MB or more of memory for Windows 95 and 32 MB for Windows NT.

As far as disk space is concerned, plan on 50 MB for the Visual C++ programs alone. Each project can require more than 6 MB (including precompiled headers, map files, and a browser database), and you'll have lots of projects. Fortunately, gigabyte hard disks are getting cheap, so you should have one. By the way, you'll also need a CD-ROM drive. Visual C++ is shipped only on CD-ROM, and you'll probably want to access sample code and online documentation directly from the CD-ROM.

Also consider a large-screen monitor with an appropriate graphics adapter. With the large monitor, you can simultaneously display the Microsoft Developer Studio with a docked help window and a Windows-based program that you're debugging.

Using the Companion CD-ROM

The companion CD-ROM bound into the inside back cover of this book contains the source code files and make files for all the sample programs. The executable program files are included, so you won't have to build the samples that you're interested in. To install the companion CD-ROM's files, insert the disc in your CD-ROM drive, and run the Setup program. Follow the on-screen instructions.

> NOTE: The Setup program copies about 17 MB of files to your hard disk. If you prefer, you can manually install only the files for individual projects. Simply tree-copy the corresponding subdirectories from the CD-ROM to *C:\VCPP32*. Each project is self-contained, so no additional files from other projects are needed. (You'll need to remove the read-only attribute from these files if you copy them using Explorer or File Manager.)

With a conventional C-language API Windows-based program, the source code files tell the whole story. With the MFC library application framework, things are not so simple. Much of the C++ code is generated by

AppWizard, and the resources originate in the graphic editor. The examples in the early chapters of this book include step-by-step instructions for using the tools to generate and customize the source code files. You'd be well advised to walk through those instructions for the first few examples; there's very little code to type. For the middle chapters, use the code from the companion CD-ROM, but read through the steps in order to appreciate the role of the graphic editor and the wizards. For the final chapters, not all the source code is listed. You'll need to examine the companion CD-ROM's files for those later examples.

Technical Notes and Sample Programs

The Visual C++ Books Online (accessible from Developer Studio) contains technical notes and sample programs that are referenced in this book. The technical notes, identified by number, are available under the heading:

Visual C++ Books

MFC 4.0

MFC Technical Notes

The Visual C++ 4.0 CD-ROM contains a number of MFC sample programs also referenced in the book and identified by name. These sample programs are documented under the heading:

Samples

MFC

WINDOWS, VISUAL C++, AND APPLICATION FRAMEWORK FUNDAMENTALS

Microsoft Windows and Visual C++

Enough has already been written about the acceptance of Microsoft Windows and the benefits of the graphical user interface (GUI). This chapter summarizes the Windows programming model (Win32 in particular) and shows you how the Visual C++ components work together to help you write applications for Windows. Along the way, you'll learn some new things about Windows.

The Windows Programming Model

No matter which development tools you use, programming for Windows is different from old-style batch-oriented or transaction-oriented programming. To get started, you need to know some Windows fundamentals. As a frame of reference, we'll use the well-known MS-DOS programming model. Even if you don't currently program for plain MS-DOS, you're probably familiar with it.

Message Processing

When you write an MS-DOS application in C, the only absolute requirement is a function named *main*. The operating system calls *main* when the user runs the program, and from that point on, you can use any programming structure you want. If your program needs to get user keystrokes or otherwise use operating system services, it calls an appropriate function, such as *getchar*, or perhaps uses a character-based windowing library.

When the Windows operating system launches a program, it calls the program's *WinMain* function. Somewhere your application must have *WinMain*, which performs some specific tasks. Its most important task is creating the

3

application's main window, which must have its own code to process messages that Windows sends it. An essential difference between a program written for MS-DOS and a program written for Windows is that an MS-DOS program calls the operating system to get user input, but a Windows program processes user input via messages from the operating system.

> NOTE: Many development environments for Windows, including Microsoft Visual C++ version 4.0 with the Microsoft Foundation Class (MFC) Library version 4.0, simplify programming by hiding the *WinMain* function and structuring the message-handling process. When you use the MFC library, you need not write a *WinMain* function, but it is essential that you understand the link between the operating system and your programs.

Many messages in Windows are strictly defined and apply to all programs. For example, a WM_CREATE message is sent when a window is being created, a WM_LBUTTONDOWN message is sent when the user presses the left mouse button, a WM_CHAR message is sent when the user types a character, and a WM_CLOSE message is sent when the user closes a window. All messages have two 32-bit parameters that convey information such as cursor coordinates, key code, and so forth. WM_COMMAND messages are sent to the appropriate window in response to user menu choices, dialog button clicks, and so on. Command message parameters vary depending on the window's menu layout. The programmer can define still other messages, known as "user messages."

Don't worry yet about how your code processes these messages. That's the job of the application framework. Be aware, though, that the Windows message processing requirement imposes a lot of structure on your program. Don't try to force your Windows programs to look like your old MS-DOS programs. Study the examples in this book, and then be prepared to start fresh.

The Windows Graphics Device Interface (GDI)

Many MS-DOS programs wrote directly to the video memory and the printer port. The disadvantage of this technique was the need to supply driver software for every video board and every printer model. Windows introduced a layer of abstraction called the Graphics Device Interface (GDI). Windows provides the video and printer drivers, so your program doesn't need to know the type of video board and printer attached to the system. Instead of addressing the hardware, your program calls GDI functions that reference a data structure called a <u>device context</u>. Windows maps the device context structure to a physical device and issues the appropriate input/output instructions. The GDI is almost as fast as direct video access, and it allows different applications written for Windows to share the display.

Resource-Based Programming

To do data-driven programming in MS-DOS, you must either code the data as initialization constants or provide separate data files for your program to read. When you program for Windows, you store data in a resource file using a number of established formats. The linker combines this binary resource file with the C++ compiler's output to generate an executable program. Resource files can include bitmaps, icons, menu definitions, dialog box layouts, and strings. They can even include custom resource formats that you define.

You use a text editor to edit a program, but you generally use wysiwyg (what you see is what you get) tools to edit resources. If you're laying out a dialog box, for example, you select elements (buttons, list boxes, and so forth) from an array of icons called a control palette, and you position and size the elements with the mouse. The Visual C++ graphic editor lets you effectively edit all standard resource formats.

Memory Management

With each new version of Windows, memory management gets easier. If you've heard horror stories about locking memory handles, thunks, and burgermasters, don't worry. That's all in the past. Today you simply allocate the memory you need, and Windows takes care of the details. Chapter 9 describes current memory management techniques for Win32, including virtual memory and memory-mapped files.

Dynamic Link Libraries (DLLs)

In the MS-DOS environment, all of a program's object modules are statically linked during the build process. Windows allows dynamic linking, which means that specially constructed libraries can be loaded and linked at runtime. Multiple applications can share dynamic link libraries (DLLs), which saves memory and disk space. Dynamic linking increases program modularity because you can compile and test DLLs separately.

Designers originally created DLLs for use with the C language, and C++ has added some complications. The MFC developers succeeded in combining all the application framework classes into a few ready-built DLLs. This means that you can statically or dynamically link the application framework classes into your application. In addition, you can create your own <u>extension</u> DLLs that build on the MFC DLLs. Chapter 21 includes information about creating MFC extension DLLs and conventional DLLs.

The Win32 Application Programming Interface (API)

Early Windows programmers wrote applications in C for the Win16 application programming interface (API). Today, if you want to write 32-bit applications, you must use the new Win32 API, either directly or indirectly. Most Win16 functions have Win32 equivalents, but many of the parameters are different—16-bit parameters are often replaced with 32-bit parameters, for example. The Win32 API offers many new functions, including functions for disk I/O, which was formerly handled by MS-DOS calls. With the 16-bit versions of Visual C++, MFC programmers were largely insulated from these API differences because they wrote to the MFC standard, which was designed to work with either Win16 or Win32 underneath.

The Visual C++ Components

Microsoft Visual C++ is two complete Windows application development systems in one product. If you so choose, you can develop C-language Windows programs using the Win32 API. Win32 programming is an extension of Win16 programming. Many familiar Win16 books, including Charles Petzold's *Programming Windows 3.1* (Microsoft Press, 1992), are being upgraded for Win32. (The book's new title is *Programming Windows 95,* to be published by Microsoft Press in 1996.) You can use many Visual C++ tools, including the graphic editor, to make low-level Win32 programming easier.

This book is not about C-language Win32 programming, however. It's about C++ programming within the MFC library application framework that's part of Visual C++. You'll be using the C++ classes that are documented in the *Microsoft Foundation Class Library Reference,* and you'll also be using application framework–specific Visual C++ tools such as AppWizard and ClassWizard.

> NOTE: Use of the MFC library programming interface doesn't cut you off from the Win32 functions. In fact, you'll almost always need some direct Win32 calls in your MFC library programs.

A quick run-through of the Visual C++ components will help you get your bearings before you zero in on the application framework. Figure 1-1 shows an overview of the Visual C++ application build process.

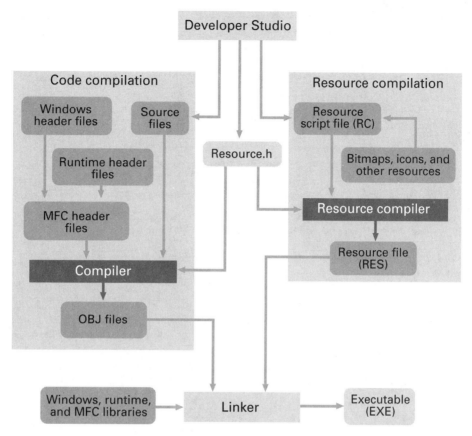

Figure 1-1.
The Visual C++ application build process.

The Microsoft Developer Studio and the Build Process

The Developer Studio is a Windows-hosted integrated development environment (IDE) that's shared by Visual C++, Microsoft FORTRAN, and some other products. This IDE has come a long way from the original Visual Workbench, which was based on QuickC for Windows. Now there are docking windows and configurable toolbars, plus a customizable editor that runs macros. The online help system is based on technology used in the Microsoft Developer Network (MSDN) and is much more powerful than the old WINHELP. Figure 1-2 on the following page shows the Developer Studio in action.

Source code
Online documentation
Build target

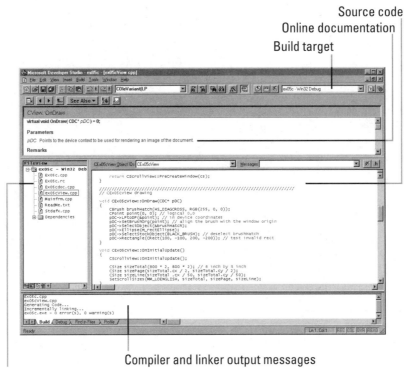

Compiler and linker output messages
Project Workspace (build view)

Figure 1-2.
The Visual C++ Developer Studio.

If you've used earlier versions of Visual C++ or the Borland IDE, you already understand how the Developer Studio operates. But if you're new to IDEs, you'll need to know what a <u>project</u> is. A project is a collection of interrelated source files that are compiled and linked to make up an executable Windows-based program or a DLL. Project source files are generally stored in a separate subdirectory. A project depends on many files outside the project subdirectory too, such as include files and library files.

Experienced programmers are familiar with make files. A <u>make</u> <u>file</u> expresses all the interrelationships among source files. (A source code file needs specific include files, an executable file requires certain object modules and libraries, and so forth.) A <u>make</u> <u>program</u> reads the make file and then invokes the compiler, assembler, linker, and resource compiler to produce the final output, which is generally an executable file. The make program uses built-in "inference rules" that tell it, for example, to invoke the compiler to generate an OBJ file from a specified CPP file.

For eachVisual C++ project, there is a make file (MAK extension) and a project Workspace file (MDP extension). The make file is an ASCII file that is built and maintained by Visual C++. You can edit the make file directly, but if you're not careful, Visual C++ can no longer maintain it, and it is designated as an "external" make file. The project Workspace file is a binary file that duplicates much of the information in the make file, including compiler and linker switch settings. The Workspace file also specifies the windows open on the desktop (when you close the project) together with other project attributes. You generally open a project by opening the MDP file, but if the MDP file is lost or corrupted, you can open the MAK file instead (by choosing Open Workspace from the Developer Studio's File menu). Once the project is open, you build the executable by choosing Build from the Build menu.

The Graphic Editor

With Visual C++, you use the graphic editor to edit all standard resources. When you double-click the project's ASCII resource script file (which has an RC extension), you are switched immediately to graphic editor mode. Chapter 3 shows some graphic editor windows. (See pages 34, 35, and 40.) The graphic editor includes a wysiwyg menu editor, a powerful dialog box editor, and tools for editing icons, bitmaps, and strings. The dialog box editor allows you to insert OLE controls in addition to standard Windows controls and the new Windows 95 controls.

Each project usually has one RC file that contains *#include* statements to bring in resources from other subdirectories. These resources include project-specific items, such as BMP files, and resources common to all Visual C++ programs, such as error message strings. Editing the RC file outside the graphic editor is not recommended. The graphic editor can also process EXE and DLL files, so you can use the clipboard to "steal" resources, such as bitmaps and icons, from other Windows applications.

The graphic editor compares favorably to the best applications written for Windows, so it's significant that the graphic editor was written using the Visual C++ tools and the MFC library.

The C/C++ Compiler

The Visual C++ compiler can process both C source code and C++ source code. It determines the language by looking at the source code's filename extension. A C extension indicates C source code, and CPP or CXX indicates C++ source code. The compiler is compliant with ANSI version 2.1 and has additional Microsoft extensions. Templates, exceptions, and runtime type identification (RTTI) are fully supported in Visual C++ version 4.0. The new C++ Standard Template Library (STL) is also included.

The Resource Compiler

The Visual C++ resource compiler reads an ASCII resource script (RC) file from the graphic editor and writes a binary RES file for the linker.

The Linker

The linker reads the OBJ and RES files produced by the C/C++ compiler and the resource compiler, and it accesses LIB files for MFC code, runtime library code, and Windows code. It then writes the project's EXE file. An incremental link option minimizes the execution time for cases in which only minor changes have been made to the source files. The MFC header files contain *#pragma* statements (special compiler directives) that specify the required library files, so you don't have to tell the linker explicitly which libraries to read.

The Debugger

If your program works the first time, you don't need the debugger. The rest of us might need one from time to time. The Visual C++ debugger has been steadily improving, but it still doesn't actually fix the bugs yet. The debugger works closely with the Developer Studio to ensure that breakpoints are saved on disk. Toolbar buttons toggle breakpoints and control single-step execution. Figure 1-3 illustrates the Visual C++ debugger in action. Note that the Variables and Watch windows can expand an object pointer to show all data members of the derived class and base classes. To debug a program, you must build the program with the compiler and linker options set to generate debugging information.

AppWizard

AppWizard is a code generator that creates a working skeleton of a Windows application with features, class names, and source code filenames that you specify through dialog boxes. You'll use AppWizard extensively as you work through the examples in this book. Don't confuse AppWizard with older code generators that generate all the code for an application. AppWizard code is minimalist code; the functionality is inside the application framework base classes. Its purpose is to get you started quickly with a new application.

AppWizard now is capable of generating an OLE control project. There is no longer a separate Control Development Kit (CDK) as there was in earlier Visual C++ versions.

Call stack
Debug toolbar

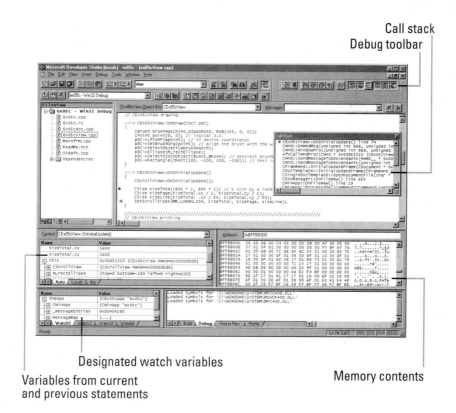

Designated watch variables

Variables from current
and previous statements

Memory contents

Figure 1-3.
The Visual C++ debugger window.

Advanced developers can now build custom AppWizards. Microsoft Corporation has exposed its macro-based system for generating projects. If you discover that your team needs to develop multiple projects with, say, a telecommunications interface, you can build a special wizard that automates the process.

ClassWizard

ClassWizard is a program (implemented as a DLL) that's accessible from the Developer Studio's View menu. ClassWizard takes the drudgery out of maintaining Visual C++ class code. Need a new class, a new virtual function, or a new message handler function? ClassWizard writes the prototypes, the function bodies, and (if necessary) the code to link the Windows message to the function. ClassWizard can update class code that you write, so you avoid the maintenance problems common to ordinary code generators. As Figure 1-2 (on page 8) illustrates, some ClassWizard features are available on a dialog bar at the top of your source code window.

The Source Browser

If you write an application from scratch, you probably have a good mental picture of your source code files, classes, and member functions. If you take over someone else's application, you'll need some assistance. The Visual C++ Source Browser (the browser, for short) lets you examine (and edit) an application from the class or function viewpoint instead of from the file viewpoint. It's a little like the "inspector" tools available with other object-oriented libraries such as Smalltalk. The browser has the following viewing modes:

■ **Definitions and References**—You select any function, variable, type, macro, or class and then see where it's defined and used in your project.

■ **Call Graph/Caller Graph**—For a selected function, you get a graphical representation of the functions it calls or the functions that call it.

■ **Derived Class Graph/Base Class Graph**—These are graphics class hierarchy diagrams. For a selected class, you see the derived classes or the base classes. You can control the hierarchy expansion with the mouse.

A typical browser window is shown on page 35 in Chapter 3.

NOTE: If you rearrange the lines in any source code file, the Developer Studio regenerates the browser database when you rebuild the project. This increases the build time.

In addition to the browser, the Developer Studio has a new Classes view option that does not depend on the browser database. You get a tree view of all the classes in your project, showing member functions and data members. Click on an element, and you see the source code immediately. The Classes view does not, however, show hierarchy information, whereas the browser does.

Online Help

The Visual C++ documentation team worked very hard to develop a brand-new online help system for version 4.0. This system, which is called InfoView, uses technology from the MSDN CDs and includes help for the Developer

Studio, the C++ language, the MFC library, the runtime library, and the Win32 API. You can access help either from the CD-ROM or from the files copied to your hard disk. You can use help in four ways:

- **By Book**—When you choose Contents from the Developer Studio's Help menu, the project Workspace switches to InfoView mode, in which one of your options is Visual C++ Books. Here the Visual C++ documentation is organized hierarchically by books and chapters.

- **By Topic**—Another InfoView option is Key Visual C++ Topics. Here information is organized by topic instead of by book.

- **F1 help**—This is the programmer's best friend. Just move the cursor inside a function name, macro, or class name and press the F1 key, and the help system goes to work. If the name is found in several places—in the MFC and Win32 help files, for example—you choose the help topic you want from a list box. With this version of online help, you can copy any help text to the clipboard for inclusion in your program.

- **Search help**—With this type of help, everything is located in one place. If you choose Search from the Help menu, you can access one alphabetic list of all the indexed terms in the entire help system.

Windows Diagnostic Tools

Visual C++ contains a number of useful diagnostic tools. SPY++ gives you a tree view of your system's processes, threads, and windows. It also lets you view messages and examine the windows of running applications. You'll find PVIEW95 (PVIEW for Windows NT) useful for killing errant processes that aren't visible from Windows. Visual C++ also includes a whole suite of OLE utilities, an OLE control test program, the HC31 help compiler, a library manager, binary file viewers and editors, a source code profiler, and other utilities.

What's missing, however, is the DBWIN utility from the 16-bit version of Visual C++. If you want to see your program's debug messages, you'll have to run the program through the debugger. If you can figure out how to write a 32-bit version of DBWIN, please let me know!

Source Code Control

Microsoft recently bought the rights to an established source code control product named SourceSafe. This product is sold separately from Visual C++, but it can be integrated into the Developer Studio so that you can coordinate large software projects. The master copy of the project's source code is stored in a central place on the network, and individual programmers can check out modules for update. These checked-out modules are usually stored on the programmer's local hard disk. After a programmer checks in modified files, other team members can synchronize their hard disks to the master copy.

The Component Gallery

The Component Gallery is a new feature that lets you share software components among different projects. The Component Gallery manages three types of modules:

- **OLE Controls**—When you install an OLE Control (OCX), an entry is made in the Windows registry. All registered OCXs appear in the Component Gallery's window, so you can select them in any project.

- **C++ source modules**—When you write a new class, you can add the code to the Component Gallery. You can then select and copy the code into other projects. You can also add resources to the Component Gallery.

- **Wizard modules**—The Component Gallery can contain tools that let you add features to your project. Such a tool could insert new member functions and data members into an existing class. Some wizard modules are supplied by Microsoft as part of Visual C++. Others will be supplied by third-party software firms.

All Component Gallery items can be imported from and exported to OGX files. These files are the new distribution and sharing medium for Visual C++ components.

The Microsoft Foundation Class Library Version 4.0

The Microsoft Foundation Class Library version 4.0 (the MFC library, for short) is really the subject of this book. It defines the application framework that you'll be getting to know intimately. Chapter 2 gets you started with actual code and some important concepts.

The Microsoft Foundation Class Library Application Framework

This chapter introduces the Microsoft Foundation Class Library version 4.0 (the MFC library) application framework by explaining its benefits. Starting on page 20, you'll see a stripped-down but fully operational MFC library program for Microsoft Windows that should help you understand what application framework programming is all about. Theory is kept to a minimum here, but the message mapping and document–view sections contain important information that will help you with the examples that follow in later chapters.

Why Use the Application Framework?

If you're going to develop applications for Windows, you've got to choose a development environment. Assuming that you've already rejected non-C options such as Microsoft Visual Basic and Borland Delphi, here are some of your options:

- Program in C with the Win32 API
- Write your own C++ Windows class library that uses Win32
- Use the MFC application framework
- Use another Windows-based application framework such as Borland's Object Windows Library (OWL)

If you're starting from scratch, any option involves a big learning curve. If you're already a Win16 or Win32 programmer, you'll still have a learning curve with the MFC library. So what benefits can justify this effort?

In earlier editions of this book, I ended up sounding like a Microsoft evangelist. Now MFC has been accepted and even used by other compiler publishers such as Symantec. It's still a good idea, though, to step through the features of this programming choice.

MFC library version 4.0 is the C++ Microsoft Windows API.   If you accept the premise that the C++ language is now the standard for serious application development, you'd have to say that it's natural for Windows to have a C++ programming interface. What better interface is there than the one produced by Microsoft, creator of Windows? That interface is the MFC library.

Application framework applications use a standard structure.   Any programmer starting on a large project develops some kind of structure for the code. The problem is that each programmer's structure is different, and for a new team member to learn the structure and conform to it is difficult. The MFC library application framework includes its own application structure— one that's been proven in many software environments and in many projects. If you write a program for Windows that uses the MFC library, you can safely retire to a Caribbean island, knowing that your minions can easily maintain and enhance your code back home.

Don't think that the MFC library's structure makes your programs inflexible. With the MFC library, your program can call Win32 functions at any time, and that means that you can take maximum advantage of Windows.

Application framework applications are small and fast.   Back in the 16-bit days, you could build a self-contained Windows EXE file that was less than 20 kilobytes (KB). Today, Windows programs are larger. One reason is that 32-bit code is fatter. Even with the large memory model, a Win16 program used 16-bit addresses for stack variables and many globals. Win32 programs use 32-bit addresses for everything, and they often use 32-bit integers because they're more efficient than 16-bit integers. In addition, the new C++ exception-handling code consumes a lot of memory.

That old 20-KB program didn't have a docking toolbar, splitter windows, a print preview mode, control container support—features that users expect in modern programs. MFC programs are bigger because they do more and look better. Fortunately, it's now easy to build applications that dynamically link to the MFC code (and to C runtime code), so the size goes back down again—from 192 KB to about 20 KB! Of course, you'll need some big support DLLs in the background, but those are a fact of life these days.

As far as speed is concerned, you're working with machine code produced by an optimizing compiler. Execution is fast, but you might notice a startup delay while the support DLLs are loaded.

The Visual C++ tools reduce coding drudgery. The graphic editor, App-Wizard, and ClassWizard significantly reduce the time needed to write code that is specific to your application. For example, the graphic editor creates a header file that contains assigned values for *#define* constants. AppWizard generates skeleton code for your entire application, and ClassWizard generates prototypes and function bodies for message handlers.

The MFC library application framework is feature-rich. The MFC library version 1.0 classes, supplied with Microsoft C/C++ version 7.0, were essentially a C++ programming interface for Windows. Some significant features were added to MFC version 1.0 classes, however:

- General-purpose (non-Windows-specific) classes, including
    - Collection classes for lists, arrays, and maps
    - A useful and efficient string class
    - Time, time span, and date classes
    - File access classes for operating system independence
    - Support for systematic object storage and retrieval to and from disk
- A "common root object" class hierarchy
- Streamlined Multiple Document Interface (MDI) application support
- Some support for OLE version 1.0

The MFC library version 2.0 classes (in Visual C++ version 1.0) picked up where the version 1.0 classes left off by supporting many user interface features that are found in current Windows-based applications, plus it introduced the application framework architecture. Here's a summary of the important new features:

- Full support for File Open, Save, and Save As menu items and the most recently used file list
- Print preview and printer support
- Support for scrolling windows and splitter windows
- Support for toolbars and status bars
- Access to Microsoft Visual Basic controls
- Support for context-sensitive help

17

■ Support for automatic processing of data entered in a dialog box

■ An improved interface to OLE version 1.0

■ DLL support

The version 2.5 classes (in Visual C++ version 1.5) contributed the following:

■ ODBC (Open Database Connectivity) support that allows your application to access and update data stored in many popular databases such as Microsoft Access, FoxPro, and SQL Server

■ An interface to OLE version 2.01, with support for in-place editing, linking, drag and drop, and OLE Automation

Visual C++ version 2.0 was the first 32-bit version of the product, which included support for Windows NT version 3.5. It contained MFC version 3.0, which had the following new features:

■ Tab dialog (property sheet) support (which was also added to Visual C++ version 1.51, included on the same CD-ROM)

■ Docking control bars that were implemented within MFC

■ Support for thin-frame windows

■ A separate Control Development Kit (CDK) for building 16-bit and 32-bit OLE controls, although no OLE control container support was provided

A subscription release, Visual C++ 2.1 with MFC 3.1, added the following:

■ Support for the new Windows 95 (beta) common controls

■ A new ODBC Level 2 driver integrated with the Access Jet database engine

Microsoft decided to skip Visual C++ version 3.0 and proceeded directly to 4.0 in order to synchronize the product version with the MFC version. MFC 4.0 contains these additional features:

■ New OLE-based Data Access Objects (DAO) classes for use with the Jet engine

■ Use of the Windows 95 docking control bars instead of the MFC control bars

■ Full support for the common controls in the released version of Windows 95, with new tree view and rich-edit view classes

■ New classes for thread synchronization

■ OLE control container support

The Learning Curve

All the benefits listed above sound great, don't they? You're probably thinking, "You don't get something for nothing." Yes, that's true. To use the application framework effectively, you have to learn it thoroughly, and that takes time. If you have to learn C++, Windows, and the MFC library (without OLE) all at the same time, it will take at least six months before you're really productive. Interestingly, that's close to the learning time for the Win32 API alone.

How can that be if the MFC library offers so much more? For one thing, you can avoid many programming details that C-language Win32 programmers are forced to learn. From my own experience, I can say that an object-oriented application framework makes programming for Windows easier to learn—that is, once you understand object-oriented programming.

The MFC library won't bring real Windows programming down to the masses. Windows programmers have usually commanded higher salaries than other programmers, and that situation will continue. The MFC library's learning curve, together with the application framework's power, should ensure that MFC library programmers will continue to be in strong demand.

What's an Application Framework?

One definition of an application framework is "an integrated collection of object-oriented software components that offers all that's needed for a generic application." That isn't a very useful definition, is it? If you really want to know what an application framework is, you'll have to read the rest of this book. The application framework example that you'll familiarize yourself with later in this chapter is a good starting point.

An Application Framework vs. a Class Library

One reason that C++ is a popular language is that it can be "extended" with class libraries. Some class libraries are delivered with C++ compilers, others are sold by third-party software firms, and still others are developed in-house. A class library is a set of related C++ classes that can be used in an application. A matrix class library, for example, might perform common mathematics operations involving matrices, and a communications class library might support the transfer of data over a serial link. Sometimes you construct objects of the supplied classes; sometimes you derive your own classes—it all depends on the design of the particular class library.

An application framework is a superset of a class library. An ordinary library is an isolated set of classes designed to be incorporated into any program, but an application framework defines the structure of the program itself. Microsoft didn't invent the application framework concept. It appeared first in the academic world, and the first commercial version was MacApp for the Apple Macintosh. Since MFC 2.0 was introduced, other companies, including Borland, have released similar products.

An Application Framework Example

Enough generalizations. It's time to look at some code—not pseudocode but real code that actually compiles and runs with the MFC library. Guess what? It's the good old "Hello, world!" application with a few additions. (If you've used version 1.0 of the MFC library, this code will be familiar except for the frame window base class.) It's about the minimum amount of code for a working MFC library application for Windows. Contrast it with an equivalent pure Win32 application such as you would see in a Petzold book! You don't have to understand every line now. Don't bother to type it in and test it. Wait for the next chapter, where you'll start using the "real" application framework.

NOTE: By convention, MFC library class names begin with the letter C.

Following is the source code for the header and implementation files for our MYAPP application. The two classes, *CMyApp* and *CMyFrame*, are each derived from the MFC library base classes. First, here is the MYAPP.H header file for the MYAPP application:

```
// application class
class CMyApp : public CWinApp
{
public:
    virtual BOOL InitInstance();
};

// frame window class
class CMyFrame : public CFrameWnd
{
public:
    CMyFrame();
```

```
protected:
    // 'afx_msg' indicates that the next two functions are part
    //  of the MFC library message dispatch system
    afx_msg void OnLButtonDown(UINT nFlags, CPoint point);
    afx_msg void OnPaint();
    DECLARE_MESSAGE_MAP()
};
```

And here is the MYAPP.CPP implementation file for the MYAPP application:

```
#include <afxwin.h> // MFC library header file declares base classes
#include "myapp.h"

CMyApp theApp; // the one and only CMyApp object

BOOL CMyApp::InitInstance()
{
    m_pMainWnd = new CMyFrame();
    m_pMainWnd->ShowWindow(m_nCmdShow);

    m_pMainWnd->UpdateWindow();
    return TRUE;
}


BEGIN_MESSAGE_MAP(CMyFrame, CFrameWnd)
    ON_WM_LBUTTONDOWN()
    ON_WM_PAINT()
END_MESSAGE_MAP()


CMyFrame::CMyFrame()
{
    Create(NULL, "MYAPP Application");
}


void CMyFrame::OnLButtonDown(UINT nFlags, CPoint point)
{
    TRACE("Entering CMyFrame::OnLButtonDown - %lx, %d, %d\n",
          (long) nFlags, point.x, point.y);
}


void CMyFrame::OnPaint()
{
    CPaintDC dc(this);
    dc.TextOut(0, 0, "Hello, world!");
}
```

Here are some of the program elements:

The *WinMain* function—Remember that Windows requires that your application have a *WinMain* function. You don't see *WinMain* here because it's hidden inside the application framework.

The *CMyApp* class—An object of class *CMyApp* represents an application. The program defines a single global *CMyApp* object, *theApp*. The *CWinApp* base class determines most of *theApp*'s behavior.

Application startup—When the user starts the application, Windows calls the application framework's built-in *WinMain* function, and *WinMain* looks for your globally constructed application object of a class derived from *CWinApp*. Don't forget that, in a C++ program, global objects are constructed <u>before</u> the main program is executed.

The *CMyApp::InitInstance* member function—When *WinMain* finds the application object, it calls the virtual *InitInstance* member function, which makes the calls needed to construct and display the application's main frame window. You must override *InitInstance* in your derived application class because the *CWinApp* base class doesn't have the slightest idea of what kind of main frame window you want.

The *CWinApp::Run* member function—The *Run* function is hidden in the base class, but it dispatches the application's messages to its windows, thus keeping the application running. *WinMain* calls *Run* after it calls *InitInstance*.

The *CMyFrame* class—An object of class *CMyFrame* represents the application's main frame window. When the constructor calls the *Create* member function of the base class *CFrameWnd*, Windows creates the actual window structure and the application framework links it to the C++ object. The *ShowWindow* and *UpdateWindow* functions, also member functions of the base class, must be called in order to display the window.

The *CMyFrame::OnLButtonDown* function—This is a sneak preview of the MFC library's message-handling capability. We've elected to "map" the left mouse button down event to a *CMyFrame* member function. You'll learn the details of the MFC library's message mapping in Chapter 4. For the time being, accept that this function gets called when the user presses the left mouse button. The function invokes the MFC library *TRACE* macro to display a message in the debugging window.

The *CMyFrame::OnPaint* **function**—The application framework calls this important mapped member function of class *CMyFrame* every time it's necessary to repaint the window: at the start of the program, when the user resizes the window, and when all or part of the window is newly exposed. The *CPaintDC* statement relates to the Graphics Device Interface (GDI) and is explained in later chapters. The *TextOut* function displays "Hello, world!"

Application shutdown—The user shuts down the application by closing the frame window. This action initiates a sequence of events, which ends with the destruction of the *CMyFrame* object, the exit from *Run*, the exit from *Win-Main*, and the destruction of the *CMyApp* object.

Look at the example again. This time try to get the big picture. Most of the application's functionality is in the MFC library base classes *CWinApp* and *CFrameWnd*. In writing MYAPP, we've followed a few simple structure rules, and we've written key functions in our derived classes. C++ lets us "borrow" a lot of code without copying it. Think of it as a partnership between us and the application framework. The application framework provided the structure, and we provided the code that made the application unique.

Now you're beginning to see why the application framework is more than a class library. Not only does the application framework define the application structure but it also encompasses more than C++ base classes. You've already seen the hidden *WinMain* function at work. Other elements support message processing, diagnostics, DLLs, and so forth.

MFC Library Message Mapping

Refer to the *OnLButtonDown* member function in the previous example. You might think that *OnLButtonDown* would be an ideal candidate for a virtual function. A window base class would define virtual functions for mouse event messages and other standard messages, and derived window classes could override the functions as necessary. Some Windows class libraries do work this way.

The MFC library application framework doesn't use virtual functions for Windows messages. Instead, it uses macros to "map" specified messages to derived class member functions. Why the rejection of virtual functions? Suppose MFC used virtual functions for messages. MFC has a hierarchy of maybe 20 window classes derived from *CWnd*, and *CWnd* declares virtual functions for more than 140 messages. C++ requires a virtual function dispatch table, called a <u>vtable</u>, for each derived class used in a program. Each vtable needs one 4-byte entry for each virtual function, regardless of whether the functions are actually overridden in the derived class. Thus, for each distinct type of window or control, the application would need an 11,280-byte table to support virtual message handlers.

What about message handlers for menu command messages and messages from button clicks? You couldn't define these as virtual functions in a window base class because each application might have a different set of menu commands and buttons. The MFC library message map system avoids large vtables, and it accommodates application-specific command messages in parallel with ordinary Windows messages. It also allows selected nonwindow classes, such as document classes and the application class, to handle command messages. MFC uses macros to connect (or map) Windows messages to C++ member functions. No extensions to the C++ language are necessary.

An MFC message handler requires a function prototype, a function body, and an entry (macro invocation) in the message map. ClassWizard helps you add message handlers to your classes. You select a Windows message ID from a list box, and the Wizard generates the code with the correct function parameters and return values.

Documents and Views

The previous example used an application object and a frame window object. Most of your MFC library applications will be more complex. Typically, they'll contain application and frame classes plus two other classes that represent the "document" and the "view." This document–view architecture is the core of the application framework and is loosely based on the Model/View/Controller classes from the Smalltalk world.

In simple terms, the document–view architecture separates data from the user's view of the data. One obvious benefit is multiple views of the same data. Consider a document that consists of a month's worth of stock quotes stored on disk. Suppose a table view and a chart view of the data are available. The user updates values through the table view window, and the chart view window changes because both windows display the same information (but in different views).

In the MFC library, documents and views are represented by C++ classes and objects. Figure 2-1 shows three objects of class *CStockDoc* corresponding to three companies: AT&T, IBM, and GM. All three documents have a table view attached, and one document also has a chart view. As you can see, there are four view objects—three objects of class *CStockListView* and one of class *CStockChartView*.

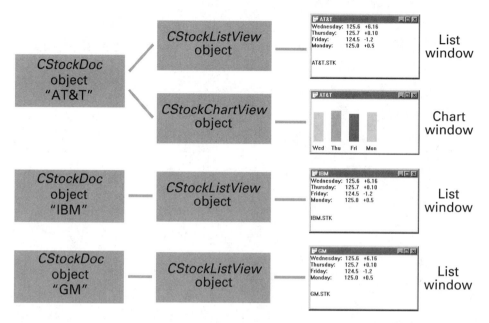

Figure 2-1.
The document–view relationship.

The document base-class code interacts with the File Open and File Save menu items; the derived document class does the actual reading and writing of the document object's data. (The application framework does most of the work of displaying the File Open and File Save dialog boxes and opening, closing, reading, and writing files.) The view base class represents a window that is contained inside a frame window; the derived view class interacts with its associated document class and does the application's display and printer I/O. The derived view class and its base classes handle Windows messages. The MFC library orchestrates all interactions among documents, views, and frame windows and the application object, mostly through virtual functions.

Don't think that a document object must be associated with a disk file that is read entirely into memory. If a "document" were really a database, for example, you could override selected document class member functions, and the File Open menu item would bring up a list of databases instead of a list of files.

THE MFC
LIBRARY
VIEW CLASS

CHAPTER THREE

Getting Started with AppWizard—"Hello, world!"

Chapter 2 sketched the MFC library version 4.0 document–view architecture. This hands-on chapter shows you how to build a functioning MFC library application, but it insulates you from the complexities of the class hierarchy and object interrelationships. You'll work with only one document–view program element, the "view class" that is closely associated with a window. For the time being, you can ignore elements such as the application class, the frame window, and the document. Of course, your application won't be able to save its data on disk, and it won't support multiple views, but Part III of this book provides plenty of opportunity to exploit those features.

> TIP: It's easy to copy a whole project, either with the Windows 95 Explorer or from the DOS prompt (XCOPY/S). There's a trap that's easy to fall into, though. If your original project has open child windows associated with source files, the child windows in the new project will be associated with files in the original project. If you're not careful, you'll change the original project inadvertently when you meant to change the copy. (I've fallen into this trap too many times.) To avoid this problem, close all the project's child windows, either before or after the copy.

Because resources are so important in Windows-based applications, you'll use the graphic editor to visually explore the resources of your new program. You'll also get some hints for setting up your Windows environment for maximum build speed and optimal debugging output.

REQUIREMENTS: To compile and run the examples presented in this chapter and in the following chapters, you must have successfully installed the released version of Microsoft Windows 95 or Microsoft Windows NT version 3.51 or later, plus all the Microsoft Visual C++ version 4.0 components. Be sure that the Developer Studio's executable, include, and library directories are set correctly. (You can change the directories by choosing Options from the Tools menu.) If you have any problems with the following steps, please refer to your Visual C++ documentation and README files for troubleshooting instructions.

What's a View?

From the user's standpoint, a <u>view</u> is an ordinary window that he or she can size, move, and close in the same way as any other Windows-based application window. From the programmer's perspective, a view is a C++ object of a class derived from the MFC library *CView* class. Like any C++ object, the view object's behavior is determined by the member functions (and data members) of the class—both the application-specific functions in the derived class and the standard functions inherited from the base classes.

With Visual C++, you can produce interesting applications for Windows by simply adding code to the derived view class that the AppWizard code generator produces. When your program runs, the MFC library application framework constructs an object of the derived view class and displays a window that is tightly linked to the C++ view object. As is customary in C++ programming, the MFC library view class is divided into two source modules—the header file (H) and the implementation file (CPP).

Single Document Interface (SDI) vs. Multiple Document Interface (MDI)

The MFC library supports two distinct application types: Single Document Interface (SDI) and Multiple Document Interface (MDI). An SDI application has, from the user's point of view, only one window. If the application depends on disk-file "documents," only one document can be loaded at a time. The original Windows Notepad is an example of an SDI application. An MDI application has multiple <u>child</u> <u>windows</u>, each of which corresponds to an individual document. Microsoft Word is a good example of an MDI application.

When you run AppWizard to create a new project, MDI is the default application type. For the early examples in this book, you'll be generating SDI applications because fewer classes and features are involved. Be sure you select the Single Document option (on the first AppWizard screen) for these examples. Starting with Chapter 17, you'll be generating MDI applications. The MFC library application framework architecture ensures that most SDI examples can be upgraded easily to MDI applications.

The "Do-Nothing" Application—EX03A

The AppWizard program generates the code for a functioning MFC library application. This working application simply brings up an empty window with a menu attached. Later you'll add code that draws inside the window. Follow these steps to build the application:

1. **Run AppWizard to generate SDI application source code.**   Choose New from the Developer Studio's File menu, and then select Project Workspace from the list box. When AppWizard starts, you'll see a dialog box, as shown here:

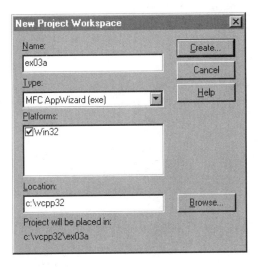

Type the program name as shown in the Name edit box, type the directory as shown in the Location edit box, and then click the Create button. Now you will step through a sequence of AppWizard screens, the first of which is shown at the top of the following page:

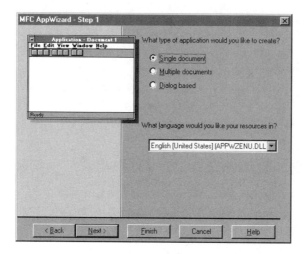

Be sure to select the Single Document option as illustrated. Accept the defaults in the next four screens. The last screen should look like this:

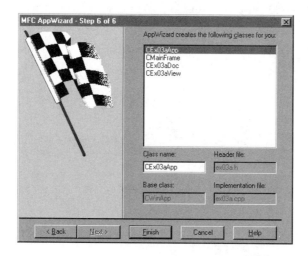

Notice that the class names and source-file names have been generated based on the project name EX03A. You could make changes to these names at this point if you wanted to. Click the Finish button. Just before AppWizard generates your code, it displays the New Project Information dialog box shown here:

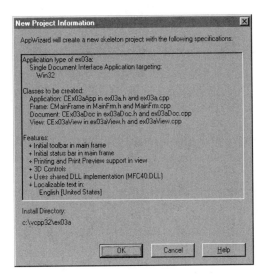

When you click the OK button, AppWizard begins to create your application's subdirectory (EX03A under\VCPP32) and a series of files in that subdirectory. When AppWizard is finished, look in the application's subdirectory. The following files are of interest (for now):

File	Description
ex03a.mak	A make file that allows the Developer Studio to build your application
ex03a.rc	An ASCII resource script file
ex03aView.cpp	A view class implementation file that contains *CEx03aView* class member functions
ex03aView.h	A view class header file that contains the *CEx03aView* class declaration
ex03a.mdp	A project file that tells the Developer Studio which files are open for this project and how the windows are arranged
ReadMe.txt	A text file that explains the purpose of all generated files
resource.h	A header file that contains #*define* constant definitions

Open the ex03aView.cpp and ex03aView.h files and look at the source code. Together these files define the *CEx03aView* class, which is central to the application. An object of class *CEx03aView* corresponds to the application's view window, where all the "action" takes place.

2. Compile and link the generated code. AppWizard, in addition to generating code, creates custom project and make files for your application. The make file, ex03a.mak, specifies all the file dependencies together with the compile and link option flags. Because the new project becomes the Developer Studio's current project, you can now build the application by choosing Build Ex03a.exe from the Build menu or by clicking the Build toolbar button.

If the build is successful, an executable program named ex03a.exe is created in a new DEBUG subdirectory underneath \VCPP32\EX03A. The OBJ files and other working files are also stored in DEBUG. Compare the file structure on disk with the structure in the project Workspace window (FileView), which is shown here:

FileView button

The Workspace window contains a logical view of your project. The header files show up under Dependencies, even though they are in the same subdirectory as the CPP files. The logical top level, Win32 Debug, represents the DEBUG subdirectory on disk.

3. Test the resulting application. Choose Execute Ex03a from the Build menu. Experiment with the program. It really doesn't do much, does it? (What do you expect for no coding, anyway?) Actually, as you might guess, the program has a lot of features—you simply haven't activated them yet. Close the program window when you've finished experimenting.

4. Browse the application.   You can use the Visual C++ browser only after you have successfully compiled an application with browse information. Choose Browse from the Tools menu, and the Browser window appears. Choose Base Classes And Members, and then select CEx03aView. After you expand the hierarchy, you should see output similar to this:

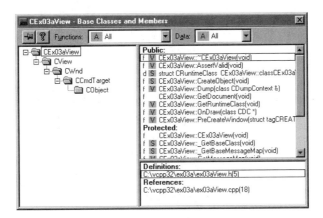

Compare the browser output to ClassView in the Workspace window, as shown below:

ClassView button

Class View doesn't show the class hierarchy, but it also doesn't involve the extra overhead of the browser. If Class View is sufficient for you, don't bother building the browser database.

The *CEx03aView* View Class

AppWizard generated the *CEx03aView* view class, and this class is specific to the EX03A application. (AppWizard generates classes based on the project name you entered in the first AppWizard dialog box.) *CEx03aView* is at the bottom of a long inheritance chain of MFC library classes, as illustrated previously in the Browser window. The class picks up member functions and data members all along the chain. You can learn about these classes in the *Microsoft Foundation Class Library Reference* (online or printed version), but you must be sure to look at the descriptions for every base class because the descriptions of inherited member functions aren't generally repeated for derived classes.

The most important *CEx03aView* base classes are *CWnd* and *CView*. *CWnd* provides *CEx03aView*'s "windowness," and *CView* provides the hooks to the rest of the application framework, particularly to the document and to the frame window that you'll see in Part III of this book.

Drawing Inside the View Window— The Windows Graphics Device Interface

Now you're ready to write code to draw inside the view window. You'll be making a few changes directly to the EX03A source code.

The *OnDraw* Member Function

Specifically, you'll be fleshing out *OnDraw* in ex03aView.cpp. *OnDraw* is a virtual member function of the *CView* class that the application framework calls every time the view window needs to be repainted. A window needs repainting if the user resizes the window or reveals a previously hidden part of the window, or if the application changes the window's data. If the user resizes the window or reveals a hidden area, the application framework calls *OnDraw*, but if a function in your program changes the data, it must inform Windows of the change by calling the view's inherited *Invalidate* (or *InvalidateRect*) member function. This call to *Invalidate* triggers a later call to *OnDraw*.

Even though you can draw inside a window at any time, it's strongly recommended that you let window changes accumulate and then process them all together in the *OnDraw* function. That way your program can respond to program-generated events and to Windows-generated events such as size changes.

The Windows Device Context

Recall from Chapter 1 that Windows doesn't allow direct access to the display hardware but communicates through an abstraction called a "device context" that is associated with the window. In the MFC library, the device context is a C++ object of class *CDC* that is passed (by pointer) as a parameter to *OnDraw*. After you have the device context pointer, you can call the many *CDC* member functions that do the work of drawing.

Adding Draw Code to the EX03A Program

Now let's write the code to draw some text and a circle inside the view window. Be sure that the project file ex03a.mdp is open in the Developer Studio. You can use the Workspace window's ClassView to locate the code for the function (double-click on *OnDraw*), or you can open the source code file ex03aView.cpp from FileView and locate the function yourself.

1. Edit the *OnDraw* function in ex03aView.cpp. Find the AppWizard-generated *OnDraw* function in ex03aView.cpp:

```
void CEx03aView::OnDraw(CDC* pDC)
{
    CEx03aDoc* pDoc = GetDocument();
    ASSERT_VALID(pDoc);

    // TODO: add draw code here
}
```

The following shaded code (which you type in) replaces the previous code:

```
void CEx03aView::OnDraw(CDC* pDC)
{
    pDC->TextOut(0, 0, "Hello, world!"); // prints in default font
                                         //   & size, top left corner
    pDC->SelectStockObject(GRAY_BRUSH);  // selects a brush for the
                                         //   circle interior
    pDC->Ellipse(CRect(0, 20, 100, 120)); // draws a gray circle 100
                                          //   units in diameter
}
```

You can safely remove the call to *GetDocument* because we're not dealing with documents yet. The functions *TextOut, SelectStockObject,* and *Ellipse* are all member functions of the application framework's device context class *CDC*. The *Ellipse* function draws a circle if the bounding rectangle's length is equal to its width.

The MFC library provides a handy utility class, *CRect*, for Windows rectangles. A temporary *CRect* object serves as the bounding rectangle argument for the ellipse drawing function. You'll see more of the *CRect* class later in this book.

2. Recompile and test EX03A.   Choose Build from the Project menu, and, if there are no compile errors, test the application again. Now you have a program that visibly does something!

For Win32 Programmers

Rest assured that the standard Windows *WinMain* and *WndProc* functions are hidden away inside the application framework. You'll see those functions later in this book, when the MFC library frame and application classes are examined. In the meantime, you're probably wondering what happened to the WM_PAINT message, aren't you? You would expect to do your window drawing in response to this Windows message, and you would expect to get your device context handle from a *PAINTSTRUCT* structure that the Windows *BeginPaint* function returns.

It so happens that the application framework has done all the dirty work for you and served up a device context (in object pointer form) in the virtual function *OnDraw*. As explained in Chapter 2, true virtual functions in window classes are an MFC library rarity. MFC library message map functions dispatched by the application framework handle most Windows messages. MFC version 1.0 programmers always defined an *OnPaint* message map function for their derived window classes. Beginning with version 2.5, however, *OnPaint* was mapped in the *CView* class, and that function made a polymorphic call to *OnDraw*. Why? Because *OnDraw* needs to support the printer as well. Both *OnPaint* and *OnPrint* call *OnDraw*, thus enabling the same drawing code to accommodate both the printer and the display.

A Preview of the Graphic Editor—
Resources Introduced

Now that you have a complete application program, it's a good time for a quick look at the graphic editor. Although the application's resource script, ex03a.rc, is an ASCII file, modifying it with a text editor is not a good idea. That's the graphic editor's job.

The Contents of ex03a.rc

The resource file determines much of the EX03A application's "look and feel." The file ex03a.rc contains (or points to) the Windows resources listed here:

Resource	Description
Accelerators	Definitions for keys that simulate menu and toolbar selections
Dialog	Layout and contents of dialog boxes—the About dialog box for EX03A
Icon	The MFC logo (32-by-32-pixel and 16-by-16-pixel versions) you see in Windows Explorer and in the application's About dialog box
Menu	The application's top-level menu and associated pop-up menus
String table	Strings that are not part of the C++ source code
Toolbar bitmap	The row of buttons immediately below the menu
Version	Program description, version number, language, and so on

In addition to the resources listed above, ex03a.rc contains the statement

```
#include "afxres.h"
```

which brings in some MFC library resources common to all applications. These resources include strings, graphical buttons, and elements needed for printing and OLE.

> **N O T E :** If you're using the shared DLL version of the MFC library, the common resources are stored inside the DLL.

The ex03a.rc file also contains the statement

```
#include "resource.h"
```

This statement brings in the application's two *#define* constants, which are *IDR_MAINFRAME* (identifying the menu, icon, string list, and accelerator table) and *IDD_ABOUTBOX* (identifying the About dialog box). This same resource.h file is included indirectly by the application's source code files. If you use the graphic editor to add more constants (symbols), the definitions ultimately show up in resource.h. If you use a text editor to add your own constants to resource.h, the graphic editor does not disturb them.

Running the Graphic Editor

1. Open the project's RC file. From the workspace window (FileView), double-click on ex03a.rc or click the ResourceView button. If you expand each item, you will see the following in the graphic editor window:

ResourceView button

2. Examine the application's resources. Now take some time to explore the individual resources. When you select a resource by double-clicking on it, another window opens with tools appropriate for the selected resource. (The control palette might also appear.)

3. Modify the IDD_ABOUTBOX dialog box. Make some changes to the About dialog box, shown here:

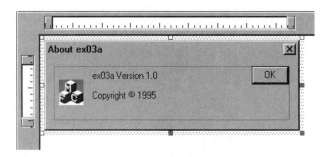

You can change the size of the window by dragging the right and bottom borders, move the OK button, change the text, and so forth. Simply click on an element to select it.

4. **Rebuild the project with the modified resource file.**   In the Developer Studio, choose Build Ex03a.exe from the Build menu. Notice that no actual C++ recompilation is necessary. The Developer Studio saves the edited resource file on disk, and then the Resource Compiler (rc.exe) processes ex03a.rc to produce a compiled version, ex03a.res, which is fed to the linker. The linker runs quickly because it can link the project incrementally.

5. **Test the new version of the application.**   Run the EX03A program again, and then choose About from the application's Help menu to confirm that your dialog box was changed as expected.

Win32 Debug Target vs. Win32 Release Target

If you open the drop-down list on the toolbar in the Workspace window, you'll notice two items: Win32 Debug and Win32 Release. These items are <u>targets</u> that represent distinct sets of build options. When AppWizard generates a project, it creates two default targets with different settings. These settings are summarized in the following table:

	Release Build	Debug Build
Source code debugging	Disabled	Enabled for both compiler and linker
MFC diagnostic macros	Disabled (*NDEBUG* defined)	Enabled (*_DEBUG* defined)
Library linkage	MFC Release libraries	MFC Debug libraries
Compiler optimization	Speed optimization	No optimization (faster compile)

You develop your application in Debug mode, and then you rebuild in Release mode prior to delivery. The Release build EXE will be smaller and faster, but it's assumed that you have fixed all the bugs. You select the configuration from the build target window in the Build toolbar as shown in Figure 1-2 on page 8. By default, the Debug output files and intermediate files are stored in the project's DEBUG subdirectory; the Release files are stored in the RELEASE subdirectory. You can change these directories from the General tab in the Settings dialog box.

You can create your own custom configurations if you need to by choosing Projects from the Developer Studio's Build menu.

Enabling the Diagnostic Macros

The application framework *TRACE* macros are particularly useful for monitoring program status. These macros, together with the *ASSERT* and *VERIFY* macros, require the Debug build option (but do not require sample code debugging information). In addition, the *TRACE* macros require that tracing be enabled. You can enable tracing by inserting the statement

```
afxtrace = TRUE;
```

in your program. Alternatively, you can insert the statement

```
TraceEnabled = 1
```

in the [Diagnostics] section of the AFX.INI file in your WINDOWS subdirectory. You can control this trace option, together with other trace options, with the TRACER utility that is included with Visual C++. You must use the debugger to get *TRACE* output, which appears in the output window's Debug view or on your auxiliary monitor.

Speeding Up the Build Process

If you've read the earlier editions of this book, you will have noticed a section on using a RAM drive to speed the build process. I tried those techniques with Windows 95 but noticed no speed improvement. When I analyzed the situation, I felt rather stupid. With the 32-bit virtual memory architecture (as described in Chapter 9 in this book), the RAM drive could be nothing other than a "virtual RAM drive" backed by the system page file. So forget about RAM drives, and SMARTDRV too.

I also recommended disabling source code debugging for faster links and loads. Now that AppWizard's default behavior is to configure projects to work with the shared DLL versions of MFC, the debugging information has little effect on code size. The Visual C++ Setup program copies large PDB files into your WINDOWS\SYSTEM directory. These files allow you to trace into the MFC source code, so that information is not rebuilt for each project. If you do decide to statically link to the MFC libraries, you can save time by disabling source code debugging, but you must do it for both the compiler and the linker.

If you find you're not using the browser, you will save some time by disabling the building of the browser database. (By default, the browser database is not built for a new Visual C++ project.) For each project, go to the C/C++ tab in the Settings dialog box and deselect Generate Browse Info.

The only sure way to speed the build process is to buy a faster machine with more memory!

Understanding Precompiled Headers

When AppWizard generates a project, it generates switch settings and files for precompiled headers. You must understand how the make system processes precompiled headers in order to effectively manage your projects.

> N O T E : Visual C++ has two precompiled header "systems": automatic and manual. Automatic precompiled headers, activated with the /Yx compiler switch, store compiler output in a "database" file. Manual precompiled headers are activated by the /Yc and /Yu switch settings and are central to all AppWizard-generated projects.

Precompiled headers represent compiler "snapshots" taken at a particular source code line. In MFC library programs, the snapshot is generally taken immediately after the statement

```
#include  "StdAfx.h"
```

The file StdAfx.h contains *#include* statements for the MFC library header files. The file's contents depend on the options that you select when you run AppWizard, but the file always contains the following statements:

```
#include <afxwin.h>
#include <afxext.h>
```

If you're using OLE, StdAfx.h also contains the statement

```
#include <afxole.h>
```

or

```
#include <afxdisp.h>
```

Occasionally you'll need other header files—for example, the header for template-based collection classes that is accessed by the statement

```
#include <afxtempl.h>
```

The source file StdAfx.cpp contains only the statement

```
#include  "StdAfx.h"
```

and is used to generate the precompiled header file in the project directory. The MFC library headers included by StdAfx.h never change, but they do take a long time to compile. The compiler switch /Yc, used only with StdAfx-.cpp, causes <u>creation</u> of the precompiled header (PCH) file. The switch /Yu, used with all the other source code files, causes <u>use</u> of an existing PCH file. The switch /Fp specifies the PCH filename that would otherwise default to the project name (with PCH extension) in the target's output files subdirectory. Figure 3-1 illustrates the whole process.

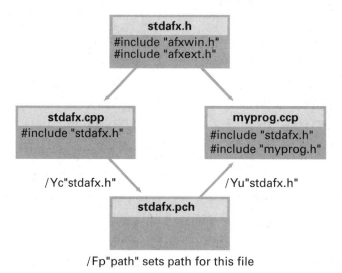

Figure 3-1.
The Visual C++ precompiled header process.

AppWizard sets the /Yc and /Yu switches for you, but you can make changes if you need to. This illustrates that it's possible to define compiler switch settings for individual files. With the Settings dialog box open, if you select only StdAfx.cpp, you'll see the /Yc setting. This overrides the /Yu setting that is defined for the target.

Be aware that PCH files are big—4 MB is typical. If you're not careful, you'll fill up your hard disk. You could keep things clean by periodically cleaning out your projects' DEBUG directories, or you could use the /Fp compiler option to reroute PCH files to a common directory.

The Windows Debug Kernel

The Windows Debug kernel is a set of DLLs and other files that replace key components of Windows. If you install the Debug kernel, you can get important error messages when you debug your programs. For example, you can detect the failure to delete GDI objects, the failure to deselect a GDI object from a device context, and the failure to free Windows heap memory. Some of these errors are not as serious in Win32 as they were in Win16, but they do indicate logic errors that you should fix.

The Debug kernel was a part of earlier versions of Visual C++. Now, however, it's provided on the Microsoft Developer Network (MSDN) CD-ROM. There are separate versions for Windows NT and Windows 95, and the Debug kernel code must be matched to the right version of Windows. I recommend that you get the Debug kernel and install it on your development machine. Instructions are included on the MSDN CD-ROM.

> F Y I: For more information about the MSDN, in the United States and Canada, call 800-759-5474 from 6:30 a.m. to 5:30 p.m. Pacific time, Monday through Friday. In Europe, call +31 10 258 88 64. Everywhere else, call 303-684-0914.
>
> Information about the MSDN program is also posted in the Dev-Only section on Microsoft's Web site (http://www.microsoft.com).

CHAPTER FOUR

Basic Event Handling, Mapping Modes, and a Scrolling View

In Chapter 3, you saw how the Microsoft Foundation Class (MFC) Library application framework called the view class's virtual *OnDraw* function. Take a look at the online help for the Microsoft Foundation Class Library now. If you look at the documentation for the *CView* class and its base class, *CWnd*, you'll see several hundred member functions. Functions with names beginning with *On*—such as *OnKeyDown* and *OnLButtonUp*—are member functions that the application framework calls in response to various Windows "events" such as keystrokes and mouse clicks.

Most of these application framework–called functions, such as *OnDraw*, aren't virtual functions and thus require more programming steps. This chapter explains how to use the Visual C++ ClassWizard to set up the <u>message map</u> structure necessary for connecting the application framework to your functions' code. You'll see the practical application of message map functions.

The first two examples use an ordinary *CView* class. In EX04A, you'll learn about the interaction between user-driven events and the *OnDraw* function. In EX04B, you'll see the effects of different Windows mapping modes.

More often than not, you'll want a <u>scrolling</u> view. The last example, EX04C, uses *CScrollView* in place of the *CView* base class. This allows the MFC library application framework to insert scroll bars and "hook them up" to the view.

Getting User Input—Message Map Functions

Your EX03A application from Chapter 3 did not accept user input (other than the standard Microsoft Windows resizing and window close commands). The window contained menus and a toolbar, but these were not "connected" to the view code. The menus and the toolbar won't be discussed until Part III of this book because they depend on the frame class, but plenty of other Windows input sources will keep you busy until then. Before you can process any Windows event, even a mouse click, however, you must learn how to use the MFC message map system.

The Message Map

When the user presses the left mouse button in a view window, Windows sends a message—specifically WM_LBUTTONDOWN—to that window. If your program needs to take action in response to WM_LBUTTONDOWN, your view class must have a member function that looks like this:

```
void CMyView::OnLButtonDown(UINT nFlags, CPoint point)
{
    // event processing code here
}
```

Your class header file must also have the corresponding prototype:

```
afx_msg void OnLButtonDown(UINT nFlags, CPoint point);
```

The *afx_msg* notation is a "no-op" that alerts you that this is a prototype for a message map function. Finally, your code file needs a message map macro that connects your *OnLButtonDown* function to the application framework:

```
BEGIN_MESSAGE_MAP(CMyView, CView)
    ON_WM_LBUTTONDOWN() // entry specifically for OnLButtonDown
    // other message map entries
END_MESSAGE_MAP()
```

and your class header file needs the statement

```
DECLARE_MESSAGE_MAP()
```

How do you know which function goes with which Windows message? Appendix B (and the MFC library's Books Online) includes a table that lists all standard Windows messages and corresponding member function prototypes. You can manually code the message-handling functions—indeed, that is still necessary for certain messages. Fortunately, Visual C++ provides a tool, ClassWizard, that automates the coding of most message map functions.

Saving the View's State–Class Data Members

If your program accepts user input, you'll want the user to have some visual feedback. The view's *OnDraw* function draws an image based on the view's current "state," and user actions can alter that state. In a full-blown MFC application, the document object holds the state of the application, but you're not to that point yet. For now, you'll use two view class <u>data</u> <u>members</u>, *m_rectEllipse* and *m_nColor*. The first is an object of class *CRect*, which holds the current bounding rectangle of an ellipse, and the second is an integer that holds the current ellipse color value. You'll make a message-mapped member function toggle the ellipse color (the view's state) between gray and white. (The toggle is activated by pressing the left mouse button.) The initial values of *m_rectEllipse* and *m_nColor* are set in the view's constructor, and the color is changed in the *OnLButtonDown* member function.

NOTE: By convention, MFC library nonstatic class data member names begin with *m_*.

TIP: Why not use a global variable for the view's state? Because if you did, you'd be in trouble if your application had multiple views. Besides, encapsulating data in objects is a big part of what object-oriented programming is all about.

Initializing a View Class Data Member

As Appendix A points out, the most efficient place to initialize a class data member is in the constructor, like this:

```
CMyView::CMyView() : m_rectEllipse(0, 0, 200, 200) { }
```

You could initialize *m_nColor* with the same syntax. Because we're using a built-in type (integer), the generated code is the same if you use an assignment statement in the constructor body.

Invalid Rectangle Theory

The *OnLButtonDown* function could toggle the value of *m_nColor* all day, but the *OnDraw* function won't get called unless the user resizes the view window. The *OnLButtonDown* function must call the *InvalidateRect* function (a member function that the view class inherits from *CWnd*). *InvalidateRect* triggers a Windows WM_PAINT message, which is mapped in the *CView* class to call to the virtual *OnDraw* function. If necessary, *OnDraw* can access the "invalid rectangle" parameter that was passed to *InvalidateRect*.

> ### For Win32 Programmers
>
> The MFC library makes it easy to attach your own <u>state</u> <u>variables</u> to a window through C++ class data members. In Win32 programming, the *WNDCLASS* members *cbClsExtra* and *cbWndExtra* are available for this purpose, but the code for using this mechanism is so complex that developers tend to use global variables instead.

There are two ways to optimize painting in Windows. First of all, you must be aware that Windows updates only those pixels that are inside the invalid rectangle. Thus, the smaller you make the invalid rectangle (in the *OnLButtonDown* handler, for instance), the quicker it can be repainted. Second, it's a waste of time to execute drawing instructions outside the invalid rectangle. Your *OnDraw* function could call the *CDC* member function *GetClipBox* to determine the invalid rectangle, and then it could avoid drawing objects outside it. Remember that *OnDraw* is being called not only in response to your *InvalidateRect* call but also when the user resizes or exposes the window. Thus, *OnDraw* is responsible for all drawing in a window, and it has to adapt to whatever invalid rectangle it gets.

The Window's Client Area

A window has a rectangular <u>client</u> <u>area</u> that excludes the border, caption bar, and menu bar. The *CWnd* member function *GetClientRect* supplies you with the client-area dimensions. Normally, you're not allowed to draw outside the client area, and most mouse messages are received only when the mouse cursor is in the client area.

CRect, *CPoint*, and *CSize* Arithmetic

The *CRect*, *CPoint*, and *CSize* classes are derived from the Windows *RECT*, *POINT*, and *SIZE* structures, and thus they inherit public integer data members as follows:

CRect	*left, top, right, bottom*
CPoint	*x, y*
CSize	*cx, cy*

If you look in the *Microsoft Foundation Class Library Reference,* you will see that these three classes have a number of overloaded operators. (Overloaded operators are explained in Appendix A.) You can, among other things, do the following:

- Add a *CSize* object to a *CPoint* object

- Subtract a *CSize* object from a *CPoint* object

- Subtract one *CPoint* object from another, yielding a *CSize* object

- Add a *CPoint* object to a *CRect* object

- Subtract a *CPoint* object from a *CRect* object

The *CRect* class has member functions that relate to the *CSize* and *CPoint* classes. For example, the *TopLeft* member function returns a *CPoint* object, and the *Size* member function returns a *CSize* object. From this, you can begin to see that a *CSize* object is the "difference between two *CPoint* objects" and that you can "bias" a *CRect* object by a *CPoint* object. The C++ compiler enforces the rules above; it will not, for example, let you add a *CSize* object to a *CRect* object.

Is a Point Inside a Rectangle?

The *CRect* class has a member function *PtInRect* that tests a point to see whether it's inside a rectangle. The second *OnLButtonDown* parameter (*point*) is an object of class *CPoint* that represents the cursor location in the client area of the window. If you want to know whether that point is inside the *m_rectEllipse* rectangle, you can use *PtInRect* like this:

```
if (m_rectEllipse.PtInRect(point)) {
    // point is inside rectangle
}
```

As you'll soon see, however, this simple logic applies only if you're working in device coordinates (which you are at this stage).

The *CRect LPRECT* Operator

If you read the *Microsoft Foundation Class Library Reference* carefully, you will notice that *CWnd::InvalidateRect* takes an *LPRECT* parameter (a pointer to a *RECT* structure), not a *CRect* parameter. A *CRect* parameter is allowed because the *CRect* class defines an overloaded operator, *LPRECT()*, that takes the address of a *CRect* object, which is equivalent to the address of a *RECT* object. Thus, the compiler converts *CRect* arguments to *LPRECT* arguments when necessary. You call functions as though they had *CRect* reference parameters. The view member function code

```
CRect rectClient;
GetClientRect(rectClient);
```

retrieves the client rectangle coordinates and stores them in *rectClient*.

Is a Point Inside an Ellipse?

The EX04A code checks to see whether the mouse hit is inside the rectangle. If you want to make a better test, you can find out whether the hit is inside the ellipse. To do this, you must construct an object of class *CRgn* that corresponds to the ellipse, and then use the *PtInRegion* function instead of *PtInRect*. Here's the code:

```
CRgn rgn;
rgn.CreateEllipticRgnIndirect(m_rectEllipse);
if (rgn.PtInRegion(point)) {
    // point is inside ellipse
}
```

Note that the *CreateEllipticRgnIndirect* function is another function that takes an *LPRECT* parameter. It builds a special region structure within Windows that represents an elliptical or a polygonal region inside a window. That structure is then attached to the C++ *CRgn* object in your program.

The EX04A Example

In the EX04A example, an ellipse (which happens to be a circle) changes color when the user presses the left mouse button while the mouse cursor is inside the rectangle that bounds the ellipse. You'll see the use of view class data members to hold the view's state, and you'll use the *InvalidateRect* function.

In the Chapter 3 example, drawing in the window depended on only one function, *OnDraw*. The EX04A example requires three customized functions (including the constructor) and two data members. The complete *CEx04aView* header and source code files are listed in Figure 4-1. (The steps for creating the program are shown after the program listings.) All changes to the original AppWizard output are shaded in gray.

EX04AVIEW.H

```
class CEx04aView : public CView
{
private:
    CRect m_rectEllipse;
    int   m_nColor;
protected: // create from serialization only
    CEx04aView();
    DECLARE_DYNCREATE(CEx04aView)
```

Figure 4-1. *(continued)*
The CEx04aView *header and source code files.*

Figure 4-1. *continued*

```
// Attributes
public:
    CEx04aDoc* GetDocument();

// Operations
public:

// Overrides
    // ClassWizard generated virtual function overrides
    //{{AFX_VIRTUAL(CEx04aView)
    public:
    virtual void OnDraw(CDC* pDC);  // overridden to draw this view
    virtual BOOL PreCreateWindow(CREATESTRUCT& cs);
    protected:
    virtual BOOL OnPreparePrinting(CPrintInfo* pInfo);
    virtual void OnBeginPrinting(CDC* pDC, CPrintInfo* pInfo);
    virtual void OnEndPrinting(CDC* pDC, CPrintInfo* pInfo);
    //}}AFX_VIRTUAL

// Implementation
public:
    virtual ~CEx04aView();
#ifdef _DEBUG
    virtual void AssertValid() const;
    virtual void Dump(CDumpContext& dc) const;
#endif

protected:

// Generated message map functions
protected:
    //{{AFX_MSG(CEx04aView)
    afx_msg void OnLButtonDown(UINT nFlags, CPoint point);
    //}}AFX_MSG
    DECLARE_MESSAGE_MAP()
};

#ifndef _DEBUG  // debug version in ex04aView.cpp
inline CEx04aDoc* CEx04aView::GetDocument()
    { return (CEx04aDoc*)m_pDocument; }
#endif
```

(continued)

Figure 4-1. *continued*

EX04AVIEW.CPP

```cpp
// ex04aView.cpp : implementation of the CEx04aView class
//

#include "StdAfx.h"
#include "ex04a.h"

#include "ex04aDoc.h"
#include "ex04aView.h"

#ifdef _DEBUG
#undef THIS_FILE
static char THIS_FILE[] = __FILE__;
#endif

/////////////////////////////////////////////////////////////////////
// CEx04aView

IMPLEMENT_DYNCREATE(CEx04aView, CView)

BEGIN_MESSAGE_MAP(CEx04aView, CView)
    //{{AFX_MSG_MAP(CEx04aView)
    ON_WM_LBUTTONDOWN()
    //}}AFX_MSG_MAP
    // Standard printing commands
    ON_COMMAND(ID_FILE_PRINT, CView::OnFilePrint)
    ON_COMMAND(ID_FILE_PRINT_DIRECT, CView::OnFilePrint)
    ON_COMMAND(ID_FILE_PRINT_PREVIEW, CView::OnFilePrintPreview)
END_MESSAGE_MAP()

/////////////////////////////////////////////////////////////////////
// CEx04aView construction/destruction

CEx04aView::CEx04aView() : m_rectEllipse(0, 0, 200, 200)
{
    m_nColor = GRAY_BRUSH;
}

CEx04aView::~CEx04aView()
{
}

BOOL CEx04aView::PreCreateWindow(CREATESTRUCT& cs)
{
```

(continued)

Figure 4-1. *continued*

```
        // TODO: Modify the Window class or styles here by modifying
        //   the CREATESTRUCT cs

        return CView::PreCreateWindow(cs);
}


/////////////////////////////////////////////////////////////////////////
// CEx04aView drawing

void CEx04aView::OnDraw(CDC* pDC)
{
        pDC->SelectStockObject(m_nColor);
        pDC->Ellipse(m_rectEllipse);
}


/////////////////////////////////////////////////////////////////////////
// CEx04aView printing

BOOL CEx04aView::OnPreparePrinting(CPrintInfo* pInfo)
{
        // default preparation
        return DoPreparePrinting(pInfo);
}


void CEx04aView::OnBeginPrinting(CDC* /*pDC*/, CPrintInfo* /*pInfo*/)
{
        // TODO: add extra initialization before printing
}


void CEx04aView::OnEndPrinting(CDC* /*pDC*/, CPrintInfo* /*pInfo*/)
{
        // TODO: add cleanup after printing
}


/////////////////////////////////////////////////////////////////////////
// CEx04aView diagnostics

#ifdef _DEBUG
void CEx04aView::AssertValid() const
{
        CView::AssertValid();
}


void CEx04aView::Dump(CDumpContext& dc) const
```

(continued)

Figure 4-1. *continued*

```
{
    CView::Dump(dc);
}


CEx04aDoc* CEx04aView::GetDocument() // non-debug version is inline
{
    ASSERT(m_pDocument->IsKindOf(RUNTIME_CLASS(CEx04aDoc)));
    return (CEx04aDoc*)m_pDocument;
}
#endif //_DEBUG


/////////////////////////////////////////////////////////////////////
// CEx04aView message handlers

void CEx04aView::OnLButtonDown(UINT nFlags, CPoint point)
{
    if (m_rectEllipse.PtInRect(point)) {
      if (m_nColor == GRAY_BRUSH) {
        m_nColor = WHITE_BRUSH;
      }
      else {
        m_nColor = GRAY_BRUSH;
      }
      InvalidateRect(m_rectEllipse);
    }
}
```

Using ClassWizard with EX04A

Look at the following ex04aView.h source code:

```
//{{AFX_MSG(CEx04aView)
afx_msg void OnLButtonDown(UINT nFlags, CPoint point);
//}}AFX_MSG
```

Now look at the following ex04aView.cpp source code:

```
//{{AFX_MSG_MAP(CEx04aView)
ON_WM_LBUTTONDOWN()
//}}AFX_MSG_MAP
```

AppWizard generated the funny-looking comment lines for the benefit of ClassWizard. ClassWizard adds message handler prototypes between the *AFX_MSG* "brackets," and it also adds message map entries between the

AFX_MSG_MAP brackets. In addition, ClassWizard generates a skeleton *OnLButtonDown* member function in ex04aView.cpp, complete with the correct parameter declarations and return type.

Notice how the AppWizard–ClassWizard combination is different from a conventional code generator. You run a conventional code generator only once and then edit the resulting code. You run AppWizard to generate the application only once, but you can run ClassWizard as many times as necessary, and you can edit the code at any time. You're safe as long as you don't alter what's inside the *AFX_MSG* and *AFX_MSG_MAP* brackets.

Using AppWizard and ClassWizard Together

The following steps illustrate how you use AppWizard and ClassWizard together to create this application:

1. **Run AppWizard to create EX04A.** Use AppWizard to generate a project named EX04A in the \VCPP32\EX04A subdirectory. The options and the default class names are shown here:

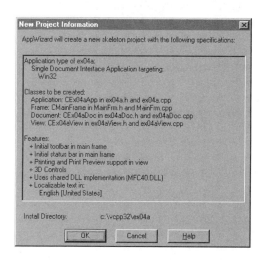

2. **Add the *m_rectEllipse* and *m_nColor* data members in ex04a-View.h.** Insert the following code at the start of the *CEx04aView* class declaration:

```
private:
    CRect m_rectEllipse;
    int m_nColor;
```

3. Use ClassWizard to add a *CEx04aView* class message handler. Be sure you have opened the EX04A project, and choose ClassWizard from the View menu of the Developer Studio or click the toolbar button shown here:

When the ClassWizard dialog box appears, be sure that the *CEx04aView* class is selected, as shown in the illustration below. Now click on *CEx04a-View* at the top of the Object IDs list box, and then scroll down past the virtual functions in the Messages list box and double-click on WM_LBUT-TONDOWN. The *OnLButtonDown* function name should appear in the Member Functions list box, and the message name should be displayed in bold in the Messages list box.

Here's the ClassWizard dialog box:

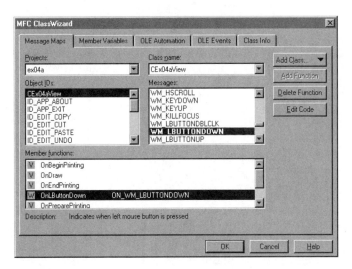

NOTE: Instead of using ClassWizard, you can map the function from the "wizard bar" at the top of the ex04aView.cpp source code window.

4. Edit the *OnLButtonDown* code in ex04aView.cpp. Click the Edit Code button. ClassWizard opens an edit window for ex04aView.cpp in the Developer Studio and positions the cursor on the newly generated

OnLButtonDown member function. The following shaded code (that you type in) replaces the previous code:

```
void CEx04aView::OnLButtonDown(UINT nFlags, CPoint point)
{
    if (m_rectEllipse.PtInRect(point)) {
        if (m_nColor == GRAY_BRUSH) {
          m_nColor = WHITE_BRUSH;
        }
        else {
          m_nColor = GRAY_BRUSH;
        }
        InvalidateRect(m_rectEllipse);
    }
}
```

5. Edit the constructor and the *OnDraw* function in ex04aView.cpp.
The following shaded code (that you type in) replaces the previous code:

```
CEx04aView::CEx04aView() : m_rectEllipse(0, 0, 200, 200)
{
    m_nColor = GRAY_BRUSH;
}
    ⋮
void CEx04aView::OnDraw(CDC* pDC)
{
    pDC->SelectStockObject(m_nColor);
    pDC->Ellipse(m_rectEllipse);
}
```

6. Build and run the EX04A program. In the Developer Studio, choose
Build from the Build menu, or click the button shown here:

and then choose Execute Ex04a.exe from the Build menu. The resulting
program responds to presses of the left mouse button by changing the
color of the circle in the view window. (Don't press the mouse's left button
quickly in succession; Windows interprets this as a double click rather
than two single clicks.)

For Win32 Programmers

A conventional Windows-based application registers a series of <u>window classes</u> (not the same as a C++ classes) and, in the process, assigns a unique function, known as a *WndProc* function, to the class. Each time the application calls *CreateWindow* to create a window, it specifies a window class as a parameter and thus links the newly created window to a *WndProc* function. This function, called each time Windows sends a message to the window, tests the message code that is passed as a parameter and then executes the appropriate code to handle the message.

The MFC application framework has a single window class and *WndProc* function for most window types. This *WndProc* function looks up the window handle (passed as a parameter) in the MFC <u>handle map</u> to get the corresponding C++ window object pointer. The *WndProc* function then uses the MFC <u>runtime class</u> system (see Appendix C) to determine the C++ class of the window object. Next it locates the handler function in static tables created by the dispatch map functions, and last it calls the handler function with the correct window object selected.

Mapping Modes

Up to now, your drawing units have been display pixels, also known as <u>device coordinates</u>. The EX04A drawing units are pixels because the device context has the default <u>mapping mode</u>, *MM_TEXT*, assigned to it. The statement

```
pDC->Rectangle(CRect(0, 0, 200, 200));
```

draws a square of 200 by 200 pixels, with its top left corner at the top left of the window's client area. (Positive *y* values increase as you move down the window.) This square would look smaller on a high-resolution display of 1024 by 768 pixels than it would on a standard VGA display that is 640 by 480 pixels, and it would look tiny if printed on a laser printer with 600-dpi resolution. (Try EX04A's Print Preview feature to see for yourself.)

What if you want the square to be 4 by 4 centimeters (cm), regardless of the display device? Windows provides a number of other mapping modes, or coordinate systems, that can be associated with the device context. If you assign the *MM_HIMETRIC* mapping mode, for example, a logical unit is 1/100 millimeter (mm) instead of 1 pixel. In the *MM_HIMETRIC* mapping mode, the *y* axis runs in the opposite direction to that in the *MM_TEXT* mode: *y* values decrease as you move down. Thus, a 4-by-4-cm square is drawn in logical coordinates this way:

```
pDC->Rectangle(CRect(0, 0, 4000, -4000));
```

Looks easy, doesn't it? Well, it isn't, because you can't work only in logical coordinates. Your program is always switching between device coordinates and logical coordinates, and you need to know when to convert between them. This section gives you a few rules that could make your programming life easier. First you need to know what mapping modes Windows gives you.

The *MM_TEXT* Mapping Mode

At first glance, *MM_TEXT* appears to be no mapping mode at all, but rather another name for device coordinates. Almost. In *MM_TEXT*, coordinates map to pixels, values of x increase as you move right, and values of y increase as you move down, but you're allowed to change the origin through calls to the *CDC* functions *SetViewportOrg* and *SetWindowOrg*. Here's some code that sets the window origin to (*100, 100*) in logical coordinate space and then draws a 200-by-200-pixel square offset by (*100, 100*). (An illustration of the output is shown in Figure 4-2.) The logical point (*100, 100*) maps to the device point (*0, 0*). This is the kind of transformation that a scrolling window uses.

```
void CMyView::OnDraw(CDC* pDC)
{
    pDC->SetMapMode(MM_TEXT);
    pDC->SetWindowOrg(CPoint(100, 100));
    pDC->Rectangle(CRect(100, 100, 300, 300));
}
```

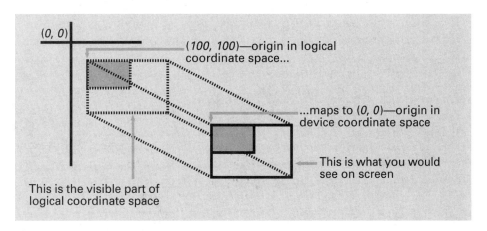

Figure 4-2.
A square drawn after the origin has been moved to (100, 100).

The Fixed Scale Mapping Modes

One important group of Windows mapping modes provides fixed scaling. You have already seen that, in the *MM_HIMETRIC* mapping mode, *x* values increase as you move right, and *y* values decrease as you move down. All fixed mapping modes follow this convention, and you can't change it. The only difference among the fixed mapping modes is the actual scale factor, listed in the table shown here:

Mapping Mode	Logical Unit
MM_LOENGLISH	0.01 inch
MM_HIENGLISH	0.001 inch
MM_LOMETRIC	0.1 mm
MM_HIMETRIC	0.01 mm
MM_TWIPS	1/1440 inch

The last mapping mode, *MM_TWIPS*, is most often used with printers. One <u>twip</u> unit is 1/20 point. (A point is a type measurement unit that equals approximately 1/72 inch.) If the mapping mode is *MM_TWIPS* and you want, for example, 12-point type, set the character height to 12 × 20, or 240 twips.

The Variable Scale Mapping Modes

Windows provides two mapping modes, *MM_ISOTROPIC* and *MM_ANISO-TROPIC*, that allow you to change the scale factor as well as the origin. With these mapping modes, your drawing can change size as the user changes the size of the window. Also, if you invert the scale of one axis, you can "flip" an image about the other axis, and you can define your own arbitrary fixed scale factors.

With the *MM_ISOTROPIC* mode, a 1:1 aspect ratio is always preserved. In other words, a circle is always a circle as the scale factor changes. With the *MM_ANISOTROPIC* mode, the *x* and *y* scale factors can change independently. Circles can be squished into ellipses.

Here's an *OnDraw* function that draws an ellipse that fits exactly in its window:

```
void CMyView::OnDraw(CDC* pDC)
{
    CRect rectClient;

    GetClientRect(rectClient);
    pDC->SetMapMode(MM_ANISOTROPIC);
```

```
    pDC->SetWindowExt(1000, 1000);
    pDC->SetViewportExt(rectClient.right, -rectClient.bottom);
    pDC-SetViewportOrg(rectClient.right / 2, rectClient.bottom / 2);

    pDC->Ellipse(CRect(-500, -500, 500, 500));
}
```

What's going on here? The functions *SetWindowExt* and *SetViewportExt* work together to set the scale, based on the window's current client rectangle returned by the *GetClientRect* function. The resulting window size is exactly 1000 by 1000 logical units. The *SetViewportOrg* function sets the origin to the center of the window. Thus, a centered ellipse with a radius of 500 logical units fills the window exactly, as illustrated in Figure 4-3.

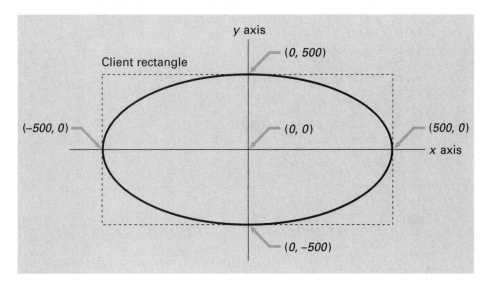

Figure 4-3.
A centered ellipse drawn in the MM_ANISOTROPIC *mapping mode.*

Here are the formulas for converting logical units to device units:

x scale factor = *x* viewport extent / *x* window extent

y scale factor = *y* viewport extent / *y* window extent

device *x* = logical *x* × *x* scale factor + *x* origin offset

device *y* = logical *y* × *y* scale factor + *y* origin offset

Suppose the window is 448 pixels wide (*clientRect.right*). The right edge of the ellipse's client rectangle is 500 logical units from the origin. The *x* scale factor is 448/1000, and the *x* origin offset is 448/2 device units. If you use the formulas above, the right edge of the ellipse's client rectangle comes out to

448 device units, the right edge of the window. The *x* scale factor is expressed as a ratio (viewport extent/window extent) because Windows device coordinates are integers, not floating-point values. The extent values are meaningless by themselves.

If you substitute *MM_ISOTROPIC* for *MM_ANISOTROPIC* in the preceding example, the "ellipse" is always a circle, as shown in Figure 4-4. It expands to fit the smallest dimension of the window rectangle.

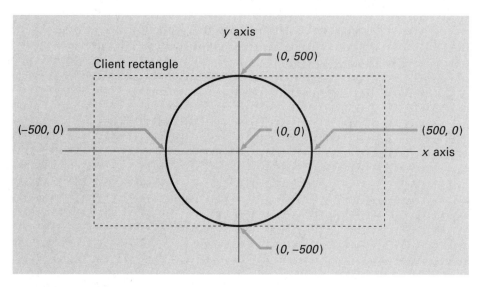

Figure 4-4.
A centered ellipse drawn in the MM_ISOTROPIC *mapping mode.*

Coordinate Conversion

Once you set the mapping mode (plus the origin) of a device context, you can use logical coordinate parameters for most *CDC* member functions. If you get the mouse cursor coordinates from a WM_MOUSEMOVE message (the *point* parameter in *OnLButtonDown*), for example, you're dealing with device coordinates. Many other MFC functions, particularly the member functions of class *CRect*, work correctly only with device coordinates.

Furthermore, you're likely to need a third set of coordinates that we will call <u>physical</u> <u>coordinates</u>. Why another set? Suppose you're using the *MM_LOENGLISH* mapping mode in which a logical unit is 0.01 inch, but an inch on the screen represents a foot (12 inches) in the real world. Now suppose the user works in inches and decimal fractions. A user measurement of 26.75 inches translates into 223 logical units, which must be ultimately translated to device coordinates. You will want to store the physical coordinates as either floating-point numbers or scaled long integers to avoid rounding-off errors.

For the physical-to-logical translation you're on your own, but the Windows GDI takes care of the logical-to-device translation for you. The *CDC* functions *LPtoDP* and *DPtoLP* translate between the two systems, assuming the device context mapping mode and associated parameters have already been set. Your job is to decide when to use each system. Here are a few rules of thumb:

- Assume that *CDC* member functions take logical coordinate parameters.

- Assume that *CWnd* member functions take device coordinate parameters.

- Do all hit-test operations in device coordinates. Define regions in device coordinates. Functions such as *CRect::PtInRect* work only with non-negative coordinates. Windows, not the MFC library, imposes this last restriction.

- Store long-term values in logical or physical coordinates. If you store a point in device coordinates and the user scrolls a window, that point is no longer valid.

Suppose you need to know whether the mouse cursor is inside a rectangle when the user presses the left mouse button. Here's the code:

```
// m_rect is CRect data member of the derived view class in MM_LOENGLISH
//   logical coordinates

void CMyView::OnLButtonDown(UINT nFlags, CPoint point)
{
    CRect rect = m_rect; // rect is a temporary copy of m_rect;
    CClientDC dc(this);  // this is how we get a device context
            // for SetMapMode and LPtoDP -- more in next chapter
    dc.SetMapMode(MM_LOENGLISH);
    dc.LPtoDP(rect);     // rect is now in device coordinates
    if (rect.PtInRect(point)) {
      TRACE("mouse cursor is inside the rectangle\n");
    }
}
```

Notice the use of the *TRACE* macro (discussed in Chapter 3).

> **N O T E :**   As you'll soon see, it's better to set the mapping mode in the virtual *CView* function *OnPrepareDC* instead of in the *OnDraw* function.

The EX04B Example—
Converting to the *MM_HIMETRIC* Mapping Mode

EX04B is EX04A converted to *MM_HIMETRIC* coordinates. The EX04B project on the companion CD-ROM uses new class names and filenames, but the instructions here take you through modifying the EX04A code. EX04B also performs a hit test so that the ellipse changes color only when you click inside the bounding rectangle.

1. Use ClassWizard to override the virtual *OnPrepareDC* function.

ClassWizard can override virtual functions for selected MFC base classes, including *CView*. It generates the correct function prototype in the class's header file and a skeleton function in the CPP file. Just select the class name in the Object IDs list, and then double-click on the *OnPrepareDC* function in the Messages list. Edit the function as shown here:

```
void CEx04aView::OnPrepareDC(CDC* pDC, CPrintInfo* pInfo)
{
    pDC->SetMapMode(MM_HIMETRIC);
    CView::OnPrepareDC(pDC, pInfo);
}
```

The application framework calls the virtual *OnPrepareDC* function just before it calls *OnDraw*.

2. Edit the view class constructor.
You must change the coordinate values for the ellipse rectangle. That rectangle is now 4 by 4 centimeters instead of 200 by 200 pixels. Note that the *y* value must be negative; otherwise, the ellipse will be drawn on the "virtual screen" right above your monitor! Change the values as shown here:

```
CEx04aView::CEx04aView() : m_rectEllipse(0, 0, 4000, -4000)
{
    m_nColor = GRAY_BRUSH;
}
```

3. Edit the *OnLButtonDown* function.
This function must now convert the ellipse rectangle to device coordinates in order to do the hit test. Change the function as shown here:

```
void CEx04aView::OnLButtonDown(UINT nFlags, CPoint point)
{
    CClientDC dc(this);
    OnPrepareDC(&dc);
    CRect rectDevice = m_rectEllipse;
    dc.LPtoDP(rectDevice);
```

```
if (rectDevice.PtInRect(point)) {
  if (m_nColor == GRAY_BRUSH) {
    m_nColor = WHITE_BRUSH;
  }
  else {
    m_nColor = GRAY_BRUSH;
  }
  InvalidateRect(rectDevice);
}
}
```

4. Build and run the EX04B program. The output should look similar to the output from EX04A, except that the ellipse size will be different. If you try using Print Preview again, the ellipse should appear much larger than it did before.

A Scrolling View Window

As the lack of scroll bars in EX04A and EX04B indicates, the MFC *CView* class, the base class of *CEx04bView*, doesn't directly support scrolling. The MFC library has another class, *CScrollView*, that does support scrolling. *CScrollView* is derived from *CView*. We'll create a new program, EX04C, that uses *CScrollView* in place of *CView*. All the coordinate conversion code you added in EX04B "sets you up" for scrolling.

The *CScrollView* class supports scrolling from the scroll bars but not from the keyboard. It's easy enough to add keyboard scrolling, so we'll do it.

A Window Is Larger than What You See

If you use the mouse to shrink the size of an ordinary window, the contents of the window remain anchored at the top left of the window, and items at the bottom and/or on the right of the window disappear. When you expand the window, the items reappear. You can correctly conclude that a window is larger than the <u>viewport</u> that you see on the screen. The viewport doesn't have to be anchored at the top left of the window area. Through the use of the *CWnd* functions *ScrollWindow* and *SetWindowOrg*, the *CScrollView* class allows you to move the viewport anywhere within the window, including areas above and to the left of the origin.

Scroll Bars

Microsoft Windows makes it easy to display scroll bars at the edges of a window, but Windows by itself doesn't make any attempt to connect those scroll bars to their window. That's where the *CScrollView* class fits in. *CScrollView* member functions process the WM_HSCROLL and WM_VSCROLL messages sent by the scroll bars to the view. Those functions move the viewport within the window and do all the necessary housekeeping.

Scrolling Alternatives

The *CScrollView* class supports a particular kind of scrolling—one in which there is one big window and a small viewport. Each item is assigned a unique position in this big window. But what if you have 10,000 address lines to display? Instead of having a window 10,000 lines long, you probably want a smaller window with scrolling logic that selects only as many lines as the screen can display. In that case, you should write your own scrolling view class derived from *CView*.

> NOTE: As you'll see in Chapter 29, a *CScrollView*-derived view can easily and efficiently accommodate as many as 2000 lines.

The *OnInitialUpdate* Function

You'll be seeing more of the *OnInitialUpdate* function when you study the document–view architecture, starting in Chapter 15. The virtual *OnInitialUpdate* function is important here because it is the first function the framework calls after your view window is fully created but before it calls *OnDraw* for the first time. It's the place for setting the logical size and mapping mode for a scrolling view. You set these parameters with a call to the *CScrollView::SetScrollSizes* function.

Accepting Keyboard Input

Keyboard input is really a two-step process. Windows sends WM_KEYDOWN and WM_KEYUP messages, with virtual key codes, to a window, but before they get to the window, they are translated. If an ANSI character is typed (resulting in a WM_KEYDOWN message), the translation function checks the keyboard shift status and then sends a WM_CHAR message with the proper code, either uppercase or lowercase. Cursor keys and function keys don't have codes, so there's no translation to do. The window gets only the WM_KEYDOWN and WM_KEYUP messages.

You can use ClassWizard to map all these messages to your view. If you're expecting characters, map WM_CHAR; if you're expecting other keystrokes, map WM_KEYDOWN. The MFC library neatly supplies the code or virtual key code as a handler function parameter.

The EX04C Example—Scrolling

The goal of EX04C is to make a logical window 20 centimeters wide by 30 centimeters high. The program draws the same ellipse that it drew in the EX04B project. You could edit the EX04B source files to convert the *CView* base class to a *CScrollView* base class, but it's easier to start over with AppWizard. AppWizard generates the *OnInitialUpdate* override function for you. Here are the steps:

1. **Run AppWizard to create EX04C.** Use AppWizard to generate a program named EX04C in the \VCPP32\EX04C subdirectory. In AppWizard Step 6, set the *CEx04cView* base class to *CScrollView*, as shown here:

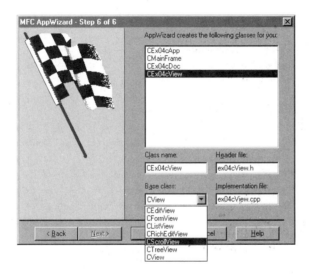

2. **Add the *m_rectEllipse* and *m_nColor* data members in ex04c-View.h.** Insert the following code at the start of the *CEx04cView* class declaration:

```
private:
    CRect m_rectEllipse;
    int m_nColor;
```

These are the same data members that were added in the EX04A and EX04B projects.

3. **Modify the AppWizard-generated *OnInitialUpdate* function.** Edit *OnInitialUpdate* in ex04cView.cpp as shown on the following page.

```
void CEx04cView::OnInitialUpdate()
{
    CScrollView::OnInitialUpdate();
    CSize sizeTotal(20000, 30000); // 20 by 30 cm
    CSize sizePage(sizeTotal.cx / 2, sizeTotal.cy / 2);
    CSize sizeLine(sizeTotal.cx / 50, sizeTotal.cy / 50);
    SetScrollSizes(MM_HIMETRIC, sizeTotal, sizePage, sizeLine);
}
```

4. **Use ClassWizard to add a message handler for the WM_KEYDOWN
   message.**   ClassWizard generates the member function *OnKeyDown*
   along with the necessary message map entries and prototypes. Edit the
   code as follows:

```
void CEx04cView::OnKeyDown(UINT nChar, UINT nRepCnt, UINT nFlags)
{
    switch (nChar) {
    case VK_HOME:
        OnVScroll(SB_TOP, 0, NULL);
        OnHScroll(SB_LEFT, 0, NULL);
        break;
    case VK_END:
        OnVScroll(SB_BOTTOM, 0, NULL);
        OnHScroll(SB_RIGHT, 0, NULL);
        break;
    case VK_UP:
        OnVScroll(SB_LINEUP, 0, NULL);
        break;
    case VK_DOWN:
        OnVScroll(SB_LINEDOWN, 0, NULL);
        break;
    case VK_PRIOR:
        OnVScroll(SB_PAGEUP, 0, NULL);
        break;
    case VK_NEXT:
        OnVScroll(SB_PAGEDOWN, 0, NULL);
        break;
    case VK_LEFT:
        OnHScroll(SB_LINELEFT, 0, NULL);
        break;
    case VK_RIGHT:
        OnHScroll(SB_LINERIGHT, 0, NULL);
        break;
    default:
        break;
    }
}
```

5. Edit the constructor and the *OnDraw* function. Change the AppWizard-generated constructor and the *OnDraw* function in ex04cView.cpp as follows:

```
CEx04cView::CEx04cView() : m_rectEllipse(0, 0, 4000, -4000)
{
    m_nColor = GRAY_BRUSH;
}
    ⋮
void CEx04cView::OnDraw(CDC* pDC)
{
    pDC->SelectStockObject(m_nColor);
    pDC->Ellipse(m_rectEllipse);
}
```

These functions are identical to those in the EX04B project.

6. Map the WM_LBUTTONDOWN message and edit the handler. Make the following changes to the AppWizard-generated code:

```
void CEx04cView::OnLButtonDown(UINT nFlags, CPoint point)
{
    CClientDC dc(this);
    OnPrepareDC(&dc);
    CRect rectDevice = m_rectEllipse;
    dc.LPtoDP(rectDevice);
    if (rectDevice.PtInRect(point)) {
      if (m_nColor == GRAY_BRUSH) {
        m_nColor = WHITE_BRUSH;
      }
      else {
        m_nColor = GRAY_BRUSH;
      }
      InvalidateRect(rectDevice);
    }
}
```

This function is identical to the *OnLButtonDown* handler in the EX04B project. It calls *OnPrepareDC* as before, but there is something different. The *CEx03aView* class doesn't have an overridden *OnPrepareDC* function, so the call goes to *CScrollView::OnPrepareDC*. That function sets the mapping mode based on the first parameter to *SetScrollSizes*, and it sets the window origin based on the current scroll position. Even if your scroll view used the *MM_TEXT* mapping mode, you'd still need the coordinate conversion logic to adjust for the origin offset.

7. Build and run the EX04C program. Check to be sure the mouse hit logic is working even if the circle is scrolled partially out of the window. Also check the keyboard logic. The output should look like this:

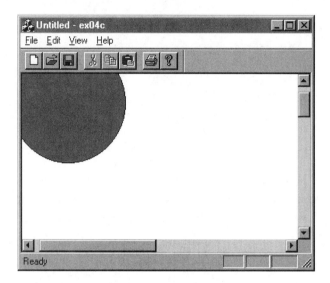

Other Windows Messages

The MFC library directly supports about 140 Windows message-handling functions. In addition, you can define your own messages. You will see plenty of message-handling examples in later chapters, including handlers for menu items, child window controls, and so forth. In the meantime, five special Windows messages deserve special attention.

The WM_CREATE Message

This is the first message that Windows sends to a view. It is sent when the window's *Create* function is called by the framework, so the window creation is not finished and the window is not visible. Therefore, your *OnCreate* handler cannot call Windows functions that depend on the window being completely alive. You can call such functions in an overridden *OnInitialUpdate* function, but you must be aware that in an SDI application, *OnInitialUpdate* can be called more than once in a view's lifetime.

The WM_CLOSE Message

Windows sends the WM_CLOSE message when the user closes a window from the system menu and when a parent window is closed. If you implement the *OnClose* message map function in your derived view class, you can control the closing process. If, for example, you need to prompt the user to save changes to a file, you do it in *OnClose*. Only when you have determined that it is safe to close the window do you call the base class *OnClose* function, which continues the close process. The view object and the corresponding window are both still active.

> **TIP:** When you're using the full application framework, you probably won't use the WM_CLOSE message handler. You can override the *CDocument::SaveModified* virtual function instead, as part of the application framework's highly structured program exit procedure.

The WM_QUERYENDSESSION Message

Windows sends the WM_QUERYENDSESSION message to all running applications when the user exits Windows. The *OnQueryEndSession* message map function handles it. If you write a handler for WM_CLOSE, write one for WM_QUERYENDSESSION too.

The WM_DESTROY Message

Windows sends this message after the WM_CLOSE message, and the *OnDestroy* message map function handles it. When your program receives this message, it should assume that the view window is no longer visible on the screen but that it is still active and its child windows are still active. Use this message handler to do cleanup that depends on the existence of the underlying window. Be sure to call the base class *OnDestroy* function. You cannot "abort" the window destruction process in your view's *OnDestroy* function. *OnClose* is the place to do that.

The WM_NCDESTROY Message

This is the last message that Windows sends when the window is being destroyed. All child windows have already been destroyed. You can do final processing in *OnNcDestroy* that doesn't depend on a window being active. Be sure to call the base class *OnNcDestroy* function.

> **TIP:** Do not try to destroy a dynamically allocated window object in *OnNcDestroy*. That job is reserved for a special *CWnd* virtual function, *PostNcDestroy*, that the base class *OnNcDestroy* calls. MFC Technical Note #17 in Books Online gives hints on when it's appropriate to destroy a window object.

The Graphics Device Interface (GDI), Colors, and Fonts

You've already seen some elements of the GDI. Any time your program draws directly on the display or the printer, it must use the GDI functions. The GDI has functions for drawing points, lines, rectangles, polygons, ellipses, bitmaps, and text. This chapter gives you the information you need to use the GDI effectively in the Visual C++ environment. You can draw circles and squares intuitively once you study the available functions, but text programming is more difficult. In this chapter, you'll see how to use fonts effectively on both the display and the printer. You must wait until Chapter 18, however, to see the details of how the framework controls the printer.

The Device Context Classes

In Chapters 3 and 4, the view class's *OnDraw* member function was passed a pointer to a device context object. *OnDraw* selected a brush and then drew an ellipse. The Windows device context is the key GDI element that represents a physical device. Each C++ device context object has an associated Windows device context, identified by a handle of type *HDC*.

Microsoft Foundation Class (MFC) Library version 4.0 has a number of device context classes. The base class *CDC* has all the member functions (including some virtual functions) that you'll need for drawing. Except for the oddball *CMetaFileDC* class, derived classes are distinct only in their constructors and destructors. If you (or the application framework) construct an object of a derived device context class, you can pass a *CDC* pointer to a function such as *OnDraw*. For the display, the usual derived classes are *CClientDC* and *CWindowDC*. For other devices, such as a printer or a memory buffer, you construct an object of the base class *CDC*.

The "virtualness" of the *CDC* class is an important feature of the application framework. In Chapter 18, you'll see how easy it is to write code that works with both the printer and the display. A statement in *OnDraw* such as

```
pDC->TextOut(0, 0, "Hello");
```

sends text to the display, the printer, or the Print Preview window depending on the class of the object referenced by the *CView::OnDraw* function's *pDC* parameter.

For display and printer device context objects, the application framework attaches the handle to the object. For other device contexts, such as the memory device context that you'll see in Chapter 10, you must call a member function after construction in order to attach the handle.

The Display Context Classes *CClientDC* and *CWindowDC*

Recall that a window's client area excludes the border, the caption bar, and the menu bar. If you create a *CClientDC* object, you have a device context that is mapped only to this client area—you can't draw outside it. The point (*0, 0*) usually refers to the upper left corner of the client area. As you'll see later, an MFC *CView* object corresponds to a <u>child</u> <u>window</u> that is contained inside a separate frame window, often along with a toolbar, a status bar, and scroll bars. The client area of the view, then, does <u>not</u> include these other windows. If the window contains a docked toolbar, for example, (*0, 0*) refers to the point immediately <u>under</u> the left edge of the toolbar.

If you construct an object of class *CWindowDC*, point (*0, 0*) is at the upper left corner of the nonclient area of the window. With this "whole-window" device context, you can draw in the window's border, in the caption area, and so forth. Don't forget that the view window doesn't have a nonclient area, so *CWindowDC* is more applicable to frame windows than to view windows.

Constructing and Destroying *CDC* Objects

After you construct a *CDC* object, it is important to destroy it promptly when you're done with it. Windows limits the number of available device contexts, and if you fail to release a Windows device context object, the Debug kernel gives you a nasty message in the Debug window. Most frequently you'll construct a device context object inside a message handler function such as *OnLButtonDown*. The easiest way to ensure that the device context object is destroyed (and that the underlying Windows device context is released) is to construct the object on the stack in this way:

```
void CMyView::OnLButtonDown(UINT nFlags, CPoint point)
{
    CRect rect;

    CClientDC dc(this);  // constructs dc on the stack
    dc.GetClipBox(rect); // retrieves the clipping rectangle
} // dc automatically released
```

Notice that the *CClientDC* constructor takes a window pointer as a parameter. The destructor for the *CClientDC* object is called upon return from the function. You can also get a device context pointer by using the *CWnd::GetDC* member function, as shown in the following code. You must be careful here to call the *ReleaseDC* function to release the device context.

```
void CMyView::OnLButtonDown(UINT nFlags, CPoint point)
{
    CRect rect;

    CDC* pDC = GetDC();      // a pointer to an internal dc
    pDC->GetClipBox(rect);  // retrieves the clipping rectangle
    ReleaseDC(pDC);         // don't forget this
}
```

> **WARNING:** You must not destroy the *CDC* object passed by the pointer to *OnDraw*. The application framework handles the destruction for you.

The State of the Device Context

You already know that a device context is required for drawing. When you use a *CDC* object to draw an ellipse, for example, what you see on the screen (or on the printer's hard copy) depends on the current "state" of the device context. This state includes the following:

- Attached GDI drawing objects such as pens, brushes, and fonts.

- The mapping mode that determines the scale of items when they are drawn. (You've already experimented with the mapping mode in Chapter 4.)

- Various details such as text alignment parameters and polygon filling mode.

You have already seen, for example, that choosing a gray brush prior to drawing an ellipse results in the ellipse having a gray interior. When you create a device context object, it has certain default characteristics such as a black pen for shape boundaries. All other state characteristics are assigned through *CDC* class member functions. GDI objects are selected into the device context by means of the overloaded *SelectObject* functions. A device context can, for example, have one pen, one brush, or one font selected at any given time.

The *CPaintDC* Class

You'll need the *CPaintDC* class only if you override your view's *OnPaint* function. The default *OnPaint* calls *OnDraw* with a properly set up device context, but sometimes you'll need display-specific drawing code. The *CPaintDC* class is special because its constructor and destructor do housekeeping unique to *OnPaint.* Once you have a *CDC* pointer, however, you can use it as you would any other device context pointer.

Here's a sample *OnPaint* function that creates a *CPaintDC* object:

```
void CMyView::OnPaint()
{
    CPaintDC dc(this);
    OnPrepareDC(&dc); // explained later
    dc.TextOut(0, 0, "for the display, not the printer");
    OnDraw(&dc);       // stuff that's common to display and printer
}
```

For Win32 Programmers

The *CPaintDC* constructor calls *BeginPaint* for you, and the destructor calls *EndPaint.* If you construct your device context on the stack, the *EndPaint* call is completely automatic.

GDI Objects

A Windows GDI object type is represented by an MFC library class. *CGdiObject* is the abstract base class for the GDI object classes. A Windows GDI object is represented by a C++ object of a class derived from *CGdiObject.* Here's a list of the GDI derived classes:

- *CBitmap*—A bitmap is an array of bits in which one or more bits correspond to each display pixel. You can use bitmaps to represent images, including icons and cursors, and you can use them to create brushes.

- **CBrush**—A brush defines a bitmapped pattern of pixels that is used to fill areas with color.

- **CFont**—A font is a complete collection of characters of a particular typeface and a particular size. Fonts are generally stored on disk as resources, and some are device-specific.

- **CPalette**—A palette is a color mapping interface that allows an application to take full advantage of the color capability of an output device without interfering with other applications.

- **CPen**—A pen is a tool for drawing lines and shape borders. You can specify a pen's color and thickness and whether it draws solid, dotted, or dashed lines.

- **CRgn**—A region is an area that is a combination of polygons and ellipses. You can use regions for filling, clipping, and mouse hit-testing.

Constructing and Destroying GDI Objects

You never construct an object of class *CGdiObject;* instead, you construct objects of the derived classes. Constructors for some GDI derived classes, such as *CPen* and *CBrush*, allow you to specify enough information to create the object in one step. Others, such as *CFont* and *CRgn*, require a second creation step. For these classes you first construct the C++ object with the default constructor, and then you call a create function such as the *CreateFont* or *CreatePolygonRgn* function.

The *CGdiObject* class has a virtual destructor. The derived class destructors delete the Windows GDI objects that are attached to the C++ objects. If you construct an object of a class derived from *CGdiObject*, you must delete it prior to exiting the program. If you don't delete it, the Windows Debug kernel gives you another nasty message in the Debug window. To delete a GDI object, you must first separate it from the device context. You'll see an example in the next section.

> **N O T E :** Failure to delete a GDI object was a much more serious offense with Win16. GDI memory was not released until the user restarted Windows. With Win32, however, the GDI memory is owned by the process and is released when your program terminates.

Tracking GDI Objects

OK, so you know that you have to delete your GDI objects and that they must first be disconnected from their device context. How do you disconnect them? Members of the *CDC SelectObject* family of functions do the work of selecting a GDI object into the device context and, in the process, return a pointer to the previously selected object (which gets deselected in the process). Trouble is, you can't deselect the old object without selecting a new object. One easy way to track the objects is to "save" the original GDI object when you select your own GDI object and "restore" the original object when you're finished. Then you'll be ready to delete your own GDI object. Here's an example:

```
void CMyView::OnDraw(CDC* pDC)
{
    CPen newPen(PS_DASHDOTDOT, 2, (COLORREF) 0);  // black pen,
                                                  //  2 pixels wide
    CPen* pOldPen = pDC->SelectObject(&newPen);

    pDC->MoveTo(10, 10);
    pDC->Lineto(110, 10);
    pDC->SelectObject(pOldPen);                   // newPen is deselected
} // newPen automatically destroyed on exit
```

When a device context object is destroyed, all its GDI objects are deselected. Thus, if you know that a device context will be destroyed before its selected GDI objects are destroyed, you don't have to deselect the objects. If, for example, you declare a pen as a view class data member (and you initialize it when you initialize the view), you don't have to deselect the pen inside *OnDraw* because the device context, controlled by the view base class's *OnPaint* handler, will be destroyed first.

Stock GDI Objects

Windows contains a number of stock GDI objects that you can use. Because these objects are part of Windows, you don't have to worry about deleting them. (Windows ignores requests to delete stock objects.) The MFC library function *SelectStockObject* gives you a *CGdiObject* pointer that you can select into a device context. These stock objects are handy when you want to deselect your own nonstock GDI object prior to its destruction. You can use a stock object as an alternative to the "old" object you used in the previous example, as shown here:

```
void CMyView::OnDraw(CDC* pDC)
{
    CPen newPen(PS_DASHDOTDOT, 2, (COLORREF) 0);  // black pen,
                                                  //  2 pixels wide

    pDC->SelectObject(&newPen);
    pDC->MoveTo(10, 10);
    pDC->Lineto(110, 10);
    pDC->SelectStockObject(BLACK_PEN);            // newPen is deselected
} // newPen destroyed on exit
```

The *Microsoft Foundation Class Library Reference* lists the stock objects available for pens, brushes, fonts, and palettes.

The Lifetime of a GDI Selection

For the display device context, you get a fresh device context at the beginning of each message handler function. No GDI selections (or mapping modes or other device context settings) persist after your function exits. You must, therefore, set up your device context from scratch each time. The *CView* class virtual member function *OnPrepareDC* is useful for setting the mapping mode, but you must manage your own GDI objects.

For other device contexts, such as those for printers and memory buffers, your assignments can last longer. For these long-life device contexts, things get a little more complicated. The complexity results from the temporary nature of GDI C++ object pointers returned by the *SelectObject* function. (The temporary "object" will be destroyed by the application framework during the idle loop processing of the application, sometime after the handler function returns the call. See MFC Technical Note #3 in Books Online.) You can't simply store the pointer in a class data member; instead, you must convert it to a Windows handle (the only permanent GDI identifier) with the *GetSafeHdc* member function. Here's an example:

```
// m_pPrintFont is a CFont pointer initialized in CMyView constructor
// m_hOldFont is a CMyView data member of type HFONT, initialized to 0

void CMyView::SwitchToCourier(CDC* pDC)
{
    m_pPrintFont->CreateFont(30, 10, 0, 0, 400, FALSE, FALSE,
                        0, ANSI_CHARSET, OUT_DEFAULT_PRECIS,
                        CLIP_DEFAULT_PRECIS, DEFAULT_QUALITY,
                        DEFAULT_PITCH | FF_MODERN,
                        "Courier New"); // TrueType
    CFont* pOldFont = pDC->SelectObject(m_pPrintFont);
```

(continued)

```
    // m_hObject is the CGdiObject public data member that contains
    //  the handle
    m_hOldFont = (HFONT) pOldFont->GetSafeHandle();
}

void CMyView:SwitchToOriginalFont(CDC* pDC)
{
    // FromHandle is a static member function that returns an
    //  object pointer
    if (m_hOldFont) {
      pDC->SelectObject(CFont::FromHandle(m_hOldFont));
    }
}

// m_pPrintFont is deleted in the CMyView destructor
```

> NOTE: Be careful when you delete an object whose pointer is returned by *SelectObject*. If you've allocated the object yourself, you can delete it. If the pointer is temporary, as it will be for the object initially selected into the device context, you cannot delete the C++ object.

Windows Color Mapping

The Windows GDI provides a hardware-independent color interface. Your program supplies an "absolute" color code, and the GDI maps that code to a suitable color or color combination on your computer's video display. Most programmers of applications for Windows try to optimize their applications' color display for a few common video card categories.

Standard Video Graphics Array (VGA) Video Cards

A standard VGA video card uses 18-bit color registers and thus has a palette of 262,144 colors. Because of video memory constraints, however, the standard VGA board accommodates 4-bit color codes, which means it can display only 16 colors at a time. Because Windows needs fixed colors for captions, borders, scroll bars, and so forth, your programs can use only 16 "standard" pure colors. You cannot conveniently access the other colors that the board can display.

Each Windows color is represented by a combination of 8-bit "red," "green," and "blue" values. The 16 standard VGA "pure" (nondithered) colors are shown in the following table:

Red	Green	Blue	Color
0	0	0	Black
0	0	255	Blue
0	255	0	Green
0	255	255	Cyan
255	0	0	Red
255	0	255	Magenta
255	255	0	Yellow
255	255	255	White
0	0	128	Dark blue
0	128	0	Dark green
0	128	128	Dark cyan
128	0	0	Dark red
128	0	128	Dark magenta
128	128	0	Dark yellow
128	128	128	Dark gray
192	192	192	Light gray

Color-oriented GDI functions accept 32-bit *COLORREF* parameters that contain 8-bit color codes each for red, green, and blue. The Windows *RGB* macro converts 8-bit red, green, and blue values to a *COLORREF* parameter. The following statement, when executed on a system with a standard VGA board, constructs a brush with a dithered color (one that consists of a pattern of pure-color pixels):

```
CBrush brush(RGB(128, 128, 192));
```

The following statement (in your view's *OnDraw* function) sets the text background to red:

```
pDC->SetBkColor(RGB(255, 0, 0));
```

The *CDC* functions *SetBkColor* and *SetTextColor* don't always display dithered colors as the brush-oriented drawing functions do. If the dithered color pattern is too complex, the closest matching pure color is displayed.

256-Color Video Cards

Many video cards can accommodate 8-bit color codes, which means they can display 256 colors simultaneously. If you have one of these super VGA (SVGA) boards, you need to install a special Windows display driver, supplied by Microsoft or your card's manufacturer, to activate the 256-color mode.

If Windows is configured for a 256-color display card, your programs are limited to 20 standard pure colors unless you activate the Windows color palette system as supported by the MFC library *CPalette* class and the Windows API, in which case you can choose your 256 colors from a total of 16.7 million. Windows color palette programming is covered in Chapter 10. In this chapter, we'll assume that the Windows default color mapping is in effect.

With an SVGA 256-color display driver installed, you get the 16 VGA colors listed in the table on the previous page, plus 4 more, for a total of 20. The following table lists the 4 additional colors:

Red	Green	Blue	Color
192	220	192	Money green
166	202	240	Sky blue
255	251	240	Cream
160	160	164	Medium gray

The *RGB* macro works much the same as it does with the standard VGA. If you specify one of the 20 standard colors for a brush, you get a pure color; otherwise, you get a dithered color. If you use the *PALETTERGB* macro instead, you don't get dithered colors; you get the closest matching standard pure color as defined by the current palette.

16-Bit–Color Video Cards

Most modern video cards support a resolution of 1024 by 768 pixels. 1 MB of video memory can support 8-bit color at this resolution. If a card has 2 MB of memory, it can support "16-bit color," with 5 bits each for red, green, and blue. This means that it can display 32,768 colors simultaneously. That sounds like a lot, but there are only 32 shades each of pure red, green, and blue. Often, a picture will look better in 8-bit color mode with an appropriate palette selected. A forest scene, for example, can use up to 236 shades of green. Palettes are not supported in 16-bit–color mode.

24-Bit–Color Video Cards

High-end cards (which are becoming more widely used) support 24-bit color. This 24-bit capability enables the display of 16.7 million pure colors. If you're using a 24-bit card, you have direct access to all the colors. The *RGB* macro allows you to specify the exact colors you want. You'll need 4 MB of video memory, though, if you want 24-bit color at 1024-by-768-pixel resolution.

Fonts

Old-fashioned character-mode applications could display only the boring system font on the screen. Windows provides multiple device-independent fonts in variable sizes. The effective use of these Windows fonts can significantly energize an application with minimum programming effort. TrueType fonts, first introduced with Windows version 3.1, are even more effective and are easier to program than the previous device-dependent fonts. You'll see several example programs that use fonts later in this chapter.

Fonts Are GDI Objects

Fonts are an integral part of the Windows GDI. This means that fonts behave in the same way as other GDI objects. They can be scaled and clipped, and they can be selected into a device context as a pen or a brush can be selected. All GDI rules about deselection and deletion apply to fonts.

Choosing a Font

Choosing a Windows font used to be like going to a fruit stand and asking for "a piece of reddish-yellow fruit, with a stone inside, that weighs about 4 ounces." You might have gotten a peach or a plum or even a nectarine, and you could be sure that it wouldn't have weighed exactly 4 ounces. Once you took possession of the fruit, you could weigh it and check the fruit type. Now, with TrueType, you can specify the fruit type, but you still can't specify the exact weight.

Today you can choose between two font types—device-independent TrueType fonts and device-dependent fonts such as the Windows display System font and the LaserJet LinePrinter font—or you can specify a font category and size and let Windows select the font for you. If you let Windows select the font, it will choose a TrueType font if possible. The MFC library provides a font selection dialog box tied to the currently selected printer, so there's little need for printer font guesswork. You let the user select the exact font and size for the printer, and then you approximate the display the best you can.

Printing with Fonts

For text-intensive applications, you'll probably want to specify printer font sizes in points. (1 point = 1/72 inch.) Why? Most, if not all, built-in printer fonts are defined in terms of points. The LaserJet LinePrinter font, for example, comes in one size, 8.5 point. You can specify TrueType fonts in any point size. If you work in points, you need a mapping mode that easily accommodates points. That's what *MM_TWIPS* is for. An 8.5-point font is 8.5 × 20, or 170, twips, and that's the character height you'll want to specify.

Displaying Fonts

If you're not worried about the display matching the printed output, you have a lot of flexibility. You can choose any of the scalable Windows TrueType fonts, or you can choose the fixed-size system fonts (stock objects). With the TrueType fonts, it doesn't much matter what mapping mode you use; simply choose a font height and go for it. No need to worry about points.

Matching printer fonts to make printed output match the screen presents some problems, but TrueType makes it easier than it used to be. Even if you're printing with TrueType fonts, however, you'll never quite get the display to match the printer output. Why? Characters are ultimately displayed in pixels (or dots), and the width of a string of characters is equal to the sum of the pixel widths of its characters, possibly adjusted for kerning. The pixel width of the characters depends on the font, the mapping mode, and the resolution of the output device. Only if both the printer and the display were set to *MM_TEXT* mode (1 pixel or dot = 1 logical unit) would you get an exact correspondence. If you're using the *CDC::GetTextExtent* function to calculate line breaks, the screen breakpoint will occasionally be different from the printer breakpoint.

> **NOTE:** In the MFC Print Preview mode, which we'll examine closely in Chapter 18, line breaks occur exactly as they do on the printer, but the print quality suffers in the process.

If you're matching a printer-specific font on the screen, TrueType again makes the job easier. Windows substitutes the closest matching TrueType font. For the 8.5-point LinePrinter font, Windows comes pretty close with its Courier New font.

Logical Inches and Physical Inches on the Display

If you've read Charles Petzold's *Programming Windows 3.1* (Microsoft Press, 1992) or the earlier editions of this book, you might remember something about logical inches and logical twips. The idea was that you could measure the screen in both physical units and logical units, which, under Windows 3.1, were different. If you had used the *CDC::GetDeviceCaps* function under Windows 3.1, you would have retrieved the following information for a standard VGA display:

Index	Description	Value
HORZSIZE	Width in millimeters	208
VERTSIZE	Height in millimeters	156
HORZRES	Width in pixels	640
VERTRES	Height in raster lines	480
LOGPIXELSX	Horizontal dots per logical inch	96
LOGPIXELSY	Vertical dots per logical inch	96

If you crunch the above numbers, you'll find out that the display size is 8.18 by 6.14 in physical inches, and 6.65 by 5.00 in logical inches. If your painting code was supposed to work on both the printer and the display, you were supposed to use different mapping modes on the two devices in order to make physical printer inches match logical display inches, thus magnifying the display output.

Well, things have changed in Windows 95 and the newer versions of Windows NT. If you make the same *GetDeviceCaps* call for a VGA display (with a standard VGA monitor), the physical dimensions will now be different:

Index	Description	Value
HORZSIZE	Width in millimeters	169
VERTSIZE	Height in millimeters	127

If you do the math again, you'll see that the display size is 6.65 by 5.00 physical inches, the same as the logical size. That means that you can use the same mapping mode for both the printer and the display. If you use *MM_TWIPS* and 10-point type, for example, the screen will correspond to a paper area of 6.65 by 5.00 inches, or 479 by 360 points.

NOTE: The Windows 95 Control Panel lets you adjust the display resolution and display font size. If you have a high-resolution video card and monitor, you can set the resolution to 1024 by 768 pixels. In that case, *HORZSIZE* is 270 and *VERTSIZE* is 203, but the dots-per-inch value is still 96. Thus the physical size is still the same as the logical size. If you change the display font size from the default 100 percent to 200 percent, *HORZSIZE* becomes 135, *VERTSIZE* becomes 101, and the dots-per-inch value becomes 192. The physical size is still the same as the logical size, but everything gets magnified by 2.

The Control Panel also lets you specify the monitor. You would expect that the physical dimensions would change when you switched from a 15-inch to a 17-inch monitor, but that is not the case.

Computing Character Height

Five font height measurement parameters are available through the *CDC* function *GetTextMetrics*, but only three are significant. The *tmHeight* parameter represents the full height of the font, including descenders (for the characters *g*, *j*, *p*, *q*, and *y*) and any diacritics that appear over capital letters. The *tmExternalLeading* parameter is the distance between the top of the diacritic and the bottom of the descender from the line above. The sum of *tmHeight* and *tmExternalLeading* is the total character height. The value of *tmExternalLeading* is often 0 for a display device context.

You would think that *tmHeight* would represent the font size in points. Wrong! Another *GetTextMetrics* parameter, *tmInternalLeading*, comes into play. The point size corresponds to the difference between *tmHeight* and *tmInternalLeading*. With the *MM_TWIPS* mapping mode in effect, a selected 12-point font might have a *tmHeight* value of 295 logical units and a *tmInternalLeading* value of 55. The font's net height of 240 corresponds to the point size of 12. Figure 5-1 shows the important font measurements.

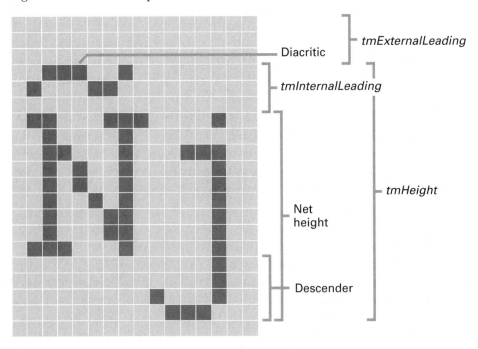

Figure 5-1.
Font height measurements.

The EX05A Example

This example sets up a view window with the logical twips mapping mode. A text string is displayed in 10 point sizes with the Arial TrueType font. Here are the steps for building the application:

1. Run AppWizard to generate the EX05A project.   Start by choosing New from the File menu, and then select Project Workspace. The options and the default class names are shown here:

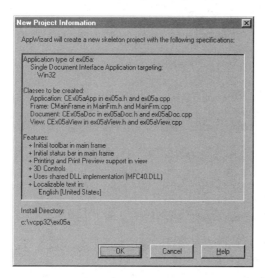

Notice that this time we're accepting the default Printing And Print Preview option.

2. Use ClassWizard to override the *OnPrepareDC* function in the *CEx05aView* class.   Edit the code in ex05aView.cpp as follows:

```
void CEx05aView::OnPrepareDC(CDC* pDC, CPrintInfo* pInfo /* = NULL */)
{
    pDC->SetMapMode(MM_TWIPS);
}
```

3. Add a private *ShowFont* helper function to the view class.   Add the prototype shown on the following page in ex05aView.h.

```
private:
    void ShowFont(CDC* pDC, int& nPos, int nPoints);
```

Then add the function itself in ex05aView.cpp:

```
void CEx05aView::ShowFont(CDC* pDC, int& nPos, int nPoints)
{
    TEXTMETRIC  tm;
    CFont       fontText;
    CString     strText;
    CSize       sizeText;

    fontText.CreateFont(-nPoints * 20, 0, 0, 0, 400, FALSE, FALSE, 0,
                        ANSI_CHARSET, OUT_DEFAULT_PRECIS,
                        CLIP_DEFAULT_PRECIS, DEFAULT_QUALITY,
                        DEFAULT_PITCH | FF_SWISS, "Arial");
    CFont* pOldFont = (CFont*) pDC->SelectObject(&fontText);
    pDC->GetTextMetrics(&tm);
    TRACE("points = %d, tmHeight = %d, tmInternalLeading = %d,"
         " tmExternalLeading = %d\n", nPoints, tm.tmHeight,
        tm.tmInternalLeading, tm.tmExternalLeading);
    strText.Format("This is %d-point Arial", nPoints);
    sizeText = pDC->GetTextExtent(strText);
    TRACE("string width = %d, string height = %d\n", sizeText.cx,
        sizeText.cy);
    pDC->TextOut(0, nPos, strText);
    pDC->SelectObject(pOldFont);
    nPos -= tm.tmHeight + tm.tmExternalLeading;
}
```

4. **Edit the *OnDraw* function in ex05aView.cpp.**   AppWizard always generates a skeleton *OnDraw* function for your view class. Find the function, and edit the code as follows:

```
void CEx05aView::OnDraw(CDC* pDC)
{
    int nPosition = 0;

    for (int i = 6; i <= 24; i += 2) {
        ShowFont(pDC, nPosition, i);
    }
}
```

5. Build and run the EX05A program. You must run the program from the debugger if you want to see the output from the *TRACE* statements. Choose Debug Go from the Developer Studio's Build menu or click the

icon in the standard toolbar. The resulting output (assuming the use of a standard VGA card) looks like the screen shown here:

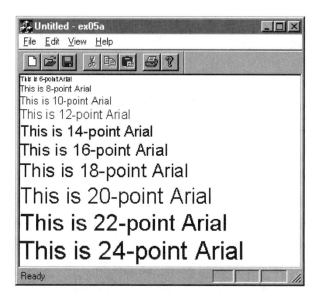

Notice that the output string sizes don't quite correspond to the point sizes. This discrepancy results from the font engine's conversion of logical units to pixels. The program's trace output, partially shown below, shows the display of font metrics. (The numbers depend on your display driver and your video driver.)

```
points = 6, tmHeight = 134, tmInternalLeading = 14, tmExternalLeading = 5
string width = 1032, string height = 134
points = 8, tmHeight = 182, tmInternalLeading = 24, tmExternalLeading = 5
string width = 1325, string height = 182
points = 10, tmHeight = 226, tmInternalLeading = 24, tmExternalLeading = 5
string width = 1829, string height = 226
points = 12, tmHeight = 274, tmInternalLeading = 34, tmExternalLeading = 10
string width = 2208, string height = 274
```

Try Print Preview. Notice, as shown below, that the printer font metrics are different from the display font metrics, particularly for the value of *tmInternalLeading*:

```
points = 6, tmHeight = 150, tmInternalLeading = 30, tmExternalLeading = 0
string width = 1065, string height = 150
points = 8, tmHeight = 210, tmInternalLeading = 45, tmExternalLeading = 0
string width = 1380, string height = 210
points = 10, tmHeight = 240, tmInternalLeading = 45, tmExternalLeading = 0
string width = 1770, string height = 240
points = 12, tmHeight = 270, tmInternalLeading = 30, tmExternalLeading = 15
string width = 2130, string height = 270
```

The EX05A Program Elements

Following is a discussion of the important elements in the EX05A example.

Setting the Mapping Mode in the *OnPrepareDC* Function

The application framework calls *OnPrepareDC* prior to calling *OnDraw*, so the *OnPrepareDC* function is the logical place to prepare the device context. If you had other message handlers that needed the correct mapping mode, those functions would have contained calls to *OnPrepareDC*.

The *ShowFont* Private Member Function

ShowFont contains code that is executed 10 times in a loop. With C, you would have made this a global function, but with C++ it's better to make it a private class member function, sometimes known as a <u>helper</u> <u>function</u>.

This function creates the font, selects it into the device context, prints a string to the window, and then deselects and deletes the font. If you choose to include debug information in the program, *ShowFont* also displays useful font metrics information, including the actual width of the string.

Calling *CFont::CreateFont*

This call includes lots of parameters, but the important ones are the first two—the font height and width. A width value of 0 means that the aspect ratio of the selected font will be set to a value specified by the font designer. If you put a nonzero value here, as you'll see in the next example, you can change the font's aspect ratio.

TIP: If you want your font to be a specific point size, then the *CreateFont* font height parameter (the first parameter) must be <u>nega-</u><u>tive</u>. If you're using the *MM_TWIPS* mapping mode, for example, a height parameter of −240 ensures a 12-point font, with *tmHeight* − *tmInternalLeading* = 240. A +240 height parameter gives you a smaller font, with *tmHeight* = 240.

The last *CreateFont* parameter specifies the font name, in this case the Arial TrueType font. If you had used *NULL* for this parameter, the *FF_SWISS* specification (which indicates a proportional font without serifs) would have caused Windows to choose the best matching font, which, depending on the specified size, might have been the System font or the Arial TrueType font. The font name takes precedence. If you had specified *FF_ROMAN* (which indicates a proportional font with serifs) with Arial, for example, you would have gotten Arial.

The EX05B Example

This program is similar to EX05A except that it shows multiple fonts. The mapping mode is *MM_ANISOTROPIC*, with the scale dependent on the window size. The characters change size along with the window. This program effectively shows off some TrueType fonts and contrasts them with the old-style fonts. Here are the steps for building the application:

1. Run AppWizard to generate the EX05B project. The options and the default class names are shown here:

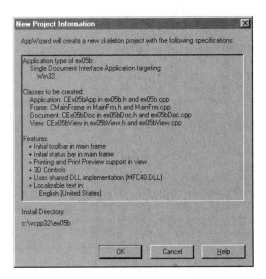

93

Notice that again we're accepting the default Printing And Print Preview option.

2. **Use ClassWizard to override the *OnPrepareDC* function in the *CEx05bView* class.** Edit the code in ex05bView.cpp as follows:

```
void CEx05bView::OnPrepareDC(CDC* pDC, CPrintInfo* pInfo /* = NULL */)
{
    CRect clientRect;

    GetClientRect(clientRect);
    pDC->SetMapMode(MM_ANISOTROPIC); // +y = down
    pDC->SetWindowExt(400, 450);
    pDC->SetViewportExt(clientRect.right, clientRect.bottom);
    pDC->SetViewportOrg(0, 0);
}
```

3. **Add a private *TraceMetrics* helper function to the view class.** Add the following prototype in ex05bView.h:

```
private:
    void TraceMetrics(CDC* pDC);
```

Then add the function itself in ex05bView.cpp:

```
void CEx05bView::TraceMetrics(CDC* pDC)
{
    TEXTMETRIC tm;
    char       szFaceName[100];

    pDC->GetTextMetrics(&tm);
    pDC->GetTextFace(99, szFaceName);
    TRACE("font = %s, tmHeight = %d, tmInternalLeading = %d,"
          " tmExternalLeading = %d\n", szFaceName, tm.tmHeight,
          tm.tmInternalLeading, tm.tmExternalLeading);
}
```

4. **Edit the *OnDraw* function in ex05bView.cpp.** AppWizard always generates a skeleton *OnDraw* function for your view class. Find the function, and edit the code as follows:

```
void CEx05bView::OnDraw(CDC* pDC)
{
    CFont fontTest1, fontTest2, fontTest3, fontTest4;

    fontTest1.CreateFont(50, 0, 0, 0, 400, FALSE, FALSE, 0,
                         ANSI_CHARSET, OUT_DEFAULT_PRECIS,
                         CLIP_DEFAULT_PRECIS, DEFAULT_QUALITY,
                         DEFAULT_PITCH | FF_SWISS, "Arial");
    CFont* pOldFont = pDC->SelectObject(&fontTest1);
    TraceMetrics(pDC);
    pDC->TextOut(0, 0, "This is Arial, default width");

    fontTest2.CreateFont(50, 0, 0, 0, 400, FALSE, FALSE, 0,
                         ANSI_CHARSET, OUT_DEFAULT_PRECIS,
                         CLIP_DEFAULT_PRECIS, DEFAULT_QUALITY,
                         DEFAULT_PITCH | FF_MODERN, "Courier");
    // not TrueType
    pDC->SelectObject(&fontTest2);
    TraceMetrics(pDC);
    pDC->TextOut(0, 100, "This is Courier, default width");

    fontTest3.CreateFont(50, 10, 0, 0, 400, FALSE, FALSE, 0,
                         ANSI_CHARSET, OUT_DEFAULT_PRECIS,
                         CLIP_DEFAULT_PRECIS, DEFAULT_QUALITY,
                         DEFAULT_PITCH | FF_ROMAN, NULL);
    pDC->SelectObject(&fontTest3);
    TraceMetrics(pDC);
    pDC->TextOut(0, 200, "This is generic Roman, variable width");

    fontTest4.CreateFont(50, 0, 0, 0, 400, FALSE, FALSE, 0,
                         ANSI_CHARSET, OUT_DEFAULT_PRECIS,
                         CLIP_DEFAULT_PRECIS, DEFAULT_QUALITY,
                         DEFAULT_PITCH | FF_MODERN, "LinePrinter");
    pDC->SelectObject(&fontTest4);
    TraceMetrics(pDC);
    pDC->TextOut(0, 300, "This is LinePrinter, default width");
    pDC->SelectObject(pOldFont);
}
```

5. **Build and run the EX05B program.** Run the program from the
debugger to see the *TRACE* output. The program's window is shown
at the top of the following page:

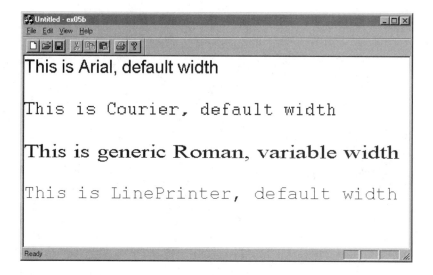

Resize the window to make it smaller, and watch the font sizes change. Compare this window with the previous one:

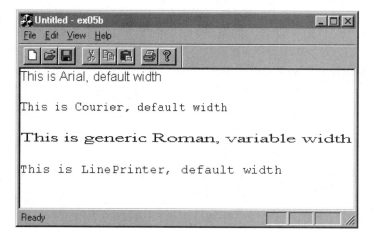

If you continue to downsize the window, notice how the Courier font stops shrinking after a certain size and how the Roman font width changes.

Now choose Print Preview from the File menu. The output, as shown in Figure 5-2, is very different from the window display output because the Courier and LinePrinter fonts are not TrueType fonts. The Windows

Courier font maps to one of the printer's built-in fixed-size Courier fonts, and the printer's LinePrinter font is available only in 8.5 point. The other fonts appear small because the *MM_TEXT* mapping mode causes printer dots to be mapped directly to display pixels—which is clearly undesirable. In Chapter 18, you'll learn more about scaling your printer output.

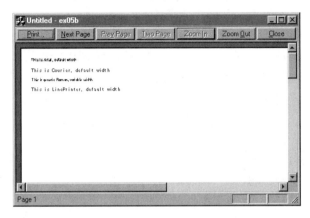

Figure 5-2.
The EX05B Print Preview output.

The EX05B Program Elements

Following is a discussion of the important elements in the EX05B example.

The *OnDraw* Member Function

The *OnDraw* function displays character strings in four fonts, as follows:

- ■ *fontTest1*—The TrueType font Arial with default width selection.

- ■ *fontTest2*—The old-style font Courier with default width selection. Notice how jagged the font is in larger sizes.

- ■ *fontTest3*—The generic Roman font for which Windows supplies the TrueType font Times New Roman with programmed width selection. The width is tied to the horizontal window scale, so the font stretches to fit the window.

- ■ *fontTest4*—The LinePrinter font is specified, but because this is not a Windows font for the display, the font engine falls back on the *FF_MODERN* specification and chooses the TrueType Courier New font.

97

The *TraceMetrics* Helper Function

The *TraceMetrics* helper function calls *CDC::GetTextMetrics* and *CDC::GetText-Face* to get the current font's parameters, which it prints in the Debug window.

The EX05C Example—*CScrollView* Revisited

You saw the *CScrollView* class in Chapter 4 (in EX04C). The EX05C program allows the user to move an ellipse with a mouse by "capturing" the mouse, using a scrolling window with the *MM_LOENGLISH* mapping mode. Keyboard scrolling is left out, but you can add it by borrowing the *OnKeyDown* member function from EX04C.

Instead of a stock brush, we'll use a pattern brush for the ellipse—a real GDI object. There's one complication with pattern brushes: you must reset the origin as the window scrolls; otherwise, strips of the pattern don't line up, and the effect is ugly.

As with EX04C, this example involves a view class derived from *CScrollView.* Here are the steps to create the application:

1. **Run AppWizard to generate the EX05C project.** Be sure to set the view base class to *CScrollView.* The options and the default class names are shown here:

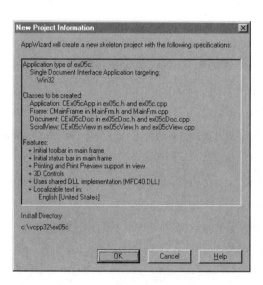

2. **Edit the *CEx05cView* class header in the file ex05cView.h.** Add the following lines in the class *CEx05cView* declaration:

```
private:
    CRect  m_rectEllipse; // logical
    CPoint m_pointMouse;  // logical
    BOOL   m_bCaptured;
```

3. Use ClassWizard to add three message handlers. Add the message handlers as follows:

Message	Member Function Name
WM_LBUTTONDOWN	*OnLButtonDown*
WM_LBUTTONUP	*OnLButtonUp*
WM_MOUSEMOVE	*OnMouseMove*

4. Edit the *CEx05cView* message handler functions. ClassWizard generated the skeletons for the functions listed above. Find the functions in ex05cView.cpp, and code them as follows:

```
void CEx05cView::OnLButtonDown(UINT nFlags, CPoint point)
{
    CRect rectEllipse;
    CRgn  circle;

    rectEllipse = m_rectEllipse;
    CClientDC dc(this);
    OnPrepareDC(&dc);
    dc.LPtoDP(rectEllipse);
    circle.CreateEllipticRgnIndirect(rectEllipse);
    if (circle.PtInRegion(point)) {
      // capturing the mouse ensures subsequent LButtonUp message
      SetCapture();
      m_bCaptured = TRUE;
      dc.DPtoLP(&point);
      m_pointMouse = point;
      // new mouse cursor is active while mouse is captured
      ::SetCursor(::LoadCursor(NULL, IDC_CROSS));
    }
}

void CEx05cView::OnLButtonUp(UINT nFlags, CPoint point)
{
```

(continued)

99

```
    if (m_bCaptured) {
      ::ReleaseCapture();
      m_bCaptured = FALSE;
    }
}

void CEx05cView::OnMouseMove(UINT nFlags, CPoint point)
{
    CSize  sizeOffset;
    CPoint pointMouse;
    CRect  rectOld, rectNew;

    CClientDC dc(this);
    OnPrepareDC(&dc);
    if (m_bCaptured) {
      rectOld = m_rectEllipse;
      pointMouse = m_pointMouse;
      dc.LPtoDP(rectOld);
      InvalidateRect(rectOld, TRUE);
      dc.LPtoDP(&pointMouse);
      sizeOffset = point - pointMouse;
      rectNew = rectOld + (CPoint(0, 0) + sizeOffset);
      InvalidateRect(rectNew, TRUE);
      dc.DPtoLP(&point);
      dc.DPtoLP(rectNew);
      m_pointMouse = point;
      m_rectEllipse = rectNew;
    }
}
```

5. Edit the _CEx05cView_ constructor, the _OnDraw_ function, and the _OnInitialUpdate_ function.   AppWizard generated these skeleton functions. Find them in ex05cView.cpp, and code them as follows:

```
CEx05cView::CEx05cView() : m_rectEllipse(0, 0, 100, -100)
{
    m_pointMouse = CPoint(0, 0);
    m_bCaptured = FALSE;
}

void CEx05cView::OnDraw(CDC* pDC)
{
    CBrush brushHatch(HS_DIAGCROSS, RGB(255, 0, 0));
    CPoint point(0, 0);                    // logical 0,0

    pDC->LPtoDP(&point);                   // In device coordinates,
```

```
        pDC->SetBrushOrg(point);                // align the brush with
                                                //  the window origin
    pDC->SelectObject(&brushHatch);
    pDC->Ellipse(m_rectEllipse);
    pDC->SelectStockObject(BLACK_BRUSH); // deselect brushHatch
    pDC->Rectangle(CRect(100, -100, 200, -200)); // test invalid rect
}

void CEx05cView::OnInitialUpdate
{
    CScrollView::OnInitialUpdate();

    CSize sizeTotal(800 * 2, 800 * 2); // 8 by 8 inch
    CSize sizePage(sizeTotal.cx / 2, sizeTotal.cy / 2);
    CSize sizeLine(sizeTotal.cx / 50, sizeTotal.cy / 50);
    SetScrollSizes(MM_LOENGLISH, sizeTotal, sizePage, sizeLine);
}
```

6. **Build and run the EX05C program.**   The program allows an ellipse to be dragged with the mouse, and it allows the window to be scrolled. The program's window should look like the one below:

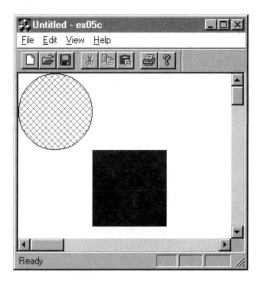

As you move the ellipse, observe the black rectangle. You should be able to see the effects of invalidating the rectangle.

The EX05C Program Elements

Following is a discussion of the important elements in the EX05C example.

The *m_pointMouse* Data Member

The *OnMouseMove* member function must compare the current mouse position with the previous mouse position to calculate how far to move the ellipse. The *m_pointMouse* object, of class *CPoint*, stores the previous mouse position.

The *m_bCaptured* Data Member

The *m_bCaptured* Boolean variable is set to TRUE when mouse tracking is in progress.

The *SetCapture* and *ReleaseCapture* Functions

SetCapture is the *CWnd* member function that "captures" the mouse, such that mouse movement messages are sent to this window even if the mouse cursor is outside the window. An unfortunate side effect of this function is that the ellipse can be moved outside the window and "lost." A desirable and necessary effect is that all subsequent mouse messages are sent to the window, including the WM_LBUTTONUP message, which would otherwise be lost. The Win32 *ReleaseCapture* function turns off mouse capture.

The *SetCursor* and *LoadCursor* Win32 Functions

The MFC library does not "wrap" some Win32 functions. By convention, we use the C++ scope resolution operator (::) when calling Win32 functions directly. In this case, there is no potential for conflict with a *CView* member function, but you can deliberately choose to call a Win32 function in place of a class member function with the same name. In that case, the :: operator ensures that you call the globally scoped Win32 function.

When the first parameter is *NULL*, the *LoadCursor* function creates a cursor resource from the specified predefined mouse cursor that Windows uses. The *SetCursor* function activates the specified cursor resource. This cursor remains active as long as the mouse is captured.

The *CScrollView::OnPrepareDC* Member Function

The *CView* class has a virtual *OnPrepareDC* function that does nothing. The *CScrollView* class implements the function for the purpose of setting the view's mapping mode, scale factor, and origin, based on the parameters that you passed to *SetScrollSizes* in *OnCreate*. The application framework calls

OnPrepareDC for you prior to calling *OnDraw*, so you don't need to worry about it. You must call *OnPrepareDC* yourself in any other message handler function that uses the view's device context, such as *OnLButtonDown* and *OnMouseMove*.

The *OnMouseMove* Coordinate Transformation Code

As you can see, this function contains quite a few translation statements. The logic can be summarized by the following steps:

1. Convert the previous ellipse rectangle and mouse point (stored in data members) from logical to device coordinates.

2. Invalidate the previous rectangle.

3. Update the mouse point and the ellipse rectangle.

4. Invalidate the new rectangle.

5. Convert the new ellipse rectangle and mouse point to logical coordinates.

The function calls *InvalidRect* twice. Windows "saves up" the two invalid rectangles and computes a new invalid rectangle that is the union of the two, intersected with the client rectangle.

The *OnDraw* Function

The *SetBrushOrg* call is necessary to ensure that all of the ellipse's interior pattern lines up when the view is scrolled. The brush is aligned with a reference point, which is at the top left of the logical window, converted to device coordinates. This is a notable exception to the rule that *CDC* member functions require logical coordinates.

The *CScrollView SetScaleToFitSize* Mode

The *CScrollView* class has a stretch-to-fit mode that displays the entire scrollable area in the view window. The Windows *MM_ANISOTROPIC* mapping mode comes into play, with one restriction: positive *y* values always increase in the down direction, as in *MM_TEXT* mode.

To use the stretch-to-fit mode, make the following call in your view's function in place of the call to *SetScrollSizes*:

```
SetScaleToFitSize(totalSize);
```

The example in Chapter 10 makes this call in *OnInitialUpdate*, and it also makes it in response to a Shrink To Fit menu command. Thus, the display can toggle between scrolling mode and shrink-to-fit mode.

The Modal Dialog and Windows 95 Common Controls

Almost every Windows program uses a dialog window to interact with the user. The dialog might be a simple OK message box, or it might be a complex data entry form. Calling this powerful element a dialog "box" is an injustice. As you'll see, a dialog is truly a window that receives messages, that can be moved and closed, and that can even accept drawing instructions in its client area.

The two kinds of dialogs are <u>modal</u> and <u>modeless</u>. This chapter explores the most common type, the modal dialog. In the first of this chapter's two examples, you'll use all the familiar "old" controls, such as the edit control and the list box, inherited from Win16. In the second example, you'll use the new Windows 95 common controls. Chapter 7 introduces the modeless dialog and the special-purpose Windows 95 common dialogs for opening files, selecting fonts, and so forth.

Modal vs. Modeless Dialogs

The *CDialog* base class supports both modal and modeless dialogs. With a modal dialog, such as the Open File dialog, the user cannot work elsewhere in the same application (more correctly, in the same user-interface thread) until the dialog is closed. With a modeless dialog, the user can work in another window in the application while the dialog remains on the screen. The Developer Studio's Find dialog is a good example of a modeless dialog; you can edit your program during a global search (once the search is started).

Your choice of a modal or a modeless dialog depends on the application. Modal dialogs are much easier to program, which might influence your decision.

FYI: The 16-bit versions of Windows support a special kind of modal dialog called a system modal dialog, which prevents the user from switching to another application. Win32 also supports system modal dialogs but with weird results: the user can switch to another application, but the dialog remains as the top window. You probably don't want to use system modal dialogs in Win32 applications.

Resources and Controls

So now you know a dialog is a window. What makes the dialog different from the *CView* windows you've seen already? For one thing, a dialog window is almost always tied to a Windows resource that identifies the dialog's elements and specifies their layout. Because you can use the graphic editor to create and edit a dialog resource, you can quickly and efficiently produce dialogs in a visual manner.

A dialog consists of a number of elements called controls. Dialog controls include edit controls (aka text boxes), buttons, list boxes, combo boxes, static text (aka labels), tree views, progress indicators, sliders, and so forth. Windows manages these controls using special grouping and tabbing logic, and that relieves you of a major programming burden. The dialog controls can be referenced either by a *CWnd* pointer (because they themselves are really windows) or by an index number (with an associated *#define* constant) assigned in the resource. Controls send messages to their parent dialog in response to user actions such as typing text or clicking a button.

The MFC library and ClassWizard work together to enhance the dialog logic that Windows provides. ClassWizard generates a class derived from *CDialog* and then lets you associate dialog class data members with dialog controls. You can specify editing parameters such as maximum text length and numeric high and low limits. ClassWizard generates calls to the MFC data exchange and data validation functions that move information back and forth between the screen and the data members.

Programming a Modal Dialog

Modal dialogs are the most frequently used dialogs. A user action (a menu choice, for example) brings up a dialog on the screen, the user enters data in the dialog, and then the user closes the dialog. Here's a summary of the steps to add a modal dialog to an existing project:

1. Use the graphic editor to create a dialog resource that contains various controls. The graphic editor updates the project's resource script (RC) file to include your new dialog resource, and it updates the project's resource.h file with corresponding #*define* constants.

2. Use ClassWizard to create a dialog class that is derived from *CDialog* and attached to the resource created in step 1. ClassWizard adds the associated code and header file to the Developer Studio project.

> **NOTE:** When ClassWizard generates your derived dialog class, it generates a public constructor that invokes the *CDialog* protected constructor, which takes a resource ID as a parameter. Your generated dialog header file contains a class *enum IDD* that is set to the dialog resource ID. In the CPP file, the constructor implementation looks like this:

```
CMyDialog::CMyDialog(CWnd* pParent /*=NULL*/)
    : CDialog(CEx07aDialog::IDD, pParent)
{
    // initialization code here
}
```

> The use of *enum IDD* decouples the CPP file from the resource IDs that are defined in the project's resource.h file.

3. Use ClassWizard to add data members, exchange functions, and validation functions to the dialog class.

4. Use ClassWizard to add message handlers for the dialog's buttons and other event-generating controls.

5. Write the code for special control initialization (in *OnInitDialog*) and for the message handlers. Be sure the *CDialog* virtual member function *OnOK* is called when the user closes the dialog (unless the user cancels the dialog). (Note: *OnOK* is called by default.)

6. Write the code in your view class to activate the dialog. This code consists of a call to your dialog class's constructor followed by a call to the *DoModal* dialog class member function. *DoModal* returns only when the user exits the dialog window.

Now we'll proceed with a real example, one step at a time.

The Dialog That Ate Cincinnati—
The EX06A Example

Let's not mess around with wimpy little dialogs. We'll build a monster dialog that contains almost every kind of control. The job will be easy because the Developer Studio's graphic editor is there to help us. The finished product is shown in Figure 6-1.

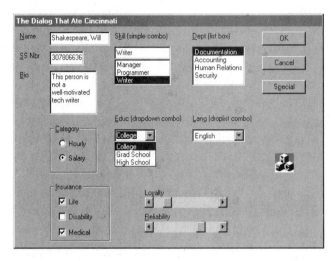

Figure 6-1.
The finished dialog in action.

As you can see, the dialog supports a human resources application. These kinds of business programs are fairly boring, so the challenge is to produce something that could not have been done with 80-column punched cards. The program is brightened a little by the use of scroll bar controls for "loyalty" and "reliability." Here is a classic example of direct action and visual representation of data! OLE controls could add more interest, but they aren't covered until Chapter 8.

Building the Dialog Resource

Here are the steps for building the dialog resource:

1. **Run AppWizard to generate a project called EX06A.** Choose New from the Developer Studio's File menu, and then select Project Workspace. Accept the defaults, but select Single Document Interface and deselect Printing And Print Preview. The options and the default class names are shown here:

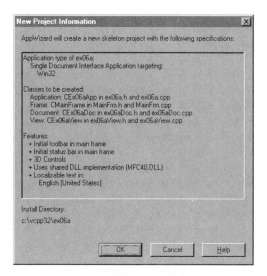

As usual, AppWizard sets the new project as the current project.

2. **Create a new dialog resource with ID *IDD_DIALOG1*.** Choose Resource from the Developer Studio's Insert menu. The Insert Resource dialog appears. Click on Dialog, and then click OK. The graphic editor creates a new dialog resource, as shown here:

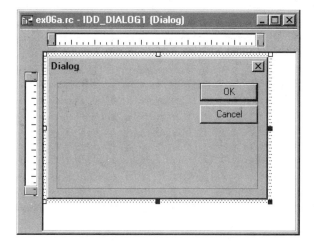

The graphic editor assigns the resource ID *IDD_DIALOG1* to the new dialog. Notice that the graphic editor inserts OK and Cancel buttons for the new dialog.

3. Size the dialog and assign a caption. When you double-click on the new dialog, or when you choose Properties from the graphic editor's Edit menu, the Dialog Properties dialog appears. Type in the caption for the new dialog as shown in the following screen. The state of the pushpin button determines whether the Dialog Properties dialog stays on top of other windows. (When the pushpin is "pushed," the dialog stays on top of other windows.) Click the Toggle Grid button (on the Dialog toolbar) to reveal the grid and to help align controls.

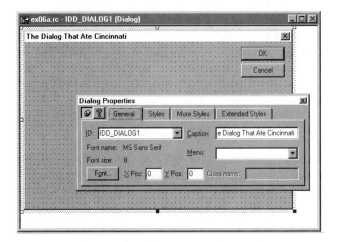

4. Set the dialog style. Click the Styles tab at the top of the Dialog Properties dialog, and then set the style properties as shown here:

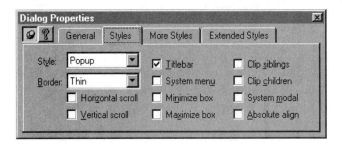

5. Set additional dialog styles. Click the More Styles tab at the top of the Dialog Properties dialog, and then set the style properties as shown at the top of the facing page:

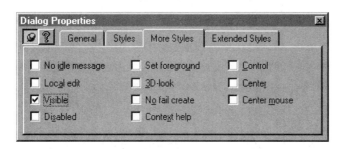

6. **Add the dialog's controls.**   Use the control palette to add each control. Drag controls from the control palette to the new dialog with the mouse, and then position and size the controls, as shown in Figure 6-1 on page 108. (You don't have to be precise when positioning the controls.) Here are the control palette's controls:

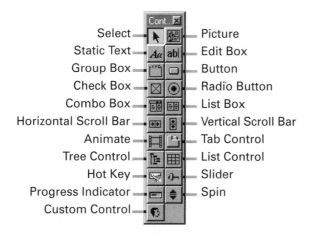

NOTE: The graphic editor displays the position and size of each control in the status bar. The position units are special "dialog units," or DLUs, <u>not</u> device units. A horizontal DLU is the average width of the dialog font divided by 4. A vertical DLU is the average height of the font divided by 8. The dialog font is normally 8-point MS Sans Serif.

Here's a brief description of the dialog's controls:

■ **The static text control for the Name field.**   A static text control simply paints characters on the screen. No user interaction occurs

111

at runtime. You can type the text after you position the bounding rectangle, and you can resize the rectangle as needed. This is the only static text control you'll see listed in text, but you should also create the other static text controls as shown in Figure 6-1. Follow the same procedure for the other static text controls in the dialog. All static text controls have the same ID, but that doesn't matter because the program doesn't need to access any of them.

■ **The Name edit control.** An edit control is the primary means of entering text in a dialog. Change this control's ID from *IDC_EDIT1* to *IDC_NAME*. Accept the defaults for the rest of the properties. Notice that the default sets Auto HScroll, which means that the text scrolls horizontally when the box is filled.

■ **The SS Nbr (social security number) edit control.** As far as the graphic editor is concerned, this control is exactly the same as the Name edit control. Simply change its ID to *IDC_SSN*. Later you will use ClassWizard to make this a numeric field.

■ **The Bio (biography) edit control.** This is a multiline edit control. Change its ID to *IDC_BIO*, and then set its properties as shown here:

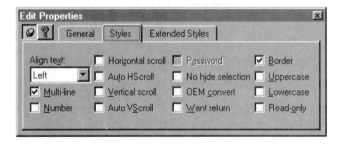

■ **The Category group box.** This control serves only to group two radio buttons visually. Type in the caption *Category*. The default ID is sufficient.

■ **The Hourly and Salary radio buttons.** Position these radio buttons inside the Category group box. Set the Hourly button's ID to *IDC_CAT*, and set the other properties as shown at the top of the facing page:

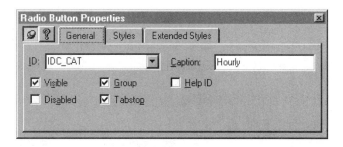

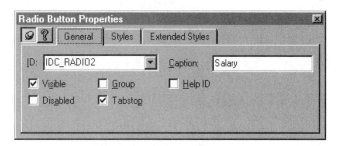

Be sure that both buttons have the Auto property on the Styles tab set (the default) and that only the Hourly button has the Group property set. When these properties are set correctly, Windows ensures that only one of the two buttons can be selected at a time. The Category group box has no effect on the buttons' operation.

■ **The Insurance group box.** This control holds three check boxes. Type in the caption *Insurance*.

> NOTE: Later, when you set the dialog's tab order, you'll ensure that the Insurance group box follows the last radio button of the Category group. Set the Insurance control's Group property now in order to "terminate" the previous group. If you fail to do this, it isn't a serious problem, but you'll get a warning message when you run the program through the debugger.

■ **The Life, Disability, and Medical check boxes.** Place these controls inside the Insurance group box. Accept the default properties, but change the IDs to *IDC_LIFE*, *IDC_DIS*, and *IDC_MED*. Unlike radio buttons, check boxes are independent; the user can set any combination.

■ **The Skill combo box.** This is the first of three types of combo boxes. Change the ID to *IDC_SKILL*; otherwise, accept all the defaults. Add three skills (terminating each line with Ctrl-Enter) in the Enter Listbox Items box, as shown here:

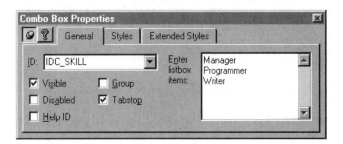

This is a combo box of type Simple (the default). The user can type anything in the top edit control, use the mouse to select an item from the attached list box, or use the Up or Down direction key to select an item from the attached list box.

Aligning Controls

To align two or more controls, select the controls by clicking on the first control and then Shift-clicking on the other controls you want aligned. Next choose one of the alignment commands (Left, Right, Top, or Bottom) from the Align Controls pop-up menu on the graphic editor's Layout menu.

■ **The Educ (education) combo box.** Change the ID to *IDC_EDUC*, and then select the Styles tab and set the Type option to Dropdown. Add the three education levels in the Enter Listbox Items box, as shown in Figure 6-1. With this combo box, the user can type anything in the edit box, click on the arrow, and then select an item from the drop-down list box, or use the Up or Down direction key to select an item from the attached list box.

NOTE: To set the size for the drop-down portion of a combo box, click on the box's arrow and drag down from the bottom center of the rectangle.

■ **The Dept (department) list box.** Change the ID to *IDC_DEPT*; otherwise, accept all the defaults. In this list box, the user can select only a single item by using the mouse, by using the Up or Down direction key, or by typing the first character of a selection. Note that you can't enter the initial choices in the graphic editor. You'll see how to set these choices later.

■ **The Lang (language) combo box.** Change the ID to *IDC_LANG*, and then select the Styles tab and set the Type option to Drop List. Add three languages (English, French, and Spanish) to the Enter Listbox Items box. With this combo box, the user can select only from the attached list box. To select, the user can click the arrow and then select an entry from the drop-down list, or the user can type in the first letter of the selection and then refine the selection with the Up or Down direction key.

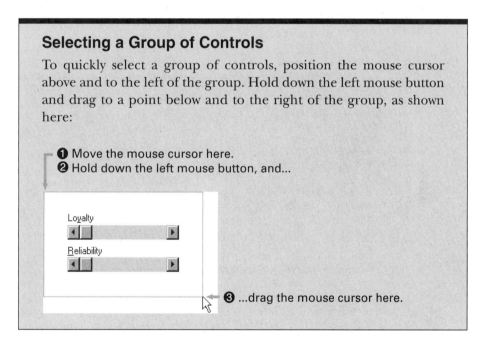

Selecting a Group of Controls

To quickly select a group of controls, position the mouse cursor above and to the left of the group. Hold down the left mouse button and drag to a point below and to the right of the group, as shown here:

❶ Move the mouse cursor here.
❷ Hold down the left mouse button, and...

Loyalty

Reliability

❸ ...drag the mouse cursor here.

■ **The Loyalty and Reliability scroll bars.** Do not confuse scroll bar controls with a window's built-in scroll bars as seen in scrolling views. A scroll bar control behaves in the same manner as do other controls and can be resized at design time. Position and size the horizontal scroll bar controls as shown in Figure 6-1, and then assign the IDs *IDC_LOYAL* and *IDC_RELY*.

■ **The OK, Cancel, and Special pushbuttons.** Be sure the button captions are *OK, Cancel,* and *Special,* and then assign the *IDC_SPECIAL* ID to the Special button. Later you'll learn about special meanings that are associated with the default *IDOK* and *IDCANCEL* IDs.

■ **Any icon. (The MFC icon is shown as an example.)** You can display any icon in a dialog, as long as the resource script defines the icon. We'll use the program's MFC icon, identified as *IDR_MAINFRAME.* Set the Type option to Icon, and set the icon to *IDR_MAINFRAME.* Leave the ID as *IDC_STATIC.*

7. Check the dialog's tabbing order. Choose Tab Order from the graphic editor's Layout menu. Use the mouse to set the tabbing order, as shown here:

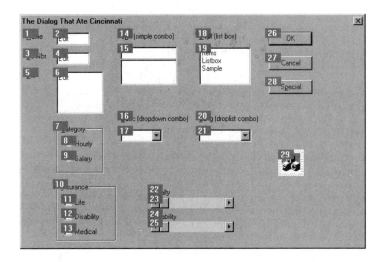

Click on each control in the order shown, and then press Enter.

TIP: If you mess up the tab sequence part way through, you can recover with a Ctrl-left mouse click on the last correctly sequenced control. Subsequent mouse clicks will start with the next sequence number.

NOTE: Static text controls (such as Name and Skill) have ampersands (&) embedded in the text for their captions. At runtime,
the ampersands will appear as underscores under the characters
that follow. (See Figure 6-1 on page 108.) This enables the user to
jump to selected controls by holding down the Alt key and pressing the key corresponding to the underlined character. (The related control must immediately follow the static text in the
tabbing order.) Thus, Alt-N jumps to the Name edit control, and
Alt-K jumps to the Skill combo box. Needless to say, designated
jump characters should be unique within the dialog. The Skill
control uses Alt-*K* because the SS Nbr control uses Alt-*S*.

8. **Save the resource file on disk.**   For safety's sake, choose Save from
the File menu or click the Save button on the toolbar to save ex06a.rc.
Keep the graphic editor running, and keep the newly built dialog on
the screen.

ClassWizard and the Dialog Class

You have now built a dialog resource, but you can't use it without a corresponding dialog class. (The section titled "Understanding the EX06A Application" beginning on page 123 explains the relationship between the dialog
window and the underlying classes.) ClassWizard works in conjunction with
the graphic editor to create that class as follows:

1. **Choose ClassWizard from the Developer Studio's View menu.**   Be
sure that you still have the newly built dialog, *IDD_DIALOG1*, selected in
the graphic editor and that \VCPP32\EX06A\EX06A.MAK is the current
Developer Studio project.

2. **Add the *CEx06aDialog* class.**   ClassWizard detects the fact that you've
just created a dialog resource without an associated C++ class. It politely
asks whether you want to create a class, as shown below:

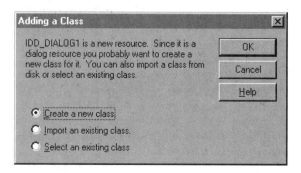

117

Click OK, and then fill in the top field of the Create New Class dialog, as shown here:

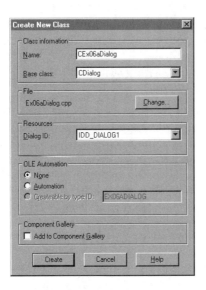

3. **Add the *CEx06aDialog* variables.** After ClassWizard creates the *CEx06aDialog* class, the MFC ClassWizard dialog appears. Click the Member Variables tab, and the Member Variables page appears, as shown here:

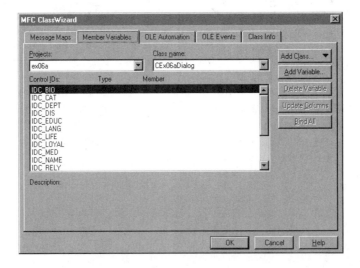

You need to associate data members with each of the dialog's controls. To associate a data member with one of the dialog's controls, click on a control ID and then click the Add Variable button. The Add Member Variable dialog appears, as shown here:

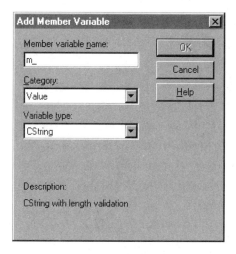

Type in the member variable name and choose the variable type according to the following table. Be sure to type in the member variable name exactly as shown; the case of each letter is important. Click OK to return to the MFC Class Wizard dialog. Repeat this process for each of the listed controls.

Control ID	Data Member	Type
IDC_BIO	m_strBio	CString
IDC_CAT	m_nCat	int
IDC_DEPT	m_strDept	CString
IDC_DIS	m_bInsDis	BOOL
IDC_EDUC	m_strEduc	CString
IDC_LANG	m_strLang	CString
IDC_LIFE	m_bInsLife	BOOL
IDC_LOYAL	m_nLoyal	int
IDC_MED	m_bInsMed	BOOL
IDC_NAME	m_strName	CString
IDC_RELY	m_nRely	int
IDC_SKILL	m_strSkill	CString
IDC_SSN	m_nSsn	int

As you select controls in the MFC ClassWizard dialog, various edit boxes appear at the bottom of the dialog. If you select a *CString* variable, you can set its maximum number of characters; if you select a numeric variable, you can set its high and low limits. Set the minimum value for *IDC_SSN* to *0* and the maximum value to *999999999*.

Most relationships between control types and variable types are obvious. The way in which radio buttons correspond to variables is not so intuitive, however. The *CDialog* class associates an integer variable with each radio button *group*, with the first button corresponding to value 0, the second to 1, and so forth.

4. Add the message-handling function for the Special button.

CEx06aDialog doesn't need many message-handling functions because the *CDialog* base class, with the help of Windows, does most of the dialog management. When you specify the *IDOK* ID for the OK button (Class-Wizard's default), for example, the virtual *CDialog* function *OnOK* gets called when the user clicks the button. For other buttons, however, you need message handlers. Click the Message Maps tab.

The ClassWizard dialog should contain an entry for *IDC_SPECIAL* in the Object IDs list box. Click on this entry, and double-click on the BN_CLICKED message that appears in the Messages list box. ClassWizard invents a member function name, *OnSpecial*, and opens the Add Member Function dialog, as shown here:

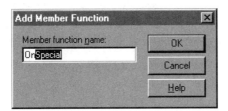

You could type in your own function name here, but this time accept the default and click OK. Next click the Edit Code button in the MFC ClassWizard dialog. This opens the file ex06aDialog.cpp and moves to the *OnSpecial* function. Insert a *TRACE* statement in the *OnSpecial* function by typing in the shaded code, which replaces the existing code.

```
void CEx06aDialog::OnSpecial()
{
    TRACE("CEx06aDialog::OnSpecial\n");
}
```

5. Use ClassWizard to add an *OnInitDialog* message-handling function. As you'll see in a moment, ClassWizard generates code that initializes a dialog's controls. This DDX (Dialog Data Exchange) code won't initialize the list box choices, however, so you must override the *CDialog::OnInitDialog* function. Although *OnInitDialog* is a virtual member function, ClassWizard generates the prototype and skeleton if you map the WM_INITDIALOG message in the derived dialog class. To do so, click on *CEx06aDialog* in the Object IDs list box, and then double-click on the WM_INITDIALOG message in the Messages list box. Click the Edit Code button in the MFC ClassWizard dialog to edit the *OnInit-Dialog* function. Type in the shaded code, which replaces the existing code:

```
BOOL CEx06aDialog::OnInitDialog()
{
    // be careful to call CDialog::OnInitDialog
    // only once in this function
    CListBox* pLB = (CListBox*) GetDlgItem(IDC_DEPT);
    pLB->InsertString(-1, "Documentation");
    pLB->InsertString(-1, "Accounting");
    pLB->InsertString(-1, "Human Relations");
    pLB->InsertString(-1, "Security");

    // call after initialization
    return CDialog::OnInitDialog();
}
```

You could use the same initialization technique for the combo boxes if you wanted, in place of the initialization in the resource.

Connecting the Dialog to the View

Now we've got the resource and the code for a dialog, but it's not connected to the view. In most applications, you would probably use a menu choice to activate a dialog, but we haven't studied menus yet. Here we'll use the familiar mouse click message WM_LBUTTONDOWN to start the dialog. The steps are as follows:

1. In ClassWizard, select the *CEx06aView* class. At this point, be sure that \VCPP32\EX06A\EX06A.MDP is the Developer Studio's current project.

2. Use ClassWizard to add the *OnLButtonDown* member function. You've done this in the examples in earlier chapters. Simply select the *CEx06aView* class name, click on the *CEx06aView* object ID, and then double-click on WM_LBUTTONDOWN.

3. Add code to the virtual *OnDraw* function in file ex06aView.cpp.
To prompt the user to press the left mouse button, code the *CEx06aView*
OnDraw function. (The skeleton was generated by AppWizard.) The fol-
lowing shaded code (which you type in) replaces the existing code:

```
void CEx06aView::OnDraw(CDC* pDC)
{
    pDC->TextOut(0, 0, "Press the left mouse button here.");
}
```

4. Write the code for *OnLButtonDown* in file ex06aView.cpp.   Add the
shaded code as shown below. Most of the code consists of *TRACE* statements to print the dialog data members after the user exits the dialog.
The *CEx06aDialog* constructor call and the *DoModal* call are the critical
statements, however:

```
void CEx06aView::OnLButtonDown(UINT nFlags, CPoint point)
{
    CEx06aDialog dlg;
    dlg.m_strName  = "Shakespeare, Will";
    dlg.m_nSsn     = 307806636;
    dlg.m_nCat     = 1;  // 0 = hourly, 1 = salary
    dlg.m_strBio   = "This person is not a well-motivated tech writer";
    dlg.m_bInsLife = TRUE;
    dlg.m_bInsDis  = FALSE;
    dlg.m_bInsMed  = TRUE;
    dlg.m_strDept    = "Documentation";
    dlg.m_strSkill   = "Writer";
    dlg.m_strLang    = "English";
    dlg.m_strEduc    = "College";
    dlg.m_nLoyal   = dlg.m_nRely = 50;
    int ret = dlg.DoModal();
    TRACE("DoModal return = %d\n", ret);
    TRACE("name = %s, ssn = %d, nCat = %d\n",
        (const char*) dlg.m_strName, dlg.m_nSsn, dlg.m_nCat);
    TRACE("dept = %s, skill = %s, lang = %s, educ = %s\n",
        (const char*) dlg.m_strDept, (const char*) dlg.m_strSkill,
        (const char*) dlg.m_strLang, (const char*) dlg.m_strEduc);
    TRACE("life = %d, dis = %d, med = %d, bio = %s\n",
        dlg.m_bInsLife, dlg.m_bInsDis, dlg.m_bInsMed,
        (const char*) dlg.m_strBio);
    TRACE(" loyalty = %d, reliability = %d\n",
        dlg.m_nLoyal, dlg.m_nRely);
}
```

5. To ex06aView.cpp, add the dialog class include statement. The *OnLButtonDown* function above depends on the declaration of class *CEx06aDialog*. You must insert the include statement

```
#include "ex06aDialog.h"
```

at the top of the *CEx06aView* class source code file (ex06aView.cpp), after the statement

```
#include "ex06aView.h"
```

6. Build and test the application. If you have done everything correctly, you should be able to build and run the EX06A application through the Developer Studio. Try entering data in each control, and then click the OK button and observe the *TRACE* results in the Debug window. Notice that the scroll bar controls don't do much yet; we'll attend to them later. Notice what happens when you press Enter while typing in text data in a control: the dialog closes immediately.

Understanding the EX06A Application

When your program calls *DoModal*, control is returned to your program only when the user closes the dialog. If you understand that, you understand modal dialogs. When you get to modeless dialogs, you'll begin to appreciate the programming simplicity of modal dialogs. A lot happens "out of sight" as a result of that *DoModal* call, however. Here's a "what calls what" summary:

CDialog::DoModal

   CEx06aDialog::OnInitDialog

     …additional initialization…

    CDialog::OnInitDialog

      CWnd::UpdateData(FALSE)

       CEx06aDialog::DoDataExchange

   user enters data…

   user clicks the OK button

   CEx06aDialog::OnOK

     …additional validation…

(continued)

123

CDialog::OnOK

CWnd::UpdateData(TRUE)

CEx06aDialog::DoDataExchange

CDialog::EndDialog(IDOK)

OnInitDialog and *DoDataExchange* are virtual functions overridden in the *CEx06a Dialog* class. Windows calls *OnInitDialog* as part of the dialog initialization process, and that results in a call to *DoDataExchange*, a *CWnd* virtual function that was overridden by ClassWizard. Here is a listing of that function:

```
void CEx06aDialog::DoDataExchange(CDataExchange* pDX)
{
    CDialog::DoDataExchange(pDX);
    //{{AFX_DATA_MAP(CEx06aDialog)
    DDX_Text(pDX, IDC_BIO, m_strBio);
    DDX_Radio(pDX, IDC_CAT, m_nCat);
    DDX_LBString(pDX, IDC_DEPT, m_strDept);
    DDX_Check(pDX, IDC_DIS, m_bInsDis);
    DDX_CBString(pDX, IDC_LANG, m_strLang);
    DDX_Check(pDX, IDC_LIFE, m_bInsLife);
    DDX_Scroll(pDX, IDC_LOYAL, m_nLoyal);
    DDX_Check(pDX, IDC_MED, m_bInsMed);
    DDX_Text(pDX, IDC_NAME, m_strName);
    DDX_Scroll(pDX, IDC_RELY, m_nRely);
    DDX_CBString(pDX, IDC_SKILL, m_strSkill);
    DDV_MinMaxInt(pDX, IDC_SSN, m_nSsn, 0, 999999999);
    DDX_CBString(pDX, IDC_EDUC, m_strEduc);
    //}}AFX_DATA_MAP
}
```

DoDataExchange and the *DDX_* (exchange) and *DDV_* (validation) functions are "bi-directional." If *UpdateData* is called with a *FALSE* parameter, the functions transfer data from the data members to the dialog controls. If the parameter is *TRUE*, the functions transfer data from the dialog controls to the data members. *DDX_Text* is overloaded to accommodate a variety of data types.

The *EndDialog* function is critical to the dialog exit procedure. *DoModal* returns the parameter passed to *EndDialog*. *IDOK* accepts the dialog's data, and *IDCANCEL* cancels the dialog.

TIP: You can write your own "custom" DDX functions and wire them into the Developer Studio. This feature is useful if you're using a unique data type throughout your application. See MFC Technical Note #26 in Books Online.

Enhancing the Dialog Program

The EX06A program required little coding for a lot of functionality. Now we'll make a new version of this program that uses some hand-coding to add extra features. We'll eliminate EX06A's rude habit of dumping the user in response to a press of the Enter key, and we'll hook up the scroll bar controls.

Taking Control of the *OnOK* Exit

In the original EX06A program, the *CDialog::OnOK* virtual function handled the OK button, which triggered data exchange and the exit from the dialog. The Enter key happens to have the same effect, and that might or might not be what you want. If the user presses Enter in the Name edit control, for example, he or she is immediately bounced out of the dialog.

What's going on here? When the user presses Enter, Windows looks to see which pushbutton has the input focus as indicated on the screen by a dotted rectangle. If no button has the focus, Windows looks for the default pushbutton that the program or the resource specifies. (The default pushbutton has a thicker border.) If the dialog has no default button, the virtual *OnOK* function is called, even if the dialog does not contain an OK button.

You can disable the Enter key simply by writing a do-nothing *CEx06aDialog::OnOK* function and adding the exit code to a new function that responds to the OK button. Here are the steps:

1. **Use ClassWizard to "map" the IDOK button to the virtual *OnOK* function.** With the *IDD_DIALOG1* resource selected in the graphic editor, choose *IDOK* from the *CEx06aDialog* Object IDs list, and then double-click on *BN_CLICKED*. This generates the prototype and skeleton for *OnOK.*

2. **Use the graphic editor to change the OK button ID.** Select the OK button, change its ID from *IDOK* to *IDC_OK*, and then uncheck its Default Button property. Leave the *OnOK* function alone.

For Win32 Programmers

Dialog controls send WM_COMMAND <u>notification messages</u> to their parent dialogs. For a single button click, for example, the bottom 16 bits of *wParam* contain the button ID, the top 16 bits of *wParam* contain the BN_CLICKED notification code, and *lParam* contains the button handle. Most *WndProc* programs process these notification messages with a nested switch statement. MFC "flattens out" the message processing logic by "promoting" control notification messages to the same level as other Windows messages.

ClassWizard generates notification message map entries similar to this:

```
ON_BN_CLICKED(IDC_DELETE, OnDeleteButtonClicked)
ON_BN_DOUBLECLICKED(IDC_DELETE, OnDeleteButtonDblClicked)
```

Button events are special because they generate <u>command messages</u> if your dialog class doesn't have notification handlers like the ones above. As Chapter 13 explains, the application framework "routes" these command messages to various objects in your application. You could also map control notifications with a more generic ON_COMMAND message-handling entry like this:

```
ON_COMMAND(IDC_DELETE, OnDelete)
```

In this case, the *OnDelete* function is unable to distinguish between a single click and a double click, but that's no problem because few Windows-based programs utilize double clicks for buttons.

3. **Use ClassWizard to create a member function called *OnClickedOk*.**
   This *CEx06aDialog* class member function is keyed to the BN_CLICKED message from the newly renamed control *IDC_OK*.

4. **Edit the body of the *OnClickedOk* function in ex06aDialog.cpp.**
   This function calls the base class *OnOK* function, as did the original *CEx06aDialog::OnOK* function. Here is the code:

```
void CEx06aDialog::OnClickedOk()
{
    TRACE("CEx06aDialog::OnClickedOk\n");
    CDialog::OnOK();
}
```

5. Edit the original *OnOK* function in ex06aDialog.cpp.   This function is a "leftover" handler for the old *IDOK* button. Edit the code as follows:

```
void CEx06aDialog::OnOK()
{
    // dummy OnOK function -- do NOT call CDialog::OnOK()
    TRACE("CEx06aDialog::OnOK\n");
}
```

6. Build and test the application.   Try pressing the Enter key now. Nothing should happen, but *TRACE* output should appear in the Debug window. Clicking the OK button should exit the dialog as before, however.

OnCancel Processing

Just as pressing the Enter key triggers a call to *OnOK*, pressing the Esc key triggers a call to *OnCancel*, which results in an exit from the dialog with a *DoModal* return code of *IDCANCEL*. EX06A does no special processing for *IDCANCEL*; therefore, pressing the Esc key (and double-clicking the Close box in Windows 95 and selecting the system menu Close command in Windows NT) closes the dialog. You can circumvent this process by substituting a dummy *OnCancel* function, following the same procedure you used for the OK button.

Hooking Up the Scroll Bar Controls

The graphic editor allows you to put scroll bar controls in your dialog, and ClassWizard lets you add integer data members. You must add code to make the Loyalty and Reliability scroll bars work.

Scroll bar controls have position and range values that can be read and written. If you set the range to (0, 100), for example, a corresponding data member with a value of 50 positions the scroll box at the center of the bar. (The function *CScrollBar::SetScrollPos* also sets the scroll box position.) The scroll bars send the WM_HSCROLL and WM_VSCROLL messages to the dialog when the user drags the scroll box or clicks the arrows. The dialog's message handlers must decode these messages and position the scroll box accordingly.

One tricky thing about scroll bar controls is that all horizontal bars send the same message, WM_HSCROLL, and all vertical bars send the WM_VSCROLL message. Because this monster dialog contains two horizontal scroll bars, the one and only WM_HSCROLL message handler must figure out which scroll bar sent the scroll message.

Here are the steps for adding the scroll bar logic to EX06A:

1. **Add the class *enum* statements for the minimum and maximum scroll range.** In ex06aDialog.h, add the following lines at the top of the class declaration:

```
enum { nMin = 0 };
enum { nMax = 100 };
```

2. **Edit the *OnInitDialog* function to initialize the scroll ranges.** The *OnInitDialog* function must set the minimum and maximum scroll values such that the *CEx06aDialog* data members represent percentage values. A value of 100 means "Set the scroll box to the extreme right"; a value of 0 means "Set the scroll box to the extreme left."

Add the following code to the *CEx06aDialog* member function *OnInit-Dialog* in the file ex06aDialog.cpp:

```
CScrollBar* pSB = (CScrollBar*) GetDlgItem(IDC_LOYAL);
pSB->SetScrollRange(nMin, nMax);

pSB = (CScrollBar*) GetDlgItem(IDC_RELY);
pSB->SetScrollRange(nMin, nMax);
```

3. **Use ClassWizard to add a scroll bar message handler to *CEx06aDialog*.** Choose the WM_HSCROLL message, and then add the member function *OnHScroll*. Enter the following shaded code:

```
void CEx06aDialog::OnHScroll(UINT nSBCode, UINT nPos,
                             CScrollBar* pScrollBar)
{
    int nTemp1, nTemp2;

    nTemp1 = pScrollBar->GetScrollPos();
    switch(nSBCode) {
    case SB_THUMBPOSITION:
        pScrollBar->SetScrollPos(nPos);
        break;
    case SB_LINELEFT: // left arrow button
        nTemp2 = (nMax - nMin) / 10;
        if ((nTemp1 - nTemp2) > nMin) {
          nTemp1 -= nTemp2;
          }
```

```
        else {
          nTemp1 = nMin;
        }
        pScrollBar->SetScrollPos(nTemp1);
        break;
  case SB_LINERIGHT: // right arrow button
        nTemp2 = (nMax - nMin) / 10;
        if ((nTemp1 + nTemp2) < nMax) {
          nTemp1 += nTemp2;
        }
        else {
          nTemp1 = nMax;
        }
        pScrollBar->SetScrollPos(nTemp1);
        break;
  }
}
```

NOTE: The scroll bar functions use 16-bit integers for both range and position.

4. **Build and test the application.** Build and run EX06A again. Do the scroll bars work this time? The scroll boxes should "stick" after you drag them with the mouse, and they should move when you click the scroll bars' arrows. (Notice that we haven't yet added logic to cover the user's click on the scroll bar itself.)

Identifying Controls:
CWnd Pointers and Control IDs

When you lay out a dialog resource in the graphic editor, you identify controls by IDs such as *IDC_SSN*. In your program code, however, you often need access to a control's underlying window object. The MFC library provides the *CWnd::GetDlgItem* function for converting an ID to a *CWnd* pointer. You've seen this already in the *OnInitDialog* and *OnClickedOK* member functions of class *CEx06aDialog*. The application framework "manufactured" this returned *CWnd* pointer because there never was a constructor call for the control objects. This pointer is temporary and should not be stored for later use.

TIP: If you need to convert a *CWnd* pointer to a control ID, use the MFC library *GetDlgCtrlID* member function of class *CWnd*.

Setting the Color for the
Dialog Background and for Controls

It's very easy to select a new color for <u>all</u> the dialogs in your application. Just edit the call to *SetDialogBkColor* in your derived application class *InitInstance* function. The following line applies a green background and white static text to all dialogs:

```
SetDialogBkColor(RGB(0, 255, 0), RGB(255, 255, 255));
```

If you want to change the background color of individual dialogs or specific controls in a dialog, you have to work a little harder. There is no *SetDlgItemColor* function. Instead, each control sends a WM_CTLCOLOR message to the parent dialog immediately before the control is displayed. A WM_CTLCOLOR message is also sent on behalf of the dialog itself. If you map this message in your derived dialog class, you can set the foreground and background text colors and can select a brush for the control or dialog nontext area.

Here's a sample *OnCtlColor* function that sets all edit control backgrounds to yellow and the dialog background to red. The *m_hYellowBrush* and *m_hRedBrush* variables are data members of type *HBRUSH*, initialized in the dialog's *OnInitDialog* function. The *nCtlColor* parameter indicates the type of control, and the *pWnd* parameter identifies the specific control. If you wanted to set the color for an individual edit control, you would convert *pWnd* to a child window ID and test it.

```
HBRUSH CMyDialog::OnCtlColor(CDC* pDC, CWnd* pWnd, UINT nCtlColor)
{
    if (nCtlColor == CTLCOLOR_EDIT) {
        pDC >SetBkColor(RGB(255, 255, 0));  // yellow
        return m_hYellowBrush;
    }
    if (nCtlColor == CTLCOLOR_DLG) {
        pDC->SetBkColor(RGB(255, 0, 0));     // red
        return m_hRedBrush;
    }
    return CDialog::OnCtlColor(pDC, pWnd, nCtlColor);
}
```

> NOTE: The dialog does not post the WM_CTLCOLOR message in the message queue; instead, it calls the Win32 *SendMessage* function to send the message immediately. Thus the message handler can return a parameter, in this case a handle to a brush. This is not an MFC *CBrush* object but rather a Win32 *HBRUSH*. You can create the brush by calling the Win32 functions *CreateSolidBrush*, *CreateHatchBrush*, and so forth.

For Win32 Programmers

Actually, Win32 doesn't have a WM_CTLCOLOR message anymore. It was replaced by control-specific messages such as WM_CTLCOLOR-BTN, WM_CTLCOLORDLG, and so on. MFC and ClassWizard process these messages invisibly, so your programs look as though they're mapping the old 16-bit WM_CTLCOLOR messages. This trick makes debugging more complex, but it makes portable code easier to write.

Painting Inside the Dialog Window

You can paint directly in the client area of the dialog window, but you'll avoid overwriting dialog elements if you paint only inside a control window. If you want to display only text, use the graphic editor to create a blank static control with a unique ID, and then call the *CWnd::SetDlgItemText* function in a dialog member function such as *OnInitDialog* to place text in the control.

Displaying graphics is more complicated. You must use ClassWizard to add an *OnPaint* member function to the dialog; this function converts the static control's ID to a *CWnd* pointer and gets its device context. The trick is to draw inside the control window while preventing Windows from overwriting your work later. The *Invalidate/UpdateWindow* sequence achieves this. Here is an *OnPaint* function that paints a small black square in a static control:

```
void CMyDialog::OnPaint()
{
    CPaintDC dc(this);                      // keeps Windows happy
    CWnd* pWnd = GetDlgItem(IDC_STATIC1);   // IDC_STATIC1 specified
                                            //  in the graphic editor

    CDC* pControlDC = pWnd->GetDC();

    pWnd->Invalidate();
    pWnd->UpdateWindow();
    pControlDC->SelectStockObject(BLACK_BRUSH);
    pControlDC->Rectangle(0, 0, 10, 10);    // black square bullet
    pWnd->ReleaseDC(pControlDC);
}
```

As with all windows, the dialog's *OnPaint* function is called only if some part of the dialog is invalidated. You can force the *OnPaint* call from another dialog member function with the following statement:

```
Invalidate();
```

Adding Dialog Controls at Runtime

You've seen how to use the graphic editor to create dialog controls at build time. If you need to add a dialog control at runtime, here are the programming steps:

1. Add an embedded control window data member to your dialog class. The MFC control window classes include *CButton*, *CEdit*, *CListBox*, and *CComboBox*. An embedded control C++ object is constructed and destroyed along with the dialog object.

2. With the graphic editor active, choose Resource Symbols from the Developer Studio's View menu. Add an ID constant for the new control.

3. Use ClassWizard to map the WM_INITDIALOG message, thus overriding *CDialog::OnInitDialog*. This function should call the embedded control window's *Create* member function. This call displays the new control in the dialog. Windows will destroy the control window when it destroys the dialog window.

4. In your derived dialog class, manually add the necessary notification message handlers for your new control.

In Chapter 12, you'll be adding a rich edit control to a view at runtime.

Using Other Control Features

You've seen how to customize one control class, *CScrollBar*, by adding code in the dialog's *OnInitDialog* member function. You can program the other controls in a similar fashion. Look in the *Microsoft Foundation Class Library Reference* at the control classes, particularly *CListBox* and *CComboBox*. Each has a number of features that ClassWizard does not directly support. List boxes and some combo boxes, for example, can support multiple selections. If you want to use these features, don't try to use ClassWizard to add data members, but define your own data members and add your own exchange code in *OnInitDialog* and *OnClickedOK*.

For Win32 Programmers

If you've programmed controls in Win32, you'll know that parent windows communicate to controls via Windows messages. So what does a function like *CListBox::InsertString* do? (You've seen this function called in your *OnInitDialog* function.) If you look at the MFC source code, you'll see that *InsertString* sends an LB_INSERTSTRING message to the designated list box control. Other control class member functions don't send messages because they apply to all window types. The *CScrollView::SetScrollRange* function, for example, calls the Win32 *SetScrollRange* function, specifying the correct *hWnd* as a parameter.

Windows 95 Common Controls

The controls you used in EX06A are a good place to start learning about controls because they're easy to program. Now you're ready for some more "interesting" controls. We'll look at some important Windows 95 common controls, including the progress indicator, trackbar, spinner, list control, and tree control. The code for these controls is inside the Windows COMCTL32.DLL file. This code includes the window procedures for each control, together with code that registers a window class for each control. The registration code is called when the DLL is loaded. When your program initializes a dialog, it uses the symbolic class name in the dialog resource to connect to the window procedure in the DLL. Thus your program owns the control's window, but the code is in the DLL. Except for OCXs, most controls work this way.

Example EX06B uses the aforementioned controls. Figure 6-2 on the following page shows the dialog from that example. Refer to it when you read the control descriptions that follow.

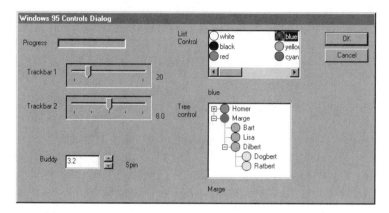

Figure 6-2.
Windows 95 common controls.

Be aware that ClassWizard offers no member variable support for the common controls. You'll have to add code to your *OnInitDialog* and *OnOK* functions to initialize and read control data. ClassWizard will, however, allow you to map notification messages from common controls.

The Progress Indicator Control

The progress indicator is the easiest common control to program and is represented by the MFC *CProgressCtrl* class. It is generally used only for output. This control, together with the trackbar, can effectively replace the scroll bar controls you saw in the previous example. To initialize the progress indicator, call the *SetRange* and *SetPos* member functions in your *OnInitDialog* function, and then call *SetPos* any time in your message handlers. The progress indicator shown in Figure 6-2 has a range of 0 through 100, which is the default range.

The Trackbar Control

The trackbar control (class *CSliderCtrl*), sometimes called a slider, allows the user to set an "analog" value. If you specify a large range for this control—0 through 100 or more, for example—the trackbar's motion appears continuous. If you specify a small range, such as 0 through 5, the tracker moves in discrete increments. You can program tick marks to match the increments. In this discrete mode, you can use a trackbar to set such items as the display screen resolution, lens f-stop values, and so forth. The trackbar does not have a default range.

The trackbar is easier to program than the scroll bar because you don't have to map the WM_HSCROLL or WM_VSCROLL messages in the dialog class. As long as you set the range, the tracker moves when the user slides it or clicks in the body of the trackbar. You might choose to map the scroll messages anyway if you want to show the position value in another control. The *GetPos* member function returns the current position value. The top trackbar in Figure 6-2 operates continuously over the range 0 through 100. The bottom trackbar has a range of 0 through 4, and those indexes are mapped to a series of double-precision values (3.5, 5.5, 8.0, 11.0, and 16.0).

The Spinner Control

The spinner control (class *CSpinButtonCtrl*) is an itsy-bitsy scroll bar that's most often used in conjunction with an edit control. The edit control, located just ahead of the spinner in the dialog's tabbing order, is known as the spinner's "buddy." The idea is that the user holds down the left mouse button on the spinner to raise or lower the value in the edit control. The spin speed accelerates as the user continues to hold down the mouse button.

If your program uses an integer in the buddy, you can avoid C++ programming entirely. Just use ClassWizard to attach an integer data member to the edit control. The spinner's range defaults to 0 through 100. Don't forget to select Auto Buddy and Set Buddy Integer in the spinner's style dialog page. You can call the *SetRange* and *SetAccel* member functions in your *OnInitDialog* function to change the range and the acceleration profile.

If you want your edit control to display a noninteger such as a time or a floating-point number, you must map the spinner's WM_VSCROLL (or WM_HSCROLL) messages to call the *GetPos* and *GetBuddy* member functions. Your handler code converts the spinner's integer to the buddy's value.

The List Control

Use the list control (class *CListCtrl*) if you want a list that contains images as well as text. Figure 6-2 shows a list control with a "list" view style and small icons. The elements are arranged in a grid, and the control includes horizontal scrolling. When the user selects an item, the control sends a notification message, which you map in your dialog class. That message handler can determine which item the user selected. Items are identified by a zero-based integer index.

Both the list control and the tree control get their graphic images from a common control element called an image list (class *CImageList*). Your program must assemble the image list from icons or bitmaps and then pass an image list pointer to the list control. Your *OnInitDialog* function is a good place to create and attach the image list and to assign text strings. The *InsertItem* member function serves this purpose.

List control programming is straightforward if you stick with strings and icons. If you implement drag-and-drop or if you need custom owner-drawn graphics, you've got more work to do.

The Tree Control

You're already familiar with tree controls if you've used the Windows 95 Explorer or the Developer Studio's workspace view and graphic editor. The MFC *CTreeCtrl* class makes it easy to add this same functionality to your own programs. Figure 6-2 illustrates a tree control that shows a modern American combined family. The user can expand and collapse elements by clicking the + and − buttons or by double-clicking the elements. The icon next to each item is programmed to change when the user selects the item with a single click.

The list control and the tree control have some things in common: they can use the same image list, and they share some of the same notification messages. The method of identifying items is different, however. The tree control uses an *HTREEITEM* handle instead of an integer index. To insert an item, you call the *InsertItem* member function, but first you must build up a *TV_INSERTSTRUCT* structure that identifies (among other things) the string, the image list index, and the handle of the parent item (null for top-level items).

As with list controls, there are infinite customization possibilities for the tree control. For example, you can allow the user to edit items and to insert and delete items.

The WM_NOTIFY Message

The original Windows controls sent their notifications in WM_COMMAND messages. The standard 32-bit *wParam* and *lParam* message parameters are not sufficient, however, for the information that a common control needs to send to its parent. Microsoft solved this "bandwidth" problem by defining a new message, WM_NOTIFY. With the WM_NOTIFY message, *wParam* is the control ID and *lParam* is a pointer to an *NMHDR* structure, which is managed by the control. This C structure is defined as follows:

```
typedef struct tagNMHDR {
    HWND hwndFrom; // handle to control sending the message
    UINT idFrom;   // ID of control sending the message
    UINT code;     // control-specific notification code
} NMHDR;
```

Many controls, however, send WM_NOTIFY messages with pointers to structures larger than *NMHDR*. Those structures contain the three members above plus appended control-specific members. Many tree control notifications, for example, pass a pointer to an *NM_TREEVIEW* structure that contains *TV_ITEM* structures, a drag point, and so forth. When ClassWizard maps a WM_NOTIFY message, it generates a pointer to the appropriate structure.

The EX06B Example

I won't try to contrive a business-oriented example that uses all the custom controls. I'll just slap the controls in a modal dialog and trust that you'll see what's going on. The steps are shown below and on the following pages. After step 3, the instructions are oriented to the individual controls rather than to the Visual C++ components you'll be using.

1. Run AppWizard to generate the EX06B project. Choose New from the Developer Studio's File menu, and then select Project Workspace. Accept the defaults, but select Single Document Interface and deselect Printing And Print Preview. The options and the default class names are shown here:

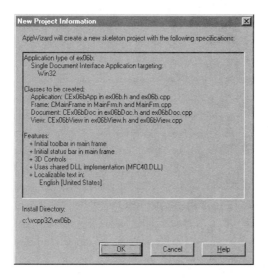

2. Create a new dialog resource with ID *IDD_DIALOG1*. Place the controls as shown in Figure 6-2 on page 134, and set the tab order as shown here:

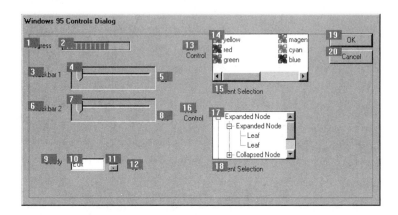

You can drag the controls from the control palette that is shown on page 111. The following table lists the control types and their IDs:

Tab Sequence	Control Type	Child Window ID
1	Static	IDC_STATIC
2	Progress	IDC_PROGRESS1
3	Static	IDC_STATIC
4	Trackbar	IDC_TRACKBAR1
5	Static	IDC_STATIC_TRACK1
6	Static	IDC_STATIC
7	Trackbar	IDC_TRACKBAR2
8	Static	IDC_STATIC_TRACK2
9	Static	IDC_STATIC
10	Edit	IDC_BUDDY_SPIN1
11	Spin button	IDC_SPIN1
12	Static	IDC_STATIC
13	Static	IDC_STATIC
14	List control	IDC_LISTVIEW1
15	Static	IDC_STATIC_LISTVIEW1
16	Static	IDC_STATIC

Tab Sequence	Control Type	Child Window ID
17	Tree control	*IDC_TREEVIEW1*
18	Static	*IDC_STATIC_TREEVIEW1*
19	Pushbutton	*IDOK*
20	Pushbutton	*IDCANCEL*

Don't worry about the other properties now—you'll set those in the following steps.

3. **Use ClassWizard to create a new class, *CWin95Dialog*, derived from *CDialog*.** ClassWizard will automatically prompt you to create this class because it knows that the *IDD_DIALOG1* resource exists without an associated C++ class. Map the WM_INITDIALOG message, the WM_HSCROLL message, and the WM_VSCROLL message.

4. **Program the progress control.** Because ClassWizard won't generate a data member for this control, you must do it yourself. Add a public integer data member named *m_nProgress* in the *CWin95Dialog* class header, and set it to 0 in the constructor. Also, add the following code in the *OnInitDialog* member function:

```
CProgressCtrl* pProg =
    (CProgressCtrl*) GetDlgItem(IDC_PROGRESS1);
pProg->SetRange(0, 100);
pProg->SetPos(m_nProgress);
```

5. **Program the "continuous" trackbar control.** Add a public integer data member named *m_nTrackbar1* to the *CWin95Dialog* header, and set it to 0 in the constructor. Next add the following code in the *OnInitDialog* member function to set the trackbar's range, to initialize its position from the data member, and to set the neighboring static control to the tracker's current value:

```
CString strText1;
CSliderCtrl* pSlide1 =
    (CSliderCtrl*) GetDlgItem(IDC_TRACKBAR1);
pSlide1->SetRange(0, 100);
pSlide1->SetPos(m_nTrackbar1);
strText1.Format("%d", pSlide1->GetPos());
SetDlgItemText(IDC_STATIC_TRACK1, strText1);
```

To keep the static control updated, you need to map the WM_H-SCROLL message that the trackbar sends to the dialog. Here is the code for the handler:

```
void CWin95Dialog::OnHScroll(UINT nSBCode, UINT nPos,
                             CScrollBar* pScrollBar)
{
    CSliderCtrl* pSlide = (CSliderCtrl*) pScrollBar;
    CString strText;
    strText.Format("%d", pSlide->GetPos());
    SetDlgItemText(IDC_STATIC_TRACK1, strText);
}
```

Finally, you need to update the trackbar's *m_nTrackbar1* data member when the user clicks OK. Your natural instinct would be to put this code in the *OnOK* button handler. You would have a problem, however, if there were a data exchange validation error on any other control in the dialog. Your handler would set *m_nTrackbar1* even though the user might choose to cancel the dialog. To avoid this problem, add your code in the *DoData-Exchange* function as shown here. If you do your own validation and detect a problem, call the *CDataExchange::Fail* function, which alerts the user with a message box.

```
if (pDX->m_bSaveAndValidate) {
    TRACE("updating trackbar data members\n");
    CSliderCtrl* pSlide1 =
        (CSliderCtrl*) GetDlgItem(IDC_TRACKBAR1);
    m_nTrackbar1 = pSlide1->GetPos();
}
```

6. Program the "discrete" trackbar control.   Add a public integer data member named *m_nTrackbar2* to the *CWin95Dialog* header, and set it to 0 in the constructor. This data member represents a zero-based index into *dValue*, a private static member variable that is an array of numbers (3.5, 5.5, 8.0, 11.0, and 16.0). Next add code in the *OnInitDialog* member function to set the trackbar's range, tick marks, and initial position.

```
CString strText2;
CSliderCtrl* pSlide2 =
    (CSliderCtrl*) GetDlgItem(IDC_TRACKBAR2);
pSlide2->SetRange(0, 4);
pSlide2->SetTic(1);
pSlide2->SetTic(2);
pSlide2->SetTic(3);
pSlide2->SetPos(m_nTrackbar2);
strText2.Format("%3.1f", dValue[pSlide2->GetPos()]);
SetDlgItemText(IDC_STATIC_TRACK2, strText2);
```

If you had only one trackbar, the WM_HSCROLL handler in step 5 would work. But you have two trackbars that send WM_HSCROLL messages, so the handler must differentiate. Here is the new code:

```
void CWin95Dialog::OnHScroll(UINT nSBCode, UINT nPos,
                             CScrollBar* pScrollBar)
{
    CSliderCtrl* pSlide = (CSliderCtrl*) pScrollBar;
    CString strText;
    // two trackbars are sending
    //  HSCROLL messages (different processing)

    switch(pScrollBar->GetDlgCtrlID()) {
    case IDC_TRACKBAR1:
        strText.Format("%d", pSlide->GetPos());
        SetDlgItemText(IDC_STATIC_TRACK1, strText);
        break;
    case IDC_TRACKBAR2:
        CSliderCtrl* pSlide =
            (CSliderCtrl*) pScrollBar; // watch it!
    strText.Format("%3.1f", dValue[pSlide->GetPos()]);
    SetDlgItemText(IDC_STATIC_TRACK2, strText);
    break;
    }
}
```

This trackbar needs tick marks, so you must check the control's Tick Marks property back in the graphic editor. The same data exchange considerations apply to this trackbar as applied to the previous trackbar. Add the following code in the dialog class *DoDataExchange* member function:

```
if (pDX->m_bSaveAndValidate) {
    CSliderCtrl* pSlide2 =
        (CSliderCtrl*) GetDlgItem(IDC_TRACKBAR2);
    m_nTrackbar2 = pSlide2->GetPos();
}
```

Use the graphic editor to set the Point property of both trackbars to Bottom/Right.

7. **Program the spinner control.** The spinner depends on its buddy edit control, located immediately before it in the tab order. Use ClassWizard to add a double-precision data member called *m_dSpin* to the *IDC_BUD-DY_SPIN1* edit control. We're using a *double* instead of an *int* because the *int* would require no programming, and that would be too easy. We want the edit control range to be 0.0 through 10.0, but the spinner itself needs an integer range. Add the following code to *OnInitDialog* to set the spinner range to 0 through 100 and to set its initial value to *m_dSpin * 10.0*:

```
CSpinButtonCtrl* pSpin =
    (CSpinButtonCtrl*) GetDlgItem(IDC_SPIN1);
pSpin->SetRange(0, 100);
pSpin->SetPos((int) (m_dSpin * 10.0));
```

To display the current value in the buddy edit control, you need to map the WM_VSCROLL message that the spinner sends to the dialog. Here's the code:

```
void CWin95Dialog::OnVScroll(UINT nSBCode, UINT nPos,
                             CScrollBar* pScrollBar)
{
    CString strValue;
    CSpinButtonCtrl* pSpin = (CSpinButtonCtrl*) GetDlgItem(IDC_SPIN1);
    strValue.Format("%3.1f", (double) (pSpin->GetPos()) / 10.0);
    pSpin->GetBuddy()->SetWindowText(strValue);
}
```

There's no need for you to add code in *OnOK* because the dialog data exchange code processes the contents of the edit control. Select the spinner's Auto Buddy property in the graphics editor.

8. **Set up an image list.** Both the list control and the tree control need an image list, and the image list needs icons.

About Icons

You probably know that a bitmap is an array of bits that represent pixels on the display. (You'll learn more about bitmaps in Chapter 10.) In Windows 95, an icon is a "bundle" of bitmaps. First of all, an icon has different bitmaps for different sizes. Typically, small icons are 16 by 16 pixels, and large icons are 32 by 32 pixels. Within each size are two separate bitmaps: one 4-bit-per-pixel bitmap for the color image and one monochrome (1-bit-per-pixel) bitmap for the "mask." If a mask bit is 0, the corresponding image pixel represents an opaque color. If the mask bit is 1, an image color of black (0) means that the pixel is transparent and an image color of white (0xF) means that the background color is inverted at the pixel location. Windows 95 seems to process inverted colors a little differently than Windows 3.x did—the inverted pixels show up black against the desktop, transparent against a Windows Explorer window background, and white against list and tree control backgrounds. Don't ask me why.

Small icons are new with Windows 95. They're used in the task bar, in the Windows Explorer, and in your list and tree controls, if you want them there. If an icon doesn't have a 16-by-16-pixel bitmap, Windows manufactures a small icon out of the 32-by-32-pixel bitmap, but it won't be as neat as one you draw yourself.

The graphic editor lets you create and edit icons. Look at the color palette shown here:

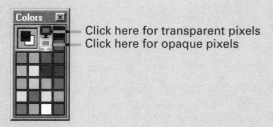

The top square in the upper-left portion shows you the main color for brushes, shape interiors, and so on, and the square under it shows the border color for shape outlines. You select a main color by left-clicking on a color, and you select a border color by right-clicking. Now look at the top center portion of the color palette. You click on the upper "monitor" to paint transparent pixels, which are drawn in dark cyan. You click on the lower monitor to paint inverted pixels, which are drawn in red.

First, use the graphic editor to add icons to the project's RC file. On the companion CD-ROM, these icons are circles with black outlines and different-colored interiors. Use fancier icons if you have them. For this example, the icon resource IDs are as follows:

IDI_BLACK

IDI_BLUE

IDI_CYAN

IDI_GREEN

IDI_PURPLE

IDI_RED

IDI_WHITE

IDI_YELLOW

Next, add a *CImageList* data member called *m_imageList* in the *CWin95Dialog* class header, and then add the following code to *OnInitDialog*:

```
HICON hIcon[8];
int n;
m_imageList.Create(16, 16, 0,
                   0, 8); // 32, 32 for large icons
hIcon[0] = AfxGetApp()->LoadIcon(IDI_WHITE);
hIcon[1] = AfxGetApp()->LoadIcon(IDI_BLACK);
hIcon[2] = AfxGetApp()->LoadIcon(IDI_RED);
hIcon[3] = AfxGetApp()->LoadIcon(IDI_BLUE);
hIcon[4] = AfxGetApp()->LoadIcon(IDI_YELLOW);
hIcon[5] = AfxGetApp()->LoadIcon(IDI_CYAN);
hIcon[6] = AfxGetApp()->LoadIcon(IDI_PURPLE);
hIcon[7] = AfxGetApp()->LoadIcon(IDI_GREEN);
for (n = 0; n < 8; n++) {
  m_imageList.Add(hIcon[n]);
}
```

9. **Program the list control.** In the graphic editor, set the list control's style attributes as shown here:

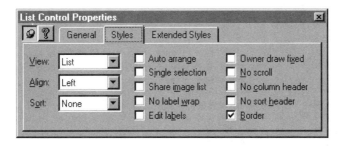

Next, add the following code to *OnInitDialog*:

```
static char* color[] = {"white", "black", "red",
                        "blue", "yellow", "cyan",
                        "purple", "green"};
CListCtrl* pList =
    (CListCtrl*) GetDlgItem(IDC_LISTVIEW1);
pList->SetImageList(&m_imageList, LVSIL_SMALL);
for (n = 0; n < 8; n++) {
  pList->InsertItem(n, color[n], n);
}
pList->SetBkColor(RGB(0, 255, 255)); // UGLY!
```

As the last line illustrates, you don't use the WM_CTLCOLOR message with common controls; you just call a function to set the background color. As you'll see when you run the program, however, the icons' transparent pixels look shabby.

If you use ClassWizard to map the list control's LVN_ITEMCHANGED notification message, you'll be able to track the user's selection of items. The code in the following handler displays the selected items' text in a static control:

```
void CWin95Dialog::OnItemchangedListview1(NMHDR* pNMHDR,
                                          LRESULT* pResult)
{
    NM_LISTVIEW* pNMListView = (NM_LISTVIEW*)pNMHDR;
    CListCtrl* pList =
        (CListCtrl*) GetDlgItem(IDC_LISTVIEW1);
    int nSelected = pNMListView->iItem;
    if (nSelected >= 0) {
      CString strItem = pList->GetItemText(nSelected, 0);
      SetDlgItemText(IDC_STATIC_LISTVIEW1, strItem);
    }
    *pResult = 0;
}
```

The *NM_LISTVIEW* structure has a data member called *iItem* that contains the index number of the selected item.

10. **Program the tree control.** In the graphic editor, set the tree control's style attributes as shown here:

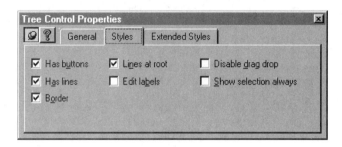

Next, add the following lines to *OnInitDialog*:

```
    CTreeCtrl* pTree = (CTreeCtrl*) GetDlgItem(IDC_TREEVIEW1);
    pTree->SetImageList(&m_imageList, TVSIL_NORMAL);
// tree structure common values
    TV_INSERTSTRUCT tvinsert;
    tvinsert.hParent = NULL;
    tvinsert.hInsertAfter = TVI_LAST;
    tvinsert.item.mask = TVIF_IMAGE ! TVIF_SELECTEDIMAGE !
                         TVIF_TEXT;
    tvinsert.item.hItem = NULL;
    tvinsert.item.state = 0;
    tvinsert.item.stateMask = 0;
    tvinsert.item.cchTextMax = 6;
    tvinsert.item.iSelectedImage = 1;
    tvinsert.item.cChildren = 0;
    tvinsert.item.lParam = 0;
// top level
    tvinsert.item.pszText = "Homer";
    tvinsert.item.iImage = 2;
    HTREEITEM hDad = pTree->InsertItem(&tvinsert);
    tvinsert.item.pszText = "Marge";
    HTREEITEM hMom = pTree->InsertItem(&tvinsert);
// second level
    tvinsert.hParent = hDad;
    tvinsert.item.pszText = "Bart";
    tvinsert.item.iImage = 3;
    pTree->InsertItem(&tvinsert);
    tvinsert.item.pszText = "Lisa";
    pTree->InsertItem(&tvinsert);
```

```
// second level
   tvinsert.hParent = hMom;
   tvinsert.item.pszText = "Bart";
   tvinsert.item.iImage = 4;
   pTree->InsertItem(&tvinsert);
   tvinsert.item.pszText = "Lisa";
   pTree->InsertItem(&tvinsert);
   tvinsert.item.pszText = "Dilbert";
   HTREEITEM hOther = pTree->InsertItem(&tvinsert);
// third level
   tvinsert.hParent = hOther;
   tvinsert.item.pszText = "Dogbert";
   tvinsert.item.iImage = 7;
   pTree->InsertItem(&tvinsert);
   tvinsert.item.pszText = "Ratbert";
   pTree->InsertItem(&tvinsert);
```

As you can see, this code sets TV_INSERT text and image indexes and calls *InsertItem* to add nodes to the tree.

Finally, use ClassWizard to map the TVN_SELCHANGED notification for the tree control. Here is the handler code to display the selected text in a static control:

```
void CWin95Dialog::OnSelchangedTreeview1(NMHDR* pNMHDR,
                                         LRESULT* pResult)
{
   NM_TREEVIEW* pNMTreeView = (NM_TREEVIEW*)pNMHDR;
   CTreeCtrl* pTree = (CTreeCtrl*) GetDlgItem(IDC_TREEVIEW1);
   HTREEITEM hSelected = pNMTreeView->itemNew.hItem;
   if (hSelected != NULL) {
     char text[31];
     TV_ITEM item;
     item.mask = TVIF_HANDLE | TVIF_TEXT;
     item.hItem = hSelected;
     item.pszText = text;
     item.cchTextMax = 30;
     VERIFY(pTree->GetItem(&item));
     SetDlgItemText(IDC_STATIC_TREEVIEW1, text);
   }
   *pResult = 0;
}
```

The *NM_TREEVIEW* structure has a data member called *hItem* that contains the handle of the selected node. The *GetItem* function retrieves the node's data, storing the text using a pointer supplied in the *TV_ITEM* structure. The *mask* variable tells Windows that the *hItem* handle is valid going in and that text output is desired.

11. Add code to the virtual *OnDraw* function in file ex06bView.cpp.
The following shaded code replaces the previous code:

```
void CEx06bView::OnDraw(CDC* pDC)
{
    pDC->TextOut(0, 0, "Press the left mouse button here.");
}
```

12. Use ClassWizard to add the *OnLButtonDown* member function.
Edit the AppWizard-generated code as follows:

```
void CEx06bView::OnLButtonDown(UINT nFlags, CPoint point)
{
    CWin95Dialog dlg;

dlg.m_nTrackbar1 = 20;
dlg.m_nTrackbar2 = 2; // index for 8.0
dlg.m_nProgress = 70; // write-only
dlg.m_dSpin = 3.2;

    int ret = dlg.DoModal();
}
```

Add a statement to include Win95Dialog.h in file ex06bView.cpp.

13. Compile and run the program.   Experiment with the controls to see how they work. We haven't added code to make the progress indicator functional; we'll cover that in Chapter 11.

Other Windows 95 Common Controls

You've seen most of the common controls that appear on the graphic editor control palette. I've skipped the animation control because this book doesn't cover multimedia, and I've skipped the hot key control because it isn't very interesting. The tab control <u>is</u> interesting, but you seldom use it inside another dialog. Chapter 12 shows you how to construct a tabbed dialog, sometimes known as a property sheet.

Two common controls that aren't in the control palette are the rich text edit control and the column heading control. In Chapter 12, you'll see an application that is built around the *CRichEditView* class, which incorporates the Windows 95 rich text edit control. A column heading control shows up inside a list control if you specify the Report property.

The Modeless Dialog and Windows 95 Common Dialogs

In Chapter 6, you saw the ordinary modal dialog and most of the controls for Microsoft Windows. Now you'll move on to the modeless dialog and the Windows 95 common dialogs (which are also available in Windows NT version 3.51). Modeless dialogs, as you'll remember, allow the user to work elsewhere in the application while the dialog is active. The common dialog classes are the C++ programming interface to the group of Windows utility dialogs that include File Open, Printer Setup, Color Selection, and so forth, which are supported by the dynamic link library COMDLG32.DLL.

In this chapter's first example, you'll build a simple modeless dialog that is controlled from a view. In the second example, you'll derive a class from the COMDLG32 *CFileDialog* class, which allows file deletion.

Modeless Dialogs

In Microsoft Foundation Class (MFC) Library version 4.0, modal and modeless dialogs share the same base class, *CDialog*, and they both use a dialog resource that you can build with the graphic editor. If you're using a modeless dialog with a view, you'll need some specialized programming techniques.

Creating Modeless Dialogs

For modal dialogs, you've already learned that you use the protected *CDialog* constructor to construct a dialog object with an attached resource, and then you display the modal dialog window by calling the *DoModal* member function. The window ceases to exist as soon as *DoModal* returns. Thus, you can construct a modal dialog object on the stack, knowing that the Windows dialog has been destroyed by the time the C++ dialog object goes out of scope.

Modeless dialogs are more complicated. You start by invoking the *CDialog* public default constructor to construct the dialog object, but then to create the dialog window you need to call the protected *CDialog::Create* member function instead of *DoModal*. That means you must write a member function that calls *Create*, which takes the resource ID as a parameter and returns immediately with the dialog still on the screen. Now you must worry about exactly when to construct the dialog object, when to create the dialog window, when to destroy the dialog, and when to process user-entered data.

Here's a summary of the differences between creating a modal dialog and a modeless dialog:

	Modal Dialog	**Modeless Dialog**
Constructor used	Protected with resource ID param	Public default
Function used to create window	*DoModal*	Protected *Create* with resource ID param

User-Defined Messages

Suppose you want the modeless dialog window to be destroyed when the user clicks the dialog's OK button. This presents a problem. How does the view know that the user has clicked the OK button? The dialog could call a view class member function directly, but that would "marry" the dialog to a particular view class. A better solution is for the dialog to send the view a user-defined message as the result of a call to the OK button message handler function. When the view gets the message, it can destroy the dialog window (but not the object). This sets the stage for the creation of a new dialog.

You have two options for sending Windows messages. You can use the *CWnd::SendMessage* function or the *PostMessage* function. The former causes an immediate call to the message-handling function, and the latter posts a message in the Windows message queue. With the *PostMessage* option, there's a slight delay, so it's reasonable to expect that the handler function has returned by the time the view gets the message.

Dialog Ownership

Now suppose you've accepted the dialog default pop-up style, which means that the dialog isn't confined to the view's client area. As far as Windows is concerned, the dialog's "owner" is the application's main frame window (introduced in Chapter 12), not the view. You need to know the dialog's view to send the view a message. Therefore, your dialog class must track its own view through a data member that the constructor sets. The *CDialog* constructor's *pParent* parameter doesn't have any effect here, so don't bother to use it.

A Modeless Dialog Example—EX07A

We could convert the Chapter 6 monster dialog to a modeless dialog, but starting from scratch with a simpler dialog is easier. Example EX07A uses a dialog with one edit control, an OK button, and a Cancel button. As in the Chapter 6 example, pressing the left mouse button while the mouse cursor is inside the view window brings up the dialog, but now we have the option of destroying it in response to another event—pressing the <u>right</u> mouse button when the mouse cursor is inside the view window. We'll allow only one dialog at a time, so we must be sure that a second left button press doesn't bring up a duplicate dialog.

To summarize the upcoming steps, the EX07A view class has a single associated dialog object that is constructed on the heap when the view is constructed. The dialog window is created and destroyed in response to user actions, but the dialog object is not destroyed until the application terminates.

Here are the steps to create the EX07A example:

1. Run AppWizard to produce \VCPP32\EX07A\EX07A. Accept the defaults, but select Single Document Interface and deselect Printing And Print Preview. The options and the default class names are shown here:

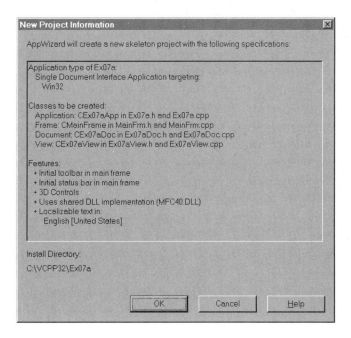

2. Use the graphic editor to create a new dialog resource. Choose Resource from the Developer Studio's Insert menu, and then select Dialog. The graphic editor assigns the ID *IDD_DIALOG1* to the new dialog. Change the dialog caption to *Modeless Dialog*. Accept the default OK and Cancel buttons with IDs *IDOK* and *IDCANCEL*, and then add a static text control and an edit control with the default ID *IDC_EDIT1*. Change the static text control's caption to *Edit 1*. Here is the completed dialog:

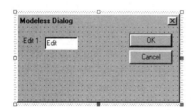

NOTE: Be sure to select the dialog's Visible property.

3. Use ClassWizard to create the *CEx07aDialog* class. Choose ClassWizard from the Developer Studio's View menu. Fill in the Create New Class dialog as shown here, and then click the Create button.

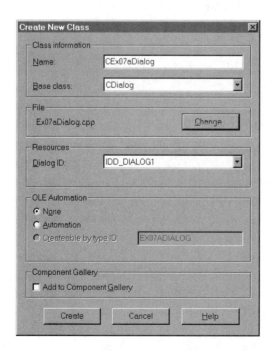

Add the message-handling functions shown below. To add a message-handling function, click on an object ID, click on a message, and then click the Add Function button. The Add Member Function dialog box appears. Type the function name, and click the OK button.

Object ID	Message	Member Function Name
IDCANCEL	BN_CLICKED	*OnCancel*
IDOK	BN_CLICKED	*OnOK*

4. **Add a variable to the *CEx07aDialog* class.** While in ClassWizard, click the Member Variables tab, and then click the Add Variable button to add the *CString* variable *m_strEdit1* to the *IDC_EDIT1* control.

5. **Edit ex07aDialog.h to add a view pointer and function prototypes.** Type in the following shaded code in the *CEx07aDialog* class declaration:

```
private:
    CView* m_pView;
```

Also, add the function prototypes as follows:

```
public:
    CEx07aDialog(CView* pView);
    BOOL Create();
```

NOTE: Using the *CView* class rather than the *CEx07aView* class allows the dialog class to be used with any view class.

6. **Edit ex07aDialog.h to define the WM_GOODBYE message ID.** Add the following line of code:

```
#define WM_GOODBYE    WM_USER + 5
```

The Windows constant WM_USER is the first message ID available for user-defined messages. The application framework uses a few of these messages, so we'll skip over the first five messages.

NOTE: The graphic editor maintains a list of symbol definitions in your project's resource.h file, but the graphic editor does
not understand constants based on other constants. You could
manually add *WM_GOODBYE* to resource.h, but it's easier to put
it in the dialog class header.

7. **Add the modeless constructor in the file ex07aDialog.cpp.** You
could modify the existing *CEx07aDialog* constructor, but if you add a separate one, the dialog class can serve for both modal and modeless dialogs.
Add the following lines:

```
CEx07aDialog::CEx07aDialog(CView* pView)   // modeless constructor
{
    m_pView = pView;
}
```

You should also add the following line to the AppWizard-generated
modal constructor:

```
m_pView = NULL;
```

The C++ compiler is clever enough to distinguish between the modeless constructor *CEx07aDialog(CView*)* and the modal constructor *CEx-
07aDialog(CWnd*)*. If the compiler sees an argument of class *CView* or a
derived *CView* class, it generates a call to the modeless constructor. If it
sees an argument of class *CWnd* or another derived *CWnd* class, it generates a call to the modal constructor.

8. **Add the *Create* function in ex07aDialog.cpp.** This derived dialog
class *Create* function calls the base class function with the dialog resource
ID as a parameter. Add the following lines:

```
BOOL CEx07aDialog::Create()
{
    return CDialog::Create(CEx07aDialog::IDD);
}
```

NOTE: *Create* is not a virtual function. You could have chosen a
different name if you had wanted to.

9. **Edit the *OnOK* and *OnCancel* functions in ex07aDialog.cpp.** These virtual functions generated by ClassWizard are called in response to dialog button clicks. Add the following shaded code:

```
void CEx07aDialog::OnOK()         // not really a message handler
{   // Do not call base class OnOK
    UpdateData(TRUE);
    if (m_pView != NULL) {
      m_pView->PostMessage(WM_GOODBYE, IDOK);
    }
}

void CEx07aDialog::OnCancel()      // not really a message handler
{   // Do not call base class OnCancel
    if (m_pView != NULL) {
      m_pView->PostMessage(WM_GOODBYE, IDCANCEL);
    }
}
```

If the dialog is being used as a modeless dialog, it sends the user-defined message WM_GOODBYE to the view. We'll worry about handling the message later.

NOTE: For a modeless dialog, be sure you do <u>not</u> call the *CDialog::OnOK* or *CDialog::OnCancel* function. This means you <u>must</u> override these virtual functions in your derived class; otherwise, using the Esc key, the Enter key, or a button click would result in a call to the base class functions, which call the Windows *EndDialog* function. *EndDialog* is appropriate only for modal dialogs. In a modeless dialog, you must call *DestroyWindow* instead, and, if necessary, you must call *UpdateData* to transfer data from the dialog controls to the class data members.

10. **Edit the ex07aView.h header file.** You need a data member to hold the dialog pointer:

```
private:
    CEx07aDialog* m_pDlg;
```

If you add the forward declaration

```
class CEx07aDialog;
```

at the beginning of ex07aView.h, you won't have to include ex07aDialog.h in every module that includes ex07aView.h.

11. **Modify the *CEx07aView* constructor and destructor in ex07aView-.cpp.** The *CEx07aView* class has a data member *m_pDlg* that points to the view's *CEx07aDialog* object. The view constructor constructs the dialog object on the heap, and the view destructor deletes it. Add the following shaded code:

```
CEx07aView::CEx07aView()
{
    m_pDlg = new CEx07aDialog(this);
}

CEx07aView::~CEx07aView()
{
    delete m_pDlg; // destroys window if not already destroyed
}
```

12. **Add code to the virtual *OnDraw* function in file ex07aView.cpp.** The *CEx07aView OnDraw* function (whose skeleton was generated by AppWizard) should be coded as follows in order to prompt the user to press the mouse button:

```
void CEx07aView::OnDraw(CDC* pDC)
{
    pDC->TextOut(0, 0, "Press the left mouse button here.");
}
```

13. **Use ClassWizard to add *CEx07aView* mouse message handlers.** Add handlers for the WM_LBUTTONDOWN and WM_RBUTTONDOWN messages. Now edit the code in file ex07aView.cpp as follows:

```
void CEx07aView::OnLButtonDown(UINT nFlags, CPoint point)

{
    // creates the dialog if not created already
    if (m_pDlg->GetSafeHwnd() == 0) {
      m_pDlg->Create(); // displays the dialog window
    }
}

void CEx07aView::OnRButtonDown(UINT nFlags, CPoint point)
{
    m_pDlg->DestroyWindow();
    // no problem if window was already destroyed
}
```

For almost all window types except main frame windows, the *Destroy-Window* function does not destroy the C++ object. We want this behavior because we'll take care of the dialog object's destruction in the view destructor.

14. Add the dialog header include statement to file ex07aView.cpp.
While you're in ex07aView.cpp, add the following dialog header include statement after the view header include statement:

```
#include "ex07aView.h"
#include "ex07aDialog.h"
```

15. Add your own message code for the WM_GOODBYE message.
Because ClassWizard does not support user-defined messages, you must write the code yourself. This task makes you appreciate the work Class-Wizard does for the other messages.

❑ In ex07aView.cpp, add the following line after the *BEGIN_MES-SAGE_MAP* statement but outside the *AFX_MSG_MAP* brackets:

```
ON_MESSAGE(WM_GOODBYE, OnGoodbye)
```

❑ Also in ex07aView.cpp, add the message handler function itself:

```
long CEx07aView::OnGoodbye(UINT wParam, long lParam)
{
    // message received in response to modeless dialog OK
    //   and Cancel buttons
    TRACE("CEx07aView::OnGoodbye %x, %lx\n", wParam, lParam);
    TRACE("Dialog edit1 contents = %s\n",
        (const char*) m_pDlg->m_strEdit1);
    m_pDlg->DestroyWindow();
    return 0L;
}
```

❑ In ex07aView.h, add the function prototype:

```
long OnGoodbye(UINT wParam, long lParam);
```

With Win32, the *wParam* and *lParam* parameters are the usual means of passing message data. In a mouse button down message, for example, the mouse *x* and *y* coordinates are packed into the *lParam* value. With the MFC library, message data is passed in more meaningful parameters. The mouse position is passed as a *CPoint* object. User-defined messages must use *wParam* and *lParam*, so you can use these two variables however you want. In this example, we've put the button ID in *wParam*.

16. **Build and test the application.**   Build and run EX07A. Try pressing the mouse's left button and then its right button. (Be sure the mouse cursor is outside the dialog window when you press the right mouse button.) Also, enter some data and then click the dialog's OK button. Does the view's *TRACE* statement correctly list the edit control's contents?

> N O T E: If you use the EX07A view and dialog classes in an MDI application, each MDI child window can have one modeless dialog. When the user closes an MDI child window, the child's modeless dialog is destroyed because the view's destructor calls the dialog destructor, which, in turn, destroys the dialog window.

The *CFormView* Class— A Modeless Dialog Alternative

If you need an application based on a single modeless dialog, the *CFormView* class will save you a lot of work. You'll have to wait until Chapter 15, however, because the *CFormView* class is most useful when coupled with the *CDocument* class, and we haven't progressed that far in our exploration of the application framework.

The Windows 95 Common Dialogs

Windows provides a group of standard user interface dialogs, and these are supported by the MFC classes. You are probably familiar with all or most of these dialogs because so many Windows-based applications, including Visual C++, already use them. All the common dialog classes are derived from a common base class, *CCommonDialog*. A list of the COMDLG32 classes is shown in the following table:

Class	Purpose
CColorDialog	Allows the user to select or create a color
CFileDialog	Allows the user to open a new file or an existing file
CFindReplaceDialog	Allows the user to substitute one string for another
CPageSetupDialog	Allows the user to input page measurement parameters
CFontDialog	Allows the user to select a font from a list of available fonts
CPrintDialog	Allows the user to set up the printer and print a document

The resources for these dialogs are buried inside the COMDLG32.DLL dynamic link library in the \WINDOWS\SYSTEM directory. You can access these resources through the graphic editor, but you shouldn't update them directly. You can use the clipboard to copy the dialogs to your own resource script if you want to.

There's one characteristic that all common dialogs share: they gather information from the user, but they don't do anything with it. The file dialog can help the user select a file to open, but it really just provides your program with the pathname—your program must make the call that opens the file. Similarly, a font dialog fills in a structure that describes a font, but it doesn't create the font.

Using the *CFileDialog* Class Directly

Using the *CFileDialog* class to open a file is easy. Here is some code that opens a file that the user has selected through the dialog:

```
CFileDialog dlg(TRUE, "bmp", "*.bmp");
if (dlg.DoModal() == IDOK){
  CFile file;
  VERIFY(file.Open(dlg.GetPathName(), CFile::modeRead)));
}
```

The first constructor parameter (*TRUE*) specifies that this object is a "File Open" dialog instead of a "File Save" dialog and that "bmp" is the default file extension. The *CFileDialog::GetPathName* function returns a *CString* object that contains the full pathname of the selected file.

Deriving from the Common Dialog Classes

Most of the time, you can use the common dialog classes directly. If you derive your own classes, you can add functionality without duplicating code. Each COMDLG32 dialog works a little differently, however. The next example is specific to the file dialog, but it should give you some ideas for customizing the other common dialogs.

NOTE: In previous editions of this book, the EX07B example dynamically created controls inside the standard file dialog. That technique doesn't work in Win32, but the new nested dialog method described here has the same effect.

Nested Dialogs

Win32 provides a way to "nest" one dialog inside another such that multiple dialogs appear as one seamless whole. You must first create a dialog resource template with a "hole" in it—typically a group box control—with the specific child window ID *stc32=0x045f*. Your program sets some parameters that tell COMDLG32 to use your template. In addition, your program must hook into the COMDLG32 message loop so that it gets first crack at selected notifications. When you're done with all of this, you'll notice that you have a dialog window that is a child of the COMDLG32 dialog window, even though your template wraps COMDLG32's template.

This sounds difficult, and it is unless you use MFC. With MFC, you build the dialog resource template as described above, derive a class from one of the common dialog base classes, add the class-specific connection code in *OnInitDialog*, and then happily use ClassWizard to map the messages that originate from your template's new controls.

A *CFileDialog* Example—EX07B

In this example, you will derive a class *CEx07bDialog* that adds a working "Delete all matching files" button to the standard file dialog. It also changes the dialog's title and changes the Open button's caption to Delete (to delete a single file). The example illustrates how you can use nested dialogs to add new controls to standard common dialogs. The new file dialog is activated as in the previous examples—by pressing the left mouse button when the mouse cursor is in the view window. Because you should be gaining skill with Visual C++, the following steps won't be as detailed as those for the earlier examples. Figure 7-1 shows what the dialog looks like.

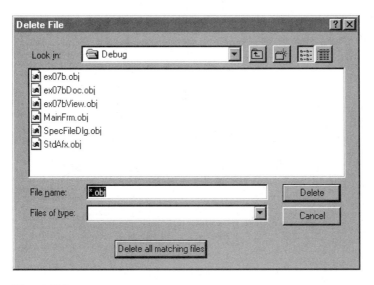

Figure 7-1.
The Delete File dialog in action.

Follow these steps to build the EX07B application:

1. Run AppWizard to produce \VCPP32\EX07B\EX07B. Accept the
defaults, but select Single Document Interface and deselect Printing And
Print Preview. The options and the default class names are shown here:

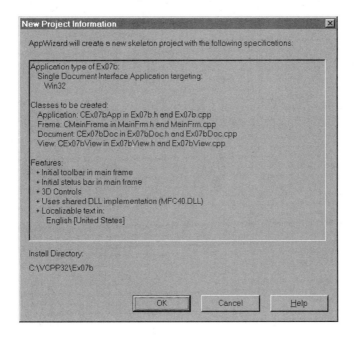

2. **Use the graphic editor to create a dialog resource *IDD_FILE-SPECIAL*.** Create the template with a group box, using ID *stc32=0x045f* and a button with ID *IDC_DELETE*, as shown here:

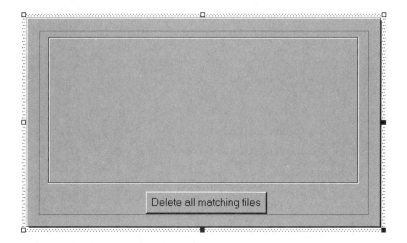

Set the dialog box's Style property to Child, its Border property to None, and select its Clip Siblings and Visible properties.

3. **Use ClassWizard to create the *CSpecialFileDialog* class.** ClassWizard won't let you specify *CFileDialog* as a base class, so you'll have to choose *CDialog* instead. Fill in the Create New Class dialog, as shown here:

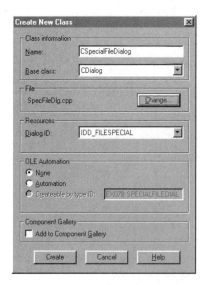

Use the Change button to change the names to SpecFileDlg.h and SpecFileDlg.cpp.

4. Edit the file SpecFileDlg.h.   Change the line

```
class CSpecialFileDialog : public CDialog
```

to

```
class CSpecialFileDialog : public CFileDialog
```

Also, add the following public data member:

```
BOOL m_bDeleteAll;
```

Finally, edit the constructor declaration:

```
CSpecialFileDialog(BOOL bOpenFileDialog,
    LPCTSTR lpszDefExt = NULL,
    LPCTSTR lpszFileName = NULL,
    DWORD dwFlags = OFN_HIDEREADONLY | OFN_OVERWRITEPROMPT,
    LPCTSTR lpszFilter = NULL,
    CWnd* pParentWnd = NULL);
```

5. Replace *CDialog* with *CFileDialog* in SpecFileDlg.cpp.   Choose Replace from the Developer Studio's Edit menu, and replace this name globally.

6. Edit the *CSpecialFileDialog* constructor in SpecFileDlg.cpp.   The derived class destructor must invoke the base class constructor and initialize the *m_bDeleteAll* data member. In addition, it must set some members of the *CFileDialog* base class data member *m_ofn*, which is an instance of the Win32 *OPENFILENAME* structure. The *Flags* and *lpTemplateName* members control the coupling to your *IDD_FILESPECIAL* template, and the *lpstrTitle* member changes the main dialog box title. Edit the constructor as follows:

```
CSpecialFileDialog::CSpecialFileDialog(BOOL bOpenFileDialog,
    LPCTSTR lpszDefExt, LPCTSTR lpszFileName, DWORD dwFlags,
    LPCTSTR lpszFilter, CWnd* pParentWnd) : CFileDialog(
    bOpenFileDialog, lpszDefExt, lpszFileName, dwFlags,
    lpszFilter, pParentWnd)
{
```

(continued)

163

```
//{{AFX_DATA_INIT(CSpecialFileDialog)
    // NOTE: the ClassWizard will add member initialization here
//}}AFX_DATA_INIT
m_ofn.Flags |= OFN_ENABLETEMPLATE;
m_ofn.lpTemplateName = MAKEINTRESOURCE(IDD_FILESPECIAL);
m_ofn.lpstrTitle = "Delete File";
m_bDeleteAll = FALSE;
}
```

7. Map the WM_INITDIALOG message in the *CSpecialDialog* class.

The *OnInitDialog* member function needs to change the common dialog's Open caption to Delete. The child window ID is *IDOK*.

```
BOOL bRet = CFileDialog::OnInitDialog();
if (bRet == TRUE) {
    GetParent()->GetDlgItem(IDOK)->SetWindowText("Delete");
}
return bRet;
```

8. Map the new IDC_DELETE button (Delete All Matching Files) in the *CSpecialDialog* class.

The *OnDelete* member function sets the *m_bDeleteAll* flag and then forces the main dialog to exit as if the Cancel button had been pressed. The client program (in this case, the view) gets the IDCANCEL return from *DoModal* and reads the flag to see whether it should delete all files. Here is the function:

```
void CSpecialFileDialog::OnDelete()
{
    m_bDeleteAll = TRUE;
    GetParent()->SendMessage(WM_COMMAND, IDCANCEL);
    // IDOK means delete selected file only
}
```

9. Add code to the virtual *OnDraw* function in file ex07bView.cpp.

The *CEx07bView OnDraw* function (whose skeleton was generated by AppWizard) should be coded as follows to prompt the user to press the mouse button:

```
void CEx07bView::OnDraw(CDC* pDC)
{
    pDC->TextOut(0, 0, "Press the left mouse button here.");
}
```

**10. Add the *OnLButtonDown* message handler to the *CEx07bView*
class.** Use ClassWizard to create the message handler for WM_LBUT-
TONDOWN, and then edit the code as follows:

```
void CEx07bView::OnLButtonDown(UINT nFlags, CPoint point)
{
    CString strFile = "*.obj";
    CSpecialFileDialog dlgFile(TRUE, "bmp", strFile);
    CString strMessage;
    int nModal = dlgFile.DoModal();
    if ((nModal == IDCANCEL) && (dlgFile.m_bDeleteAll)) {
      strMessage.Format(
        "Are you sure you want to delete all %s files?", strFile);
      if (AfxMessageBox(strMessage, MB_YESNO) == IDYES) {
        HANDLE h;
        WIN32_FIND_DATA fData;
        while ((h = ::FindFirstFile(strFile, &fData))
            != (HANDLE) 0xFFFFFFFF) { // no MFC equivalent
          if (::DeleteFile(fData.cFileName) == FALSE) {
            strMessage.Format("Unable to delete file %s\n",
                fData.cFileName);
            AfxMessageBox(strMessage);
            break;
          }
        }
      }
    }
    else if (nModal == IDOK) {
      CString strFilename = dlgFile.GetPathName();
      strMessage.Format(
          "Are you sure you want to delete %s?", strFilename);
      if (AfxMessageBox(strMessage, MB_YESNO) == IDYES) {
        CFile::Remove(strFilename);
      }
    }
}
```

Remember that common dialogs just gather data. Since the view is the
client of the dialog, it must call *DoModal* for the file dialog object and
then figure out what to do with the information it gets back. In this case,
it has the return value from *DoModal* (*IDOK* or *IDCANCEL*), the value of
the public *m_bDeleteAll* data member, and various *CFileDialog* member
functions such as *GetPathName*. If *DoModal* returns *IDCANCEL* and the
flag is *TRUE*, the function makes the Win32 file system calls necessary to
delete all matching files. If *DoModal* returns *IDOK*, the function can use
the MFC *CFile* functions to delete an individual file.

Using the global *AfxMessageBox* function is a convenient way to pop up a simple dialog that displays some text and that queries the user for a *Yes/No* answer. The *Microsoft Foundation Class Library Reference* describes all the message box variations and options.

Of course, you'll need the statement

```
#include "SpecFileDlg.h"
```

after the line

```
#include "ex07bView.h"
```

11. **Build and test the application.**   Build and run EX07B. Pressing the left mouse button should bring up the Delete File dialog, and you should be able to use it to navigate through the disk directory and to delete files. Be careful not to delete your important source files!

Other Customization for *CFileDialog*

In the EX07B example, you added a pushbutton to the dialog. It's easy to add other controls too. Just put them in the resource template, and, if they are standard Windows controls such as edit controls or list boxes, you can use ClassWizard to add data members and DDX/DDV code to your derived class. The client program can set the data members before calling *DoModal*, and it can retrieve the updated values after *DoModal* returns.

> NOTE: Even if you don't use nested dialogs, there are still two windows associated with a *CFileDialog* object. Suppose you have overridden *OnInitDialog* in a derived class, and you want to assign an icon to the file dialog. You must call *CWnd::GetParent* to get the top-level window, just as you did in the EX07B example. Here's the code:
>
> ```
> HICON hIcon = AfxGetApp()->LoadIcon(ID_MYICON);
> GetParent()->SetIcon(hIcon, TRUE);        // Set big icon
> GetParent()->SetIcon(hIcon, FALSE);       // Set small icon
> ```

CHAPTER EIGHT

Using OLE Controls (OCXs)

Microsoft Visual Basic (VB) was introduced in 1991 and has proven to be a very popular and successful application development system for Microsoft Windows. Part of its success is attributable to its open-ended nature. The 16-bit versions of VB (versions 1 through 3) supported Visual Basic controls (VBXs), which were ready-to-run software components that VB developers could buy or write themselves. VBXs became the center of a whole industry, and pretty soon there were hundreds of them. The MFC team figured out a way for Visual C++ programmers to use VBXs in their programs too.

The VBX standard, which was highly dependent on the 16-bit segment architecture, did not make it to the 32-bit world. Now there are OLE Controls (OCXs), which are an industrial-strength replacement for VBXs based on Microsoft OLE technology. OCXs can be used both by VB 4.0 developers and by Visual C++ 4.0 developers. While VBXs were written mostly in plain C, OCXs can be written in C++ with the help of the MFC library.

This chapter is not about writing OCXs; it's about using them in an application. The premise here is that you can learn to use OCXs without knowing much about OLE—after all, Microsoft doesn't require that VB programmers be OLE experts. To effectively write OCXs, however, you need to know a bit more, starting with the fundamentals of OLE. Consider picking up a copy of Adam Denning's *OLE Controls Inside Out* (Microsoft Press, 1995) if you're serious about underlineing OCXs. Of course, knowing some OLE theory won't hurt you when you're using OCXs in your programs. Chapters 23 and 24 of this book would be a good place to start.

OCXs vs. Ordinary Windows Controls

An OCX is a software module that plugs into your C++ program the same way a Windows control does. At least that's the way it seems at first. It's worthwhile to analyze the similarities and differences between OCXs and the controls you already know.

Ordinary Controls—A Frame of Reference

In Chapter 6, you used ordinary Windows controls such as the edit control and the list box, and you saw the new Windows 95 controls, which work much the same way. These controls are all child windows that you use mostly in a dialog, and they are represented by MFC classes such as *CEdit* and *CTreeCtrl*. The client program is always responsible for the creation of the control's child window.

Ordinary controls send notification command messages (standard Windows messages), such as BN_CLICKED, to the dialog. If you want to perform an action on the control, you call a C++ control class member function, which sends a Windows message to the control. The controls are all windows in their own right. All the MFC control classes are derived from *CWnd*, so if you want to get the text from an edit control, you call *CWnd::GetWindowText*. But even that function works by sending a message to the control.

The Windows controls are an integral part of Windows, even though the Windows 95 common controls are in a separate DLL. There is another species of ordinary controls, the so-called <u>custom</u> <u>controls</u>. (A custom control is a programmer-created control that acts as an ordinary control in that it sends WM_COMMAND notifications to its parent window and receives user-defined messages.) You'll see one of these in Chapter 21.

How OCXs Are Similar to Ordinary Controls

You can consider an OCX to be a child window, just as an ordinary control is. If you want an OCX in a dialog, you use the graphic editor to place it there, and the OCX identifier turns up in the resource template. If you're creating an OCX on the fly, you call a *Create* member function for a class that represents the OCX, usually in the WM_CREATE handler for the parent window. When you want to manipulate an OCX, you call a C++ member function, just as you do for a Windows control. The window that contains OCXs is called a <u>container</u>.

How OCXs Are Different from Ordinary Controls—
Properties and Methods

The most obvious OCX features are properties and methods. Those C++ member functions you call to manipulate an OCX all revolve around properties and methods. Properties have symbolic names that are matched to integer indexes. For each property, the OCX designer assigns a property name, such as BackColor or GridLineWidth, and a property type, such as string, integer, or double. There's even a picture type for bitmaps and icons. The client program can set individual OCX properties by specifying the property's integer index and its value. The client can get a property by specifying the index and accepting the appropriate return value. In certain cases, ClassWizard lets you define data members in your client window class that are associated with the properties of the OCXs the client class contains. The generated Dialog Data Exchange (DDX) code exchanges data between the OCX properties and the client class data members.

OCX methods are like functions. A method has a symbolic name, a set of parameters, and a return value. You call a method by calling a C++ member function of the class that represents the OCX. An OCX designer can define any methods he or she needs, such as *AddRow*, *LowerControlRods*, and so forth.

The OCX doesn't send WM_ notification messages to its container the way ordinary controls do; instead, it "fires events." An event has a symbolic name and can have an arbitrary sequence of parameters—it's really a container function that the OCX calls. Like ordinary control notification messages, events don't return a value to the OCX. Examples of events are Click, KeyDown, and RowColChange. Events are mapped in your client class just as control notification messages are.

In the MFC world, OCXs act just like child windows, but there's a significant layer of code between the container window and the OCX window. In fact, the OCX might not even have a window. When you call *Create*, the OCX window isn't created directly; instead, the OCX is loaded and given the command for "in-place activation." The OCX then creates its own window, which MFC lets you access through a *CWnd* pointer. It's not a good idea for the client to use the OCX's *hWnd*, however.

OCXs are stored in individual DLLs. As a matter of fact, an OCX <u>is</u> a DLL. Your container program loads the OCXs when it needs them, using sophisticated OLE techniques that rely on the Windows registry. For the time being, simply accept the fact that once you specify an OCX at design time, it will be loaded for you at runtime. Obviously, when you ship a program that requires special OCXs, you'll have to include the OCX files and an appropriate setup program.

16-Bit OCXs and 32-Bit OCXs

Because OCXs are DLLs, you can't use a 32-bit OCX with a 16-bit container program or vice versa. Microsoft provides tools for building 16-bit OCXs for use with 16-bit applications, but it's doubtful that these OCXs will become widespread. Developers of 16-bit applications will probably continue using VBXs. This chapter focuses on 32-bit OCXs.

Installing OCXs

Let's assume you've found a nifty OCX that you want to use in your project. Your first step is to copy the OCX to your hard disk. You could put it anywhere, but it's easier to track your OCXs if you put them in one place, such as the WINDOWS\SYSTEM directory. Some OCXs have licensing requirements, which may involve separate LIC files or extra entries to the registry. (See Chapters 14, 16, 23, and 24 for information about how the Windows registry works.) Licensed OCXs usually come with a setup program that takes care of those details.

The next step is to install the OCX in the Developer Studio and in your project. This is a two-part process. Choose Component from the Insert menu and click the OLE Controls tab, and you'll see the OCXs that are installed in the Component Gallery. Figure 8-1 shows the Component Gallery OLE Controls page.

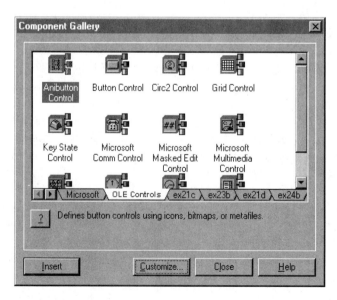

Figure 8-1.
The Component Gallery OLE Controls page.

If your OCX is already installed in the Developer Studio, you'll see it as an icon. (You might have to scroll to see it.) If it isn't there, you must click the Customize button and then the Import button in the next dialog. In the third dialog, you can browse your hard disk to find the OCX file and then click another Import button. When you return to the Component Gallery OLE Controls page, you should see the icon for your OCX.

N O T E :   The Developer Studio's OCX install process enters the OCX in four places in the Windows registry:

```
\HKEY_CLASSES_ROOT\CLSID
\HKEY_CLASSES_ROOT\TypeLib
\HKEY_LOCAL_MACHINE\SOFTWARE\Classes\CLSID
\HKEY_LOCAL_MACHINE\SOFTWARE\Classes\TypeLib
```

Actually, the OCX registers itself when the Developer Studio calls a special exported function. Other registration utilities, such as Regsvr32 and \vcpp32\regserv, do exactly the same thing.

After you install your OCX in the Developer Studio, you must install it in each project that uses it. That doesn't mean that the OCX itself gets copied. It means that ClassWizard generates a copy of a C++ class that's specific to that OCX, and it means that the OCX shows up in the graphic editor control palette for that project. You do the per-project installation by clicking the Component Gallery Insert button, shown in Figure 8-1.

The GRID32 Control

The GRID32 control is one of the OCXs included with Visual C++ 4.0. It's a kind of spreadsheet that's useful for learning about OCXs, but it's not really good enough to include in a commercial product, even though Microsoft grants you a redistribution license. Actually, it's a rework of the old GRID VBX included with the 16-bit versions of Visual C++.

If you run the Visual C++ Setup program, the grid32.ocx file is copied to your WINDOWS\SYSTEM directory, and the registry is updated with license information.

Figure 8-2 on the following page shows the GRID32 control inside a modal dialog.

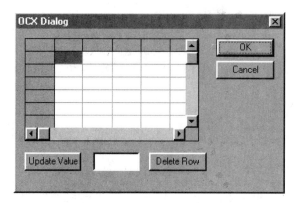

Figure 8-2.
The GRID32 control in use.

The best way to get to know an OCX is to examine its properties, methods, and events. But first, here's a list of types most commonly used for properties, method return values, and parameters:

Type	Description
BSTR	Special double-byte-character OLE string
I2	2-byte integer
I4	4-byte integer
UI4	Unsigned 4-byte integer
R4	4-byte floating point
R8	8-byte IEEE double
BOOL	Boolean (2-byte integer)
VARIANT	Special OLE all-purpose type (see Chapter 24)
PTR	Pointer to object (font, bitmap, icon)

Now here's a list of the GRID32 control's ordinary properties. The integer index, called the dispatch ID, is what your C++ program uses to access the property. If you need to, you can call a function that converts a symbolic name to an index. The negative numbers identify "stock" properties that have the same ID for all OCXs.

ID	Type	Name
0	BSTR	_Text
1	BSTR	Text
2	BSTR	FontName
3	R4	FontSize
4	BOOL	FontBold
5	BOOL	FontItalic
6	BOOL	FontStrikethru
7	BOOL	FontUnderline
8	I2	Rows
9	I2	Cols
10	I2	FixedRows
11	I2	FixedCols
12	I2	Row
13	I2	Col
14	I4	ScrollBars
15	BOOL	CellSelected
16	BSTR	Clip
17	I2	SelStartRow
18	I2	SelEndRow
19	I2	SelStartCol
20	I2	SelEndCol
21	PTR	Picture
22	BOOL	GridLines
23	I2	TopRow
24	I2	LeftCol
25	BOOL	HighLight
26	I2	GridLineWidth
27	I4	FillStyle
28	I4	BorderStyle
39	I4	MousePointer
40	PTR	MouseIcon
-501	UI4	BackColor
-512	PTR	Font
-513	UI4	ForeColor
-514	BOOL	Enabled
-515	I4	hWnd

Some properties are indexed. The RowHeight property, for example, has a value for each row in the spreadsheet. The indexes shown here are all short integers, but properties can be indexed by other types, and they can have multiple index parameters.

ID	Type	Name and Parameters
31	I4	RowHeight(I2 Index)
32	I4	ColWidth(I2 Index)
33	I2	ColAlignment(I2 Index)
34	I2	FixedAlignment(I2 Index)
35	I4	RowPos(I2 Index)
36	I4	ColPos(I2 Index)
37	BOOL	RowIsVisible(I2 Index)
38	BOOL	ColIsVisible(I2 Index)

The control's methods are shown below. (Remember that the container calls the methods and the OCX implements them.) The *AddItem* method adds a new row with the Item string in column 0, and the *RemoveItem* method removes a row. These methods, by the way, are left over from the VBX days, when there was a restricted set of method names. An OCX developer could choose method names such as *AddRow, AddColumn, DeleteRow*, and *DeleteColumn*.

ID	Return Type	Name and Parameters
29	I2	AddItem(BSTR Item, VARIANT Index)
30	I2	RemoveItem(I2 RemRow) // row
-550	VOID	Refresh()
-552	VOID	AboutBox()

Last is the list of events that the GRID32 control fires. These are functions that the container implements and the GRID32 control calls. (If the container doesn't implement a function for an event, the event is ignored.)

ID	Return Type	Name and Parameters
1	VOID	RowColChange()
2	VOID	SelChange()
-600	VOID	Click()
-601	VOID	DblClick()
-602	VOID	KeyDown(I2* KeyCode, I2* Shift)
-603	VOID	KeyPress(I2* KeyAscii)
-604	VOID	KeyUp(I2* KeyCode, I2* Shift)
-605	VOID	MouseDown(I2 Button, I2 Shift, I4 X, I4 Y)
-606	VOID	MouseMove(I2 Button, I2 Shift, I4 X, I4 Y)
-607	VOID	MouseUp(I2 Button, I2 Shift, I4 X, I4 Y)

The GRID32 control looks like a spreadsheet, and it lets the user select cells. It does not, however, allow the user to enter numbers directly into cells. Cell access works this way: you set the Row property to the row number, you set the Col property to the column number, and then you set or get the string Text property.

OCX Container Programming

MFC and ClassWizard support OCXs both in dialogs and as "child windows." To use OCXs, you must understand how an OCX grants access to properties, and you must understand the interactions between your DDX code and those property values.

Property Access

The OCX developer designates certain properties for access at design time. Those properties are specified in the OCX's property pages that the control displays for the graphic editor when you double-click on a control. The GRID32 control's one property page looks like the one shown at the top of the following page:

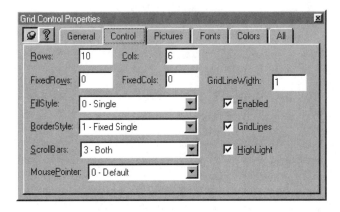

When you click on the All tab, you see a list of all the design-time–accessible properties, which might include a few properties not on the Control tab. For the GRID32 control, the All page looks like this:

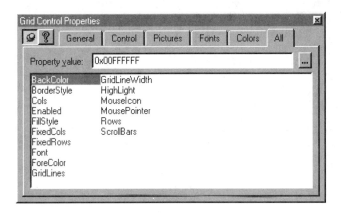

All the OCXs properties, including the design-time properties, are accessible at runtime. Some, however, might be designated as read-only.

ClassWizard's C++ Wrapper Classes for OCXs

When you install an OCX in a project, ClassWizard generates one or more C++ wrapper classes, derived from *CWnd*, that are tailored to your control's methods and properties. The class has member functions for all properties and methods, and it has constructors that you can use to dynamically create an instance of an OCX. Here are a few typical member functions from the CPP file that ClassWizard generates for the GRID32 control:

```
CString CGridCtrl::GetText()
{
    CString result;
    GetProperty(0x1, VT_BSTR, (void*)&result);
    return result;
}

void CGridCtrl::SetText(LPCTSTR propVal)
{
    SetProperty(0x1, VT_BSTR, propVal);
}

BOOL CGridCtrl::GetFontUnderline()
{
    BOOL result;
    GetProperty(0x7, VT_BOOL, (void*)&result);
    return result;
}

void CGridCtrl::SetFontUnderline(BOOL propVal)
{
    SetProperty(0x7, VT_BOOL, propVal);
}

long CGridCtrl::GetRowHeight(short Index)
{
    long result;
    static BYTE parms[] =
        VTS_I2;
    InvokeHelper(0x1f, DISPATCH_PROPERTYGET, VT_I4, (void*)&result,
                parms, Index);
    return result;
}

void CGridCtrl::SetRowHeight(short Index, long nNewValue)
{
    static BYTE parms[] =
        VTS_I2 VTS_I4;
    InvokeHelper(0x1f, DISPATCH_PROPERTYPUT, VT_EMPTY, NULL, parms,
                Index, nNewValue);
}

short CGridCtrl::RemoveItem(short RemRow)
{
    short result;
```

(continued)

```
static BYTE parms[] =
    VTS_I2;
InvokeHelper(0x1e, DISPATCH_METHOD, VT_I2, (void*)&result, parms,
            RemRow);
return result;
}
```

You don't have to worry too much about the code inside these functions, but you can match up the first parameters of *GetProperty*, *SetProperty*, and *Invoke* with the dispatch IDs in the GRID32 control property list. As you can see, there are always separate *Set* and *Get* functions for properties. As you do for events, you simply call the function. For example, to call the *RemoveItem* method from a dialog class function, you write code such as this:

```
m_grid->RemoveItem(3);
```

In this case, *m_grid* is an object of class *CGridCtrl*.

AppWizard Support for OCXs

When you check the AppWizard OLE Controls option, AppWizard inserts the following line in your application class *InitInstance* member function:

```
AfxEnableControlContainer();
```

It also inserts the following line in the project's StdAfx.h file:

```
#include <afxdisp.h>
```

If you decide to add OCXs to an existing project, you can simply add the two lines above.

ClassWizard and the Container Dialog

Once you've used the graphic editor to generate a dialog template, you already know that you can use ClassWizard to generate a C++ class for the dialog window. If that template contains one or more OCXs, you can use ClassWizard to add data members and event handler functions.

Dialog Class Data Members vs. Wrapper Class Usage

What kind of data members can you add to the dialog for an OCX? If you want to set an OCX property before you call *DoModal* for the dialog, you can add a dialog data member for that property. If you want to change properties inside the dialog member functions, you must take another approach: you add a data member that is an object of the wrapper class for the OCX.

Now is a good time to review the MFC DDX logic. Look back at the Cincinnati dialog in Chapter 6. The *CDialog::OnInitDialog* function calls *CWnd::UpdateData(FALSE)* to read the dialog class data members, and the *CDialog::OnOK* function calls *UpdateData(TRUE)* to write the members. Suppose you added a data member for each OCX property and you needed to get the Text property value in a button handler. If you called *UpdateData(FALSE)* in the button handler, it would read <u>all</u> the property values from <u>all</u> the dialog's controls—clearly a waste of time. It's more effective to avoid using a data member and to call the wrapper class *Get* function instead. To call that function, you must tell ClassWizard to add a wrapper class object data member.

Suppose you have a GRID32 wrapper class *CGridCtrl* and you have an *m_grid* data member in your dialog class. If you want to get the Text property, you do it like this:

```
CString str = m_grid.GetText();
```

Now consider another case: you want to set underline mode before the control is displayed. Ask ClassWizard to add a data member *m_bUnderline* that corresponds to the control's FontUnderline property. Here's how you construct and display the dialog:

```
CMyDialog dlg;
dlg.m_bUnderline = TRUE;
dlg.DoModal();
```

The DDX code takes care of setting the property value from the data member before the control is displayed. No other programming is needed. As you would expect, the DDX code sets the data member from the property value when the user clicks the OK button.

> NOTE: ClassWizard can't necessarily generate data members for all of a control's properties. In particular, it can't handle indexed properties such as the GRID32 ColWidth property. You'll have to use the wrapper class for these properties.

Mapping OCX Events

ClassWizard lets you map OCX events the same way you map Windows messages and command messages from controls. If a dialog class contains one or more OCXs, ClassWizard adds and maintains an <u>event</u> <u>sink</u> <u>map</u> that connects mapped events to their handler functions. It works something like a message map. You can see the code in Figure 8-3 beginning on page 183.

Locking OCXs in Memory

Normally, an OCX remains mapped in your process as long as its parent dialog is active. That means it must be reloaded each time the user opens a modal dialog. The reloads are usually quicker than the initial load because of disk caching, but you can lock the OCX into memory for better performance. To do so, add the following line in the overridden *OnInitDialog* function after the base class call:

```
AfxOleLockControl(m_grid.GetClsid());
```

The OCX remains mapped until your program exits or until you call the *AfxUnlockControl* or *AfxUnlockAllControls* function.

The EX08A Example—An OCX Dialog Container

Now it's time to build an application that uses a GRID32 control in a dialog. Here are the steps to create the EX08A example:

1. **Verify that the GRID32 OCX is installed.** If the control does not appear in the Developer Studio's Component Gallery OLE Controls page, install the control by following the instructions on pages 170–71.

2. **Run AppWizard to produce \VCPP32\EX08A\EX08A.** Accept the default settings, but select Single Document Interface and deselect Printing And Print Preview. This time, be sure to check the OLE Controls option in the AppWizard Step 3 dialog, as shown here:

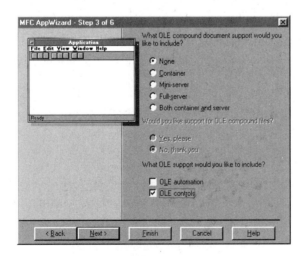

3. Install the GRID32 OCX in the EX08A project. Choose Component from the Developer Studio's Insert menu, select the grid icon, and then click the Insert button. ClassWizard generates three classes in the EX08A directory, as shown here:

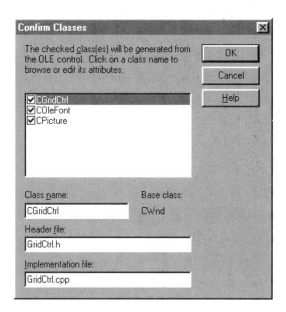

4. Use the graphic editor to create a new dialog resource. Choose Resource from the Developer Studio's Insert menu, and then select Dialog. The graphic editor assigns the ID *IDD_DIALOG1* to the new dialog. Change the ID to *IDD_OCXDIALOG*, and change the dialog caption to *OCX Dialog*. Accept the default OK and Cancel buttons with the IDs *IDOK* and *IDCANCEL*, and then add the other controls as shown in Figure 8-2 on page 172. Make the Update Value button the default button. Drag the grid control from the control palette, and then open the Control property page. Set the Rows property to *8* and the Cols property to *6*. Assign control IDs as shown in this table:

Control	ID
Grid OCX control	*IDC_GRID1*
Update Value button	*IDC_UPDATEVALUE*
Edit control	*IDC_VALUE*
Delete Row button	*IDC_DELETEROW*

5. Use ClassWizard to create the *COcxDialog* class. If you run
ClassWizard directly from the graphic editor window, it will know that
you want to create a *CDialog*-derived class based on the *IDD_OCXDIALOG*
template. Simply accept the default options.

Click on the Message Maps tab, and then add the message handler
functions shown below. To add a message handler function, click on an
object ID, click on a message, and click the Add Function button. The
Add Member Function dialog box appears. Type the function name,
and click the OK button.

Object ID	Message	Member Function Name
COcxDialog	WM_INITDIALOG	*OnInitDialog* (virtual function)
IDC_GRID1	SelChange event	*OnSelChangeGrid1*
IDC_UPDATEVALUE	BN_CLICKED	*OnUpdatevalue*
IDC_DELETEROW	BN_CLICKED	*OnDeleterow*
IDOK	BN_CLICKED	*OnOK* (virtual function)

6. Use ClassWizard to add data members to the *COcxDialog* class.
Click on the Member Variables tab, and then add the data members as
shown here:

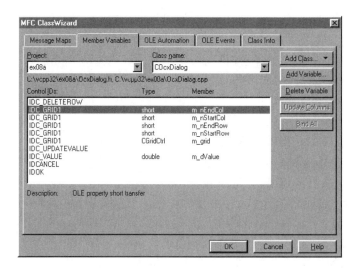

NOTE: You might think that the OLE Events tab is for mapping
OCX events in a container. That's not true: it's for OCX developers who are <u>defining</u> events for a control.

The screen on the previous page shows the process of adding dialog member variables for the GRID32 control. The top item in the Category combo box is always Control. This is what you select to declare the data member that represents the control itself. The other items represent individual control properties.

7. **Edit the *COcxDialog* class.** An array of doubles holds numeric values for the grid cells. Add the *m_dArray* data member in OcxDialog.h, and initialize it in the constructor in OcxDialog.cpp. Add code for the three handler functions *OnSelChangeGrid1*, *OnInitDialog*, and *OnDeleterow*. When the user changes the selected cell, the cell value is copied to the edit control, and when the user clicks the Update Value button, the edit control contents are copied to the selected cell. Both buttons are initially disabled because there is no selected cell until the user selects one. Figure 8-3 shows all the code for the dialog class, with new code shaded.

OCXDIALOG.H

```
//{{AFX_INCLUDES()
#include "gridctrl.h"
//}}AFX_INCLUDES

class COcxDialog : public CDialog
{
// Construction
public:
    COcxDialog(CWnd* pParent = NULL);   // standard constructor

// Dialog Data
    //{{AFX_DATA(COcxDialog)
    enum { IDD = IDD_OCXDIALOG };
    CGridCtrl m_grid;
    double    m_dValue;
    short     m_nStartRow;
    short     m_nEndRow;
    short     m_nStartCol;
    short     m_nEndCol;
    //}}AFX_DATA
    double m_dArray[7][5];

// Overrides
    // ClassWizard generated virtual function overrides
    //{{AFX_VIRTUAL(COcxDialog)
    protected:
    virtual void DoDataExchange(CDataExchange* pDX);  // DDX/DDV support
    //}}AFX_VIRTUAL
```

Figure 8-3. *(continued)*

The COcxDialog *class listing.*

Figure 8-3. *continued*

```
// Implementation
protected:

    // Generated message map functions
    //{{AFX_MSG(COcxDialog)
    afx_msg void OnSelChangeGrid1();
    virtual BOOL OnInitDialog();
    afx_msg void OnUpdatevalue();
    afx_msg void OnDeleterow();
    virtual void OnOK();
    DECLARE_EVENTSINK_MAP()
    //}}AFX_MSG
    DECLARE_MESSAGE_MAP()
};
```

OCXDIALOG.CPP

```
#include "StdAfx.h"
#include "ex08a.h"
#include "OcxDialog.h"

#ifdef _DEBUG
#define new DEBUG_NEW
#undef THIS_FILE
static char THIS_FILE[] = __FILE__;
#endif


/////////////////////////////////////////////////////////////////////////////
// COcxDialog dialog


COcxDialog::COcxDialog(CWnd* pParent /*=NULL*/)
    : CDialog(COcxDialog::IDD, pParent)
{
    //{{AFX_DATA_INIT(COcxDialog)
    m_dValue = 0.0;
    m_nStartRow = 0;
    m_nEndRow = 0;
    m_nStartCol = 0;
    m_nEndCol = 0;
    //}}AFX_DATA_INIT
    memset(m_dArray, 0, sizeof(m_dArray));
}

void COcxDialog::DoDataExchange(CDataExchange* pDX)
```

(continued)

Figure 8-3. *continued*

```
{
    CDialog::DoDataExchange(pDX);
    //{{AFX_DATA_MAP(COcxDialog)
    DDX_Control(pDX, IDC_GRID1, m_grid);
    DDX_Text(pDX, IDC_VALUE, m_dValue);
    DDX_OCShort(pDX, IDC_GRID1, DISPID(17), m_nStartRow);
    DDX_OCShort(pDX, IDC_GRID1, DISPID(18), m_nEndRow);
    DDX_OCShort(pDX, IDC_GRID1, DISPID(19), m_nStartCol);
    DDX_OCShort(pDX, IDC_GRID1, DISPID(20), m_nEndCol);
    //}}AFX_DATA_MAP
}


BEGIN_MESSAGE_MAP(COcxDialog, CDialog)
    //{{AFX_MSG_MAP(COcxDialog)
    ON_BN_CLICKED(IDC_UPDATEVALUE, OnUpdatevalue)
    ON_BN_CLICKED(IDC_DELETEROW, OnDeleterow)
    //}}AFX_MSG_MAP
END_MESSAGE_MAP()

////////////////////////////////////////////////////////////////////
// COcxDialog message handlers

BEGIN_EVENTSINK_MAP(COcxDialog, CDialog)
    //{{AFX_EVENTSINK_MAP(COcxDialog)
    ON_EVENT(COcxDialog, IDC_GRID1, 2 /* SelChange */,
            OnSelChangeGrid1, VTS_NONE)
    //}}AFX_EVENTSINK_MAP
END_EVENTSINK_MAP()

void COcxDialog::OnSelChangeGrid1()
{
    int i = m_grid.GetRow();
    int j = m_grid.GetCol();
    CString str = m_grid.GetText();
    m_dValue = atof(str);
    CDataExchange dx(this, FALSE);
    DDX_Text(&dx, IDC_VALUE, m_dValue);
    GetDlgItem(IDC_UPDATEVALUE)->EnableWindow(TRUE);
    GetDlgItem(IDC_DELETEROW)->EnableWindow(TRUE);
}

void COcxDialog::OnUpdatevalue() // button
{
    CString str;
```

(continued)

Figure 8-3. *continued*

```
    int i = m_grid.GetRow();
    int j = m_grid.GetCol();
    CDataExchange dx(this, TRUE);
    DDX_Text(&dx, IDC_VALUE, m_dValue);
    str.Format("%8.1f", m_dValue);
    m_grid.SetText(str);
}

BOOL COcxDialog::OnInitDialog()
{
    int i, j;
    CString str;
    CDialog::OnInitDialog();
    m_grid.SetCol(0); // row labels
    for (i = 1; i < 8; i++) {
      m_grid.SetRow(i);
      str.Format("%d", i);
      m_grid.SetText(str);
    }
    m_grid.SetRow(0); // column labels
    for (j = 1; j < 6; j++) {
      m_grid.SetCol(j);
      str = 'A' + j - 1;
      m_grid.SetText(str);
    }
    for (i = 1; i < 8; i++) {
      m_grid.SetRow(i);
      for (j = 1; j < 6; j++) {
        m_grid.SetCol(j);
        str.Format("%8.1f", m_dArray[i - 1][j - 1]);
        m_grid.SetText(str);
      }
    }
    GetDlgItem(IDC_UPDATEVALUE)->
        EnableWindow(FALSE); // no initial selection
    GetDlgItem(IDC_DELETEROW)->
        EnableWindow(FALSE); // no initial selection
    return TRUE;
}

void COcxDialog::OnDeleterow()
{
    int i = m_grid.GetRow();
    m_grid.RemoveItem(i);
}
```

(continued)

Figure 8-3. *continued*

```
void COcxDialog::OnOK()
{
    CString str;
    int i, j;
    for (i = 1; i < 8; i++) {
      m_grid.SetRow(i);
       for (j = 1; j < 6; j++) {
         m_grid.SetCol(j);
         str = m_grid.GetText();
         m_dArray[i - 1][j - 1] = atof(str);
       }
    }
    CDialog::OnOK();
}
```

8. **Connect the dialog to the view.**   Use ClassWizard to map the
   WM_LBUTTONDOWN message, and then edit the handler function
   as follows:

```
void CEx08aView::OnLButtonDown(UINT nFlags, CPoint point)
{
    int i, j;
    COcxDialog dlg;
    for (i = 0; i < 7; i++) {
      for (j = 0; j < 5; j++) {
         dlg.m_dArray[i][j] = i + j;
      }
    }
    // zero-based row and column numbers
    // row 0 and column 0 have headings
    dlg.m_nStartRow = 3;
    dlg.m_nStartCol = 3;
    dlg.m_nEndRow = 4;
    dlg.m_nEndCol = 4;
    dlg.DoModal();
    TRACE("new selection = (%d, %d, %d, %d)\n",
          dlg.m_nStartRow, dlg.m_nStartCol,
          dlg.m_nEndRow, dlg.m_nEndCol);
}
```

You'll need to include OcxDialog.h in ex08aView.cpp.

Notice that the handler sets and reads four data members that define
the grid's selected range. This range appears blue when the program runs,
but the range is independent of the selected cell, which is indicated by a
dotted rectangle. You can't set the selected cell from outside the control—
at least, I haven't found a way to do it.

For Win32 Programmers

If you used a text editor to look inside the ex08a.rc file, you'd be quite mystified. Here's the entry for the GRID32 control in the OCX dialog template:

```
CONTROL    "",IDC_GRID1,"{A8C3B720-0B5A-101B-B22E-00AA0037B2FC}",
                 WS_TABSTOP,7,7,152,79
```

There's a 32-digit number sequence where the window class name should be. What's going on? Actually, the resource template isn't the one that Windows sees. The *CDialog::DoModal* function "preprocesses" the resource template before passing it on to the dialog box procedure within Windows. It strips out all the OCXs and creates the dialog window without them. Then it loads the OCXs (based on their 32-digit identification numbers, called CLSIDs) and activates them in place, causing them to create their own windows in the correct places. The initial values for the properties that you set in the graphic editor are stored in binary form inside the project's custom DLGINIT resource.

When the modal dialog runs, the MFC code coordinates the messages sent to the dialog window both by the ordinary controls and by the OCXs. This allows the user to tab between all the controls in the dialog, even though the OCXs are not part of the actual dialog template.

When you call the member functions for the OCX object, you might think you're calling functions for a child window. The OCX window is quite far removed, but MFC steps in to make it seem as if you're communicating with a real child window. In OLE terminology, the container owns a <u>site</u>, which is not a window. You call functions for the site, and OLE and MFC make the connection to the underlying window in the OCX.

The container window is an object of a class derived from *CWnd*. The control site is also an object of a class derived from *CWnd*—the OCX wrapper class. That means that the *CWnd* class has built-in support for both containers and sites.

What you're seeing here is MFC OCX support grafted onto regular Windows. Maybe some future Windows version will have more direct support for OCXs. Imagine new Windows common controls being implemented as OCXs!

9. **Edit the virtual *OnDraw* function in the file ex08aView.cpp.** To prompt the user to press the left mouse button, add the following line to the view class *OnDraw* function:

```
pDC->TextOut(0, 0, "Click the left mouse button here");
```

10. **Build and test the EX08A application.** Open the dialog, click in a grid cell to select it, type a number in the edit control, and then click the Update Value button. The new value should appear in the cell.

Creating OCXs at Runtime

You've seen how to use the graphic editor to create OCXs at design time. If you need to create an OCX at runtime without a resource template entry, here are the programming steps:

1. Add an embedded OCX wrapper class data member to your dialog class or other C++ window class. An embedded C++ object is constructed and destroyed along with the window object.

2. With the graphic editor active, choose Resource Symbols from the Developer Studio's View menu. Add an ID constant for the new control.

3. If the parent window is a dialog, use ClassWizard to map the dialog's WM_INITDIALOG message, thus overriding *CDialog::OnInitDialog*. For other windows, use ClassWizard to map the WM_CREATE message. The new function should call the embedded OCX class's *Create* member function. This call indirectly displays the new control in the dialog. The control will be properly destroyed when the parent window is destroyed.

4. In the parent window class, manually add the necessary event message handlers and prototypes for your new control. Don't forget to add the event sink map macros.

TIP: ClassWizard doesn't help you with event sink maps when you add a dynamic OCX to a project. Consider inserting the target OCX in a dialog in another temporary project. After you're finished, simply copy the event sink map code to the parent window class in your main project.

The EX08B Example—A Dynamic OCX

This example uses the TIME OCX from the MFC library sample programs. This OCX doesn't have its own window; once enabled, it fires events at a fixed interval, just as the Windows timer does. You must associate the TIME OCX with a parent window because the MFC OCX container support is built into the *CWnd* base class. The view class is as good a place as any to put the control.

When the EX08B application runs, it immediately enables its TIME control, and then an event handler adds a dot to a *CString* data member and calls *CWnd::Invalidate*. The *OnDraw* function draws the growing line of dots. Here are the steps to create the EX08B example:

1. **Install the TIME control.** This control is located in the Visual C++ CD-ROM's \MSDEV\SAMPLES\MFC\CONTROLS\TIME directory. Copy the file time.ocx to your WINDOWS\SYSTEM directory, and then install it from the Developer Studio's Component Gallery screen by following the procedure on pages 170–71.

2. **Run AppWizard to produce \VCPP32\EX08B\EX08B.** Accept the default settings, but select Single Document Interface and deselect Printing And Print Preview. Check the OLE Controls option as you did in EX08A.

3. **Install the TIME OCX in the EX08B project.** Choose Component from the Developer Studio's Insert menu, click the OLE Controls tab, select the Time Control icon, and then click the Insert button. ClassWizard generates the *CTime1* wrapper class in the EX08B directory. (ClassWizard chooses the name *CTime1* because the MFC library already contains a *CTime* class.)

4. **Add two data members to the *CEx08bView* class.** Add the following private data members in ex08bView.h:

```
CTime1 m_time;
CString m_strDots;
```

Also, add this line in both the ex08bView.cpp and ex08b.cpp files:

```
#include "time.h"
```

before the line

```
#include "ex08bView.h"
```

5. **Edit the view's *OnDraw* function.** Add the following line in the *OnDraw* member function in ex08bView.cpp:

```
pDC->TextOut(0, 0, m_strDots);
```

6. **Use ClassWizard to map the view's WM_CREATE message.** Edit the handler code in ex08bView.cpp as follows:

```
int CEx08bView::OnCreate(LPCREATESTRUCT lpCreateStruct)
{
    if (CView::OnCreate(lpCreateStruct) == -1)
        return -1;
    BOOL bRet = m_time.Create(NULL, WS_DISABLED,
                        CRect(0, 0, 0, 0), this, IDC_TIMECTRL1);
    m_time.SetInterval(500);
    m_time.SetEnabled(TRUE);
    return bRet;
}
```

IDC_TIMECTRL1 is the child window ID for the control. You will have to add this to the project's symbol list by choosing Resource Symbols from the Developer Studio's View menu.

7. **Add the event sink macros in the *CEx08bView* files.** Add the following line inside the class declaration in ex08bView.h:

```
DECLARE_EVENTSINK_MAP()
```

and add the following code in ex08bView.cpp:

```
BEGIN_EVENTSINK_MAP(CEx08bView, CView)
    ON_EVENT(CEx08bView, IDC_TIMECTRL1, 1 /* Timer */,
            OnTimerTimectrl1, VTS_NONE)
END_EVENTSINK_MAP()
```

8. **Add the event handler function.** ClassWizard can't map events from a dynamic OCX, so you must do it manually. Add the following function in ex08bView.cpp, and add a corresponding declaration in ex08bView.h:

```
void CEx08bView::OnTimerTimectrl1()
{
    m_strDots += '.';
    Invalidate();
}
```

9. Build and test the EX08B application. When you start the application, you should see a growing row of dots. New dots appear at 0.5-second intervals.

Picture Properties

Some OCXs, including GRID32, support picture properties, which can accommodate bitmaps, metafiles, and icons. If an OCX has at least one picture property, ClassWizard generates a *CPicture* class in your project during the control's installation. You must use the MFC class *CPictureHolder* in conjunction with *CPicture*. To access the *CPictureHolder* class declaration and code, you must add the following line to StdAfx.h:

```
#include <afxctl.h>
```

The GRID32 control has a picture property named (coincidentally) Picture. If you set the Row and Col properties, you can set and get a picture in the selected cell. The generated *CGridCtrl* class has *GetPicture* and *SetPicture* functions. You can use the *SetPicture* function to put a bitmap in cell (0, 0) like this:

```
m_grid.SetRow(0);
m_grid.SetCol(0);
CPictureHolder pict;
pict.CreateFromBitmap(IDB_MYBITMAP); // from project's resources
CPicture picture(pict.GetPictureDispatch());
m_grid.SetPicture(picture);
```

> NOTE: If you include the AfxCtl.h file, you can't statically link your program with the MFC library. If you need a stand-alone program that supports picture properties, you'll have to borrow code from the *CPictureHolder* class, located in the mfc\src\ctlpict.cpp file.

Bindable Properties—Change Notifications

If an OCX has a property designated as "bindable," the OCX will send change notifications to its container when the value of the property changes inside the OCX. The OCX sends an OnChange notification when the bindable property value changes. In addition, the OCX can send an OnRequestEdit notification for a property whose value is about to change but has not yet changed. If the container returns FALSE from its OnRequestEdit handler, the OCX should not change the property value.

MFC fully supports property change notifications in OCX containers, but as of Visual C++ version 4.0, there was no ClassWizard support. That means you must manually add entries to your container class's event sink map.

Suppose you have an OCX with a bindable property named Note with a dispatch ID of 4. You add an *ON_PROPNOTIFY* macro to the EVENTSINK macros like this:

```
BEGIN_EVENTSINK_MAP(CAboutDlg, CDialog)
    //{{AFX_EVENTSINK_MAP(CAboutDlg)
    // other event notification macros here
    ON_PROPNOTIFY(CAboutDlg, IDC_MYOCXCTRL1, 4, OnNoteRequestEdit,
                OnNoteChanged)
    //}}AFX_EVENTSINK_MAP
END_EVENTSINK_MAP()
```

You must then code the *OnNoteRequestEdit* and *OnNoteChanged* functions with return types and parameter types exactly as shown here:

```
BOOL CMyDlg::OnNoteRequestEdit(BOOL* pb)
{
    TRACE("CMyDlg::OnNoteRequestEdit\n");
    *pb = TRUE; // TRUE means change request granted
    return TRUE;
}

BOOL CMyDlg::OnNoteChanged()
{
    TRACE("CMyDlg::OnNoteChanged\n");
    return TRUE;
}
```

Of course, you'll need corresponding prototypes in the class header, as shown here:

```
afx_msg BOOL OnNoteRequestEdit(BOOL* pb);
afx_msg BOOL OnNoteChanged();
```

Other OCXs

The Visual C++ REDIST\OCX directory contains six OCXs in addition to GRID32. The Setup program installs all of these on your hard disk. The file ctlref.hlp in the HELP directory documents these OCXs. Here's a summary of what's there:

ANIBTN32	Animated button control—allows the use of any icon, bitmap, or metafile to define a button control
KEYSTA32	Key state control—displays the CAPS LOCK, NUM LOCK, INS, and SCROLL LOCK keyboard states and allows the user to modify those states
MCI32	Multimedia MCI control—manages the recording and playback of multimedia files on Media Control Interface (MCI) devices
MSCOMM32	Communications control—provides serial communications for an application by allowing the transmission and reception of data through a serial port
MSMASK32	Masked edit control—provides restricted data input as well as formatted data output
PICCLP32	Picture clip control—allows the selection of an area of a source bitmap and then displays the image of that area in a form or a picture box

CHAPTER NINE

Win32 Memory Management

If you compared the memory management specs for Win32 with those for Win16, you would conclude that you were looking at two completely unrelated operating systems. It's amazing, then, that Microsoft has made the two programming interfaces so consistent. At least that's the way it appears on the surface. If you probe more deeply, however, you'll soon discover that you must change your programming techniques if you want to fully exploit the power of Win32.

In this chapter, I will try to persuade you to start writing true Win32 code, thus abandoning Win16 "backward compatibility." Unfortunately, this job isn't easy because there's still so much old code that's based on Win16 strategies. Along the way, you'll get a dose of Win32 memory management theory, and you'll learn specific Win32 programming techniques that will make your applications more efficient.

In no way do I intend this chapter to be a definitive description of Win32 memory management. For that, you'll have to get Jeffrey Richter's *Advanced Windows* book (Microsoft Press, 1995). (Be sure it's the second edition or later—the one with the CD-ROM bound in.) This chapter does, however, give you a jumping-off point for further study, and it gives you the MFC slant. For example, you'll learn what happens when you invoke the C++ *new* operator, and you'll learn when not to use *new*.

Like the rest of this book, this chapter is oriented toward Windows 95. If there are specific differences for Windows NT, I try to point them out parenthetically, but I'm excluding Win32s entirely. Don't assume that anything in this chapter applies to Win32s.

Processes and Memory Space

Before you study how Windows manages memory, you must first understand what a process is. If you already know what a program is, you're on your way. A program is an EXE file that you can launch in various ways from Windows. Once a program is running, it's a process. A process owns its own memory, file handles, and other system resources. If you launch the same program twice in a row, you have two separate processes. Pressing Ctrl-Alt-Del gives you a list of "ordinary" processes that are currently running; the PView 95 (PView in Windows NT) and Spy++ utilities list these along with some hidden system processes.

> NOTE: The Windows 95 Task Bar and the Alt-Tab screen list main windows. A single process (such as Windows 95 Explorer) might have several main windows, each supported by its own thread. See Chapter 11 for a discussion of threads.

The important thing to know about a process is that it has its own "private" 4-gigabyte (GB) virtual memory address space, which I'll describe in detail in a moment. For now, pretend that your computer has hundreds of gigabytes of RAM, and that each process gets 4 GB. Your program can access any byte of this space with a single 32-bit linear address. Each process's memory space contains a variety of items, including:

- Your program's EXE image

- Any nonsystem DLLs that your program loads, including the MFC DLLs

- Your program's global data (both read-only and read/write)

- Your program's stack

- Dynamically allocated memory, including both the Windows and CRT heaps

- Memory-mapped files

- Interprocess shared memory blocks

- Memory local to specific executing threads

- All sorts of special system memory blocks, including virtual memory tables

- The Windows kernel and executive, plus DLLs that are part of Windows

When I said that a process's address space was private, I lied. The top 2 GB isn't private at all; the contents are the same for all processes. The bottom 2 GB is truly private, particularly the stack, the heaps, and the read/write global memory. It wouldn't make sense, though, for each of two identical processes to have its own copy of the code and read-only data in the EXE file. And indeed, that's not what happens; the EXE image is "mapped" separately into each process's memory space at the same address, usually starting at 0x400000. The same is true for the DLLs, assuming that it's possible to load the DLLs at the same address for each process. This process-private memory is in the lower 2 GB (0 to 0x7FFFFFFF), but the bottom 4 MB (the bottom 64 KB in Windows NT) is off-limits.

A program's read/write data can't be mapped to the EXE or the DLL file because each process might assign different values to the variables. In Windows NT, all data is at first mapped to the program file. If the program changes the data, however, the corresponding pages are copied, with the copies backed by the swap file. This activity is called <u>copy-on-write.</u> In Windows 95, separate pages are allocated for read/write data when the program is loaded. Each process, then, has its own set of pages for read/write data, all backed by the swap file.

Let's take a closer look at the top 2 GB. The Windows kernel, executive, VxDs, and file system code, along with important tables such as page tables, are mapped to the top 1 GB (0xC0000000 to 0xFFFFFFFF) of the address space and thus can be shared by all processes. Windows DLLs and memory-mapped files are located in the range 0x80000000 to 0xBFFFFFFF, also shared by all processes. (Memory-mapped files are located in the private address space below 0x80000000 in Windows NT.) Figure 9-1 on the following page shows a memory map of two processes using the same program.

How safe is all this? It's next to impossible for one process to overwrite another process's stack, global, or heap memory because this memory, located in the bottom 2 GB of virtual memory space, is assigned only to that process. EXEs and DLLs in that space are flagged as read-only, so there's no problem if they're mapped in several processes. There is a problem with the top 1 GB, however, because important Windows read/write data is mapped there. An errant program could wipe out important system tables located in this region. (This is not a problem in Windows NT because the entire top 2 GB is protected.) There is also the possibility that one process could mess up another process's memory-mapped files in the range 0x80000000 through 0xBFFFFFFF because this region is shared by all processes. (This is also not a problem in Windows NT because memory-mapped files are located below 0x80000000.)

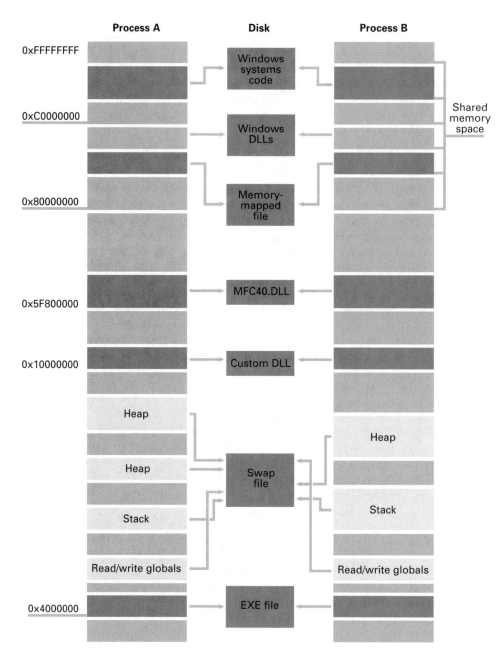

Figure 9-1.
Typical Windows 95 virtual memory map for two processes linked to the same EXE file.

How Virtual Memory Works

OK, so your computer doesn't really have hundreds of gigabytes of RAM. And it doesn't have hundreds of gigabytes of disk space either. Windows uses some smoke and mirrors here. First of all, a process's 4-GB address space is going to be sparsely used. Various programs and data elements will be scattered throughout the 4-GB address space in 4-KB blocks starting on 4-KB boundaries. Each 4-KB unit is called a <u>page</u> and can hold either code or data. When a page is actually being used, it occupies physical memory, but you never see the physical memory address. The Intel microprocessor chip efficiently maps a 32-bit virtual address to both a physical page and an offset within the page, using two levels of 4-KB page tables, as shown in Figure 9-2. Note that individual pages can be flagged as either read-only or read/write. Also note that each process has its own set of page tables. The chip's CR3 register holds a pointer to the directory page, so when Windows switches from one process to another, it just updates CR3.

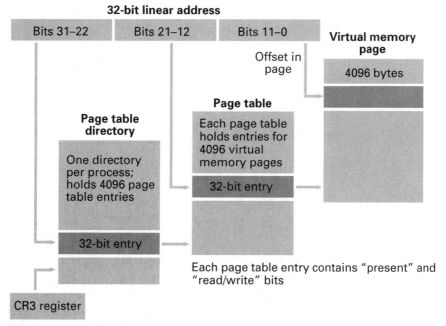

Figure 9-2.
Win32 virtual memory management (Intel).

So now our process is down from 4 GB to maybe 5 MB—a definite improvement. But if we're running several programs, together with Windows itself, we'll still run out of RAM. If you look at Figure 9-2 again, you'll notice that the page table entry has a "present" bit that indicates whether the 4-KB page is currently in RAM. If we try to access a page that's not in RAM, an interrupt fires and Windows analyzes the situation by checking its internal tables. If the memory reference was bogus, we'll get the dreaded "page fault" message, and the program will exit. Otherwise, Windows reads the page from a disk file into RAM and updates the page table by loading the physical address and setting the present bit. This is the essence of Win32 virtual memory.

The Windows virtual memory manager figures out how to read and write 4-KB pages so that it optimizes performance. If one process hasn't used a page for a while and another process needs memory, the first page is swapped out or discarded, and the RAM is used for the new process's page. Your program isn't normally aware that this going on. The more disk I/O that goes on, however, the worse the performance will be, so it stands to reason that more RAM is better.

I mentioned the word "disk," but I haven't talked about files yet. All processes share a big systemwide <u>swap file</u> that's used for all read/write data and some read-only data. (Windows NT supports multiple swap files.) Windows determines the swap file size based on available RAM and free disk space, but there are ways to fine-tune the swap file's size and specify its physical location on disk.

The swap file isn't the only file used by the virtual memory manager, however. It wouldn't make much sense to write code pages back to the swap file. Instead of using the swap file, Windows maps EXE and DLL files directly to their files on disk. Because the code pages are marked read-only, there's never a need to write them back to disk. If two processes use the same EXE file, that file is mapped into each process's address space. Memory-mapped files, which I'll talk about later, are also mapped directly. These can be flagged as read/write and made available for sharing among processes.

> NOTE: A dynamic link library can be mapped directly to its DLL
> file only if the DLL can be loaded at its designated base address. If a
> DLL were statically linked to load at, say, 10000000 but that address
> range is already occupied by another DLL, Windows would copy
> the DLL to the swap file and relocate the DLL code to another ad-
> dress. Only then can the DLL be dynamically linked to the process.
> Needless to say, it's important to build your DLLs with nonover-
> lapping address ranges. If you're using the MFC DLLs, set the base
> address of your own DLLs outside the range 0x5F800000 through
> 0x5FFFFFFF. Chapter 21 provides more details on writing DLLs.

For Win32 Programmers: Segment Registers in Win32

If you've experimented with the debugger in Win32, you may have noticed the segment registers, particularly CS, DS, and SS. Yes, these 16-bit relics haven't gone away, but you can mostly ignore them. In 32-bit mode, the Intel microprocessor still uses segment registers, which are 16 bits long, to translate addresses prior to sending them through the virtual memory system. The contents of a segment register is called a selector. There is a table in RAM, called the descriptor table, that has entries that contain the virtual memory base address and block size for code, data, and stack segments. In 32-bit mode, these segments can be up to 4 GB in size and can be flagged read-only or read/write. For every memory reference, the chip uses the selector to look up the descriptor table entry for the purpose of translating the address.

Under Win32 each process has two segments—one for code and one for data and the stack. You can assume that both have a base value of 0 and a size of 4 GB, so they overlap. The net result is no translation at all, but there are some tricks Windows plays to exclude the bottom 16 KB from the data segment. If you try to access memory down there, you get a protection fault instead of a page fault, which is useful for debugging null pointers.

Maybe some future operating system will use segments to get around that annoying 4-GB size limitation, but by then we'll have Win64 to worry about!

The *VirtualAlloc* Function—
Committed and Reserved Memory

If your program needs dynamic memory, sooner or later the Win32 *VirtualAlloc* function will be called. Chances are that you will never call *VirtualAlloc* yourself, but you'll rely on the Windows heap or the C runtime (CRT) heap functions to call it for you. Knowing how it works will help you better understand the functions that call it.

First, however, you must know the meaning of reserved and committed memory. When memory is reserved, a contiguous virtual address range is set aside. If, for example, you know that your program is going to use a single 5-MB memory block (known as a region) but you don't need to use it all right away, you call *VirtualAlloc* with a *MEM_RESERVE* allocation type parameter and a 5-MB size parameter. Windows rounds the start and end addresses of the region to 64-KB boundaries and prevents your process from reserving other memory in the same range. You can specify a starting address for your region, but more often you'll let Windows assign it for you. Nothing else happens. No RAM is allocated, and no swap file space is set aside.

When you get more serious about needing memory, you call *VirtualAlloc* again to commit the memory, using a *MEM_COMMIT* allocation type parameter. Now the start and end addresses of the region are rounded to 4-KB boundaries, and corresponding swap file pages are set aside together with the required page table. The block is designated either read-only or read/write. Still no RAM is allocated, however; that happens only when you try to write to the memory. If the memory was not previously reserved, no problem. If the memory was previously committed, still no problem. The rule is that memory must be committed before you can use it.

You call the *VirtualFree* function to "decommit" committed memory, thereby returning the designated pages back to reserved status. *VirtualFree* can also free a reserved region of memory, but you have to specify the base address you got from a previous *VirtualAlloc* reservation call.

The Windows Heap and the *GlobalAlloc* Function Family

A heap is a memory pool for a specific process. When your program needs a block of memory, it calls a heap allocation function, and it calls a companion function to free the memory. There's no assumption about 4-KB page boundaries; the heap manager uses space in existing pages or calls *VirtualAlloc* to get more pages. One of the two heaps you'll use is the Windows heap. The *HeapAlloc* function allocates memory in the Windows heap, and *HeapFree* releases it. *HeapAlloc* is particularly useful for "large" blocks of memory.

You might never call *HeapAlloc* yourself, but it will be called for you by the *GlobalAlloc* function that's left over from Win16. In the ideal 32-bit world, you wouldn't have to use *GlobalAlloc*, but this is the real world. We're stuck with a lot of code ported from Win16, including OLE, that uses "memory handle" (HGLOBAL) parameters instead of 32-bit memory addresses.

GlobalAlloc does two different things, depending on its attribute parameter. If you specify *GMEM_FIXED*, it simply calls *HeapAlloc* and returns the address cast as a 32-bit HGLOBAL value. If you specify *GMEM_MOVEABLE*, the returned HGLOBAL value is a pointer to a "handle table" entry in your process. That entry contains a pointer to the actual memory, which is allocated with *HeapAlloc*.

Why bother with "moveable" memory if it adds an extra level of indirection? You're looking at an artifact from Win16, in which, once upon a time, the operating system actually moved memory blocks around. In Win32, moveable blocks exist only to support the *GlobalReAlloc* function, which allocates a new memory block, copies bytes from the old block to the new, frees the old block, and assigns the new block address to the existing handle table entry. If nobody ever called *GlobalReAlloc*, we could use *HeapAlloc* instead of *GlobalAlloc*.

Unfortunately, many library functions use HGLOBAL return values and parameters instead of memory addresses. If such a function returns an HGLOBAL value, you should assume that memory was allocated with the *GMEM_MOVEABLE* attribute, and that means you must call the *GlobalLock* function to get the memory address. (If the memory was fixed, the *GlobalLock* call just returns the handle as an address.) If you're required to supply an HGLOBAL parameter, to be absolutely safe you should generate it with a *GlobalAlloc(GMEM_MOVEABLE...)* call just in case the called function decides to call *GlobalReAlloc* and expects the handle value to be unchanged.

In practice, you can assume that the Windows Clipboard uses fixed memory; thus you can pass an address returned by *HeapAlloc*, and you can cast returned HGLOBAL values to void pointers. You can also pass a fixed address to an OLE function that takes an HGLOBAL parameter, but the HGLOBAL values returned by OLE are moveable, so you have to call *GlobalLock*.

The CRT Heap, the C++ *new* and *delete* Operators, and *_heapmin*

You've seen the Windows heap (used by the *HeapAlloc* function), but that's not the heap you'll use most often. There's a separate heap that's managed by the CRT (the C runtime library). The CRT heap is accessed by the *malloc* and *free* functions, which are called directly by the C++ *new* and *delete* operators. This heap is optimized for small allocations, and there's a debug version that tells you where *malloc* (or *new*) was called. (This debugging feature was moved from MFC to the CRT starting with Visual C++ version 4.0.)

The *malloc* function, of course, calls *VirtualAlloc*, but it does so very cleverly. On the first call by a process, it reserves a 1-MB region (these numbers are subject to change in future versions of Visual C++) and commits a memory block whose size is a multiple of 64 KB (one 64-KB block if the *malloc* request was for 64 KB or less). Subsequent requests are satisfied from this block if possible; otherwise, the heap manager calls *VirtualAlloc* to commit more memory. If the 1-MB region is filled, *malloc* reserves a separate 2-MB region, then a 4-MB region, and so forth, committing the memory as necessary.

When you call *free*, the heap manager puts memory block descriptors on a singly linked, circular "free list" that exists outside the CRT heap itself. The *malloc* function uses the free list for later allocations if possible. Because this list is fairly compact, free pages can be found quickly without accessing a lot of virtual memory pages.

NOTE: In previous versions of the CRT, the free list pointers were stored inside the heap pages. This strategy required the *malloc* function to "touch" (read from the swap file) many pages to find free space, and this degraded performance. The current system is faster and minimizes the need for third-party heap management software.

If your process allocated a lot of CRT heap memory and then freed most of it, all the pages would remain committed. Even though RAM wouldn't necessarily be allocated, other processes would be locked out of your process's swap file pages. If you call another CRT function, *_heapmin*, the heap manager decommits all the free pages that it can and, furthermore, frees any regions that have been completely decommitted.

Memory-Mapped Files

Just in case you don't think you have enough memory management options already, I'll toss you another one. Suppose your program needs to read a DIB (device-independent bitmap) file. Your instinct would be to allocate a buffer of the correct size, open the file, and then call a read function to copy the whole disk file into the buffer. The Windows memory-mapped file is a much more elegant tool for handling this problem. You simply map an address range directly to the file. When the process accesses a memory page, Windows allocates RAM and reads the data from disk. Here's what the code looks like:

```
HANDLE hFile = ::CreateFile(strPathname, GENERIC_READ,
    FILE_SHARE_READ,NULL, OPEN_EXISTING, FILE_ATTRIBUTE_NORMAL, NULL);
ASSERT(hFile);
HANDLE hMap = ::CreateFileMapping(hFile, NULL, PAGE_READONLY,
    0, 0, NULL);
ASSERT(hMap);
LPVOID lpvFile = ::MapViewOfFile(hMap, FILE_MAP_READ,
    0, 0, 0); // map whole file
DWORD dwFileSize = ::GetFileSize(hFile, NULL);  // useful info
```

Here you're using virtual memory backed by the DIB file. Windows figures out the file size and commits a corresponding area of virtual memory. In this case, *lpvFile* is the starting address. The *hMap* variable contains the handle for the "file mapping object," which can be shared among processes if desired.

The DIB in the example above is a small file that you would read entirely into a buffer. Imagine a larger file (less than 1 GB, of course), for which you would normally issue seek commands. A memory-mapped file works for such a file too because of the underlying virtual memory system. RAM is allocated, and pages are read only when you access them.

> **NOTE:** By default, the entire file is committed when you map it, although it's possible to map only part of a file. If you intend to access only a few random pages of the file, you can use a technique that Jeffrey Richter describes in *Advanced Windows* under the heading "Sparsely Committed Memory-Mapped Files." In this case, you call *CreateFileMapping* with a special flag, and then you commit specific address ranges later with the *VirtualAlloc* function.

If two processes (or two threads) share a file mapping object (such as *hMap* in the sample code above), the file itself is, in effect, shared memory, and the virtual addresses will be the same in all processes (although this is not true for Windows NT). Indeed, this is the preferred Win32 method of sharing memory because the *GlobalAlloc* function doesn't support the GMEM_SHARE flag as it did in Win16. If memory sharing is all you want to do and you don't need a permanent disk file, you can omit the call to *CreateFile* and pass 0xFFFFFFFF as the *CreateFileMapping hFile* parameter. Now the shared memory will be backed by pages in the swap file. Better consult Richter for details on memory-mapped files. There's a lot to learn.

Unfortunately, there's no direct support for memory-mapped files or shared memory in MFC or OLE because these elements were designed with Win16 compatibility in mind.

Accessing Resources

Resources are contained inside EXEs and DLLs and thus occupy virtual memory space that doesn't change during the life of the process. This fact makes it easy to read a resource directly. If you need to access a bitmap, for example, you can get the DIB address with code like this:

```
LPVOID lpvResource = (LPVOID) ::LoadResource(NULL, ::FindResource(NULL,
    MAKEINTRESOURCE(IDB_ARCHES), RT_BITMAP));
```

The *LoadResource* function returns an HGLOBAL value, but you can safely cast it to a pointer.

Some Tips for Managing Dynamic Memory

The more you use the heap, the more fragmented it gets, and the slower your program runs. If your program is supposed to run for hours or days at a time, you have to be careful. It's better to allocate all the memory you need when your program starts and then free it when the program exits, but that's not always possible. The *CString* class is a nuisance because it's constantly allocating and freeing little bits of memory. The MFC developers have recently made some improvements, however.

If you generally use small memory blocks but occasionally use relatively large blocks with a different retention time, consider allocating the large blocks with *HeapAlloc* instead of *new*. This keeps the CRT heap a little cleaner. Don't forget to call *_heapmin* every once in a while. Be careful to keep track of where heap memory comes from. You'd have a big problem, for instance, if you called *HeapFree* on a pointer you got from *new*.

Be aware that your stack can be as big as it needs to be. Because you no longer have a 64-KB size limit, you can put large objects on the stack, thereby reducing the need for heap allocations.

As in Win16, your program doesn't run at full speed and then suddenly throw an exception when Windows runs out of virtual memory. It just slowly grinds to a halt, making your customer unhappy. There's not much you can do except try to figure out which program is eating memory and why. Because the Windows 95 USER and GDI modules still have 16-bit components, there is still some possibility of exhausting the 64-KB heaps that hold GDI objects and window structures. This possibility is pretty remote, however, and if it happens, it probably indicates a bug in your program.

Optimizing Storage for Constant Data

Remember that the code in your program is backed not by the swap file but directly by its EXE and DLL files. If several instances of your program are running, the same EXE and DLL files will be mapped to each process's virtual address space. What about constant data? You would want that data to be part of the program rather than have it copied to another block of virtual memory that's backed by the swap file.

You've got to work a little bit to ensure that constant data gets stored with the program. First consider string constants, which often permeate your programs. You would think that these would be read-only data, but guess again. Because you're allowed to write code like this,

```
char* pch = "test";
*pch = 'x';
```

"test" can't possibly be constant data, and it isn't. If you want "test" to be a constant, you must declare it as an initialized *const* static or global variable. Here's the global definition:

```
const char g_pch[] = "test";
```

Now *g_pch* is stored with the code, but where, specifically? To answer that, you must understand the "data sections" that the Visual C++ linker generates. If you set the link options to generate a map file, you'll see a long list of the sections (memory blocks) in your program. Individual sections can be designated for code or data, and they can be read-only or read/write. The important sections and their characteristics are listed here:

Name	Type	Access	Contents
.text	Code	Read-only	Program code
.rdata	Data	Read-only	Constant initialized data
.data	Data	Read/write	Nonconstant initialized data
.bss	Data	Read/write	Nonconstant uninitialized data

The .rdata section is part of the EXE file, and that's where the linker puts the *g_pch* variable. The more stuff you put in the .rdata section, the better. The use of the *const* modifier does the trick.

You can put built-in types and even structures in the .rdata section, but you can't put C++ objects there if they have a constructor. If you write a statement like this,

```
const CRect g_rect(0, 0, 100, 100);
```

the linker puts the object into the .bss section, and it will be backed separately to the swap file for each process. When you think about it, this makes sense because the compiler must invoke the constructor function after the program is loaded.

Now suppose you wanted to do the worst possible thing. You'd declare a *CString* global variable (or static class data member) like this:

```
const CString g_str("this is the worst thing I can do");
```

Now you've got the *CString* object (which is quite small) in the .bss section, and you've also got a character array in the .data section, neither of which can be backed by the EXE file. To make matters worse, when the program starts, the *CString* class must allocate heap memory for a copy of the characters. You would be much better off using a *const* character array instead of a *CString* object.

CHAPTER TEN

Bitmaps

Without graphics images, Windows-based applications would be pretty dull. Some applications depend on images for their usefulness, but any application can be spruced up with the addition of decorative clip art from a variety of sources. Windows bitmaps are arrays of bits mapped to display pixels. That might sound simple, but you have to learn a lot about bitmaps before you can use them to create professional Windows-based applications.

This chapter starts with the "old" way of programming bitmaps—creating the device-dependent GDI bitmaps that work with a memory device context. You'll need to know these techniques because many programmers are still using them and you'll need them yourself on occasion.

Next you'll graduate to the modern way of programming bitmaps— creating device-independent bitmaps (DIBs). If you use DIBs, you'll have an easier time with colors and the printer, and in some cases you'll get better performance. A new Win32 function, *CreateDIBSection*, gives you the benefits of DIBs combined with all the features of GDI bitmaps.

Finally, you'll learn how to use the MFC *CBitmapButton* class to put bitmaps on pushbuttons. This has nothing to do with DIBs, but it's a useful technique that would be difficult to master without an example.

GDI Bitmaps and Device-Independent Bitmaps (DIBs)

There are two kinds of Windows bitmaps: GDI bitmaps and DIBs. GDI bitmap objects are represented by the Microsoft Foundation Class (MFC) Library version 4.0 *CBitmap* class. The GDI bitmap object has an associated Windows data structure, maintained inside the Windows GDI module, that is device-dependent. Your program can get a copy of the bitmap data, but the bit arrangement depends on the display hardware. GDI bitmaps can be freely transferred among programs on a single computer, but because of their device dependency, transferring them by disk or modem doesn't make sense.

> **NOTE:** In Win32, you're allowed to put a GDI bitmap handle on the clipboard for transfer to another process, but behind the scenes Windows converts the device-dependent bitmap to a DIB and copies the DIB to shared memory. That's a good reason to consider using DIBs.

DIBs offer many programming advantages over GDI bitmaps. Because a DIB carries its own color information, color palette management is easier. DIBs also make it easy to control gray shades when printing. Any computer running Windows can process DIBs, which are usually stored in BMP disk files or as a resource in your program's EXE or DLL file. The wallpaper background on your monitor is read from a BMP file when you start Windows. The primary storage format for Windows Paint is the BMP file, and the Developer Studio's graphic editor uses BMP files for toolbar buttons and other images. Other graphic interchange formats are available, such as TIFF, GIF, and JPEG, but the DIB format is the only one that is supported directly by the Win32 API.

Color Bitmaps and Monochrome Bitmaps

Now might be a good time to reread the "Windows Color Mapping" section in Chapter 5. As you'll see here, Windows deals with color bitmaps a little differently from the way it deals with brush colors.

Many color bitmaps are 16-color. A standard VGA board has four contiguous color planes, with 1 corresponding bit from each plane combining to represent a pixel. The 4-bit color values are set when the bitmap is created. With a standard VGA board, bitmap colors are limited to the standard 16 colors. Windows does not use dithered colors in bitmaps.

A monochrome bitmap has only one plane. Each pixel is represented by a single bit that is either on (1) or off (0). The *CDC::SetTextColor* function sets the "off" display color, and *SetBkColor* sets the "on" color. You can specify both of these pure colors with the Windows *RGB* macro.

Using GDI Bitmaps

A GDI bitmap is simply another GDI object, such as a pen or a font. You must somehow create a bitmap, and then you must select it into a device context. When you're finished with the object, you must deselect it and delete it. You know the drill.

There's a catch, though, because the "bitmap" of the display or printer device is effectively the display surface or the printed page itself. Therefore, you can't select a bitmap into a display device context or a printer device context. You have to create a special <u>memory</u> <u>device</u> <u>context</u> for your bitmaps, using the *CDC::CreateCompatibleDC* function. You must then use the *CDC* member function *StretchBlt* or *BitBlt* to copy the bits from the memory device context to the "real" device context. These "bit-blitting" functions are generally called in your view class's *OnDraw* function. Of course, you mustn't forget to clean up the memory display context when you're finished.

Loading a GDI Bitmap from a Resource

The easiest way to use a bitmap is to load it from a resource. If you open a resource script with the graphic editor, you'll find a list of the project's bitmap resources. If you select a bitmap and examine its properties, you'll see a filename. Here's an example entry in an RC file, when viewed by a text editor:

```
IDB_REDBLOCKS              BITMAP  DISCARDABLE    "res\\Red Blocks.bmp"
```

IDB_REDBLOCKS is the resource ID, and the file is Red Blocks.bmp in the project's RES subdirectory. (This is one of the Microsoft Windows 95 wallpaper bitmaps, normally located in the WINDOWS directory.) The resource compiler reads the DIB from disk and stores it in the project's RES file. The linker copies the DIB into the program's EXE file. You know that the Red Blocks bitmap must be in device-independent format because the EXE can be run with any display board that Windows supports.

The *CDC::LoadBitmap* function converts a resource-based DIB to a GDI bitmap. Below is the simplest possible self-contained *OnDraw* function that displays the Red Blocks bitmap:

```
CMyView::OnDraw(CDC* pDC)
{
    CBitmap bitmap; // sequence is important
    CDC dcDisplayMemory;
    bitmap.LoadBitmap(IDB_REDBLOCKS);
    dcDisplayMemory.CreateCompatibleDC(pDC);
    dcDisplayMemory.SelectObject(&bitmap);
    pDC->BitBlt(100, 100, 54, 96, &dcDisplayMemory, 0, 0, SRCCOPY);
    // dcDisplayMemory is deleted; bitmap is deselected
    // bitmap is deleted
}
```

The *BitBlt* function copies the Red Blocks pixels from the memory display context to the display (or printer) device context. The bitmap is 54 bits wide by 96 bits high, and on a VGA display it occupies a rectangle 54 logical units by 96 logical units, offset 100 units down and to the right of the upper left corner of the window's client area.

> NOTE: The code shown on the previous page works fine for the display. As you'll see in Chapter 18, the application framework calls the *OnDraw* function for printing, in which case *pDC* points to a printer device context. The bitmap here, unfortunately, is configured specifically for the display and thus cannot be selected into the printer-compatible memory device context. If you want to print a bitmap, you can create a display-compatible memory device context in the view's *OnInitialUpdate* function and then call *BitBlt* in *OnDraw* to copy the bits to the printer device context. The EX10A program in this chapter demonstrates this technique. Even this technique isn't perfect, however, because bitmap colors aren't converted to gray shades on the printer. This is one of the problems that DIBs solve.

The Effect of the Display Mapping Mode

If the display mapping mode in the Red Blocks example is *MM_TEXT*, each bitmap pixel maps to a display pixel, and the bitmap looks nice. If the mapping mode is *MM_LOENGLISH*, the bitmap size is 0.54 inch by 0.96 inch, or 42 pixels by 75 pixels on a VGA screen, and the GDI must do some bit crunching to make the bitmap fit. Consequently, the bitmap won't look as good with the *MM_LOENGLISH* mapping mode.

Stretching the Bits

What if we want Red Blocks to occupy a rectangle exactly 54 pixels by 96 pixels, even though the mapping mode is <u>not</u> *MM_TEXT*? The *StretchBlt* function is the solution. If we replace the *BitBlt* call with the following three statements, Red Blocks is displayed cleanly, whatever the mapping mode:

```
CSize size(54, 96);
pDC->DPtoLP(&size);
pDC->StretchBlt(0, 0, size.cx, -size.cy,
                &dcDisplayMemory, 0, 0, 54, 96, SRCCOPY);
```

With either *BitBlt* or *StretchBlt*, the display update is slow if the GDI has to actually stretch or compress bits. If, as in the case above, the GDI determines that no conversion is necessary, the update is fast.

The EX10A Example

The EX10A example displays a resource-based bitmap in a scrolling view with mapping mode set to *MM_LOENGLISH*. The program uses the *StretchBlt* logic described above except that the memory device context and the bitmap are created in the view's *OnInitialUpdate* member function and last for the life of the program. Also, the program reads the bitmap size through a call to the *CGdiObject* member function *GetObject*, so it's not using hard-coded values as in the examples above.

Here are the steps for building the example:

1. **Run AppWizard to produce \VCPP32\EX10A\EX10A.** Accept the default settings, but select Single Document Interface and the *CScrollView* view base class. The options and the default class names are shown here:

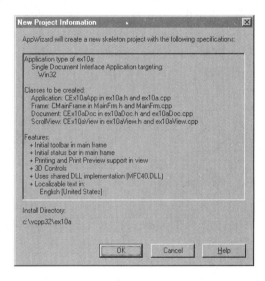

2. **Import the *IDB_GOLDWEAVE* bitmap.** Choose Resource from the Developer Studio's Insert menu. Import the bitmap Gold Weave.bmp from the WINDOWS directory. (If your version of Windows doesn't have this bitmap, load it from the companion CD-ROM.) The Developer Studio will copy this bitmap file into your project's RES subdirectory. Assign the ID *IDB_GOLDWEAVE*, and save the changes.

3. Add the following private data members to the class *CEx10aView*.
Edit the file ex10aView.h. The bitmap and the memory device context last for the life of the view. The *CSize* objects are the source (bitmap) dimensions and the destination (display) dimensions.

```
CDC*     m_pdcDisplayMemory;
CBitmap* m_pBitmap;
CSize    m_sizeSource, m_sizeDest;
```

4. Edit the following member functions in the class *CEx10aView*. Edit the file ex10aView.cpp. The constructor and destructor do C++ house-keeping for the embedded objects. You want to keep the constructor as simple as possible because failing constructors cause problems. The *OnInitialUpdate* function sets up the memory display context and the bitmap, and it computes output dimensions that map each bit to a pixel. The *OnDraw* function calls *StretchBlt* twice—once by using the special computed dimensions and once by mapping each bit to a 0.01-by-0.01-inch square. Add the following shaded code:

```
CEx10aView::CEx10aView()
{
    m_pdcDisplayMemory = new CDC;
    m_pBitmap = new CBitmap;
}


CEx10aView::~CEx10aView()
{
    // cleans up the memory display context and the bitmap
    delete m_pdcDisplayMemory; // deselects bitmap
    delete m_pBitmap;
}
void CEx10aView::OnDraw(CDC* pDC)
{
    pDC->StretchBlt(20, -20, m_sizeDest.cx, -m_sizeDest.cy,
        m_pdcDisplayMemory, 0, 0,
        m_sizeSource.cx, m_sizeSource.cy, SRCCOPY);

    pDC->StretchBlt(320, -20, m_sizeSource.cx, -m_sizeSource.cy,
        m_pdcDisplayMemory, 0, 0,
        m_sizeSource.cx, m_sizeSource.cy, SRCCOPY);
}


void CEx10aView::OnInitialUpdate()
{
    CScrollView::OnInitialUpdate();
```

```
    CSize totalSize(800, 1050); // 8 by 10.5 inches
    CSize lineSize = CSize(totalSize.cx / 100, totalSize.cy / 100);
    SetScrollSizes(MM_LOENGLISH, totalSize, totalSize, lineSize);

    BITMAP bm; // Windows BITMAP data structure; see Win32 help
    if (m_pdcDisplayMemory->GetSafeHdc() == NULL) {
      CClientDC dc(this);
      OnPrepareDC(&dc); // necessary
      m_pBitmap->LoadBitmap(IDB_GOLDWEAVE);
      m_pdcDisplayMemory->CreateCompatibleDC(&dc);
      m_pdcDisplayMemory->SelectObject(m_pBitmap);
      m_pBitmap->GetObject(sizeof(bm), &bm);
      m_sizeSource.cx = bm.bmWidth;
      m_sizeSource.cy = bm.bmHeight;
      m_sizeDest = m_sizeSource;
      dc.DPtoLP(&m_sizeDest);
    }
}
```

5. Build and test the EX10A application.   Your screen should look like this:

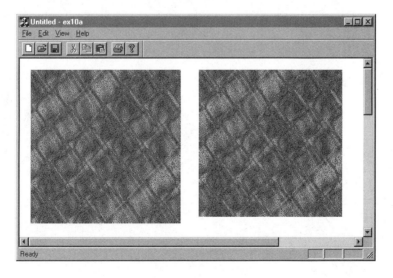

Notice that the bitmap on the right (without the adjusted dimensions) shows the effects of dropped bits.

6. Try the Print Preview and Print functions.   The bitmap prints to scale because the application framework applies the *MM_LOENGLISH* mapping mode to the printer device context just as it does to the display device context. The output looks great in print preview mode, but it looks like a dog's breakfast on the printer! We'll fix that soon.

Using Bitmaps to Improve the Screen Display

You've seen an example program that displayed a bitmap that originated outside the program. Now you'll see an example program that generates its own bitmap to support smooth motion on the screen. The principle is simple: you draw on a memory device context with a bitmap selected, and then you zap the bitmap onto the screen.

The EX10B Example

In the EX05C example in Chapter 5, the user dragged a circle with the mouse. As the circle moved, the display flickered because the circle was erased and redrawn on every mouse move message. EX10B uses a GDI bitmap to correct this problem. The EX05C custom code for mouse message processing carries over almost intact; most of the new code is in the *OnPaint* and *OnInitialUpdate* functions.

In summary, the EX10B *OnInitialUpdate* function creates a memory device context and a bitmap that are compatible with the display. The *OnPaint* function prepares the memory device context for drawing, passes *OnDraw* a handle to the memory device context, and copies the resulting bitmap from the memory device context to the display.

Here are the steps to build EX10B from scratch:

1. **Run AppWizard to produce \VCPP32\EX10B\EX10B.** Accept the default settings, but select Single Document Interface and the *CScrollView* view base class. The options and the default class names are shown here:

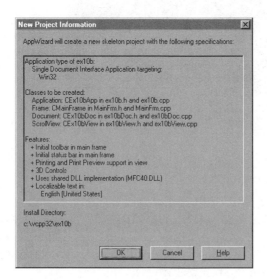

2. Use ClassWizard to add *CEx10bView* message handlers. Add messages handlers for the following messages:

❑ WM_LBUTTONDOWN

❑ WM_LBUTTONUP

❑ WM_MOUSEMOVE

❑ WM_PAINT

3. Edit the ex10bView.h header file. Add the private data members shown here to the *CEx10bView* class:

```
private:
    CRect    m_rectEllipse;
    CPoint   m_pointMouse;
    BOOL     m_bCaptured;
    CDC*     m_pdcDisplayMemory;
    CBitmap* m_pBitmap;
```

4. Code the *CEx10bView* constructor and destructor in ex10bView.cpp.
You need a memory device context object and a bitmap GDI object.
These are constructed in the view's constructor and destroyed in the
view's destructor. Add the following shaded code:

```
CEx10bView::CEx10bView() : m_rectEllipse(10, -10, 110, -110),
                           m_pointMouse(10, -10)
{
    m_bCaptured         = FALSE;
    m_pdcDisplayMemory  = new CDC;
    m_pBitmap           = new CBitmap;
}
CEx10bView::~CEx10bView()
{
    delete m_pBitmap;          // already deselected
    delete m_pdcDisplayMemory;
}
```

5. Add code for the *OnInitialUpdate* function in ex10bView.cpp. The
C++ memory device context and bitmap objects are already constructed.
This function creates the corresponding Windows objects. Both the device context and the bitmap are compatible with the display context *dc*,
but you must explicitly set the memory display context's mapping mode
to match the display context. You could create the bitmap in the *OnPaint*

217

function, but the program runs faster if you create it once here. Add the following shaded code:

```
void CEx10bView::OnInitialUpdate()
{
    CScrollView::OnInitialUpdate();

    CSize sizeTotal(800, 1050); // 8 by 10.5 inches
    CSize sizePage(sizeTotal.cx / 2, sizeTotal.cy / 2);
    CSize sizeLine(sizeTotal.cx / 50, sizeTotal.cy / 50);
    SetScrollSizes(MM_LOENGLISH, sizeTotal, sizePage, sizeLine);
    // creates the memory device context and the bitmap
    if (m_pdcDisplayMemory->GetSafeHdc() == NULL) {
      CClientDC dc(this);
      OnPrepareDC(&dc);
      CRect rectMax(0, 0, sizeTotal.cx, -sizeTotal.cy);
      dc.LPtoDP(rectMax);
      m_pdcDisplayMemory->CreateCompatibleDC(&dc);
      // makes bitmap same size as display window
      m_pBitmap->CreateCompatibleBitmap(&dc, rectMax.right,
                                        rectMax.bottom);
      m_pdcDisplayMemory->SetMapMode(MM_LOENGLISH);
    }
}
```

6. **Add code for the *OnPaint* function in ex10bView.cpp.**   Normally, it isn't necessary to override *OnPaint* in your new class. The *CView* version of *OnPaint* contains the following code:

```
CPaintDC dc(this);
OnPrepareDC(&dc);
OnDraw(&dc);
```

In this example, you will be overriding *OnPaint* to reduce screen flicker through the use of a memory display context. *OnDraw* is passed this memory display context for the display, and it is passed the printer device context for printing. Thus, *OnDraw* can perform tasks common to the display and the printer. You don't need to use the bitmap with the printer because the printer has no speed constraint.

The overridden *OnPaint* must perform in order the following three steps to prepare the memory device context for drawing:

❑ Select the bitmap into the memory device context.

❑ Transfer the invalid rectangle (as calculated by *OnMouseMove*) from the display context to the memory device context. There is no *SetClipRect* function, but the *CDC::IntersectClipRect* function, when called after the *CDC::SelectClipRgn* function (with a *NULL* parameter), has the same effect. If you don't set the clipping rectangle to the minimum size, the program runs more slowly.

❑ Initialize the bitmap to the current window background color. The *CDC::PatBlt* function fills the specified rectangle with a pattern. In this case, the pattern is the brush pattern for the current window background. That brush must first be constructed and selected into the memory device context.

After the memory device context is prepared, *OnPaint* can call *OnDraw* with a memory device context parameter. Then the *CDC::BitBlt* function copies the updated rectangle from the memory device context to the display device context. Add the following shaded code:

```
void CEx10bView::OnPaint()
{
    CRect rectUpdate;
    CPaintDC dc(this);
    OnPrepareDC(&dc);
    dc.GetClipBox(&rectUpdate);
    CBitmap* pOldBitmap =
    m_pdcDisplayMemory->SelectObject(m_pBitmap);
    m_pdcDisplayMemory->SelectClipRgn(NULL);
    m_pdcDisplayMemory->IntersectClipRect(&rectUpdate);
    CBrush backgroundBrush(
        (COLORREF) ::GetSysColor(COLOR_WINDOW));
    CBrush* pOldBrush =
        m_pdcDisplayMemory->SelectObject(&backgroundBrush);
    m_pdcDisplayMemory->PatBlt(rectUpdate.left, rectUpdate.top,
        rectUpdate.Width(), rectUpdate.Height(), PATCOPY);
    OnDraw(m_pdcDisplayMemory);
    dc.BitBlt(rectUpdate.left, rectUpdate.top,
        rectUpdate.Width(), rectUpdate.Height(),
        m_pdcDisplayMemory, rectUpdate.left, rectUpdate.top,
        SRCCOPY);
    m_pdcDisplayMemory->SelectObject(pOldBitmap);
    m_pdcDisplayMemory->SelectObject(pOldBrush);
}
```

7. Code the *OnDraw* function in ex10bView.cpp. This *CEx10bView* member function is similar to the EX05C *OnDraw* function except that it draws a stationary black square in addition to the moving circle. In EX10B, *OnDraw* is passed a pointer to a memory device context by the *OnPaint* function. For printing, *OnDraw* is passed a pointer to the printer device context. Add the following shaded code:

```
void CEx10bView::OnDraw(CDC* pDC)
{
    pDC->SelectStockObject(BLACK_BRUSH);
    pDC->Rectangle(100, -100, 200, -200);
    pDC->SelectStockObject(GRAY_BRUSH);
    pDC->Ellipse(m_rectEllipse);
}
```

8. Copy mouse message–handling code from ex05cView.cpp. Copy the functions shown below from ex05cView.cpp to ex10bView.cpp. Be sure to change the functions' class names from *CEx05cView* to *CEx10bView*.

❑ *OnLButtonDown*

❑ *OnLButtonUp*

❑ *OnMouseMove*

9. Change two lines in the *OnMouseMove* function in ex10bView.cpp. Change the following two lines:

```
InvalidateRect(rectOld, TRUE);
InvalidateRect(rectNew, TRUE);
```

to

```
InvalidateRect(rectOld, FALSE);
InvalidateRect(rectNew, FALSE);
```

If the second *CWnd::InvalidateRect* parameter is *TRUE* (the default), Windows erases the background before repainting the invalid rectangle. That's what you needed in EX05C, but the background erasure is what causes the flicker. Because the entire invalid rectangle is being copied from the bitmap, you no longer need to erase the background. The *FALSE* parameter prevents this erasure.

10. Build and run the application. Here is the EX10B program output:

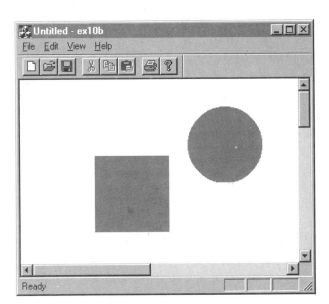

Is the circle's movement smoother now? The problem is that the bitmap is only 8 by 10.5 inches, and if the scrolling window is big enough, the circle goes off the edge. One solution to this problem is to make the bitmap as big as the largest display.

Windows Animation

EX10B is a crude attempt at Windows animation. What if you wanted to move an angelfish instead of a circle? Win32 doesn't have an *Angelfish* function ... ep your angelfish in its own bitmap and use the ... s to merge the fish with the background. You'd ... und in its own bitmap too. Now things are getting ... Better run out and get Nigel Thompson's *Anima-* ... icrosoft Press, 1995). After you read it, you can get ... r Windows!

... **ss**

... I bitmaps (*CBitmap*), but there's no MFC class for ... ing you one here. It's a complete rewrite of the ... editions of this book, and it takes advantage of

221

Win32 features such as memory-mapped files, improved memory management, and DIB sections. It also includes palette support. Before you examine the *CDib* class, however, you need a little background on DIBs.

DIBs, Windows 95, and Windows NT

Optimized DIB processing is a major feature of Windows 95. Modern video cards have frame buffers that conform to the standard DIB image format. If you have one of these cards, your programs can take advantage of the new Windows 95 DIB engine, which speeds up the process of drawing directly from DIBs. If you're still running in VGA mode, however, you're out of luck; your programs will still work, but not as fast.

Windows 95 is optimized for the direct display of DIBs, but Windows NT is not. There's a client-server boundary within the Windows NT operating system. The frame buffer is on the server side, and the DIB is on the client side, so all communication is through shared memory. The new Win32 DIB section bridges the gap and lets you use *BitBlt* or *StretchBlt* to directly transfer DIB bits to the display, so you should plan to use DIB sections if you want your program to run fast under Windows NT.

A Few Words About Palette Programming

Windows palette programming is quite complex, but you've got to deal with it if you expect your users to run their displays in the 8-bpp (bits per pixel) mode—and many users will if they have video cards with 1 MB or less of memory. Suppose you're displaying a single DIB in a window. The first thing you must do is create a <u>logical</u> palette, a GDI object that contains the colors in the DIB. Then you must "realize" this logical palette into the hardware <u>system palette</u>, which is a table of the 256 colors the video card can display at that instant. If your program is the foreground program, the realization process tries to copy all your colors into the system palette, but it doesn't touch the 20 standard Windows colors that are always there. For the most part, your DIB looks just like you want it to.

But what if another program is the foreground program, and what if that program has a forest scene DIB with 236 shades of green? Your program still realizes its palette, but something different happens this time. Now the system palette won't change, but Windows sets up a new mapping between your logical palette and the system palette. If your DIB contains a neon pink color, for example, Windows maps it to the standard red color. If your program forgot to realize its palette, your neon pink stuff would turn green when the other program went active.

The forest scene example is extreme because we assumed that the other program grabbed 236 colors. If instead the other program realized a logical palette with only 200 colors, Windows would let your program load 36 of its own colors, including, hopefully, neon pink.

So when is a program supposed to realize its palette? The Windows message WM_PALETTECHANGED is sent to your program's main window whenever a program, including yours, realizes its palette. Another message, WM_QUERYNEWPALETTE, is sent whenever your program becomes the foreground program. Your program should realize its palette in response to both these messages. These palette messages are not sent to your view window, however. You must map them in your application's main frame window and then notify the view. Chapter 12 discusses the relationship between the frame window and the view.

You call the Win32 *RealizePalette* function to perform the realization, but first you must call *SelectPalette* to select your DIB's logical palette into the device context. *SelectPalette* has a flag parameter that you normally set to *FALSE* in your WM_PALETTECHANGED and WM_QUERYNEWPALETTE handlers. This flag ensures that your palette is realized as a foreground palette if your application is indeed running in the foreground. If you use a *TRUE* flag parameter here, you can force Windows to realize the palette as though the application were in the background.

You must also call *RealizePalette* for each DIB that you display in your *OnDraw* function. Of course, you must call *SelectPalette* first, but this time you call it with a *TRUE* flag parameter. Things do get complicated if you're displaying several DIBs, each with its own palette. Basically, you've got to choose a palette for one of the DIBs and realize it (by selecting it with the *FALSE* parameter) in the palette message handlers. That chosen DIB will end up looking better than the other DIBs. There are ways of merging palettes, but it might be easier to go out and buy more video memory.

DIBs, Pixels, and Color Tables

A DIB consists of a two-dimensional array of elements called <u>pixels</u>. In many cases, each DIB pixel will be mapped to a display pixel, but the DIB pixel might be mapped to some logical area on the display, depending on the mapping mode and the display function stretch parameters. You've already seen the effects of a mismatch between bitmap pixels and display pixels.

A pixel consists of 1, 4, 8, 16, 24, or 32 contiguous bits, depending on the color resolution of the DIB. For 16-bpp, 24-bpp, and 32-bpp DIBs, each pixel represents an RGB color. In a 16-bpp DIB, there are typically 5 bits each for red, green, and blue values, and in the more common 24-bpp DIB, there are 8 bits for each color value. The 16-bpp and 24-bpp DIBs are optimized for video cards that can display 65,536 or 16.7 million simultaneous colors.

A 1-bpp DIB is really a monochrome DIB, but these DIBs don't have to be black and white—they can contain any two colors chosen from the color table that is built into the DIB. A monochrome bitmap has two 32-bit color table entries, each containing 8 bits for red, green, and blue values plus another 8 bits for flags. Zero (0) pixels use the first entry, and one (1) pixels use the second. If you have a 65,536-color video card or a 16.7-million–color card, Windows can display the two colors directly. (Windows truncates 8-bits-per-color values to 5 bits for 65,536-color displays.) If your video card is running in 256-color palettized mode, your program can adjust the system palette to load the two specified colors.

Eight-bpp DIBs are quite common. Like a monochrome DIB, an 8-bpp DIB has a color table, but the color table has 256 (or fewer) 32-bit entries. Each pixel is an index into this color table. If you have a palettized video card, your program can create a logical palette from the 256 entries. If another program (running in the foreground) has control of the system palette, Windows does its best to match your logical palette colors to the system palette.

What if you're trying to display a 24-bpp DIB with a 256-color palettized video card? If the DIB author were nice, he or she would have included a color table containing the most important colors in the DIB. Your program could then build a logical palette from that table, and the DIB would look OK. If the DIB has no color table, you can build a logical palette from the current system palette and use that. It's better than the 20 standard colors you'd get with no palette at all. Another option is to analyze the DIB to identify the most important colors, but you can buy a utility to do that.

The Structure of a DIB Within a BMP File

You know that the DIB is the standard Windows bitmap format and that a BMP file contains a DIB. So let's look inside a BMP file to see what's there. Figure 10-1 shows a layout for a BMP file. The *BITMAPFILEHEADER* structure contains the offset to the image bits, which you can use to compute the combined size of the *BITMAPINFOHEADER* structure and the color table that follows. The *BITMAPFILEHEADER* structure contains a file size member, but you can't depend on it because you don't know whether the size is measured in bytes, words, or double words.

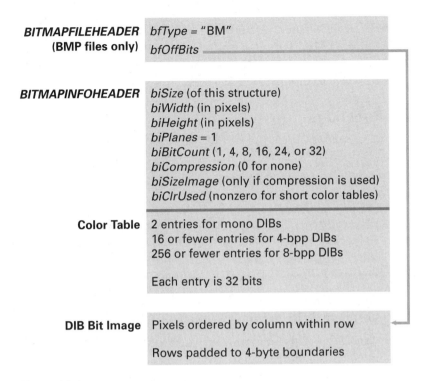

BITMAPFILEHEADER (BMP files only)	bfType = "BM" bfOffBits
BITMAPINFOHEADER	biSize (of this structure) biWidth (in pixels) biHeight (in pixels) biPlanes = 1 biBitCount (1, 4, 8, 16, 24, or 32) biCompression (0 for none) biSizeImage (only if compression is used) biClrUsed (nonzero for short color tables)
Color Table	2 entries for mono DIBs 16 or fewer entries for 4-bpp DIBs 256 or fewer entries for 8-bpp DIBs Each entry is 32 bits
DIB Bit Image	Pixels ordered by column within row Rows padded to 4-byte boundaries

Figure 10-1.
The layout for a BMP file.

The *BITMAPINFOHEADER* structure contains the bitmap dimensions, the bits per pixel, compression information for 4-bpp and 8-bpp bitmaps, and the number of color table entries. If the DIB is compressed, this header contains the size of the pixel array; otherwise, you can compute the size from the dimensions and the bits per pixel. Immediately following the header is the color table (if the DIB has a color table). The DIB image comes after that. The DIB image consists of pixels arranged by column within rows, starting with the bottom row. Each row is padded to a 4-byte boundary.

The only place you'll find a *BITMAPFILEHEADER* structure, however, is in a BMP file. If you get a DIB from the clipboard, for example, there will not be a file header. You can always count on the color table to follow the *BITMAPINFOHEADER* structure, but you can't count on the image to follow the color table. If you're using the *CreateDIBSection* function, for example, you must allocate the bitmap info header and color table and then let Windows allocate the image somewhere else.

NOTE: This chapter and all the associated code are specific to Windows DIBs. There's also a well-documented variation of the DIB format for OS/2. If you need to process these OS/2 DIBs, you'll have to modify the *CDib* class.

DIB Access Functions

Windows supplies some important DIB access functions. None of these functions is wrapped by MFC, so you'll need to refer to the Win32 documentation (or Books Online) for details. Here's a summary:

- **SetDIBitsToDevice**—This function displays a DIB directly on the display or printer. No scaling occurs; one bitmap bit corresponds to one display pixel or one printer dot. This scaling restriction limits the function's usefulness. The function doesn't work like *BitBlt* because *BitBlt* uses logical coordinates.

- **StretchDIBits**—This function displays a DIB directly on the display or printer in a manner similar to that of *StretchBlt*.

- **GetDIBits**—This function constructs a DIB from a GDI bitmap, using memory that you allocate. You have some control over the format of the DIB because you can specify the number of color bits per pixel and the compression. If you are using compression, you have to call *GetDIBits* twice—once to calculate the memory needed and again to generate the DIB data.

- **CreateDIBitmap**—This function creates a GDI bitmap from a DIB. As for all these DIB functions, you must supply a device context pointer as a parameter. A display device context will do; you don't need a memory device context.

- **CreateDIBSection**—This function creates a special kind of DIB known as a <u>DIB</u> <u>section</u>. It then returns a GDI bitmap handle. This is the new Win32 function that gives you the best features of DIBs and GDI bitmaps. You have direct access to the DIB's memory, and with the bitmap handle and a memory device context, you can call GDI functions to draw into the DIB. While *StretchBlt* and *StretchDIBits* are equally fast under Windows 95, *StretchBlt* is faster under Windows NT. Thus, you can use *CreateDIBSection* to optimize your application's performance.

The *CDib* Class

If DIBs look intimidating, don't worry. The *CDib* class makes DIB programming easy. The best way to get to know the *CDib* class is to look at the public member functions and data members. Figure 10-2 shows the *CDib* header file. You'll have to look at the companion CD-ROM for the implementation code.

CDIB.H

```
class CDib : public CObject
{
    enum Alloc {noAlloc, crtAlloc,
                heapAlloc}; // applies to BITMAPINFOHEADER
    DECLARE_SERIAL(CDib)
public:
    LPVOID   m_lpvColorTable;
    HBITMAP m_hBitmap;
    LPBYTE   m_lpImage;   // starting address of DIB bits
    LPBITMAPINFOHEADER m_lpBMIH; // buffer containing the
                                 //  BITMAPINFOHEADER
private:
    HGLOBAL m_hGlobal; // for external windows we need to free
                       // could be allocated by this class or
                       //  allocated externally
    Alloc m_nBmihAlloc;
    Alloc m_nImageAlloc;
    DWORD m_dwSizeImage; // of bits -- not BITMAPINFOHEADER
                         //  or BITMAPFILEHEADER
    int m_nColorTableEntries;

    HANDLE m_hFile;
    HANDLE m_hMap;
    LPVOID m_lpvFile;
    HPALETTE m_hPalette;
public:
    CDib();
    CDib(CSize size, int nBitCount);  // builds BITMAPINFOHEADER
    ~CDib();
    int GetSizeImage() {return m_dwSizeImage;}
    int GetSizeHeader()
        {return sizeof(BITMAPINFOHEADER) +
                sizeof(RGBQUAD) * m_nColorTableEntries;}
    CSize GetDimensions();
```

Figure 10-2.   *(continued)*
The CDib *class declaration.*

Figure 10-2. *continued*

```
        BOOL AttachMapFile(const char* strPathname, BOOL bShare = FALSE);
        BOOL CopyToMapFile(const char* strPathname);
        BOOL AttachMemory(LPVOID lpvMem, BOOL bMustDelete = FALSE,
            HGLOBAL hGlobal = NULL);
        BOOL Draw(CDC* pDC, CPoint origin,
            CSize size); // until we implement CreateDibSection
        HBITMAP CreateSection(CDC* pDC = NULL);
        UINT UsePalette(CDC* pDC, BOOL bBackground = FALSE);
        BOOL MakePalette();
        BOOL SetSystemPalette(CDC* pDC);
        BOOL Compress(CDC* pDC,
            BOOL bCompress = TRUE); // FALSE means decompress
        HBITMAP CreateBitmap(CDC* pDC);
        BOOL Read(CFile* pFile);
        BOOL Write(CFile* pFile);
        void Serialize(CArchive& ar);
        void Empty();
private:
        void DetachMapFile();
        void ComputePaletteSize(int nBitCount);
        void ComputeMetrics();
};
```

Here's a rundown of the *CDib* member functions, starting with the constructors and the destructor:

■ **Default constructor**—You'll use the default constructor in preparation for loading a DIB from a file or for attaching to a DIB in memory. The default constructor creates an empty DIB object.

■ **DIB section constructor**—If you need a DIB section that is created by the *CreateDIBSection* function, use this constructor. Its parameters determine DIB size and number of colors. The constructor allocates info header memory but not image memory.

Parameter	Description
size	*CSize* object that contains the width and height of the *DIB*.
nBitCount	Bits per pixel; should be 1, 4, 8, 16, 24, or 32.

■ **Destructor**—The *CDib* destructor frees all allocated DIB memory.

■ *AttachMapFile*—This function opens a memory-mapped file in read mode and attaches it to the *CDib* object. The return is immediate because the file isn't actually read into memory until it is used. When you access the DIB, however, there could be a delay as the file is paged in. The *AttachMapFile* function releases existing allocated memory and closes any previously attached memory-mapped file.

Parameter	Description
strPathname	Pathname of the file to be mapped.
bShare	Flag that is *TRUE* if the file is to be opened in share mode. The default value is *FALSE*.
Return value	*TRUE* if successful.

■ *AttachMemory*—This function associates an existing *CDib* object with a DIB in memory. This memory could be in the program's resources, or it could be clipboard or OLE data object memory. Memory might have been allocated from the CRT heap with the *new* operator, or it might have been allocated from the Windows heap with *GlobalAlloc*.

Parameter	Description
lpvMem	Address of the memory to be attached.
bMustDelete	Flag that is *TRUE* if the *CDib* class is responsible for deleting this memory. The default value is *FALSE*.
hGlobal	If memory was obtained with a call to the Win32 *GlobalAlloc* function, the *CDib* object needs to keep the handle in order to free it later, assuming that *bMustDelete* was set to *TRUE*.
Return value	*TRUE* if successful.

■ *Compress*—This function regenerates the DIB as a compressed or an uncompressed DIB. Internally, it converts the existing DIB to a GDI bitmap and then makes a new compressed or an uncompressed DIB. Compression is supported only for 4-bpp and 8-bpp DIBs. You can't compress a DIB section.

229

Parameter	Description
pDC	Pointer to the display device context.
bCompress	*TRUE* (default) to compress the DIB, *FALSE* to uncompress it.
Return value	*TRUE* if successful.

■ *CopyToMapFile*—This function creates a new memory-mapped file and copies the existing *CDib* data to the file's memory, releasing any previously allocated memory and closing any existing memory-mapped file. The data isn't actually written to disk until the new file is closed, but that happens when the *CDib* object is reused or destroyed.

Parameter	Description
strPathname	Pathname of the file to be mapped.
Return value	*TRUE* if successful.

■ *CreateBitmap*—This function creates a GDI bitmap from an existing DIB and is called by the *Compress* function. Don't confuse this function with *CreateSection*, which generates a DIB and stores the handle.

Parameter	Description
pDC	Pointer to the display or printer device context.
Return value	Handle to a GDI bitmap—*NULL* if unsuccessful. This handle is <u>not</u> stored as a public data member.

■ *CreateSection*—This function creates a DIB section by calling the Win32 *CreateDIBSection* function.

Parameter	Description
pDC	Pointer to the display or printer device context.
Return value	Handle to a GDI bitmap—*NULL* if unsuccessful. This handle is also stored as a public data member.

■ **Draw**—This function outputs this *CDib* object to the display (or the printer) with a call to the Win32 *StretchDIBits* function. The bitmap will be stretched as necessary to fit the specified rectangle.

Parameter	Description
pDC	Pointer to the display or printer device context that will receive the DIB image.
origin	*CPoint* object that holds the logical coordinates at which the DIB will be displayed.
size	*CSize* object that represents the display rectangle's width and height in logical units.
Return value	*TRUE* if successful.

■ **Empty**—This function empties the DIB, freeing allocated memory and closing the map file if necessary.

■ **GetDimensions**—This function returns the width and height of the DIB in pixels.

Parameter	Description
Return value	*CSize* object.

■ **GetSizeHeader**—This function returns the number of bytes in the info header and color table combined.

Parameter	Description
Return value	32-bit integer.

■ **GetSizeImage**—This function returns the number of bytes in the DIB image (excluding the info header and the color table).

Parameter	Description
Return value	32-bit integer.

■ *MakePalette*—This function reads the DIB's color table and (if the color table exists) creates a Windows palette. The *HPALETTE* handle is stored in a data member.

Parameter	Description
Return value	*TRUE* if successful.

■ *Read*—This function reads a DIB from a file into the *CDib* object. The file must have been successfully opened. If the file is a BMP file, reading starts from the beginning of the file. If the file is a document, reading starts from the current file pointer.

Parameter	Description
pFile	Pointer to a *CFile* object. The corresponding disk file contains the DIB.
Return value	*TRUE* if successful.

■ *Serialize*—Serialization is covered in Chapter 16. The *CDib::Serialize* function, which overrides the MFC *CObject::Serialize* function, calls the *Read* and *Write* member functions. See the *Microsoft Foundation Class Library Reference* for a description of the parameters.

■ *SetSystemPalette*—If you have a 16-bpp, 24-bpp, or 32-bpp DIB that doesn't have a color table, you can call this function to create for your *CDib* object a logical palette that matches the system palette. If your program is running on a 256-color palettized display and you don't call *SetSystemPalette*, you'll have no palette at all, and you'll see only the 20 standard Windows colors in your DIB.

Parameter	Description
pDC	Pointer to the display context.
Return value	*TRUE* if successful.

■ *UsePalette*—This function selects the *CDib* object's logical palette into the device context and then realizes the palette. The *Draw* member function calls *UsePalette* prior to painting the DIB.

Parameter	Description
pDC	Pointer to the display device context for realization.
bBackground	If this flag is *FALSE* (the default value) and the application is running in the foreground, Windows realizes the palette as the foreground palette (copies as many colors as possible into the system palette). If this flag is *TRUE*, Windows realizes the palette as a background palette (maps the logical palette to the system palette as best as it can).
Return value	Number of entries in the logical palette mapped to the system palette. If the function fails, the return value is *GDI_ERROR*.

■ *Write*—This function writes a DIB from the *CDib* object to a file. The file must have been successfully opened or created.

Parameter	Description
pFile	Pointer to a *CFile* object. The DIB will be written to the corresponding disk file.
Return value	*TRUE* if successful.

For your convenience, four public data members give you access to the DIB memory and to the DIB section handle. These members should give you a clue about the structure of a *CDib* object. It's just a bunch of pointers to heap memory. That memory might be owned by the DIB or by someone else. Additional private data members determine whether the *CDib* class frees the memory.

The EX10C Example

Now you'll put the *CDib* class to work in an application. The EX10C program displays two DIBs, one from a resource and the other loaded from a BMP file that you select at runtime. The program manages the system palette and displays the DIBs correctly on the printer. Compare the EX10C code with the GDI bitmap code in EX10A. Notice that you're not dealing with a memory device context and all the GDI selection rules!

Here are the steps to build EX10C. It's a good idea to type in the view class code, but you'll want to use the cdib.h and cdib.cpp files from the companion CD-ROM.

1. **Run AppWizard to produce \VCPP32\EX10C\EX10C.** Accept the defaults, but select Single Document Interface and the *CScrollView* view base class. The options and the default class names are shown here:

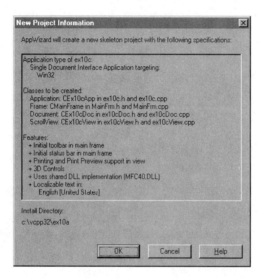

2. **Import the *IDB_REDBLOCKS* bitmap.** Choose Resource from the Developer Studio's Insert menu. Import the Red Blocks.bmp bitmap from the WINDOWS directory. (If your version of Windows doesn't have this bitmap, load it from the companion CD-ROM.) The Developer Studio will copy this bitmap file into your project's RES subdirectory. Assign the ID *IDB_REDBLOCKS*, and save the changes.

3. **Add the following private data members to the class *CEx10cView*.** Edit the file ex10cView.h. This embeds two *CDib* objects in the view. Add the following shaded code:

```
CDib m_dibResource;
CDib m_dibFile;
```

4. Edit the *OnInitialUpdate* member function in the file ex10cView.cpp.
This function sets the mapping mode to *MM_HIMETRIC* and loads the
m_dibResource object directly from the *IDB_REDBLOCKS* resource. Note
that we're not calling *LoadBitmap* to load a GDI bitmap as we were in
EX10A. The *CDib::AttachMemory* function connects the object to the
resource in your EXE file. Add the following shaded code:

```
void CEx10cView::OnInitialUpdate()
{
    CScrollView::OnInitialUpdate();

    CSize totalSize(30000, 40000); // 30 by 40 cm
    CSize lineSize = CSize(totalSize.cx / 100,
                           totalSize.cy / 100);
    SetScrollSizes(MM_HIMETRIC, totalSize,
                   totalSize, lineSize);

    LPVOID lpvResource = (LPVOID) ::LoadResource(NULL,
        ::FindResource(NULL, MAKEINTRESOURCE(IDB_REDBLOCKS),
        RT_BITMAP));
    m_dibResource.AttachMemory(lpvResource); // no need for
                                             //  ::LockResource
    CClientDC dc(this);
    TRACE("bits per pixel = %d\n", dc.GetDeviceCaps(BITSPIXEL));
}
```

5. Edit the *OnDraw* member function in the file ex10cView.cpp. This
code calls *CDib::Draw* for each of the DIBs. The *UsePalette* call should really
be made by message handlers for the WM_QUERYNEWPALETTE and
WM_PALETTECHANGED messages. These messages are hard to deal
with because they don't go to the view directly, so we'll take a shortcut.
Add the following shaded code:

```
void CEx10cView::OnDraw(CDC* pDC)
{
    BeginWaitCursor();
    m_dibResource.UsePalette(pDC);
    m_dibFile.UsePalette(pDC); // should be in palette message
                               //  handlers, not here
```

(continued)

```
        pDC->TextOut(0, 0,
        "Click the left mouse button here to load a file");
        CSize sizeResourceDib = m_dibResource.GetDimensions();
        sizeResourceDib.cx *= 20;
        sizeResourceDib.cy *= -20;
        m_dibResource.Draw(pDC, CPoint(0, -500), sizeResourceDib);
        CSize sizeFileDib = m_dibFile.GetDimensions();
        sizeFileDib.cx *= 20;
        sizeFileDib.cy *= -20;
        m_dibFile.Draw(pDC, CPoint(1200, -500), sizeFileDib);
        EndWaitCursor();
}
```

6. Map the WM_LBUTTONDOWN message in the *CEx10cView* class.

Edit the file ex10cView.cpp. *OnLButtonDown* contains code to read a DIB
in two different ways. If you leave the MEMORY_MAPPED_FILES definition intact, the *AttachMapFile* code is activated to read a memory-mapped
file. If you comment out the first line, the *Read* call is activated. The
SetSystemPalette call is there for DIBs that don't have a color table. Add
the following shaded code:

```
#define MEMORY_MAPPED_FILES
void CEx10cView::OnLButtonDown(UINT nFlags, CPoint point)
{
    CFileDialog dlg(TRUE, "bmp", "*.bmp");
    if (dlg.DoModal() != IDOK) return;
#ifdef MEMORY_MAPPED_FILES
    if (m_dibFile.AttachMapFile(dlg.GetPathName(),
        TRUE) == TRUE) { // share
      Invalidate();
    }
#else
    CFile file;
    file.Open(dlg.GetPathName(), CFile::modeRead);
    if (m_dibFile.Read(&file) == TRUE) {
        Invalidate();
    }
#endif
    CClientDC dc(this);
    m_dibFile.SetSystemPalette(&dc);
}
```

7. **Integrate the *CDib* class with this project.** If you've created this project from scratch, copy the cdib.h and cdib.cpp files from \VCPP32\EX10C on the companion CD-ROM. Simply copying the files to disk isn't enough; you must also add the cdib.cpp file to the project: choose Files Into Project from the Developer Studio's Insert menu, and then select cdib.cpp. Finally, you must add the line

```
#include "cdib.h"
```

immediately above the line

```
#include "ex10cView.h"
```

in <u>two</u> files: ex10c.cpp and ex10cView.cpp. This lets the compiler see the *CDib* class declaration before it sees the embedded objects.

8. **Build and run the application.** The EX10C project directory on the companion CD-ROM contains several interesting bitmaps. The chicago.bmp file is an 8-bpp DIB with 256 color table entries; the forest.bmp and clouds.bmp files are also 8 bpp, but they have smaller color tables. The balloons.bmp is a 24-bpp DIB with no color table. Try some other BMP files if you have them. Note that Red Blocks is a 16-color DIB that uses standard colors, which are always included in the system palette.

Putting Bitmaps on Pushbuttons

The MFC library makes it easy to display a bitmap (instead of text) on a pushbutton. If you were to program this from scratch, you would set the Owner Draw property for your button, and then you would write a message handler in your dialog class that would paint a bitmap on the button control's window. If you use the MFC *CBitmapButton* class instead, you end up doing a lot less work, but you have to follow a kind of "cookbook" procedure. Don't worry too much about how it all works, but be glad you don't have to write much code.

To make a long story short, you lay out your dialog resource as usual with unique text captions for the buttons you designate for bitmaps. Next you add some bitmap resources to your project, and you identify those resources by <u>name</u> rather than by numeric ID. Finally you add some *CBitmapButton* data members to your dialog class, and you call the *AutoLoad* member function for each one, which matches a bitmap name to a button caption. If the button caption is "COPY", you add two bitmaps: "COPYU" for the up state and

"COPYD" for the down state. Oh, by the way, you must still set the button's Owner Draw property. This will all make more sense when you write a program.

> **N O T E :** If you look at the MFC source code for the *CBitmapButton* class, you'll see that the bitmap is an ordinary GDI bitmap painted with a *BitBlt* call. Thus, you can't expect any palette support. That's usually not a problem because bitmaps for buttons are usually 16-color bitmaps that depend on standard VGA colors.

The EX10D Example

Here are the steps to build EX10D.

1. **Run AppWizard to produce \VCPP32\EX10D\EX10D.** Accept the defaults, but select Single Document Interface, deselect Printing And Print Preview, and select Context-Sensitive Help. The options and the default class names are shown here:

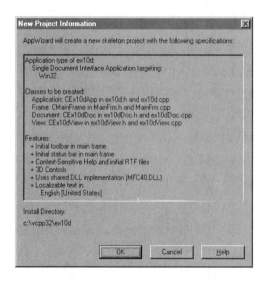

The Context-Sensitive Help option was selected for one reason only—it causes AppWizard to copy some bitmap files into your project's HLP subdirectory. These bitmaps are supposed to be bound into your project's help file, but we won't study help files until Chapter 20.

2. **Modify the project's IDD_ABOUTBOX dialog resource.** It's too much hassle to create a new dialog resource for a few buttons, so we'll use the About dialog that AppWizard generates for every project. Add three

pushbuttons with captions, as shown below, accepting the default IDs *IDC_BUTTON1*, *IDC_BUTTON2*, and *IDC_BUTTON3*. The size of the buttons isn't important because the framework adjusts the button size at runtime to match the bitmap size.

Select the Owner Draw property for all three buttons.

3. Import three bitmaps from the project's HLP subdirectory. Choose Resource from the Developer Studio's Insert menu, and then click the Import button. Start with EditCopy.bmp, as shown here:

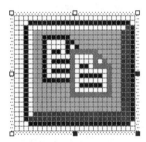

Assign the name "COPYU" as shown:

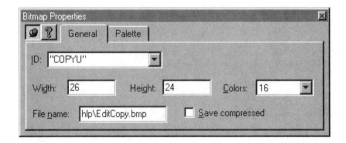

Be sure to use quotes around the name in order to identify the resource by name rather than by ID. This is now the bitmap for the button's up state. Close the bitmap window and, from the ResourceView window, use the clipboard (or drag and drop) to make a copy of the bitmap. Rename the copy "COPYD" (down state), and then edit this bitmap. Choose Invert Colors from the Image menu. There are other ways of making a variation of the up image, but inversion is the quickest.

Repeat the steps above for the EditCut and EditPast bitmaps. When you're finished, you should have the following bitmap resources in your project:

Resource Name	Original File	Invert Colors
"COPYU"	EditCopy.bmp	no
"COPYD"	EditCopy.bmp	yes
"CUTU"	EditCut.bmp	no
"CUTD"	EditCut.bmp	yes
"PASTEU"	EditPast.bmp	no
"PASTED"	EditPast.bmp	yes

4. **Edit the code for the *CAboutDlg* class.** Both the declaration and the implementation for this class are contained in the ex10d.cpp file. First you add the three private data members shown here in the class declaration:

```
CBitmapButton m_editCopy;
CBitmapButton m_editCut;
CBitmapButton m_editPaste;
```

Then you use ClassWizard to map the WM_INITDIALOG message in the dialog class. (Be sure that the *CAboutDlg* class is selected.) The message handler (actually a virtual function) is coded as follows:

```
BOOL CAboutDlg::OnInitDialog()
{
    CDialog::OnInitDialog();
    VERIFY(m_editCopy.AutoLoad(IDC_BUTTON1, this));
    VERIFY(m_editCut.AutoLoad(IDC_BUTTON2, this));
    VERIFY(m_editPaste.AutoLoad(IDC_BUTTON3, this));
    return TRUE;    // return TRUE unless you set the focus to a control
                    // EXCEPTION: OCX Property Pages should return FALSE
}
```

The *AutoLoad* function connects the button with the two matching resources. The *VERIFY* macro is an MFC diagnostic aid that displays a message box if you didn't code the bitmap names correctly.

5. **Build and test the application.**   When the program starts, choose About from the Help menu, and observe the button behavior. The image below shows the CUT button in the down state:

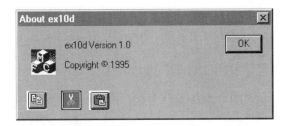

Note that bitmap buttons send BN_CLICKED notification messages just as ordinary buttons do. ClassWizard can, of course, map those messages in your dialog class.

Going Further with Bitmap Buttons

You've seen bitmaps for the buttons' up and down states. The *CBitmapButton* class also supports bitmaps for the focused and disabled states. For the COPY button, the focused bitmap name would be "COPYF", and the disabled bitmap name would be "COPYX". If you want to test the disabled option, make a "COPYX" bitmap, possibly with a red line through it, and then add the following line to your program:

```
m_editCopy.EnableWindow(FALSE);
```

CHAPTER ELEVEN

Windows Message Processing and Multithreaded Programming

Win32 has revolutionized Windows-based programming with its new preemptive multitasking and multithreading API. If you've seen magazine articles and advanced programming books on these subjects, you might have been intimidated by their complexity. So far in this book, we've managed to avoid all mention of threads. Indeed, you could stick with single-threaded programming for a long time and still write useful Win32 applications. If you learn the fundamentals of threads, however, you'll be able to write more efficient and capable programs, and you'll be on your way to a better understanding of the Win32 programming model.

Windows Message Processing

To understand threads, you must first understand how 32-bit Windows processes messages. The best starting point is a single-threaded program that shows the importance of the message translation and dispatch process. You'll improve that program by adding a second thread to it, which you'll control with a global variable and a simple message. Then you'll experiment with events and critical sections. For the heavy-duty multithreading elements such as mutexes and semaphores, however, you'll need to refer to another book, such as Jeffrey Richter's *Advanced Windows* (Microsoft Press, 1995).

How a Single-Threaded Program Processes Messages

All your programs so far have been <u>single-threaded</u>, which means that there is only one execution path through your code. With ClassWizard's help, you've written handler functions for various Windows messages, and you've written *OnDraw* code that is called in response to the WM_PAINT message. It's easy to think that Windows magically calls your handler when the message floats in, but it doesn't work that way. Deep inside the MFC code (which is linked to your program) are instructions that look something like this:

```
MSG message;
while (::GetMessage(&message, NULL, 0, 0)) {
    ::TranslateMessage(&message);
    ::DispatchMessage(&message);
}
```

Windows determines which messages belong to your program, and the *GetMessage* function returns when there is a message to process. If there is no message, your program is suspended, and other programs can run. When a message eventually comes in, your program "wakes up." The *TranslateMessage* function translates WM_KEYDOWN messages into WM_CHAR messages containing ASCII characters, and the *DispatchMessage* function passes control (via the window class) to the MFC message pump, which calls your function via the message map. When your handler is finished, it returns to the MFC code, which eventually causes *DispatchMessage* to return.

Yielding Control

What would happen if one of your handler functions were a pig and chewed up 10 seconds of CPU time? Back in the 16-bit days, that would have hung up the whole computer for the duration. Only cursor tracking and a few other interrupt-based tasks would have run. With Win32, multitasking has gotten a whole lot better. Other applications can run because of preemptive multitasking—Windows simply interrupts your pig function when it needs to. However, even in Win32, your program would be locked out for 10 seconds. It couldn't process any messages because *DispatchMessage* doesn't return until the pig returns.

There is a way around this problem, however, which works with both Win16 and Win32. You simply train your pig function to be nice and yield control once in a while by inserting the following instructions inside the pig's main loop:

```
MSG message;
if (::PeekMessage(&message, NULL, 0, 0, PM_REMOVE)) {
  ::TranslateMessage(&message);
  ::DispatchMessage(&message);
}
```

The *PeekMessage* function works like *GetMessage*, except that it returns immediately even if there is no message for your program. In that case, the pig keeps on chewing. If there is a message, however, the handler is called, and the pig starts up again after the handler exits.

Timers

A Windows timer is a useful programming element that sometimes makes multithreaded programming unnecessary. If you need to read a communication buffer, for example, you could set up a timer to retrieve the accumulated characters every 100 milliseconds. You could also use a timer to control animation because the timer is independent of CPU clock speed.

Timers are easy to use. You simply call the *CWnd* member function *SetTimer* with an interval parameter, and then you provide, with the help of ClassWizard, a message handler function for the resulting WM_TIMER messages. Once you start the timer with a specified interval in milliseconds, WM_TIMER messages will be sent continuously to your window until you call *CWnd::KillTimer* or until the timer's window is destroyed. You can have multiple timers if you want, each identified by an integer. Because Windows isn't a real-time operating system, things get imprecise if you specify an interval much less than 100 milliseconds.

Timer messages are just like other Windows messages in that they can be blocked by other handler functions in your program. Fortunately, timer messages don't stack up. Windows won't put a timer message in the queue if a message for that timer is already present.

The EX11A Program

We're going to write a program that contains a CPU-intensive computation loop. We want to let the program process messages after the user starts the computation; otherwise, the user couldn't cancel the job. Also we'd like to display the percent complete status by using a progress indicator control, as shown in Figure 11-1 on the following page. The EX11A program allows message processing by yielding control in the compute loop. A timer handler updates the progress control based on compute parameters. The WM_TIMER messages could not be processed if the compute process didn't yield control.

245

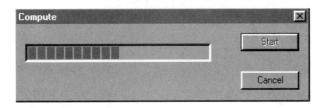

Figure 11-1.
The Compute dialog box.

Here are the steps for building the EX11A application:

1. Run AppWizard to generate \VCPP32\EX11A\EX11A. Accept the
default settings, but select Single Document Interface and deselect Printing And Print Preview. The options and the default class names are
shown here:

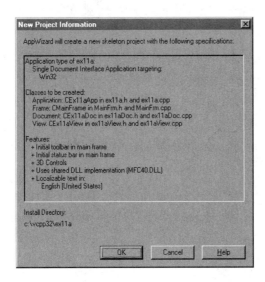

2. Use the graphic editor to create the dialog resource *IDD_COMPUTE*.
Use the resource shown here as a guide:

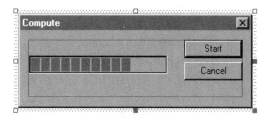

Keep the default control ID for the Cancel button, but use *IDC_START*
for the Start button. For the progress indicator, accept the default ID
IDC_PROGRESS1.

3. Use ClassWizard to create the *CComputeDlg* class. ClassWizard
connects the new class to the *IDD_COMPUTE* resource you just created.
  After the class is generated, add message handler functions for
IDC_START, *IDCANCEL*, and WM_TIMER. (Add BN_CLICKED message
handlers for *IDC_START* and *IDCANCEL*. Accept the default names
OnStart and *OnCancel*.)

4. Edit the file ComputeDlg.h. Add the following private data members:

```
int m_nTimer;
int m_nCount;
enum { nMaxCount = 100000 };
```

The *m_nCount* data member of class *CComputeDlg* is incremented during
the compute process. It serves as a percent complete measurement when
divided by the "constant" *nMaxCount.*

**5. Add initialization code to the *CComputeDlg* constructor in
ComputeDlg.cpp.** Add the following line to the constructor to ensure
that the Cancel button will work if the compute process has not been
started:

```
m_nCount = 0;
```

Be sure to add the line outside the //{{AFX_DATA_INIT comments generated by ClassWizard.

6. Code the *OnStart* function in ComputeDlg.cpp. This code is executed when the user clicks the Start button. Add the following shaded code:

```
void CControlDlg::OnStart()
{
    MSG message;

    m_nTimer = SetTimer(1, 100, NULL); // 1/10 second
    ASSERT(m_nTimer != 0);
    GetDlgItem(IDC_START)->EnableWindow(FALSE);
    volatile int nTemp;
    for (m_nCount = 0; m_nCount < nMaxCount; m_nCount++) {
      for (nTemp = 0; nTemp < 1000; nTemp++)
        {} // uses up CPU cycles
      if (::PeekMessage(&message, NULL, 0, 0, PM_REMOVE)) {
        ::TranslateMessage(&message);
        ::DispatchMessage(&message);
      }
    }
    CDialog::OnOK();
}
```

The main *for* loop is controlled by the value of *m_nCount*. Each time it moves through the loop, *PeekMessage* allows other messages, including WM_TIMER, to be processed. The *EnableWindow(FALSE)* call disables the Start button during the computation. If we didn't take this precaution, the *OnStart* function could be reentered.

7. Code the *OnTimer* function in ComputeDlg.cpp. When the timer fires, the scroll bar's scroll box is set according to the value of *m_nCount*. Add the following shaded code:

```
void CComputeDlg::OnTimer(UINT nIDEvent)
{
    CProgressCtrl* pBar =
        (CProgressCtrl*) GetDlgItem(IDC_PROGRESS1);
    pBar->SetPos(m_nCount * 100 / nMaxCount);
}
```

8. Update the *OnCancel* function in ComputeDlg.cpp. When the user clicks the Cancel button during computation, we don't destroy the dialog, but we set *m_nCount* to its maximum value, which causes *OnStart* to exit the dialog. If the computation hasn't started, it's OK to exit directly. Add the following shaded code:

```
void CControlDlg::OnCancel()
{
    TRACE("entering CComputeDlg::OnCancel\n");
    if (m_nCount == 0) {    // prior to Start button
      CDialog::OnCancel();
    }
    else { // computation in progress
      m_nCount = nMaxCount;  // force exit from OnStart
    }
}
```

9. **Add a WM_LBUTTONDOWN message handler to *CEx11aView* in ex11aView.cpp.**   First edit the virtual *OnDraw* function to display a message, as shown here:

```
void CEx11aView::OnDraw(CDC* pDC)
{
    pDC->TextOut(0, 0, "Press the left mouse button here.");
}
```

Then use ClassWizard to add the *OnLButtonDown* function, and add the following shaded code:

```
void CEx11aView::OnLButtonDown(UINT nFlags, CPoint point)
{
    CComputeDlg dlg;
    dlg.DoModal();
}
```

This code displays the modal dialog whenever the user presses the left mouse button while the mouse cursor is in the view window.

While you're in ex11aView.cpp, add the following *#include* statement:

```
#include "ComputeDlg.h"
```

10. **Build and run the application.**   Press the left mouse button while the mouse cursor is inside the view window to display the dialog. Click the Start button, and then click Cancel. The progress indicator should show the status of the computation.

On-Idle Processing

Before multithreaded programming came along, Windows developers used on-idle processing for "background" tasks such as pagination. Now on-idle processing is not so important, but there are still uses for it. The application framework calls a virtual member function *OnIdle* of class *CWinApp*, and you can override this function to do background processing. *OnIdle* is called from the framework's message processing loop, which is actually a little more complicated than the simple *GetMessage/TranslateMessage/DispatchMessage* sequence you've seen. Generally, the *OnIdle* function is called once after the application's message queue has been emptied. If you override this function, your code will be called, but it won't be called continuously unless there is a constant stream of messages. The base class *OnIdle* updates the toolbar buttons and status indicators, and it cleans up various temporary object pointers. It makes sense for you to override *OnIdle* to update the user interface. The fact that your code won't be executed when there are no messages is not important because the user interface shouldn't be changing.

> NOTE: If you do override *CWinApp::OnIdle*, don't forget to call the base class *OnIdle*. Otherwise, your toolbar buttons won't be updated and temporary objects won't be deleted.

OnIdle isn't called at all if the user is working in a modal dialog or is using a menu. If you need to use background processing for modal dialogs and menus, you'll have to add a message handler function for the WM_ENTER-IDLE message, but you must add it to the <u>frame</u> class rather than to the view class. That's because pop-up dialogs are always "owned" by the application's main frame window, not by the view window. Chapter 14 explores the relationship between the frame window and the view window.

Multithreaded Programming

As you'll recall from Chapter 9, a <u>process</u> is a running program that owns its own memory file handles and other system resources. An individual process can contain separate execution paths, called <u>threads</u>. Don't look for separate code for separate threads, however, because a single function could be called from many threads. For the most part, all of a process's code and data space is available to all of the threads in the process. Two threads, for example, can access the same global variables. Threads are managed by the operating system, and each thread has its own stack.

There are two kinds of threads, <u>worker threads</u> and <u>user-interface threads</u>, and both are supported by the MFC library. The user-interface thread has its own message loop, but the worker thread doesn't. Worker threads are easier to program and are generally more useful. The remaining examples in this chapter illustrate worker threads. At the end of the chapter, however, an application for a user-interface thread is described.

Don't forget that even a single-threaded application has one thread—the main thread. In the MFC hierarchy, *CWinApp* is derived from *CWinThread*. Back in Chapter 3, I told you that *InitInstance* and *m_pMainWnd* are members of *CWinApp*. Well, I lied. The members are declared in *CWinThread*, but of course they're inherited by *CWinApp*. The important thing to remember here is that an application is a thread.

Writing the Worker Thread Function and Starting the Thread

If you haven't guessed already, using a worker thread for a long computation is more efficient than using a message handler that contains a *PeekMessage* call. Before you worry about starting a worker thread, however, you must write a global function for your thread's main program. This global function should return a *UINT*, and it should take a single 32-bit value (declared *LPVOID*) as a parameter. You can use the parameter to pass anything at all to your thread when you start it. The thread does its computation, and when the global function returns, the thread terminates. The thread would also be terminated if the process terminated, but it's preferable to ensure that the worker thread terminates first to guarantee that you'll have no memory leaks.

To start the thread (with function name *ComputeThreadProc*), your program makes the following call:

```
CWinThread* pThread =
    AfxBeginThread(ComputeThreadProc, GetSafeHwnd(),
                   THREAD_PRIORITY_NORMAL);
```

The *AfxBeginThread* return value is a pointer to the newly created thread object. You can use that pointer to suspend and resume the thread (*CWinThread::SuspendThread* and *ResumeThread*), but you shouldn't use it to kill the thread. The second parameter is the 32-bit value that gets passed to the global function, and the third parameter is the thread's priority code. Once the worker thread starts, both threads run independently. Windows divides the time between the two threads (and among the threads that belong to other processes) according to their priority. If the main thread is waiting for a message, the compute thread can still run.

How the Main Thread Talks to a Worker Thread

The main thread (your application program) can communicate with the subsidiary worker thread in many different ways. One option that will not work, however, is a Windows message; the worker thread doesn't have a message loop. The simplest means of communication is a global variable because all the threads in the process have access to all the globals. Suppose the worker thread increments and tests a global integer as it computes and then exits when the value reaches 100. The main thread could force the worker thread to terminate by setting the global variable to 100 or higher. The code below looks as though it should work, and when you test it, it probably will:

```
UINT ComputeThreadProc(LPVOID pParam)
{
    g_nCount = 0;
    while (g_nCount++ < 100) {
        // do some computation here
    }
    return 0;
}
```

There's a problem, however, that you could detect only by looking at the generated assembly code. The value of *g_nCount* gets loaded into a register, the register is incremented, and then the register value is stored back in *g_nCount*. Suppose *g_nCount* is 40 and Windows interrupts the worker thread just after the worker thread loads 40 into the register. Now the main thread gets control and sets *g_nCount* to 100. When the worker thread resumes, it increments the register value and stores 41 back into *g_nCount*, obliterating the previous value of 100. The thread loop doesn't terminate!

But suppose you rewrote the thread procedure as shown here:

```
UINT ComputeThreadProc(LPVOID pParam)
{
    g_nCount = 0;
    while (g_nCount < 100) {
        // do some computation here
        g_nCount++;
    }
    return 0;
}
```

Now the main thread can terminate the worker thread because the ++ operator increments *g_nCount* directly in memory, using the value that the main thread might have stored there. A single instruction can't be interrupted by another thread. But if you turned on the compiler's optimization switch, you'd have another problem. The compiler would use a register for *g_nCount*, and the register would stay loaded for the duration of the loop. If the main thread changes the value of *g_nCount* in memory, it would have no effect on the worker thread's compute loop. You can ensure that the counter isn't stored in a register, however, by declaring *g_nCount* as *volatile*.

Now you've seen some of the pitfalls of using global variables for communication. Using global variables is sometimes appropriate, as the next example illustrates, but there are alternative methods that require less knowledge of assembly language, as you'll see later in this chapter.

How the Worker Thread Talks to the Main Thread

It makes sense for the worker thread to check a global variable in a loop, but what if the main thread did that? Remember the pig function? You definitely don't want your main thread to enter a loop because that would waste CPU cycles and stop your program's message processing. A Windows message is the preferred way for a worker thread to communicate with the main thread because the main thread always has a message loop. This implies, however, that the main thread has a window (visible or invisible) and that the worker thread has a handle to that window.

How does the worker thread get the handle? That's what the 32-bit thread function parameter discussed on page 9 is for. You simply pass the handle in the *AfxBeginThread* call. Why not pass the C++ window pointer instead? Doing so would be dangerous because you can't depend on the continued existence of the object, and you're not allowed to share objects of MFC classes among threads. (This rule does not apply to objects derived directly from *CObject* or to simple classes such as *CRect* and *CString*.)

Do you send the message or post it? Better to post it because sending it could cause reentry of the main thread's MFC message pump code, and that would create major problems. What kind of message do you post? Any user-defined message will do.

The EX11B Program

The EX11B program looks exactly like the EX11A program when you run it. When you look at the code, however, you'll see some differences. The computation is done in a worker thread instead of in the main thread. The count value is stored in a global variable *g_nCount*, which is set to the maximum value in the dialog window's Cancel button handler. When the thread exits, it posts a message to the dialog, which causes *DoModal* to exit.

The document, view, frame, and application classes are the same except for their names, and the dialog resource is the same. The modal dialog class is still named *CComputeDlg*, but the code inside is quite different. The constructor, timer handler, and data exchange functions are pretty much the same. The code at the top of the following page shows the global variable definition and the global thread function as given in the \vcpp32\ex11b\ComputeDlg-.cpp file on the companion CD-ROM. Note that the function exits (and the thread terminates) when *g_nCount* is greater than a constant maximum value. Before it exits, however, the function posts a user-defined message to the dialog window.

```
volatile int g_nCount = 0; // volatile necessary if you optimize

UINT ComputeThreadProc(LPVOID pParam)
{
    volatile int nTemp; // volatile else compiler
                        //    optimizes too much
    for (g_nCount = 0; g_nCount < CComputeDlg::nMaxCount;
        g_nCount++) {
      for (nTemp = 0; nTemp < 1000; nTemp++)
        {} // uses up CPU cycles
    }
    // WM_THREADFINISHED is user-defined message
    ::PostMessage((HWND) pParam, WM_THREADFINISHED, 0, 0);
    g_nCount = 0;
    return 0; // ends the thread
}
```

The *OnStart* handler below is mapped to the dialog's Start button. Its job is to start the timer and the worker thread. You can change the worker thread's priority by changing the third parameter of *AfxBeginThread*—for example, the computation runs a little more slowly if you set the priority to *THREAD_PRIORITY_NORMAL*.

```
void CComputeDlg::OnStart()
{
    m_nTimer = SetTimer(1, 100, NULL); // 1/10 second
    ASSERT(m_nTimer != 0);
    GetDlgItem(IDC_START)->EnableWindow(FALSE);
    AfxBeginThread(ComputeThreadProc, GetSafeHwnd(),
                THREAD_PRIORITY_HIGHEST);
}
```

The *OnCancel* handler below is mapped to the dialog's Cancel button. It sets the *g_nCount* variable to the maximum value, causing the thread to terminate.

```
void CComputeDlg::OnCancel()
{
    if (g_nCount == 0) { // prior to Start button
      CDialog::OnCancel();
    }
    else { // computation in progress
      g_nCount = nMaxCount;  // force thread to exit
    }
}
```

The *OnThreadFinished* handler below is mapped to the dialog's WM-_THREADFINISHED user-defined message. It causes the dialog's *DoModal* function to exit.

```
LONG CComputeDlg::OnThreadFinished(UINT wParam, LONG lParam)
{
    CDialog::OnOK();
    return 0;
}
```

Using Events for Thread Synchronization

The global variable is a crude but effective means of interthread communication. Now let's try something more sophisticated. We want to think in terms of thread synchronization instead of simple communication. Our threads must carefully synchronize their interactions with one another.

An event is one type of kernel object (processes and threads are also kernel objects) that Windows provides for thread synchronization. An event is identified by a unique 32-bit handle within a process and can be identified by name for sharing among processes. An event can be either in the signaled (or true) state or in the unsignaled (or false) state. There are two types of events, manual reset and autoreset; we'll be looking at autoreset events here because they're ideal for the synchronization of two processes.

Let's go back to our worker thread example. We want the main (user interface) thread to "signal" the worker thread to make it start or stop, so we'll need a "start" event and a "kill" event. MFC provides a handy *CEvent* class that's derived from *CSyncObject*. The default constructor creates a Win32 autoreset event object in the nonsignaled state. If you declare your events as global objects, any thread can easily access them. When the main thread wants to start or kill the worker thread, it sets the appropriate event to the signaled state by calling *CEvent::SetEvent*.

Now the worker thread must monitor the two events and respond when either is signaled. MFC provides the *CSingleLock* class for this purpose, but it's easier to use the Win32 *WaitForSingleObject* function. This function suspends the thread until the specified object becomes signaled. When the thread is suspended, it's not using any CPU cycles—which is good. The first *WaitForSingleObject* parameter is the event handle, which is stored in the *m_hObject* public data member of *CSyncObject*. The second parameter is the time-out interval. If you set this parameter to *INFINITE*, the function waits forever until the event becomes signaled. If you set the time-out to 0, *WaitForSingleObject* returns immediately, with a return value of *WAIT_OBJECT_0* if the event was signaled.

The EX11C Program

The EX11C program uses two events to synchronize the worker thread with the main thread. Most of the EX11C code is the same as EX11B, but the *CComputeDlg* class is quite different. The StdAfx.h file contains the following line for the *CEvent* class:

```
#include <afxmt.h>
```

There are two global event objects, as shown below. Note that the constructors create the Windows events prior to the execution of the main program.

```
CEvent g_eventStart; // creates autoreset events
CEvent g_eventKill;
```

It's best to look at the worker thread global function first. The function increments *g_nCount* just as it did in EX11B. The worker thread is started by the *OnInitDialog* function instead of by the Start button handler. The first *WaitForSingleObject* call waits for the start event, which is signaled by the Start button handler. The *INFINITE* parameter means that the thread waits as long as necessary. The second *WaitForSingleObject* call is different—it has a 0 time-out value. It's located in the main compute loop and simply makes a quick test to see whether the kill event was signaled by the Cancel button handler. If the event was signaled, the thread terminates.

```
UINT ComputeThreadProc(LPVOID pParam)
{
    volatile int nTemp;
    ::WaitForSingleObject(g_eventStart.m_hObject, INFINITE);
    TRACE("starting computation\n");
    for (g_nCount = 0; g_nCount < CComputeDlg::nMaxCount;
        g_nCount++) {
      for (nTemp = 0; nTemp < 1000; nTemp++)
        {} // simulate computation
      if (::WaitForSingleObject(g_eventKill.m_hObject, 0) ==
          WAIT_OBJECT_0)
        break;
    }
    // tell owner window we're finished
    ::PostMessage((HWND) pParam, WM_THREADFINISHED, 0, 0);
    g_nCount = 0;
    return 0; // ends the thread
}
```

Here is the *OnInitDialog* function that's called when the dialog is initialized. Note that it starts the worker thread, which doesn't do anything until the start event is signaled.

```
BOOL CComputeDlg::OnInitDialog()
{
    CDialog::OnInitDialog();
    AfxBeginThread(ComputeThreadProc, GetSafeHwnd());
    return TRUE;   // return TRUE unless you set the
                   //   focus to a control
                   // EXCEPTION: OCX Property Pages
                   //   should return FALSE
}
```

The following Start button handler sets the start event to the signaled state, thereby starting the worker thread's compute loop:

```
void CComputeDlg::OnStart()
{
    m_nTimer = SetTimer(1, 100, NULL); // 1/10 second
    ASSERT(m_nTimer != 0);
    GetDlgItem(IDC_START)->EnableWindow(FALSE);
    g_eventStart.SetEvent();
}
```

The following Cancel button handler sets the kill event to the signaled state, causing the worker thread's compute loop to terminate:

```
void CComputeDlg::OnCancel()
{
    if (g_nCount == 0) { // prior to Start button
      // must start it before we can kill it
        g_eventStart.SetEvent();
    }
    g_eventKill.SetEvent();
}
```

Note the awkward use of the start event when the user cancels without starting the compute process. It might be neater to define a new cancel event and then replace the first *WaitForSingleObject* call with a *WaitForMultipleObjects* call in the *ComputeThreadProc* function. If *WaitForMultipleObjects* detected a cancel event, it could cause an immediate thread termination.

Thread Blocking

The first *WaitForSingleObject* call in the *ComputeThreadProc* function on the facing page is an example of thread blocking. The thread simply stops executing until an event becomes signaled. There are many other ways a thread could be blocked. You could call the Win32 *Sleep* function, for example, to put your thread to "sleep" for 500 milliseconds. Many other functions block threads, particularly those functions that access devices such as communication ports and disk drives. Back in the Win16 days, those functions took over the CPU until they were finished. In Win32, they allow other processes and threads to run.

You should avoid putting blocking calls in your main user-interface thread. Remember that if your main thread is blocked, it can't process its messages, and that makes the program appear sluggish. If you have a task that requires heavy disk I/O, put the code in a worker thread and synchronize it with your main thread.

Critical Sections

Remember the problems with access to the *g_nCount* global variable? If you want to share global data among threads but you don't want to learn assembly language, <u>critical</u> <u>sections</u> might be the synchronization tools for you. Events are good for signaling, but critical sections (sections of code that require exclusive access to shared data) are good for controlling access to data.

Suppose your program tracks time values as hours, minutes, and seconds, each stored in a separate integer, and suppose two threads are sharing time values. Thread A is changing a time value but is interrupted by thread B after it has updated hours but before it has updated minutes and seconds. Thread B will have an invalid time value.

If you write a C++ class for your time format, it's easy to control data access by making the data members private and providing public member functions. The *CHMS* class, shown in Figure 11-2, does exactly that. Notice that the class has a data member of type *CRITICAL SECTION*. (There is no MFC support here.) The constructor calls the Win32 *InitializeCriticalSection* function, and the destructor calls *DeleteCriticalSection*. Thus, there is a critical section object associated with each *CHMS* object.

Notice that the other member functions call the *EnterCriticalSection* and *LeaveCriticalSection* functions. If thread A is executing in the middle of *SetTime*, thread B will be blocked by the *EnterCriticalSection* call in *GetTotalSecs* until thread A calls *LeaveCriticalSection*. The *IncrementSecs* function calls *SetTime*, which means that there are nested critical sections. That's OK because Windows keeps track of the nesting level.

The *CHMS* class works well if you use it to construct global objects. If you share pointers to objects on the heap, you have another set of problems. Each thread must determine whether another thread has deleted the object, and that means you must synchronize access to the pointers.

HMS.H

```
#include "StdAfx.h"
class CHMS
{
private:
    int m_nHr, m_nMn, m_nSc;
    CRITICAL_SECTION m_cs;
public:
    CHMS() : m_nHr(0), m_nMn(0), m_nSc(0)
    {
        ::InitializeCriticalSection(&m_cs);
    }

    ~CHMS()
    {
        ::DeleteCriticalSection(&m_cs);
    }

    void SetTime(int nSecs)
    {
        ::EnterCriticalSection(&m_cs);
        m_nSc = nSecs % 60;
        m_nMn = (nSecs / 60) % 60;
        m_nHr = nSecs / 3600;
        ::LeaveCriticalSection(&m_cs);
    }

    int GetTotalSecs()
    {
        int nTotalSecs;
        ::EnterCriticalSection(&m_cs);
        nTotalSecs = m_nHr * 3600 + m_nMn * 60 + m_nSc;
        ::LeaveCriticalSection(&m_cs);
        return nTotalSecs;
    }

    void IncrementSecs()
    {
        ::EnterCriticalSection(&m_cs);
        SetTime(GetTotalSecs() + 1);
        ::LeaveCriticalSection(&m_cs);
    }
};
```

Figure 11-2.
The CHMS class listing.

No sample program is provided that uses the *CHMS* class, but the file hms.h is included in the \VCPP32\EX11C subdirectory on the companion CD-ROM. If you write a multithreaded program, you can share global objects of the class. You don't need any other calls to the thread-related functions.

Mutexes and Semaphores

As I mentioned, I'm leaving these synchronization objects to Jeffrey Richter's *Advanced Windows.* You might need a mutex or a semaphore if you're controlling access to data across different processes because a critical section is accessible only within a single process. Mutexes and semaphores (along with events) are shareable by name.

User-Interface Threads

The MFC library provides good support for UI threads. You derive a class from *CWinThread,* and you use an overloaded version of *AfxBeginThread* to start the thread. Your derived *CWinThread* class has its own *InitInstance* function, and most important, it has its own message loop. You can construct windows and map messages as required.

Why do you want a user-interface thread? If you want multiple top-level windows, you can create and manage them from your main thread. Suppose you allow the user to run multiple instances of your application, but you want all instances to share memory. You can configure a single process to run multiple UI threads such that users think they are running separate processes. That's exactly what the Windows 95 Explorer does. Check it out with Spy++.

It's a little tricky starting the second and subsequent threads because the user actually launches a new process each time. When the second process starts, it signals the first process to start a new thread, and then it exits. The second process can locate the first process either by calling the Win32 *FindWindow* function or by declaring a shared data section. Shared data sections are explained in detail in Jeffrey Richter's book.

PART III

THE DOCUMENT–VIEW ARCHITECTURE

Menus, Keyboard Accelerators, the Rich Edit Control, and Property Sheets

In all the examples to this point, mouse clicks have triggered most program activity. Even though menu selections might have been more appropriate, you've used mouse clicks because mouse click messages are handled simply and directly within the Microsoft Foundation Class (MFC) Library version 4.0 view window. If you want program activity to be triggered when the user chooses a command from a menu, you must first become familiar with the other application framework elements.

This chapter concentrates on menus and the command routing architecture. Along the way, it introduces frames and documents, explaining the relationships between these new application framework elements and the already-familiar view element. You'll use the graphic editor to lay out a menu visually, and you'll use ClassWizard to link document and view member functions to menu items. You'll learn how to use special update command user interface (UI) member functions to check and disable menu items, and you'll see how to use keyboard accelerators as menu shortcut keys.

Because you're probably tired of circles and dialogs, you'll see two other MFC building blocks. The rich edit common control can add powerful text editing features to your application, and property sheets are ideal for setting edit options.

The Main Frame Window and Document Classes

Up to now, you've been using a view window as if it were the application's only window. In an SDI application, the view window sits inside another window—the application's main frame window. It's the main frame window that has the title bar and the menu bar. Various child windows, including the view window, the toolbar window, and the status bar window, occupy the main frame window's client area, as shown in Figure 12-1. The application framework controls the interaction between the frame and the view by routing messages from the frame to the view.

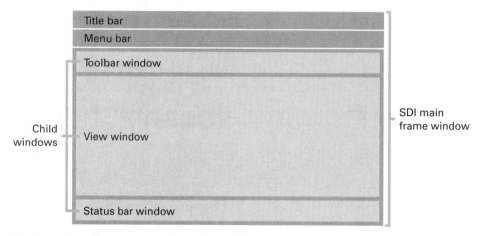

Figure 12-1.
The child windows within an SDI main frame window.

Look again at any project files generated by AppWizard. The MainFrm.h and MainFrm.cpp files contain the code for the application's main frame window class, derived from the class *CFrameWnd*. Other files, with names such as ex12aDoc.h and ex12aDoc.cpp, contain code for the application's document class, which is derived from *CDocument*. Starting with this chapter, you'll be modifying those frame and document files a lot.

Windows Menus

A Windows menu is a familiar application element that consists of a top-level horizontal list of items with associated pop-up menus that appear when the user selects a top-level item. Most of the time, you define a default menu resource for a frame window that loads when the window is created. You can also define a menu resource independent of a frame window. In that case, your program must call the functions necessary to load and activate the menu.

A menu resource completely defines the initial appearance of a menu. Menu items can be grayed or have check marks, and bars can separate groups of menu items. Multiple levels of pop-up menus are possible. If a first-level menu item is associated with a subsidiary popup, the menu item carries a right-pointing arrow symbol, as shown next to the Debug menu item in Figure 12-2.

The graphic editor includes an easy-to-use menu resource editing tool. This tool lets you edit menus in a wysiwyg environment. Each menu item has a properties dialog that defines all the characteristics of that item. The resulting resource definition is stored in the application's resource script (RC) file. Each menu item is associated with an ID, such as *ID_FILE_OPEN*, that is defined in the resource.h file.

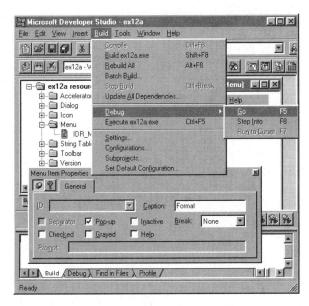

Figure 12-2.
Multilevel pop-up menus (from Microsoft Visual C++).

The MFC library extends the functionality of the standard menus for Windows. Each menu item can have a prompt string that appears in the frame's status bar when the item is highlighted. These prompts are really Windows string resource elements linked to the menu item by a common ID. From the point of view of the graphic editor and your program, the prompts appear to be part of the menu item definition.

265

Keyboard Accelerators

You've probably noticed that one letter is underlined in most menu items. In the Developer Studio (and most other applications), pressing Alt-F followed by S activates the File Save menu item. This shortcut system is the standard Windows method of using the keyboard to choose commands from menus. If you looked at the application's menu resource script (or the graphic editor's properties dialog), you would see an ampersand (&) preceding each of the characters that are underlined in the application's menu items.

Windows offers an alternative way of linking keystrokes to menu items. The keyboard accelerator resource consists of a table of key combinations with associated command IDs. The Edit Copy menu item (with command ID *ID_EDIT_COPY*), for example, might be linked to the Ctrl-C key combination through a keyboard accelerator entry. A keyboard accelerator entry does not have to be associated with a menu item. If no Edit Copy menu item were present, the Ctrl-C key combination would nevertheless activate the *ID_EDIT-_COPY* command.

> NOTE: If a keyboard accelerator is associated with a menu item, the accelerator key is disabled when the menu item is disabled.

Command Processing

As you saw in Chapter 2, the application framework provides a sophisticated routing system for command messages. These messages originate from menu selections, keyboard accelerators, and toolbar and dialog button clicks. Command messages can also be sent by calls to the *CWnd::SendMessage* or *PostMessage* function. Each message is identified by a *#define* constant that is often assigned by the graphic editor. The application framework has its own set of internal command message IDs, such as *ID_FILE_PRINT* and *ID_FILE-_OPEN*. Your project's resource.h file contains IDs that are unique to your application.

Most command messages originate in the application's frame window, and without the application framework in the picture, that's where you would put the message handlers. With command routing, however, you can handle the message almost anywhere. When the application framework sees a frame window command message, it starts looking for message handlers in one of the sequences listed here:

SDI Application	MDI Application
View	View
Document	Document
SDI main frame window	MDI child frame window
Application	MDI main frame window
	Application

Most applications have a particular command handler in only one class, but suppose your one-view application has an identical handler in both the view class and the document class. Because the view is higher in the command route, only the view's command handler function will be called.

What is needed to install a command handler function? The installation requirements are similar to those of the window message handlers you've already seen. You need the function itself, a corresponding message map entry, and the function prototype. Suppose you have a menu item named Zoom (with *IDM_ZOOM* as the associated ID) that you want your view class to handle. First you add the following code to your view implementation file:

```
BEGIN_MESSAGE_MAP(CMyView, CView)
    ON_COMMAND(IDM_ZOOM, OnZoom)
END_MESSAGE_MAP()

void CMyView::OnZoom()
{
    // command message processing code
}
```

Now add the following function prototype to the *CMyView* class header file:

```
afx_msg void OnZoom();
```

Of course, ClassWizard automates the process of inserting command message handlers the same way it facilitates the insertion of window message handlers. You'll learn how in the next example, EX12A, on page 272.

Command Message Handling in Derived Classes

The command routing system is one dimension of command message handling. The class hierarchy is a second dimension. If you look at the source code for the MFC library classes, you'll see lots of *ON_COMMAND* message map entries. When you derive a class from one of these base classes—for example, *CView*—the derived class inherits all the *CView* message map functions, including the command message functions. To override one of the base class message map functions, you must add both a function and a message map entry to your derived class.

Update Command User Interface (UI) Handlers

You often need to change the appearance of a menu item to match the internal state of your application. If you have a Clear All item on your application's Edit menu, for example, you might want to disable that item if there's nothing to clear. You've undoubtedly seen such grayed menu items in Windows-based applications, and you've probably also seen check marks next to menu items.

With Win32 programming, it's difficult to keep menu items synchronized with the application's state. Every piece of code that changes the internal state must contain statements to update the menu. The MFC library takes a different approach by calling a special update command UI handler function whenever a pop-up menu is first displayed. The handler function's argument is a *CCmdUI* object, which contains a pointer to the corresponding menu item. The handler function can then use this pointer to modify the menu item's appearance. Update command UI handlers apply only to items on pop-up menus, not to top-level menu items that are permanently displayed. You couldn't use an update command UI handler to disable the File menu item, for example.

The update command UI coding requirements are similar to those for commands. You need the function itself, a special message map entry, and of course the prototype. The associated ID—in this case, *IDM_ZOOM*—is the same constant used for the command. Here is an example of the necessary additions to the view class code file:

```
BEGIN_MESSAGE_MAP(CMyView, CView)
    ON_UPDATE_COMMAND_UI(IDM_ZOOM, OnUpdateZoom)
END_MESSAGE_MAP()

void CMyView::OnUpdateZoom(CCmdUI* pCmdUI)
{
    pCmdUI->SetCheck(m_bZoomed); // m_bZoomed is a class data member
}
```

Here is the function prototype that you must add to the class header:

```
afx_msg void OnUpdateZoom(CCmdUI* pCmdUI);
```

Needless to say, ClassWizard automates the process of inserting update command UI handlers.

Commands That Originate in Dialogs

Suppose you have a pop-up dialog with buttons and you want a particular button to send a command message. Command IDs must be in the range 0x8000 through 0xDFFF, the same ID range that the graphic editor uses for your menu items. If you assign an ID in this range to a dialog button, the button will generate a routable command. The application framework first routes this command to the main frame window because the frame window owns all pop-up dialogs. The command routing then proceeds normally; if your view has a handler for the button's command, that's where it will be handled. To ensure that the ID is in the range 0x8000 through 0xDFFF, you must use the graphic editor's symbol editor to enter the ID prior to assigning it to a button.

The Application Framework's Built-In Menu Items

You don't have to start each frame menu from scratch—the MFC library defines some useful menu items for you, along with all the command handler functions, as shown in Figure 12-3.

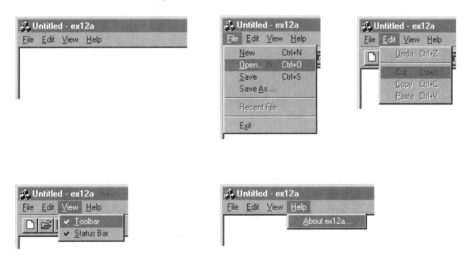

Figure 12-3.
The standard SDI frame menus.

The menu items and command message handlers you get depend on the options you choose in AppWizard. If you deselect Printing And Print Preview, for example, you don't get the Print and Print Preview menu items. Because printing is optional, the message map entries are not defined in

269

the *CView* class but are generated in your derived view class. That's why entries such as the following are defined in the *CMyView* class instead of in the *CView* class:

```
ON_COMMAND(ID_FILE_PRINT, CView::OnFilePrint)
ON_COMMAND(ID_FILE_PRINT_PREVIEW, CView::OnFilePrintPreview)
```

Enabling/Disabling Menu Items

The application framework can disable a menu item if it does not find a command message handler in the current command route. This feature saves you the trouble of having to write *ON_UPDATE_COMMAND_UI* handlers. You can disable the feature if you set the *CFrameWnd* data member *m_bAutoMenu-Enable* to *FALSE* (the default).

Suppose you have two views for one document, but only the first view class has a message handler for the *IDM_ZOOM* command. The Zoom item on the frame menu will be enabled only when the first view is active. Or consider the application framework–supplied Edit Cut, Copy, and Paste menu items. These will be disabled if you have not provided message handlers in your derived view or document class.

MFC Text Editing Options

Windows itself supplies two text editing tools: the original edit control and the new Windows 95 rich edit common control. Both can be used as controls within dialogs, but both can also be made to look like view windows. The MFC library supports this versatility with the *CEditView* and *CRichEditView* classes.

The *CEditView* Class

This class is based on the Windows edit control, and so it inherits all the edit control's limitations. Text size is limited to 64 KB, and you can't mix fonts. AppWizard gives you the option of making *CEditView* the base class of your view class. When the framework gives you an edit view object, you can use all the member functions of both *CView* and *CEdit*. There's no multiple inheritance here, just some magic that involves window subclassing. The *CEditView* class implements and maps the clipboard cut, copy, and paste functions, so they appear active on the Edit menu.

The *CRichEditView* Class

This class uses the rich edit control, so it supports mixed formats and large quantities of text. The *CRichEditView* class is designed to be used with the *CRichEditDoc* and *CRichEditCntrItem* classes to implement a complete OLE container application. (Maybe that's a little too much for right now.)

The *CRichEditCtrl* Class

This class wraps the rich edit control class, and you can use it to make a fairly decent text editor. That's exactly what we'll do in the EX12A example. We'll use an ordinary view class derived from *CView*, and we'll cover the view's client area with a big rich edit control that resizes itself when the view size changes. The *CRichEditCtrl* class has dozens of useful member functions, and it picks up other functions from its *CWnd* base class. The functions we'll use in this chapter are as follows:

Function	Description
Create	Creates the rich edit control window (called from the parent's WM_CREATE handler)
SetWindowPos	Sets the size and position of the edit window (sizes the control to cover the view's client area)
GetWindowText	Retrieves plain text from the control (other functions available to retrieve the text with rich text formatting codes)
SetWindowText	Stores plain text in the control
GetModify	Gets a flag that is *TRUE* if the text has been modified (text modified if the user types in the control or if the program calls *SetModify(TRUE)*)
SetModify	Sets the modify flag to *TRUE* or *FALSE*
GetSel	Gets a flag that indicates whether the user has selected text
SetDefaultCharFormat	Sets the control's default format characteristics
SetSelectionCharFormat	Sets the format characteristics of the selected text

The EX12A Example

This example illustrates the routing of menu and keyboard accelerator commands to both documents and views. The application's view class is derived from *CView* and contains a rich edit control. View-directed menu commands, originating from a new pop-up menu, Transfer, move data between the view object and the document object, and a Clear Document menu item erases the document's contents. On the Transfer menu, the Store Data In Document item is grayed when the view is empty. The Clear Document item, located on the Edit menu, is grayed when the document is empty. Figure 12-4 shows the first iteration of the EX12A program in use.

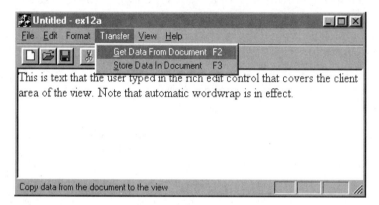

Figure 12-4.
The EX12A program in use.

If we exploited the document–view architecture fully, we would tell the rich edit control to keep its text inside the document, but that's rather difficult to do. Instead, we'll define a document *CString* data member named *m_strText*, the contents of which the user can transfer to and from the control. The initial value of *m_strText* is Hello; choosing Clear Document from the Edit menu sets it to empty. By running this example, you'll start to understand the separation of the document and the view.

The first part of the EX12A example exercises the graphic editor's wysiwyg menu editor and keyboard accelerator editor together with Class-Wizard. You'll need to do very little C++ coding. Simply follow these steps:

1. Run AppWizard to generate \VCPP32\EX12A\EX12A. Accept the default settings, but select Single Document Interface and deselect Printing And Print Preview.

2. Use the graphic editor to edit the application's main menu.

Click the ResourceView tab in the Project Workspace window. Edit the *IDR_MAINFRAME* menu resource to add a separator and a Clear Document item to the Edit menu, as shown here:

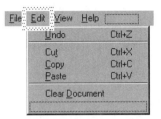

TIP: The graphic editor's menu resource editor is intuitive, but you might need some help the first time you insert an item in the middle of a menu. Each menu has a blank item at the bottom. Using the mouse, drag the blank item to the insertion position to define a new item. A new blank item will appear at the bottom when you're finished.

Now add a Transfer menu, and then define the underlying items, as shown here:

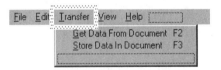

Use the following command IDs for your new menu items:

Menu	Item	Command ID
Edit	Clear &Document	*ID_EDIT_CLEAR_ALL*
Transfer	&Get Data From Document\tF2	*ID_TRANSFER_GETDATA*
Transfer	&Store Data In Document\tF3	*ID_TRANSFER_STOREDATA*

The MFC library has defined the first item, *ID_EDIT_CLEAR_ALL*. (Note: \t is a tab character—but type \t; don't press the Tab key.)

When you add the menu items, type appropriate prompt strings in the Menu Item Properties dialog. These prompts will appear in the application's status window when the menu item is highlighted.

3. Use the graphic editor to add keyboard accelerators. Open the *IDR_MAINFRAME* accelerator table, and then use the insert key to add the following items:

Accelerator ID	Key
ID_TRANSFER_GETDATA	VK_F2
ID_TRANSFER_STOREDATA	VK_F3

Be sure to turn off the Ctrl, Alt, and Shift modifiers. The Accelerator edit screen and properties dialog are shown here:

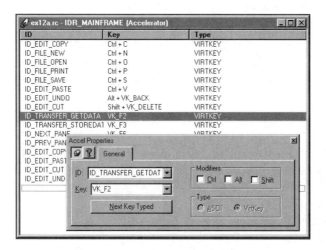

4. Use ClassWizard to add the view class command and update command UI message handlers. Select the *CEx12aView* class, and then add the following member functions:

Object ID	Message	Member Function Name
ID_TRANSFER_GETDATA	COMMAND	*OnTransferGetdata*
ID_TRANSFER_STOREDATA	COMMAND	*OnTransferStoredata*
ID_TRANSFER_STOREDATA	UPDATE_COMMAND_UI	*OnUpdateTransferStoredata*

5. Use ClassWizard to add the document class command and update command UI message handlers. Select the *CEx12aDoc* class, and then add the following member functions:

Object ID	Message	Member Function Name
ID_EDIT_CLEAR_ALL	COMMAND	*OnEditClearDocument*
ID_EDIT_CLEAR_ALL	UPDATE_COMMAND_UI	*OnUpdateEditClearDocument*

6. Add a data member in the file ex12aDoc.h. Add the following public data member in the *CEx12aDoc* class definition:

```
public:
    CString m_strText;
```

7. Edit the document class member functions in ex12aDoc.cpp. The *OnNewDocument* function was generated by ClassWizard. As you'll see in Chapter 15, the framework calls this function after it first constructs the document and when the user chooses New from the File menu. Your version sets some text in the string data member. Add the following shaded code:

```
BOOL CEx12aDoc::OnNewDocument()
{
    if (!CDocument::OnNewDocument())
        return FALSE;
    m_strText = "Hello (from CEx12aDoc::OnNewDocument)";
    return TRUE;
}
```

The Edit Clear Document message handler sets *m_strText* to empty, and the update command UI handler grays the menu item if the string is already empty. Remember that the framework calls *OnUpdateEditClearDocument* when the Edit menu pops up. Add the following shaded code:

```
void CEx12aDoc::OnEditClearDocument()
{
    m_strText.Empty();
}
```

(continued)

```
void CEx12aDoc::OnUpdateEditClearDocument(CCmdUI* pCmdUI)
{
    pCmdUI->Enable(!m_strText.IsEmpty());
}
```

8. **Add a data member in the file ex12aView.h.**   Add the following public data member in the *CEx12aView* class definition:

```
public:
    CRichEditCtrl m_rich;
```

9. **Use ClassWizard to map the WM_CREATE and WM_SIZE messages in the *CEx12aView* class.**   The *OnCreate* function creates the rich edit control. The control's size is 0 here because the view window doesn't have a size yet. Here is the code for the two handlers:

```
int CEx12aView::OnCreate(LPCREATESTRUCT lpCreateStruct)
{
    CRect rect(0, 0, 0, 0);
    if (CView::OnCreate(lpCreateStruct) == -1)
        return -1;
    m_rich.Create(ES_AUTOVSCROLL | ES_MULTILINE | ES_WANTRETURN |
                  WS_CHILD | WS_VISIBLE | WS_VSCROLL, rect, this, 1);
    return 0;
}
```

Windows sends the WM_SIZE message to the view as soon as the view's initial size is determined and again each time the user changes the frame size. This handler simply adjusts the rich edit control's size to fill the view client area. Add the following shaded code:

```
void CEx12aView::OnSize(UINT nType, int cx, int cy)
{
    CRect rect;
    CView::OnSize(nType, cx, cy);
    GetClientRect(rect);
    m_rich.SetWindowPos(&wndTop, 0, 0, rect.right - rect.left,
                        rect.bottom - rect.top, SWP_SHOWWINDOW);
}
```

10. **Edit the menu command handler functions in ex12aView.cpp.**
    ClassWizard generated these skeleton functions when you mapped the menu commands in step 4. The *OnTransferGetdata* function gets the text from the rich edit control and puts it in the document data member. There is no update command UI handler. Add the following shaded code:

```
void CEx12aView::OnTransferGetdata()
{
    CEx12aDoc* pDoc = GetDocument();
    m_rich.SetWindowText(pDoc->m_strText);
}
```

The *OnTransferStoredata* function copies the text from the document string to the view's rich edit control and resets the control's modified flag. The corresponding update command UI handler grays the menu item if the control has not been changed since it was last copied to the document. Add the following shaded code:

```
void CEx12aView::OnTransferStoredata()
{
    CEx12aDoc* pDoc = GetDocument();
    m_rich.GetWindowText(pDoc->m_strText);
    m_rich.SetModify(FALSE);
}

void CEx12aView::OnUpdateTransferStoredata(CCmdUI* pCmdUI)
{
    pCmdUI->Enable(m_rich.GetModify());
}
```

11. **Build and test the EX12A application.**   When the application starts, the Clear Document item on the Edit menu should be enabled. Choose Get Data From Document from the Transfer menu. Some text should appear. Edit the text, and then choose Store Data In Document. That menu item should now appear gray. Try choosing the Clear Document command, and then choose Get Data From Document again.

Property Sheets

You've already seen property sheets in the Developer Studio and in many other modern Windows-based programs. Property sheets are a nice UI element that allows you to cram lots of categorized information into a small dialog. The user selects pages by clicking on their tabs. Windows 95 offers a tab control that you can insert in a dialog, but it's more likely that you'll want to put dialogs inside the tab control. The MFC library supports this, and the result is called a property sheet. The individual dialogs are called property pages.

Building a Property Sheet

Follow these general steps to build a property sheet using the Visual C++ tools:

1. Use the graphic editor to create a series of dialog templates that are all approximately the same size. The captions are the strings that you want to display on the tabs.

2. Use ClassWizard to generate a class for each template. Choose *CPropertyPage* as the base class. Add data members for the controls.

3. Use ClassWizard to generate a single class derived from *CPropertySheet*.

4. To the sheet class, add one data member for each page class.

5. In the sheet class constructor, call the *AddPage* member function for each page, specifying the address of the embedded page object.

6. In your application, construct an object of the derived *CPropertySheet* class, and then call *DoModal*. You must specify a caption in the constructor call, but you can change the caption later by calling *CPropertySheet::SetTitle*.

7. Take care of programming for the Apply button.

Property Sheet Data Exchange

The property sheet buttons, shown in Figure 12-5, were put there by the framework. Be aware that the framework calls the DDX (Dialog Data Exchange) code for a property page every time the user switches to and from that page. As you would expect, the framework calls the DDX code for a page when the user clicks OK, thus updating that page's data members. From these statements, you can conclude that all data members for all pages are updated when the user clicks OK to exit the sheet. All this with no C++ programming on your part!

> NOTE: With a normal modal dialog, if the user clicks the Cancel button, the changes are discarded and the dialog class data members are unchanged. With a property sheet, however, the data members are updated if the user changes one page and then moves to another, even if the user exits by clicking the Cancel button.

What does the Apply button do? Nothing at all if you don't write some code. It won't even be enabled. To enable it for a given page, you must set the page's modified flag by calling *SetModified(TRUE)* when you detect that the user has made changes on the page.

If you've enabled the Apply button, you can write a handler function for it in your page class by overriding the virtual *CPropertyPage::OnApply* function. Don't try to understand property page message processing in the context of normal modal dialogs; it's quite different. The framework gets a WM_NOTIFY message for all button presses. It then calls the DDX code for the page if the OK or Apply button was pressed. It then calls the virtual *OnApply* functions <u>for</u> <u>all</u> <u>the</u> <u>pages</u>, and it resets the modified flag, which disables the Apply button. Don't forget that the DDX code has already been called to update the data members in all pages, so you need to override *OnApply* in only one page class.

What you put in your *OnApply* function is your business, but one option is to send a user-defined message to the object that created the property sheet. The message handler can get the property page data members and process them. Meanwhile, the property sheet stays on the screen.

The EX12A Example Revisited

Now we'll add a property sheet to EX12A that allows the user to change the rich edit control's font characteristics. Of course, we could have used the standard MFC *CFontDialog* function, but then you wouldn't have learned how to create property sheets. Figure 12-5 shows the property sheet that you'll build as you continue with EX12A.

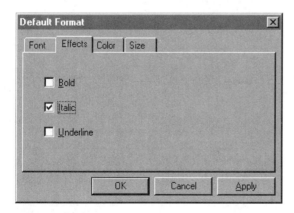

Figure 12-5.
The property sheet from EX12A.

If you haven't built EX12A, follow the instructions beginning on page 272 to build it. If you already have EX12A working with the Transfer menu commands, just continue on with these steps:

1. Use the graphic editor to edit the application's main menu. Click on the ResourceView tab in the Project Workspace window. Edit the *IDR_MAINFRAME* menu resource to add a Format menu that looks like this:

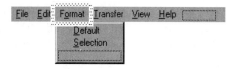

Use the following command IDs for the new Font menu items:

Item	Command ID
&Default	*ID_FORMAT_DEFAULT*
&Selection	*ID_FORMAT_SELECTION*

2. Use ClassWizard to add the view class command and update command UI message handlers. Select the *CEx12aView* class, and then add the following member functions:

Object ID	Message	Member Function Name
ID_FORMAT_DEFAULT	COMMAND	*OnFormatDefault*
ID_FORMAT_DEFAULT	UPDATE_COMMAND_UI	*OnUpdateFormatDefault*
ID_FORMAT_SELECTION	COMMAND	*OnFormatSelection*
ID_FORMAT_SELECTION	UPDATE_COMMAND_UI	*OnUpdateFormatSelection*

3. Use the graphic editor to add four property page dialog templates. The four templates are shown here with their associated IDs:

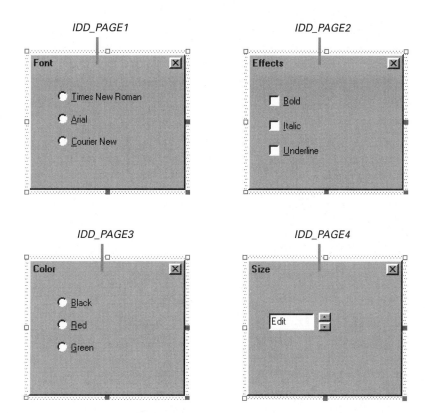

Use the following IDs for the controls in the dialogs, and then use ClassWizard to create the classes *CPage1*, *CPage2*, *CPage3*, and *CPage4*, derived from *CPropertyPage*. Implement these classes in Property.h and Property.cpp. Add the data members shown here:

Dialog	Control	ID	Type	Data Member
IDD_PAGE1	First radio button	*IDC_FONT*	*int*	*m_nFont*
IDD_PAGE2	Bold check box	*IDC_BOLD*	*BOOL*	*m_bBold*
IDD_PAGE2	Italic check box	*IDC_ITALIC*	*BOOL*	*m_bItalic*
IDD_PAGE2	Underline check box	*IDC_UNDERLINE*	*BOOL*	*m_bUnderline*
IDD_PAGE3	First radio button	*IDC_COLOR*	*int*	*m_nColor*
IDD_PAGE4	Edit control	*IDC_FONTSIZE*	*int*	*m_nFontSize*
IDD_PAGE4	Spin control	*IDC_SPIN1*		

The spin control has its Auto Buddy and Set Buddy properties set. The *IDC_FONT* and *IDC_COLOR* radio buttons have their Group property set. Set the minimum value of *IDC_FONTSIZE* to *8* and its maximum value to *24*.

4. Use ClassWizard to create a class derived from *CPropertySheet*. Choose the name *CFontSheet*. Also, use ClassWizard to add an *OnInitDialog* message handler function for *CPage4*. In the EX12A example, all the property page classes and the property sheet class are combined into two files, Property.h and Property.cpp. Figure 12-6 shows these files with the added code shaded.

PROPERTY.H

```
// Property.h : header file
//
#define WM_USERAPPLY WM_USER + 5
extern CView* g_pView;
/////////////////////////////////////////////////////////////////////////////
// CPage1 dialog

class CPage1 : public CPropertyPage
{
    DECLARE_DYNCREATE(CPage1)

// Construction
public:
    CPage1();
    ~CPage1();

// Dialog Data
    //{{AFX_DATA(CPage1)
    enum { IDD = IDD_PAGE1 };
    int  m_nFont;
    //}}AFX_DATA


// Overrides
    // ClassWizard generated virtual function overrides
```

Figure 12-6.   *(continued)*

The EX12A header and implementation file listings for the property page and property sheet classes.

Figure 12-6. *continued*

```
//{{AFX_VIRTUAL(CPage1)
    protected:
    virtual BOOL OnApply();
    virtual BOOL OnCommand(WPARAM wParam, LPARAM lParam);
    virtual void DoDataExchange(CDataExchange* pDX);  // DDX/DDV support
    //}}AFX_VIRTUAL
// Implementation
protected:
    // Generated message map functions
    //{{AFX_MSG(CPage1)
    //}}AFX_MSG
    DECLARE_MESSAGE_MAP()

};
/////////////////////////////////////////////////////////////////////////////
// CPage2 dialog

class CPage2 : public CPropertyPage
{
    DECLARE_DYNCREATE(CPage2)

// Construction
public:
    CPage2();
    ~CPage2();

// Dialog Data
    //{{AFX_DATA(CPage2)
    enum { IDD = IDD_PAGE2 };
    BOOL m_bBold;
    BOOL m_bItalic;
    BOOL m_bUnderline;
    //}}AFX_DATA


// Overrides
    // ClassWizard generated virtual function overrides
    //{{AFX_VIRTUAL(CPage2)
    protected:
    virtual BOOL OnCommand(WPARAM wParam, LPARAM lParam);
    virtual void DoDataExchange(CDataExchange* pDX); // DDX/DDV support
    //}}AFX_VIRTUAL
```

(continued)

283

Figure 12-6. *continued*

```
// Implementation
protected:
    // Generated message map functions
    //{{AFX_MSG(CPage2)
        // NOTE: the ClassWizard will add member functions here
    //}}AFX_MSG
    DECLARE_MESSAGE_MAP()

};
/////////////////////////////////////////////////////////////////////////
// CPage3 dialog

class CPage3 : public CPropertyPage
{
    DECLARE_DYNCREATE(CPage3)

// Construction
public:
    CPage3();
    ~CPage3();

// Dialog Data
    //{{AFX_DATA(CPage3)
    enum { IDD = IDD_PAGE3 };
    int m_nColor;
    //}}AFX_DATA


// Overrides
    // ClassWizard generated virtual function overrides
    //{{AFX_VIRTUAL(CPage3)
    protected:
    virtual BOOL OnCommand(WPARAM wParam, LPARAM lParam);
    virtual void DoDataExchange(CDataExchange* pDX);   // DDX/DDV support
    //}}AFX_VIRTUAL

// Implementation
protected:
    // Generated message map functions
    //{{AFX_MSG(CPage3)
        // NOTE: the ClassWizard will add member functions here
    //}}AFX_MSG
    DECLARE_MESSAGE_MAP()

};
```

(continued)

Figure 12-6. *continued*

```
//////////////////////////////////////////////////////////////////
// CPage4 dialog

class CPage4 : public CPropertyPage
{
    DECLARE_DYNCREATE(CPage4)

// Construction
public:
    CPage4();
    ~CPage4();

// Dialog Data
    //{{AFX_DATA(CPage4)
    enum { IDD = IDD_PAGE4 };
    int m_nFontSize;
    //}}AFX_DATA


// Overrides
    // ClassWizard generated virtual function overrides
    //{{AFX_VIRTUAL(CPage4)
    protected:
    virtual BOOL OnCommand(WPARAM wParam, LPARAM lParam);
    virtual void DoDataExchange(CDataExchange* pDX);  // DDX/DDV support
    //}}AFX_VIRTUAL

// Implementation
protected:
    // Generated message map functions
    //{{AFX_MSG(CPage4)
    virtual BOOL OnInitDialog();
    //}}AFX_MSG
    DECLARE_MESSAGE_MAP()

};
//////////////////////////////////////////////////////////////////
// CFontSheet

class CFontSheet : public CPropertySheet
{
```

(continued)

Figure 12-6. *continued*

```
        DECLARE_DYNAMIC(CFontSheet)
public:
    CPage1 m_page1;
    CPage2 m_page2;
    CPage3 m_page3;
    CPage4 m_page4;
// Construction
public:
    CFontSheet(UINT nIDCaption, CWnd* pParentWnd = NULL,
            UINT iSelectPage = 0);
    CFontSheet(LPCTSTR pszCaption, CWnd* pParentWnd = NULL,
            UINT iSelectPage = 0);

// Attributes
public:

// Operations
public:

// Overrides
    // ClassWizard generated virtual function overrides
    //{{AFX_VIRTUAL(CFontSheet)
    //}}AFX_VIRTUAL

// Implementation
public:
    virtual ~CFontSheet();

    // Generated message map functions
protected:
    //{{AFX_MSG(CFontSheet)
        // NOTE - ClassWizard will add and remove member functions here.
    //}}AFX_MSG
    DECLARE_MESSAGE_MAP()
};
```

PROPERTY.CPP

```
// Property.cpp : implementation file
//

#include "StdAfx.h"
#include "ex12a.h"
#include "Property.h"
```

(continued)

Figure 12-6. *continued*

```
#ifdef _DEBUG
#define new DEBUG_NEW
#undef THIS_FILE
static char THIS_FILE[] = __FILE__;
#endif

CView* g_pView;
/////////////////////////////////////////////////////////////////////
// CPage1 property page

IMPLEMENT_DYNCREATE(CPage1, CPropertyPage)

CPage1::CPage1() : CPropertyPage(CPage1::IDD)
{
    //{{AFX_DATA_INIT(CPage1)
    m_nFont = -1;
    //}}AFX_DATA_INIT
}


CPage1::~CPage1()
{
}


BOOL CPage1::OnApply()
{
    TRACE("CPage1::OnApply\n");
    g_pView->SendMessage(WM_USERAPPLY);
    return TRUE;
}


BOOL CPage1::OnCommand(WPARAM wParam, LPARAM lParam)
{
    SetModified(TRUE);
    return CPropertyPage::OnCommand(wParam, lParam);
}

void CPage1::DoDataExchange(CDataExchange* pDX)
{
    TRACE("Entering CPage1::DoDataExchange -- %d\n",
          pDX->m_bSaveAndValidate);
    CPropertyPage::DoDataExchange(pDX);
    //{{AFX_DATA_MAP(CPage1)
    DDX_Radio(pDX, IDC_FONT, m_nFont);
    //}}AFX_DATA_MAP
}
```

(continued)

Figure 12-6. *continued*

```
BEGIN_MESSAGE_MAP(CPage1, CPropertyPage)
    //{{AFX_MSG_MAP(CPage1)
    //}}AFX_MSG_MAP
END_MESSAGE_MAP()


/////////////////////////////////////////////////////////////////////////
// CPage2 property page

IMPLEMENT_DYNCREATE(CPage2, CPropertyPage)

CPage2::CPage2() : CPropertyPage(CPage2::IDD)
{
    //{{AFX_DATA_INIT(CPage2)
    m_bBold = FALSE;
    m_bItalic = FALSE;
    m_bUnderline = FALSE;
    //}}AFX_DATA_INIT
}


CPage2::~CPage2()
{
}

BOOL CPage2::OnCommand(WPARAM wParam, LPARAM lParam)
{
    SetModified(TRUE);
    return CPropertyPage::OnCommand(wParam, lParam);
}


void CPage2::DoDataExchange(CDataExchange* pDX)
{
    TRACE("Entering CPage2::DoDataExchange -- %d\n",
        pDX->m_bSaveAndValidate);
    CPropertyPage::DoDataExchange(pDX);
    //{{AFX_DATA_MAP(CPage2)
    DDX_Check(pDX, IDC_BOLD, m_bBold);
    DDX_Check(pDX, IDC_ITALIC, m_bItalic);
    DDX_Check(pDX, IDC_UNDERLINE, m_bUnderline);
    //}}AFX_DATA_MAP
}


BEGIN_MESSAGE_MAP(CPage2, CPropertyPage)
    //{{AFX_MSG_MAP(CPage2)
        // NOTE: the ClassWizard will add message map macros here
    //}}AFX_MSG_MAP
END_MESSAGE_MAP()
```

(continued)

Figure 12-6. *continued*

```
///////////////////////////////////////////////////////////////////
// CPage3 property page

IMPLEMENT_DYNCREATE(CPage3, CPropertyPage)

CPage3::CPage3() : CPropertyPage(CPage3::IDD)
{
    //{{AFX_DATA_INIT(CPage3)
    m_nColor = -1;
    //}}AFX_DATA_INIT
}

CPage3::~CPage3()
{
}

BOOL CPage3::OnCommand(WPARAM wParam, LPARAM lParam)
{
    SetModified(TRUE);
    return CPropertyPage::OnCommand(wParam, lParam);
}

void CPage3::DoDataExchange(CDataExchange* pDX)
{
    TRACE("Entering CPage3::DoDataExchange -- %d\n",
        pDX->m_bSaveAndValidate);
    CPropertyPage::DoDataExchange(pDX);
    //{{AFX_DATA_MAP(CPage3)
    DDX_Radio(pDX, IDC_COLOR, m_nColor);
    //}}AFX_DATA_MAP
}

BEGIN_MESSAGE_MAP(CPage3, CPropertyPage)
    //{{AFX_MSG_MAP(CPage3)
        // NOTE: the ClassWizard will add message map macros here
    //}}AFX_MSG_MAP
END_MESSAGE_MAP()

///////////////////////////////////////////////////////////////////
// CPage4 property page

IMPLEMENT_DYNCREATE(CPage4, CPropertyPage)
```

(continued)

289

Figure 12-6. *continued*

```
CPage4::CPage4() : CPropertyPage(CPage4::IDD)
{
    //{{AFX_DATA_INIT(CPage4)
    m_nFontSize = 0;
    //}}AFX_DATA_INIT
}

CPage4::~CPage4()
{
}

BOOL CPage4::OnCommand(WPARAM wParam, LPARAM lParam)
{
    SetModified(TRUE);
    return CPropertyPage::OnCommand(wParam, lParam);
}

void CPage4::DoDataExchange(CDataExchange* pDX)
{
    TRACE("Entering CPage4::DoDataExchange -- %d\n",
        pDX->m_bSaveAndValidate);
    CPropertyPage::DoDataExchange(pDX);
    //{{AFX_DATA_MAP(CPage4)
    DDX_Text(pDX, IDC_FONTSIZE, m_nFontSize);
    DDV_MinMaxInt(pDX, m_nFontSize, 8, 24);
    //}}AFX_DATA_MAP
}

BEGIN_MESSAGE_MAP(CPage4, CPropertyPage)
    //{{AFX_MSG_MAP(CPage4)
    //}}AFX_MSG_MAP
END_MESSAGE_MAP()

/////////////////////////////////////////////////////////////////////
// CFontSheet

IMPLEMENT_DYNAMIC(CFontSheet, CPropertySheet)

CFontSheet::CFontSheet(LPCTSTR pszCaption, CWnd* pParentWnd,
                    UINT iSelectPage)
    : CPropertySheet(pszCaption, pParentWnd, iSelectPage)
{
```

(continued)

Figure 12-6. *continued*

```
        AddPage(&m_page1);
        AddPage(&m_page2);
        AddPage(&m_page3);
        AddPage(&m_page4);
    }

    CFontSheet::~CFontSheet()
    {
    }

    BEGIN_MESSAGE_MAP(CFontSheet, CPropertySheet)
        //{{AFX_MSG_MAP(CFontSheet)
        // NOTE - the ClassWizard will add and remove mapping macros here.
        //}}AFX_MSG_MAP
    END_MESSAGE_MAP()

    BOOL CPage4::OnInitDialog()
    {
        CPropertyPage::OnInitDialog();
        ((CSpinButtonCtrl*) GetDlgItem(IDC_SPIN1))->SetRange(8, 24);
        return TRUE;  // return TRUE unless you set the focus to a control
                      // EXCEPTION: OCX Property Pages should return FALSE
    }
```

5. Add data members in the file ex12aView.h.   Add the following private data members in the *CEx12aView* class definition:

```
private:
    CFontSheet m_sh;
    BOOL m_bDefault; // TRUE default format, FALSE selection
```

Also add the following function prototypes:

```
void Format(CHARFORMAT& cf);
afx_msg LRESULT OnUserApply(WPARAM wParam, LPARAM lParam);
```

6. Edit and add code in the file ex12aView.cpp.   Add the following line to include the property page and property sheet classes:

```
#include "Property.h"
```

(You'll need to add this statement to ex12a.cpp as well.)

Map the user-defined WM_USERAPPLY message, as shown here:

```
ON_MESSAGE(WM_USERAPPLY, OnUserApply)
```

Add the following lines to the *OnCreate* function:

```
CHARFORMAT cf;
Format(cf);
m_rich.SetDefaultCharFormat(cf);
```

Edit the view constructor to set default values for the property sheet data members, as follows:

```
CEx12aView::CEx12aView() : m_sh("")
{
    m_sh.m_page1.m_nFont = 0;
    m_sh.m_page2.m_bBold = FALSE;
    m_sh.m_page2.m_bItalic = FALSE;
    m_sh.m_page2.m_bUnderline = FALSE;
    m_sh.m_page3.m_nColor = 0;
    m_sh.m_page4.m_nFontSize = 12;
    g_pView = this;
    m_bDefault = TRUE;
}
```

Edit the format command handlers, as shown here:

```
void CEx12aView::OnFormatDefault()
{
    m_sh.SetTitle("Default Format");
    m_bDefault = TRUE;
    m_sh.DoModal();
}

void CEx12aView::OnFormatSelection()
{
    m_sh.SetTitle("Selection Format");
    m_bDefault = FALSE;
    m_sh.DoModal();
}

void CEx12aView::OnUpdateFormatSelection(CCmdUI* pCmdUI)
{
    long nStart, nEnd;
    m_rich.GetSel(nStart, nEnd);
    pCmdUI->Enable(nStart != nEnd);
}
```

Add the following handler for the user-defined WM_USERAPPLY message:

```
LRESULT CEx12aView::OnUserApply(WPARAM wParam, LPARAM lParam)
{
    TRACE("CEx12aView::OnUserApply--wParam = %x\n", wParam);
    CHARFORMAT cf;
    Format(cf);
    if (m_bDefault) {
      m_rich.SetDefaultCharFormat(cf);
    }
    else {
      m_rich.SetSelectionCharFormat(cf);
    }
    return 0;
}
```

Add the *Format* helper function, as shown here, to set a *CHARFORMAT* structure based on the values of the property sheet data members:

```
void CEx12aView::Format(CHARFORMAT& cf)
{
    cf.cbSize = sizeof(CHARFORMAT);
    cf.dwMask = CFM_BOLD | CFM_COLOR | CFM_FACE |
                CFM_ITALIC | CFM_SIZE | CFM_UNDERLINE;
    cf.dwEffects = (m_sh.m_page2.m_bBold ? CFE_BOLD : 0) |
                   (m_sh.m_page2.m_bItalic ? CFE_ITALIC : 0) |
                   (m_sh.m_page2.m_bUnderline ? CFE_UNDERLINE : 0);
    cf.yHeight = m_sh.m_page4.m_nFontSize * 20;
    switch(m_sh.m_page3.m_nColor) {
    case -1:
    case 0:
      cf.crTextColor = RGB(0, 0, 0);
      break;
    case 1:
      cf.crTextColor = RGB(255, 0, 0);
      break;
    case 2:
      cf.crTextColor = RGB(0, 255, 0);
      break;
    }
    switch(m_sh.m_page1.m_nFont) {
    case -1:
    case 0:
```

(continued)

293

```
      strcpy(cf.szFaceName, "Times New Roman");
      break;
    case 1:
      strcpy(cf.szFaceName, "Arial");
      break;
    case 2:
      strcpy(cf.szFaceName, "Courier New");
      break;
    }
    cf.bCharSet = 0;
    cf.bPitchAndFamily = 0;
}
```

7. **Build and test the enhanced EX12A application.** Type some text, and then choose Default from the Format menu. Observe the *TRACE* messages in the Debug window as you select property sheet tabs and click the Apply button. Try highlighting some text and then formatting the selection.

Apply Button Processing

You might be curious about the way the property sheet classes process the Apply button. The *OnCommand* virtual overrides in all the page classes enable the Apply button whenever a control sends a message to the page. This works fine for pages 1 through 3 in EX12A, but for page 4, *OnCommand* is called during the initial conversation between the spin control and its buddy.

The *OnApply* virtual override in the *CPage1* class sends a user-defined message to the view. The function finds the view in an expedient way—by using a global variable set by the view class. A better approach would be to pass the view pointer to the sheet constructor and then to the page constructor.

The view class calls the property sheet's *DoModal* function for both default formatting and selection formatting. It sets the *m_bDefault* flag to indicate the mode. We don't need to check the return from *DoModal* because the user-defined message is sent for both the OK button and the Apply button. If the user clicks Cancel, no message is sent.

The *CMenu* Class

Up to this point, the application framework and the graphic editor have shielded you from the menu class, *CMenu*. A *CMenu* object can represent each Windows menu, including the top-level menu items and associated popups. Most of the time, the menu's resource is directly attached to a frame window when the window's *Create* function is called, and a *CMenu* object is never explicitly constructed. The *CWnd* member function *GetMenu* returns a temporary *CMenu* pointer. Once you have this pointer, you can freely access and update the menu object.

Suppose you want to switch menus after the application starts. *IDR_MAINFRAME* always identifies the initial menu in the resource script. If you want a second menu, you use the graphic editor to create a menu resource with your own ID. Then, in your program, you construct a *CMenu* object, use the *CMenu::LoadMenu* function to load the menu from the resource, and call the *CWnd::SetMenu* function to attach the new menu to the frame window.

You can use a resource to define a menu, and then your program can modify the menu items at runtime. If necessary, however, you can build the whole menu at runtime, without benefit of a resource. In either case, you can use *CMenu* member functions such as *ModifyMenu*, *InsertMenu*, and *DeleteMenu*. Each of these functions operates on an individual menu item identified by ID or by a relative position index.

A menu object is actually composed of a nested structure of submenus. You can use the *GetSubMenu* member function to get a *CMenu* pointer to a pop-up menu contained in the main *CMenu* object. The *CMenu::GetMenuString* function returns the menu item string using a zero-based index or a command ID. If you use the command ID option, the menu is searched, together with any submenus.

Creating Floating Pop-Up Menus

Floating pop-up menus are one of the latest trends in user interface design. The user clicks the right mouse button, and a floating menu offers choices that relate to the current selection. It's easy to create these menus using the graphic editor and the MFC library *CMenu::TrackPopupMenu* function. Just follow these steps:

1. Use the graphic editor to insert a new, empty menu in your project's resource file.

2. Type some characters in the left top-level item, and then add your menu items in the resulting popup.

3. Add a WM_CONTEXTMENU message handler in your view class or in some other window class that receives mouse click messages.
   Code the handler as shown on the following page:

```
void CMyView::OnContextMenu(CWnd *pWnd, CPoint point)
{
    CMenu menu;
    menu.LoadMenu(IDR_MYFLOATINGMENU);
    menu.GetSubMenu(0)->TrackPopupMenu(TPM_LEFTALIGN |
        TPM_RIGHTBUTTON, point.x, point.y, this);
}
```

You can use ClassWizard to map the floating menu's command IDs the same way you would map the frame menu's command IDs.

Extended Command Processing

In addition to the *ON_COMMAND* message map macro, the MFC library provides an extended variation, *ON_COMMAND_EX*. The extended command message map macro provides two features not supplied by the regular command message—a command ID function parameter and the ability to reject a command at runtime, sending it to the next object in the command route. If the extended command handler returns *TRUE*, the command goes no further; if it returns *FALSE*, the application framework looks for another command handler.

The command ID parameter is useful when you want one function to handle several related command messages. The rejection feature is used in the Help system (introduced in Chapter 20). If a view can't handle a help request, for example, the request can be passed to the document or the application. You might invent some of your own uses for this feature.

ClassWizard can't help you with extended command handlers, so you'll have to do the coding yourself, outside the *AFX_MSG_MAP* brackets. Assume that *IDM_ZOOM_1* and *IDM_ZOOM_2* are related command IDs defined in resource.h. Here's the class code you'll need to process both messages with one function, *OnZoom*:

```
BEGIN_MESSAGE_MAP(CMyView, CView)
    ON_COMMAND_EX(IDM_ZOOM_1, OnZoom)
    ON_COMMAND_EX(IDM_ZOOM_2, OnZoom)
END_MESSAGE_MAP()

BOOL CMyView::OnZoom(UINT nID)
{
    if (nID == IDM_ZOOM_1) {
      // code specific to first zoom command
    }
```

```
    else {
      // code specific to second zoom command
    }
    // code common to both commands
    return TRUE; // command goes no further
}
```

Here's the function prototype:

```
afx_msg BOOL OnZoom(UINT nID);
```

There are other MFC message map macros that are helpful for processing ranges of commands, as you might see in dynamic menu applications. These macros include:

> *ON_COMMAND_RANGE*
>
> *ON_COMMAND_EX_RANGE*
>
> *ON_UPDATE_COMMAND_UI_RANGE*

If the values of *IDM_ZOOM_1* and *IDM_ZOOM_2* were consecutive, you then could rewrite the *CMyView* message map as follows:

```
BEGIN_MESSAGE_MAP(CMyView, CView)
    ON_COMMAND_EX_RANGE(IDM_ZOOM_1, IDM_ZOOM_2, OnZoom)
END_MESSAGE_MAP()
```

Now *OnZoom* is called for both menu choices, and the handler can determine the choice from the integer parameter.

CHAPTER THIRTEEN

Toolbars and Status Bars

All the Visual C++ examples up to this point have included toolbars and status bars. AppWizard generated the code that initialized these application framework elements as long as you accepted the AppWizard default options Dockable Toolbar and Initial Status Bar. The default toolbar provides graphics equivalents for many of the standard application framework menu selections, and the default status bar displays menu prompts together with the keyboard state indicators CAP, NUM, and SCRL.

This chapter shows you how to customize the toolbar and the status bar for your application. You'll be able to add your own toolbar graphical buttons and control their appearance. You'll also learn how to disable the status bar's normal display of menu prompts and keyboard indicators. This allows your application to take over the status bar for its own use.

Control Bars and the Application Framework

The toolbar is an object of class *CToolBar*, and the status bar is an object of class *CStatusBar*. Both these classes are derived from class *CControlBar*, which is itself derived from *CWnd*. The *CControlBar* class supports control bar windows that are positioned inside frame windows. These control bar windows resize and reposition themselves as the parent frame moves and changes size. The application framework takes care of the construction, window creation, and destruction of the control bar objects. AppWizard generates control bar code for its derived frame class located in the files MainFrm.cpp and MainFrm.h.

In a typical SDI application, a *CToolBar* object occupies the top portion of the *CMainFrame* client area, and a *CStatusBar* object occupies the bottom portion. The view occupies the remaining (middle) part of the frame.

In Microsoft Foundation Class (MFC) Library version 4.0, the toolbar is built around the Windows 95 toolbar common control and thus is fully dockable. The programming interface is much the same as it was in earlier versions of the MFC library, however. The button images are easier to work with now because a special resource type is supported by the graphic editor. The old global *buttons* array is gone now.

Assuming that AppWizard has generated the control bar code for your application, the user can enable and disable the toolbar and the status bar individually by choosing commands from the application's View menu. When a control bar is disabled, it disappears and the view size is recalculated. Apart from the common behavior just described, toolbar and status bar objects operate independently of each other and have rather different characteristics.

The Toolbar

A toolbar consists of a number of horizontally (or vertically) arranged graphical buttons that might be clustered in groups. The programming interface determines the grouping. The graphical images for the buttons are stored in a single bitmap that is attached to the application's resource file. When the buttons are clicked, they send command messages, as do menus and keyboard accelerators. Update command UI message handlers are used to update the buttons' states, which in turn are used by the application framework to modify the buttons' graphical images.

The Toolbar Bitmap

Each button on a toolbar appears to have its own bitmap, but actually there is a single bitmap for the entire toolbar. The toolbar bitmap has a tile, 15 pixels high and 16 pixels wide, for each button. The application framework supplies the button borders, and it modifies those borders, together with the button's bitmap tile color, to reflect the current button state. Figure 13-1 shows the relationship between the toolbar bitmap and the corresponding toolbar. (The question mark in each toolbar is for a context-sensitive Help button, which has not yet been discussed.)

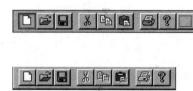

Figure 13-1.
A toolbar bitmap and an actual toolbar.

The toolbar bitmap is stored in the file Toolbar.bmp in the application's RES subdirectory. It's identified in the RC file as *IDR_MAINFRAME*. You don't edit the toolbar bitmap directly; instead you use the graphic editor's special toolbar editing facility.

Button States

Each button can assume the following states:

State	Meaning
0	Normal, unpressed state (up)
TBBS_PRESSED	Currently selected (pressed) with the mouse
TBBS_CHECKED	In the checked (down) state
TBBS_DISABLED	Unavailable for use
TBBS_INDETERMINATE	Enabled, but neither up nor down
*TBBS_CHECKED	TBBS_DISABLED*	In the checked state, but unavailable for use

A button can behave in either of two ways. It can be a pushbutton, which is down only when currently selected by the mouse, or it can be a check box button, which can be toggled up and down with mouse clicks. All buttons in the standard application framework toolbar are pushbuttons.

The Toolbar and Command Messages

When the user clicks a toolbar button with the mouse, a command message is generated. This message is routed like the menu command messages you saw in Chapter 12. Most of the time, a toolbar button matches a menu option. In the standard application framework toolbar, for example, the Disk button is equivalent to the File Save menu option because both generate the *ID_FILE_SAVE* command. The object receiving the command message doesn't need to know whether the message was produced by a click on the toolbar or by a selection from the menu.

A toolbar button doesn't have to mirror a menu item. If you don't provide the equivalent menu item, however, you are advised to define a keyboard accelerator for the button so that the user can activate the command with the keyboard or with a Windows keyboard macro product. If your application has toolbar buttons without corresponding menu items, ClassWizard can't define command and update command UI message handlers. You'll have to add the functions, message map entries, and prototypes yourself.

A toolbar has an associated bitmap resource and a companion TOOL-BAR resource that defines the menu commands associated with the buttons. Both the bitmap and the TOOLBAR resource have the same ID, typically *IDR_MAINFRAME*. The text of the AppWizard-generated TOOLBAR resource is shown below:

```
IDR_MAINFRAME TOOLBAR DISCARDABLE  16, 15
BEGIN
     BUTTON       ID_FILE_NEW
     BUTTON       ID_FILE_OPEN
     BUTTON       ID_FILE_SAVE
     SEPARATOR
     BUTTON       ID_EDIT_CUT
     BUTTON       ID_EDIT_COPY
     BUTTON       ID_EDIT_PASTE
     SEPARATOR
     BUTTON       ID_FILE_PRINT
     BUTTON       ID_APP_ABOUT
END
```

The *SEPARATOR* constants serve to group the buttons by inserting corresponding spaces on the toolbar. If the number of toolbar bitmap panes exceeds the number of resource elements (excluding separators), the extra buttons are not displayed.

When you edit the toolbar with the graphic editor, you're editing both the bitmap resource and the TOOLBAR resource. You select a button image, and then you double-click on the left panel to edit the properties, including the button's ID.

Toolbar Update Command UI Message Handlers

You remember from Chapter 12 that update command UI message handlers were used to disable or check menu items. These same message handlers apply to toolbar buttons. If your update command UI message handler calls the *CCmdUI::Enable* member function with a *FALSE* parameter, the corresponding button is set to the disabled (grayed) state and no longer responds to mouse clicks.

With menu items, the *CCmdUI::SetCheck* member function displays a check mark next to the menu item. For the toolbar, the *SetCheck* function implements check box buttons. If the update command UI message handler calls *SetCheck* with a parameter value of 1, the button is toggled to the down (checked) state; if the parameter is 0, the button is toggled up (unchecked).

NOTE: If the *SetCheck* parameter value is 2, the button is set to the <u>indeterminate</u> state. This state looks like the disabled state, but the button is still active and its color is a bit brighter. Microsoft Word for Windows uses the up, down, and indeterminate states for its boldface toolbar button. If the user has selected some text that contains only boldface characters, the boldface button is down. If no selected characters are boldface, the button is up; but if the selected characters are mixed, the button is indeterminate.

The update command UI message handlers for menu items are called only when the items' drop-down menu is painted. The toolbar is displayed all the time, so when are its update command UI message handlers called? They're called during the application's idle processing, so the buttons can be updated continuously. If the same handler covers a menu item and a toolbar button, it is called both during idle processing and when the drop-down menu is displayed.

NOTE: Even though a toolbar button is disabled, keyboard accelerators can still send the associated command message if there is no corresponding menu item. Your command handlers, therefore, must be able to ignore these accelerator keys and other spurious commands. In other words, you can't count on the command UI message handler to totally disable the command.

ToolTips

You've seen ToolTips in various Windows applications, including the Developer Studio. When the user positions the mouse on a toolbar button for a certain interval, text is displayed in a little box next to the button. In Chapter 12, you learned that menu items can have associated prompt strings, which are string resource elements with matching IDs. To create a ToolTip, you simply add the tip text to the end of the menu prompt, preceded by a newline (\n) character. The graphic editor lets you edit the prompt string while you are editing the toolbar images. Just double-click in the left panel.

Locating the Main Frame Window

The toolbar and status bar objects you'll be working with are attached to the application's main frame window, not to the view window. How does your view find its main frame window? In an SDI application, you can use the

CWnd::GetParentFrame function. Unfortunately, this function won't work in an MDI application because the view's parent frame is the MDI child frame, not the MDI frame window.

If you want your view class to work in both SDI and MDI applications, you must find the main frame window through the application object. The *AfxGetApp* global function returns a pointer to the application object, and you can use that pointer to get the *CWinApp* data member *m_pMainWnd*. In an MDI application, AppWizard generates code that sets *m_pMainWnd*, but in an SDI application, the framework sets *m_pMainWnd* during the view creation process. Once *m_pMainWnd* is set, you can use it in a view class to get the frame's toolbar with statements such as this:

```
CMainFrame* pFrame = (CMainFrame*) AfxGetApp()->m_pMainWnd;
CToolBar* pToolBar = &pFrame->m_wndToolBar;
```

> **NOTE:** You'll need to cast *m_pMainWnd* from *CFrameWnd** to *CMainFrame** because *m_wndToolBar* is a member of that derived class. You'll also have to make *m_wndToolBar* public or make your class a friend of *CMainFrame*.

You can use similar logic to locate menu objects, status bar objects, and dialog objects.

> **NOTE:** In an SDI application, the value of *m_pMainWnd* is not set when the view's *OnCreate* message handler is called. If you need to access the main frame window in your *OnCreate* function, you must use the *GetParentFrame* function.

The EX13A Toolbar Example

In this example, you will replace the standard application framework Edit Cut, Copy, and Paste toolbar buttons with three special-purpose buttons that control drawing in the view window. You will also construct a Draw menu with three corresponding menu items, as follows:

Menu Item	Function
Circle	Draws a circle in the view window
Square	Draws a square in the view window
Pattern	Toggles a diagonal line fill pattern for new squares and circles

The menu and toolbar options force the user to alternate between drawing circles and squares. After the user draws a circle, the Circle menu item and toolbar button are disabled; after the user draws a square, the Square menu item and toolbar button are disabled.

On the application's Draw menu, the Pattern menu item gets a check mark when pattern fill is active. On the toolbar, the corresponding button is a check box button that is down when pattern fill is active and up when it is not active.

Figure 13-2 shows the application in action. The user has drawn a circle with pattern fill. Notice the states of the three drawing buttons.

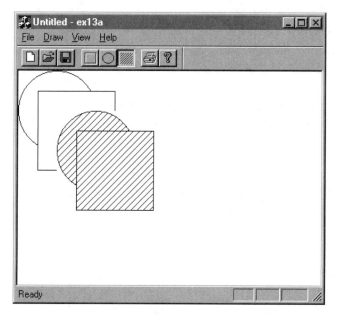

Figure 13-2.
The EX13A program in action.

The EX13A example introduces the graphic editor's toolbar capabilities. You'll need to do very little C++ coding. Simply follow these steps:

1. **Run AppWizard to generate VCPP32\EX13A\EX13A.** Accept the default settings, but select Single Document Interface and deselect Printing And Print Preview. The options and the default class names are shown at the top of the following page:

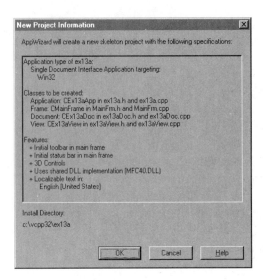

2. Use the graphic editor to edit the application's main menu. Select ex13a.rc, and then double-click on IDR_MAINFRAME under Menu. Edit the *IDR_MAINFRAME* menu resource to create a menu that looks like this (which means you'll need to change the Edit menu):

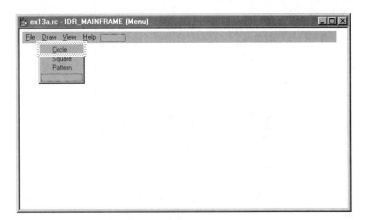

Use the following command IDs for your new menu items:

Menu	Menu Item	Command ID
Draw	Circle	*ID_DRAW_CIRCLE*
Draw	Square	*ID_DRAW_SQUARE*
Draw	Pattern	*ID_DRAW_PATTERN*

When you're in the Menu Item Properties dialog, add some appropriate prompt strings and ToolTips (after a newline character). The string for *ID_DRAW_CIRCLE* might be "Draw a circle\nCircle".

3. **Use the graphic editor to update the application's toolbar.** Edit the *IDR_MAINFRAME* bitmap resource to create a bitmap that looks like this:

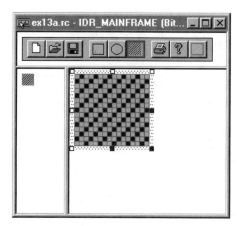

You'll be erasing the Edit Cut, Copy, and Paste tiles (fourth, fifth, and sixth from the left) and replacing them with new tiles. The toolbar editor is fairly intuitive. You simply move the buttons around with the mouse. The Del key erases a button's pixels. If you want to eliminate a button entirely, just drag it off the toolbar. Use the rectangle and ellipse tools from the bitmap editor's palette. Experiment with different line widths. Save the resource file when you're done—just in case.

Assign the IDs *ID_DRAW_CIRCLE*, *ID_DRAW_SQUARE*, and *ID_DRAW_PATTERN* to the three new buttons.

4. **Use ClassWizard to add *CEx13aView* view class message handlers.** Add message handlers for the following command and update command UI messages, and accept the default function names in the table on the following page:

Object ID	Member Message	Function Name
ID_DRAW_CIRCLE	COMMAND	*OnDrawCircle*
ID_DRAW_CIRCLE	UPDATE_COMMAND_UI	*OnUpdateDrawCircle*
ID_DRAW_PATTERN	COMMAND	*OnDrawPattern*
ID_DRAW_PATTERN	UPDATE_COMMAND_UI	*OnUpdateDrawPattern*
ID_DRAW_SQUARE	COMMAND	*OnDrawSquare*
ID_DRAW_SQUARE	UPDATE_COMMAND_UI	*OnUpdateDrawSquare*

5. **Edit the ex13aView.h file.** Add the following private data members to the *CEx13aView* class header:

```
CRect m_rect;
BOOL  m_bCircle;
BOOL  m_bPattern;
```

6. **Edit the ex13aView.cpp file.** The *CEx13aView* constructor simply initializes the class data members. Add the following shaded code:

```
CEx13aView::CEx13aView() : m_rect(0, 0, 100, 100)
{
    m_bCircle = TRUE;
    m_bPattern = FALSE;
}
```

The *OnDraw* function draws an ellipse or a rectangle, depending on the value of the *m_bCircle* flag. The brush is plain white or a diagonal pattern, depending on the value of *m_bPattern*.

```
void CEx13aView::OnDraw(CDC* pDC)
{
    CBrush brush(HS_BDIAGONAL, 0L); // brush with diagonal
                                    //  pattern

    if (m_bPattern) {
      pDC->SelectObject(&brush);
    }
    else {
      pDC->SelectStockObject(WHITE_BRUSH);
    }
```

```
  if (m_bCircle) {
    pDC->Ellipse(m_rect);
  }
  else {
    pDC->Rectangle(m_rect);
  }
  pDC->SelectStockObject(WHITE_BRUSH); // deselects brush
                                       //  if selected
}
```

The *OnDrawCircle* function handles the *ON_DRAW_CIRCLE* command message, and the *OnDrawSquare* function handles the *ON_DRAW-_SQUARE* command message. These two functions move the drawing rectangle down and to the right, and then they invalidate the rectangle, causing the *OnDraw* function to redraw it. The effect of this invalidation strategy is a diagonal cascading of alternating squares and circles.

```
void CEx13aView::OnDrawCircle()
{
    m_bCircle = TRUE;
    m_rect += CPoint(25, 25);
    InvalidateRect(m_rect);
}
```

```
void CEx13aView::OnDrawSquare()
{
    m_bCircle = FALSE;
    m_rect += CPoint(25, 25);
    InvalidateRect(m_rect);
}
```

The following two update command UI functions alternately enable and disable the Circle and Square buttons and corresponding menu items. Only one item can be enabled at a time.

```
void CEx13aView::OnUpdateDrawCircle(CCmdUI* pCmdUI)
{
    pCmdUI->Enable(!m_bCircle);
}
```

```
void CEx13aView::OnUpdateDrawSquare(CCmdUI* pCmdUI)
{
    pCmdUI->Enable(m_bCircle);
}
```

The *OnDrawPattern* function toggles the state of the *m_bPattern* flag.

```
void CEx13aView::OnDrawPattern()
{
    m_bPattern ^= 1;
}
```

The *OnUpdateDrawPattern* function updates the Pattern button and menu item according to the state of the *m_bPattern* flag. The toolbar button appears to move in and out, and the menu item check mark appears and disappears.

```
void CEx13aView::OnUpdateDrawPattern(CCmdUI* pCmdUI)
{
    pCmdUI->SetCheck(m_bPattern);
}
```

7. **Build and test the EX13A application.** Notice the behavior of the toolbar buttons. Try the corresponding menu items, and notice that they too are enabled, disabled, and checked as the application's state changes. Observe the ToolTip when you stop the mouse on one of the new toolbar buttons.

The Status Bar

The status bar window neither accepts user input nor generates command messages. Its job is simply to display text in panes under program control. The status bar supports two types of text panes—a message line pane and a status indicator pane. To use the status bar for application-specific data, you must first disable the standard status bar that displays the menu prompt and keyboard status.

The Status Bar Definition

The static *indicators* array that AppWizard generates in the MainFrm.cpp file defines the application's status bar. The constant *ID_SEPARATOR* identifies a message line pane; the other constants are string resource IDs that identify indicator panes. Figure 13-3 shows the *indicators* array and its relationship to the standard framework status bar.

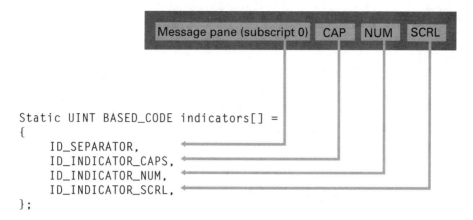

```
Static UINT BASED_CODE indicators[] =
{
    ID_SEPARATOR,
    ID_INDICATOR_CAPS,
    ID_INDICATOR_NUM,
    ID_INDICATOR_SCRL,
};
```

Figure 13-3.
The status bar and the indicators *array.*

The *CStatusBar::SetIndicators* member function, called in the application's derived frame class, configures the status bar according to the contents of the *indicators* array.

The Message Line

A message line pane displays a string that the program supplies dynamically. To set the value of the message line, you must first get access to the status bar object, and then you must call the *CStatusBar::SetPaneText* member function with a zero-based index parameter. Pane 0 is the leftmost pane, 1 is the next pane to the right, and so forth.

The following code fragment is part of a view class member function. Note that you must navigate up to the application object and then back down to the main frame window.

```
CMainFrame* pFrame = (CMainFrame*) AfxGetApp()->m_pMainWnd;
CStatusBar* pStatus = &pFrame->m_wndStatusBar;
pStatus->SetPaneText(0, "message line for first pane");
```

Normally, the length of a message line pane is exactly one-fourth the width of the display. If, however, the message line is the first (index 0) pane, it is a stretchy pane without a beveled border. Its minimum length is one-fourth the display width, and it expands if room is available in the status bar.

The Status Indicator

A status indicator pane is linked to a single resource-supplied string that is displayed or hidden by logic in an associated update command UI message handler function. Indicators are identified by a string resource ID, and that same ID is used to route update command UI messages. The Caps Lock indicator is handled in the frame class by the following message map entry and handler function. The *Enable* function turns on the indicator if the Caps Lock mode is set.

```
ON_UPDATE_COMMAND_UI(ID_INDICATOR_CAPS, OnUpdateKeyCapsLock)

void CMainFrame::OnUpdateKeyCapsLock(CCmdUI* pCmdUI)
{
    pCmdUI->Enable(::GetKeyState(VK_CAPITAL) & 1);
}
```

The status bar update command UI functions are called during idle processing so that the status bar is updated whenever your application receives messages.

The length of a status indicator pane is the exact length of the corresponding resource string.

Taking Control of the Status Bar

In the standard application framework implementation, the status bar has the child window ID *AFX_IDW_STATUS_BAR*. The application framework looks for this ID when it wants to display a menu prompt. The update command UI handlers for the keyboard state indicators, embedded in the frame window base class, are linked to three string IDs: *ID_INDICATOR_CAPS*, *ID_INDICATOR_NUM*, and *ID_INDICATOR_SCRL*. To take control of the status bar, you must use a different child window ID, and you must use different indicator ID constants.

> NOTE: The only reason to change the status bar's child window ID is to prevent the framework from writing menu prompts in pane 0. If you like the menu prompts, you can ignore the following instructions.

The status bar window ID is assigned in the *CStatusBar::Create* function called by the derived frame class *OnCreate* member function. That function is contained in the MainFrm.cpp file that AppWizard generates. The window ID is the third *Create* parameter, and it defaults to *AFX_IDW_STATUS_BAR*.

To assign your own ID, you must replace this call:

```
m_wndStatusBar.Create(this);
```

with this call:

```
m_wndStatusBar.Create(this, WS_CHILD | WS_VISIBLE | CBRS_BOTTOM,
                 ID_MY_STATUS_BAR);
```

You must also, of course, define the *ID_MY_STATUS_BAR* constant in the resource.h file (using the Developer Studio's resource symbol editor).

We forgot one thing. The standard application framework's View menu allows the user to turn the status bar on and off. That logic is pegged to the *AFX_IDW_STATUS_BAR* window ID, so you'll have to change the menu logic too. In your derived frame class, you must write message map entries and handlers for the *ID_VIEW_STATUS_BAR* command and update command UI messages. *ID_VIEW_STATUS_BAR* is the ID of the Status Bar menu item. The derived class handlers override the standard handlers in the *CFrameWnd* base class. See the EX13B example for code details.

The EX13B Status Bar Example

The EX13B example replaces the standard application framework status bar with a new status bar that has the following text panes:

Pane Index	String ID	Type	Description
0	*ID_SEPARATOR* (0)	Message line	*x* cursor coordinate
1	*ID_SEPARATOR* (0)	Message line	*y* cursor coordinate
2	*ID_INDICATOR_LEFT*	Status indicator	Left mouse button status
3	*ID_INDICATOR_RIGHT*	Status indicator	Right mouse button status

The resulting status bar is shown in Figure 13-4 on the following page.

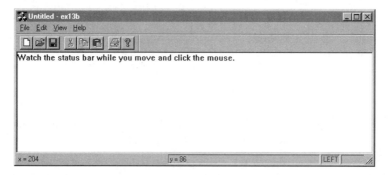

Figure 13-4.
The status bar of the EX13B example.

The leftmost pane stretches past its normal ¼-screen length as the displayed frame window expands to fill more than ¾-screen width.

Follow these steps to produce the EX13B example:

1. Run AppWizard to generate \VCPP32\EX13B\EX13B. Accept the default settings, but select Single Document Interface and deselect Printing And Print Preview. The options and the default class names are shown here:

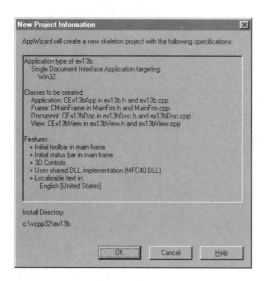

2. **Use the graphic editor to edit the application's string table resource.** The application has a single string table resource with artificial "segment" divisions left over from the 16-bit era. You can insert new entries by choosing New String from the Developer Studio's Insert menu. A dialog allows you to assign the ID and the string value as shown below:

Add two strings as follows:

String ID	String Caption
ID_INDICATOR_LEFT	LEFT
ID_INDICATOR_RIGHT	RIGHT

3. **Use the Developer Studio to edit the application's symbols.** Be sure that the ex13b.rc resource file is open, and then select Resource Symbols from the View menu. Add the new status bar identifier, ID_MY-_STATUS_BAR, and accept the default value.

4. **Use ClassWizard to add View menu command handlers in the class *CMainFrame*.** Add the following command message handlers:

Object ID	Message	Member Function Name
ID_VIEW_STATUS_BAR	COMMAND	*OnViewStatusBar*
ID_VIEW_STATUS_BAR	UPDATE_COMMAND_UI	*OnUpdateViewStatusBar*

5. **Add the following function prototypes to MainFrm.h.** You must add these *CMainFrame* message handler prototypes manually because ClassWizard doesn't recognize the associated command message IDs.

```
afx_msg void OnUpdateLeft(CCmdUI* pCmdUI);
afx_msg void OnUpdateRight(CCmdUI* pCmdUI);
```

Add the message handler statements <u>inside</u> the *AFX_MSG* brackets so
that ClassWizard will let you access and edit the code later. Also make
m_wndToolBar public rather than protected

6. Edit the MainFrm.cpp file. Replace the original *indicators* array with
the following shaded code:

```
static UINT BASED_CODE indicators[] =
{
    ID_SEPARATOR,   // first message line pane
    ID_SEPARATOR,   // second message line pane
    ID_INDICATOR_LEFT,
    ID_INDICATOR_RIGHT,
};
```

Next edit the *OnCreate* member function. Replace the following
statement:

```
if (!m_wndStatusBar.Create(this) ||
    !m_wndStatusBar.SetIndicators(indicators,
      sizeof(indicators)/sizeof(UINT)))
{
    TRACE0("Failed to create status bar\n");
    return -1;      // fail to create
}
```

with

```
if (!m_wndStatusBar.Create(this,
    WS_CHILD | WS_VISIBLE | CBRS_BOTTOM, ID_MY_STATUS_BAR) ||
    !m_wndStatusBar.SetIndicators(indicators,
      sizeof(indicators)/sizeof(UINT)))
{
    TRACE0("Failed to create status bar\n");
    return -1;      // fail to create
}
```

The modified call to *Create* uses our own status bar ID, *ID_MY_STATUS-
_BAR*, instead of *AFX_IDW_STATUS_BAR* (the application framework's
status bar object).

Now add the following message map entries for the class *CMainFrame*.
ClassWizard can't add these for you because it doesn't recognize the
string table IDs and the constant *ID_VIEW_STATUS_BAR* as object IDs.

```
ON_UPDATE_COMMAND_UI(ID_INDICATOR_LEFT, OnUpdateLeft)
ON_UPDATE_COMMAND_UI(ID_INDICATOR_RIGHT, OnUpdateRight)
```

Next add the following *CMainFrame* member functions that update the three status indicators:

```
void CMainFrame::OnUpdateLeft(CCmdUI* pCmdUI)
{
    pCmdUI->Enable(::GetKeyState(VK_LBUTTON) < 0);
}

void CMainFrame::OnUpdateRight(CCmdUI* pCmdUI)
{
    pCmdUI->Enable(::GetKeyState(VK_RBUTTON) < 0);
}
```

Note that the left and right mouse buttons have virtual key codes like keys on the keyboard have. You don't have to depend on mouse click messages to determine the button status.

Finally, edit the following View menu functions that ClassWizard originally generated in MainFrm.cpp:

```
void CMainFrame::OnViewStatusBar()
{
    m_wndStatusBar.ShowWindow((m_wndStatusBar.GetStyle() &
                               WS_VISIBLE) == 0);
    RecalcLayout();
}
void CMainFrame::OnUpdateViewStatusBar(CCmdUI* pCmdUI)
{
pCmdUI->SetCheck((m_wndStatusBar.GetStyle() &
                 WS_VISIBLE) != 0);
}
```

These functions ensure that the View menu Status Bar command is properly linked to the new status bar.

7. Edit the *OnDraw* function in Ex13bView.cpp. The *OnDraw* function displays a message in the view window. Add the following shaded code:

```
void CEx13bView::OnDraw(CDC* pDC)
{
    pDC->TextOut(0, 0,
      "Watch the status bar while you move and click the mouse.");
}
```

8. Add a WM_MOUSEMOVE handler in the *CEx13bView* class. Use ClassWizard to map the message to *OnMouseMove*, and then edit the function as shown below. This function gets a pointer to the status bar object and then calls the *SetPaneText* function to update the first and second message line panes.

```
void CEx13bView::OnMouseMove(UINT nFlags, CPoint point)
{
    CString str;
    CMainFrame* pFrame = (CMainFrame*) AfxGetApp()->m_pMainWnd;
    CStatusBar* pStatus = &pFrame->m_wndStatusBar;
    if (pStatus) {
      str.Format("x = %d", point.x);
      pStatus->SetPaneText(0, str);
      str.Format("y = %d", point.y);
      pStatus->SetPaneText(1, str);
    }
}
```

9. Build and test the EX13B application. Move the mouse, and observe that the left two status bar panes accurately reflect the mouse cursor's position. Try the left and right mouse buttons. Can you toggle the status bar on and off from the View menu?

NOTE: If you want the first (0th) status bar pane to have a beveled border like the other panes, include the following line in the *CMainFrame::OnCreate* function, after the call to the status bar *Create* function:

```
m_wndStatusBar.SetPaneInfo(0, 0, SBPS_STRETCH, 0);
```

CHAPTER FOURTEEN

A Reusable Frame Window Base Class

C++ promises the ability to produce "software Lego blocks" that can be taken "off the shelf" and fitted easily into an application. The Microsoft Foundation Class (MFC) Library version 4.0 classes are a good example of this kind of reusable software. This chapter shows you how to build your own reusable base class by taking advantage of what the MFC library already provides.

In the process of building the reusable class, you'll learn a few more things about Windows and the MFC library. In particular, you'll see how the application framework allows access to the Windows registry, you'll learn more about the mechanics of the *CFrameWnd* class, and you'll get more exposure to static class variables and the *CString* class.

Why Reusable Base Classes Are Difficult to Write

In a normal application, you write code for software components that solve particular problems. It's usually a simple matter of meeting the project specification. With reusable base classes, however, you must anticipate future programming needs, both your own and those of others. You have to write a class that's general and complete yet efficient and easy to use.

This chapter's example showed me the difficulty in building reusable software. I started out with the intention of writing a frame class that would "remember" its window size and position. When I got into the job, I discovered that existing Windows-based programs remember whether they have been iconized or whether they have been maximized to full screen. Then there was the oddball case of a window that was both iconized and maximized. After that, I had to worry about the toolbar and the status bar, plus the class had to work in a dynamic link library (DLL). In short, it was surprisingly difficult to write a frame class that would do everything that a programmer might expect.

In a production programming environment, reusable base classes might fall out of the normal software development cycle. A class written for one project might be extracted and further generalized for another project. There's always the temptation, though, to cut and paste existing classes without asking, "What can I factor out into a base class?" If you're in the software business for the long term, it's beneficial to start building your library of truly reusable components.

The *CPersistentFrame* Class

In this chapter, you'll be using a class named *CPersistentFrame* that is derived from the *CFrameWnd* class. This *CPersistentFrame* class supports a persistent SDI (Single Document Interface) frame window that remembers the following characteristics:

- Window size

- Window position

- Maximized status

- Iconized status

- Toolbar and status bar enablement

When you terminate an application that's built with the *CPersistentFrame* class, the above information is saved on disk in the Windows registry. When the application starts again, it reads the registry and restores the frame to its state at the previous exit.

You can use the persistent view class in any SDI application, including the examples in this book. All you have to do is substitute *CPersistentFrame* for *CFrameWnd* in your application's derived frame class files.

The *CFrameWnd* Class and the *ActivateFrame* Member Function

Why choose *CFrameWnd* as the base class for a persistent window? Why not have a persistent view class instead? In an MFC SDI application, the main frame window is always the parent of the view window. This frame window is created first, and then the control bars and the view are created as child windows. The application framework ensures that the child windows shrink and expand appropriately as the user changes the size of the frame window. It wouldn't make sense to change the view size after the frame was created.

The key to controlling the frame's size is the *CFrameWnd::ActivateFrame* member function. The application framework calls this virtual function (declared in *CFrameWnd*) during the SDI main frame window creation process (and in response to the File New and File Open commands). The framework's job is to call the *CWnd::ShowWindow* function with the parameter *nCmd-Show*. *ShowWindow* makes the frame window visible along with its menu, view window, and control bars. The *nCmdShow* parameter determines whether the window is maximized or iconized or both.

If you override *ActivateFrame* in your derived frame class, you can change the value of *nCmdShow* before passing it to the *CFrameWnd::ActivateFrame* function. You can also call the *CWnd::SetWindowPlacement* function, which sets the size and position of the frame window, and you can set the visible status of the control bars. Because all changes are made before the frame window becomes visible, there is no annoying flash on the screen.

You must be careful not to reset the frame window's position and size after every File New or File Open command. A first-time flag data member ensures that your *CPersistentFrame::ActivateFrame* function operates only when the application starts.

The *PreCreateWindow* Member Function

PreCreateWindow, declared at the *CWnd* level, is another virtual function that you can override to change the characteristics of your window before it's displayed. The framework calls this function before it calls *ActivateFrame*. Starting with Visual C++ version 4.0, AppWizard generates an overridden *PreCreateWindow* function in your project's view and frame window classes.

This function has a *CREATESTRUCT* structure as a parameter, and this structure has two data members, *style* and *dwExStyle*. You can change these data members before passing the structure on to the base class *PreCreate-Window* function. The *style* flag determines whether the window has a border, scroll bars, a minimize box, and so on. The *dwExStyle* flag controls other characteristics, such as always-on-top status. See Books Online for Window Styles and Extended Window Styles for details. The EX14A program gives an example of an overridden *PreCreateWindow* function.

The *CREATESTRUCT* member *lpszClass* is also useful if you want to change the window's background brush, cursor, or icon. It doesn't make sense to change the brush or cursor in a frame window because the client area is covered by the view window. If you register a window class yourself, you don't have to call the base class *PreCreateWindow* function. If you want an ugly red view window, for example, you could override your <u>view's</u> *PreCreateWindow* function like this:

```
BOOL CMyView::PreCreateWindow(CREATESTRUCT& cs)
{
    HBRUSH hBrushRed = ::CreateSolidBrush(RGB(255, 0, 0));
    HCURSOR hCursor = ::LoadCursor(NULL, IDC_ARROW);
    cs.lpszClass = AfxRegisterWndClass(CS_HREDRAW | CS_VREDRAW,
                                       hCursor, hBrushRed);
    ::DeleteObject(hBrushRed);
    ::DeleteObject(hCursor);
    return TRUE;
}
```

If you overrode the *PreCreateWindow* function in your persistent frame class, windows of all derived classes would share the characteristics you programmed in the base class. Of course, derived classes could have their own overridden *PreCreateWindow* functions, but then you'd have to be careful about the interaction between the two functions.

The Windows Registry

If you've used Win16-based applications, you've probably seen INI files. You can still use INI files in Win32-based applications, but Microsoft recommends that you use the Windows registry instead. The registry is a set of system files, managed by Windows, in which Windows and individual applications can store and access permanent information. The registry is organized as a kind of hierarchical database in which string and integer data is accessed by a multipart key.

For example, a text processing application, TEXTPROC, might need to store the most recent font and point size in the registry. Suppose that the program name forms the root of the key (a simplification) and that the application maintains two hierarchy levels below the name. The structure looks something like this:

TEXTPROC

   Text formatting

     Font = Times Roman

     Points = 10

The MFC library provides four *CWinApp* member functions, holdovers from the days of INI files, for accessing the registry. In fact, your application will use an INI file unless you specifically add a call to *CWinApp::SetRegistryKey* in your application's *InitInstance* function. The *SetRegistryKey* function's string parameter establishes the top of the hierarchy, and the following registry functions define the bottom two levels, called heading name and entry name:

- *GetProfileInt*
- *WriteProfileInt*
- *GetProfileString*
- *WriteProfileString*

These functions treat registry data as either *CString* objects or unsigned integers. If you need floating-point values as entries, you must use the string functions and do the conversion yourself. All the functions take a heading name and an entry name as parameters. In the example above, the heading name is Text Formatting and the entry names are Font and Points.

To use the registry access functions, you need a pointer to the application object. The global function *AfxGetApp* does the job. With the previous sample registry, the Font and Points entries were set with the following code:

```
AfxGetApp()->WriteProfileString("Text formatting", "Font",
                                "Times Roman");

AfxGetApp()->WriteProfileInt("Text formatting", "Points", 10);
```

You'll see a real registry example in EX14A, and you'll learn to use the Windows Regedit program to examine and edit the registry.

NOTE: The application framework stores a list of most recently used files in the registry (only if you call *SetRegistryKey*) under the heading Recent File List.

Using the *CString* Class

The MFC *CString* class is a significant de facto extension to the C++ language. As the *Microsoft Foundation Class Library Reference* points out, the *CString* class has many useful operators and member functions, but perhaps its most important feature is its dynamic memory allocation. You never have to worry about the size of a *CString* object. The statements on the following page represent typical uses of *CString* objects.

```
CString strFirstName("Elvis");
CString strLastName("Presley");
CString strTruth = strFirstName + " " +
        strLastName; // concatenation
strTruth += " is alive";
ASSERT(strTruth == "Elvis Presley is alive");
ASSERT(strTruth.Left(5) == strFirstName);
ASSERT(strTruth[2] == 'v'); // subscript operator
```

In a perfect world, C++ programs would always use all *CString* objects and never use ordinary zero-terminated character arrays. Unfortunately, many runtime library functions still use character arrays, so programs must always mix and match their string representations. Fortunately, the *CString* class provides a *const char* ()* operator that converts a *CString* object to a character pointer. Many of the MFC library functions have *const char** parameters. Take the global *AfxMessageBox* function, for example. Here is one of the function's prototypes:

```
int AFXAPI AfxMessageBox(LPCTSTR lpszText, UINT nType = MB_OK,
                        UINT nIDHelp = 0);
```

(Note: LPCTSTR is not a pointer to a *CString* object but rather is a replacement for *const char**.)

You can call *AfxMessageBox* this way:

```
char szMessageText[] = "Unknown error";
AfxMessageBox(szMessageText);
```

Or you can call it this way:

```
CString strMessageText("Unknown error");
AfxMessageBox(strMessageText);
```

Now suppose you want to generate a formatted string. *CString::Format* does the job, as shown here:

```
int nError = 23;
CString strMessageText;
strMessageText.Format("Error number %d", nError);
AfxMessageBox(strMessageText);
```

NOTE: Suppose you want direct write access to the characters in a *CString* object. If you write code like this

```
CString strTest("test");
strncpy(strTest, "T", 1);
```

you'll get a compile error because the first parameter of *strncpy* is declared *char**, not *const char**. The *CString::GetBuffer* function "locks down" the buffer with a specified size and returns a *char**. You must call the *ReleaseBuffer* member function later to make the string dynamic again. Here's the correct way capitalize the *T*:

```
CString strTest("test");
strncpy(strTest.GetBuffer(5), "T", 1);
strText.ReleaseBuffer();
ASSERT(strText == "Test");
```

The *const char** operator takes care of converting a *CString* object to a constant character pointer; but what about conversion in the other direction? It so happens that the *CString* class has a constructor that converts a constant character pointer to a *CString* object, and it has a set of overloaded operators for these pointers. That's why statements such as this work:

```
truth += " is alive";
```

The special constructor works with functions that take a *CString* reference parameter, such as *CDC::TextOut*. In the following statement, a temporary *CString* object is created on the calling program's stack, and then the object's address is passed to *TextOut*:

```
pDC->TextOut(0, 0, "Hello, world!");
```

It's more efficient to use the other overloaded version of *CDC::TextOut* if you're willing to count the characters:

```
pDC->TextOut(0, 0, "Hello, world!", 13);
```

If you're writing a function that takes a string parameter, you've got some design choices. Here are some programming rules:

- If the function doesn't change the contents of the string, and you're willing to use C runtime functions such as *strcpy*, use a *const char** parameter.

- If the function doesn't change the contents of the string, but you want to use *CString* member functions inside the function, use a *const CString&* parameter.

- If the function changes the contents of the string, use a *CString&* parameter.

The Position of a Maximized Window

As a Windows user, you know that you can maximize a window from the system menu or by clicking a button at the top right corner of the window. You can return a maximized window to its original size in a similar fashion. It's obvious that a maximized window remembers its original size and position.

The *CWnd* function *GetWindowRect* retrieves the screen coordinates of a window. If a window is maximized, *GetWindowRect* returns the coordinates of the screen rather than the window's unmaximized coordinates. If a persistent frame class is to work for maximized windows, it has to know the window's unmaximized coordinates. *CWnd::GetWindowPlacement* retrieves the window's unmaximized coordinates together with some flags that indicate whether the window is currently iconized or maximized or both.

The companion *SetWindowPlacement* function lets you set both the maximized and minimized size and the position of the window. To calculate the position of the top left corner of a maximized window, you need to account for the window's border size, obtainable from the Win32 *GetSystemMetrics* function. See Figure 14-1 for the *CPersistentFrame::ActivateFrame* code.

Control Bar Status and the Registry

The MFC library provides two *CFrameWnd* member functions, *LoadBarState* and *SaveBarState*, for loading and saving control bar status from and to the registry. These functions process the size and position of docking toolbars.

Static Data Members

The *CPersistentFrame* class stores its Registry key values in *static const char* array data members. What were the other storage choices? String resource entries won't work because the strings need to be defined with the class itself. (String resources make sense if *CPersistentFrame* is made into a DLL, however.) Global variables are generally not recommended because they defeat encapsulation. Static *CString* objects don't make sense because the characters must be copied to the heap when the program starts.

An obvious choice would have been regular data members. But static data members are better because, as constants, they are segregated into the program's read-only data section and can be mapped to multiple instances of the same program. If the *CPersistentFrame* class is part of a DLL, the character arrays can be mapped by all processes that are using the DLL. Static data members are really global variables, but they are scoped to their class, so there's no chance of name collisions.

The Default Window Rectangle

You're used to defining rectangles with device or logical coordinates. A *CRect* object constructed with the statement

```
CRect rect(CW_USEDEFAULT, CW_USEDEFAULT, 0, 0);
```

has a special meaning. When Windows creates a new window with this special rectangle, it positions the window in a cascade pattern with the top left corner below and to the right of the window most recently created. The right and bottom edges of the window are always within the display's boundaries.

The *CFrameWnd* class's static *rectDefault* data member contains the special rectangle in the previous example. The *CPersistentFrame* class declares its own *rectDefault* default window rectangle with a fixed size and position as a static data member, thus hiding the base class member.

The EX14A Example

The EX14A program illustrates the use of a persistent frame window class, *CPersistentFrame*. Figure 14-1 shows the contents of the files persist.h and persist.cpp, which are included in the EX14A project on the companion CD-ROM. In this example, you'll insert the new frame class into an AppWizard-generated SDI application. EX14A is a "do-nothing" application, but you can easily insert the persistent frame class into any of your own SDI "do-something" applications.

PERSIST.H

```
class CPersistentFrame : public CFrameWnd
{ // remembers where it was on the desktop
    DECLARE_DYNAMIC(CPersistentFrame)
private:
    static const CRect s_rectDefault;
    static const char s_profileHeading[];
    static const char s_profileRect[];
    static const char s_profileIcon[];
    static const char s_profileMax[];
    static const char s_profileTool[];
    static const char s_profileStatus[];
    BOOL m_bFirstTime;
protected: // created from serialization only
    CPersistentFrame();
    ~CPersistentFrame();
```

Figure 14-1. *(continued)*

The CPersistentView *class listing.*

Figure 14-1. *continued*

```
    //{{AFX_VIRTUAL(CPersistentFrame)
    public:
    virtual void ActivateFrame(int nCmdShow = -1);
    protected:
    virtual BOOL PreCreateWindow(CREATESTRUCT& cs);
    //}}AFX_VIRTUAL

    //{{AFX_MSG(CPersistentFrame)
    afx_msg void OnDestroy();
    //}}AFX_MSG

    DECLARE_MESSAGE_MAP()
};
```

PERSIST.CPP

```
#include "StdAfx.h"
#include "persist.h"

#ifdef _DEBUG
#undef THIS_FILE
static char BASED_CODE THIS_FILE[] = __FILE__;
#endif
/////////////////////////////////////////////////////////////////
// CPersistentFrame

const CRect CPersistentFrame::s_rectDefault(10, 10,
                                        500, 400);  // static
const char CPersistentFrame::s_profileHeading[] - "Window size";
const char CPersistentFrame::s_profileRect[] = "Rect";
const char CPersistentFrame::s_profileIcon[] = "icon";
const char CPersistentFrame::s_profileMax[] = "max";
const char CPersistentFrame::s_profileTool[] = "tool";
const char CPersistentFrame::s_profileStatus[] = "status";
IMPLEMENT_DYNAMIC(CPersistentFrame, CFrameWnd)

BEGIN_MESSAGE_MAP(CPersistentFrame, CFrameWnd)
    //{{AFX_MSG_MAP(CPersistentFrame)
    ON_WM_DESTROY()
    //}}AFX_MSG_MAP
END_MESSAGE_MAP()


/////////////////////////////////////////////////////////////////
CPersistentFrame::CPersistentFrame()
```

(continued)

Figure 14-1. *continued*

```
{
    m_bFirstTime = TRUE;
}


//////////////////////////////////////////////////////////////
CPersistentFrame::~CPersistentFrame()
{
}


//////////////////////////////////////////////////////////////
void CPersistentFrame::OnDestroy()
{
    CString strText;
    BOOL bIconic, bMaximized;

    WINDOWPLACEMENT wndpl;
    wndpl.length = sizeof(WINDOWPLACEMENT);
    // gets current window position and
    //  iconized/maximized status
    BOOL bRet = GetWindowPlacement(&wndpl);
    if (wndpl.showCmd == SW_SHOWNORMAL) {
      bIconic = FALSE;
      bMaximized = FALSE;
    }
    else if (wndpl.showCmd == SW_SHOWMAXIMIZED) {
      bIconic = FALSE;
      bMaximized = TRUE;
    }
    else if (wndpl.showCmd == SW_SHOWMINIMIZED) {
      bIconic = TRUE;
      if (wndpl.flags) {
        bMaximized = TRUE;
      }
      else {
        bMaximized = FALSE;
      }
    }
    strText.Format("%04d %04d %04d %04d",
                    wndpl.rcNormalPosition.left,
                    wndpl.rcNormalPosition.top,
                    wndpl.rcNormalPosition.right,
                    wndpl.rcNormalPosition.bottom);
    AfxGetApp()->WriteProfileString(s_profileHeading,
                                    s_profileRect, strText);
```

(continued)

Figure 14-1. *continued*

```
    AfxGetApp()->WriteProfileInt(s_profileHeading,
                                 s_profileIcon, bIconic);
    AfxGetApp()->WriteProfileInt(s_profileHeading,
                                 s_profileMax, bMaximized);
    SaveBarState(AfxGetApp()->m_pszProfileName);
    CFrameWnd::OnDestroy();
}


/////////////////////////////////////////////////////////////////
void CPersistentFrame::ActivateFrame(int nCmdShow)
{
    CString strText;
    BOOL bIconic, bMaximized;
    UINT flags;
    WINDOWPLACEMENT wndpl;
    CRect rect;

    if (m_bFirstTime) {
      m_bFirstTime = FALSE;
      strText = AfxGetApp()->GetProfileString(s_profileHeading,
                                              s_profileRect);
        if (!strText.IsEmpty()) {
          rect.left = atoi((const char*) strText);
          rect.top = atoi((const char*) strText + 5);
          rect.right = atoi((const char*) strText + 10);
          rect.bottom = atoi((const char*) strText + 15);
        }
        else {
          rect = s_rectDefault;
        }

        bIconic = AfxGetApp()->GetProfileInt(s_profileHeading,
                                             s_profileIcon, 0);
        bMaximized = AfxGetApp()->GetProfileInt(s_profileHeading,
                                                s_profileMax, 0);
        TRACE("CPersistentFrame::ActivateFrame--bIconic = %d,");
        TRACE(" bMaximized = %d\n", bIconic, bMaximized);

        if (bIconic) {
          nCmdShow = SW_SHOWMINNOACTIVE;
          if (bMaximized) {
            flags = WPF_RESTORETOMAXIMIZED;
          }
```

(continued)

Figure 14-1. *continued*

```
            else {
                flags = WPF_SETMINPOSITION;
            }
        }
        else {
            if (bMaximized) {
                nCmdShow = SW_SHOWMAXIMIZED;
                flags = WPF_RESTORETOMAXIMIZED;
            }
            else {
                nCmdShow = SW_NORMAL;
                flags = WPF_SETMINPOSITION;
            }
        }
        wndpl.length = sizeof(WINDOWPLACEMENT);
        wndpl.showCmd = nCmdShow;
        wndpl.flags = flags;
        wndpl.ptMinPosition = CPoint(0, 0);
        wndpl.ptMaxPosition =
            CPoint(-::GetSystemMetrics(SM_CXBORDER),
                   -::GetSystemMetrics(SM_CYBORDER));
        wndpl.rcNormalPosition = rect;
        LoadBarState(AfxGetApp()->m_pszProfileName);
        // sets window's position and iconized/maximized status
        BOOL bRet = SetWindowPlacement(&wndpl);
    }
    CFrameWnd::ActivateFrame(nCmdShow);
}


BOOL CPersistentFrame::PreCreateWindow(CREATESTRUCT& cs)
{
    // TODO: add your specialized code here
    //  and/or call the base class
//    cs.dwExStyle != WS_EX_TOPMOST; // window always on top!
    return CFrameWnd::PreCreateWindow(cs);
}
```

Here are the steps for building the EX14A example program:

1. **Run AppWizard to generate \VCPP32\EX14A\EX14A.** Accept the default settings, but select Single Document Interface and deselect Printing And Print Preview. The options and the default class names are shown on the following page.

2. **Modify MainFrm.h.**   You must change the base class of *CMainFrame*. To do this, simply change the line

```
class CMainFrame : public CFrameWnd
```

to

```
class CMainFrame : public CPersistentFrame
```

3. **Modify MainFrm.cpp.**   Globally replace all occurrences of *CFrameWnd* with *CPersistentFrame*. Also, add the line

```
#include "persist.h"
```

immediately <u>before</u> the line

```
#include "MainFrm.h"
```

4. **Modify ex14a.cpp.**   Add the line

```
SetRegistryKey("Inside Visual C++");
```

immediately <u>before</u> the line

```
LoadStdProfileSettings();
```

Also, add the line

```
#include "persist.h"
```

immediately <u>before</u> the line

```
#include "MainFrm.h"
```

> NOTE: As an alternative to modifying ex14a.cpp, you can in-
> sert the line
>
> ```
> #include "persist.h"
> ```
>
> at the top of the MainFrm.h file. If you do this, you won't need to
> add the #include statements in MainFrm.cpp and ex14a.cpp.

5. **Add the persist.cpp file to the project.**   You could type in the persist.h
   and persist.cpp files from Figure 14-1, or you could copy the files from
   the companion CD-ROM. Having the files in the \VCPP32\EX14A directory is not sufficient. You must add the name of the implementation file
   to the project's make file. Choose Files Into Project from the Developer
   Studio's Insert menu. Select persist.cpp from the list.

6. **Use ClassWizard to import the new *CPersistentFrame* class.**   Click
   the Add Class button in the main ClassWizard dialog, and then select
   From A File. Fill in the Import Class Information dialog as shown here:

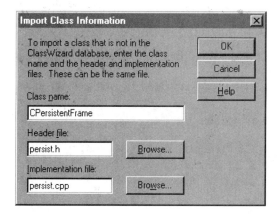

   Be sure that the class header file is persist.h and that the implementation file is persist.cpp. After you complete this step, you'll be able to map
   messages and override virtual functions in the *CPersistentFrame* class.

7. **Build and test the EX14A application.**   Size and move the application's frame window, and then close the application. When you restart
   the application, does its window open at the same location at which it was

closed? Experiment with maximizing and iconizing, and then change the status of the control bars. Does the persistent frame remember its settings?

> **NOTE:** If you run the program through the debugger, you'll notice some memory leaks from the Registry key strings. Comments in the MFC library source code indicate that this is normal.

8. Examine the Windows registry. Run the Windows regedit.exe program. (It is named regedt32 under Microsoft Windows NT 3.51.) Navigate to the HKEY_CURRENT_USER\Software\Inside Visual C++\ex14a key. You should see data values similar to those shown below:

Notice the relationship between the Registry key and the *SetRegistryKey* function parameter, *Inside Visual C++*. If you supply an empty string as the *SetRegistryKey* parameter, the program name (ex14a, in this case) is positioned directly below *Software*.

Persistent Frames in MDI Applications

You won't get to MDI applications until Chapter 17, but if you're using this book as a reference, you might want to apply the persistent frame technique to MDI applications.

The *CPersistentFrame* class, as presented in this chapter, won't work in an MDI application because the MDI main frame window's *ShowWindow* function is called, not by a virtual *ActivateFrame* function, but directly by the application class's *InitInstance* member function. If you need to control the characteristics of an MDI main frame window, add the necessary code to *InitInstance*.

The *ActivateFrame* function is called, however, for *CMDIChildWnd* objects. This means your MDI application could remember the sizes and positions of its child windows. You could store the information in the INI file, but you would have to accommodate multiple windows. You would have to modify the *CPersistentFrame* class for this purpose.

Separating the Document from Its View

Now you're finally going to see the interaction between documents and views. Chapter 12 gave you a preview of this interaction when it showed the routing of command messages to both view objects and document objects. In this chapter, you'll see how the document maintains the application's data and how the view presents the data to the user. You'll also learn how the document and view objects talk to each other while the application executes.

The two examples in this chapter both use the *CFormView* class as the base class for their views. The first example is as simple as possible, with the document holding only one simple object of class *CStudent*, which represents a single student record. The view shows the student's name and grade and allows editing. With the *CStudent* class, you'll get some practice writing classes to represent real-world entities. You'll also get to use the Microsoft Foundation Class (MFC) Library version 4.0 diagnostic dump functions.

The second example goes further by introducing pointer collection classes—the *CObList* and *CTypedPtrList* classes in particular. Now the document holds a collection of student records, and the view allows the sequencing, insertion, and deletion of individual records.

Document–View Interaction Functions

You already know that the document object holds the data and that the view object displays the data and allows editing. An SDI application has a document class derived from *CDocument*, and it has one or more view classes, each ultimately derived from *CView*. A complex handshaking process takes place among the document, the view, and the rest of the application framework.

To understand this process, you need to know about five important member functions in the document and view classes. Two are nonvirtual base class functions that you call in your derived classes; three are virtual functions that you often override in your derived classes. Let's look at these functions one at a time.

The *CView::GetDocument* Function

A view object has one and only one associated document object. The *GetDocument* function allows an application to navigate from a view to its document. Suppose a view object gets a message that the user has entered new data into an edit control. The view must tell the document object to update its internal data accordingly. The *GetDocument* function provides the document pointer that can be used to access document class member functions or public data members.

> NOTE: The *CDocument::GetNextView* function navigates from the document to the view, but because a document can have more than one view, it's necessary to call this member function once for each view, inside a loop. You'll seldom call *GetNextView* because the application framework provides a better method of iterating through a document's views.

When AppWizard generates a derived *CView* class, it creates a special type-safe version of the *GetDocument* function that returns not a *CDocument* pointer but a pointer to an object of your derived class. This function is an inline function, and it looks something like this:

```
CMyDoc* GetDocument()
{
    return (CMyDoc*) m_pDocument;
}
```

When the compiler sees a call to *GetDocument* in your view class code, it uses the derived class version instead of the *CDocument* version, so you do not have to cast the returned pointer to your derived document class. Because the *CView::GetDocument* function is <u>not</u> a virtual function, a statement such as

```
pView->GetDocument(); // pView is declared CView*
```

calls the base class *GetDocument* function and thus returns a pointer to a *CDocument* object.

The *CDocument::UpdateAllViews* Function

If the document data changes for any reason, all views must be notified so that they can update their representations of that data. If *UpdateAllViews* is called from a member function of a derived document class, its first parameter, *pSender*, is *NULL*. If *UpdateAllViews* is called from a member function of a derived view class, set the *pSender* parameter to the current view, like this:

```
GetDocument()->UpdateAllViews(this);
```

The non-null parameter prevents the application framework from notifying the current view. The assumption is that the current view has already updated itself.

The function has optional <u>hint</u> parameters that can be used to give the view specific and application-dependent information about which parts of the view to update. This is an advanced use of the function.

How exactly is a view notified when *UpdateAllViews* gets called? Take a look at the next function, *OnUpdate*.

The *CView::OnUpdate* Function

This is a virtual function that the application framework calls in response to your application's call to the *CDocument::UpdateAllViews* function. You can, of course, call it directly within your derived *CView* class. Typically, your derived view class's *OnUpdate* function accesses the document, gets the document's data, and then updates the view's data members or controls to reflect the changes. Alternatively, *OnUpdate* can invalidate a portion of the view, causing the view's *OnDraw* function to use document data to draw in the window. The *OnUpdate* function might look something like this:

```
void CMyView::OnUpdate(CView* pSender, LPARAM lHint, CObject* pHint)
{
    CMyDocument* pMyDoc = GetDocument();
    CString lastName = pMyDoc->GetLastName();
    m_pNameStatic->SetWindowText(lastName); // m_pNameStatic is
                                            //   a CMyView data member
}
```

The hint information is passed through directly from the call to *Update-AllViews*. The default *OnUpdate* implementation invalidates the entire window rectangle. In your overridden version, you can choose to define a smaller invalid rectangle as specified by the hint information.

If the *CDocument* function *UpdateAllViews* is called with the *pSender* parameter pointing to a specific view object, *OnUpdate* is called for all the document's views <u>except</u> the specified view.

339

The *CView::OnInitialUpdate* Function

This virtual *CView* function is called when the application starts, when the user chooses New from the File menu, and when the user chooses Open from the File menu. The *CView* base class version of *OnInitialUpdate* does nothing but call *OnUpdate*. If you override *OnInitialUpdate* in your derived view class, be sure that the view class calls the base class's *OnInitialUpdate* function or the derived class's *OnUpdate* function.

You can use your derived class's *OnInitialUpdate* function to initialize your view object. When the application starts, the application framework calls *OnInitialUpdate* immediately after *OnCreate* (if you've mapped *OnCreate* in your view class). *OnCreate* is called only once, but *OnInitialUpdate* can be called many times.

The *CDocument::OnNewDocument* Function

The framework calls this virtual function after a document object is first constructed and when the user chooses New from the File menu in an SDI application. This is a good place to set the initial values of your document's data members. AppWizard generates an overridden *OnNewDocument* function in your derived document class. Be sure to retain the call to the base class function.

The Simplest Document–View Application

Suppose you don't need multiple views of your document but you plan to take advantage of the application framework's file support. In this case, you can forget about the *UpdateAllViews* and *OnUpdate* functions. Simply follow these steps when you develop the application:

1. In your derived document class header file (generated by AppWizard), declare your document's data members. These data members are the primary data storage for your application. You can make these data members public, or you can declare the derived view class a <u>friend</u> of the document class.

2. In your derived view class, override the *OnInitialUpdate* virtual member function. The application framework calls this function after the document data has been initialized or read from disk. (Chapter 16 discusses disk file I/O.) *OnInitialUpdate* should update the view to reflect the current document data.

3. In your derived view class, let your window message and command message handlers update the document data members directly, using *GetDocument* to access the document object.

The sequence of events for this simplified document–view environment is as follows:

Application starts   *CMyDocument* object constructed

                         CMyView object constructed

                         View window created

                         CMyView::OnCreate called (if mapped)

                         CMyDocument::OnNewDocument called

                         CMyView::OnInitialUpdate called

                             View object initialized

                             View window invalidated

User edits data   *CMyView* functions update *CMyDocument* data members

User exits application *CMyView* object destroyed

                         CMyDocument object destroyed

The *CFormView* Class

The *CFormView* class is a useful view class that has many of the characteristics of a modeless dialog window. Like a class derived from *CDialog*, a derived *CFormView* class is associated with a dialog resource that defines the frame characteristics and enumerates the controls. The *CFormView* class supports the same dialog data exchange and validation (DDX and DDV) functions that you saw in the *CDialog* examples in Chapter 6.

> WARNING: If AppWizard generates a Form View dialog, the properties are set correctly, but if you use the graphic editor to make a dialog for a form view, you <u>must</u> specify the following items in the Dialog Properties dialog:
>
> Style = Child
> Border = None
> Visible = unchecked

A *CFormView* object receives notification messages directly from its controls, and it receives command messages from the application framework. This application framework command-processing ability clearly separates

CFormView from *CDialog*, and it makes controlling the view from the frame's main menu or toolbar easy.

The *CFormView* class is derived from *CView* (actually, from *CScrollView*) and not from *CDialog*. You can't, therefore, assume that *CDialog* member functions are supported. *CFormView* does <u>not</u> have virtual *OnInitDialog*, *OnOK*, and *OnCancel* functions. *CFormView* member functions do not call *UpdateData* and the DDX functions. You have to call *UpdateData* yourself at the appropriate times, usually in response to control notification messages or command messages.

Even though the *CFormView* class is not derived from the *CDialog* class, it is built around the Windows dialog. For this reason, you can use many of the *CDialog* class member functions such as *GotoDlgCtrl* and *NextDlgCtrl*. All you have to do is cast your *CFormView* pointer to a *CDialog* pointer. The following statement, extracted from a member function of a class derived from *CFormView*, sets the focus to a specified control. *GetDlgItem* is a *CWnd* function and is thus inherited by the derived *CFormView* class.

```
((CDialog*) this)->GotoDlgCtrl(GetDlgItem(IDC_NAME));
```

AppWizard gives you the option of using *CFormView* as the base class for your view. When you select *CFormView*, AppWizard generates an empty dialog with the correct style properties set. The next step is to use ClassWizard to add control notification message handlers, command message handlers, and update command UI handlers. (The example steps beginning on page 350 show you what to do.) You can also define data members and validation criteria.

NOTE: If you want ClassWizard to add menu command message handlers to a *CFormView* derived class, you must run ClassWizard from the graphic editor after selecting the appropriate menu.

The *CObject* Class

If you study the MFC library hierarchy, you'll notice that the *CObject* class is at the top. All other classes, except *CString* and trivial classes such as *CRect* and *CPoint*, are derived from the *CObject* <u>root</u> class. When a class is derived from *CObject*, it inherits a number of important characteristics. The many benefits of *CObject* derivation will become clear as you read the chapters that follow.

In this chapter, you'll see how *CObject* derivation allows objects to participate in the diagnostic dumping scheme and to be elements in the collection classes.

Diagnostic Dumping

The MFC library gives you some useful tools for diagnostic dumping. You enable these tools when you select the Debug target. When you select the Win32 Release target, diagnostic dumping is disabled, and the diagnostic code is not linked to your program. All diagnostic output goes to the Debug view in the debugger's output window.

TIP: To clear diagnostic output from the debugger's output window, position the cursor in the output window and click the right mouse button, and then select Clear from the pop-up menu.

The *TRACE* Macro

You've seen the *TRACE* macro used throughout the preceding examples in this book. *TRACE* statements are active whenever the constant *_DEBUG* is defined (when you select the Debug target and when the *afxTraceEnabled* variable is set to *TRUE*). *TRACE* statements work like C language *printf* statements, but they're completely disabled in the release version of the program. Here's a typical *TRACE* statement:

```
int nCount = 9;
CString strDesc("total");
TRACE("Count = %d, Description = %s\n", nCount, (const char*) strDesc);
```

NOTE: You must use the *(const char*)* cast for *CString* objects in a *TRACE* statement. Be careful to match all *TRACE* format strings to variables because the compiler's type checking is turned off in this situation. If the formats are mismatched, the *TRACE* statement will give you incorrect results and hinder your debugging efforts.

NOTE: The *TRACE* macro takes a variable number of parameters and is thus easy to use. If you look at the MFC source code, you won't see *TRACE* macros but rather *TRACE0*, *TRACE1*, *TRACE2*, and *TRACE3* macros. These macros take 0, 1, 2, and 3 parameters, respectively, and are leftovers from the 16-bit environment, when it was necessary to conserve space in the data segment.

The *afxDump* Object

An alternative to the *TRACE* statement is more compatible with the C++ language. The MFC *afxDump* object accepts program variables with a syntax similar to that of *cout*, the C++ output stream object. You don't need complex formatting strings; instead, overloaded operators control the output format.

343

(Overloaded operators are explained in Appendix A.) The *afxDump* output goes to the same destination as the *TRACE* output, but the *afxDump* object is defined only in the Debug version of the MFC library. Here is a typical stream-oriented diagnostic statement that produces the same output as the *TRACE* statement above:

```
int nCount = 9;
CString strDesc("total");
#ifdef _DEBUG
    afxDump << "Count = " << nCount << ", Description = " << strDesc <<
"\n";
#endif
```

Although both *afxDump* and *cout* use the same insertion operator (<<), they don't share any code. The *cout* object is part of the Visual C++ iostream library, and *afxDump* is part of the MFC library. Don't assume that any of the *cout* formatting capability is available through *afxDump*.

Classes that aren't derived from *CObject*, such as *CString*, *CTime*, and *CRect*, contain their own overloaded insertion operators for *CDumpContext* objects. The *CDumpContext* class, of which *afxDump* is an instance, includes the overloaded insertion operators for the native C++ data types (*int*, *double*, *char∗*, and so on). The *CDumpContext* class also contains insertion operators for *CObject* references and pointers, and that's where things get interesting.

The Dump Context and the *CObject* Class

If the *CDumpContext* insertion operator accepts *CObject* pointers and references, it must also accept pointers and references to derived classes. Consider a trivial class, *CAction*, that is derived from *CObject*, as shown here:

```
class CAction : public CObject
{
public:
    int m_nTime;
};
```

What happens when the following statement executes?

```
#ifdef _DEBUG
    afxDump << action; // action is an object of class CAction
#endif
```

The virtual *CObject::Dump* function gets called. If you haven't overridden *Dump* for *CAction*, you don't get much except for the address of the object. If you have overridden *Dump*, however, you can get the internal state of your object. Here's a *CAction::Dump* function:

```
#ifdef _DEBUG
void CAction::Dump(CDumpContext& dc) const
{
    CObject::Dump(dc); // always call base class function
    dc << "\ntime = " << m_nTime << "\n";
}
#endif
```

The base class (*CObject*) *Dump* function prints a line such as this:

```
a CObject at $4498
```

If you have called the *DECLARE_DYNAMIC* macro in your *CAction* class definition and the *IMPLEMENT_DYNAMIC* macro in your *CAction* declaration, you will see the name of the class in your dump, like this:

```
a CAction at $4498
```

even if your dump statement looks like this:

```
#ifdef _DEBUG
    afxDump << (CObject*) pAction;
#endif
```

The two macros work together to include the MFC library runtime class code in your derived *CObject* class. With this code in place, your program can determine an object's class name at runtime (for the dump, for example), and it can obtain class hierarchy information.

NOTE: The (*DECLARE_SERIAL*, *IMPLEMENT_SERIAL*) and (*DECLARE_DYNCREATE, IMPLEMENT_DYNCREATE*) macro pairs provide the same runtime class features as those provided by the (*DECLARE_DYNAMIC, IMPLEMENT_DYNAMIC*) macro pair.

Automatic Dump of Undeleted Objects

With the Debug target selected, the application framework dumps all objects that are undeleted when your program exits. This dump is a useful diagnostic aid, but if you want it to be really useful, you must be sure to delete <u>all</u> your objects, even the ones that would normally disappear after the exit. This object cleanup is good programming discipline.

NOTE: The code that adds debug information to allocated memory blocks is now in the Debug version of the C runtime (CRT) library rather than in the MFC library. If you choose to dynamically link MFC, the MSVCR40D DLL is loaded along with the necessary MFC DLLs. When you add the line

```
#define new DEBUG_NEW
```

at the top of a CPP file, the CRT library lists the filename and line number at which the allocations were made.

Window Subclassing for Enhanced Data Entry Control

What if you want an edit control (in a dialog or a form view) that accepts only numeric characters? The MFC library provides a convenient way to change the behavior of any standard control, including the edit control. Actually, there are several ways. You can derive your own classes from *CEdit*, *CListBox*, and so forth (with their own message handler functions) and then create control objects at runtime. Or you can register a special window class, as a Win32 programmer would do, and integrate it into the project's resource file with a text editor. Neither of these methods, however, allows you to use the graphic editor to position controls in the dialog resource.

The easy way to modify a control's behavior is to use the MFC library's <u>window</u> <u>subclassing</u> feature. You use the graphic editor to position a normal control in a dialog resource, and then you write a new C++ class that contains message handlers for the events that you want to handle yourself. Here are the steps for subclassing an edit control:

1. With the graphic editor, position an edit control in your dialog resource. Assume that it has the child window ID *IDC_EDIT1*.

2. Write a new class—for example, *CNumericEdit*—derived from *CEdit*. Map the WM_CHAR message, and write a handler like this:

```
void CNumericEdit::OnChar(UINT nChar, UINT nRepCnt,
                          UINT nFlags)
{
    if (isdigit(nChar)) {
        CEdit::OnChar(nChar, nRepCnt, nFlags);
    }
}
```

3. In your derived dialog or form view class header, declare a data member of class *CNumericEdit* in this way:

```
private:
    CNumericEdit m_numericEdit;
```

4. If you're working with a dialog class, add the following line to your *OnInitDialog* override function:

```
m_numericEdit.SubclassDlgItem(IDC_EDIT1, this);
```

5. If you're working with a form view class, add the following code to your *OnInitialUpdate* override function:

```
if (m_numericEdit.m_hWnd == NULL) {
    m_numericEdit.SubclassDlgItem(IDC_EDIT1, this);
}
```

The *CWnd SubclassDlgItem* member function ensures that all messages are routed through the application framework's message dispatch system before being sent to the control's built-in window procedure. This technique is called <u>dynamic</u> <u>subclassing</u> and is explained in more detail in Technical Note #1.

A word of caution here: Your ability to change the behavior of a control depends on the code inside the control's window procedure. The edit control, for example, appears to read the keyboard after it receives the WM_CHAR message. If you change the values of the character before calling *CEdit::OnChar*, the change has no effect.

The EX15A Example

The first of this chapter's two examples shows a very simple document–view interaction. The *CEx15aDoc* document class, derived from *CDocument*, allows for a single embedded *CStudent* object. The *CStudent* class represents a student record that is composed of a *CString* name and an integer grade. The *CEx15aView* view class is derived from *CFormView*. It is a visual representation of a student record that has edit controls for the name and grade. The default Enter pushbutton updates the document with data from the edit controls. Figure 15-1 on the following page shows the EX15A window.

Figure 15-2 beginning on the following page shows the code for the *CStudent* class. Most of the class's features serve EX15A, but a few items carry forward to EX15B and the programs discussed in Chapter 16. For now, take note of the two data members, the default constructor, the operators, and the *Dump* function declaration. The *DECLARE_DYNAMIC* and *IMPLEMENT_DYNAMIC* macros ensure that the class name is available for the diagnostic dump.

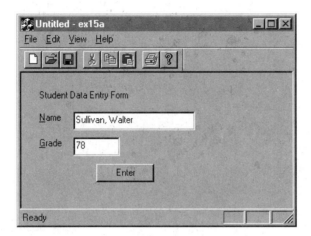

Figure 15-1.
The EX15A program in action.

STUDENT.H

```
class CStudent : public CObject
{
    DECLARE_DYNAMIC(CStudent)
public:
    CString m_strName;
    int m_nGrade;

    CStudent() {
        m_nGrade = 0;
    }

    CStudent(const char* szName, long nGrade) : m_strName(szName) {
        m_nGrade = nGrade;
    }

    CStudent(const CStudent& s) : m_strName(s.m_strName) {
        // copy constructor m_nGrade = s.m_nGrade;
    }
```

Figure 15-2.   *(continued)*
The CStudent *class listing.*

Figure 15-2. *continued*

```
    const CStudent& operator =(const CStudent& s) {
        m_strName = s.m_strName;
        m_nGrade = s.m_nGrade;
        return *this;
    }

    BOOL operator ==(const CStudent& s) const
    {
        if ((m_strName == s.m_strName) &&
                (m_nGrade == s.m_nGrade)) {
          return TRUE;
        }
        else {
            return FALSE;
         }
    }

    BOOL operator !=(const CStudent& s) const
    {
        // Let's make use of the operator we just defined!
        return !(*this == s);
    }
#ifdef _DEBUG
    void Dump(CDumpContext& dc) const;
#endif
};
```

STUDENT.CPP

```
#include "StdAfx.h"
#include "student.h"

IMPLEMENT_DYNAMIC(CStudent, CObject)

#ifdef _DEBUG
void CStudent::Dump(CDumpContext& dc) const
{
    CObject::Dump(dc);
    dc << "\nm_strName = " << m_strName << "\nm_nGrade = " <<
m_nGrade;
}
#endif
```

Follow these steps to build the EX15A example:

1. Run AppWizard to generate \VCPP32\EX15A\EX15A. In the Step 6 dialog, change the view's base class to *CFormView,* as shown here:

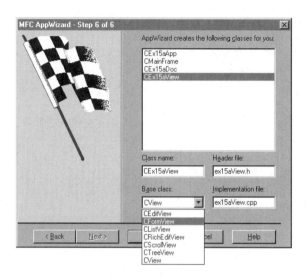

The options and the default class names are shown here:

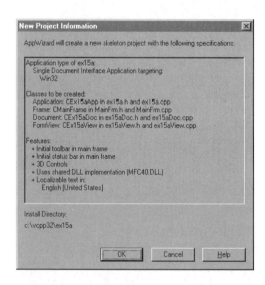

2. Use the graphic editor to replace the Edit menu options. Delete the current Edit menu items, and replace them with a Clear All option, as shown here:

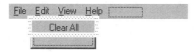

Use the default constant *ID_EDIT_CLEAR_ALL*, which is assigned by the application framework. A menu prompt automatically appears.

3. Use the graphic editor to modify the *IDD_EX15A_FORM* dialog.
Open the AppWizard-generated dialog *IDD_EX15A_FORM*, and add controls as shown here:

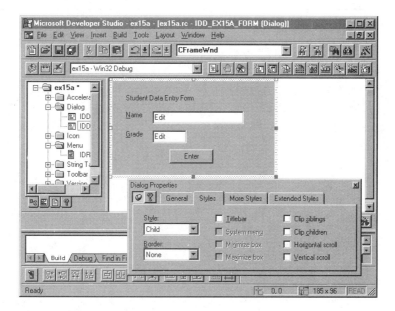

Be sure that the Style properties are set <u>exactly</u> as shown in the Dialog Properties dialog (Style = Child; Border = None) and that Visible is unchecked.

Use the following IDs for the controls:

Control	ID
Name edit control	*IDC_NAME*
Grade edit control	*IDC_GRADE*
Enter pushbutton	*IDC_ENTER*

4. Use ClassWizard to add message handlers for *CEx15aView*.

> NOTE: You must run ClassWizard from the graphic editor (with the menu *IDR_MAINFRAME* selected) to see the menu's Object IDs.

Select the *CEx15aView* class, and then add handlers for the following messages. Accept the default function names.

Object ID	Message	Member Function Name
IDC_ENTER	BN_CLICKED	*OnEnter*
ID_EDIT_CLEAR_ALL	COMMAND	*OnEditClearAll*
ID_EDIT_CLEAR_ALL	UPDATE_COMMAND_UI	*OnUpdateEditClearAll*

5. Use ClassWizard to add variables for *CEx15aView*. Click on the Member Variables tab in the MFC ClassWizard dialog, and then add the following variables:

Control	Member Variable Name	Property Type	Variable Type
IDC_GRADE	*m_nGrade*	*Value*	*int*
IDC_NAME	*m_strName*	*Value*	*CString*

For *m_nGrade*, enter a minimum value of *0* and a maximum value of *100*. Notice that ClassWizard generates the code necessary to validate data entered by the user.

6. Use ClassWizard to override the virtual *OnInitialUpdate* function in the view class.

7. In Ex15aView.h, add a prototype for the helper function *Update-ControlsFromDoc*. Add the following code:

```
private:
    void UpdateControlsFromDoc();
```

8. Edit Ex15aView.cpp. Because the view class uses the *CStudent* class, you must include the *CStudent* class declaration. ClassWizard generated the skeleton *OnInitialUpdate* function, but you must enter the *UpdateControlsFromDoc* function from scratch. This function is a private <u>helper</u> member function that transfers data from the document to the *CEx15aView* data members and then to the dialog edit controls. Edit the code as shown here:

```
void CEx15aView::OnInitialUpdate()
{    // called on startup
    UpdateControlsFromDoc();
}

void CEx15aView::UpdateControlsFromDoc()
{    // called from OnInitialUpdate and OnEditClearAll
    CEx15aDoc* pDoc = GetDocument();
    m_nGrade = pDoc->m_student.m_nGrade;
    m_strName = pDoc->m_student.m_strName;
    UpdateData(FALSE); // calls DDX
}
```

Add the statement

```
#include "student.h"
```

<u>before</u> the statement

```
#include "ex15aDoc.h"
```

The *OnEnter* function replaces the *OnOK* function you'd expect to see in a dialog class. The function transfers data from the edit controls to the view's data members and then to the document. Add the following shaded code:

```
void CEx15aView::OnEnter()
{
    CEx15aDoc* pDoc = GetDocument();
    UpdateData(TRUE);
    pDoc->m_student.m_nGrade = m_nGrade;
    pDoc->m_student.m_strName = m_strName;
}
```

In a complex multiview application, the Edit Clear All command would be routed directly to the document. In this simple example, it's routed to the view. The update command UI handler disables the menu item if the document's student object is already blank. Add the following shaded code:

```
void CEx15aView::OnEditClearAll()
{
    GetDocument()->m_student = CStudent(); // "blank" student object
    UpdateControlsFromDoc();
}
void CEx15aView::OnUpdateEditClearAll(CCmdUI* pCmdUI)
{
    pCmdUI->Enable(GetDocument()->m_student != CStudent()); // blank?
}
```

9. **Edit the Ex15aDoc.h file.** The *CEx15aDoc* class provides for an embedded *CStudent* object. The *CStudent* constructor is called when the document object is constructed, and the *CStudent* destructor is called when the document object is destroyed. Add the following code:

```
public:
    CStudent m_student;
```

10. **Edit the Ex15aDoc.cpp file.** Because the document class incorporates the *CStudent* class, you must include its declaration. <u>Before</u> the statement

```
#include "ex15aDoc.h"
```

add the statement

```
#include "student.h"
```

Let's use the *CEx15aDoc* constructor to initialize the student object, as shown here:

```
CEx15aDoc::CEx15aDoc() : m_student("default value", 0)
{
    TRACE("Document object constructed\n");
}
```

We can't tell whether the EX15A program worked properly unless we dump the document when the program exits. We'll use the destructor to call the document's *Dump* function, which calls the *CStudent::Dump* function.

```
CEx15aDoc::~CEx15aDoc()
{
#ifdef _DEBUG
    Dump(afxDump);
#endif
}


void CEx15aDoc::Dump(CDumpContext& dc) const
{
    CDocument::Dump(dc);
    dc << "\n" << m_student << "\n";
}
```

11. Edit the ex15a.cpp file.   <u>Before</u> the statement

```
#include "ex15aDoc.h"
```

add the statement

```
#include "student.h"
```

12. Edit the EX15A project to add Student.cpp.   You must tell the make processor that you are adding the *CStudent* code to the project. Choose Files Into Project from the Insert menu, and select the Student.cpp source code file. The Developer Studio will analyze the other project files and establish the Student.h dependencies.

13. Build and test the EX15A application.   Type a name and a grade, and then click the Enter button. Now exit the application. Does the Debug window show messages similar to those shown here?

```
a CEx15aDoc at $4472
m_strTitle = Untitled
m_strPathName =
m_bModified = 0
m_pDocTemplate = $438E

a CStudent at $4498

m_strName = default value
m_nGrade = 0
```

> N O T E :   To see these messages, you must compile the application with the Win32 Debug target selected, and you must run the program from the debugger.

355

A More Advanced Document–View Interaction

If you're laying the groundwork for a multiview application, the document–view interaction must be more complex than the simple interaction in example EX15A. The fundamental problem is this: the user edits in view #1, so view #2 (and any other views) must be updated to reflect the changes. Now you need the *UpdateAllViews* and *OnUpdate* functions because the document is going to act as the clearinghouse for all view updates. The development steps are as follows:

1. In your derived document class header file (generated by App-Wizard), declare your document's data members. If you want, you can make these data members private, and you can define member functions to access them or declare the view class as a friend of the document class.

2. In your derived view class, use ClassWizard to override the *OnUpdate* virtual member function. The application framework calls this function whenever the document data has changed for any reason. *OnUpdate* should update the view to reflect the current document data.

3. Evaluate all your command messages. Determine whether each is document-specific or view-specific. (A good example of a document-specific command is the Clear All command on the Edit menu.) Now map the commands to the appropriate classes.

4. In your derived view class, allow the appropriate command message handlers to update the document data. Be sure that these message handlers call the *CDocument::UpdateAllViews* function before they exit. Use the type-safe version of the *CView::GetDocument* member function to access the view's document.

5. In your derived document class, allow the appropriate command message handlers to update the document data. Be sure that these message handlers call the *CDocument::UpdateAllViews* function before they exit.

The sequence of events for the complex document–view interaction is shown here:

Application starts   *CMyDocument* object constructed

                               CMyView object constructed

	Other view objects constructed
	View windows created
	CMyView::OnCreate called (if mapped)
	CDocument::OnNewDocument called
	CView::OnInitialUpdate called
	Calls *CMyView::OnUpdate*
	Initializes the view
User executes view command	*CMyView* functions update *CMyDocument* data members
	Calls *CDocument::UpdateAllViews*
	Other views' *OnUpdate* function called
User executes document command	*CMyDocument* functions update data members
	Calls *CDocument::UpdateAllViews*
	CMyView::OnUpdate called
	Other views' *OnUpdate* called
User exits application	View objects destroyed
	CMyDocument object destroyed

The *CDocument::DeleteContents* Function

At some point, you'll need a function to delete the contents of your document. You could write your own private member function, but it happens that the application framework declares a virtual *DeleteContents* function for the *CDocument* class. The application framework calls your overridden *Delete-Contents* function when the document is closed and, as you'll see in the next chapter, at other times as well.

The *CObList* Collection Class

Once you get to know the collection classes, you'll wonder how you ever got along without them. The *CObList* class is a useful representative of the collection class family. If you're familiar with this class, it's easy to learn the other list classes, the array classes, and the map classes.

You might think that collections are something new, but the C programming language has always supported one kind of collection—the array. C arrays must be fixed in size, and they do not support insertion of elements. Many C programmers have written function libraries for other collections,

357

including linked lists, dynamic arrays, and indexed dictionaries. For implementing collections, the C++ class is an obvious and better alternative than a C function library. A list object, for example, neatly encapsulates the list's internal data structures.

The *CObList* class supports ordered lists of pointers to objects of classes derived from *CObject*. Another MFC collection class, *CPtrList*, stores *void* pointers instead of *CObject* pointers. Why not use *CPtrList* instead? The *CObList* class offers advantages for diagnostic dumping, which you'll see in this chapter, and for serialization, which you'll see in the next chapter. One important feature of *CObList* is that it can contain <u>mixed</u> pointers. In other words, a *CObList* collection can hold pointers to both *CStudent* objects and *CTeacher* objects, assuming that both *CStudent* and *CTeacher* were derived from *CObject*.

Using the *CObList* Class for a First-In, First-Out (FIFO) List

One of the easiest ways to use a *CObList* object is to add new elements to the tail, or bottom, of the list, and to remove elements from the head, or top, of the list. The first element added to the list will always be the first element removed from the head of the list. Suppose you're working with element objects of class *CAction*, which is your own custom class derived from *CObject*. A command-line program that puts five elements into a list and then retrieves them in the same sequence is shown here:

```
#include <afx.h>
#include <afxcoll.h>
class CAction : public CObject
{
private:
    int m_nTime;
public:
    CAction(int nTime) { m_nTime = nTime; } // constructor
                                    //  stores integer time value
    void PrintTime() { TRACE("time = %d\n", m_nTime); }
};

int main()
{
    CAction* pAction;
    CObList actionList; // action list constructed on stack
    int     i;

    // inserts action objects in sequence {0, 1, 2, 3, 4}
```

```
for (i = 0; i < 5; i++) {
  pAction = new CAction(i);
  actionList.AddTail(pAction); // no cast necessary for pAction
}

// retrieves and removes action objects in sequence {0, 1, 2, 3, 4}
while (!actionList.IsEmpty()) {
  pAction = (CAction*) actionList.RemoveHead(); // cast required for
                                                //  return value
  pAction->PrintTime();
  delete pAction;
}

return 0;
}
```

Here's what's going on in the program. First a *CObList* object, *actionList*, is constructed. Then the *CObList::AddTail* member function inserts pointers to newly constructed *CAction* objects. No casting is necessary for *pAction* because *AddTail* takes a *CObject* pointer parameter and *pAction* is a pointer to a derived class.

Next the *CAction* object pointers are removed from the list of the objects deleted. A cast is necessary for the returned value of *RemoveHead* because *RemoveHead* returns a *CObject* pointer that is <u>higher</u> in the class hierarchy than *CAction*.

When you remove an object pointer from a collection, the object is not automatically deleted. The *delete* statement is necessary for deleting the *CAction* objects.

CObList Iteration—The *POSITION* Variable

Suppose you want to iterate through the elements in a list. The *CObList* class provides a *GetNext* member function that returns a pointer to the "next" list element, but using it is a little tricky. *GetNext* takes a parameter of type *POSITION*, which is simply an integer. The *POSITION* variable is an internal representation of the retrieved element's position in the list. Because the *POSITION* parameter is declared as a reference (&), the function can change its value.

GetNext does the following:

1. It returns a pointer to the "current" object in the list, identified by the incoming value of the *POSITION* parameter.

2. It increments the value of the *POSITION* parameter to the next list element.

359

Here's what a *GetNext* loop looks like, assuming you're using the list generated in the previous example:

```
CAction* pAction;
POSITION pos = actionList.GetHeadPosition();
while (pos != NULL) {
  pAction = (CAction*) actionList.GetNext(pos);
  pAction->PrintTime();
}
```

Now suppose you have an interactive Windows application that uses toolbar buttons to sequence forward and backward through the list, one element at a time. You can't use *GetNext* to retrieve the entry because *GetNext* always <u>increments</u> the *POSITION* variable, and you don't know in advance whether the user is going to want the next element or the previous element. Here's a sample view class command message handler function that gets the next list entry. In the *CMyView* class, *m_actionList* is an embedded *CObList* object, and the *m_position* data member is a *POSITION* variable that holds the current list position.

```
CMyView::OnCommandNext()
{
    POSITION pos;
    CAction*  pAction;

    if ((pos = m_position) != NULL) {
      m_actionList.GetNext(pos);
      if (pos != NULL) { // pos is NULL at end of list
        pAction = (CAction*) m_actionList.GetAt(pos);
        pAction->PrintTime();
        m_position = pos;
      }
      else {
        AfxMessageBox("End of list reached");
      }
    }
}
```

GetNext is now called first to increment the list position, and the *CObList::GetAt* member function is called to retrieve the entry. The *m_position* variable is updated only when we're sure we're not at the tail of the list.

The *CTypedPtrList* Template Collection Class

The *CObList* class works fine if you want a collection to contain mixed pointers. If on the other hand you want a type-safe collection that contains only one type of object pointer, you should look at the MFC library template pointer collection classes. *CTypedPtrList* is a good example. Templates are a relatively new C++ language element, introduced by Microsoft in Visual C++ version 2.0. *CTypedPtrList* is a template class that you can use to create a list of any pointers to objects of any specified class. To make a long story short, you use the template to create a custom derived list class, using either *CPtrList* or *CObList* as a base class.

To declare an object for *CAction* pointers, you write this line of code:

```
CTypedPtrList< CObList, CAction* > m_actionList;
```

The first parameter is the base class for the collection, and the second parameter is the type for parameters and return values. Only *CPtrList* and *CObList* are permitted for the base class because those are the only two MFC library pointer collection classes. If you are storing objects of classes derived from *CObject*, you should use *CObList* as your base class; otherwise, use *CPtrList*.

By using the template as shown above, the compiler ensures that all list member functions return a *CAction* pointer. Thus, you can write the following code:

```
pAction = m_actionList.GetAt(pos); // no cast required
```

If you want to clean up the notation a little, use a *typedef* to generate what looks like a class, as shown here:

```
typedef CTypedPtrList< CObList, CAction* > CActionList;
```

Now you can declare *m_actionList* as follows:

```
CActionList m_actionList;
```

The Dump Context and Collection Classes

The *Dump* function for *CObList* and the other collection classes has a useful property. If you call *Dump* for a collection object, you can get a display of each object in the collection. If the element objects use the *DECLARE_DYNAMIC* and *IMPLEMENT_DYNAMIC* macros, the dump will show the class name for each object.

The default behavior of the collection *Dump* functions is to display only class names and addresses of element objects. If you want the collection *Dump* functions to call the *Dump* function for each element object, you must, some-where at the start of your program, make the following call:

```
#ifdef _DEBUG
    afxDump.SetDepth(1);
#endif
```

Now the statement

```
#ifdef _DEBUG
    afxDump << actionList;
#endif
```

produces output such as this:

```
a CObList with 4 elements

    a CAction at $4CD6
time = 0
    a CAction at $5632
time = 1
    a CAction at $568E
time = 2
    a CAction at $56EA
time = 3
```

If the collection contains mixed pointers, the virtual *Dump* function is called for the object's class and the appropriate class name is printed.

The EX15B Example

This second SDI example improves on EX15A in the following ways:

- Instead of a single embedded *CStudent* object, the document now contains a list of *CStudent* objects. (Now you see the reason for using the *CStudent* class instead of making *m_strName* and *m_nGrade* data members of the document.)

- Toolbar buttons allow the user to sequence through the list.

- The application is structured to allow the addition of extra views. The Edit Clear All command is now routed to the document object, so the document's *UpdateAllViews* function and the view's *OnUpdate* function are brought into play.

- The student-specific view code is isolated so that the *CEx15bView* class can later be transformed into a base class that contains only general-purpose code. Derived classes can override selected functions to accommodate lists of application-specific objects.

The EX15B window, shown in Figure 15-3, looks a little different from the EX15A window (shown in Figure 15-1 on page 348). The toolbar buttons are enabled only when appropriate. The Next (arrow-down graphic) button, for example, is disabled when we're positioned at the bottom of the list.

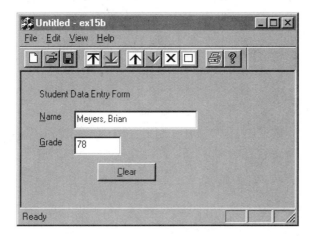

Figure 15-3.
The EX15B program in action.

The toolbar buttons function as follows:

Button	Function
![first]	Retrieves the first student record
![last]	Retrieves the last student record
![previous]	Retrieves the previous student record
![next]	Retrieves the next student record
![delete]	Deletes the current student record
![insert]	Inserts a new student record

The Clear button in the view window clears the contents of the Name and Grade edit controls. The Clear All command on the Edit menu deletes all the student records in the list and clears the view's edit controls.

This example deviates from the step-by-step format in the previous examples. Because there's now more code, we'll simply list selected code and the resource requirements. (You'll need to include AfxTempl.h in the StdAfx.h file.) In the listing figures, shaded code indicates where you enter additional code or enter other changes to the output from AppWizard and ClassWizard. The frequent use of *TRACE* statements lets you follow the program's execution in the debugging window.

Here's a list of the files and classes in the EX15B example:

Header File	Source Code File	Classes	Description
ex15b.h	ex15b.cpp	*CEx15bApp*	Application class (from AppWizard)
		CAboutDlg	About dialog
MainFrm.h	MainFrm.cpp	*CMainFrame*	SDI main frame
StuDoc.h	StuDoc.cpp	*CStudentDoc*	Student document
StuView.h	StuView.cpp	*CStudentView*	Student form view (derived from *CFormView*)
Student.h	Student.cpp	*CStudent*	Student record (similar to EX15A)
StdAfx.h	StdAfx.cpp		Includes the standard pre-compiled headers

CEx15bApp

ex15b.cpp is standard AppWizard output except for the following line:

```
#include "student.h"
```

included immediately <u>before</u> the statement

```
#include "studoc.h"
```

CMainFrame

The code for the *CMainFrame* class in MainFrm.cpp is standard AppWizard output.

CStudent

This is the code from EX15A except for the following line added at the end of Student.h:

```
typedef CTypedPtrList< CObList, CStudent* > CStudentList;
```

NOTE: Use of the MFC template collection classes requires the following statement in StdAfx.h:

```
#include <afxtempl.h>
```

CStudentDoc

AppWizard originally generated the *CStudentDoc* class. Figure 15-4 shows the code used in the EX15B example.

STUDOC.H

```
class CStudentDoc : public CDocument
{
private:
    CStudentList m_studentList;
protected: // create from serialization only
    CStudentDoc();
    DECLARE_DYNCREATE(CStudentDoc)

// Attributes
public:
    CStudentList* GetList() {
        return &m_studentList;
    }

// Operations
public:

// Overrides
    // ClassWizard generated virtual function overrides
    //{{AFX_VIRTUAL(CStudentDoc)
    public:
    virtual BOOL OnNewDocument();
    virtual void Serialize(CArchive& ar);
    virtual void DeleteContents();
    //}}AFX_VIRTUAL
```

Figure 15-4. *(continued)*
The CStudentDoc *class listing.*

Figure 15-4. *continued*

```
// Implementation
public:
    virtual ~CStudentDoc();
#ifdef _DEBUG
    virtual void AssertValid() const;
    virtual void Dump(CDumpContext& dc) const;
#endif

protected:

// Generated message map functions
protected:
    //{{AFX_MSG(CStudentDoc)
    afx_msg void OnEditClearAll();
    afx_msg void OnUpdateEditClearAll(CCmdUI* pCmdUI);
    //}}AFX_MSG
    DECLARE_MESSAGE_MAP()
};
```

STUDOC.CPP

```
#include "StdAfx.h"
#include "resource.h"

#include "Student.h"
#include "StuDoc.h"

#ifdef _DEBUG
#undef THIS_FILE
static char THIS_FILE[] = __FILE__;
#endif

/////////////////////////////////////////////////////////////////////////
// CStudentDoc

IMPLEMENT_DYNCREATE(CStudentDoc, CDocument)

BEGIN_MESSAGE_MAP(CStudentDoc, CDocument)
    //{{AFX_MSG_MAP(CStudentDoc)
    ON_COMMAND(ID_EDIT_CLEAR_ALL, OnEditClearAll)
    ON_UPDATE_COMMAND_UI(ID_EDIT_CLEAR_ALL, OnUpdateEditClearAll)
    //}}AFX_MSG_MAP
END_MESSAGE_MAP()

/////////////////////////////////////////////////////////////////////////
// CStudentDoc construction/destruction
```

(continued)

Figure 15-4. *continued*

```
CStudentDoc::CStudentDoc()
{
#ifdef _DEBUG
    afxDump.SetDepth(1); // ensure dump of list elements
#endif
}

CStudentDoc::~CStudentDoc()
{
}

BOOL CStudentDoc::OnNewDocument()
{
    TRACE("Entering CStudentDoc::OnNewDocument\n");
    if (!CDocument::OnNewDocument())
        return FALSE;

    // TODO: add reinitialization code here
    // (SDI documents will reuse this document)

    return TRUE;
}

/////////////////////////////////////////////////////////////////////////
// CStudentDoc serialization

void CStudentDoc::Serialize(CArchive& ar)
{
    if (ar.IsStoring())
    {
        // TODO: add storing code here
    }
    else
    {
        // TODO: add loading code here
    }
}

/////////////////////////////////////////////////////////////////////////
// CStudentDoc diagnostics

#ifdef _DEBUG
void CStudentDoc::AssertValid() const
{
    CDocument::AssertValid();
}
```

(continued)

Figure 15-4. *continued*

```
void CStudentDoc::Dump(CDumpContext& dc) const
{
    CDocument::Dump(dc);
    dc << "\n" << m_studentList << "\n";
}
#endif //_DEBUG


/////////////////////////////////////////////////////////////////////////
// CStudentDoc commands

void CStudentDoc::DeleteContents()
{
#ifdef _DEBUG
    Dump(afxDump);
#endif
    while (m_studentList.GetHeadPosition()) {
      delete m_studentList.RemoveHead();
    }
}


void CStudentDoc::OnEditClearAll()
{
    DeleteContents();
    UpdateAllViews(NULL);
}

void CStudentDoc::OnUpdateEditClearAll(CCmdUI* pCmdUI)
{
    pCmdUI->Enable(!m_studentList.IsEmpty());
}
```

ClassWizard and *CStudentDoc*

The Edit Clear All command is handled in the document class. The following message handlers were added through ClassWizard:

Object ID	Message	Member Function Name
ID_EDIT_CLEAR_ALL	COMMAND	*OnEditClearAll*
ID_EDIT_CLEAR_ALL	ON_UPDATE_COMMAND_UI	*OnUpdateEditClearAll*

Data Members

The document class provides for an embedded *CStudentList* object, the *m_studentList* data member, that holds pointers to *CStudent* objects. The list object is constructed when the *CStudentDoc* object is constructed, and it is destroyed at program exit. *CStudentList* is a *typedef* for a *CTypedPtrList* for *CStudent* pointers.

Constructor

The document constructor sets the depth of the dump context so that a dump of the list causes a dump of the individual list elements.

GetList

The inline *GetList* function helps isolate the view from the document. The document class must be specific to the type of object in the list—in this case, objects of the class *CStudent*. A generic list view base class, however, can use a member function to get a pointer to the list without knowing the name of the list object.

DeleteContents

The *DeleteContents* function is a virtual override function that is called by other document functions and by the application framework. Its job is to remove all student object pointers from the document's list and to delete those student objects. An important point to remember here is that SDI document objects are reused after they are closed. *DeleteContents* also dumps the student list.

Dump

AppWizard generates the *Dump* function skeleton between the lines *#ifdef _DEBUG* and *#endif*. Because the *afxDump* depth was set to *1* in the document constructor, all the *CStudent* objects contained in the list are dumped.

CStudentView

Figure 15-5 shows the code for the *CStudentView* class. This code will be carried over into the next two chapters.

STUVIEW.H

```
// StuView.h : interface of the CStudentView class
//
```

Figure 15-5.   *(continued)*
The CStudentView *class listing.*

Figure 15-5. *continued*

//

```cpp
class CStudentView : public CFormView
{
protected:
    POSITION        m_position; // current position in document list
    CStudentList* m_pList;       // copied from document
protected: // create from serialization only
    CStudentView();
    DECLARE_DYNCREATE(CStudentView)

public:
    //{{AFX_DATA(CStudentView)
    enum { IDD = IDD_EX15B_FORM };
    int         m_nGrade;
    CString     m_strName;
    //}}AFX_DATA

// Attributes
public:
    CStudentDoc* GetDocument();

// Operations
public:

// Overrides
    // ClassWizard generated virtual function overrides
    //{{AFX_VIRTUAL(CStudentView)
    public:
    virtual BOOL PreCreateWindow(CREATESTRUCT& cs);
    virtual void OnInitialUpdate();
    protected:
    virtual void DoDataExchange(CDataExchange* pDX);    // DDX/DDV
support
    virtual void OnUpdate(CView* pSender, LPARAM lHint, CObject* pHint);
    //}}AFX_VIRTUAL

// Implementation
public:
    virtual ~CStudentView();
#ifdef _DEBUG
    virtual void AssertValid() const;
    virtual void Dump(CDumpContext& dc) const;
#endif

protected:
```

(continued)

Figure 15-5. *continued*

```
    // Generated message map functions
protected:
    //{{AFX_MSG(CStudentView)
    afx_msg void OnCommandHome();
    afx_msg void OnUpdateCommandHome(CCmdUI* pCmdUI);
    afx_msg void OnCommandEnd();
    afx_msg void OnUpdateCommandEnd(CCmdUI* pCmdUI);
    afx_msg void OnCommandPrev();
    afx_msg void OnUpdateCommandPrev(CCmdUI* pCmdUI);
    afx_msg void OnCommandNext();
    afx_msg void OnUpdateCommandNext(CCmdUI* pCmdUI);
    afx_msg void OnCommandDel();
    afx_msg void OnUpdateCommandDel(CCmdUI* pCmdUI);
    afx_msg void OnCommandIns();
    afx_msg void OnClear();
    //}}AFX_MSG
protected:
    virtual void GetEntry(POSITION position);
    virtual void InsertEntry(POSITION position);
    virtual void ClearEntry();

    DECLARE_MESSAGE_MAP()
};

#ifndef _DEBUG  // debug version in StuView.cpp
inline CStudentDoc* CStudentView::GetDocument()
    { return (CStudentDoc*)m_pDocument; }
#endif
```

STUVIEW.CPP

```
// StuView.cpp : implementation of the CStudentView class
//

#include "StdAfx.h"
#include "ex15b.h"

#include "Student.h"
#include "StuDoc.h"
#include "StuView.h"

#ifdef _DEBUG
#undef THIS_FILE
static char THIS_FILE[] = __FILE__;
#endif
```

(continued)

Figure 15-5. *continued*

```
/////////////////////////////////////////////////////////////////////
// CStudentView

IMPLEMENT_DYNCREATE(CStudentView, CFormView)
BEGIN_MESSAGE_MAP(CStudentView, CFormView)
    //{{AFX_MSG_MAP(CStudentView)
    ON_COMMAND(ID_STUDENT_HOME, OnCommandHome)
    ON_UPDATE_COMMAND_UI(ID_STUDENT_HOME, OnUpdateCommandHome)
    ON_COMMAND(ID_STUDENT_END, OnCommandEnd)
    ON_UPDATE_COMMAND_UI(ID_STUDENT_END, OnUpdateCommandEnd)
    ON_COMMAND(ID_STUDENT_PREV, OnCommandPrev)
    ON_UPDATE_COMMAND_UI(ID_STUDENT_PREV, OnUpdateCommandPrev)
    ON_COMMAND(ID_STUDENT_NEXT, OnCommandNext)
    ON_UPDATE_COMMAND_UI(ID_STUDENT_NEXT, OnUpdateCommandNext)
    ON_COMMAND(ID_STUDENT_DEL, OnCommandDel)
    ON_UPDATE_COMMAND_UI(ID_STUDENT_DEL, OnUpdateCommandDel)
    ON_COMMAND(ID_STUDENT_INS, OnCommandIns)
    ON_BN_CLICKED(IDC_CLEAR, OnClear)
    //}}AFX_MSG_MAP
END_MESSAGE_MAP()


/////////////////////////////////////////////////////////////////////
// CStudentView construction/destruction

CStudentView::CStudentView()
    : CFormView(CStudentView::IDD)
{
    TRACE("Entering CStudentView constructor\n");
    //{{AFX_DATA_INIT(CStudentView)
    m_nGrade = 0;
    m_strName = _T("");
    //}}AFX_DATA_INIT
    m_position = NULL;

}


CStudentView::~CStudentView()
{
}

void CStudentView::DoDataExchange(CDataExchange* pDX)
{
    CFormView::DoDataExchange(pDX);
    //{{AFX_DATA_MAP(CStudentView)
    DDX_Text(pDX, IDC_GRADE, m_nGrade);
    DDV_MinMaxInt(pDX, m_nGrade, 0, 100);
```

(continued)

Figure 15-5. *continued*

```
    DDX_Text(pDX, IDC_NAME, m_strName);
    DDV_MaxChars(pDX, m_strName, 20);
    //}}AFX_DATA_MAP
}


BOOL CStudentView::PreCreateWindow(CREATESTRUCT& cs)
{
    // TODO: Modify the Window class or styles here by modifying
    //   the CREATESTRUCT cs

    return CFormView::PreCreateWindow(cs);
}


/////////////////////////////////////////////////////////////////////////
// CStudentView diagnostics

#ifdef _DEBUG
void CStudentView::AssertValid() const
{
    CFormView::AssertValid();
}


void CStudentView::Dump(CDumpContext& dc) const
{
    CFormView::Dump(dc);
}


CStudentDoc* CStudentView::GetDocument() // non-debug version is inline
{
    ASSERT(m_pDocument->IsKindOf(RUNTIME_CLASS(CStudentDoc)));
    return (CStudentDoc*) m_pDocument;
}
#endif //_DEBUG


/////////////////////////////////////////////////////////////////////////
// CStudentView message handlers

/////////////////////////////////////////////////////////////////////////
void CStudentView::OnCommandHome()
{
    // need to deal with list empty condition
    TRACE("Entering CStudentView::OnCommandHome\n");
    if (!m_pList->IsEmpty()) {
      m_position = m_pList->GetHeadPosition();
      GetEntry(m_position);
    }
```

(continued)

373

Figure 15-5. *continued*

```
}

//////////////////////////////////////////////////////////////////////////
void CStudentView::OnCommandNext()
{
    POSITION pos;

    TRACE("Entering CStudentView::OnCommandNext\n");
    if ((pos = m_position) != NULL) {
      m_pList->GetNext(pos);
      if (pos) {
        GetEntry(pos);
        m_position = pos;
      }
    }
}

//////////////////////////////////////////////////////////////////////////
void CStudentView::OnCommandEnd()
{
    TRACE("Entering CStudentView::OnCommandEnd\n");
    if (!m_pList->IsEmpty()) {
      m_position = m_pList->GetTailPosition();
      GetEntry(m_position);
    }
}

//////////////////////////////////////////////////////////////////////////
void CStudentView::OnCommandPrev()
{
    POSITION pos;

    TRACE("Entering CStudentView::OnCommandPrev\n");
    if ((pos = m_position) != NULL) {
      m_pList->GetPrev(pos);
      if (pos) {
        GetEntry(pos);
        m_position = pos;
      }
    }
}

//////////////////////////////////////////////////////////////////////////
void CStudentView::OnCommandDel()
{
    // deletes current entry and positions to next one or head
    POSITION pos;
```

(continued)

Figure 15-5. *continued*

```
      TRACE("Entering CStudentView::OnCommandDel\n");
    if ((pos = m_position) != NULL) {
      m_pList->GetNext(pos);
      if (pos == NULL) {
        pos = m_pList->GetHeadPosition();
        TRACE("GetHeadPos = %ld\n", pos);
        if (pos == m_position) {
          pos = NULL;
        }
      }
      GetEntry(pos);
      CStudent* ps = m_pList->GetAt(m_position);
      m_pList->RemoveAt(m_position);
      delete ps;
      m_position = pos;
      GetDocument()->SetModifiedFlag();
      GetDocument()->UpdateAllViews(this);
    }
}

/////////////////////////////////////////////////////////////////////////
void CStudentView::OnCommandIns()
{
    TRACE("Entering CStudentView::OnCommandIns\n");
    InsertEntry(m_position);
    GetDocument()->SetModifiedFlag();
    GetDocument()->UpdateAllViews(this);
}

/////////////////////////////////////////////////////////////////////////
void CStudentView::OnUpdateCommandHome(CCmdUI* pCmdUI)
{
    // called during idle processing
    POSITION pos;

    // enables button if list not empty and not at home already
    pos = m_pList->GetHeadPosition();
    pCmdUI->Enable((m_position != NULL) && (pos != m_position));
}

/////////////////////////////////////////////////////////////////////////
void CStudentView::OnUpdateCommandEnd(CCmdUI* pCmdUI)
{
    // called during idle processing
    POSITION pos;
```

(continued)

Figure 15-5. *continued*

```
    // enables button if list not empty and not at end already
    pos = m_pList->GetTailPosition();
    pCmdUI->Enable((m_position != NULL) && (pos != m_position));
}


/////////////////////////////////////////////////////////////////////
void CStudentView::OnUpdateCommandPrev(CCmdUI* pCmdUI)
{
    // called during idle processing
    POSITION pos;

    // enables button if list not empty and previous item(s) exist
    if ((pos = m_position) != NULL) {
      m_pList->GetPrev(pos);
    }
    pCmdUI->Enable((m_position != NULL) && (pos != NULL));
}


/////////////////////////////////////////////////////////////////////
void CStudentView::OnUpdateCommandNext(CCmdUI* pCmdUI)
{
    // called during idle processing
    POSITION pos;

    // enables button if list not empty and following item(s) exist
    if ((pos = m_position) != NULL) {
      m_pList->GetNext(pos);
    }
    pCmdUI->Enable((m_position != NULL) && (pos != NULL));
}


/////////////////////////////////////////////////////////////////////
void CStudentView::OnUpdateCommandDel(CCmdUI* pCmdUI)
{
    // called during idle processing
    pCmdUI->Enable(m_position != NULL);
}


/////////////////////////////////////////////////////////////////////
void CStudentView::OnClear()
{
    TRACE("Entering CStudentView::OnClear\n");
    ClearEntry();
}


/////////////////////////////////////////////////////////////////////
// protected virtual functions
```

(continued)

Figure 15-5. *continued*

```
void CStudentView::GetEntry(POSITION position)
{
    if (position) {
      CStudent* pStudent = m_pList->GetAt(position);
      m_strName = pStudent->m_strName;
      m_nGrade = pStudent->m_nGrade;
    }
    else {
      ClearEntry();
    }
    UpdateData(FALSE);
}


///////////////////////////////////////////////////////////////////////////
void CStudentView::InsertEntry(POSITION position)
{
    if (UpdateData(TRUE)) {
      // UpdateData returns FALSE if it detects a user error
      CStudent* pStudent = new CStudent;
      pStudent->m_strName = m_strName;
      pStudent->m_nGrade = m_nGrade;
      m_position = m_pList->InsertAfter(m_position, pStudent);
    }
}


///////////////////////////////////////////////////////////////////////////
void CStudentView::ClearEntry()
{
    m_strName = "";
    m_nGrade = 0;
    UpdateData(FALSE);
    ((CDialog*) this)->GotoDlgCtrl(GetDlgItem(IDC_NAME));
}


void CStudentView::OnUpdate(CView* pSender, LPARAM lHint,
    CObject* pHint)
{
    // called by OnInitialUpdate and by UpdateAllViews
    TRACE("Entering CStudentView::OnUpdate\n");
    m_pList = GetDocument()->GetList();
    m_position = m_pList->GetHeadPosition();
    GetEntry(m_position); // initial data for view
}
```

(continued)

Figure 15-5. *continued*

```
void CStudentView::OnInitialUpdate()
{
    TRACE("Entering CStudentView::OnInitialUpdate\n");
    CFormView::OnInitialUpdate();

    // TODO: add your specialized code here and/or call the base class

}
```

ClassWizard and *CStudentView*

ClassWizard was used to map the *CStudentView* Clear pushbutton notification message as follows:

Object ID	Message	Member Function Name
IDC_CLEAR	BN_CLICKED	*OnClear*

Because *CStudentView* is derived from *CFormView*, ClassWizard supports the definition of dialog data members. The variables shown here were added with the Edit Variables button:

Control ID	Member Variable Name	Property Type	Variable Type
IDC_GRADE	*m_nGrade*	*Value*	*int*
IDC_NAME	*m_strName*	*Value*	*CString*

Set the minimum value of the *m_nGrade* data member to *0* and its maximum value to *100*. Set the maximum length of the *m_strName* data member to 20 characters.

Because the toolbar buttons aren't duplicated by menu items, Class-Wizard won't help you with the message handlers. You must add the command and update command UI function prototypes manually.

Data Members

The *m_position* data member is a kind of cursor for the document's collection. It points to the *CStudent* object that is currently displayed. The *m_pList* variable provides a quick way to get at the student list in the document.

OnInitialUpdate

The virtual *OnInitialUpdate* function is called when you start the application. It sets the view's *m_pList* data member for subsequent access to the document's list object.

OnUpdate

The virtual *OnUpdate* function is called both by the *OnInitialUpdate* function and by the *CDocument::UpdateAllViews* function. It resets the list position to the head of the list, and it displays the head entry. In this example, the *UpdateAllViews* function is called only in response to the Edit Clear All command. In a multiview application, you might need a different strategy for setting the *CStudentView m_position* variable in response to document updates from another view.

Toolbar Button (and Menu) Command Message Handlers

These functions are called in response to toolbar button clicks and menu selections:

> *OnCommandHome*
> *OnCommandEnd*
> *OnCommandPrev*
> *OnCommandNext*
> *OnCommandDel*
> *OnCommandIns*

Each function has built-in error checking.

Toolbar Button (and Menu) Update Command UI Message Handlers

These functions are called during idle processing to update the state of the toolbar buttons:

> *OnUpdateCommandHome*
> *OnUpdateCommandEnd*
> *OnUpdateCommandPrev*
> *OnUpdateCommandNext*
> *OnUpdateCommandDel*

For example, this button,

which retrieves the first student record, is disabled when the list is empty and when the *m_position* variable is already set to the head of the list. Because a delay sometimes occurs in calling the update command UI functions, the command message handlers must check for error conditions.

Protected Virtual Functions

These three functions are protected virtual functions that deal specifically with *CStudent* objects:

> *GetEntry*
> *InsertEntry*
> *ClearEntry*

Move these functions to a derived class if you want to isolate the general-purpose list-handling features in a base class.

Resource Requirements

The file ex15b.rc defines the application's resources as follows.

Student Menu

Having menu options that correspond to the new toolbar buttons isn't absolutely necessary, but it sure makes programming easier. When you add the menu options, the graphic editor defines the symbols for you, and you can use ClassWizard to map the commands to view class member functions.

Toolbar

The toolbar (visible in Figure 15-3 on page 363) was created by erasing the Edit Cut, Copy, and Paste tiles (fourth, fifth, and sixth from the left) and replacing them with six new patterns. The Flip Vertical command (on the Image menu) was used to duplicate some of the tiles. The ex15b.rc file defines the linkage between the command IDs and the toolbar buttons.

Edit Menu

On the Edit menu, the clipboard menu items are replaced by the Clear All menu item. See step 2 on page 351 for an illustration of the Edit menu.

The *IDD_STUDENT* Dialog Template

The *IDD_STUDENT* dialog template, shown here, is similar to the EX15A dialog shown in Figure 15-1 on page 348 except that the Enter pushbutton has been replaced by the Clear pushbutton:

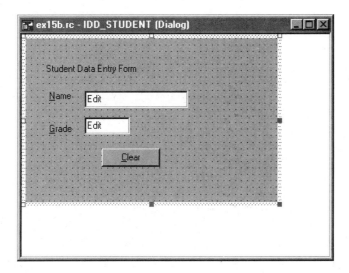

The following IDs identify the controls:

Control	ID
Name edit control	*IDC_NAME*
Grade edit control	*IDC_GRADE*
Clear pushbutton	*IDC_CLEAR*

The controls' styles are the same as for the EX15A program.

Testing the EX15B Application

Fill in the student name and grade fields, and then click this button

to insert the entry into the list. Repeat this action several more times, using the Clear pushbutton to erase the data from the previous entry. When you exit the application, the debug output should look similar to this:

```
a CStudentDoc at $48EE
m_strTitle = Ex15b
m_strPathName =
m_bModified = 0
m_pDocTemplate = $46AE
a CObList with 4 elements

    a CStudent at $4DC2
m_strName = Fisher, Lon
m_nGrade = 67
    a CStudent at $50FA
m_strName = Meyers, Brian
m_nGrade = 80
    a CStudent at $5152
m_strName = Seghers, John
m_nGrade = 92
    a CStudent at $51AA
m_strName = Anderson, Bob
m_nGrade = 87
```

Two Exercises for the Reader

You might have noticed the absence of a modify toolbar button. Without such a button, you can't modify an existing student record. Can you add the necessary toolbar button and message handlers? The most difficult task might be designing a graphic for the button's tile.

Recall that the *CStudentView* class is just about ready to be a general-purpose base class. Try separating the *CStudent*-specific virtual functions into a derived class. After that, make another derived class that uses a new element class other than *CStudent*.

Reading and Writing Documents—SDI

As you've probably noticed, every AppWizard-generated program has a File menu that contains the familiar New, Open, Save, and Save As commands. In this chapter, you'll learn how to make your application respond to read and write documents.

Here we'll stick with the Single Document Interface (SDI) application because it's familiar territory. Chapter 17 introduces the Multiple Document Interface (MDI) application, which is more flexible in its handling of documents and files. In both chapters, you'll get a heavy but necessary dose of application framework theory; you'll learn a lot about the various helper classes that have been concealed up to this point. The going will be rough, but believe me, you really have to know the details to get the most out of the application framework.

This chapter's example, EX16A, is an SDI application based on the EX15B example in the previous chapter. It uses the student list document with a *CFormView*-derived view class minus some of the frills such as the Edit Clear All command. Now the student list can be written to and read from disk through a process called <u>serialization</u>. Chapter 17 shows you how to use the same view and document classes to make an MDI application.

Serialization—What Is It?

The term "serialization" might be new to you, but it's already seen some use in the world of object-oriented programming. The idea is that objects can be persistent, which means they can be saved on disk when a program exits and then can be restored when the program is restarted. The process of saving and restoring objects is called serialization. In the MFC library, designated classes have a member function named *Serialize*. When the application framework calls *Serialize* for a particular object—for example, an object of class *CStudent*—the data for the student is either saved on disk or read from disk.

In the MFC library, serialization is not a substitute for a database management system. All the objects associated with a document are <u>sequentially</u> read from or written to a single disk file. It's not possible to access individual objects at random disk file addresses. If you need database capability in your application, consider using the Microsoft Open Database Connectivity (ODBC) software or Data Access Objects (DAO). Chapters 28 and 29 show you how to use ODBC and DAO with the MFC application framework.

> NOTE: There's a new storage option that fits between sequential files and a database: OLE structured storage, described in Chapter 26. The framework already uses structured storage for embedded objects. In a future version of Visual C++, structured storage will be fully integrated into the serialization process.

Disk Files and Archives

How do you know whether *Serialize* should read or write data? How is *Serialize* connected to a disk file? With the MFC library, disk files are represented by objects of class *CFile*. A *CFile* object encapsulates the binary file handle that you get through the Win32 function *CreateFile*. This is <u>not</u> the buffered *FILE* pointer that you'd get with a call to the C runtime *fopen* function; rather, it's a handle to a binary file. This file handle is used by the application framework for Win32 *ReadFile*, *WriteFile*, and *SetFilePointer* calls.

If your application does no direct disk I/O but instead relies on the serialization process, you can avoid direct use of *CFile* objects. Between the *Serialize* function and the *CFile* object is an archive object (of class *CArchive*), as shown in Figure 16-1.

The *CArchive* object buffers data for the *CFile* object, and it maintains an internal flag that indicates whether the archive is storing (writing to disk) or loading (reading from disk). Only one active archive is associated with a file at any one time. The application framework takes care of constructing the *CFile* and *CArchive* objects, opening the disk file for the *CFile* object, and associating the archive object with the file. All you have to do, in your *Serialize* function, is load data from or store data in the archive object. The application framework calls the document's *Serialize* function during the File Open and File Save processes.

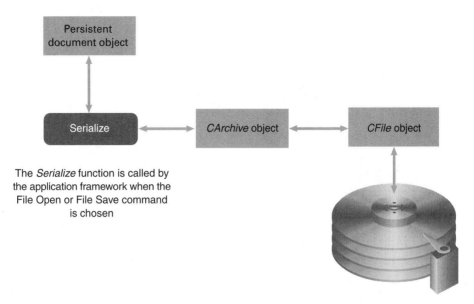

Figure 16-1.
The serialization process.

Making a Class Serializable

A serializable class must be derived directly or indirectly from *CObject.* In addition, the class declaration must contain the *DECLARE_SERIAL* macro call, and the class implementation file must contain the *IMPLEMENT_SERIAL* macro call. (See the *Microsoft Foundation Class Library Reference* for a description of these macros.) The *CStudent* class, which you'll be using in this chapter's examples, already includes these macros.

Writing a *Serialize* Function

In Chapter 15, you saw a *CStudent* class, derived from *CObject*, with these data members:

```
public:
    CString m_strName;
    int     m_nGrade;
```

Now your job is to write a *Serialize* member function for *CStudent.* Because *Serialize* is a virtual member function of class *CObject*, you must be sure that the return value and parameter types match the *CObject* declaration. Here's the *Serialize* function for the *CStudent* class:

```
void CStudent::Serialize(CArchive& ar)
{
    if (ar.IsStoring()) {
      ar << m_strName << (LONG) m_nGrade;
    }
    else {
      ar >> m_strName >> (LONG&) m_nGrade;
    }
}
```

Serialization functions generally call the *Serialize* function of their base class. If *CStudent* were derived from *CPerson*, for example, the first line of the *Serialize* function would be

```
CPerson::Serialize(ar);
```

The *Serialize* functions for *CObject* and *CDocument* don't do anything useful, so there's no need to call them.

Making Persistent Object Data Portable

You can't help noticing the *int*-to-*LONG* casts in the *Serialize* function above. An MFC library design goal was to make persistent object data portable between Win16 and Win32 programs. For this reason, *CArchive* does not have overloaded insertion operators and extraction operators for word-width–dependent types such as *int*. *CArchive* does support the following types, however:

Type	Description
BYTE	8 bits, unsigned
WORD	16 bits, unsigned
LONG	32 bits, signed
DWORD	32 bits, unsigned
float	32 bits
double	64 bits, IEEE standard

If you need to use word-width–dependent types, you must cast them to one of the supported types.

Notice that *ar* is a *CArchive* reference parameter that identifies the application's archive object. The *CArchive::IsStoring* member function tells us whether the archive is currently being used for storing or loading. The *CArchive* class has overloaded insertion operators (<<) and extraction operators (>>) for many of the C++ built-in types. MFC classes that are not derived from *CObject*, such as *CString* and *CRect*, have their own overloaded insertion and extraction operators for *CArchive*.

Loading from an Archive—Embedded Objects vs. Pointers

Now suppose your *CStudent* object has other objects embedded in it and these objects are not instances of standard classes such as *CString*, *CSize*, and *CRect*. Let's add a new data member to the *CStudent* class:

```
public:
    CTranscript m_transcript;
```

Assume that *CTranscript* is a custom class, derived from *CObject*, with its own *Serialize* member function. There's no overloaded << or >> operator for *CObject*, so the *CStudent::Serialize* function now becomes

```
void CStudent::Serialize(CArchive& ar)
{
    if (ar.IsStoring()) {
      ar << m_strName << (LONG) m_nGrade;
    }
    else {
      ar >> m_strName >> (LONG&) m_nGrade;
    }
    m_transcript.Serialize(ar);
}
```

Before the *CStudent::Serialize* function can be called to load a student record from the archive, a *CStudent* object must exist somewhere. The embedded *CTranscript* object *m_transcript* is constructed along with the *CStudent* object before the call to the *CTranscript::Serialize* function. When the virtual *CTranscript::Serialize* function does get called, it can load the archived transcript data into the embedded *m_transcript* object. If you're looking for a rule, here it is: always make a direct call to *Serialize* for embedded objects of classes derived from *CObject*.

Suppose that, instead of an embedded object, your *CStudent* object contained a *CTranscript* <u>pointer</u> data member such as this:

```
public:
    CTranscript* m_pTranscript;
```

You could use the *Serialize* function as shown below, but as you can see, you must construct a new *CTranscript* object yourself:

```
void CStudent::Serialize(CArchive& ar)

{
    if (ar.IsStoring())
      ar << m_strName << (LONG) m_nGrade;
    else {
      m_pTranscript = new CTranscript;
      ar >> m_strName >> (LONG&) m_nGrade;
    }
    m_pTranscript->Serialize(ar);
}
```

Because the *CArchive* insertion and extraction operators are indeed overloaded for *CObject* <u>pointers</u>, you could write *Serialize* this way instead:

```
void CStudent::Serialize(CArchive& ar)
{
    if (ar.IsStoring())
      ar << m_strName << (LONG) m_nGrade << m_pTranscript;
    else
      ar >> m_strName >> (LONG&) m_nGrade >> m_pTranscript;
}
```

But how is the *CTranscript* object constructed when the data is loaded from the archive? That's where the *DECLARE_SERIAL* and *IMPLEMENT-_SERIAL* macros in the *CTranscript* class come in. When the *CTranscript* object is written to the archive, the macros ensure that the class name is written along with the data. When the archive is read, the class name is read in, and an object of the correct class is dynamically constructed, under the control of code generated by the macros. Once the *CTranscript* object is constructed, the overridden *Serialize* function for *CTranscript* can be called to do the work of reading the student data from the disk file. Finally, the *CTranscript* pointer is stored in the *m_pTranscript* data member. To avoid a memory leak, you must be sure that *m_pTranscript* does not already contain a pointer to a *CTranscript* object. If the *CStudent* object was just constructed and thus was not previously loaded from the archive, the transcript pointer will be null.

The insertion and extraction operators do <u>not</u> work with embedded objects of classes derived from *CObject*, as shown here:

```
ar >> m_strName >> (LONG&) m_nGrade >> &m_transcript; // don't try this
```

Serializing Collections

Because all collection classes are derived from the *CObject* class and the collection class declarations contain the *DECLARE_SERIAL* macro call, you can conveniently serialize collections with a call to the collection class's *Serialize* member function. If you call *Serialize* for a *CObList* collection of *CStudent* objects, for example, the *Serialize* function for each *CStudent* object will be called in turn. You should, however, remember the following specifics about loading collections from an archive:

■ If a collection contains pointers to objects of mixed classes (all derived from *CObject*), the individual class names are in essence stored in the archive so that the objects can be properly constructed with the appropriate class constructor.

■ If a container object, such as a document, contains an embedded collection, loaded data is appended to the existing collection.

   You might need to empty the collection before loading from the archive. This is usually done in the virtual *DeleteContents* function, which is called by the application framework.

■ When a collection of *CObject* pointers is loaded from an archive, the following processing steps take place for each object in the collection:

   ❑ The object's class is identified.

   ❑ Heap storage is allocated for the object.

   ❑ The object's data is loaded into the newly allocated storage.

   ❑ A pointer to the new object is stored in the collection.

The EX16A example beginning on page 398 shows serialization of an embedded collection of *CStudent* records.

The *Serialize* Function and the Application Framework

OK, so you know how to write *Serialize* functions, and you know that these function calls can be nested. But do you know when the first *Serialize* function gets called to start the serialization process? With the application framework, everything is keyed to the document (the object of a class derived from *CDocument*). When you choose Save or Open from the File menu, the application framework creates a *CArchive* object (and an underlying *CFile* object) and then calls your document class's *Serialize* function, passing a reference to the

CArchive object. Your derived document class *Serialize* function then serializes each of its nontemporary data members.

> **NOTE:** If you take a close look at any AppWizard-generated document class, you'll notice that the class includes the *DECLARE-_DYNCREATE* and *IMPLEMENT_DYNCREATE* macros instead of the *DECLARE_SERIAL* and *IMPLEMENT_SERIAL* macros. The *SERIAL* macros are not needed because document objects are never used in conjunction with the *CArchive* extraction operator or included in collections; the application framework calls the document's *Serialize* member function directly. You should include the *DECLARE_SERIAL* and *IMPLEMENT_SERIAL* macros in all other serializable classes.

The SDI Application

You've seen many SDI applications that have one document class and one view class. We'll stick to a single view class in this chapter, but we'll explore the interrelationships among the application object, the main frame window, the document, the view, the document template object, and the associated string and menu resources.

The Windows Application Object

For each of your applications, AppWizard has been quietly generating a class derived from *CWinApp*. It has also been generating a statement such as this:

```
CMyApp theApp;
```

What you're seeing here is the mechanism that starts an MFC application. The class *CMyApp* is derived from the class *CWinApp*, and *theApp* is a globally declared instance of the class. This global object is called the Windows application object. Here's a summary of the startup steps in a Microsoft Windows MFC library application:

1. Windows loads your program into memory.

2. The global object *theApp* is constructed. (All globally declared objects are constructed immediately when the program is loaded.)

3. Windows calls the global function *WinMain*, which is part of the MFC library. (*WinMain* is equivalent to the non-Windows *main* function—each is a main program entry point.)

4. *WinMain* searches for the one and only instance of a class derived from *CWinApp*.

5. *WinMain* calls the *InitInstance* member function for *theApp*, which is overridden in your derived application class.

6. Your overridden *InitInstance* function starts the process of loading a document and displaying the main frame and view windows.

7. *WinMain* calls the *Run* member function for *theApp*, which starts the processes of dispatching window messages and command messages.

You can override another important *CWinApp* member function. The *ExitInstance* function is called when the application terminates, after all its windows are closed.

NOTE: Windows allows multiple instances of programs to run. The *InitInstance* function is called each time a program instance starts up. In Win32, each instance runs as an independent process. It's only incidental that the same code is mapped to the virtual memory address space of each process. If you want to locate other running instances of your program, you must either call the Win32 *FindWindow* function or set up a shared data section or memory-mapped file for communication.

The Document Template Class

If you look at the *InitInstance* function that AppWizard generates for your derived application class, you'll see that the following statements are featured prominently:

```
CSingleDocTemplate* pDocTemplate;
pDocTemplate = new CSingleDocTemplate(
    IDR_MAINFRAME,
    RUNTIME_CLASS(CStudentDoc),
    RUNTIME_CLASS(CMainFrame),          // main SDI frame window
    RUNTIME_CLASS(CStudentView));
AddDocTemplate(pDocTemplate);
```

Unless you start doing fancy things with splitter windows and multiple views, this is the only time you'll actually see a document template object. In this case, it's an object of class *CSingleDocTemplate*, which is derived from *CDocTemplate*. The *CSingleDocTemplate* class applies only to SDI applications because SDI applications are limited to one document object. *AddDocTemplate* is a member function of class *CWinApp*.

The *AddDocTemplate* call, together with the document template constructor call, establishes the relationships among <u>classes</u>—the application class, the document class, the view window class, and the main frame window class. The application object exists, of course, before template construction, but the document, view, and frame objects are <u>not</u> constructed at this time. The application framework later dynamically constructs these objects when they are needed.

This dynamic construction is a sophisticated use of the C++ language. Through the use of the *DECLARE_DYNCREATE* and *IMPLEMENT_DYNCREATE* macros in the class declaration and implementation, the MFC library is able to construct objects of specified classes dynamically. If this dynamic construction capability weren't present, more relationships among your application's classes would have to be hard-coded. Your derived application class, for example, would need code for constructing document, view, and frame objects of your specific derived classes. This would compromise the object-oriented nature of your program.

> NOTE: The MFC library dynamic construction capability was designed before the runtime type identification (RTTI) feature was added to the C++ language. The original MFC implementation goes beyond RTTI, and the MFC library continues to use it for dynamic object construction. See Appendix C for a description of MFC library dynamic construction.

With the template system, all that's required in your application class is use of the *RUNTIME_CLASS* macro. Notice that the target class's declaration must be included for this macro to work.

Figure 16-2 illustrates the relationships among the various classes, and Figure 16-3 illustrates the object relationships. The application can have more than one template (and associated class groups), but when the SDI program is running, there can be only one document object and only one main frame window object.

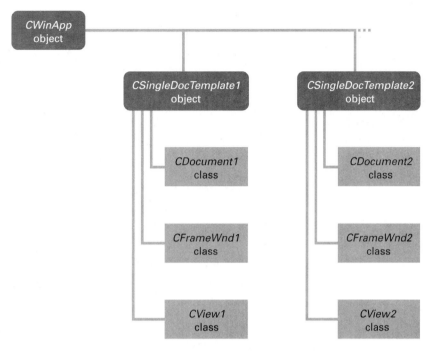

Figure 16-2.
Class relationships.

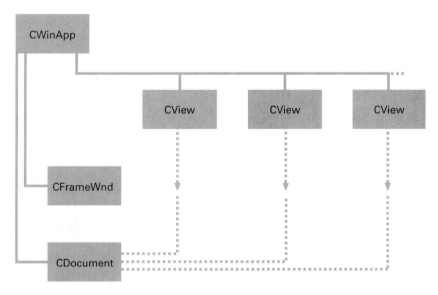

Figure 16-3.
Object relationships.

The Document Template Resource

The first *AddDocTemplate* parameter is *IDR_MAINFRAME*, the identifier for a string table resource. Here is the corresponding string that AppWizard might generate in the application's RC file:

```
IDR_MAINFRAME
    "MYAPP Windows Application\n"     // application window caption
    "MYAPP\n"                         // root for default document name
    "MYAPP Document\n"                // document type name
    "MYAPP Files (*.xyz)\n"           // document type description and
                                      //  filter
    ".xyz"                            // extension for documents of this
                                      //  type
```

> **NOTE:** The resource compiler won't accept the string concatenations as shown above. If you examine the ex16a.rc file, you'll see the substrings combined in one long string.

IDR_MAINFRAME specifies one string that is separated into substrings by newline characters (\n). The substrings show up in various places when the application executes. The string *xyz* is the default document file extension specified to AppWizard.

The *IDR_MAINFRAME* ID, in addition to specifying the application's strings, identifies the application's icon, toolbar resources, and menu. AppWizard generates these resources, and you can maintain them with the graphic editor.

So now you've seen how the *AddDocTemplate* call ties all the application elements together. Be aware, though, that no windows have been created yet, and therefore nothing appears on the screen.

Multiple Views of an SDI Document

Providing multiple views of an SDI document is a little more complicated. You could simply provide a menu item that allows the user to choose a view, or you could allow multiple views in a splitter window. Chapter 19 shows you how to use a splitter window.

Creating an Empty Document—The *CWinApp::OnFileNew* Function

After your application class's *InitInstance* function calls the *AddDocTemplate* member function, it calls *OnFileNew* (indirectly through *CWinApp::Process-ShellCommand*), another important *CWinApp* member function. *OnFileNew*, through a call to *CWinApp::OpenDocumentFile*, sorts through the web of interconnected class names and does the following:

1. Constructs the document object but does not attempt to read data from disk.

2. Constructs the main frame object (of class *CMainFrame*); also creates the main frame window but does not show it. The main frame window includes the *IDR_MAINFRAME* menu, the toolbar, and the status bar.

3. Constructs the view object; also creates the view window but doesn't show it.

4. Establishes connections among the document, main frame, and view <u>objects</u>. Do not confuse these object connections with the <u>class</u> connections established by the call to *AddDocTemplate*.

5. Calls the virtual *CDocument::OnNewDocument* member function for the document object, which calls the virtual *DeleteContents* function.

6. Calls the virtual *CView::OnInitialUpdate* member function for the view object.

7. Calls the virtual *CFrameWnd::ActivateFrame* for the frame object to show the main frame window together with the menus, view window, and control bars.

NOTE: Some of the functions listed above are not called directly by *OpenDocument* but are called indirectly through the application framework.

In an SDI application, the document, main frame, and view objects are created only once, and they last for the life of the program. The *CWinApp::OnFileNew* function is called by *InitInstance*. It's also called in response to the File New menu item. In this case, *OnFileNew* must behave a little differently. It can't construct the document, frame, and view objects because they're already constructed. Instead, it reuses the existing document object and performs steps 5, 6, and 7 above. Notice that *OnFileNew* always calls *DeleteContents* to empty the document.

The Document Class's *OnNewDocument* Function

You've seen the view class *OnInitialUpdate* member function and the document class *OnNewDocument* member function in Chapter 15. If an SDI application didn't reuse the same document object, you wouldn't need *OnNewDocument* because you could perform all document initialization in your document class constructor. Now you must override *OnNewDocument* to initialize your document object each time the user chooses File New or File Open. AppWizard helps you by providing a skeleton function in the derived document class it generates.

NOTE: It's a good idea to minimize the work you do in constructor functions. The fewer things you do, the less chance there is for the constructor to fail—and constructor failures are messy. Functions such as *CDocument::OnNewDocument* and *CView::OnInitial-Update* are excellent places to do initial housekeeping. If things aren't right, you can pop up a message box and, in the case of *OnNewDocument*, you can return *FALSE*. Be advised that both functions can be called more than once for the same object. If you need certain instructions executed only once, declare a "first time" flag data member.

Connecting File Open to Your Serialization Code— The *OnFileOpen* Function

When AppWizard generates an application, it maps the File Open menu item to the *CWinApp OnFileOpen* member function, which, through a call to the *CWinApp* function *OpenDocumentFile*, does the following:

1. Calls the virtual *CDocument::OnOpenDocument* member function for the already existing document object. This function prompts the user to select a file and then opens the file, constructs a *CArchive* object set for loading, and calls *CDocument::DeleteContents*.

2. Calls the document's *Serialize* function, which loads data from the archive.

3. Calls the view's *OnInitialUpdate* function.

NOTE: Some of the functions listed above are not called directly by *OpenDocument* but are called indirectly through the application framework.

The Most Recently Used (MRU) file list is a handy alternative to the File Open menu item. The application framework tracks the four most recently used files and displays their names on the File menu. These filenames are stored in the application's INI file or Windows registry between program executions.

The Document Class's *DeleteContents* Function

When you load an existing SDI document object from a disk file, you must somehow erase the existing contents of the document object. The best way to do this is to override the *CDocument::DeleteContents* virtual function in your derived document class. The overridden function, as you've seen in Chapter 15, does whatever is necessary to clean up your document class's data members. In response to both the File New and File Open menu items, the *CDocument OnFileNew* and *OnFileOpen* functions both call the *DeleteContents* function, which means *DeleteContents* is called immediately after the document object is first constructed. It's called again when you close a document.

If you want your document classes to work in SDI applications, plan on emptying the document's contents in the *DeleteContents* member function rather than in the destructor. Use the destructor only to clean up items that last for the life of the object.

Connecting File Save and File Save As to Your Serialization Code

When AppWizard generates an application, it maps the File Save menu item to the *OnFileSave* member function of the *CDocument* class. *OnFileSave* calls the *CDocument* function *OnSaveDocument*, which in turn calls your document's *Serialize* function with an archive object set for storing. The File Save As menu item is handled in a similar manner; it is mapped to the *CDocument* function *OnFileSaveAs*, which calls *OnSaveDocument*. Here the application framework does all the file management necessary to save a document on disk.

> N O T E : Yes, it is true that the File New and File Open menu options are mapped to <u>application</u> class member functions, but File Save and File Save As are mapped to <u>document</u> class member functions. File New is mapped to *OnFileNew*. The SDI version of *InitInstance* also calls *OnFileNew* (indirectly). No document object exists when the application framework calls *InitInstance*, so *OnFileNew* can't possibly be a member function of *CDocument*. When a document is saved, however, a document object certainly exists.

The Document's "Dirty" Flag

Many document-oriented applications for Windows track the user's modification of a document. If the user tries to close a document or exit the program, a message box asks whether the user wants to save the document. The MFC application framework directly supports this behavior with the *CDocument* data member *m_bModified*. This Boolean variable is *TRUE* if the document has been modified (has become "dirty"); otherwise, it is *FALSE*.

The protected *m_bModified* flag is accessed through the *CDocument* member functions *SetModifiedFlag* and *IsModified*. A document object's flag is set to *FALSE* when the document is created or read from disk and when it is saved on disk. You, the programmer, must use the *SetModifiedFlag* function to set the flag to *TRUE* when the document data changes.

In the EX16A example, you'll see how a one-line update command UI function can use *IsModified* to control the state of the disk button and the corresponding menu item. When the user modifies the file, the disk button changes to black; when the user saves the file, the button changes to gray.

NOTE: In one respect, MFC SDI applications behave a little differently from other Windows SDI applications such as Paint. Here's a typical sequence of events:

1. The user creates a document and saves it on disk under the name, say, test.dat.

2. The user modifies the document.

3. The user chooses File Open and then specifies test.dat.

When the user chooses File Open, Paint asks whether the user wants to save the changes made to the document (in step 2 above). If the user answers no, the program rereads the document from disk. An MFC application, on the other hand, assumes that the changes are permanent and does not reread the file.

The EX16A Example—SDI with Serialization

The EX16A example is similar to example EX15B. The student dialog and bitmaps are the same, and the view class is the same. Serialization has been added, together with an update command UI function for File Save. The header and implementation files for the view and document classes will be reused in example EX17A in the next chapter.

All the new code (code that is different from EX15B) is listed, with additions and changes to the AppWizard-generated code and ClassWizard code shaded.

A list of the files and classes in the EX16A example is shown in the table on the facing page:

Header File	Source Code File	Class	Description
ex16a.h	ex16a.cpp	*CEx16aApp*	Application class (from AppWizard)
		CAboutDlg	About dialog
MainFrm.h	MainFrm.cpp	*CMainFrame*	SDI main frame
StuDoc.h	StuDoc.cpp	*CStudentDoc*	Student document (from EX15B)
StuView.h	StuView.cpp	*CStudentView*	Student form view (from EX15B)
Student.h	Student.cpp	*CStudent*	Student record
StdAfx.h	StdAfx.cpp		Precompiled headers (with afxtempl.h included)

CStudent

The EX16A Student.h file is almost the same as the file in the EX15A project (shown in Figure 15-2 on page 348). The header contains the macro

```
DECLARE_SERIAL(CStudent)
```

instead of

```
DECLARE_DYNAMIC(CStudent)
```

and the implementation file contains the macro

```
IMPLEMENT_SERIAL(CStudent, CObject, 0)
```

instead of

```
IMPLEMENT_DYNAMIC(CStudent, Cobject)
```

The virtual *Serialize* function (as shown on page 407) has also been added.

CEx16aApp

The application class files, shown in Figure 16-4, contain mostly AppWizard-generated code. The only additions are the include statement for Student.h and the *SetRegistryKey* call. You should look at the *InitInstance* function, but it's difficult to follow because it's doing most of its work in called framework functions such as *ProcessShellCommand*.

EX16A.H

```
#ifndef __AFXWIN_H__
    #error include 'StdAfx.h' before including this file for PCH
#endif

#include "resource.h"        // main symbols

/////////////////////////////////////////////////////////////////////////
// CEx16aApp:
// See ex16a.cpp for the implementation of this class
//

class CEx16aApp : public CWinApp
{
public:
    CEx16aApp();

// Overrides
    // ClassWizard generated virtual function overrides
    //{{AFX_VIRTUAL(CEx16aApp)
    public:
    virtual BOOL InitInstance();
    //}}AFX_VIRTUAL

// Implementation

    //{{AFX_MSG(CEx16aApp)
    afx_msg void OnAppAbout();
    // NOTE - the ClassWizard will add and remove member functions here.
    //    DO NOT EDIT what you see in these blocks of generated code !
    //}}AFX_MSG
    DECLARE_MESSAGE_MAP()
};
```

EX16A.CPP

```
#include "StdAfx.h"
#include "ex16a.h"

#include "Student.h"
#include "MainFrm.h"
#include "StuDoc.h"
#include "StuView.h"
```

Figure 16-4.   *(continued)*

The ex16a.h and ex16a.cpp listings.

Figure 16-4. *continued*

```
#ifdef _DEBUG
#undef THIS_FILE
static char THIS_FILE[] = __FILE__;
#endif

/////////////////////////////////////////////////////////////////////////
// CEx16aApp

BEGIN_MESSAGE_MAP(CEx16aApp, CWinApp)
    //{{AFX_MSG_MAP(CEx16aApp)
    ON_COMMAND(ID_APP_ABOUT, OnAppAbout)
    // NOTE - the ClassWizard will add and remove mapping macros here.
    //     DO NOT EDIT what you see in these blocks of generated code!
    //}}AFX_MSG_MAP
    // Standard file based document commands
    ON_COMMAND(ID_FILE_NEW, CWinApp::OnFileNew)
    ON_COMMAND(ID_FILE_OPEN, CWinApp::OnFileOpen)
END_MESSAGE_MAP()

/////////////////////////////////////////////////////////////////////////
// CEx16aApp construction

CEx16aApp::CEx16aApp()
{
    // TODO: add construction code here,
    // Place all significant initialization in InitInstance
}

/////////////////////////////////////////////////////////////////////////
// The one and only CEx16aApp object

CEx16aApp theApp;

/////////////////////////////////////////////////////////////////////////
// CEx16aApp initialization

BOOL CEx16aApp::InitInstance()
{
    AfxEnableControlContainer();

    // Standard initialization
    // If you are not using these features and wish to reduce the size
    //  of your final executable, you should remove from the following
    //  the specific initialization routines you do not need.
```

(continued)

Figure 16-4. *continued*

```
#ifdef _AFXDLL
    Enable3dControls();    // Call this when using MFC in a shared DLL
#else
    Enable3dControlsStatic();   // Call this when linking
                                //  to MFC statically
#endif

    SetRegistryKey("Inside Visual C++");
    LoadStdProfileSettings();  // Load standard INI file options
                               //  (including MRU)

    // Register the application's document templates.
    //  Document templates serve as the connection between
    //  documents, frame windows and views.

    CSingleDocTemplate* pDocTemplate;
    pDocTemplate = new CSingleDocTemplate(
        IDR_MAINFRAME,
        RUNTIME_CLASS(CStudentDoc),
        RUNTIME_CLASS(CMainFrame),         // main SDI frame window
        RUNTIME_CLASS(CStudentView));
    AddDocTemplate(pDocTemplate);

    // Enable DDE Execute open
    EnableShellOpen();
    RegisterShellFileTypes(TRUE);

    // Parse command line for standard shell commands, DDE, file open
    CCommandLineInfo cmdInfo;
    ParseCommandLine(cmdInfo);

    // Dispatch commands specified on the command line
    if (!ProcessShellCommand(cmdInfo))
        return FALSE;

    // Enable drag/drop open
    m_pMainWnd->DragAcceptFiles();

    return TRUE;
}


///////////////////////////////////////////////////////////////////
// CAboutDlg dialog used for App About
```

(continued)

Figure 16-4. *continued*

```
class CAboutDlg : public CDialog
{
public:
    CAboutDlg();

// Dialog Data
    //{{AFX_DATA(CAboutDlg)
    enum { IDD = IDD_ABOUTBOX };
    //}}AFX_DATA

// Implementation
protected:
    virtual void DoDataExchange(CDataExchange* pDX);// DDX/DDV support
    //{{AFX_MSG(CAboutDlg)
        // No message handlers
    //}}AFX_MSG
    DECLARE_MESSAGE_MAP()
};

CAboutDlg::CAboutDlg() : CDialog(CAboutDlg::IDD)
{
    //{{AFX_DATA_INIT(CAboutDlg)
    //}}AFX_DATA_INIT
}

void CAboutDlg::DoDataExchange(CDataExchange* pDX)
{
    CDialog::DoDataExchange(pDX);
    //{{AFX_DATA_MAP(CAboutDlg)
    //}}AFX_DATA_MAP
}

BEGIN_MESSAGE_MAP(CAboutDlg, CDialog)
    //{{AFX_MSG_MAP(CAboutDlg)
        // No message handlers
    //}}AFX_MSG_MAP
END_MESSAGE_MAP()

// App command to run the dialog
void CEx16aApp::OnAppAbout()
{
    CAboutDlg aboutDlg;
    aboutDlg.DoModal();
}
```

CFrameWnd

The main frame window class code, shown in Figure 16-5, is almost unchanged from the code that AppWizard generated. The toolbar button constants are added, and the overridden *ActivateFrame* function exists solely for trace purposes.

MAINFRM.H

```
class CMainFrame : public CFrameWnd
{
protected: // create from serialization only
    CMainFrame();
    DECLARE_DYNCREATE(CMainFrame)

// Attributes
public:

// Operations
public:

// Overrides
    // ClassWizard generated virtual function overrides
    //{{AFX_VIRTUAL(CMainFrame)
    virtual BOOL PreCreateWindow(CREATESTRUCT& cs);
    virtual void ActivateFrame(int nCmdShow);
    //}}AFX_VIRTUAL

// Implementation
public:
    virtual ~CMainFrame();
#ifdef _DEBUG
    virtual void AssertValid() const;
    virtual void Dump(CDumpContext& dc) const;
#endif

protected:  // control bar embedded members
    CStatusBar   m_wndStatusBar;
    CToolBar     m_wndToolBar;

// Generated message map functions
protected:
    //{{AFX_MSG(CMainFrame)
    afx_msg int OnCreate(LPCREATESTRUCT lpCreateStruct);
```

Figure 16-5. *(continued)*
The CMainFrame *class listing.*

Figure 16-5. *continued*

```
// NOTE - the ClassWizard will add and remove member functions here.
//    DO NOT EDIT what you see in these blocks of generated code!
//}}AFX_MSG
DECLARE_MESSAGE_MAP()

};
```

MAINFRM.CPP

```
#include "stdafx.h"
#include "ex16a.h"

#include "MainFrm.h"

#ifdef _DEBUG
#undef THIS_FILE
static char THIS_FILE[] = __FILE__;
#endif

/////////////////////////////////////////////////////////////////
// CMainFrame

IMPLEMENT_DYNCREATE(CMainFrame, CFrameWnd)

BEGIN_MESSAGE_MAP(CMainFrame, CFrameWnd)
    //{{AFX_MSG_MAP(CMainFrame)
    // NOTE - the ClassWizard will add and remove mapping macros here.
    //    DO NOT EDIT what you see in these blocks of generated code !
    ON_WM_CREATE()
    //}}AFX_MSG_MAP
END_MESSAGE_MAP()

static UINT indicators[] =
{
    ID_SEPARATOR,           // status line indicator
    ID_INDICATOR_CAPS,
    ID_INDICATOR_NUM,
    ID_INDICATOR_SCRL,
};

/////////////////////////////////////////////////////////////////
// CMainFrame construction/destruction

CMainFrame::CMainFrame()
{
```

(continued)

Figure 16-5. *continued*

```
      // TODO: add member initialization code here

}

CMainFrame::~CMainFrame()
{
}

int CMainFrame::OnCreate(LPCREATESTRUCT lpCreateStruct)
{
    if (CFrameWnd::OnCreate(lpCreateStruct) == -1)
        return -1;

    if (!m_wndToolBar.Create(this) ¦¦
        !m_wndToolBar.LoadToolBar(IDR_MAINFRAME))
    {
        TRACE0("Failed to create toolbar\n");
        return -1;      // fail to create
    }

    if (!m_wndStatusBar.Create(this) ¦¦
        !m_wndStatusBar.SetIndicators(indicators,
          sizeof(indicators)/sizeof(UINT)))
    {
        TRACE0("Failed to create status bar\n");
        return -1;      // fail to create
    }

    // TODO: Remove this if you don't want tool tips
    m_wndToolBar.SetBarStyle(m_wndToolBar.GetBarStyle() ¦
        CBRS_TOOLTIPS ¦ CBRS_FLYBY);

    // TODO: Delete these three lines if you don't want the toolbar to
    //   be dockable
    m_wndToolBar.EnableDocking(CBRS_ALIGN_ANY);
    EnableDocking(CBRS_ALIGN_ANY);
    DockControlBar(&m_wndToolBar);

    return 0;
}

BOOL CMainFrame::PreCreateWindow(CREATESTRUCT& cs)
{
    // TODO: Modify the Window class or styles here by modifying
    //   the CREATESTRUCT cs
```

(continued)

Figure 16-5. *continued*

```
      return CFrameWnd::PreCreateWindow(cs);
}
/////////////////////////////////////////////////////////////////////
// CMainFrame diagnostics

#ifdef _DEBUG
void CMainFrame::AssertValid() const
{
    CFrameWnd::AssertValid();
}

void CMainFrame::Dump(CDumpContext& dc) const
{
    CFrameWnd::Dump(dc);
}

#endif //_DEBUG

/////////////////////////////////////////////////////////////////////
// CMainFrame message handlers

void CMainFrame::ActivateFrame(int nCmdShow)
{
    TRACE("Entering CMainFrame::ActivateFrame\n");
    CFrameWnd::ActivateFrame(nCmdShow);
}
```

CStudentDoc

The *CStudentDoc* class is the same as the *CStudentDoc* class from the previous chapter (shown in Figure 15-4 on page 365) except for three functions: *Serialize, OnOpenDocument,* and *OnUpdateFileSave.*

Serialize

One line has been added to the AppWizard-generated function to serialize the document's student list, as shown here:

```
/////////////////////////////////////////////////////////////////////
// CStudentDoc serialization

void CStudentDoc::Serialize(CArchive& ar)
{
```

(continued)

```
    if (ar.IsStoring())
    {
        // TODO: add storing code here for other data members
    }
    else
    {
        // TODO: add loading code here for other data members
    }
    m_studentList.Serialize(ar);
}
```

OnOpenDocument

This virtual function is overridden only for the purpose of displaying a *TRACE* message, as shown here:

```
BOOL CStudentDoc::OnOpenDocument(const char* pszPathName)
{
    TRACE("Entering CStudentDoc::OnOpenDocument\n");
    if (!CDocument::OnOpenDocument(pszPathName))
        return FALSE;
    return TRUE;
}
```

OnUpdateFileSave

This is a message map function that grays the File Save toolbar button when the document is in the unmodified state. The view controls this state by calling the document's *SetModifiedFlag* function, as shown here:

```
void CStudentDoc::OnUpdateFileSave(CCmdUI* pCmdUI)
{
    // disable disk toolbar button if file is not modified
    pCmdUI->Enable(IsModified());
}
```

CStudentView

The code for the *CStudentView* class comes from the previous chapter. Figure 15-5 on page 369 shows the code.

AppWizard and EX16A

If you want a default filename extension for your application and you want Explorer launch and drag and drop, as described later in this chapter, you must do one thing when you first run AppWizard. The AppWizard Step 4 dialog has an Advanced button. When you click this button, the Advanced Options dialog appears. You must enter the filename extension in the upper left control, as shown here:

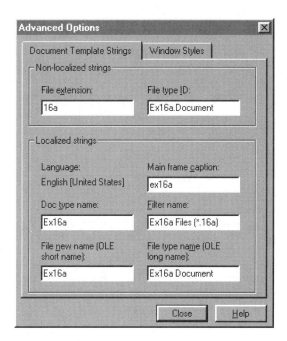

This ensures that the document template resource string contains the correct default extension and that the correct Explorer-related coded is inserted into your application class *InitInstance* member function. You can change some of the other resource substrings if you want.

Testing the EX16A Application

Build the program and start it from the debugger, and then test it by typing some data and saving it on disk with the filename TEST.16A. (You don't need to type the *.16A*.)

Exit the program, and then restart it and open the file you saved. Did the names come back? Take a look at the Debug window and observe the sequence of function calls. Is the following sequence produced when you start the application?

```
Entering CStudentDoc constructor
Entering CStudentView constructor
Entering CStudentDoc::OnNewDocument
Entering CStudentDoc::DeleteContents
Entering CStudentView::OnInitialUpdate
Entering CStudentView::OnUpdate
Entering CMainFrame::ActivateFrame
Entering CStudentDoc::OnOpenDocument
Entering CStudentDoc::DeleteContents
Entering CStudentDoc::Serialize
Entering CStudent::Serialize
Entering CStudent::Serialize
Entering CStudent::Serialize
Entering CStudentView::OnInitialUpdate
Entering CStudentView::OnUpdate
Entering CMainFrame::ActivateFrame
```

Explorer Launch and Drag and Drop

In the past, PC users were accustomed to starting up a program and then selecting a disk file (sometimes called a document) that contained data the program understood. Many MS-DOS programs worked this way; the old Windows Program Manager improved things by allowing the user to double-click on a program icon instead of typing a program name. Meanwhile, Apple Macintosh users were double-clicking on a document icon; the Macintosh operating system figured out which program to run.

The current Windows Explorer (and the Windows NT File Manager) still lets users double-click on a program, but it also lets users double-click on a document icon to run the document's program. But how does Explorer know which program to run? Explorer uses the Windows registry to make the connection between document and program. The link starts with the three-character filename extension that you typed into AppWizard, but as you'll see there's more to it than that. Once the association is made, users can launch your program by double-clicking on its document icon or by dragging the icon from Explorer to a running instance of your program. In addition, users can drag the icon to a printer, and your program will print it.

Program Registration

In Chapter 14, you saw how you could store data in the Windows registry by adding a call to *SetRegistryKey* in your *InitInstance* function. Whether or not you include the *SetRegistryKey* call, your program can write file association information in a different part of the registry on startup. To activate this feature, you must type in the filename extension when you create the application with AppWizard. After you do that, AppWizard adds the extension as a substring in your template string, and it adds the following line in your *InitInstance* function:

```
RegisterShellFileTypes();
```

Now your program adds two items to the registry. Under the HKEY_CLASSES_ROOT top-level key, it adds a subkey and a data string as shown here (for the EX16A example):

```
.16A = Ex16a.Document
```

The data item is the file type ID that AppWizard has chosen for you. Ex16a.Document, in turn, is the key for finding the program itself. The registry entries for Ex16a.Document, also beneath HKEY_CLASSES_ROOT, are shown here:

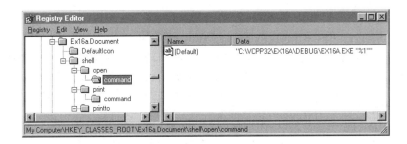

Notice that the registry contains the full pathname of the EX16A program. Now Explorer can use the registry to navigate from the extension to the file type ID to the actual program itself. After the extension is registered, Explorer finds the document's icon and displays it next to the filename as shown here:

test.16A

Enabling Embedded Launch

An embedded launch occurs when the user double-clicks a document icon in Explorer. The launch is a two-step process. First the program is executed with the */Embedding* parameter. After it's running, the program gets a message via

Windows' Dynamic Data Exchange (DDE) that tells it to load a file.

AppWizard generates the following call to a *CWinApp* member function in the *InitInstance* function:

```
EnableShellOpen();
```

This function does the setup that is required for the program to accept DDE messages.

Enabling Drag and Drop

If you want your already-running program to open files dragged from Explorer, you must call the *CWnd* function *DragAcceptFiles* for the application's main frame window. The application object's public data member *m_pMainWnd* points to the *CFrameWnd* (or *CMDIFrameWnd*) object. The following line in *InitInstance*, generated by AppWizard, enables drag and drop:

```
m_pMainWnd->DragAcceptFiles();
```

Program Startup Parameters

When an MFC library SDI program is run from Program Manager, it usually has no command-line parameter. When it's run from Explorer (an embedded launch), the program is run with the */Embedding* parameter. The *InitInstance* function processes the command line with calls to *ProcessCommandLine* and *ProcessShellCommand*.

If the command line contains something that looks like a filename, the program immediately loads that file. Thus, you create a Windows shortcut that can run your program with a specific document file.

Responding to DDE Messages

The MFC library base classes take care of the DDE messages that result from drag and drop or an Explorer embedded launch (with the */Embedding* command-line parameter). In drag and drop, the application framework calls the *CWinApp* function *OpenDocumentFile* with the filename as a parameter. In an embedded launch, the application framework calls two *CWinApp* functions: *OnDDECommand* and *OpenDocumentFile*. You normally don't need to override these functions in your derived application class. Let the application framework do the work.

Experimenting with Embedded Launch and Drag and Drop

Once you have built EX16A, you can try running it with Explorer or with the Windows NT File Manager. You must execute the program directly, however, in order to write the initial entries in the registry. Be sure that you've saved at least one 16A file to disk, and then exit EX16A. Start Explorer, and then open the \VCPP32\EX16A directory. Double-click on one of the 16A files in the right panel. Your program should start with the selected file loaded. Now, with both EX16A and Explorer open on the desktop, try dragging another file from Explorer to the EX16A window. The program should open the new file just as if you had selected File Open from the EX16A menu.

You might also want to look at the EX16A entries in the Windows registry. Run the Regedit program (possibly named Regedt32 in Windows NT), and expand the HKEY_CLASSES_ROOT key. Look under ".16A" and "Ex16a.Document." Also expand the HKEY_CURRENT_USER (or HKEY_USERS) key, and look under "Software." You should see a Recent File list under the subkey ex16a. The EX16A program called *SetRegistryKey* with an empty string, so the program name goes directly beneath "Software."

CHAPTER SEVENTEEN

Reading and Writing Documents—MDI

This chapter introduces the Microsoft Foundation Class (MFC) Library version 4.0 Multiple Document Interface (MDI) application and explains how it reads and writes its document files. The MDI application seems to be the preferred MFC library program style. It's the AppWizard default, and most of the sample programs that come with Microsoft Visual C++ are MDI applications.

Here you'll learn the similarities and differences between Single Document Interface (SDI) and MDI applications, and you'll learn how to convert an SDI application to an MDI application. Be sure you thoroughly understand the SDI application, as described in Chapter 16, before you attack the MDI application.

The MDI Application

Before you look at the MFC library code for MDI applications, you should be familiar with the operation of Windows MDI programs. Take a close look at the Visual C++ Developer Studio now. It's an MDI application whose "multiple documents" are program source code files. The Developer Studio is not the most typical MDI application, however, because it collects its documents into projects. It's better to examine Microsoft Word for Windows or, better yet, to examine a real MFC library MDI application—the kind that App-Wizard generates.

A Typical MDI Application, MFC Style

This chapter's first example, EX17A, is an MDI version of EX16A. Run the EX16A example to see an illustration of the SDI version after the user has selected a file. Now look at the MDI equivalent, shown in Figure 17-1 on the following page.

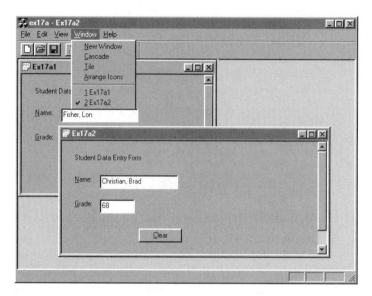

Figure 17-1.
The EX17A application with two files open and the Window menu shown.

The user has two separate document files open, each in a separate MDI child window, but only one child window is active—the lower window, which lies on top of the other child window. The application has only one menu and one toolbar, and all commands are routed to the active child window. The main window's title bar reflects the name of the active child window's document file.

The child window's minimize box allows the user to reduce the child window to an icon in the main window. The application's Window menu (shown in Figure 17-1) lets the user control the presentation through the following items:

Menu Item	Action
New Window	Opens an additional child window for the selected document
Cascade	Arranges the existing windows in an overlapped pattern
Tile	Arranges the existing windows in a nonoverlapped, tiled pattern
Arrange Icons	Arranges iconized windows in the frame window
(document names)	Selects the corresponding child window and brings it to the top

If the user saves and closes both child windows (and opens the File menu), the application looks like Figure 17-2.

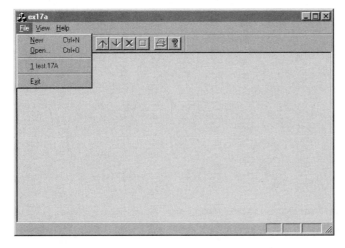

Figure 17-2.
EX17A with no child windows.

The File menu is different: most toolbar buttons are disabled, and the window caption does not show a filename. About the only thing the user can do is start a new document or open an existing document from disk.

Figure 17-3 shows the application when it first starts up and a new document is created. The single child window has been maximized.

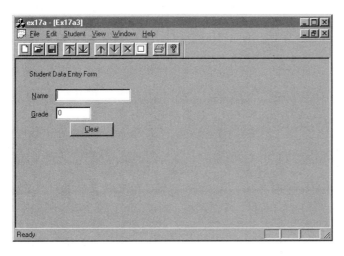

Figure 17-3.
EX17A with initial child window.

For Win32 Programmers

Starting with version 3.0, Windows has directly supported MDI applications. The MFC library builds on this Windows support to create an MDI environment that parallels the SDI environment. In a Win32 MDI application, a main application frame window contains the menu and a single client window. The client window manages various child windows that correspond to documents. The MDI client window has its own preregistered window class (not to be confused with a C++ class) with a procedure that handles special messages such as WM_MDICASCADE and WM_MDITILE. An MDI child window procedure is similar to the window procedure for an SDI main window.

In the MFC library, the *CMDIFrameWnd* class encapsulates the functions of both the main frame window and the MDI client window. This class has message handlers for all the Windows MDI messages and thus can manage its child windows, which are represented by objects of class *CMDIChildWnd*.

The single, empty child window has the default document name Ex17a1. This name is based on the Doc Type Name you selected in the AppWizard Classes dialog, Ex17a. The first new file is Ex17a1, the second is Ex17a2, and so forth. The user normally chooses a different name when saving the document.

MFC library MDI applications, like many commercial MDI applications, start up with a new, empty document. (The Developer Studio is an exception.) If you want your application to start up with a blank frame, you can remove the *OnFileNew* call in the application class file, as shown in example EX17A.

The MDI Application Object

You're probably wondering how an MDI application works and what code makes it different from an SDI application. Actually, the startup sequences are pretty much the same. An application object, of a class derived from class *CWinApp*, has an overridden *InitInstance* member function. This *InitInstance* function is somewhat different from the SDI *InitInstance* function, starting with the call to *AddDocTemplate*.

The MDI Document Template Class

The MDI template construction call in *InitInstance* looks like this:

```
CMultiDocTemplate* pDocTemplate;
pDocTemplate = new CMultiDocTemplate(
    IDR_EX17ATYPE,
    RUNTIME_CLASS(CStudentDoc),
    RUNTIME_CLASS(CChildFrame), // custom MDI child frame
    RUNTIME_CLASS(CStudentView));
AddDocTemplate(pDocTemplate);
```

Like the *CSingleDocTemplate* class you saw in Chapter 16, the *CMulti-DocTemplate* class allows an application to use multiple document types, but, unlike the *CSingleDocTemplate* class, it allows the simultaneous existence of more than one document object. This is the essence of the MDI application.

The single *AddDocTemplate* call shown above permits the MDI application to support multiple child windows, each connected to a document object and a view object. It's also possible to have several child windows (and corresponding view objects) connected to the same document object. In this chapter, we'll start with only one view class and one document class. You'll see multiple view classes and multiple document classes in Chapter 19.

NOTE: When your application is running, the document template object maintains a list of active document objects that were created from the template. The *CMultiDocTemplate* member functions *GetFirstDocPosition* and *GetNextDoc* allow you to iterate through the list. Use *CDocument::GetDocTemplate* to navigate from a document to its template.

The MDI Frame Window and the MDI Child Window

The SDI examples had only one frame window class and only one frame window object. For SDI applications, AppWizard generated a class named *CMainFrame*, which was derived from the class *CFrameWnd*. An MDI application has two frame window classes and many frame objects, as shown in the following table. The MDI frame–view window relationship is shown in Figure 17-4 on the following page.

Base Class	AppWizard-Generated Class	Number of Objects	Menu and Control Bars	Contains a View	Object Constructed
CMDIFrameWnd	*CMainFrame*	1 only	Yes	No	In application class's *InitInstance* function
CMDIChildWnd	*CChildFrame*	1 per child window	No	Yes	By application framework when a new child window is opened

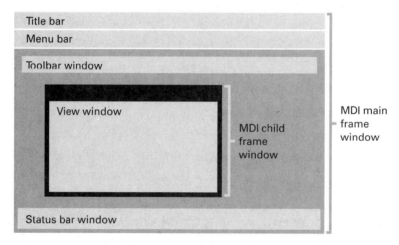

Figure 17-4.
The MDI frame–view window relationship.

In an SDI application, the *CMainFrame* object frames the application <u>and</u> contains the view object. In an MDI application, the two roles are separated. Now the *CMainFrame* object is constructed in *InitInstance,* and the *CChildFrame* object contains the view. AppWizard generates code as shown here:

```
CMainFrame* pMainFrame = new CMainFrame;
if (!pMainFrame->LoadFrame(IDR_MAINFRAME))
    return FALSE;
m_pMainWnd = pMainFrame;
pMainFrame->ShowWindow(m_nCmdShow);
pMainFrame->UpdateWindow();
```

The application framework can create the *CChildFrame* objects dynamically because the *CChildFrame* runtime class pointer is passed to the *CMultiDoc-Template* constructor.

NOTE: The MDI *InitInstance* function sets the *CWinApp* data member *m_pMainWnd* to point to the application's main frame window. This means you can access *m_pMainWnd* through the global *AfxGetApp* function anytime you need to get your application's main frame window.

The Main Frame and Document Template Resources

An MDI application (EX17A, as described later in this chapter) has two separate string and menu resources, identified by the *IDR_MAINFRAME* and *IDR_EX17ATYPE* constants. The first resource set goes with the empty main frame window; the second set goes with the occupied main frame window. Here are the two string resources with substrings broken out:

```
IDR_MAINFRAME
    "ex17a"                       // application window caption

IDR_MYDOCTYPE
    "\n"                          // application window caption
    "Ex17a\n"                     // root for default document name
    "Ex17a\n"                     // document type name
    "Ex17a Files (*.17a)\n"       // document type description and filter
    ".17a\n"                      // extension for documents of this type
    "Ex17a.Document\n"            // registry file type ID
    "Ex17a Document"              // registry file type description
```

NOTE: The resource compiler won't accept the string concatenations as shown above. If you examine the EX17A.RC file, you'll see the substrings combined in one long string.

The application window caption comes from the *IDR_MAINFRAME* string. When a document is open, the document filename is appended. The last two substrings in the *IDR_EX17ATYPE* string are there to support embedded launch and drag and drop.

Creating an Empty Document—The *CWinApp::OnFileNew* Function

The MDI *InitInstance* function calls *OnFileNew*, as did the SDI *InitInstance* function. This time, however, the main frame window has already been created. *OnFileNew*, through a call to the *CWinApp* function *OpenDocumentFile*, now does the following:

1. Constructs a document object but does not attempt to read data from disk.

2. Constructs a child frame window object (of class *CChildFrame*). Also creates the child frame window but does not show it. In the main frame window, the *IDR_MAINFRAME* menu is replaced by the *IDR_EX17ATYPE* menu. *IDR_EX17ATYPE* also identifies an icon resource that is used when the child window is minimized within the frame.

3. Constructs a view object. Also creates the view window but does not show it.

4. Establishes connections among the document, the main frame, and view <u>objects</u>. Do not confuse these object connections with the <u>class</u> associations established by the call to *AddDocTemplate*.

5. Calls the virtual *OnNewDocument* member function for the document object.

6. Calls the virtual *OnInitialUpdate* member function for the view object.

7. Calls the virtual *ActivateFrame* member function for the child frame object to show the frame window and the view window.

The *OnFileNew* function is also called in response to the File New menu command. In an MDI application, *OnFileNew* performs exactly the same steps as it does when called from *InitInstance*.

NOTE: Some functions listed above are not called directly by *OpenDocumentFile* but are called indirectly through the application framework.

Creating an Additional View for an Existing Document

If you choose the New Window command from the Window menu, the application framework opens a new child window that's linked to the currently selected document. The associated *CMDIFrameWnd* function, *OnWindowNew*, does the following:

1. Constructs a child frame object (of class *CChildFrame*). Also creates the child frame window but does not show it.

2. Constructs a view object. Also creates the view window but does not show it.

3. Establishes connections between the new view object and the existing document and main frame objects.

4. Calls the virtual *OnInitialUpdate* member function for the view object.

5. Calls the virtual *ActivateFrame* member function for the child frame object to show the frame window and the view window.

Loading and Storing Documents

In MDI applications, documents are loaded and stored the same way as in SDI applications, but with two important differences: a new document object is constructed each time a document file is loaded from disk, and the document object is destroyed when the child window is closed. Don't worry about clearing a document's contents before loading—but you should override the *CDocument::DeleteContents* function anyway to make the class portable to the SDI environment.

Multiple Document Templates

An MDI application can support multiple document templates through multiple calls to the *AddDocTemplate* function. Each template can specify a different combination of document, view, and MDI child frame classes. When the user chooses New from the File menu, the application framework displays a list box that allows the user to choose a template by name as specified in the string resource (document type substring). Multiple *AddDocTemplate* calls are not fully supported in SDI applications because the document, view, and frame objects are constructed once for the life of the application.

> **NOTE:** When your application is running, the application object maintains a list of active document template objects. The *CWinApp* member functions *GetFirstDocTemplatePosition* and *GetNextDocTemplate* allow you to iterate through the list. These functions, together with the functions that iterate through a template's documents, give you access to all the application's document objects.

If you don't want the template list box, you can edit the file menu to add a New choice for each document type. Code the command message handlers as follows, using the document type substring from each template:

```
void CMyApp::OnFileNewStudent()
{
    OpenNewDocument("Studnt");
}
void CMyApp::OnFileNewTeacher()
{
    OpenNewDocument("Teachr");
}
```

Then add the OpenNewDocument helper function as follows:

```
BOOL CMypp::OpenNewDocument(const CString& strTarget)
{
    CString strDocName;
    CDocTemplate* pSelectedTemplate;
    POSITION pos = GetFirstDocTemplatePosition();
    while (pos != NULL) {
      pSelectedTemplate =
          (CDocTemplate*) GetNextDocTemplate(pos);
      ASSERT(pSelectedTemplate != NULL);
      ASSERT(pSelectedTemplate->IsKindOf(
          RUNTIME_CLASS(CDocTemplate)));
      pSelectedTemplate->GetDocString(strDocName,
          CDocTemplate::docName);
      if (strDocName == strTarget) { // from template's
                                     //  string resource
        pSelectedTemplate->OpenDocumentFile(NULL);
        return TRUE;
      }
    }
    return FALSE;
}
void CMainFrame::SwitchToView(eView nView)
{
    CView* pOldActiveView = GetActiveView();
    CView* pNewActiveView = (CView*)GetDlgItem(nView);
    if (pNewActiveView == NULL) {
      switch(nView)  {
      case STRING:
          pNewActiveView = (CView*)new CStringView;
          break;
      case HEX:
          pNewActiveView = (CView*)new CHexView;
          break;
      }
```

```
        CCreateContext context;
        context.m_pCurrentDoc =
        pOldActiveView->GetDocument();
        pNewActiveView->Create(NULL, NULL, OL,
            CFrameWnd::rectDefault, this, nView, &context);
        pNewActiveView->OnInitialUpdate();
    }
    SetActiveView(pNewActiveView);
    pNewActiveView->ShowWindow(SW_SHOW);
    pOldActiveView->ShowWindow(SW_HIDE);
    pOldActiveView->SetDlgCtrlID(
        pOldActiveView->GetRuntimeClass()
        == RUNTIME_CLASS(CStringView) ? STRING : HEX);
    pNewActiveView->SetDlgCtrlID(AFX_IDW_PANE_FIRST);
    RecalcLayout();
}
```

Explorer Launch and Drag and Drop

Explorer launch and drag and drop work much the same way in an MDI application as they do in an SDI application. If you drag a file from Explorer to your MDI main frame window, the program opens a new child frame (with associated document and view) just as if you'd selected the File Open command. As with SDI applications, you must use the AppWizard Advanced button to specify the filename extension.

The EX17A Example

This example is the MDI version of the EX16A example in the previous chapter. It uses exactly the same document and view class code and the same resources (except the program name). The application code and main frame class code are different, however. All the new code is listed here, including the code that AppWizard generates.

A list of the files and classes in the EX17A example are shown in the table on the following page:

Header File	Source Code File	Class	Description
ex17a.h	ex17a.cpp	*CEx17aApp*	Application class (from AppWizard)
		CAboutDlg	About dialog
MainFrm.h	MainFrm.cpp	*CMainFrame*	MDI main frame
ChildFrm.h	ChildFrm.cpp	*CChildFrame*	MDI child frame
StuDoc.h	StuDoc.cpp	*CStudentDoc*	Student document (from EX16A)
StuView.h	StuView.cpp	*CStudentView*	Student form view (from EX15B)
Student.h	Student.cpp	*CStudent*	Student record (from EX16A)
StdAfx.h	StdAfx.h		Precompiled headers (with afxtempl.h included)

CEx17aApp

In the *CEx17aApp* source code listing, two functions, *OpenDocumentFile* and *OnDDECommand*, are overridden only for the purpose of inserting *TRACE* statements. Also, the *OnFileNew* call in *InitInstance* has been commented out to prevent the creation of an empty document window on startup. Figure 17-5 shows the source code.

EX17A.H

```
#ifndef __AFXWIN_H__
    #error include 'stdafx.h' before including this file for PCH
#endif

#include "resource.h"        // main symbols


/////////////////////////////////////////////////////////////////////////////
// CEx17aApp:
// See ex17a.cpp for the implementation of this class
//

class CEx17aApp : public CWinApp
{
```

Figure 17-5. *(continued)*
The CEx17aApp *source code listing.*

Figure 17-5. *continued*

```
public:
    CEx17aApp();

// Overrides
    // ClassWizard generated virtual function overrides
    //{{AFX_VIRTUAL(CEx17aApp)
    public:
    virtual BOOL InitInstance();
    //}}AFX_VIRTUAL

// Implementation

    //{{AFX_MSG(CEx17aApp)
    afx_msg void OnAppAbout();
    // NOTE - the ClassWizard will add and remove member functions here.
    //     DO NOT EDIT what you see in these blocks of generated code !
    //}}AFX_MSG
    DECLARE_MESSAGE_MAP()
};
```

EX17A.CPP

```
// ex17a.cpp : Defines the class behaviors for the application
//

#include "StdAfx.h"
#include "ex17a.h"

#include "Student.h"
#include "MainFrm.h"
#include "ChildFrm.h"
#include "StuDoc.h"
#include "StuView.h"

#ifdef _DEBUG
#undef THIS_FILE
static char THIS_FILE[] = __FILE__;
#endif

/////////////////////////////////////////////////////////////////////
// CEx17aApp

BEGIN_MESSAGE_MAP(CEx17aApp, CWinApp)
    //{{AFX_MSG_MAP(CEx17aApp)
    ON_COMMAND(ID_APP_ABOUT, OnAppAbout)
    // NOTE - the ClassWizard will add and remove mapping macros here.
```

(continued)

Figure 17-5. *continued*

```
//      DO NOT EDIT what you see in these blocks of generated code!
//}}AFX_MSG_MAP
// Standard file based document commands
ON_COMMAND(ID_FILE_NEW, CWinApp::OnFileNew)
ON_COMMAND(ID_FILE_OPEN, CWinApp::OnFileOpen)
END_MESSAGE_MAP()

/////////////////////////////////////////////////////////////////////
// CEx17aApp construction

CEx17aApp::CEx17aApp()
{
    // TODO: add construction code here,
    // Place all significant initialization in InitInstance
}

/////////////////////////////////////////////////////////////////////
// The one and only CEx17aApp object

CEx17aApp theApp;

/////////////////////////////////////////////////////////////////////
// CEx17aApp initialization

BOOL CEx17aApp::InitInstance()
{
    AfxEnableControlContainer();

    // Standard initialization
    // If you are not using these features and wish to reduce the size
    // of your final executable, you should remove from the following
    // the specific initialization routines you do not need.

#ifdef _AFXDLL
    Enable3dControls();        // Call this when using MFC in
                               // a shared DLL
#else
    Enable3dControlsStatic();  // Call this when linking to
                               // MFC statically
#endif
    SetRegistryKey("");
    LoadStdProfileSettings();  // Load standard INI file options
                               // (including MRU)
    // Register the application's document templates.  Document
    // templates serve as the connection between documents, frame
    // windows and views.
```

(continued)

Figure 17-5. *continued*

```
    CMultiDocTemplate* pDocTemplate;
    pDocTemplate = new CMultiDocTemplate(
        IDR_EX17ATYPE,
        RUNTIME_CLASS(CStudentDoc),
        RUNTIME_CLASS(CChildFrame), // custom MDI child frame
        RUNTIME_CLASS(CStudentView));
    AddDocTemplate(pDocTemplate);

    // create main MDI Frame window
    CMainFrame* pMainFrame = new CMainFrame;
    if (!pMainFrame->LoadFrame(IDR_MAINFRAME))
        return FALSE;
    m_pMainWnd = pMainFrame;

    // enable DDE execute open
    EnableShellOpen();
    RegisterShellFileTypes();

    // Parse command line for standard shell commands, DDE, file open
    CCommandLineInfo cmdInfo;
    ParseCommandLine(cmdInfo);

    // Dispatch commands specified on the command line
    if (!ProcessShellCommand(cmdInfo))
        return FALSE;

    // enable drag and drop open
    m_pMainWnd->DragAcceptFiles();

    // The main window has been initialized, so show and update it.
    pMainFrame->ShowWindow(m_nCmdShow);
    pMainFrame->UpdateWindow();

    return TRUE;
}


/////////////////////////////////////////////////////////////////////
// CAboutDlg dialog used for App About

class CAboutDlg : public CDialog
{
public:
    CAboutDlg();
```

(continued)

Figure 17-5. *continued*

```
// Dialog Data
    //{{AFX_DATA(CAboutDlg)
    enum { IDD = IDD_ABOUTBOX };
    //}}AFX_DATA

// Implementation
protected:
    virtual void DoDataExchange(CDataExchange* pDX); // DDX/DDV support
    //{{AFX_MSG(CAboutDlg)
        // No message handlers
    //}}AFX_MSG
    DECLARE_MESSAGE_MAP()
};

CAboutDlg::CAboutDlg() : CDialog(CAboutDlg::IDD)
{
    //{{AFX_DATA_INIT(CAboutDlg)
    //}}AFX_DATA_INIT
}

void CAboutDlg::DoDataExchange(CDataExchange* pDX)
{
    CDialog::DoDataExchange(pDX);
    //{{AFX_DATA_MAP(CAboutDlg)
    //}}AFX_DATA_MAP
}

BEGIN_MESSAGE_MAP(CAboutDlg, CDialog)
    //{{AFX_MSG_MAP(CAboutDlg)
        // No message handlers
    //}}AFX_MSG_MAP
END_MESSAGE_MAP()

// App command to run the dialog
void CEx17aApp::OnAppAbout()
{
    CAboutDlg aboutDlg;
    aboutDlg.DoModal();
}
```

CMainFrame

This main frame class, listed in Figure 17-6, is almost identical to the SDI version except that it is derived from *CMDIFrameWnd* instead of from *CFrameWnd*. The same toolbar definitions are included.

MAINFRM.H

```
class CMainFrame : public CMDIFrameWnd
{
    DECLARE_DYNAMIC(CMainFrame)
public:
    CMainFrame();

// Attributes
public:

// Operations
public:

// Overrides
    // ClassWizard generated virtual function overrides
    //{{AFX_VIRTUAL(CMainFrame)
    virtual BOOL PreCreateWindow(CREATESTRUCT& cs);
    //}}AFX_VIRTUAL

// Implementation
public:
    virtual ~CMainFrame();
#ifdef _DEBUG
    virtual void AssertValid() const;
    virtual void Dump(CDumpContext& dc) const;
#endif

protected:  // control bar embedded members
    CStatusBar   m_wndStatusBar;
    CToolBar     m_wndToolBar;

// generated message map functions
protected:
    //{{AFX_MSG(CMainFrame)
    afx_msg int OnCreate(LPCREATESTRUCT lpCreateStruct);
    // NOTE - the ClassWizard will add and remove member functions here.
    //     DO NOT EDIT what you see in these blocks of generated code!
    //}}AFX_MSG
    DECLARE_MESSAGE_MAP()
};
```

MAINFRM.CPP (the class implementation file)

```
#include "StdAfx.h"
#include "ex17a.h"
```

Figure 17-6.   *(continued)*
The CMainFrame *class listing.*

431

Figure 17-6. *continued*

```
#include "MainFrm.h"

#ifdef _DEBUG
#undef THIS_FILE
static char THIS_FILE[] = __FILE__;
#endif

/////////////////////////////////////////////////////////////////////////
// CMainFrame

IMPLEMENT_DYNAMIC(CMainFrame, CMDIFrameWnd)

BEGIN_MESSAGE_MAP(CMainFrame, CMDIFrameWnd)
    //{{AFX_MSG_MAP(CMainFrame)
    // NOTE - the ClassWizard will add and remove mapping macros here.
    //    DO NOT EDIT what you see in these blocks of generated code !
    ON_WM_CREATE()
    //}}AFX_MSG_MAP
END_MESSAGE_MAP()

static UINT indicators[] =
{
    ID_SEPARATOR,           // status line indicator
    ID_INDICATOR_CAPS,
    ID_INDICATOR_NUM,
    ID_INDICATOR_SCRL,
};

/////////////////////////////////////////////////////////////////////////
// CMainFrame construction/destruction

CMainFrame::CMainFrame()
{
    // TODO: add member initialization code here

}

CMainFrame::~CMainFrame()
{
}

int CMainFrame::OnCreate(LPCREATESTRUCT lpCreateStruct)
{
    if (CMDIFrameWnd::OnCreate(lpCreateStruct) == -1)
        return -1;
```

(continued)

Figure 17-6. *continued*

```
    if (!m_wndToolBar.Create(this) ||
        !m_wndToolBar.LoadToolBar(IDR_MAINFRAME))
    {
        TRACE0("Failed to create toolbar\n");
        return -1;      // fail to create
    }

    if (!m_wndStatusBar.Create(this) ||
        !m_wndStatusBar.SetIndicators(indicators,
          sizeof(indicators)/sizeof(UINT)))
    {
        TRACE0("Failed to create status bar\n");
        return -1;      // fail to create
    }

    // TODO: Delete these three lines if you don't want the toolbar to
    //  be dockable
    m_wndToolBar.EnableDocking(CBRS_ALIGN_ANY);
    EnableDocking(CBRS_ALIGN_ANY);
    DockControlBar(&m_wndToolBar);

    // TODO: Remove this if you don't want tool tips
    m_wndToolBar.SetBarStyle(m_wndToolBar.GetBarStyle() |
        CBRS_TOOLTIPS | CBRS_FLYBY);

    return 0;
}

BOOL CMainFrame::PreCreateWindow(CREATESTRUCT& cs)
{
    // TODO: Modify the Window class or styles here by modifying
    //  the CREATESTRUCT cs

    return CMDIFrameWnd::PreCreateWindow(cs);
}

/////////////////////////////////////////////////////////////////////
// CMainFrame diagnostics

#ifdef _DEBUG
void CMainFrame::AssertValid() const
{
    CMDIFrameWnd::AssertValid();
}
```

(continued)

433

Figure 17-6. *continued*

```
void CMainFrame::Dump(CDumpContext& dc) const
{
    CMDIFrameWnd::Dump(dc);
}

#endif //_DEBUG
```

CChildFrame

This child frame class, listed in Figure 17-7, lets you conveniently control the child frame window's characteristics by adding code in the *PreCreateWindow* function. You can also map messages and override other virtual functions.

CHILDFRM.H

```
class CChildFrame : public CMDIChildWnd
{
    DECLARE_DYNCREATE(CChildFrame)
public:
    CChildFrame();

// Attributes
public:

// Operations
public:

// Overrides
    // ClassWizard generated virtual function overrides
    //{{AFX_VIRTUAL(CChildFrame)
    virtual BOOL PreCreateWindow(CREATESTRUCT& cs);
    //}}AFX_VIRTUAL

// Implementation
public:
    virtual ~CChildFrame();
#ifdef _DEBUG
    virtual void AssertValid() const;
    virtual void Dump(CDumpContext& dc) const;
#endif

// Generated message map functions
protected:
    //{{AFX_MSG(CChildFrame)
    // NOTE - the ClassWizard will add and remove member functions here.
```

Figure 17-7. *(continued)*

The CChildFrame *class listing.*

Figure 17-7. *continued*

```
    //      DO NOT EDIT what you see in these blocks of generated code!
    //}}AFX_MSG
    DECLARE_MESSAGE_MAP()
};
```

CHILDFRM.CPP

```
// ChildFrm.cpp : implementation of the CChildFrame class
//

#include "StdAfx.h"
#include "ex17a.h"

#include "ChildFrm.h"

#ifdef _DEBUG
#undef THIS_FILE
static char THIS_FILE[] = __FILE__;
#endif

/////////////////////////////////////////////////////////////////////
// CChildFrame

IMPLEMENT_DYNCREATE(CChildFrame, CMDIChildWnd)

BEGIN_MESSAGE_MAP(CChildFrame, CMDIChildWnd)
    //{{AFX_MSG_MAP(CChildFrame)
    // NOTE - the ClassWizard will add and remove mapping macros here.
    //      DO NOT EDIT what you see in these blocks of generated code !
    //}}AFX_MSG_MAP
END_MESSAGE_MAP()

/////////////////////////////////////////////////////////////////////
// CChildFrame construction/destruction

CChildFrame::CChildFrame()
{
    // TODO: add member initialization code here

}

CChildFrame::~CChildFrame()
{
}
```

(continued)

Figure 17-7. *continued*

```
BOOL CChildFrame::PreCreateWindow(CREATESTRUCT& cs)
{
    // TODO: Modify the Window class or styles here by modifying
    //  the CREATESTRUCT cs

    return CMDIChildWnd::PreCreateWindow(cs);
}


/////////////////////////////////////////////////////////////////////
// CChildFrame diagnostics

#ifdef _DEBUG
void CChildFrame::AssertValid() const
{
    CMDIChildWnd::AssertValid();
}

void CChildFrame::Dump(CDumpContext& dc) const
{
    CMDIChildWnd::Dump(dc);
}

#endif //_DEBUG
```

Testing the EX17A Application

Do the build, run the program from the Developer Studio, and then make several documents. Try saving the documents on disk, closing them, and reloading them. Also, choose New Window from the Window menu. Notice that you now have two views (and child frames) attached to the same document. Now exit the program and start Explorer. The files you created should show up with document icons. Double-click on a document icon and see whether the EX17A program starts up. Now, with both Explorer and EX17A on the desktop, drag a document from Explorer to EX17A. Was the file opened?

> NOTE: If Explorer is already running when you first start EX17A, it might not recognize the changes made to the registry. You might have to choose Refresh from Explorer's View menu.

CHAPTER EIGHTEEN

Printing and Print Preview

If you're depending on the Win32 API alone, printing is one of the tougher programming jobs you'll have. If you don't believe me, just skim through the 60-page chapter "Using the Printer" in Charles Petzold's *Programming Windows 3.1* (Microsoft Press, 1992). Other books about Windows ignore the subject completely. The Microsoft Foundation Class (MFC) Library version 4.0 application framework goes a long way toward making printing easy. As a bonus, it adds a print preview capability that behaves like the print preview functions in commercial Windows-based programs such as Microsoft Word for Windows and Microsoft Excel.

In this chapter, you'll learn how to use the MFC library Print and Print Preview functions. In the process, you'll get a feeling for what's involved in Windows printing and how it's different from MS-DOS printing. First you'll do some wysiwyg printing, in which the printer output matches the screen display. This option requires careful use of Windows' mapping modes. Later you'll print a paginated data processing style report that doesn't reflect the screen display at all. In that example, you will use a template array to structure your document so that the program can print any specified range of pages on demand.

Windows Printing

In the old days, programmers had to worry about configuring their applications for dozens of printers. Now Windows makes life easy because it provides all the printer drivers you'll ever need. It also supplies a consistent user interface for printing.

Standard Printer Dialogs

When the user chooses Print from the File menu of a Windows-based application, the standard Print dialog appears, as shown in Figure 18-1.

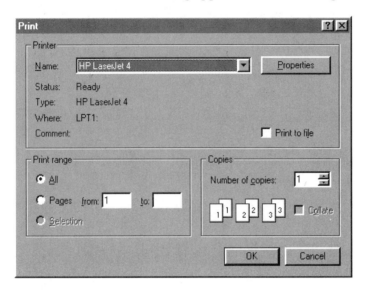

Figure 18-1.
The standard Print dialog.

If the user chooses Print Setup from the File menu, the standard Print Setup dialog appears, as shown in Figure 18-2.

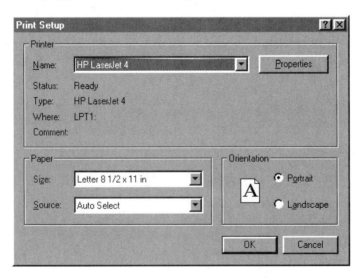

Figure 18-2.
The standard Print Setup dialog.

During the printing process, the application displays a standard printer status dialog, as shown in Figure 18-3.

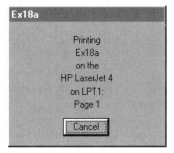

Figure 18-3.
The standard printer status dialog.

Interactive Print Page Selection

If you've worked in the data processing field, you're used to batch-mode printing. A program reads a record and then formats and prints selected information as a line in a report. Every time, say, 50 lines have been printed, the program ejects the paper and prints a new page heading. The programmer assumes that the whole report will be printed at one time and makes no allowance for interactively printing selected pages.

As Figure 18-1 shows, page numbers are important in Windows-based printing. A program must respond to a user's page selection by calculating which information to print and then printing the selected pages. If you're aware of this page selection requirement, you can design your application's data structures accordingly.

Remember the student list from Chapter 16? What if there were 1000 students and the user wanted page 5 of a student report? If you assumed that each student record required one print line and that a page held 50 lines, page 5 would include records 201 through 250. With an MFC list collection class, you're stuck iterating through the first 200 list elements before you can start printing. Maybe the list isn't the ideal data structure. How about an array collection instead? With the *CObArray* class (or with one of the template array classes), you can directly access the 201st student record.

Not every application has elements that map to a fixed number of print lines. Suppose the student record contained a multiline text biography field. Because you wouldn't know how many biography lines each record had, you'd have to search through the whole file to determine the page breaks. If your program could remember those page breaks as it calculated them, its efficiency would increase.

Display Pages vs. Printed Pages

In many cases, you'll want a printed page to correspond to a display page. As you learned in Chapter 5, you cannot guarantee that objects will be printed exactly as they are displayed. With TrueType fonts, however, you can get pretty close. If you're working with full-size paper and you want the corresponding display to be readable, you'll certainly want a display window that's larger than the screen. Thus, the *CScrollView* class is ideal for your printable views.

Sometimes, however, you might not care about display pages. Perhaps your view holds its data in a list box, or maybe you don't need to display the data at all. In these cases, your program can contain stand-alone print logic that simply extracts data from the document and sends it to the printer. Of course, the program must properly respond to a user's page range request. If you query the printer to determine the paper size and portrait/landscape configuration, you can adjust the pagination accordingly.

Print Preview

The MFC library Print Preview feature shows you on screen the <u>exact</u> page breaks and line breaks you'll get when you print your document on the selected printer. The fonts might look a little funny, especially in the smaller sizes, but it's not a problem. Look now at the print preview window that appears on page 448.

Print Preview is an MFC library feature, not a Windows feature. Don't underestimate how much effort went into programming Print Preview. The Print Preview program examines each character individually, determining its position based on the printer's device context. After selecting an approximating font, the program displays the character in the print preview window at the proper location.

Programming for the Printer

The application framework does most of the work for printing and print preview. To use the printer effectively, you must understand the sequence of function calls and know which functions to override.

The Printer Device Context and the *CView::OnDraw* Function

When your program prints on the printer, it uses a device context object of class *CDC*. Don't worry about where the object comes from; the application framework constructs it and passes it as a parameter to your view's *OnDraw* function. If your application uses the printer to duplicate the display, the *OnDraw* function can do double duty. If you're displaying, the *OnPaint* function calls *OnDraw*, and the device context is the display context. If you're printing, *OnDraw* is called by another *CView* virtual function, *OnPrint*, with a printer device context as a parameter. The *OnPrint* function is called once to print an entire page.

In print preview mode, the *CDC* object is linked to another device context object of class *CPreviewDC*, but that linkage is transparent. Your *OnPrint* and *OnDraw* functions work the same regardless of whether you're printing or previewing.

The *CView::OnPrint* Function

You've seen that the base class *OnPrint* function calls *OnDraw* and that *OnDraw* can use both a display device context and a printer device context. The mapping mode should be set before *OnPrint* is called. You can override *OnPrint* to print items that you don't need on the display, such as a title page, headers, and footers. The *OnPrint* parameters are

- A pointer to the device context
- A pointer to a print information structure (*CPrintInfo*) that includes page dimensions, the current page number, and the maximum page number

In your overridden *OnPrint* function, you can elect not to call *OnDraw* at all to support print logic that is totally independent of the display logic. The application framework calls the *OnPrint* function once for each page to be printed, with the current page number in the *CPrintInfo* structure. You're about to find out how the application framework determines the page number.

Preparing the Device Context— The *CView::OnPrepareDC* Function

If you need a display mapping mode other than *MM_TEXT* (and you usually do), that mode is generally set in the view's *OnPrepareDC* function. You override this function yourself if your view class is derived directly from *CView*, but it's already overridden if your view is derived from *CScrollView*. The *OnPrepareDC* function is called in *OnPaint* immediately before the call to *OnDraw*. If you're printing, the same *OnPrepareDC* function is called, this time immediately before the application framework calls *OnPrint*. Thus, the mapping mode is set before both the painting of the view and the printing of a page.

The second parameter of the *OnPrepareDC* function is a pointer to a *CPrintInfo* structure. This pointer is valid only if *OnPrepareDC* is being called prior to printing. You can test for this condition by calling the *CDC* member function *IsPrinting*. The *IsPrinting* function is particularly handy if you're using *OnPrepareDC* to set different mapping modes for the display and the printer.

If you do not know in advance how many pages your print job requires, your overridden *OnPrepareDC* function can detect the end of the document and reset the *m_bContinuePrinting* flag in the *CPrintInfo* structure. When this flag is *FALSE*, the *OnPrint* function won't be called, and control will pass to the end of the print loop.

The Start and End of a Print Job

When a print job starts, the application framework calls two *CView* functions, *OnPreparePrinting* and *OnBeginPrinting*. The first function, *OnPreparePrinting*, is called before the display of the Print dialog. (AppWizard generates the *OnPreparePrinting*, *OnBeginPrinting*, and *OnEndPrinting* functions for you if you select the Printing And Print Preview option.) If you know the minimum and maximum page numbers, call *CPrintInfo::SetMinPage* and *CPrintInfo::SetMaxPage* in *OnPreparePrinting*. The numbers you pass to these functions will appear in the Print dialog for the user to override.

The second function, *OnBeginPrinting*, is called after the Print dialog exits. Override this function to create Graphics Device Interface (GDI) objects, such as fonts, that you need for the entire print job. A program runs faster if you create a font once instead of creating it repetitively for each page.

The *CView* function *OnEndPrinting* is called at the end of the print job, after the last page has been printed. Override this function to get rid of GDI objects created in *OnBeginPrinting*.

The following table summarizes the important overridable *CView* print loop functions:

OnPreparePrinting	Sets minimum and maximum page numbers
OnBeginPrinting	Creates GDI objects
OnPrepareDC (for each page)	Sets mapping mode and optionally detects end of print job
OnPrint (for each page)	Does print-specific output and then calls *OnDraw*
OnEndPrinting	Deletes GDI objects

The EX18A Example—A Wysiwyg Print Program

This example displays and prints a single page of text stored in a document. The printed image should match the displayed image. The *MM_TWIPS* mapping mode is used for both printer and display. In the first iteration, the drawing rectangle is fixed; in the second iteration, the drawing rectangle is based on the printable area rectangle supplied by the printer driver.

Here are the steps for building the example:

1. **Run AppWizard to generate \VCPP32\EX18A\EX18A.** Accept the default options, and then rename the document and view classes and files as shown here:

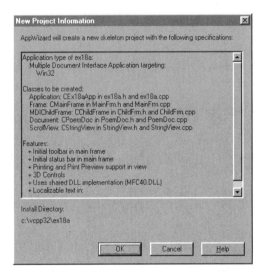

Note that this is an MDI application.

2. **Edit the PoemDoc.h header file.** The document data is stored in a string array. The MFC library *CStringArray* class holds an array of *CString* objects, accessible by a zero-based subscript. You need not set a maximum dimension in the declaration because the array is dynamic. Add the following public data member to the *CPoemDoc* class declaration:

```
public:
    CStringArray m_stringArray;
```

3. Edit the StringView.h header file. Add the following private data member to the *CStringView* class declaration:

```
private
    CRect m_rectPrint;
```

4. Edit three *CPoemDoc* member functions in the file PoemDoc.cpp. Skeleton *OnNewDocument* and *Serialize* functions were generated by AppWizard, but we'll have to use ClassWizard to override the *Delete-Contents* function. We'll initialize the poem document in the overridden *OnNewDocument* function. *DeleteContents* is called in *CDocument::On-NewDocument*, so we're sure the poem won't be deleted. (The poem, by the way, is an excerpt from the twentieth poem in Lawrence Ferlinghetti's book *A Coney Island of the Mind*.) Type 10 lines of your choice. You could use another poem or maybe your favorite Win32 function description. Add the following shaded code:

```
BOOL CPoemDoc::OnNewDocument()
{
    if (!CDocument::OnNewDocument())
        return FALSE;

    m_stringArray.SetSize(10);
    m_stringArray[0] = "The pennycandystore beyond the El";
    m_stringArray[1] = "is where I first";
    m_stringArray[2] = "                    fell in love";
    m_stringArray[3] = "                        with unreality";
    m_stringArray[4] = "Jellybeans glowed in the semi-gloom";
    m_stringArray[5] = "of that september afternoon";
    m_stringArray[6] = "A cat upon the counter moved among";
    m_stringArray[7] = "                    the licorice sticks";
    m_stringArray[8] = "                    and tootsie rolls";
    m_stringArray[9] = "              and Oh Boy Gum";

    return TRUE;
}
```

(Note: The *CStringArray* class supports dynamic arrays, but here we're using the *m_stringArray* object as though it were a static array of 10 elements.)

The application framework calls the document's virtual *DeleteContents* function when it closes the document; this action deletes the strings in the array. A *CStringArray* contains actual objects, and a *CObArray* contains pointers to objects. This distinction is important when it's time to delete the array elements. Here the *RemoveAll* function actually deletes the string objects:

```
void CPoemDoc::DeleteContents()
{
    // called before OnNewDocument and when document is closed
    m_stringArray.RemoveAll();
}
```

Serialization isn't important in this example, but the following function illustrates how easy it is to serialize strings. The application framework calls the *DeleteContents* function before loading from the archive, so you don't have to worry about emptying the array. Add the following shaded code:

```
void CPoemDoc::Serialize(CArchive& ar)
{
    m_stringArray.Serialize(ar);
}
```

5. Edit the *OnInitialUpdate* function in StringView.cpp. You must override the function for all classes derived from *CScrollView*. This function's job is to set the logical window size and the mapping mode. Add the following shaded code:

```
void CStringView::OnInitialUpdate()
{
    CScrollView::OnInitialUpdate();
    CSize sizeTotal(11520, 15120);       // 8 by 10.5 inches
    CSize sizePage(sizeTotal.cx / 2,
                   sizeTotal.cy / 2);    // page scroll
    CSize sizeLine(sizeTotal.cx / 100,
                   sizeTotal.cy / 100);  // line scroll
    SetScrollSizes(MM_TWIPS, sizeTotal, sizePage, sizeLine);
}
```

6. Edit the *OnDraw* function in StringView.cpp. The *OnDraw* function of class *CStringView* draws on both the display and the printer. In addition to displaying the poem text lines in 10-point roman font, it draws a border around the printable area and a crude ruler along the top and left margins. The function assumes an HP LaserJet printer that has a printable area of 8 by 10.5 inches offset from the upper left corner of the paper. The function also assumes the *MM_TWIPS* mapping mode, in which 1 inch = 1440 units. Add the shaded code shown on the following page.

```
void CStringView::OnDraw(CDC* pDC)
{
    int        i, j, nHeight;
    CString    str;
    CFont      font;
    TEXTMETRIC tm;

    CPoemDoc* pDoc = GetDocument();
    // draw a border 8 by 10.5 inches
    pDC->Rectangle(m_rectPrint);
    // draw horizontal and vertical rulers
    for (i = 0; i <= 8; i++) {
        str.Format("%02d", i);
        pDC->TextOut(i * 1440, 0, str);
    }
    for (i = 0; i <= 10; i++) {
        str.Format("%02d", i);
        pDC->TextOut(0, -i * 1440, str);
    }
    // print the poem 0.5 inch down and over;
    //  use 10-point roman font
    font.CreateFont(-200, 0, 0, 0, 400, FALSE, FALSE, 0, ANSI_CHARSET,
                    OUT_DEFAULT_PRECIS, CLIP_DEFAULT_PRECIS,
                    DEFAULT_QUALITY, DEFAULT_PITCH | FF_ROMAN,
                    "Times New Roman");
    CFont* pOldFont = (CFont*) pDC->SelectObject(&font);
    pDC->GetTextMetrics(&tm);
    nHeight = tm.tmHeight + tm.tmExternalLeading;
    TRACE("font height = %d, internal leading = %d\n",
        nHeight, tm.tmInternalLeading);
    j = pDoc->m_stringArray.GetSize();
    for (i = 0; i < j; i++) {
        pDC->TextOut(720, -i * nHeight - 720, pDoc->m_stringArray[i]);
    }
    pDC->SelectObject(pOldFont);
    TRACE("LOGPIXELSX = %d, LOGPIXELSY = %d\n",
        pDC->GetDeviceCaps(LOGPIXELSX),
        pDC->GetDeviceCaps(LOGPIXELSY));
    TRACE("HORZSIZE = %d, VERTSIZE = %d\n",
        pDC->GetDeviceCaps(HORZSIZE),
        pDC->GetDeviceCaps(VERTSIZE));
}
```

7. Edit the *OnPreparePrinting* function in StringView.cpp. This function sets the maximum number of pages in the print job. This example has only one page. It's absolutely necessary to call the base class *DoPreparePrinting* function in your overridden *OnPreparePrinting* function. Add the following shaded code:

```
BOOL CStringView::OnPreparePrinting(CPrintInfo* pInfo)
{
    pInfo->SetMaxPage(1);
    return DoPreparePrinting(pInfo);
}
```

8. Edit the constructor in StringView.cpp. The initial value of the print rectangle should be 8 by 10.5 inches, expressed in twips (1 inch = 1440 twips). Add the following shaded code:

```
CStringView::CStringView() : m_rectPrint(0, 0, 11505, -15105)
{
}
```

9. Build and test the application. When you start the EX18A application, your MDI child window should look like this:

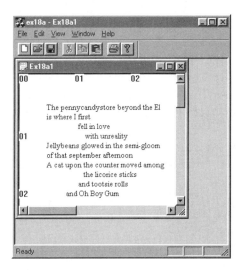

Choose Print Preview from the File menu, and then use the magnifying glass twice to enlarge the image. The print preview output is illustrated on the following page.

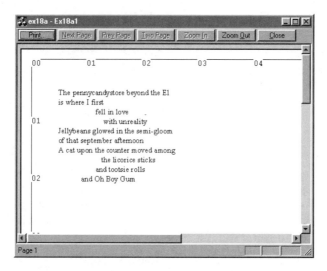

Reading the Printer Rectangle

The EX18A program prints in a fixed-size rectangle that's appropriate for a laser printer set to portrait mode with 8½-by-11-inch (letter-size) paper. But what if you loaded European-size paper or you switched to landscape mode? The program should be able to adjust accordingly.

It's relatively easy to read the printer rectangle. Remember the *CPrintInfo* pointer that's passed to *OnPrint*? That structure has a data member *m_rectDraw* that contains the rectangle in logical coordinates. Your overridden *OnPrint* function simply stuffs the rectangle in a view data member, and *OnDraw* uses it. There's only one problem: you can't get the rectangle until you start printing, so you need to set a default value for *OnDraw* to use before printing begins.

If you want the EX18A program to read the printer rectangle, use ClassWizard to override *OnPrint*, and then code the function as follows:

```
void CStringView::OnPrint(CDC* pDC, CPrintInfo* pInfo)
{
    m_rectPrint = pInfo->m_rectDraw;
    CScrollView::OnPrint(pDC, pInfo);
}
```

Template Collection Classes Revisited— The *CArray* Class

In EX15B in Chapter 15, you saw the MFC library *CTypedPtrList* template collection class, which was used to store a list of pointers to *CStudent* objects. Another collection class, *CArray*, is appropriate for the next example, EX18B. This class is different from *CTypedPtrList* in two ways. First, it's an array, with elements accessible by index, just like *CStringArray* in EX18A. Second, the array holds not pointers to objects but actual objects. In EX18B, the elements are *CRect* objects. The element's class does not have to be derived from *CObject*, and indeed *CRect* is not.

As in EX15B, a *typedef* makes the template collection easier to use. We use the statement

```
typedef CArray<CRect, CRect&> CRectArray;
```

to define an array class that holds *CRect* objects and whose functions take *CRect* reference parameters. (It's cheaper to pass a 32-bit pointer than to copy a 128-bit object.) To use the template array, you declare an instance of *CRectArray*, and then you call *CArray* member functions such as *SetSize*. You can also use the *CArray* subscript operator to get and set elements.

The template classes *CArray*, *CList*, and *CMap* are easy to use if the element class is sufficiently simple. The *CRect* class fits that description because it contains no pointer data members. Each template class uses a global function, *SerializeElements*, to serialize all the elements in the collection. The default *SerializeElements* function does a <u>bitwise</u> copy of the object to and from the archive.

If your element class contains pointers or is otherwise complex, you'll need to write your own *SerializeElements* function. If you did write this function for the rectangle array (not required), your code would look like this:

```
void AFXAPI SerializeElements(CArchive& ar, CRect* pNewRects,
    int nCount)
{
    for (int i = 0; i < nCount; i++, pNewRects++) {
      if (ar.IsStoring()) {
        ar << *pNewRects;
      }
      else {
        ar >> *pNewRects;
      }
    }
}
```

When the compiler sees this function, it uses the function to replace the *SerializeElements* function inside the template. This works, however, only if the compiler sees the *SerializeElements* prototype before it sees the template class declaration.

> NOTE: The template classes depend on two other global functions, *ConstructElements* and *DestructElements*. Starting with Visual C++ version 4.0, these functions call the element class constructor and destructor for each object. Therefore, there's no real need to replace them.

The EX18B Example—A Multipage Print Program

In this example, the document contains an array of 50 *CRect* objects that define circles. The circles are randomly positioned in a 6-by-6-inch area and have random diameters of as much as 0.5 inch. The circles, when drawn on the display, look like two-dimensional simulations of soap bubbles. Instead of drawing the circles on the printer, the application prints the corresponding *CRect* coordinates in numeric form, 12 to a page with headers and footers.

1. Run AppWizard to generate \VCPP32\EX18B\EX18B. Accept the default settings, but select Single Document Interface. The options and the default class names are shown here:

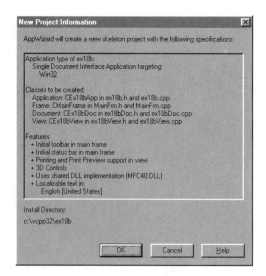

2. Edit the StdAfx.h header file. You'll need to bring in the declarations for the MFC template collection classes. Add the following statement:

```
#include <afxtempl.h>
```

3. Edit the ex18bDoc.h header file. In the EX18A example, the document data consisted of strings stored in a *CStringArray* collection. Because we're using a template collection for ellipse rectangles, we'll need a *typedef* statement outside the class declaration, as shown here:

```
typedef CArray<CRect, CRect> CRectArray;
```

Next add the following public data members to the ex18bDoc.h header file:

```
public:
    enum { nLinesPerPage = 12};
    enum { nMaxEllipses = 50};
    CRectArray m_ellipseArray;
```

The two enumerations are object-oriented replacements for *#defines*.

4. Edit the ex18bDoc.cpp implementation file. The overridden *OnNewDocument* function initializes the ellipse array with some random values, and the *Serialize* function reads and writes the whole array. App-Wizard generated the skeletons for both functions. You don't need a *DeleteContents* function because the *CArray* subscript operator writes a new *CRect* object on top of any existing one. Add the following shaded code:

```
BOOL CEx18bDoc::OnNewDocument()
{
    if (!CDocument::OnNewDocument())
        return FALSE;

    int n1, n2, n3;
    // make 50 random circles
    srand((unsigned) time(NULL));
    m_ellipseArray.SetSize(nMaxEllipses);

    for (int i = 0; i < nMaxEllipses; i++) {
      n1 = rand() * 600 / RAND_MAX;
      n2 = rand() * 600 / RAND_MAX;
```

(continued)

```
        n3 = rand() * 50  / RAND_MAX;
        m_ellipseArray[i] = CRect(n1, -n2, n1 + n3, -(n2 + n3));
    }

    return TRUE;
}
```

```
void CEx18bDoc::Serialize(CArchive& ar)
{
    m_ellipseArray.Serialize(ar);
}
```

5. **Edit the ex18bView.h header file.** The *m_nPage* data member holds
the document's current page number for printing. The private function
prototypes are for the header and footer subroutines. Add the following
code:

```
public:
    int m_nPage;
private:
    void PrintPageHeader(CDC* pDC);
    void PrintPageFooter(CDC* pDC);
```

6. **Edit the *OnDraw* function in ex18bView.cpp.** The overridden
OnDraw function simply draws the bubbles in the view window. Add the
following shaded code:

```
void CEx18bView::OnDraw(CDC* pDC)
{
    int i, j;

    CEx18bDoc* pDoc = GetDocument();
    j = pDoc->m_ellipseArray.GetUpperBound();
    for (i = 0; i < j; i++) {
      pDC->Ellipse(pDoc->m_ellipseArray[i]);
    }
}
```

7. **Insert the *OnPrepareDC* function in ex18bView.cpp.** The view class
is not a scrolling view, so the mapping mode must be set in this function.
Add the following shaded code:

```
void CEx18bView::OnPrepareDC(CDC* pDC, CPrintInfo* pInfo)
{
    pDC->SetMapMode(MM_LOENGLISH);
}
```

8. Insert the *OnPrint* function in ex18bView.cpp.   The *CView* default *OnPrint* function calls *OnDraw*. In this example, we want the printed output to be entirely different from the displayed output, so the *OnPrint* function must take care of the print output without calling *OnDraw*. *OnPrint* first sets the mapping mode to *MM_TWIPS* and then creates a fixed-pitch font. After printing the numeric contents of 12 *m_ellipseArray* elements, it deselects the font. You could have created the font once in *OnBeginPrinting*, but you wouldn't have noticed the increase in efficiency. Use ClassWizard to override the *OnPrint* function, and then add the following shaded code:

```cpp
void CEx18bView::OnPrint(CDC* pDC, CPrintInfo* pInfo)
{
    int i,      nStart, nEnd, nHeight;
    CString     str;
    CPoint      point(720, -1440);
    CFont       font;
    TEXTMETRIC tm;

    pDC->SetMapMode(MM_TWIPS);
    CEx18bDoc* pDoc = GetDocument();
    m_nPage = pInfo->m_nCurPage; // for PrintPageFooter's benefit
    nStart = (m_nPage - 1) * CEx18bDoc::nLinesPerPage;
    nEnd = nStart + CEx18bDoc::nLinesPerPage;
    // 14-point fixed-pitch font
    font.CreateFont(-280, 0, 0, 0, 400, FALSE, FALSE,
                    0, ANSI_CHARSET, OUT_DEFAULT_PRECIS,
                    CLIP_DEFAULT_PRECIS, DEFAULT_QUALITY,
                    DEFAULT_PITCH | FF_MODERN, "Courier New");
                    // Courier New is a TrueType font
    CFont* pOldFont = (CFont*) (pDC->SelectObject(&font));
    PrintPageHeader(pDC);
    pDC->GetTextMetrics(&tm);
    nHeight = tm.tmHeight + tm.tmExternalLeading;
    for (i = nStart; i < nEnd; i++) {
      if (i > pDoc->m_ellipseArray.GetUpperBound())
        break;
      str.Format("%6d %6d %6d %6d %6d", i + 1,
                 pDoc->m_ellipseArray[i].left,
                 pDoc->m_ellipseArray[i].top,
                 pDoc->m_ellipseArray[i].right,
                 pDoc->m_ellipseArray[i].bottom);
      point.y -= nHeight;
      pDC->TextOut(point.x, point.y, str);
    }
    PrintPageFooter(pDC);
    pDC->SelectObject(pOldFont);
}
```

9. **Edit the *OnPreparePrinting* function in ex18bView.cpp.** The *OnPreparePrinting* function computes the number of pages in the document and then communicates that value to the application framework through the *SetMaxPage* function. Add the following shaded code:

```
BOOL CEx18bView::OnPreparePrinting(CPrintInfo* pInfo)
{
    CEx18bDoc* pDoc = GetDocument();
    pInfo->SetMaxPage(pDoc->m_ellipseArray.GetUpperBound() /
                      CEx18bDoc::nLinesPerPage + 1);
    return DoPreparePrinting(pInfo);
}
```

10. **Insert the page header and footer functions in ex18bView.cpp.** These private functions, called from *OnPrint*, print the page headers and the page footers. The page footer includes the page number, stored by *OnPrint* in the view class data member *m_nPage*. The *CDC::GetTextExtent* function right-justifies the page number. Add the following code:

```
void CEx18bView::PrintPageHeader(CDC* pDC)
{
    CString str;

    CPoint point(0, 0);
    pDC->TextOut(point.x, point.y, "Bubble Report");
    point += CSize(720, -720);
    str.Format("%6.6s %6.6s %6.6s %6.6s %6.6s",
               "Index", "Left", "Top", "Right", "Bottom");
    pDC->TextOut(point.x, point.y, str);
}

void CEx18bView::PrintPageFooter(CDC* pDC)
{
    CString str;

    CPoint point(0, -14400); // move 10 inches down
    CEx18bDoc* pDoc = GetDocument();
    str.Format("Document %s", (LPCSTR) pDoc->GetTitle());
    pDC->TextOut(point.x, point.y, str);
    str.Format("Page %d", m_nPage);
    CSize size = pDC->GetTextExtent(str);
    point.x += 11520 - size.cx;
    pDC->TextOut(point.x, point.y, str); // right-justified
}
```

11. Build and test the application.   For one set of random numbers, the bubble child window looks like this:

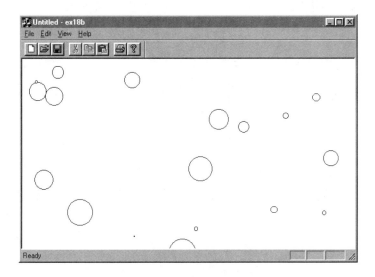

Each time you choose New from the File menu, you should see a different picture. In Print Preview, the first page of the output should look like this:

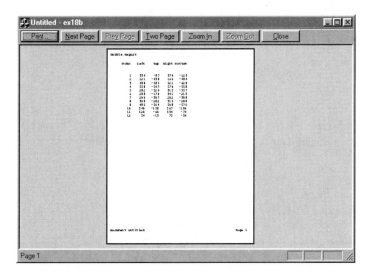

Splitter Windows and Multiple Views

Except for the EX17A example, each program you've seen has had only one view attached to a document. If you've used a Windows-based word processor, you know that it's convenient to have two windows open simultaneously on various parts of a document. Both windows might contain a normal view, or one window might contain a page layout view and another might contain an outline view.

The application framework has several ways to present multiple views—the splitter window and multiple MDI child windows. You'll learn about both presentation options here, and you'll see that in each it's easy to make multiple view <u>objects</u> of the same view class (the normal view). It's slightly more difficult, however, to use two or more view <u>classes</u> in the same application (say, the outline view and the page layout view).

This chapter emphasizes the selection and presentation of multiple views. The examples depend on a document with data initialized in the *OnNewDocument* function. Look back now to Chapter 15 for a review of document–view communication.

The Splitter Window

A splitter window appears as a special type of frame window that holds several views in panes. The application can split the window on creation, or the user can split the window by choosing a menu command or by dragging a splitter box in the splitter window's scroll bar. After the window is split, the user can move the splitter bars with the mouse to adjust the relative sizes of the panes. Splitter windows can be used in both SDI and MDI applications. You can see examples of splitter windows on pages 461, 463, and 466.

The splitter window is represented by an object of class *CSplitterWnd*. As far as Windows is concerned, a *CSplitterWnd* object is an actual window that fully occupies the frame window (*CFrameWnd* or *CMDIChildWnd*) client area. The view windows occupy the splitter window pane areas. The splitter window does not take part in the command dispatch mechanism. The active view window (in the splitter pane) is, logically, connected directly to its frame window.

View Options

When you combine multiview presentation methods with application models, you get a number of permutations. Here are some of them:

- **SDI application with splitter window, single view class**   This chapter's first example, EX19A, covers this case. Each splitter window pane can be scrolled to a different part of the document. The programmer determines the maximum number of horizontal and vertical panes; the user makes the split at runtime.

- **SDI application with splitter window, multiple view classes**   The EX19B example illustrates this case. The programmer determines the number of panes and the sequence of views; the user can change the pane size at runtime.

- **SDI application with no splitter windows, multiple view classes**   The EX19C example illustrates this case. The user switches view classes by making a selection from a menu.

- **MDI application with no splitter windows, single view class**   This is the standard MDI application you've seen already in Chapter 17. The New Window menu item lets the user open a new child window for a document that's open already.

- **MDI application with no splitter windows, multiple view classes**   A small change to the standard MDI application allows the use of multiple views. As example EX19D shows, all that's necessary is to replace the New Window menu item with menu items and functions for each of the available view classes.

- **MDI application with splitter child windows**   This case is covered thoroughly in Books Online. The SCRIBBLE example illustrates the splitting of an MDI child window.

Dynamic and Static Splitter Windows

A dynamic splitter window allows the user to split the window at any time by choosing a menu item or by dragging a splitter box located on the scroll bar. The panes in a dynamic splitter window generally use the same view class. The top left pane is initialized to a particular view when the splitter window is created. In a dynamic splitter window, scroll bars are shared among the views. In a window with a single horizontal split, for example, the bottom scroll bar controls both views. A dynamic splitter application starts with a single view object. When the user splits the frame, other view objects are constructed. When the user unsplits the frame, view objects are destroyed.

The panes of a static splitter window are defined when the window is first created, and they cannot be changed. The user can move the bars but cannot unsplit or resplit the window. Static splitter windows can accommodate multiple view classes, with the configuration set at creation time. In a static splitter window, each pane has separate scroll bars. In a static splitter window application, all view objects are constructed when the frame is constructed, and they are all destroyed when the frame is destroyed.

The EX19A Example— A Single View Class SDI Dynamic Splitter

In this example, the user can dynamically split the view into four panes. A four-way split produces four separate view objects, all managed by a single view class. We'll use the document and the view code from EX18A.

AppWizard allows you to add a dynamic splitter window to a new application. Click the Advanced button in the AppWizard Step 4 dialog, click on the Window Styles tab, and set the options as shown here:

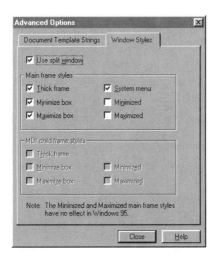

When you check the Use Split Window check box, AppWizard adds code to your *CMainFrame* class. Of course, you could add the same code to the *CMainFrame* class of an existing application to add splitter capability.

Resource Requirements

When AppWizard generates an application with a splitter frame, it includes a Split option in the project's View menu. The *ID_WINDOW_SPLIT* command ID is mapped in the *CView* class within the MFC library.

CMainFrame

The application's main frame window class needs a splitter window data member and a prototype for an overridden *OnCreateClient* function. Here are the additions that AppWizard makes to the MainFrm.h file:

```
protected:
    CSplitterWnd m_wndSplitter;
    virtual BOOL OnCreateClient(LPCREATESTRUCT lpcs,
                                CCreateContext* pContext);
```

The application framework calls the *CFrameWnd::OnCreateClient* virtual member function when the frame object is created. The base class version creates a single view window as specified by the document template. The AppWizard-generated *OnCreateClient* override shown here (in MainFrm.cpp) creates a splitter window instead, and the splitter window creates the first view:

```
BOOL CMainFrame::OnCreateClient( LPCREATESTRUCT /*lpcs*/,
    CCreateContext* pContext)
{
    return m_wndSplitter.Create( this,
        2, 2,               // TODO: adjust the number of rows, columns
        CSize( 10, 10 ), // TODO: adjust the minimum pane size
        pContext );
}
```

The *CSplitterWnd Create* member function creates a dynamic splitter window. The *CSplitterWnd* object knows the view class because its name is embedded in the *CCreateContext* structure that's passed as a parameter to *Create*.

The second and third *Create* parameters (*2, 2*) specify that the window can be split into a maximum of two rows and two columns. If you changed the parameters to (*2, 1*), you would have a single horizontal split. The parameters (*1, 2*) give you a single vertical split. The *CSize* parameter specifies the minimum pane size.

Testing the EX19A Application

When the application starts, you can split the window by choosing Split from the View menu or by dragging the splitter boxes at the left and top of the scroll bars. Figure 19-1 shows a typical single view window with a four-way split. Multiple views share the scroll bars.

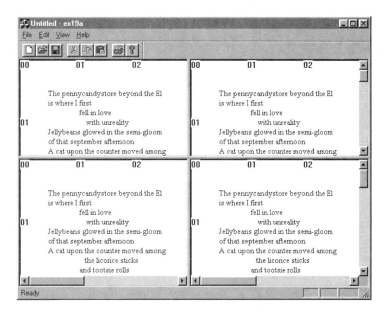

Figure 19-1.
A single view window with a four-way split.

The EX19B Example—
A Double View Class SDI Static Splitter

In EX19B, we'll extend EX19A by defining a second view class and allowing a static splitter window to show the two views. (The H and CPP files are cloned from the original view class.) This time the splitter window works a little differently. Instead of starting off as a single pane, the splitter is initialized with two panes. The user can move the bar between the panes by using the splitter box on the right scroll bar or by using the Window Split menu item.

The easiest way to generate a static splitter application is to let AppWizard generate a dynamic splitter application and then edit the generated *CMainFrame::OnCreateClient* function.

CHexView

The *CHexView* class was written to allow programmers to appreciate poetry. As shown below, it is essentially the same as *CStringView* except for the *OnDraw* member function:

```
void CHexView::OnDraw(CDC* pDC)
{
    // hex dump of document strings
    int i, j, k, l, n, nHeight;
    CString outputLine, str;
    TEXTMETRIC tm;
    CFont font;

    CPoemDoc* pDoc = GetDocument();
    font.CreateFont(-160, 80, 0, 0, 400, FALSE, FALSE, 0, ANSI_CHARSET,
                OUT_DEFAULT_PRECIS, CLIP_DEFAULT_PRECIS, DEFAULT_QUALITY,
                DEFAULT_PITCH | FF_SWISS, "Arial");
    CFont* pOldFont = pDC->SelectObject(&font);
    pDC->GetTextMetrics(&tm);
    nHeight = tm.tmHeight + tm.tmExternalLeading;

    j = pDoc->m_stringArray.GetSize();
    for (i = 0; i < j; i++) {
      outputLine.Format("%02x    ", i);
      l = pDoc->m_stringArray[i].GetLength();
      for (k = 0; k < l; k++) {
        n = pDoc->m_stringArray[i][k] & 0x00ff;
        str.Format("%02x ", n);
        outputLine += str;
      }
      pDC->TextOut(720, -i * nHeight - 720, outputLine);
    }
    pDC->SelectObject(pOldFont);
}
```

This function displays a hexadecimal dump of all strings in the document's *m_stringArray* collection. Notice the use of the subscript operator to access individual characters in a *CString* object.

CMainFrame

As in EX19A, the EX19B application's main frame window class needs a splitter window data member and a prototype for an overridden *OnCreateClient* function. You can let AppWizard generate the code by specifying Use Split Window, as in EX19A. You won't have to modify the MainFrm.h file.

The implementation file, MainFrm.cpp, needs both view class headers (and the prerequisite document header), as shown here:

```
#include "PoemDoc.h"
#include "StringView.h"
#include "HexView.h"
```

AppWizard generates dynamic splitter code in the *OnCreateClient* function, so you'll have to do some editing if you want a static splitter. Instead of calling *CSplitterWnd::Create*, you need to call the *CSplitterWnd::CreateStatic* function, which is tailored for multiple view classes. The following calls to *CSplitterWnd::CreateView* attach the two view classes. As the second two *CreateStatic* parameters (*2, 1*) dictate, this splitter window contains only two panes, with an initial horizontal split 100 device units from the top of the window. The top pane is the string view; the bottom pane is the hex dump view. The user can change the splitter bar position but cannot change the view configuration.

```
BOOL CMainFrame::OnCreateClient(LPCREATESTRUCT lpcs,
                                CCreateContext* pContext)
{
    VERIFY(m_wndSplitter.CreateStatic(this, 2, 1));
    VERIFY(m_wndSplitter.CreateView(0, 0, RUNTIME_CLASS(CStringView),
                                    CSize(100, 100), pContext));
    VERIFY(m_wndSplitter.CreateView(1, 0, RUNTIME_CLASS(CHexView),
                                    CSize(100, 100), pContext));
    return TRUE;
}
```

Testing the EX19B Application

When you start the EX19B application, the window should look like the one shown below. Notice the separate horizontal scroll bars for the two views.

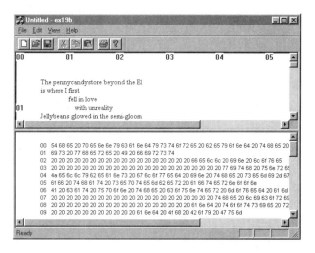

The EX19C Example— Switching View Classes Without a Splitter

Sometimes you just want to switch view classes under program control, and you don't want to be bothered with a splitter window. The EX19C example is an SDI application that switches between *CStringView* and *CHexView* in response to selections on the View menu. All you need to do is add two new menu commands and then add some code to the *CMainFrame* class. You also need to change the *CStringView* and *CHexView* constructors from protected to public.

Resource Requirements

The following two items have been added to the View menu in the *IDR_MAINFRAME* menu resource:

Menu Item	Command ID	*CMainFrame* Function
String &View	*ID_VIEW_STRINGVIEW*	*OnViewStringview* (replaces New Window item)
&Hex View	*ID_ VIEW_HEXVIEW*	*OnViewHexview*

ClassWizard was used to add the command-handling functions to the *CMainFrame* class.

CMainFrame

The *CMainFrame* class gets a new private helper function *SwitchToView*, which is called from the two menu command handlers. The *enum* parameter tells the function which view to switch to. Here are the two added items in the MainFrm.h header file:

```
private:
    enum eView {STRING = 1, HEX = 2};
    void SwitchToView(eView nView);
```

The *SwitchToView* function (in MainFrm.cpp) makes some low-level MFC calls to locate the requested view and to activate it. Don't worry about how it works. Just adapt it to your own applications when you want the view switching feature. Add the following code:

```
void CMainFrame::SwitchToView(eView nView)
{
    CView* pOldActiveView = GetActiveView();
    CView* pNewActiveView = (CView*)GetDlgItem(nView);
    if (pNewActiveView == NULL) {
      switch(nView) {
      case STRING:
          pNewActiveView = (CView*)new CStringView;
          break;
      case HEX:
          pNewActiveView = (CView*)new CHexView;
          break;
      }
      CCreateContext context;
      context.m_pCurrentDoc = pOldActiveView->GetDocument();
      pNewActiveView->Create(NULL, NULL, 0L, CFrameWnd::rectDefault,
                             this, nView, &context);
      pNewActiveView->OnInitialUpdate();
    }
    SetActiveView(pNewActiveView);
    pNewActiveView->ShowWindow(SW_SHOW);
    pOldActiveView->ShowWindow(SW_HIDE);
    pOldActiveView->SetDlgCtrlID(
        pOldActiveView->GetRuntimeClass() ==
        RUNTIME_CLASS(CStringView) ? STRING : HEX);
    pNewActiveView->SetDlgCtrlID(AFX_IDW_PANE_FIRST);
    RecalcLayout();
}
```

Finally, here are the menu command handlers and update command UI handlers that were initially generated (along with message map entries and prototypes) by ClassWizard. The update command UI handlers test the current view's class.

```
/////////////////////////////////////////////////////////////////
// CMainFrame message handlers

void CMainFrame::OnViewStringview()
{
    SwitchToView(STRING);
}

void CMainFrame::OnUpdateViewStringview(CCmdUI* pCmdUI)
{
```

(continued)

```
    pCmdUI->Enable(
        !GetActiveView()->IsKindOf(RUNTIME_CLASS(CStringView)));
}


void CMainFrame::OnViewHexview()
{
    SwitchToView(HEX);
}


void CMainFrame::OnUpdateViewHexview(CCmdUI* pCmdUI)
{
    pCmdUI->Enable(
        !GetActiveView()->IsKindOf(RUNTIME_CLASS(CHexView)));
}
```

Testing the EX19C Application

The EX19C application initially displays the *CStringView* view of the document. You can toggle between the *CStringView* and *CHexView* views by choosing the appropriate command from the View menu. The *CStringView* view and the *CHexView* view of the document are shown in Figure 19-2.

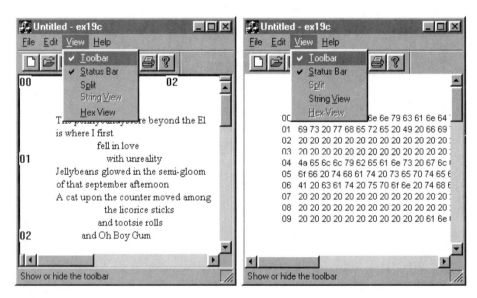

Figure 19-2.
The CStringView *view and the* CHexView *view of the document.*

The EX19D Example— A Multiple View Class MDI Application

The final example, EX19D, uses the previous document and view classes to create a multiple view class MDI application without a splitter window. The logic is different from the logic in the other multiple view class applications. This time the action takes place in the application class rather than in the main frame class. As you study EX19D, you'll gain some more insight into the use of *CDocTemplate* objects.

This example was generated with the AppWizard Context-Sensitive Help option. In Chapter 20, you'll be activating the context-sensitive help capability.

If you're starting from scratch, use AppWizard to generate an ordinary MDI application with one of the view classes. Then add the second view class to the project, and modify the application class files and main frame class files as described below.

Resource Requirements

The following two items have been added to the Window menu in the *IDR_EX19DTYPE* menu resource:

Menu Item	Command ID	*CMainFrame* Function
New &String Window	*ID_WINDOW_NEW1*	*OnWindowNew1* (replaces New Window item)
New &Hex Window	*ID_WINDOW_NEW2*	*OnWindowNew2*

ClassWizard was used to add the command-handling functions to the *CMainFrame* class.

CEx19dApp

In the application class header file, ex19d.h, the following data members and function prototype have been added:

```
public:
    CMultiDocTemplate* m_pTemplate1;
    CMultiDocTemplate* m_pTemplate2;
    int ExitInstance();
```

The implementation file, ex19d.cpp, contains the following *#include* statements:

```
#include "PoemDoc.h"
#include "StringView.h"
#include "HexView.h"
```

The *CEx19dApp InitInstance* member function has the following code inserted immediately after the *AddDocTemplate* function call:

```
m_pTemplate1 = new CMultiDocTemplate(IDR_EX19DTYPE,
    RUNTIME_CLASS(CPoemDoc),
    RUNTIME_CLASS(CChildFrame),
    RUNTIME_CLASS(CStringView));

m_pTemplate2 = new CMultiDocTemplate(IDR_EX19DTYPE,
    RUNTIME_CLASS(CPoemDoc),
    RUNTIME_CLASS(CChildFrame),
    RUNTIME_CLASS(CHexView));
```

The *AddDocTemplate* call generated by AppWizard established the primary document/frame/view combination for the application that is effective when the program starts. The two template objects above are secondary templates that can be activated in response to menu selections.

Now all you need is an *ExitInstance* member function that cleans up the secondary templates:

```
int CEx19dApp::ExitInstance()
{
    delete m_pTemplate1;
    delete m_pTemplate2;
    return CWinApp::ExitInstance(); // saves profile settings
}
```

CMainFrame

The main frame class implementation file, MainFrm.cpp, has both view class headers (and the prerequisite document header) included:

```
#include "PoemDoc.h"
#include "StringView.h"
#include "HexView.h"
```

The base frame window class, *CMDIFrameWnd,* has an *OnWindowNew* function that is normally connected to the standard New Window menu item on the Window menu. The following two command-handling functions are clones of *OnWindowNew,* adapted for the two view-specific templates that are defined in *InitInstance.* They are mapped to the new menu commands and create new child windows based on the specified view class.

```
void CMainFrame::OnWindowNew1() // ordinary text view
{
    CMDIChildWnd* pActiveChild = MDIGetActive();
    CDocument* pDocument;
    if (pActiveChild == NULL ||
      (pDocument = pActiveChild->GetActiveDocument()) == NULL)
    {
      TRACE0("Warning: No active document for WindowNew command\n");
      AfxMessageBox(AFX_IDP_COMMAND_FAILURE);
      return;          // command failed
    }

    // otherwise, we have a new frame!
    CDocTemplate* pTemplate = ((CEx19dApp*) AfxGetApp())->m_pTemplate1;
    ASSERT_VALID(pTemplate);
    CFrameWnd* pFrame = pTemplate->CreateNewFrame(pDocument,
                                                  pActiveChild);

    if (pFrame == NULL)
    {
      TRACE0("Warning: failed to create new frame\n");
      AfxMessageBox(AFX_IDP_COMMAND_FAILURE);
      return;          // command failed
    }

    pTemplate->InitialUpdateFrame(pFrame, pDocument);
}


void CMainFrame::OnWindowNew2() // hex dump view
{
    CMDIChildWnd* pActiveChild = MDIGetActive();
    CDocument* pDocument;
    if (pActiveChild == NULL ||
      (pDocument = pActiveChild->GetActiveDocument()) == NULL)
    {
      TRACE0("Warning: No active document for WindowNew command\n");
      AfxMessageBox(AFX_IDP_COMMAND_FAILURE);
      return;          // command failed
    }
```

(continued)

469

```
// otherwise, we have a new frame!
CDocTemplate* pTemplate = ((CEx19dApp*) AfxGetApp())->m_pTemplate2;
ASSERT_VALID(pTemplate);
CFrameWnd* pFrame = pTemplate->CreateNewFrame(pDocument,
                                              pActiveChild);

if (pFrame == NULL)
{
  TRACE0("Warning: failed to create new frame\n");
  AfxMessageBox(AFX_IDP_COMMAND_FAILURE);
  return;            // command failed
}


pTemplate->InitialUpdateFrame(pFrame, pDocument);
}
```

NOTE: The function cloning above is a useful MFC programming technique. You must first find a base class function that does almost what you want and then copy it from the \MSVC40\MFC\SRC subdirectory into your derived class, changing it as required. The only danger is that subsequent versions of the MFC library will implement the original function differently.

Testing the EX19D Application

When you start the EX19D application, a text view child window appears. Choose New Hex Window from the Window menu. The application should look like this:

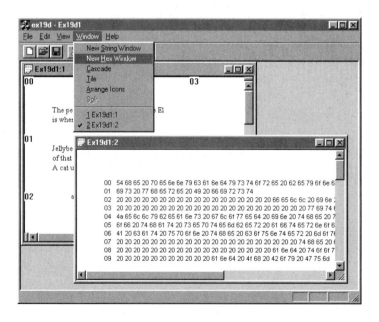

Context-Sensitive Help

Most commercial Windows programs take advantage of the powerful WinHelp help engine that's included with Windows. The Microsoft Foundation Class (MFC) Library version 4.0 application framework allows you to use this same help engine for context-sensitive help in your own applications. This chapter first shows you how to construct and process a simple stand-alone help file that has a table of contents and lets the user jump between topics. Next you'll see how your MFC library program activates WinHelp with help context IDs that are derived from window and command IDs keyed to an AppWizard-generated help file. Last you'll learn how to modify the MFC library help message-handling system to customize the help capability.

The Windows WinHelp Program

If you've used commercial Windows-based applications, you've probably marveled at their sophisticated help screens with graphics, hyperlinks, and popups. At some software firms, including Microsoft, help authoring has been elevated to a profession in its own right. This section can't turn you into a help expert, but it can get you started by showing you how to prepare a simple no-frills help file.

Rich Text Format (RTF)

The original Windows SDK documentation showed you how to format help files with an ASCII file format called rich text format (RTF). We'll be using rich text format too, but we'll be working in wysiwyg mode, thereby avoiding the direct use of awkward escape sequences. You write with the same fonts, sizes, and styles that your user sees on the help screens. You'll definitely need a word processor that handles RTF. I've used Microsoft Word for Windows for this book, but many other word processors accommodate the RTF format.

NOTE: Several commercial Windows help tools are available, including RoboHELP from Blue Sky Software and FOREHELP from the Forefront Corporation. RoboHELP is a set of templates and macros for Microsoft Word, and FOREHELP is a stand-alone package that simulates WinHelp, giving you immediate feedback as you write the help system.

Writing a Simple Help File

We're going to write a simple help file with a table of contents and three topics. This help file is designed to be run directly from WinHelp, started from Windows. No C++ programming is involved. Here are the steps:

1. Create a \VCPP32\EX20A subdirectory.

2. Write the main help text file.   Use Microsoft Word for Windows (or another RTF-compatible word processor) to type text as shown here:

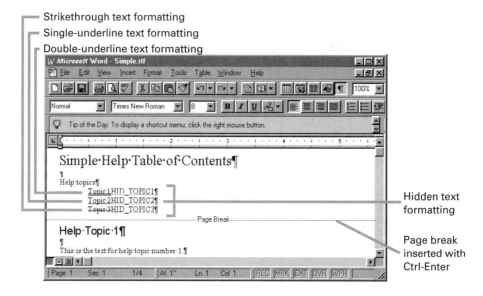

Be sure to apply the double-underline and hidden text formats correctly and to insert the page break at the correct place.

NOTE: To see hidden text, you must turn on your word processor's hidden text viewing mode. In Microsoft Word, select Options from the Tools menu, and then click on the View tab.

3. Insert footnotes for the Table Of Contents screen.   The Table Of Contents screen is the first topic screen in this help system. Turn on the word processor's footnote view, and then insert the following footnotes at the beginning of the topic title, using the specified custom footnote marks:

Footnote Mark	Text	Description
#	HID_CONTENTS	Help context ID
$	SIMPLE Help Contents	Topic title

When you're finished with this step, the document should look like this:

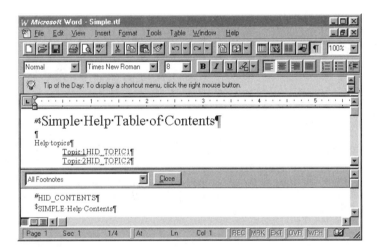

4. Insert footnotes for the Topic 1 screen.   The Topic 1 screen is the second topic screen in the help system. Insert the following footnotes, using the specified custom footnote marks:

Footnote Mark	Text	Description
#	HID_TOPIC1	Help context ID
$	SIMPLE Help Topic 1	Topic title
K	SIMPLE Topics	Keyword text

5. Clone the Topic 1 screen.   Copy the entire Topic 1 section of the document, including the page break, to the clipboard, and then paste two copies of the text into the document. The footnotes are copied along with the text. In the first copy, change all occurrences of *1* to *2*. In the second copy, change all occurrences of *1* to *3*. Don't forget to change the footnotes. With Word for Windows, it's a little difficult to see which footnote goes with which topic, so be careful. When you're finished with this step, the document text (including footnotes) should look like this:

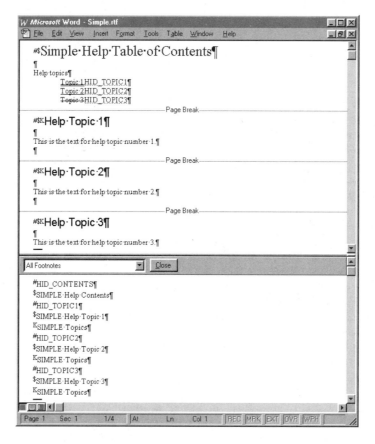

6. Save the document.   Save the document as \vcpp32\ex20a\simple.rtf. Specify Rich Text Format as the file type.

7. Write a help project file.   Using the Developer Studio or another text editor, create a file \vcpp32\ex20a\simple.hpj, as follows:

```
[OPTIONS]
CONTENTS=HID_CONTENTS
TITLE=SIMPLE Application Help
COMPRESS=true
WARNING=2

[FILES]
simple.rtf
```

This file specifies the context ID of the Table Of Contents screen and the name of the RTF file that contains the help text. Be sure to save the file in text (ASCII) format.

8. **Build the help file.**   From Windows, run the Microsoft Help Workshop (Hcrtf) utility. Open the file \vcpp32\ex20a\simple.hpj, and then click the Save And Compile button.

This step runs the Windows Help Compiler with the project file simple.hpj. The output is the Help file simple.hpj in the same directory. This example assumes that the \MSVC40\BIN subdirectory is in your computer's search path. Edit your autoexec.bat file to run the \msvc40-\bin\vcvars32.bat file to set your computer's search environment variable.

9. **Run WinHelp with the new help file.**   From Windows, run WinHelp and then open the file \vcpp32\ex20a\simple.hlp. The Table Of Contents screen should look like this:

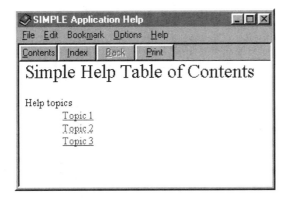

Now move the mouse cursor to Topic 1, and notice that the mouse cursor changes from an arrow to a pointing hand. When you press the left mouse button, the Topic 1 screen should appear, as shown at the top of the following page.

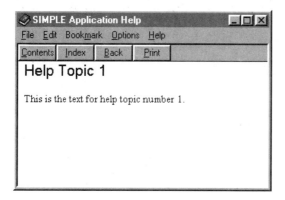

The *HID_TOPIC1* text in the Table Of Contents screen links to the corresponding context ID (the # footnote) in the topic page. This link is known as a jump.

The link to Topic 2 is coded as a pop-up jump. When you click on Topic 2, here's what you see:

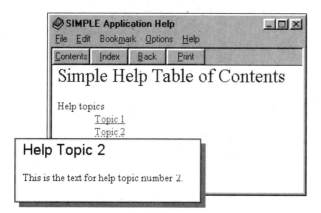

10. **Try the WinHelp Contents pushbutton.**   Clicking this button should take you to the Table Of Contents screen, as shown in step 9. WinHelp knows the ID of the Table Of Contents window because you specified it in the HPJ file.

11. **Try the WinHelp Index pushbutton.**   When you click the Index button, WinHelp opens Help's Index dialog, which displays the Help file's list of keywords. In simple.hlp, all topics (excluding the table of contents) have the same keyword (the K footnotes), SIMPLE Topics. When you double-click on this keyword, you see all associated topic titles (the $ footnotes), as shown here:

What you have here is a two-level search hierarchy. The user can type the first few letters of the keyword and then select a topic from a list box. The more carefully you select your keywords and topic titles, the more effective your help system will be.

An Improved Table of Contents

You've been looking at the "old-style" help table of contents. The latest Win32 version of WinHelp can give you a modern tree-view table of contents. All you need is a text file with a CNT extension. Add a new file, simple.cnt, in the \VCPP32\EX20A directory, as shown here:

```
:Base simple.hlp
1 Help topics
2 Topic 1=HID_TOPIC1
2 Topic 2=HID_TOPIC2
2 Topic 3=HID_TOPIC3
```

Notice the context IDs that match the help file. After compiling simple.cnt, the next time you run WinHelp with the simple.hlp file, you'll see a new contents screen similar to the one shown on the following page.

477

If you want, you can use the Microsoft Help Workshop (Hcrtf) to edit CNT files. The CNT file is independent of the HPJ file and the RTF files. If you update your RTF files, you must make corresponding changes in your CNT file.

The Application Framework and WinHelp

You've seen WinHelp running as a stand-alone program. The application framework and WinHelp cooperate to give you context-sensitive help. Here's a summary of how this works:

1. You select the Context-Sensitive Help option when you run AppWizard.

2. AppWizard generates Contents and Search items on your application's Help menu, and it creates one or more generic RTF files together with an HPJ file and a batch file that runs the Help Compiler.

3. AppWizard inserts a keyboard accelerator for the F1 key, and it maps the F1 key and the Help menu items to the *CWinApp/ CWinThread* member functions.

4. When your program runs, it calls WinHelp when the user presses F1 or chooses an item from the Help menu, passing a context ID that determines which help topic is displayed.

You now need to understand how WinHelp is called from another application and how your application generates context IDs for WinHelp.

Calling WinHelp

The *CWinApp* member function *WinHelp* activates WinHelp from within your application. If you look up *WinHelp* in the *Microsoft Foundation Class Library Reference*, you'll see a long list of actions that the optional second parameter controls. Ignore the second parameter, and pretend that *WinHelp* has only one unsigned long integer parameter, *dwData*. This parameter corresponds to a help topic. Suppose that the SIMPLE Help file is available and that your program contains the statement

```
AfxGetApp()->WinHelp(HID_TOPIC1);
```

When the statement is executed, in response to the F1 key or some other event, the Topic 1 Help screen appears, as it would if the user had clicked on Topic 1 in the Help Table Of Contents screen.

"Wait a minute," you say. "How does WinHelp know what Help file to use?" The name of the Help file matches the application name. If the executable program name is simple.exe, the Help file is named simple.hlp.

NOTE: You can force *WinHelp* to use a different Help file by setting the *CWinApp* data member *m_pszHelpFilePath*.

"And how does WinHelp match the program constant *HID_TOPIC1* to the Help file's context ID?" you ask. The Help project file must contain a MAP section that maps context IDs to numbers. If your application's resource.h file defines *HID_TOPIC1* as *101*, the simple.hpj MAP section looks like this:

```
[MAP]
HID_TOPIC1        101
```

The program's *#define* constant name doesn't have to match the help context ID; only the numbers must match. Making the names correspond, however, is good practice.

Using Search Strings

For a text-based application, you might need help based on a keyword rather than a numeric context ID. In that case, use the WinHelp *HELP_KEY* or *HELP_PARTIALKEY* option as follows:

```
CString string("find this string");
AfxGetApp()->WinHelp((DWORD) (LPCSTR) string, HELP_KEY);
```

The double cast for *string* is necessary because the first *WinHelp* parameter is multipurpose; its meaning depends on the value of the second parameter.

Calling WinHelp from the Application's Menu

AppWizard generates a Help Topics option on the Help menu, and it maps that option to *CWinApp::OnHelpFinder*, which calls WinHelp this way:

```
WinHelp(0L, HELP_FINDER);
```

If you want the old-style table of contents, call WinHelp this way instead:

```
WinHelp(0L, HELP_INDEX);
```

And if you want a "help on help" item, make this call:

```
WinHelp(0L, HELP_HELPONHELP);
```

Help Context Aliases

The ALIAS section of the HPJ file allows you to equate one context ID with another. Suppose your HPJ file contained the following statements:

```
[ALIAS]
HID_TOPIC1 = HID_GETTING_STARTED

[MAP]
HID_TOPIC1        101
```

Your RTF files could use *HID_TOPIC1* and *HID_GETTING_STARTED* interchangeably. Both would be mapped to the help context 101 as generated by your application.

Determining the Help Context

You now have enough information to add a simple context-sensitive help system to an MFC program. You define F1 (the standard MFC library Help key) as a keyboard accelerator, and then you write a command handler that maps the program's help context to a *WinHelp* parameter. You could invent your own method for mapping the program state to a context ID, but why not take advantage of the system that's already built into the application framework?

The application framework determines the help context based on the ID of the active program element. These identified program elements include menu commands, frame windows, dialog windows, message boxes, and control bars. A menu item might be identified as *ID_EDIT_CLEAR_ALL*, for example, and the main frame window usually has the identifier *IDR_MAIN-FRAME*. You might expect these identifiers to map directly to help contexts.

IDR_MAINFRAME, for example, would map to a help context of the same name. But what if a frame ID and a command ID had the same numeric value? Obviously, you need a way to prevent these overlaps.

The application framework solves the overlap problem by defining a new set of help *#define* constants that are derived from program element IDs. These help constants are the sum of the element ID and a base value, as follows:

Program Element	Element ID Prefix	Help Context ID Prefix	Base (Hexadecimal)
Menu item	*ID_*	*HID_*	10000
Frame or dialog	*IDR_, IDD_*	*HIDR_, HIDD_*	20000
Error message box	*IDP_*	*HIDP_*	30000
Nonclient areas	Other	*H...*	40000
Control bar	*IDW_*	*HIDW_*	50000

HID_EDIT_CLEAR_ALL (0x1E121) corresponds to *ID_EDIT_CLEAR_ALL* (0xE121), and *HIDR_MAINFRAME* (0x20002) corresponds to *IDR_MAIN-FRAME* (2).

Menu Access to Help

If you've selected the AppWizard Context-Sensitive Help option, your application will have an Index item on its Help menu. This item (and the corresponding toolbar button) displays the Help Table Of Contents screen, and the user can navigate the Help file through jumps and searches.

F1 Help

Two separate context-sensitive help access methods are built into an MFC application and are available if you've selected the AppWizard Context-Sensitive Help option. The first is standard F1 help. The user presses F1; the program makes its best guess about the help context and then calls WinHelp. In this mode, it is possible to determine the menu item currently selected with the keyboard or the currently selected window (frame, view, dialog, or message box).

Shift-F1 Help

This second context-sensitive help mode is more powerful than the F1 mode. With Shift-F1 help, the program can identify the help contexts listed on the following page:

- A menu item selected with the mouse cursor

- A toolbar button

- A frame window

- A view window

- A specific graphics element within a view window

- The status bar

- Various nonclient elements such as the system menu control

The user activates Shift-F1 help by pressing Shift-F1 or by clicking the Context Help toolbar button, shown here:

In either case, the mouse cursor changes to

On the next mouse click, the help topic appears, with the position of the mouse cursor determining the context.

Shift-F1 help doesn't work with modal dialogs or message boxes.

Message Box Help—The *AfxMessageBox* Function

The global function *AfxMessageBox* displays application framework error messages. This function is similar to the *CWnd::MessageBox* member function except that it has a help context ID as a parameter. The application framework maps this ID to a WinHelp context ID and then calls WinHelp when the user presses F1. If you can use the *AfxMessageBox* help context parameter, be sure to use prompt IDs that begin with *IDP_*. In your RTF file, use help contexts that begin with *HIDP_*.

There are two versions of *AfxMessageBox*. In the first version, the prompt string is specified by a character-array pointer parameter. In the second version, the prompt ID parameter specifies a string resource. If you use the second version, your executable program will be more efficient. Both *AfxMessageBox* versions take a style parameter that makes the message box display an exclamation point, a question mark, or another graphics symbol.

Generic Help

When context-sensitive help is enabled, AppWizard assembles a series of default help topics that are associated with standard MFC library program elements. Following are some of the standard topics:

- Menu and toolbar commands (File, Edit, and so forth)
- Nonclient window elements (maximize box, caption bar, and so forth)
- Status bar
- Error message boxes

These topics are contained in the files AfxCore.rtf and AfxPrint.rtf, which are contained, along with associated bitmap files, in the application's HLP subdirectory. Your job is to customize the generic help files.

NOTE: AppWizard generates AfxPrint.rtf only if you specify the Printing And Print Preview option.

A Help Example—No Programming Required

If you followed the instructions for EX19D in Chapter 19, you selected the AppWizard Context-Sensitive Help option. We'll now return to that example and explore the application framework's built-in help capability. You'll see how easy it is to link help topics to menu command IDs and frame window resource IDs. You edit RTF files, not CPP files.

Here are the steps for customizing the help for EX19D:

1. From the EX19D project directory, run the MAKEHELP batch file.

If the path environment variable were set correctly, the Developer Studio would have created the EX19D Help file when you built the project. If you have not already done so, add the following line to your autoexec.bat file:

```
c:\msvc40\bin\vcvars32 x86
```

NOTE: If Visual C++ is not installed in the C:\MSVC40 directory, edit the vcvars32 path to reflect its actual location.

You can run the MAKEHELP batch file now to generate the Help file. At the MS-DOS prompt, type the following commands:

```
CD \VCPP32\EX19D
MAKEHELP
```

The MAKEHELP batch file, generated by AppWizard, builds the application's ready-to-use HLP file from components located mostly in the project's HLP subdirectory. The project should also be on the same hard drive as Visual C++. (Some of the commands in the MAKEHELP batch file assume this.)

2. **Test the generic help file.** Run the EX19D application. Try the following experiments:

❑ Move the mouse cursor into the application's main frame window, and then press F1. You should see the generic Application Help screen, as shown here:

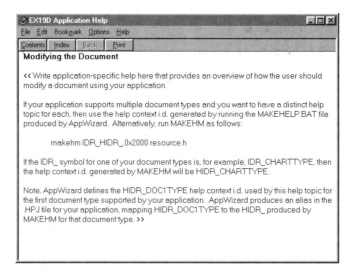

❑ Close the Help dialog, and then press Alt-F, F1. This should open the help topic for the File New command.

❑ Close the Help dialog, click the Context Help toolbar button (shown on page 482), and then choose Save from the File menu. Do you get the appropriate help topic?

❑ Click the Context Help toolbar button again, and then select the frame window's title bar. You should get an explanation of a Windows title bar.

❑ Choose New from the EX19D File menu. Select the Poem document frame, and then press F1. You should see a generic Application Help screen with the title Modifying The Document.

3. **Change the application title.** The file AfxCore.rtf, in the \VCPP32-\EX19D\HLP directory, contains the string *<<YourApp>>* throughout. Replace it globally with *EX19D*.

4. **Change the Modifying The Document Help screen.** The AfxCore.rtf file in the \VCPP32\EX19D\HLP directory contains text for the generic Application Help screen. Search for "Modifying The Document," and then change the text to something appropriate for the application. This topic has the help context ID *HIDR_DOC1TYPE*. The generated ex19d.hpj file provides the alias *HIDR_EX19DTYPE*.

5. **Add a topic for the Window New String Window menu item.** The New String Window menu item was added to EX19D and thus didn't have associated help text. Add a topic to AfxCore.rtf, as shown here:

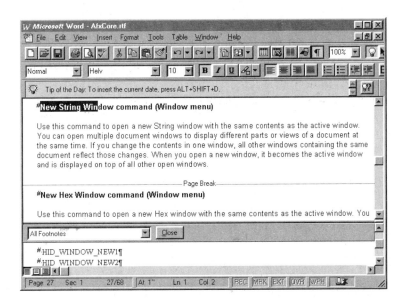

Notice the # footnote that links the topic to the context ID *HID_WINDOW_NEW1* as defined in hlp\ex19d.hm. The program's command ID for the New String Window menu item is, of course, *ID_WINDOW_NEW1*.

6. **Rebuild the Help file, and test the application.** Run the MAKEHELP batch file again, and then rerun the EX19D program. Try the two new help links.

The MAKEHELP Process

The process of building the application's HLP file is complex. Part of the complexity results from the Help Compiler's nonacceptance of statements such as

```
HID_MAINFRAME = ID_MAINFRAME + 0x20000
```

Because of this nonacceptance, a special preprocessing program named makehm.exe must read the resource.h file to produce a help map file that defines the help context values. Below is a diagram of the entire MAKEHELP process:

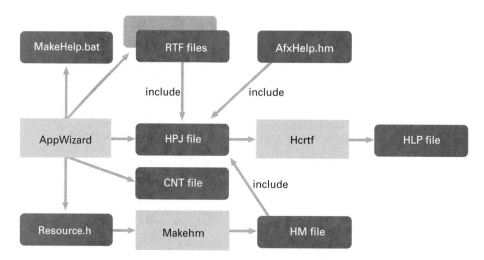

AppWizard generates the application's Help project file (HPJ) and the Help contents file (CNT). Its FILES section brings in the RTF files, and its MAP section contains *#include* statements for both the generic and the application-specific help map (HM) files. The Help Workshop (Hcrtf) processes the project file to produce the Help file that WinHelp reads.

Help Command Processing

You've seen the components of a Help file, and you've seen the effects of F1 and Shift-F1. You know how the application element IDs are linked to help context IDs. What you haven't seen is the application framework's internal processing of the help requests. Why should you be concerned? Suppose you want to provide help on a specific view window instead of a frame window.

What if you need help topics linked to specific graphics items in a view window? These and other needs can be met only by overriding the Help command processing functions.

Help command processing is different because it depends on whether the help request was an F1 request or a Shift-F1 request. The processing of each help request will be described separately.

F1 Processing

The F1 key is normally handled by a keyboard accelerator entry that App-Wizard inserts in the RC file. The accelerator associates the F1 key with an *ID_HELP* command that is mapped to the *CWinApp* member function *OnHelp*.

> NOTE: In an active modal dialog or a menu selection in progress, the F1 key is processed by a Windows <u>hook</u> that causes the same *OnHelp* function to be called. The F1 accelerator key would otherwise be disabled.

The *CWinApp::OnHelp* function sends a WM_COMMANDHELP message to the outermost frame window. In an SDI application, that message is handled by the main frame base class function, *CFrameWnd::OnCommand-Help*, which calls WinHelp with the help context ID *HIDR_MAINFRAME*. The main frame window is the top-level window, and that is the starting point for daisy-chained WM_COMMANDHELP message processing. If you need to display help for a view window or another child window, you must map WM_COMMANDHELP in your derived frame class. Your *OnCommandHelp* function should then send the WM_COMMANDHELP message down the line to the active view window. When the view window gets the message, it calls WinHelp with an appropriate help context ID.

In an MDI application, the WM_COMMANDHELP message is mapped in both the *CMDIFrameWnd* class and the *CMDIChildWnd* class. If there are no MDI children, the frame window sets the context to *HIDR_MAINFRAME*; if there are one or more children, the frame window sends the message to the active child window, which sets the help context for the document. If you need help for views, you must derive a class from *CMDIChildWnd* and then map the *OnCommandHelp* function in that derived class. This function then sends the WM_COMMANDHELP message down to the view.

Remember that F1 WM_COMMANDHELP processing is always in top-down order. The application first sends the message to the top-level window, which has the option of delegating the message to a child window. This routing is different from the normal command routing.

Shift-F1 Processing

When the user presses Shift-F1 or clicks the Context Help toolbar button, a mapped menu command message is sent to the *CWinApp* function *OnContextHelp*. When the user presses the mouse button again after positioning the mouse cursor, a WM_HELPHITTEST message is sent to the innermost window, where the mouse click is detected. If the message is not mapped in that window's class, the next outer window gets a chance at it.

In an SDI application, WM_HELPHITTEST is mapped to the *CFrameWnd* class member function *OnHelpHitTest*, which sets the help context to *HIDR_MAINFRAME*. In an MDI application, the message is mapped in both the *CMDIChildWnd* class and the *CMDIFrameWnd* class. If the mouse cursor is in the child window, the document help context is set; otherwise, the context is set to *HIDR_MAINFRAME*.

If you want a view-specific help context, simply map WM_HELPHITTEST in your view class and don't pass the message on to the frame. The *lParam* parameter of *OnHelpHitTest* contains the mouse coordinates in device units, relative to the upper left corner of the window's client area. The *y* value is in the high-order half; the *x* value is in the low-order half. You can use these coordinates to set the help context specifically for an item in the view.

Remember that Shift-F1 processing is always in bottom-up order. The message is first sent to the lowest-level window. If that window doesn't map the message, the message is sent to the parent window.

A Help Command Processing Example—EX20B

This example, EX20B, is based on example EX19D from Chapter 19. It's a two-view MDI application with view-specific help added. The purpose of the added code is as follows:

■ A new derived MDI child frame window class delegates the F1 help response to the active view object, and each of the two view classes has the necessary *OnCommandHelp* message handler.

■ Each view class has an *OnHelpHitTest* message handler to process Shift-F1 help requests.

Header Requirements

The compiler recognizes help-specific identifiers only if the following *#include* statement is present:

```
#include <afxpriv.h>
```

In EX20B, the statement is in the StdAfx.h file.

CChildFrame

The child frame class needs to map the WM_COMMANDHELP message, but ClassWizard can't do the job. You must add the handler prototype in the ChildFrm.h file:

```
afx_msg LRESULT OnCommandHelp(WPARAM wParam, LPARAM lParam);
```

Here are the message map entry and the handler implementation from ChildFrm.cpp:

```
ON_MESSAGE(WM_COMMANDHELP, OnCommandHelp)

LRESULT CChildFrame::OnCommandHelp(WPARAM wParam, LPARAM lParam)
{
    if (lParam == 0) {
        if (m_nIDTracking > 0xe001) {
            // frame's own menu (system menu)
            lParam = HID_BASE_COMMAND + m_nIDTracking;
        }
        else {
            CView* pView = GetActiveView();
            if (pView) {
                // delegate the Help command to the view
                return pView->SendMessage(WM_COMMANDHELP, wParam, 0L);
            }
            else {
                lParam = HID_BASE_RESOURCE + IDR_MAINFRAME;
            }
        }
    }
    if (lParam != 0) {
        AfxGetApp()->WinHelp(lParam);
        return TRUE;
    }
    return FALSE;
}
```

The *OnCommandHelp* function first tests the *m_nIDTracking* data member to see whether the user was asking for help on a menu item. If no menu was open, the function tries to pass the WM_COMMANDHELP command message on to the active view. If no view is available, the function displays the help topic for the MDI client window. The document-specific topic isn't needed here because a document MDI child window can't exist without a view.

489

CStringView

The modified string view in StringView.h needs message map function prototypes for both F1 help and Shift-F1 help, as shown here:

```
afx_msg LRESULT OnCommandHelp(WPARAM wParam, LPARAM lParam);
afx_msg LRESULT OnHelpHitTest(WPARAM wParam, LPARAM lParam);
```

Here are the message map entries in StringView.cpp:

```
ON_MESSAGE(WM_COMMANDHELP, OnCommandHelp)
ON_MESSAGE(WM_HELPHITTEST, OnHelpHitTest)
```

The *OnCommandHelp* message handler member function in StringView.cpp processes F1 help requests. It responds to the message sent from the MDI child frame and displays the help topic for the string view window, as shown here:

```
LRESULT CStringView::OnCommandHelp(WPARAM wParam, LPARAM lParam)
{
    if (lParam == 0) {
        lParam = HID_BASE_RESOURCE + IDR_STRINGVIEW;
    }
    // context already determined above--we don't modify it
    AfxGetApp()->WinHelp(lParam);
    return TRUE;
}
```

Last the *OnHelpHitTest* member function handles Shift-F1 help, as shown here:

```
LRESULT CStringView::OnHelpHitTest(WPARAM wParam, LPARAM lParam)
{
    return HID_BASE_RESOURCE + IDR_STRINGVIEW;
}
```

In a more complex application, you might want *OnHelpHitTest* to set the help context based on the mouse cursor position.

CHexView

The *CHexView* class processes help requests the same way the *CStringView* class does. Following is the necessary header code in HexView.h:

```
afx_msg LRESULT OnCommandHelp(WPARAM wParam, LPARAM lParam);
afx_msg LRESULT OnHelpHitTest(WPARAM wParam, LPARAM lParam);
```

Here are the message map entries in HexView.cpp:

```
ON_MESSAGE(WM_COMMANDHELP, OnCommandHelp)
ON_MESSAGE(WM_HELPHITTEST, OnHelpHitTest)
```

And here is the implementation code in HexView.cpp:

```
LRESULT CHexView::OnCommandHelp(WPARAM wParam, LPARAM lParam)
{
    if(lParam == 0) {
      lParam = HID_BASE_RESOURCE + IDR_HEXVIEW;
    }
    // context already determined above--we don't modify it
    AfxGetApp()->WinHelp(lParam);
    return TRUE;
}


LRESULT CHexView::OnHelpHitTest(WPARAM wParam, LPARAM lParam)
{
    return HID_BASE_RESOURCE + IDR_HEXVIEW;
}
```

Resource Requirements

Two new symbols were added to the resource file. Here are their values and corresponding help context IDs:

Symbol	Value	Help Context ID	Value
IDR_STRINGVIEW	101	*HIDR_STRINGVIEW*	0x20065
IDR_HEXVIEW	102	*HIDR_HEXVIEW*	0x20066

Help File Requirements

Two topics were added to the AfxCore.rtf file with the help context IDs *HIDR_STRINGVIEW* and *HIDR_HEXVIEW*, as shown on the following page.

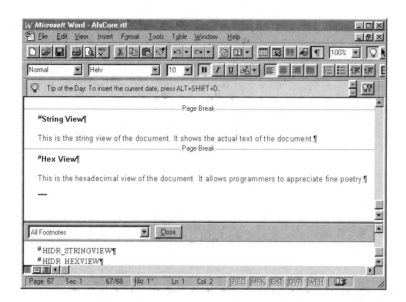

The generated ex20b.hm file, in the project's HLP subdirectory, should look like this:

```
// EX20B.HM generated Help Map file.  Used by EX20B.HPJ.

// Commands (ID_* and IDM_*)
HID_WINDOW_NEW1                         0x18003
HID_WINDOW_NEW2                         0x18004

// Prompts (IDP_*)

// Resources (IDR_*)
HIDR_STRINGVIEW                         0x20065
HIDR_HEXVIEW                            0x20066
HIDR_MAINFRAME                          0x20080
HIDR_EX20BTYPE                          0x20081

// Dialogs (IDD_*)
HIDD_ABOUTBOX                           0x20064

// Frame Controls (IDW_*)
```

Testing the EX20B Application

Open a string child window and a hexadecimal child window. Test the action of F1 help and Shift-F1 help.

CHAPTER TWENTY-ONE

Dynamic Link Libraries (DLLs)

If you want to write modular software, you'll be very interested in DLLs. You're probably thinking that you've been writing modular software all along because C++ classes are modular. The difference is that classes are build-time modular, and DLLs are runtime modular. Instead of programming giant EXEs, which you must rebuild and test each time you make the slightest change, you can build smaller DLL modules, which you can test individually. You can, for example, put a C++ class in a DLL, which might be as small as 12 KB after compiling and linking. Client programs can load and link your DLL very quickly when they run. Windows itself uses DLLs for its major functions.

DLLs are getting easier to write. Win32 has greatly simplified the programming model, and there's more and better support from AppWizard and the MFC library. This chapter shows you how to write DLLs in C++ and how to write client programs that use DLLs. You'll see how Win32 maps DLLs into your processes, and you'll learn the differences between MFC regular DLLs and MFC extension DLLs. You'll see examples of simple DLLs of each type, and you'll see a more complex DLL example that implements a custom control.

Fundamental DLL Theory

Before you look at the application framework's support for DLLs, you must understand how Win32 integrates DLLs into your process. You might want to review Chapter 9 to renew your knowledge of processes and virtual memory. Remember that a process is a running instance of a program and that the program starts out as an EXE file on disk.

Basically, a DLL is a file on disk (usually with a DLL extension), consisting of global data, compiled functions, and resources, that becomes part of your process. It is compiled to load at a preferred base address, and if there's no conflict with other DLLs, the file gets mapped to the same virtual address in your process. The DLL has various "exported" functions, and the client program (the program that loaded the DLL in the first place) imports those functions. Windows matches up the imports and exports when it loads the DLL.

NOTE: Win32 DLLs allow exported global variables as well as functions. Because this is a new feature, not too many DLL authors are using it yet.

In Win32, each process gets its own copy of the DLL's read/write global variables. If you want to share memory among processes, you must either use a memory-mapped file or declare a shared data section as described in Jeffrey Richter's *Advanced Windows* (Microsoft Press, 1995). Whenever your DLL requests heap memory, that memory is allocated from the client process's heap.

How Imports Are Matched to Exports

A DLL contains a table of exported functions. These functions are identified to the outside world by their symbolic names and (optionally) by integers called ordinal numbers. The function table also contains the addresses of the functions within the DLL. When the client program first loads the DLL, it doesn't know the addresses of the functions it needs to call, but it does know the symbols or ordinals. The dynamic linking process then builds a table that connects the client's calls to the function addresses in the DLL. If you edit and rebuild the DLL, you don't need to rebuild your client program unless you have changed function names or parameter sequences.

NOTE: In a simple world, you'd have one EXE file that imports functions from one or more DLLs. In the real world, many DLLs call functions inside other DLLs. Thus, a particular DLL can have both exports and imports. This is no problem because the dynamic linkage process can handle cross-dependencies.

In the DLL code, you must explicitly declare your exported functions like this:

```
__declspec(dllexport) int MyFunction(int n);
```

On the client side, you need to declare the corresponding imports like this:

```
__declspec(dllimport) int MyFunction(int n);
```

If you're using C++, however, the compiler generates a <u>decorated</u> name for *MyFunction* that other languages can't use. These decorated names are the long names the compiler invents based on class name, function name, and parameter types, as listed in the project's MAP file. If you want to use the plain name *MyFunction*, you have to write the declarations this way:

```
extern "C" __declspec(dllexport) int MyFunction(int n);
extern "C" __declspec(dllimport) int MyFunction(int n);
```

> NOTE: By default, the compiler uses the *__cdecl* argument pass-ing convention, which means that the calling program pops the pa-rameters from the stack. Some client languages might require the *__stdcall* convention (formerly known as Pascal), which means that the called function pops the stack. Therefore, you might have to use the *__stdcall* modifier in your DLL export declaration.

Just having import declarations isn't enough to make a client link to a DLL. The client's project must specify the import library (LIB) to the linker, <u>and</u> the client program must actually contain a call to at least one of the DLL's imported functions. That call statement doesn't have to be executed, but the compiler must see it.

Implicit Linkage vs. Explicit Linkage

As a C++ programmer, you'll probably be using implicit linkage for your DLLs. When you build your DLL, the linker produces a companion <u>import</u> LIB file, which contains all the DLLs' exported symbols and (optionally) or-dinals, but no code. The LIB file is a surrogate for the DLL that is added to the client program's project. When you build (statically link) the client, the imported symbols are matched to the exported symbols in the LIB, and those symbols (or ordinals) are bound into the EXE file. The LIB file also contains the DLL filename (but not its full pathname), which gets stored inside the EXE file. When the client is loaded, Windows finds and loads the DLL and then dynamically links it by symbol or ordinal.

Explicit linking is more appropriate for interpreted languages such as Visual Basic, but you can use it from C++ if you need to. With explicit linking, you don't use an import file; instead, you call the Win32 *LoadLibrary* func-tion, specifying the DLL's pathname as a parameter. *LoadLibrary* returns an *HINSTANCE* parameter that you can use in a call to *GetProcAddress*, which converts a symbol (or an ordinal) to an address inside the DLL. Suppose you have a DLL that exports a function like this:

```
extern "C" __declspec(dllexport) double SquareRoot(double d);
```

Here's an example of a client's explicit linkage to the function:

```
typedef double (SQRTPROC)(double);
HINSTANCE hInstance;
SQRTPROC* pFunction;
VERIFY(hInstance = ::LoadLibrary("c:\\windows\\system\\mydll.dll"));
VERIFY(pFunction = (SQRTPROC*)
    ::GetProcAddress((HMODULE) hInstance, "SquareRoot"));
double d = (*pFunction)(81.0); // call the DLL function
```

With implicit linkage, all DLLs are loaded when the client is loaded, but with explicit linkage, you can determine when DLLs are loaded and unloaded. Explicit linkage allows you to determine at runtime which DLLs to load. You could, for example, have one DLL with string resources in English and another with string resources in Spanish. Your application would load the appropriate DLL after the user chose a language.

Symbolic Linkage vs. Ordinal Linkage

In Win16, ordinal linkage was more efficient and was the preferred linkage option. In Win32, the symbolic linkage efficiency was improved, and Microsoft now recommends it over ordinal linkage. The DLL version of the MFC library, however, uses ordinal linkage. A typical MFC program might link to hundreds of functions in the MFC DLL. Ordinal linkage permits that program's EXE file to be smaller because it does not have to contain the long symbolic names of its imports. If you build your own DLL with ordinal linkage, you must specify the ordinals in the project's DEF file, which doesn't have too many other uses in the Win32 environment. If your exports are C++ functions, you must use decorated names in the DEF file. Here's a short extract from one of the MFC library DEF files:

```
?ReadClass@CArchive@@QAEPAUCRuntimeClass@@PBU2@PAIPAK@Z @ 2311 NONAME
?ReadCount@CArchive@@QAEKXZ @ 2312 NONAME
?ReadFromArchive@CEditView@@QAEXAAVCArchive@@I@Z @ 2313 NONAME
?ReadList@CRecentFileList@@UAEXXZ @ 2314 NONAME
?ReadObject@CArchive@@QAEPAVCObject@@PBUCRuntimeClass@@@Z @ 2315 NONAME
?ReadString@CArchive@@QAEHAAVCString@@@Z @ 2316 NONAME
?ReadString@CArchive@@QAEPADPADI@Z @ 2317 NONAME
```

The numbers after the at symbols (@) are the ordinals. Makes you want to use symbolic linkage instead, doesn't it?

The DLL Entry Point—*DllMain*

By default, the linker assigns the main entry point *_DllMainCRTStartup* to your DLL. When Windows loads the DLL, it calls this function, which first calls the constructors for global objects and then calls the global function *DllMain*, which you're supposed to write. *DllMain* is called not only when the DLL is attached to the process but also when it is detached, and at other times as well. Here is a skeleton *DllMain* function:

```
HINSTANCE g_hInstance;
extern "C" int APIENTRY
    DllMain(HINSTANCE hInstance, DWORD dwReason, LPVOID lpReserved)
{
    if (dwReason == DLL_PROCESS_ATTACH)
    {
      TRACE0("EX21A.DLL Initializing!\n");
      g_hInstance = hInstance;
      // do initialization here
    }
    else if (dwReason == DLL_PROCESS_DETACH)
    {
      TRACE0("EX21A.DLL Terminating!\n");
      // do cleanup here
    }
    return 1;   // ok
}
```

The *hInstance* parameter is quite important, as you'll see in the next section, so we're storing it in a DLL global variable so that we can get to it from other functions. If you don't write a *DllMain* function for your DLL, a do-nothing version is brought in from the runtime library.

The *DllMain* function is also called when individual threads are started and terminated, as indicated by the *dwReason* parameter. Richter's book tells you all you need to know about this complex subject.

Instance Handles—Loading Resources

Each DLL in a process is identified by a unique 32-bit *HINSTANCE* value. In addition, the process itself has an *HINSTANCE* value. All these instance handles are valid only within a particular process, and they represent the starting virtual address of the DLL or EXE. The process (EXE) instance handle is almost always 0x400000, and the handle for a DLL with the default base address is 0x10000000. If your program uses several DLLs, each will have a different *HINSTANCE* value, either because the DLLs had different base addresses specified at build time or because the loader copied and relocated the DLL code.

Instance handles are particularly important for loading resources. The Win32 *FindResource* function takes an *HINSTANCE* parameter. EXEs and DLLs can each have their own resources. If you want a resource from the DLL, you specify the DLL's instance handle, and if you want a resource from the EXE file, you specify the EXE's instance handle.

How do you get an instance handle? You've seen that the DLL's instance handle is passed as a parameter to the DLL's *DllMain* function. If you want the EXE's handle, you call the Win32 *GetModuleHandle* function with a *NULL* parameter. Later you'll see that the MFC library has its own method of loading resources by searching various modules in sequence.

How the Client Program Finds a DLL

If you link explicitly with *LoadLibrary*, you can specify the DLL's full pathname. If you link implicitly, Windows uses the following search sequence to locate your DLL:

1. The directory containing the EXE file

2. The process's current directory

3. The Windows system directory

4. The Windows directory

5. The directories listed in the PATH environment variable

There's a trap you can easily fall into. You build a DLL as one project, then you copy the DLL file to the \WINDOWS\SYSTEM directory, and then you run the DLL from a client program. So far, so good. Next you rebuild the DLL with some changes, but you forget to copy the DLL file to the \WINDOWS\SYSTEM directory. The next time you run the client program, it loads the old version of the DLL. Be careful!

Debugging a DLL

The Developer Studio makes it easy to debug a DLL. Just run the debugger from the DLL project. The first time you do this, the debugger asks for the pathname of the client EXE file. Every time you "run" the DLL from the debugger after this, the debugger loads the EXE, but the EXE uses the search sequence to find the DLL. This means that you must either set the PATH environment variable to point to the DLL or you must copy the DLL to a directory in the search sequence.

Extension DLLs vs. Regular DLLs

Up to now, we've been looking at Win32 DLLs that have a *DllMain* function and some exported functions. Now we'll move into the world of the MFC application framework, which adds its own support layer on top of the Win32 basics. AppWizard lets you build two kinds of DLLs with MFC library support, <u>extension</u> DLLs and <u>regular</u> DLLs. You must understand the differences between these two types before you decide which one is right for your needs.

> N O T E : Of course, the Developer Studio lets you build a pure Win32 DLL without the MFC library, just as it lets you build a Windows program without the MFC library. This is an MFC-oriented book, however, so we'll ignore the Win32 option here.

An extension DLL dynamically links to the code in the DLL version of the MFC library, so an extension DLL requires that your client program be dynamically linked to the MFC library (the AppWizard default) and that both the client program and the extension DLL be synchronized to the same version of the MFC DLLs (mfc40.dll, mfcd40.dll, and so on). An extension DLL supports a C++ interface. In other words, the DLL can export whole classes, and the client can construct objects of those classes or derive classes from them. Extension DLLs are quite small; you can build a simple extension DLL with a size of 12 KB, which loads quickly.

If you need a DLL that can be loaded by any Win32 programming environment (including Visual Basic version 4.0), you want a regular DLL. A big restriction here is that a regular DLL can export only C-style functions. It can't export C++ classes, member functions, or overloaded functions because every C++ compiler has its own method of decorating names. You can, however, use C++ classes (and MFC library classes, in particular) inside your regular DLL.

When you build an MFC regular DLL, you can choose to statically link or dynamically link to the MFC library. If you choose static linking, your DLL will include a copy of all the MFC library code it needs and will thus be self-contained. The smallest release-build statically linked regular DLL is about 110 KB. If you choose dynamic linking, the size drops to about 20 KB, but you'll have to ensure that the proper MFC DLLs are present on the target machine. That's no problem if the client program is already dynamically linked to the same version of the MFC library.

When you tell AppWizard what kind of DLL or EXE you want, compiler *#define* constants are set as shown in the following table:

	Dynamically Linked to Shared MFC Library	Statically Linked to MFC Library
Regular DLL	_AFXDLL,_USRDLL	_USRDLL
Extension DLL	_AFXEXT,_AFXDLL	unsupported option
Client EXE	_AFXDLL	no constants defined

If you look inside the MFC source code and header files, you'll see a ton of *#ifdef* statements for these constants. This means that the library code is compiled quite differently depending on the kind of project you're producing.

The Shared MFC DLLs and the Windows DLLs

If you build a Windows Debug target with the shared MFC DLL option, your program is dynamically linked to one or more of the following MFC DLLs:

MFC40D.DLL	Core MFC classes
MFCO40D.DLL	OLE classes
MFCD40D.DLL	Database classes (ODBC and DAO)
MFCN40D.DLL	Windows Sockets classes

When you build a Release target, your program is dynamically linked to MFC40.DLL only. Linkage to these MFC DLLs is implicit via import library. You might assume implicit linkage to the supporting Windows OLE and ODBC DLLs, in which case you would expect all these DLLs to be linked to your Release build client when it loads, regardless of whether it uses OLE or ODBC features. This is not what happens. Through some creative thunking, MFC loads the OLE and ODBC DLLs explicitly (by calling *LoadLibrary*) when one of their functions is first called. Your client application thus loads only the DLLs it needs.

MFC Extension DLLs—Exporting Classes

If your extension DLL contains only exported C++ classes, you'll have an easy time building and using it. The steps for building the EX21A example show you exactly how to tell AppWizard that you're building an extension DLL skeleton. That skeleton has only the *DllMain* function. You simply add your own C++ classes to the project. There's only one special thing you must do. You must add the macro *AFX_EXT_CLASS* to the class declaration, as shown here:

```
class AFX_EXT_CLASS CStudent : public CObject
```

This modification goes into the H file that's part of the DLL project, and it also goes into the H file that client programs use. In other words, the H files are exactly the same for both client and DLL. The macro generates different code depending on the situation—it exports the class in the DLL and imports the class in the client.

The MFC Extension DLL Resource Search Sequence

If you build a dynamically linked MFC <u>client</u> application, many of the MFC library's standard resources (error message strings, print preview dialog templates, and so on) are stored in the MFC DLLs (mfc40.dll, mfcd40.dll, and so on), but your application has its own resources too. When you call an MFC function such as *CString::LoadString* or *CBitmap::LoadBitmap*, the framework steps in and searches first the EXE file's resources and then the MFC DLL's resources.

If you build an extension DLL, the search sequence is first the EXE file, then the extension DLL, and then the MFC DLLs. If you have a string resource ID, for example, that's unique among all resources, the MFC library will find it. If you have duplicate string IDs in your EXE file and your extension DLL file, the MFC library loads the string in the EXE file.

You can change the search sequence if you need to. Suppose you want to search the extension DLL's resources first. Use code such as this:

```
HINSTANCE hInstResourceClient = AfxGetResourceHandle();
AfxSetResourceHandle(g_hInstance);          // uses DLL's instance
                                            //  handle, set in DllMain
CString strRes;
strRes.LoadString(IDS_MYSTRING);
AfxSetResourceHandle(hInstResourceClient); // restores client's
                                            //  instance handle
```

You might be tempted to use the MFC function *AfxGetInstanceHandle* instead of using the global variable set in *DllMain*. This won't work because in an extension DLL, *AfxGetInstanceHandle* returns the EXE's instance handle, not the DLL's handle.

The EX21A Example—An MFC Extension DLL

This example makes an extension DLL out of the *CPersistentFrame* class you saw in Chapter 14. First you'll build the ex21a.dll file, and then you'll use it in a test client program, EX21B.

Here are the steps for building the EX21A example:

1. Run AppWizard to produce \VCPP32\EX21A\EX21A. Select New from the Developer Studio's File menu, and then choose Project Workspace as before. Instead of selecting the default, MFC AppWizard (exe), choose MFC AppWizard (dll), as shown here:

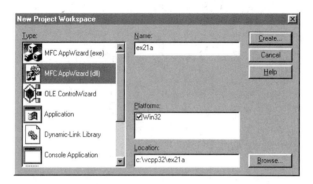

In this example, there's only one AppWizard screen. Choose MFC Extension DLL, as shown here:

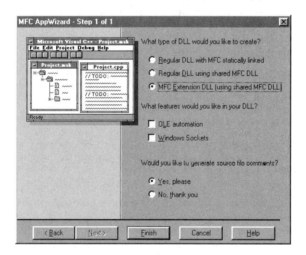

2. Examine the ex21a.cpp file. AppWizard generates the following code, which includes the *DllMain* function:

```
// ex21a.cpp : Defines the initialization routines for the DLL.
//

#include "stdafx.h"
#include <afxdllx.h>
```

```
#ifdef _DEBUG
#define new DEBUG_NEW
#undef THIS_FILE
static char THIS_FILE[] = __FILE__;
#endif

static AFX_EXTENSION_MODULE Ex21aDLL = { NULL, NULL };

extern "C" int APIENTRY
DllMain(HINSTANCE hInstance, DWORD dwReason, LPVOID lpReserved)
{
    if (dwReason == DLL_PROCESS_ATTACH)
    {
        TRACE0("EX21A.DLL Initializing!\n");

        // Extension DLL one-time initialization
        AfxInitExtensionModule(Ex21aDLL, hInstance);

        // Insert this DLL into the resource chain
        new CDynLinkLibrary(Ex21aDLL);
    }
    else if (dwReason == DLL_PROCESS_DETACH)
    {
        TRACE0("EX21A.DLL Terminating!\n");
    }
    return 1;   // ok
}
```

Typically, you don't have to change this code unless you want to capture the instance handle in a global variable.

3. **Add the files persist.h and persist.cpp to the project.**   Copy these files from the \VCPP32\EX14A directory to the \VCPP32\EX21A directory, and then choose Files Into Project from the Developer Studio's Insert menu to add persist.cpp to the project.

4. **Edit the persist.h file.**   Modify the line

```
class CPersistentFrame : public CFrameWnd
```

to read

```
class AFX_EXT_CLASS CPersistentFrame : public CFrameWnd
```

5. **Build the project and copy the DLL file.**   Copy the file ex21a.dll from the \VCPP32\EX21A\DEBUG directory to the \WINDOWS\SYSTEM (or equivalent) directory.

The EX21B Example—A DLL Test Client Program

This example starts off as a client for ex21a.dll. It imports the *CPersistentFrame* class from the DLL and uses it as a base class for the SDI frame window. Later you'll add code to load and test the other sample DLLs in this chapter.

Here are the steps for building the EX21B example:

1. **Run AppWizard to produce \VCPP32\EX21B\EX21B.** This is an ordinary MFC EXE program. Accept the default settings, but select Single Document Interface. Be absolutely sure that, in step 5, you accept the "As a shared DLL" option.

2. **Copy the file persist.h from the \VCPP32\EX21A directory.** Note that you're copying the header file, not the CPP file.

3. **Change the *CMainFrame* base class to *CPersistentFrame*.** Follow the steps from EX14A. Be sure that you insert the following line in both MainFrm.cpp and ex21b.cpp:

```
#include "persist.h"
```

4. **Add the ex21a import library to the linker's input library list.** Choose Settings from the Developer Studio's Build menu, and then fill in the Object/Library Modules control on the Link page as shown here:

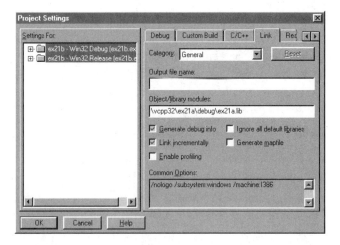

Note that you must specify the full pathname for the ex21a.lib file unless you have a copy of that file in your project directory.

5. Build and test the EX21B program. If Windows can't find the EX21A DLL, it displays a message box when EX21B starts. If all goes well, you should have a persistent frame application that works exactly like the one in EX14A. The only difference is that the *CPersistentFrame* code is in an extension DLL.

MFC Regular DLLs—The *CWinApp* Derived Class

When AppWizard generates a regular DLL, the *DllMain* function is inside the framework, and you end up with a class derived from *CWinApp* (and a global object of that class), just as you would with an EXE program. You can get control by overriding *CWinApp::InitInstance* and *CWinApp::ExitInstance*. Most of the time, you don't bother overriding those functions, though. You simply write the C functions and then export them with the _ _*declspec(dllexport)* modifier (or with entries in the project's DEF file).

The MFC Regular DLL Resource Search Sequence

If you use the MFC resource loading functions in a regular DLL, the framework looks only at the DLL's own resources. If, for some reason, you need to load resources from the client, you must write code such as this:

```
HINSTANCE hInstResourceDll = AfxGetResourceHandle();
HINSTANCE hInstResourceClient =
    (HINSTANCE) ::GetModuleHandle(NULL);
AfxSetResourceHandle(hInstResourceClient);
// uses EXE's instance handle
CString strRes;
strRes.LoadString(IDS_MYSTRING);
AfxSetResourceHandle(hInstResourceDll);
// restores client's instance handle
```

Don't try to use *AfxGetInstanceHandle* instead of *GetModuleHandle*. In a regular DLL, *AfxGetInstanceHandle* returns the DLL's instance handle, not the EXE's handle.

The EX21C Example—An MFC Regular DLL

This example makes a regular DLL that exports a single square root function. First you'll build the ex21c.dll file, and then you'll modify the test client program, EX21B, to test the new DLL.

Here are the steps for building the EX21C example:

1. Run AppWizard to produce \VCPP32\EX21C\EX21C. Proceed as you did for EX21A, but accept "Regular DLL using shared MFC DLL"

505

(instead of choosing MFC Extension DLL) from the one and only AppWizard page.

2. Examine the ex21c.cpp file. AppWizard generates the following code, which includes a derived *CWinApp* class:

```
// ex21c.cpp : Defines the initialization routines for the DLL.
//

#include "StdAfx.h"
#include "ex21c.h"

#ifdef _DEBUG
#define new DEBUG_NEW
#undef THIS_FILE
static char THIS_FILE[] = __FILE__;
#endif

/////////////////////////////////////////////////////////////////////////////
// CEx21cApp

BEGIN_MESSAGE_MAP(CEx21cApp, CWinApp)
    //{{AFX_MSG_MAP(CEx21cApp)
    // NOTE - the ClassWizard will add and remove mapping macros here.
    //    DO NOT EDIT what you see in these blocks of generated code!
    //}}AFX_MSG_MAP
END_MESSAGE_MAP()

/////////////////////////////////////////////////////////////////////////////
// CEx21cApp construction

CEx21cApp::CEx21cApp()
{
    // TODO: add construction code here,
    // Place all significant initialization in InitInstance
}

/////////////////////////////////////////////////////////////////////////////
// The one and only CEx21cApp object

CEx21cApp theApp;
/////////////////////////////////////////////////////////////////////////////
```

3. Add the code for the exported *Ex21cSquareRoot* function. It's OK to add this code in the ex21c.cpp file, although you can use a new file if you want to:

```
extern "C" __declspec(dllexport) double Ex21cSquareRoot(double d)
{
    TRACE("Entering Ex21cSquareRoot\n");
    if (d > 0.0) {
      return sqrt(d);
    }
    AfxMessageBox("Can't take square root of 0 or negative number");
    return 0.0;
}
```

You can see that there's no problem with the DLL displaying a message box or other modal dialog. You'll need to include math.h in ex21c.cpp.

4. **Build the project, and copy the DLL file.**   Copy the file ex21c.dll from the \VCPP32\EX21C\DEBUG directory to the \WINDOWS\SYSTEM (or equivalent) directory.

Updating the EX21B Example—Adding Code to Test ex21c.dll

When you first built the EX21B program, it linked dynamically to the EX21A MFC extension DLL. Now you'll update the project to implicitly link to the EX21C MFC regular DLL and to call the DLL's square root function.

Here are the steps for updating the EX21B example:

1. **Add a new dialog resource and class to \VCPP32\EX21B\EX21B.**
Use the graphic editor to create the IDD-EX21C template, as shown here:

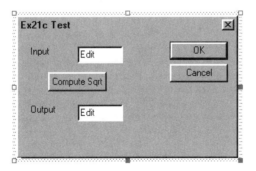

Then use ClassWizard to generate a class *CTest21cDialog*, derived from *CDialog*. The controls, data members, and message map function are shown in the table on the following page:

507

Control ID	Type	Data Member	Message Map Function
IDC_INPUT	edit	*m_dInput* (double)	
IDC_OUTPUT	edit	*m_dOutput* (double)	
IDC_COMPUTE	button		*OnCompute*

2. Code the *OnCompute* function to call the DLL's exported function.

Edit the ClassWizard-generated function in Test21cDialog.cpp as shown here:

```
void CTest21cDialog::OnCompute()
{
    UpdateData(TRUE);
    m_dOutput = Ex21cSquareRoot(m_dInput);
    UpdateData(FALSE);
}
```

You'll have to declare the *Ex21cSquareRoot* function as an imported function. Add the following line to the Test21cDialog.h file:

```
extern "C" __declspec(dllimport) double Ex21cSquareRoot(double d);
```

3. Integrate the *CTest21cDialog* class into the EX21B application.

You'll need to add a top-level menu, Test, and an Ex21c DLL option with the ID *ID_TEST_EX21CDLL*. Use ClassWizard to map this option to a member function in the *CEx21bView* class, and then code the handler in Ex21bView.cpp as follows:

```
void CEx21bView::OnTestEx21cdll()
{
    CTest21cDialog dlg;
    dlg.DoModal();
}
```

Of course, you'll have to add the following line to the Ex21bView.cpp file:

```
#include "Test21cDialog.h"
```

4. Add the ex21c import library to the linker's input library list.

Choose Settings from the Developer Studio's Build menu, and then add \vcpp32\ex21c\debug\ex21c.lib to the Object/Library Modules control on the Link page. (Use a space to separate the existing entry from the new entry.) Now the program should implicitly link to both the EX21A.DLL and the EX21C.DLL. As you can see, the client doesn't much care whether the DLL is a regular DLL or an extension DLL. You just specify the LIB name to the linker.

5. **Build and test the updated EX21B application.** Choose Ex21c DLL from the Test menu. Type a number in the Input edit control, and click the Compute Sqrt button. The result should appear in the Output control.

A Custom Control DLL

Programmers have been using DLLs for custom controls since the early days of Windows because custom controls are neatly self-contained. The original custom controls were written in pure C and configured as stand-alone DLLs. Today you can use the features of the MFC library in your custom controls, and you can use the wizards to make coding easier. A regular DLL is the best choice for a custom control because the control doesn't need a C++ interface, and the control can be used by any development system that accepts custom controls (such as the Borland C++ compiler). You'll probably want the MFC dynamic linking option because the resulting DLL will be smaller and quicker to load.

What Is a Custom Control?

You've seen ordinary controls and Windows 95 common controls in Chapter 6, and OLE Controls in Chapter 8. The custom control acts like an ordinary control, such as the edit control, in that it sends WM_COMMAND notification messages to its parent window and it receives user-defined messages. The graphic editor lets you position custom controls in dialog templates. That's what the "head" control palette item, shown here, is for:

You have a lot of freedom in designing your custom control. You can paint anything you want in its window (which is managed by the client application), and you can define any notification and inbound messages you need. You can use ClassWizard to map normal Windows messages in the control (WM_LBUTTONDOWN, for example), but you must manually map the user-defined messages, and you must manually map the notification messages in the parent window class.

A Custom Control's Window Class

A dialog resource template specifies its custom controls by their symbolic <u>window</u> <u>class</u> names. Don't confuse the Win32 window class with the C++ class; the only similarity is the name. A window class is defined by a structure that contains the following:

- the name of the class
- a pointer to the *WndProc* function that receives messages sent to windows of the class
- miscellaneous attributes, such as the background brush

The Win32 *RegisterClass* function copies the structure into process memory such that any function in the process can use the class to create a window. Now, when the dialog window is initialized, Windows creates the custom control child windows from the window class names stored in the template.

Suppose now that the control's *WndProc* function is inside a DLL. When the DLL is initialized (by a call to *DllMain*), it can call *RegisterClass* for the control. Because the DLL is part of the process, the client program can create child windows of the custom control class. To summarize, the client knows the name string of a control window class, and it uses that class name to construct the child window. All the code for the control, including the *WndProc* function, is inside the DLL. All that's necessary is that the client load the DLL prior to creating the child window.

The MFC Library and the *WndProc* Function

OK, so Windows calls the control's *WndProc* function for each message sent to that window. But you don't want to write an old-fashioned *switch-case* statement—you want to map those messages to C++ member functions, as you've been doing all along. Now, in the DLL, you must rig up a C++ class that corresponds to the control's window class. Once you've done that, you can happily use ClassWizard to map messages.

The obvious part is the writing of the C++ class for the control. You simply use ClassWizard to create a new class derived from *CWnd*. The tricky part is wiring the C++ class to the *WndProc* function and to the application framework's message pump. You'll see a real *WndProc* in the EX21D example, but here's the pseudocode for a typical control *WndProc* function:

```
LONG MyControlWndProc(HWND hWnd, UINT message
                      UINT wParam, LONG lParam)
{
```

```
    if (this is the first message for this window) {
      CWnd* pWnd = new CMyControlWindowClass();
      attach pWnd to hWnd
    }
    return AfxCallWndProc(pWnd, hWnd, message, WParam, lParam);
}
```

The MFC *AfxCallWndProc* function passes messages on to the framework, which dispatches them to the member functions mapped in *CMyControl-WindowClass*.

Custom Control Notification Messages

The control communicates with its parent window by sending it special WM_COMMAND notification messages with parameters, as shown here:

Parameter	Usage
(HIWORD) wParam	notification code
(LOWORD) wParam	child window ID
lParam	child window handle

The meaning of the notification code is arbitrary and depends on the control. The parent window must interpret the code based on its knowledge of the control. For example, the code 77 might mean that the user typed a character while positioned on the control.

The control might send a notification message such as this:

```
GetParent()->SendMessage(WM_COMMAND,
    GetDlgCtrlID() | ID_NOTIFYCODE << 16, (LONG) GetSafeHwnd());
```

On the client side, you map the message with the MFC *ON_CONTROL* macro like this:

```
ON_CONTROL(ID_NOTIFYCODE, IDC_MYCONTROL, OnClickedMyControl)
```

and you declare the handler function like this:

```
void OnClickedMyControl();
```

User-Defined Messages Sent to the Control

You have already seen user-defined messages in Chapter 7. This is the means by which the client program communicates with the control. Because a standard message returns a 32-bit value if it is sent rather than posted, the client can obtain information from the control.

The EX21D Example—A Custom Control

The EX21D program is an MFC Regular DLL that implements a traffic-light control indicating off, red, yellow, and green states. When clicked with the left mouse button, it sends a clicked notification message to its parent, and it responds to two user-defined messages, RYG_SETSTATE and RYG_GET-STATE. The state is an integer that represents the color. Credit goes to Richard Wilton, who included the original C-language version of this control in his *Windows 3 Developer's Workshop* book (Microsoft Press, 1991).

The EX21D project was originally generated using AppWizard, with linkage to the shared MFC DLL, just like EX21C. Figure 21-1 shows the code for the primary source file, with the added *InitInstance* function shaded. The dummy exported *Ex21dEntry* function exists solely to allow the DLL to be implicitly linked. The client program must include a call to this function. As an alternative, the client program could call the Win32 *LoadLibrary* in its *Init-Instance* function to explicitly link the DLL.

EX21D.CPP

```
#include "StdAfx.h"
#include "ex21d.h"
#include "RygWnd.h"

#ifdef _DEBUG
#define new DEBUG_NEW
#undef THIS_FILE
static char THIS_FILE[] = __FILE__;
#endif

extern "C" __declspec(dllexport ) void Ex21dEntry() {} // dummy function
/////////////////////////////////////////////////////////////////////////
// CEx21dApp

BEGIN_MESSAGE_MAP(CEx21dApp, CWinApp)
    //{{AFX_MSG_MAP(CEx21dApp)
    // NOTE - the ClassWizard will add and remove mapping macros here.
    //    DO NOT EDIT what you see in these blocks of generated code!
    //}}AFX_MSG_MAP
END_MESSAGE_MAP()


/////////////////////////////////////////////////////////////////////////
// CEx21dApp construction
```

Figure 21-1.   *(continued)*
The EX21D primary source listing.

Figure 21-1. *continued*

```
CEx21dApp::CEx21dApp()
{
    // TODO: add construction code here,
    // Place all significant initialization in InitInstance
}


/////////////////////////////////////////////////////////////////////////////
// The one and only CEx21dApp object

CEx21dApp theApp;
```

```
BOOL CEx21dApp::InitInstance()
{
    CRygWnd::RegisterWndClass(AfxGetInstanceHandle());
    return CWinApp::InitInstance();
}
```

Figure 21-2 shows the code for the *CRygWnd* class, including the global *RygWndProc* function. The code that paints the traffic light isn't very interesting, so we'll concentrate on the functions that are common to most custom controls. The static *RegisterWndClass* member function actually registers the RYG window class and must be called as soon as the DLL is loaded. The *OnLButtonDown* handler is called when the user presses the left mouse button in the control window. It sends the clicked notification message to the parent window. The overridden *PostNcDestroy* function is important because it deletes the *CRygWnd* object when the client program destroys the control window. The *OnGetState* and *OnSetState* functions are called in response to user-defined messages sent by the client. Remember to copy the DLL to the \WINDOWS\SYSTEM (or equivalent) directory.

RYGWND.H

```
#define RYG_SETSTATE WM_USER + 0
#define RYG_GETSTATE WM_USER + 1

LRESULT CALLBACK AFX_EXPORT
    RygWndProc(HWND hWnd, UINT message, WPARAM wParam, LPARAM lParam);

class CRygWnd : public CWnd
{
```

Figure 21-2. *(continued)*

The CRygWnd *class listing.*

Figure 21-2. *continued*

```
private:
    int m_nState; // 0=off, 1=red, 2=yellow, 3=green
    static CRect  s_rect;
    static CPoint s_point;
    static CRect  s_rColor[3];
    static CBrush s_bColor[4];

// Construction
public:
    CRygWnd();
public:
    static BOOL RegisterWndClass(HINSTANCE hInstance);

// Overrides
    // ClassWizard generated virtual function overrides
    //{{AFX_VIRTUAL(CRygWnd)
    protected:
    virtual void PostNcDestroy();
    //}}AFX_VIRTUAL

// Implementation
public:
    virtual ~CRygWnd();

    // Generated message map functions
private:
    void SetMapping(CDC* pDC);
    void UpdateColor(CDC* pDC, int n);
protected:
    //{{AFX_MSG(CRygWnd)
    afx_msg void OnPaint();
    afx_msg void OnLButtonDown(UINT nFlags, CPoint point);
    afx_msg LONG OnSetState(UINT wParam, LONG lParam);
    afx_msg LONG OnGetState(UINT wParam, LONG lParam);
    //}}AFX_MSG
    DECLARE_MESSAGE_MAP()
};


///////////////////////////////////////////////////////////////////
```

RYGWND.CPP

```
#include "StdAfx.h"
    // add additional includes here
#include "RygWnd.h"
```

(continued)

Figure 21-2. *continued*

```
#ifdef _DEBUG
#undef THIS_FILE
static char THIS_FILE[] = __FILE__;
#endif

LRESULT CALLBACK AFX_EXPORT
    RygWndProc(HWND hWnd, UINT message, WPARAM wParam, LPARAM lParam)
{
    CWnd* pWnd;

    pWnd = CWnd::FromHandlePermanent(hWnd);
    if (pWnd == NULL) {
      // assume that client created a CRygWnd window
      pWnd = new CRygWnd();
      pWnd->Attach(hWnd);
    }
    ASSERT(pWnd->m_hWnd == hWnd);
    ASSERT(pWnd == CWnd::FromHandlePermanent(hWnd));

    LRESULT lResult = AfxCallWndProc(pWnd, hWnd, message,
                                     wParam, lParam);

    return lResult;
}


/////////////////////////////////////////////////////////////////////
// CRygWnd
// static data members
CRect CRygWnd::s_rect(-500, 1000, 500, -1000); // outer rectangle
CPoint CRygWnd::s_point(300, 300); // rounded corners
CRect  CRygWnd::s_rColor[] = {CRect(-250, 800, 250, 300),
                              CRect(-250, 250, 250, -250),
                              CRect(-250, -300, 250, -800)};

CBrush  CRygWnd::s_bColor[] = {RGB(192, 192, 192),
                               RGB(0xFF, 0x00, 0x00),
                               RGB(0xFF, 0xFF, 0x00),
                               RGB(0x00, 0xFF, 0x00)};

BOOL CRygWnd::RegisterWndClass(HINSTANCE hInstance) // static member
                                                    //   function
{
    WNDCLASS wc;
    wc.lpszClassName = "RYG";  // matches classname in client
    wc.hInstance = hInstance;
    wc.lpfnWndProc = RygWndProc;
```

(continued)

515

Figure 21-2. *continued*

```
    wc.hCursor = ::LoadCursor(NULL, IDC_ARROW);
    wc.hIcon = 0;
    wc.lpszMenuName = NULL;
    wc.hbrBackground = (HBRUSH) ::GetStockObject(LTGRAY_BRUSH);
    wc.style = CS_GLOBALCLASS;
    wc.cbClsExtra = 0;
    wc.cbWndExtra = 0;
    return (::RegisterClass(&wc) != 0);
}
/////////////////////////////////////////////////////////////////////

CRygWnd::CRygWnd()
{
    m_nState = 0;
    TRACE("CRygWnd ctor\n");
}


CRygWnd::~CRygWnd()
{
    TRACE("CRygWnd dtor\n");
}



BEGIN_MESSAGE_MAP(CRygWnd, CWnd)
    //{{AFX_MSG_MAP(CRygWnd)
    ON_WM_PAINT()
    ON_WM_LBUTTONDOWN()
    ON_MESSAGE(RYG_SETSTATE, OnSetState)
    ON_MESSAGE(RYG_GETSTATE, OnGetState)
    //}}AFX_MSG_MAP
END_MESSAGE_MAP()


void CRygWnd::SetMapping(CDC* pDC)
{
    CRect clientRect;
    GetClientRect(clientRect);
    pDC->SetMapMode(MM_ISOTROPIC);
    pDC->SetWindowExt(1000, 2000);
    pDC->SetViewportExt(clientRect.right, -clientRect.bottom);
    pDC->SetViewportOrg(clientRect.right / 2, clientRect.bottom / 2);
}


void CRygWnd::UpdateColor(CDC* pDC, int n)
{
```

(continued)

Figure 21-2. *continued*

```
   if (m_nState == n + 1) {
     pDC->SelectObject(&s_bColor[n + 1]);
   }
   else {
     pDC->SelectObject(&s_bColor[0]);
   }
   pDC->Ellipse(s_rColor[n]);
}


/////////////////////////////////////////////////////////////////////
// CRygWnd message handlers

void CRygWnd::OnPaint()
{
   int i;
   CPaintDC dc(this); // device context for painting
   SetMapping(&dc);
   dc.SelectStockObject(DKGRAY_BRUSH);
   dc.RoundRect(s_rect, s_point);
   for (i = 0; i < 3; i++) {
     UpdateColor(&dc, i);
   }
}


void CRygWnd::OnLButtonDown(UINT nFlags, CPoint point)
{
   // notification code is HIWORD of wParam, 0 in this case
   GetParent()->SendMessage(WM_COMMAND, GetDlgCtrlID(),
       (LONG) GetSafeHwnd()); // 0
}


void CRygWnd::PostNcDestroy()
{
   TRACE("CRygWnd::PostNcDestroy\n");
   delete this; // CWnd::PostNcDestroy does nothing
}


LONG CRygWnd::OnSetState(UINT wParam, LONG lParam)
{
   TRACE("CRygWnd::SetState, wParam = %d\n", wParam);
   m_nState = (int) wParam;
   Invalidate(FALSE);
   return 0L;
}
```

(continued)

Figure 21-2. *continued*

```
LONG CRygWnd::OnGetState(UINT wParam, LONG lParam)
{
    TRACE("CRygWnd::GetState\n");
    return m_nState;
}
```

Revising the Updated EX21B Example— Adding Code to Test ex21d.dll

The EX21B program already links to the EX21A and EX21C DLLs. Now you'll revise the project to implicitly link to the EX21D custom control.

Here are the steps for updating the EX21B example:

1. Add a new dialog resource and class to \VCPP32\EX21B\EX21B.
Use the graphic editor to create the *IDD_EX21D* template with a custom control with child window ID *IDC_RYG*, as shown here:

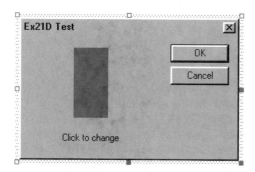

Then use ClassWizard to generate a class *CTest21dDialog*, derived from *CDialog*. Specify RYG as the window class name of the custom control, as shown here:

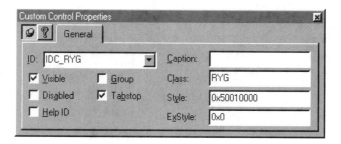

2. Edit the Test21dDialog.h file. Add the following private data member:

```
enum {OFF, RED, YELLOW, GREEN} m_nState;
```

Also, add the following import and user-defined message IDs:

```
extern "C" __declspec(dllimport) void Ex21dEntry(); // dummy function
#define RYG_SETSTATE WM_USER + 0
#define RYG_GETSTATE WM_USER + 1
```

3. Edit the constructor in Test21dDialog.cpp to initialize the state data member. Add the following shaded code:

```
CTest21dDialog::CTest21dDialog(CWnd* pParent /*=NULL*/)
    : CDialog(CTest21dDialog::IDD, pParent)
{
    //{{AFX_DATA_INIT(CTest21dDialog)
        // NOTE: the ClassWizard will add member initialization here
    //}}AFX_DATA_INIT
    m_nState = OFF;
}
```

4. Map the control's clicked notification message. You can't use ClassWizard here, so you must add the message map entry and handler function in the Test21dDialog.cpp file, as shown here:

```
ON_CONTROL(0, IDC_RYG, OnClickedRyg) // notification code is 0
void CTest21dDialog::OnClickedRyg()
{
    switch(m_nState) {
    case OFF:
      m_nState = RED;
      break;
    case RED:
      m_nState = YELLOW;
      break;
    case YELLOW:
      m_nState = GREEN;
      break;
    case GREEN:
      m_nState = OFF;
      break;
    }
```

(continued)

```
        GetDlgItem(IDC_RYG)->SendMessage(RYG_SETSTATE, m_nState);
        return;
        Ex21dEntry(); // make sure DLL gets loaded
}
```

When the dialog gets the clicked notification message, it sends the
RYG_SETSTATE message back to the control in order to change the
color. The DLL's dummy *Ex21dEntry* function isn't actually called, but
the call statement is needed to load the DLL. Don't forget to add the
following prototype in the Text21dDialog.h file:

```
afx_msg void OnClickedRyg();
```

5. **Integrate the *CTest21dDialog* class into the EX21B application.**
You'll need to add a second item on the Test menu, an Ex21d DLL option
with ID *ID_TEST_EX21DDLL*. Use ClassWizard to map this option to a
member function in the *CEx21bView* class, and then code the handler in
Ex21bView.cpp as follows:

```
void CEx21bView::OnTestEx21ddll()
{
    CTest21dDialog dlg;
    dlg.DoModal();
}
```

Of course, you'll have to add the following line to the Ex21bView.h
file:

```
#include "Test21dDialog.h"
```

6. **Add the ex21d import library to the linker's input library list.**
Choose Settings from the Developer Studio's Build menu, and then
add \wcpp32\ex21d\debug\ex21d.lib to the Object/Library Modules
control on the Link page. Now the program should implicitly link
to all three DLLs.

7. Build and test the updated EX21B application.   Choose Ex21d DLL from the Test menu. Try clicking the traffic light with the left mouse button. The traffic-light color should change. The result of clicking the traffic light several times is shown here:

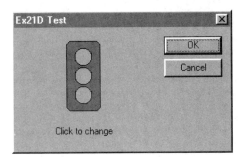

MFC Programs Without Document or View Classes

The document–view architecture is useful for many applications, but sometimes a simpler program structure is sufficient. This chapter illustrates three applications: a dialog-based program, a Single Document Interface (SDI) program, and a Multiple Document Interface (MDI) program. None of these programs use document, view, or document–template classes, but they do use command routing and some other MFC library features. You'll use App-Wizard for the first example, but you won't use it for the other two examples. You will, however, use the graphic editor and ClassWizard for all three.

These three examples don't have a lot in common, but all do use an application object of a class derived from *CWinApp*. The examples start to diverge in the application class's *InitInstance* function.

The EX22A Example—A Dialog-Based Application

When a resizable main frame window is unnecessary, a dialog can be sufficient for an application's user interface. The dialog window appears straightaway when the user starts the application. The user can minimize the dialog window, and as long as the dialog is not system modal, the user can freely switch to other applications.

In this example, the dialog functions as a simple calculator, as shown in Figure 22-1 on the following page. ClassWizard takes charge of defining the class data members and generating the DDX (Dialog Data Exchange) function calls—everything but the coding of the compute function. The application's resource script, ex22a.rc, defines an icon as well as the dialog.

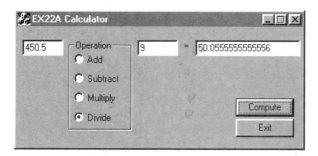

Figure 22-1.
The EX22A Calculator dialog.

AppWizard gives you the option of generating a dialog-based application. Here are the steps for building the EX22A example:

1. Run AppWizard to produce \VCPP32\EX22A\EX22A.   Select the Dialog Based option in the AppWizard Step 1 dialog, as shown here:

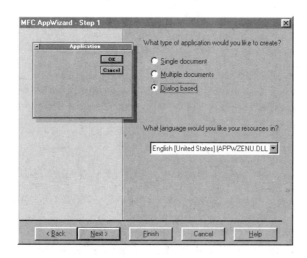

In the next dialog, enter *EX22A Calculator* as the dialog title.

2. Edit the *IDD_EX22A_DIALOG* resource.   Refer to Figure 22-1 as a guide. Use the graphic editor to assign IDs to the controls as follows:

Control	ID
Left operand edit control	IDC_LEFT
Right operand edit control	IDC_RIGHT
Result edit control	IDC_RESULT
First radio button (group property set)	IDC_OPERATION
Compute pushbutton	IDC_COMPUTE

Open the dialog's property sheet, and then click on the Styles tab. Select the System Menu and Minimize Box options.

3. **Use ClassWizard to add member variables and a command handler.** AppWizard has already generated a class *CEx22aDlg*. Add the following data members:

ID	Member Variable
IDC_LEFT	double m_dLeft
IDC_RIGHT	double m_dRight
IDC_RESULT	double m_dResult
IDC_OPERATION	int m_nOperation

Add the message handler *OnCompute* for the *IDC_COMPUTE* button.

4. **Code the *OnCompute* member function in the ex22aDlg.cpp file.** Add the following shaded code:

```
void CEx22aDlg::OnCompute()
{
    UpdateData(TRUE);
    switch (m_nOperation) {
    case 0:  // add
      m_dResult = m_dLeft + m_dRight;
      break;
    case 1:  // subtract
      m_dResult = m_dLeft - m_dRight;
      break;
    case 2:  // multiply
      m_dResult = m_dLeft * m_dRight;
      break;
```

(continued)

525

```
    case 3:  // divide
      if (m_dRight != 0.0) {
         m_dResult = m_dLeft / m_dRight;
      }
      else {
        AfxMessageBox("Divide by zero");
        m_dResult = 0.0;
      }
      break;
   default:
      TRACE("default m_nOperation = %d\n", m_nOperation);
   }
   UpdateData(FALSE);
}
```

5. Build and test the EX22A application. Notice that the program's icon appears in the Windows 95 task bar. Verify that you can minimize the dialog window.

The Application Class *InitInstance* Function

The critical element of the EX22A application is the *CEx22aApp::InitInstance* function that was generated by AppWizard. A normal *InitInstance* function creates a main frame window and returns *TRUE*, allowing the program's message loop to run. The EX22A version constructs a modal dialog object, calls *DoModal*, and then returns *FALSE*. This means that the application exits after the user exits the dialog. The *DoModal* function lets the Windows dialog procedure get and dispatch messages, as it always does. Here is the *InitInstance* code generated from ex22a.cpp:

```
BOOL CEx22aApp::InitInstance()
{
    // Standard initialization
    // If you are not using these features and wish to reduce the size
    //  of your final executable, you should remove from the following
    //  the specific initialization routines you do not need.

#ifdef _AFXDLL
    Enable3dControls(); // Call this when using MFC in a shared DLL
#else
    Enable3dControlsStatic(); // Call this when linking to MFC statically
#endif

    CEx22aDlg dlg;
    m_pMainWnd = &dlg;
    int nResponse = dlg.DoModal();
    if (nResponse == IDOK)
    {
```

```
      // TODO: Place code here to handle when the dialog is
      //  dismissed with OK
    }
    else if (nResponse == IDCANCEL)
    {
      // TODO: Place code here to handle when the dialog is
      //  dismissed with Cancel
    }

    // Since the dialog has been closed, return FALSE so that we exit the
    //  application, rather than start the application's message pump.
    return FALSE;
}
```

The Dialog Class and the Program Icon

If you look at the generated ex22aDlg class, you'll see the following three
message map entries:

```
ON_WM_SYSCOMMAND()
ON_WM_PAINT()
ON_WM_QUERYDRAGICON()
```

The associated handler functions take care of displaying the application's
icon when the user minimizes the program. This code applies only to Windows NT version 3.51, in which the icon is displayed on the desktop. You
don't need the three handlers for Windows 95 or for future versions of Windows NT because those versions of Windows display the program's icon directly on the task bar.

There is some icon code that you do need, however, even for Windows
95. It's in the dialog's handler for WM_INITDIALOG, which is generated by
AppWizard. Notice the two *SetIcon* calls in the code below. AppWizard generates code to add an About box to the System menu if you checked the About
box option. *m_hIcon* is a data member of the dialog class that is initialized in
the constructor. Here is the *OnInitDialog* function:

```
BOOL CEx22aDlg::OnInitDialog()
{
    CDialog::OnInitDialog();

    // Add "About..." menu item to system menu.

    // IDM_ABOUTBOX must be in the system command range.
    ASSERT((IDM_ABOUTBOX & 0xFFF0) == IDM_ABOUTBOX);
    ASSERT(IDM_ABOUTBOX < 0xF000);
```

(continued)

527

```
CMenu* pSysMenu = GetSystemMenu(FALSE);
CString strAboutMenu;
strAboutMenu.LoadString(IDS_ABOUTBOX);
if (!strAboutMenu.IsEmpty())
{
  pSysMenu->AppendMenu(MF_SEPARATOR);
  pSysMenu->AppendMenu(MF_STRING, IDM_ABOUTBOX, strAboutMenu);
}

// Set the icon for this dialog.  The framework does this
//  automatically when the application's main window
//  is not a dialog.
SetIcon(m_hIcon, TRUE);      // Set big icon
SetIcon(m_hIcon, FALSE);     // Set small icon

// TODO: Add extra initialization here

return TRUE;  // return TRUE unless you set the focus to a control
}
```

The EX22B Example—An SDI Application

This SDI "Hello, world!" example builds on the code you saw way back in Chapter 3. The application has only one window, an object of a class derived from *CFrameWnd*. All drawing occurs inside the frame window, and all messages are handled there. Besides the frame and application classes, here are the application's necessary elements:

- **A main menu**—You can have a Windows-based application without a menu—you don't even need a resource script. But EX22B has both. The application framework routes menu commands to message handlers in the frame class.

- **An icon**—An icon is useful if the program is to be activated from Explorer. It's also useful when the application's main frame window is minimized. The icon is stored in the resource, along with the menu.

- **Window close message command handler**—Many applications need to do special processing when their main window is closed. If you were using documents, you could override the *CDocument::SaveModified* function. Here, to take control of the Close process, you must write message handlers to process close messages sent as a result of user actions and by Windows itself when it shuts down.

■ **Precompiled headers**—Precompiled headers offer such a compile speed advantage that you can't afford not to use them. This demands two extra files in the project (StdAfx.h and StdAfx.cpp), but they are short and simple.

■ **Toolbar and status bar**—The EX22B application has these, but they present a problem. They overlap the frame window client area, so you must account for them if you are painting in the client area.

The EX22B application was originally generated with AppWizard as a normal SDI application. The document and view classes were removed, and the application class *InitInstance* function was modified. If you need an application such as this, it might be easier to copy the EX22B project and then change the class names and filenames.

The Application Class *InitInstance* Function

As in all the examples in this chapter, the *InitInstance* function plays a major role. Here the function creates a main frame window and displays it. The key function here is *CFrameWnd::LoadFrame*. It calls *Create* to create the window, and it attaches the menu and icon identified by *IDR_MAINFRAME*. It also attaches an accelerator table and gets the title string (*IDR_MAINFRAME*) from the application's string table. Here is the *InitInstance* code from ex22b.cpp:

```
BOOL CEx22bApp::InitInstance()
{
    // Standard initialization
    // If you are not using these features and wish to reduce the size
    //  of your final executable, you should remove from the following
    //  the specific initialization routines you do not need.

#ifdef _AFXDLL
    Enable3dControls();         // Call this when using MFC in a shared DLL
#else
    Enable3dControlsStatic();   // Call this when linking to MFC statically
#endif

    CMainFrame* pMainFrame = new CMainFrame;
    if (!pMainFrame->LoadFrame(IDR_MAINFRAME))
      return FALSE;
    m_pMainWnd = pMainFrame;
    m_pMainWnd->ShowWindow(m_nCmdShow);
    m_pMainWnd->UpdateWindow();
    return TRUE;
}
```

The *CMainFrame* Class

The *CMainFrame* class is a normal product of AppWizard, with only a few minor changes. It uses the *DECLARE_DYNAMIC* and *IMPLEMENT_DYNAMIC* macros instead of the *DYNCREATE* macros because dynamic construction isn't necessary. Also, the constructor must be public because we're explicitly constructing a frame window from the application class. The following message handlers were added by ClassWizard for the WM_PAINT, WM_CLOSE, and WM_QUERYENDSESSION messages:

```
void CMainFrame::OnPaint()
{
    CPaintDC dc(this); // device context for painting
    dc.TextOut(0, 50, "Hello, world!");
    // Do not call CFrameWnd::OnPaint() for painting messages
}

void CMainFrame::OnClose()
{
    if (AfxMessageBox("OK to close window?", MB_YESNO) == IDYES) {
        CFrameWnd::OnClose();
    }
}

BOOL CMainFrame::OnQueryEndSession()
{
    if (AfxMessageBox("OK to close window?", MB_YESNO) == IDYES) {
        return TRUE;
    }
    return FALSE;
}
```

The EX22C Example—An MDI Application

This bare-bones MDI example isn't as simple as the SDI example, EX22B. Remember, from Chapter 17, that an MDI application consists of a main frame window and one or more child windows. Also, a single MDI client window is attached to the main frame window, but the application framework keeps that window hidden. If you use EX22C as a prototype, you'll be doing most of your programming in a class derived from *CMDIChildWnd*. Child window objects can receive and process messages as the frame window object did in the EX22B example.

The EX22C MDI program doesn't have all the features of a full-blown document–view MDI application, but it does have these basic elements:

- **A main menu**—A full-blown MDI application has two (or more) menus. EX22C has only one menu, and that menu is attached to the main frame window. The MDI Window submenu (with the Cascade, Tile, and child selection items) is part of this main menu structure, but these items (along with the File Close item) are disabled when no child windows are present.

- **An icon**—Every Windows-based program needs an icon. The EX22C resource script defines two icons—one for the application and another for the child window.

- **Initial child window**—Many MDI applications open an empty child window on startup. EX22C is no exception. If you use EX22C as a prototype for your own MDI applications, you can easily disable this feature.

- **Window close message command handler**—MDI window close logic is more complex than SDI window close logic because of the many windows involved. Child windows can be closed individually or as a result of the main frame window's closure. In the EX22C example, the main frame window sends WM_CLOSE messages to all child windows, and the child window message handlers process these messages. The Window menu even has a Close All item, a feature not present in a standard document–view MDI application.

- **Precompiled headers**—As in the previous examples, EX22C uses precompiled headers to speed compilation.

- **Toolbar and status bar**

The EX22C application was originally generated with AppWizard as a normal MDI application. The document and view classes were removed, and the application class *InitInstance* function was modified.

The Application Class *InitInstance* Function

The EX22C *InitInstance* function is almost identical to the EX22B *InitInstance* function except for a call to create the initial child frame. The *CMDIFrameWnd::LoadFrame* call attaches the *IDR_MAINFRAME* icon and menu. In this application, *IDR_MAINFRAME* identifies a complete menu that is identical to the *IDR_EX22CTYPE* menu. This menu remains attached to the MDI frame window both when it is empty and when it contains child windows. The *InitInstance* code from ex22c.cpp is shown on the following page:

```
BOOL CEx22cApp::InitInstance()
{
    // Standard initialization
    // If you are not using these features and wish to reduce the size
    //  of your final executable, you should remove from the following
    //  the specific initialization routines you do not need.

#ifdef _AFXDLL
    Enable3dControls();          // Call this when using MFC in a shared DLL
#else
    Enable3dControlsStatic();    // Call this when linking to MFC statically
#endif

    // create main MDI Frame window
    CMainFrame* pMainFrame = new CMainFrame;
    if (!pMainFrame->LoadFrame(IDR_MAINFRAME))
        return FALSE;
    m_pMainWnd = pMainFrame;

    // The main window has been initialized, so show and update it.
    pMainFrame->ShowWindow(m_nCmdShow);
    pMainFrame->UpdateWindow();

    pMainFrame->CreateInitialChild();

    return TRUE;
}
```

The *CMainFrame* Class

The *CMainFrame* class is a normal product of AppWizard, with some changes. It uses the *DECLARE_DYNAMIC* and *IMPLEMENT_DYNAMIC* macros instead of the *DYNCREATE* macros because dynamic construction isn't necessary. It also has a private integer data member *m_nChild*, which keeps track of the child window number for the child window's caption. The following message handlers were added by ClassWizard for the WM_CLOSE and WM_QUERYENDSESSION messages:

```
void CMainFrame::OnClose()
{
    if (CloseAllChildWindows()) {
        CMDIFrameWnd::OnClose();
    }
}

BOOL CMainFrame::OnQueryEndSession()
{
    return CloseAllChildWindows();
}
```

The following command handlers (and update command UI handler) were added for the File New and Window Close All menu options. The *LoadFrame* function creates a child window. If there is an existing maximized child frame, the new child frame is created with the *WS_MAXIMIZE* style. The *CMDIChildWnd::LoadFrame* function uses the document icon, but it does not reset the main frame window's menu or set the caption.

```
void CMainFrame::OnFileNew()
{
    BOOL bMaximized = FALSE;
    // creates a new child window, maximized if active child is maximized
    CChildFrame* pActiveChild = (CChildFrame*) MDIGetActive(&bMaximized);
    CChildFrame* pChild = new CChildFrame();
    pChild->LoadFrame(IDR_EX22CTYPE,
            WS_CHILD | WS_VISIBLE | WS_OVERLAPPEDWINDOW |
            (bMaximized ? WS_MAXIMIZE : 0), this);

    CString strTitle;
    strTitle.Format("Child Window %d", m_nChild++);
    pChild->SetWindowText(strTitle);
}
void CMainFrame::OnWindowCloseall()
{
    CloseAllChildWindows();
}


void CMainFrame::OnUpdateWindowCloseall(CCmdUI* pCmdUI)
{
    pCmdUI->Enable(MDIGetActive() != NULL);
}
```

Finally, a public function is necessary for the *InitInstance* function to create the initial child window, and a helper function closes the child windows, as shown here:

```
void CMainFrame::CreateInitialChild()
{
    OnFileNew(); // call it here because it's protected
}


BOOL CMainFrame::CloseAllChildWindows()
{
    // returns TRUE if all child windows permit closure
    CChildFrame* pChild;
    CChildFrame* pPrevChild = NULL;
    while ((pChild = (CChildFrame*) MDIGetActive()) != NULL) {
```

(continued)

533

```
            if (pChild == pPrevChild)
                return FALSE; // closure not permitted
            pPrevChild = pChild;
            pChild->SendMessage(WM_CLOSE);
        }
        return TRUE;
    }
```

The *CChildFrame* Class

The *CChildFrame* class was originally generated by AppWizard. The message handlers shown here were added by ClassWizard for the WM_PAINT and WM_CLOSE messages:

```
void CChildFrame::OnPaint()
{
    CPaintDC dc(this); // device context for painting
    dc.TextOut(0, 50, "Hello, world!");
    // Do not call CFrameWnd::OnPaint() for painting messages
}

void CChildFrame::OnClose()
{
    if (AfxMessageBox("OK to close window?", MB_YESNO) == IDYES) {
        CMDIChildWnd::OnClose();
    }
}
```

The following command handler was added for the File Close menu command:

```
void CChildFrame::OnFileClose()
{
    SendMessage(WM_CLOSE);
}
```

For Win32 Programmers

The *CMDIChildWnd::LoadFrame* function calls *CMDIChildWnd::Create*, but *Create* doesn't create the child frame window directly. It loads a structure and then sends a WM_MDICREATE message to the MDI client window (owned by the main frame window). The client window then creates the child window.

Resource Requirements

The AppWizard-generated resources weren't changed much for this project. A Close All option was added to the *IDR_EX22CTYPE* Window menu, and then the *IDR_EX22CTYPE* menu was copied on top of the *IDR_MAINFRAME* menu.

Custom AppWizards

The EX22B and EX22C projects are logical candidates for custom App-Wizards. See the topic "Creating Custom AppWizards" in the *Visual C++ User's Guide* in Books Online.

PART IV

OLE

The OLE Component
Object Model (COM)

OLE used to be a separate set of libraries, but now it's an integral part of Windows, and so I've made it an integral part of this book. Soon all Windows programming will involve some OLE, so you'd better start learning it now. But where do you begin? You could start with the MFC classes for OLE documents and document items, but those classes, useful as they are, obscure the real OLE architecture. You've got to start with fundamental OLE theory, and that includes the Component Object Model (COM) and something called an interface.

This is the first of five OLE chapters that make up Part IV of this book. Here you'll get the theory that you'll need for the other four chapters. You'll learn about interfaces, and you'll also learn how the MFC library implements interfaces through its macros and interface maps.

OLE Background

Technically, OLE stands for Object Linking and Embedding, but that now-insufficient title is left over from a previous incarnation, OLE 1. For a while, there was an OLE 2, but now there's just OLE—Microsoft's continuously evolving software architecture for the future. Sounds pretty grandiose, doesn't it? If you found this book in a bookstore, you might have noticed other OLE books on the shelf, particularly Kraig Brockschmidt's 1200-page *Inside OLE,* 2d ed. (Microsoft Press, 1995) and the two volumes of the *OLE Programmer's Reference Library,* 2d ed. (Microsoft Press, 1995; also supplied as part of the Win32 SDK documentation in Books Online.) Did you get the feeling that maybe you didn't know as much as you thought you did? You should have!

Let me tell you my experience. I was feeling pretty good about myself because I had mastered the C++ language, Windows programming, and the MFC library. I thought I was ahead of the game—but then there was this obscure API for linking and embedding that had undergone a version change. No problem, I thought, because the MFC developers had promised that their OLE classes wouldn't change much. Then I started digging in. Pretty soon I began to see references to "interfaces," and I had no clue what an interface was. Shortly thereafter, I attended some OLE seminars at a conference, and I saw dozens of incomprehensible APIs on Microsoft PowerPoint slides. Suddenly it dawned on me that I was at the very bottom of yet another learning curve!

Kraig Brockschmidt, a true Microsoft insider who's also a very bright guy, refers to "six months of mental fog." He's not kidding. Perhaps it won't be as bad for you. Brockschmidt's book, these five chapters, and the MFC OLE classes are available to help you. But if your boss or client has asked for an OLE application by the middle of next week, you could be in trouble. Don't make the same mistake I did: do not depend on the MFC OLE classes to shield you from the underlying OLE architecture. That would be like using the MFC library to create Windows-based applications with no understanding of Windows messages and device contexts.

A few other words of advice:

■ Know the C++ language cold.

■ Get Brockschmidt's book.

Brockschmidt's book almost ignores the MFC library, and it goes into a lot of detail that might frustrate you as a beginning OLE programmer. Once you've gone through the five OLE chapters in this book, however, you'll be ready to make sense out of Brockschmidt and pick up the details that I don't cover. Good luck!

The Component Object Model (COM)

As far as I'm concerned, the Component Object Model (COM) is what OLE is about. OLE is a superset of COM that has some nice features, such as visual editing, drag and drop, and automation, but COM encompasses a new modular software architecture. You really need to learn COM before you can master the OLE features that build on it.

NOTE: You might see the COM acronym interpreted as "Common Object Model." Back in 1994, Microsoft Corporation and Digital Equipment Corporation announced a deal allowing the COM standard to be supported by both companies; "common" took precedence over "component" for a while, but now "component" is back.

The Problem That COM Solves

The "problem" is that there isn't a standard way for Windows program modules to communicate with one another. "But," you say, "what about the DLL with its exported functions, Dynamic Data Exchange (DDE), the Windows clipboard, and the Windows API itself, not to mention legacy standards such as VBX and OLE 1? Aren't they good enough?" Well, no. You can't build an object-oriented operating system for the future out of these ad hoc, unrelated standards. With the OLE Component Object Model, however, you can, and that's precisely what Microsoft is doing.

The Essence of COM

What's wrong with the old standards? Lots. The Windows API has too large a programming "surface area"—350 separate functions. VBXs don't work in the 32-bit world. With DDE, there's a complicated system of applications, topics, and items. How you call a DLL is totally application-specific. COM provides a unified, expandable, object-oriented communications protocol for Windows that already supports the following:

- A standard, language-independent way for a Win32 client EXE to load and call a Win32 DLL

- A general-purpose way for one EXE to control another EXE on the same computer (the DDE replacement)

- A replacement for the VBX control, called an OLE Control (OCX)

- A powerful new way for application programs to interact with the operating system

- Expansion to accommodate new protocols such as Data Access Objects (DAO), described in Chapter 29

> NOTE: COM also supports the 16-bit environment. A 16-bit EXE can use a 16-bit DLL, and 16-bit EXEs can communicate with 32-bit EXEs running on the same computer. This 16-bit capability will become less important as more users switch to the 32-bit versions of Windows.

In the immediate future, Microsoft Corporation will expand COM to handle communications between programs running on separate processors and even different processor types.

So what is COM? That's an easier question to ask than to answer. COM is a protocol that connects one software module with another and then drops out of the picture. After the connection is made, the two modules can communicate through a mechanism called an <u>interface</u>. Interfaces require no statically or dynamically linked entry points or hard-coded addresses other than the few general-purpose COM functions that get the communication process started. An interface (more precisely, a COM interface) is an OLE term that you'll be seeing a lot of. Follow along, and you'll begin to understand what an interface is.

What Is a COM Interface?

Appendix A of this book uses a planetary-motion simulation (suitable for NASA or Nintendo) to illustrate C++ inheritance and polymorphism. I'll stick with that same example here because it's useful to show what COM adds to the plain-vanilla C++ approach used in the appendix. The example here, however, is independent of Appendix A.

Imagine a spaceship that travels through our solar system under the influence of the sun's gravity. In ordinary C++, you could declare a *CSpaceship* class and write a constructor that sets the spaceship's initial position and acceleration. Then you could write a member function named *Fly* that implemented Kepler's laws in order to move the spaceship from one position to the next—say, over a period of 0.1 second. *Fly* would be an ordinary nonvirtual member function. You could also write a *Display* function that painted an image of the spaceship in a window.

If we move the example to COM, the spaceship code lives in a separate EXE or DLL (the <u>server</u>), which is a COM module. A <u>client</u> program can't call *Fly* or any *CSpaceship* constructor directly because COM provides only a standard global function to gain access to the spaceship. Before we tackle real COM, let's build a "COM simulation" in which both the server and the client code are statically linked in the same EXE file. For our standard global function, we'll invent a function named *GetClassObject*, with the following three parameters:

```
BOOL GetClassObject(int nClsid, int nIid, void** ppvObj);
```

The first *GetClassObject* parameter, *nClsid*, is a 32-bit integer that uniquely identifies the *CSpaceship* class. The second parameter, *nIid*, is the unique identifier of the interface that we want. The function returns TRUE if the call was successful.

Now let's back up to the design of *CSpaceship*. We haven't talked about spaceship interfaces yet. A COM interface is a C++ base class (actually, a C++ *struct*) that declares a group of pure virtual functions. These functions completely control some aspect of derived class behavior. For *CSpaceship*, let's write an interface named *IMotion*, which controls the spaceship object's position. For simplicity's sake, we'll declare just two functions, *Fly* and *GetPosition*, and we'll make the position value an integer. The *Fly* function moves the spaceship, and the *GetPosition* function returns a reference to the current position. Here are the declarations:

```
struct IMotion
{
    virtual void Fly() = 0;
    virtual int& GetPosition() = 0;
};

class CSpaceship : public IMotion
{
protected:
    int m_nPosition;
public:
    CSpaceship() { m_nPosition = 0; }
    void Fly();
    int& GetPosition() { return m_nPosition; }
};
```

The actual code for the spaceship-related functions, including *Get-ClassObject*, is located in the server part of the program. The client part calls the *GetClassObject* function to construct the spaceship and to obtain an *IMotion* pointer. Both parts have access to the *IMotion* declaration at compile time. Here's how the client calls *GetClassObject*:

```
IMotion* pMot;
GetClassObject(CLSID_CSpaceship, IID_IMotion, (void**) &pMot);
```

Assume for the moment that COM can use the unique identifiers *CLSID_CSpaceship* and *IID_IMotion* to find the specific *GetClassObject* function for spaceships. If the call is successful, *pMot* points to a *CSpaceship* object that *GetClassObject* somehow constructs. As you can see, the *CSpaceship* class implements the *Fly* and *GetPosition* functions, and our main program can call them for the one particular spaceship object, as shown on the following page:

```
int nPos = 50;
pMot->GetPosition() = nPos;
pMot->Fly();
nPos = pMot->GetPosition();
TRACE("new position = %d\n", nPos);
```

Now the spaceship is off and flying, and we're controlling it entirely through the *pMot* pointer. Notice that *pMot* is technically not a pointer to a *CSpaceship* object, but in this case, a *CSpaceship* pointer and an *IMotion* pointer are the same because *CSpaceship* is derived from *IMotion*. You can see how the virtual functions work here: it's classic C++ polymorphism.

Let's make things a little more complex by adding a second interface, *IVisual*, that handles the spaceship's visual representation. One function is enough—*Display*. Here's the whole base class:

```
struct IVisual
{
    virtual void Display() = 0;
};
```

Are you getting the idea that COM wants you to associate functions in groups? (You're not imagining it.) But why? Well, in your space simulation, you probably want other kinds of objects in addition to spaceships. Imagine that the *IMotion* and *IVisual* interfaces are being used for other classes. Perhaps the *CSun* class has an implementation of *IVisual* but does not have an implementation of *IMotion*, and perhaps the *CSpaceStation* class has other interfaces as well. If you "published" your *IMotion* and *IVisual* interfaces, perhaps other space simulation software companies would adopt them. Or perhaps they wouldn't.

Think of an interface as a contract between two software modules. The idea is that interface declarations never change. If you want to upgrade your spaceship code, you don't change the *IMotion* or the *IVisual* interface; rather, you add a new interface, such as *ICrew*. The existing spaceship clients can continue to run with the old interfaces, and new client programs can use the new *ICrew* interface as well. These client programs can find out, at runtime, which interfaces a particular spaceship software version supports.

Consider the *GetClassObject* function as a more powerful alternative to the C++ constructor. With the ordinary constructor, you obtain one object with one batch of member functions. With the *GetClassObject* function, you obtain the object plus your choice of interfaces. As you'll see later, you start with one interface, and then you use that interface to get other interfaces to the same object.

So how do you program <u>two</u> interfaces for *CSpaceship*? You could use C++ multiple inheritance, but that isn't the preferred way. The MFC library uses <u>nested</u> <u>classes</u> instead. Not all C++ programmers are familiar with nested classes, so I'll offer a little help. Here's a first cut at nesting interfaces within the *CSpaceship* class:

```
class CSpaceship
{
protected:
    int m_nPosition;
    int m_nAcceleration;
    int m_nColor;
public:
    CSpaceship()
        { m_nPosition = m_nAcceleration = m_nColor = 0; }
    class XMotion : public IMotion
    {
    public:
        XMotion() { }
        virtual void Fly();
        virtual int& GetPosition();
    } m_xMotion;

    class XVisual : public IVisual
    {
    public:
        XVisual() { }
        virtual void Display();
    } m_xVisual;

    friend class XVisual;
    friend class XMotion;
};
```

> **NOTE:** It might make sense to make *m_nAcceleration* a data member of *XMotion* and *m_nColor* a data member of *XVisual*. We'll make them data members of *CSpaceship* because that strategy is more compatible with the MFC macros, which you'll see later.

Notice that the implementations of *IMotion* and *IVisual* are contained within the "parent" *CSpaceship* class. Be aware that *m_xMotion* and *m_xVisual* are really embedded data members of *CSpaceship*. Indeed, you could have implemented *CSpaceship* strictly with embedding. Nesting, however, brings two things to the party: first, nested class member functions can access parent class data members without the need for separate *CSpaceship** data members, and second, the nested classes are neatly packaged along with the parent and are invisible outside the parent. Look at the following code for the *GetPosition* member function:

```
int& CSpaceship::XMotion::GetPosition()
{
    METHOD_PROLOGUE(CSpaceship, Motion) // makes pThis
    return pThis->m_nPosition;
}
```

Notice also the double scope resolution operators, which are necessary for nested class member functions. *METHOD_PROLOGUE* is a one-line MFC macro that uses the C *offsetof* operator to generate a *this* pointer to the parent class, *pThis*. The compiler always knows the offset from the beginning of parent class data to the beginning of nested class data. *GetPosition* can thus access the *CSpaceship* data member *m_nPosition*.

Now suppose you have <u>two</u> interface pointers, *pMot* and *pVis*, for a particular *CSpaceship* object. (Don't worry yet about how you got the pointers.) You can call interface member functions in the following manner:

```
pMot->Fly();
pVis->Display();
```

What's happening under the hood? In C++, each <u>class</u> (at least, each class that has virtual functions and is not an abstract base class) has a virtual function table, aka <u>vtable</u>. In this example, that means there are vtables for *CSpaceship::XMotion* and *CSpaceship::XVisual*. For each <u>object</u>, there's a pointer to the object's data, the first element of which is a pointer to the class's vtable. The pointer relationships are shown here:

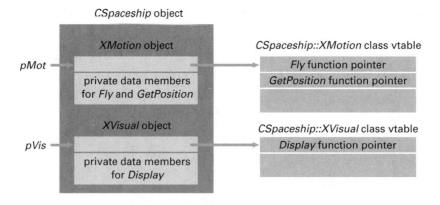

NOTE: Theoretically, it's possible to program OLE in C. If you look at the OLE header files, you'll see code such as this:

```
#ifdef __cplusplus
// C++-specific headers
#else
/* C-specific headers */
#endif
```

In C++, interfaces are declared as C++ *structs*, often with inheritance; in C, they're declared as C *typedef structs* with no inheritance. In C++, the compiler generates vtables for your derived classes; in C, you must "roll your own" vtables, and that gets tedious. It's important to realize, however, that in neither language do the interface declarations have data members, constructors, or destructors. Therefore, you can't rely on the interface having a virtual destructor—but that's not a problem because you never invoke a destructor for an interface.

The *IUnknown* Interface and the *QueryInterface* Member Function

Let's get back to the problem of obtaining your interface pointers in the first place. OLE declares a special interface named *IUnknown* for this purpose. As a matter of fact, all interfaces are derived from *IUnknown*, which has a pure virtual member function, *QueryInterface*, that returns an interface pointer based on the interface ID you feed it. All this assumes that you have one interface pointer to start with, either an *IUnknown* pointer or a pointer to a derived interface such as *IMotion*. Here is the new interface hierarchy, with *IUnknown* at the top:

```
struct IUnknown
{
    virtual BOOL QueryInterface(int nIid, void** ppvObj) = 0;
};

struct IMotion : public IUnknown
{
    virtual void Fly() = 0;
    virtual int& GetPosition() = 0;
};

struct IVisual : public IUnknown
{
    virtual void Display() = 0;
};
```

To satisfy the compiler, we must now add the following *QueryInterface* implementations in both *CSpaceship::XMotion* and *CSpaceship::XVisual*:

```
virtual BOOL QueryInterface(int& nIid, void** ppvObj);
```

What do the vtables look like now? For each derived class, the compiler builds a vtable with the base class function pointers on top, as shown here:

CSpaceship::XMotion vtable
QueryInterface function pointer
Fly function pointer
GetPosition function pointer

CSpaceship::XVisual vtable
QueryInterface function pointer
Display function pointer

Now there's a way for *GetClassObject* to get the interface pointer for a given *CSpaceship* object.

Here's the code for the *QueryInterface* function in *XMotion*:

```
BOOL CSpaceship::XMotion::QueryInterface(int nIid,
                                         void** ppvObj)
{
    METHOD_PROLOGUE(CSpaceship, Motion)
    switch (nIid) {
    case IID_IUnknown:
    case IID_IMotion:
        *ppvObj = &pThis->m_xMotion;
        break;
    case IID_IVisual:
        *ppvObj = &pThis->m_xVisual;
        break;
    default:
        *ppvObj = NULL;
        return FALSE;
    }
    return TRUE;
}
```

Because *IMotion* is derived from *IUnknown*, an *IMotion* pointer will be OK if the caller asks for an *IUnknown* pointer.

NOTE: The COM standard demands that *QueryInterface* return exactly the same *IUnknown* pointer value for *IID_IUnknown*, no matter which interface pointer you start with. Thus, if two *IUnknown* pointers match, you can assume that they refer to the same object.

Below is a *GetClassObject* function that uses the address of *m_xMotion* to obtain the first interface pointer for the newly constructed *CSpaceship* object:

```
BOOL GetClassObject(int& nClsid, int& nIid,
                    void** ppvObj)
{
    ASSERT(nClsid == CLSID_CSpaceship);
    CSpaceship* pObj = new CSpaceship();
    IUnknown* pUnk = &pObj->m_xMotion;
    return pUnk->QueryInterface(nIid, ppvObj);
}
```

Now your client program can call *QueryInterface* to obtain an *IVisual* pointer, as shown here:

```
IMotion* pMot;
IVisual* pVis;
GetClassObject(CLSID_CSpaceship, IID_IMotion, (void**) &pMot);
pMot->Fly();
pMot->QueryInterface(IID_IVisual, (void**) &pVis);
pVis->Display();
```

Notice that the client uses a *CSpaceship* object, but it <u>never</u> has an actual *CSpaceship* pointer. Thus, the client cannot directly access *CSpaceship* data members, even if they're public.

OLE has its own graphical representation for interfaces and COM classes. Interfaces are shown as small circles (or jacks) with lines attached to their class. The *IUnknown* interface, which every COM class supports, is at the top, and the others are on the left. The *CSpaceship* class can be represented like this:

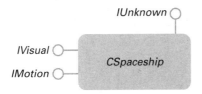

Reference Counting: The *AddRef* and *Release* Functions

COM interfaces don't have virtual destructors, so it isn't cool to write a statement such as this:

```
delete pMot;  // Don't do this.
```

OLE has a strict protocol for deleting objects, and the two other *IUnknown* virtual functions, *AddRef* and *Release*, are the key. Each COM class has a data member—*m_dwRef*, in the MFC library—that keeps track of how many "users" an object has. Each time the server program returns a new interface pointer (as in *QueryInterface*), the program calls *AddRef*, which increments *m_dwRef*. When the client program is finished with the pointer, it calls *Release*. When *m_dwRef* goes to 0, the object destroys itself. Here's an example of a *Release* function for the *CSpaceship::XMotion* class:

```
DWORD CSpaceship::XMotion::Release()
{
    METHOD_PROLOGUE(CSpaceship, Motion) // makes pThis
    if (pThis->m_dwRef == 0)
      return 0;
    if (--pThis->m_dwRef == 0) {
      delete pThis; // the spaceship object
      return 0;
    }
    return pThis->m_dwRef;
}
```

In MFC OLE programs, the object's constructor sets *m_dwRef* to 1. This means it isn't necessary to call *AddRef* after the object is first constructed.

Class Factories

Object-oriented terminology gets a little fuzzy sometimes. Smalltalk programmers, for example, talk about "objects" the way C++ programmers talk about "classes." The OLE reference documentation often uses the term "component object" when it should use "component class." What OLE calls a "class factory" is really an "object factory." A class factory is a class that supports a special OLE interface named *IClassFactory*. This interface, like all interfaces, is derived from *IUnknown*. *IClassFactory*'s principal member function is *CreateInstance*, which is declared like this:

```
virtual BOOL CreateInstance(int& nIid, void** ppvObj) = 0;
```

Why use a class factory? We've already seen that we can't call the target class constructor directly; we have to let the server decide how to construct objects. The server provides the class factory for this purpose and thus encapsulates the creation step, as it should. Locating and launching server modules, and thus establishing the class factory, is expensive, but constructing objects with *CreateInstance* is cheap. We can, therefore, allow a single class factory to create multiple objects.

What does all this mean? It means that we screwed up when we let *GetClassObject* construct the *CSpaceship* object directly. We were supposed to construct a class factory object and then call *CreateInstance* to cause the class factory (object factory) to construct the actual spaceship object.

Now let's do things the right way. First we declare a new class, *CSpaceshipFactory*. To keep things simple, we'll derive the class from *IClassFactory* so that we don't have to deal with nested classes, and in addition, we'll add the code that tracks references:

```
struct IClassFactory : public IUnknown
{
    virtual BOOL CreateInstance(int& nIid, void** ppvObj) = 0;
};


class CSpaceshipFactory : public IClassFactory
{
private:
    DWORD m_dwRef;
public:
    CSpaceshipFactory() { m_dwRef = 1; }
    // IUnknown functions
    virtual BOOL QueryInterface(int& nIid,
                                 void** ppvObj);
    virtual DWORD AddRef();
    virtual DWORD Release();
    // IClassFactory function
    virtual BOOL CreateInstance(int& nIid,
                                 void** ppvObj);
};
```

Next we write the *CreateInstance* member function:

```
BOOL CSpaceshipFactory::CreateInstance(int& nIid, void** ppvObj)
{
    CSpaceship* pObj = new CSpaceship();
    IUnknown* pUnk = &pObj->m_xMotion;
    return pUnk->QueryInterface(nIid, ppvObj);
}
```

Finally, here's the new *GetClassObject* function, which constructs a class factory object and returns an *IClassFactory* interface pointer:

```
BOOL GetClassObject(int& nClsid, int& nIid,
                     void** ppvObj)
{
    ASSERT(nClsid == CLSID_CSpaceship);
    ASSERT((nIid == IID_IUnknown) || (nIid == IID_IClassFactory));
    CSpaceshipFactory* pObj = new CSpaceshipFactory();
    *ppObj = pObj; // IUnknown* = IClassFactory* = CSpaceship*
}
```

The *CSpaceship* and *CSpaceshipFactory* classes work together and share the same class ID. Now the client code looks like this (without error-checking logic):

```
IMotion* pMot;
IVisual* pVis;
IClassFactory* pFac;
GetClassObjcct(CLSID_CSpaceship, IID_IClassFactory, (void**) &pFac);
pFac->CreateInstance(IID_IMotion, &pMot);
pMot->QueryInterface(IID_IVisual, (void**) &pVis);
pMot->Fly();
pVis->Display();
```

Notice that the *CSpaceshipFactory* class implements the *AddRef* and *Release* functions. It must do this because *AddRef* and *Release* are pure virtual functions in the *IUnknown* base class. We'll start using these functions in the next iteration of the program.

The *CCmdTarget* Class

We're still a long way from real MFC OLE code, but we can take one more step in the COM simulation before we switch to the real thing. As you might guess, there's some code and data that can be "factored out" of our spaceship COM classes into a base class. That's exactly what the MFC library does, and the base class is *CCmdTarget*, the standard base class for document and window classes. *CCmdTarget*, in turn, is derived from *CObject*. We'll use *CSimulated-CmdTarget* instead, and we won't put too much in it—only the reference counting logic and the *m_dwRef* data member. The *CCmdTarget* functions *ExternalAddRef* and *ExternalRelease* can be called in derived COM classes. Because we're using *CCmdTarget*, we'll bring *CSpaceshipFactory* in line with *CSpaceship*, and we'll use a nested class for the *IClassFactory* interface.

We can also do some factoring out inside our *CSpaceship* class. The *QueryInterface* function can be "delegated" from the nested classes to the outer class helper function *ExternalQueryInterface*, which calls *ExternalAddRef*. Each *QueryInterface* function calls *AddRef*, but *CreateInstance* calls *ExternalQueryInterface*, followed by a call to *ExternalRelease*. Now, when the first interface pointer is returned by *CreateInstance*, the spaceship object has a reference count of 1. A subsequent *QueryInterface* call increments the count to 2, and in this case, the client must call *Release* twice to destroy the spaceship object.

One last thing—we'll make the class factory object a global object. That way we won't have to call its constructor. When the client calls *Release*, there is no problem because the class factory's reference count is 2 by the time the client receives it. (The *CSpaceshipFactory* constructor set the reference count to 1, and *ExternalQueryInterface*, called by *GetClassObject*, set the count to 2.)

The EX23A Example—A Simulated COM

Figures 23-1, 23-2, 23-3, and 23-4 show code for a working "simulated OLE" program, EX23A. This is a Win32 command-line program (without the MFC library) that uses a class factory to construct an object of class *CSpaceship*, calls its interface functions, and then releases the spaceship. The Interface.h header file, shown in Figure 23-1, contains the *CSimulatedCmdTarget* base class and the interface declarations that are used by both the client and server programs. The Spaceship.h header file, shown in Figure 23-2 (beginning on page 555), contains the spaceship-specific class declarations that are used in the server program. Spaceship.cpp, shown in Figure 23-3 (beginning on page 556), is the server, which implements *GetClassObject*; and Client.cpp, shown in Figure 23-4 (beginning on page 560), is the client, which calls *GetClassObject*. What's phony here is that both client and server code are linked within the same ex23a.exe program. Thus, our simulated OLE is not required to make the connection at runtime. (You'll see how that's done later in this chapter.)

INTERFACE.H

```
// definitions that make our code look like MFC code
#define BOOL    int
#define DWORD   unsigned int
#define TRUE    1
#define FALSE   0
#define TRACE   printf
#define ASSERT  assert
//----------definitions and macros------------------------------------
#define CLSID_CSpaceship      10

#define IID_IUnknown          0
#define IID_IClassFactory     1
#define IID_IMotion           2
#define IID_IVisual           3

// this macro for 16-bit Windows only
#define METHOD_PROLOGUE(theClass, localClass) \
    theClass* pThis = ((theClass*)((char*)(this) - \
        offsetof(theClass, m_x##localClass))); \


BOOL GetClassObject(int nClsid, int nIid, void** ppvObj);
```

Figure 23-1. *(continued)*
The Interface.h file.

Figure 23-1. *continued*

```
//----------interface declarations-----------------------------------
struct IUnknown
{
    IUnknown() { TRACE("Entering IUnknown ctor %p\n", this); }
    virtual BOOL QueryInterface(int nIid, void** ppvObj) = 0;
    virtual DWORD Release() = 0;
    virtual DWORD AddRef() = 0;
};

struct IClassFactory : public IUnknown
{
    IClassFactory()
        { TRACE("Entering IClassFactory ctor %p\n", this); }
    virtual BOOL CreateInstance(int nIid, void** ppvObj) = 0;
};

struct IMotion : public IUnknown
{
    IMotion() { TRACE("Entering IMotion ctor %p\n", this); }
    virtual void Fly() = 0; // pure
    virtual int& GetPosition() = 0;
};

struct IVisual : public IUnknown
{
    IVisual() { TRACE("Entering IVisual ctor %p\n", this); }
    virtual void Display() = 0;
};

class CSimulatedCmdTarget // 'simulated' CSimulatedCmdTarget
{
public:
    DWORD m_dwRef;

protected:
    CSimulatedCmdTarget() {
      TRACE("Entering CSimulatedCmdTarget ctor %p\n", this);
      m_dwRef = 1; // implied first AddRef
    }
    virtual ~CSimulatedCmdTarget()
        { TRACE("Entering CSimulatedCmdTarget dtor %p\n", this); }
    DWORD ExternalRelease() {
TRACE("Entering CSimulatedCmdTarget::ExternalRelease--RefCount = %ld\n",
    m_dwRef);
        if (m_dwRef == 0)
          return 0;
```

(continued)

Figure 23-1. *continued*

```
        if(--m_dwRef == 0L) {
          TRACE("deleting\n");
          delete this;
          return 0;
        }
        return m_dwRef;
    }
    DWORD ExternalAddRef() { return ++m_dwRef; }
};
```

SPACESHIP.H

```
class CSpaceship;

//----------class declarations-------------------------------------
class CSpaceshipFactory : public CSimulatedCmdTarget
{
public:
    CSpaceshipFactory()
        { TRACE("Entering CSpaceshipFactory ctor %p\n", this); }
    ~CSpaceshipFactory()
        { TRACE("Entering CSpaceshipFactory dtor %p\n", this); }
    BOOL ExternalQueryInterface(int lRid, void** ppvObj);
    class XClassFactory : public IClassFactory
    {
    public:
        XClassFactory()
            { TRACE("Entering XClassFactory ctor %p\n", this); }
        virtual BOOL QueryInterface(int lRid, void** ppvObj);
        virtual DWORD Release();
        virtual DWORD AddRef();
        virtual BOOL CreateInstance(int lRid, void** ppvObj);
    } m_xClassFactory;
    friend class XClassFactory;
};

class CSpaceship : public CSimulatedCmdTarget
{
private:
    int m_nPosition; // we can access these from
                     //  all the interfaces
    int m_nAcceleration;
    int m_nColor;
```

Figure 23-2.   *(continued)*

The Spaceship.h file.

Figure 23-2. *continued*

```
public:
    CSpaceship() {
        TRACE("Entering CSpaceship ctor %p\n", this);
        m_nPosition = 100;
        m_nAcceleration = 101;
        m_nColor = 102;
    }
    ~CSpaceship()
        { TRACE("Entering CSpaceship dtor %p\n", this); }
    BOOL ExternalQueryInterface(int lRid, void** ppvObj);
    class XMotion : public IMotion
    {
    public:
        XMotion()
            { TRACE("Entering XMotion ctor %p\n", this); }
        virtual BOOL QueryInterface(int lRid, void** ppvObj);
        virtual DWORD Release();
        virtual DWORD AddRef();
        virtual void Fly();
        virtual int& GetPosition();
    } m_xMotion;

    class XVisual : public IVisual
    {
    public:
        XVisual() { TRACE("Entering XVisual ctor\n"); }
        virtual BOOL QueryInterface(int lRid, void** ppvObj);
        virtual DWORD Release();
        virtual DWORD AddRef();
        virtual void Display();
    } m_xVisual;

    friend class XVisual;  // these must be at the bottom!
    friend class XMotion;
    friend class CSpaceshipFactory::XClassFactory;
};
```

SPACESHIP.CPP

```
#include <stdio.h>
#include <stddef.h> // for offsetof in METHOD_PROLOGUE
#include <ASSERT.h>
#include "Interface.h"
#include "Spaceship.h"


CSpaceshipFactory g_factory;
```

Figure 23-3.   *(continued)*

The Spaceship.cpp file.

Figure 23-3. *continued*

```
//---------- member functions ----------------------------------------
BOOL CSpaceshipFactory::ExternalQueryInterface(int nIid,
                                                  void** ppvObj) {
TRACE("Entering CSpaceshipFactory::ExternalQueryInterface--nIid = %d\n",
     nIid);
    switch (nIid) {
    case IID_IUnknown:
    case IID_IClassFactory:
      *ppvObj = &m_xClassFactory;
      break;
    default:
      *ppvObj = NULL;
      return FALSE;
    }
    ExternalAddRef();
    return TRUE;
}


BOOL CSpaceshipFactory::XClassFactory::QueryInterface(int nIid,
                                                        void** ppvObj) {
  TRACE("Entering CSpaceshipFactory::XClassFactory::\
QueryInterface--nIid = %d\n", nIid);
    METHOD_PROLOGUE(CSpaceshipFactory, ClassFactory) // makes pThis
    return pThis->
        ExternalQueryInterface(nIid, ppvObj); // delegate to
                                               //  CSpaceshipFactory
}


BOOL CSpaceshipFactory::XClassFactory::CreateInstance(int nIid,
                                                        void** ppvObj) {
TRACE("Entering CSpaceshipFactory::XClassFactory::CreateInstance\n");
    METHOD_PROLOGUE(CSpaceshipFactory, ClassFactory) // makes pThis
    CSpaceship* pObj = new CSpaceship();
    if (pObj->ExternalQueryInterface(nIid, ppvObj)) {
      pObj->ExternalRelease(); // balance reference count
      return TRUE;
    }
    return FALSE;
}

DWORD CSpaceshipFactory::XClassFactory::Release() {
    TRACE("Entering CSpaceshipFactory::XClassFactory::Release\n");
    METHOD_PROLOGUE(CSpaceshipFactory, ClassFactory) // makes pThis
    return pThis->ExternalRelease(); // delegate to CSimulatedCmdTarget
}
```

(continued)

Figure 23-3. *continued*

```
DWORD CSpaceshipFactory::XClassFactory::AddRef() {
    TRACE("Entering CSpaceshipFactory::XClassFactory::AddRef\n");
    METHOD_PROLOGUE(CSpaceshipFactory, ClassFactory) // makes pThis
    return pThis->ExternalAddRef(); // delegate to CSimulatedCmdTarget
}

BOOL CSpaceship::ExternalQueryInterface(int nIid, void** ppvObj) {
TRACE("Entering CSpaceship::ExternalQueryInterface--nIid = %d\n",
    nIid);
    switch (nIid) {
    case IID_IUnknown:
    case IID_IMotion:
      *ppvObj = &m_xMotion; // both IMotion and IVisual are derived
      break;               //   from IUnknown, so either pointer will do
    case IID_IVisual:
      *ppvObj = &m_xVisual;
      break;
    default:
      *ppvObj = NULL;
      return FALSE;
    }
    ExternalAddRef();
    return TRUE;
}

BOOL CSpaceship::XMotion::QueryInterface(int nIid, void** ppvObj) {
TRACE("Entering CSpaceship::XMotion::QueryInterface--nIid = %d\n",
    nIid);
    METHOD_PROLOGUE(CSpaceship, Motion) // makes pThis
    return pThis->ExternalQueryInterface(nIid, ppvObj); // delegate to
                                                        // CSpaceship
}

DWORD CSpaceship::XMotion::Release() {
    TRACE("Entering CSpaceship::XMotion::Release\n");
    METHOD_PROLOGUE(CSpaceship, Motion) // makes pThis
    return pThis->ExternalRelease(); // delegate to CSimulatedCmdTarget
}

DWORD CSpaceship::XMotion::AddRef() {
    TRACE("Entering CSpaceship::XMotion::AddRef\n");
    METHOD_PROLOGUE(CSpaceship, Motion) // makes pThis
    return pThis->ExternalAddRef(); // delegate to CSimulatedCmdTarget
}
```

(continued)

Figure 23-3. *continued*

```
void CSpaceship::XMotion::Fly() {
    TRACE("Entering CSpaceship::XMotion::Fly\n");
    METHOD_PROLOGUE(CSpaceship, Motion) // makes pThis
    TRACE("this = %p, pThis = %p\n", this, pThis);
    TRACE("m_nPosition = %d\n", pThis->m_nPosition);
    TRACE("m_nAcceleration = %d\n", pThis->m_nAcceleration);
}


int& CSpaceship::XMotion::GetPosition() {
    TRACE("Entering CSpaceship::XMotion::GetPosition\n");
    METHOD_PROLOGUE(CSpaceship, Motion) // makes pThis
    TRACE("this = %p, pThis = %p\n", this, pThis);
    TRACE("m_nPosition = %d\n", pThis->m_nPosition);
    TRACE("m_nAcceleration = %d\n", pThis->m_nAcceleration);
    return pThis->m_nPosition;
}


BOOL CSpaceship::XVisual::QueryInterface(int nIid, void** ppvObj) {
TRACE("Entering CSpaceship::XVisual::QueryInterface--nIid = %d\n",
    nIid);
    METHOD_PROLOGUE(CSpaceship, Visual) // makes pThis
    return pThis->ExternalQueryInterface(nIid, ppvObj); // delegate to
                                                        //   CSpaceship
}


DWORD CSpaceship::XVisual::Release() {
    TRACE("Entering CSpaceship::XVisual::Release\n");
    METHOD_PROLOGUE(CSpaceship, Visual) // makes pThis
    return pThis->ExternalRelease(); // delegate to CSimulatedCmdTarget
}


DWORD CSpaceship::XVisual::AddRef() {
    TRACE("Entering CSpaceship::XVisual::AddRef\n");
    METHOD_PROLOGUE(CSpaceship, Visual) // makes pThis
    return pThis->ExternalAddRef(); // delegate to CSimulatedCmdTarget
}


void CSpaceship::XVisual::Display() {
    TRACE("Entering CSpaceship::XVisual::Display\n");
    METHOD_PROLOGUE(CSpaceship, Visual) // makes pThis
    TRACE("this = %p, pThis = %p\n", this, pThis);
    TRACE("m_nPosition = %d\n", pThis->m_nPosition);
    TRACE("m_nColor = %d\n", pThis->m_nColor);
}
```

(continued)

Figure 23-3. *continued*

```
//----------simulates OLE server ------------------------------------
// in real OLE, this would be DllGetClassObject, which would be called
// whenever a client called CoGetClassObject

BOOL GetClassObject(int nClsid, int nIid, void** ppvObj)
{
    ASSERT(nClsid == CLSID_CSpaceship);
    ASSERT((nIid == IID_IUnknown) || (nIid == IID_IClassFactory));
    return g_factory.ExternalQueryInterface(nIid, ppvObj);
    // refcount is 2, which prevents accidental deletion
}
```

CLIENT.CPP

```
#include <stdio.h>
#include <stddef.h> // for offsetof in METHOD_PROLOGUE
#include <assert.h>
#include "Interface.h"



//----------main program----------------------------------------------
int main() // simulates OLE client program
{
    TRACE("Entering client main\n");
    IUnknown* pUnk; // if you declare these void*, you lose type-safety
    IMotion* pMot;
    IVisual* pVis;
    IClassFactory* pClf;

    GetClassObject(CLSID_CSpaceship, IID_IClassFactory,
                   (void**) &pClf);



    pClf->CreateInstance(IID_IUnknown, (void**) &pUnk);
    pUnk->QueryInterface(IID_IMotion, (void**) &pMot); // all three
    pMot->QueryInterface(IID_IVisual, (void**) &pVis); //   pointers
                                                       //   should work
    TRACE("main: pUnk = %p, pMot = %p, pDis = %p\n", pUnk, pMot, pVis);

    // test all the interface virtual functions
    pMot->Fly();
    int nPos = pMot->GetPosition();
    TRACE("nPos = %d\n", nPos);
    pVis->Display();
```

Figure 23-4.
The Client.cpp file.

(continued)

Figure 23-4. *continued*
```
        pClf->Release();

        pUnk->Release();
        pMot->Release();
        pVis->Release();
        return 0;
    }
```

Real COM with the MFC Library

So much for simulations. Now we'll get ready to convert the spaceship example to genuine COM. There are some more things to learn before we start, though. First you must learn about the *CoGetClassObject* function, and then you have to understand the difference between a DLL server and an EXE server, and then you must learn how OLE uses the Windows registry to load the server. Finally, you must become familiar with the MFC macros that support nested classes.

The net result will be an MFC Regular DLL server that contains all the *CSpaceship* code with the *IMotion* and *IVisual* interfaces. A regular MFC library application acts as the client. It loads and runs the server when the user selects a menu item.

The OLE *CoGetClassObject* Function

In our simulation, we used a phony function named *GetClassObject*. In real OLE, we use the global *CoGetClassObject* function. (*Co* stands for "component object.") Compare the following prototype to the *GetClassObject* function you've seen already:

```
HRESULT CoGetClassObject(REFCLSID rclsid, DWORD dwClsContext,
             LPVOID pvReserved, REFIID riid, LPVOID* ppvObj)
```

The interface pointer goes in the *ppvObj* parameter, and *pvReserved* is always *NULL*. The types *REFCLSID* and *REFIID* are references to 128-bit GUIDs (globally unique identifiers for COM classes and interfaces). The standard GUIDs are defined in the OLE libraries that are dynamically linked to your program. Special-purpose GUIDs, such as the ones for spaceship objects, must be defined in your program like this:

```
// {692D03A4-C689-11CE-B337-88EA36DE9E4E}
static const IID IID_IMotion =
{0x692d03a4, 0xc689, 0x11ce, {0xb3, 0x37, 0x88, 0xea, 0x36,
 0xde, 0x9e, 0x4e}};
```

If the *dwClsContext* parameter is *CLSCTX_INPROC_SERVER*, OLE looks for a DLL. If it is *CLSCTX_INPROC_HANDLER*, OLE looks for an EXE. (The two codes can be combined to select either a DLL or an EXE.) The return value is a 32-bit *HRESULT* value, which is 0 (*NOERROR*) if there is no error.

> N O T E :   Another OLE function, *CoCreateInstance*, combines the functionality of *CoGetClassObject* and *IClassFactory::CreateInstance*.

OLE and the Windows Registry

In the EX23A example, the server was statically linked to the client, a clearly bogus circumstance. In real OLE, the server is either a DLL or a separate EXE. When the client calls the *CoGetClassObject* function, OLE steps in and finds the correct server, which might already be in process memory or might be on disk. How does OLE make the connection? It looks up the class's unique 128-bit class ID number in the Windows registry. Thus, the <u>class</u> must be registered permanently on your computer.

If you run the Windows 95 Regedit program (Regedt32 in Windows NT), you will see a screen similar to the one shown in Figure 23-5. This figure shows three class IDs, two that are associated with DLLs (InprocServer32) and one that is associated with an EXE (LocalServer32). The *CoGetClassObject* function looks up the class ID in the registry and then loads the DLL or EXE as required.

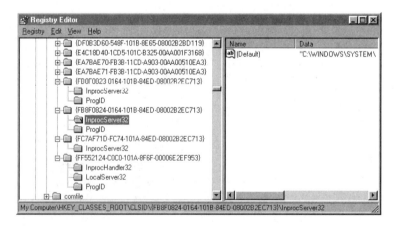

Figure 23-5.
Three class IDs in the registry.

What if you don't want to track those ugly class ID numbers in your client program? No problem. OLE supports another type of registration database entry, which translates a human-readable program ID into the corresponding class ID. Figure 23-6 shows the registry entries. The OLE function *CLSIDFromProgID* reads the database and performs the translation.

> NOTE: The first *CLSIDFromProgID* parameter is a string that holds the program ID, but it's not an ordinary string. This is your first exposure to double-byte characters in OLE. All string parameters of OLE functions (except DAO) are Unicode character string pointers of type *OLECHAR**. Your life is going to be made miserable because of the constant need to convert between double-byte strings and ordinary strings. If you need a double-byte literal string, you prefix the string with an L character, like this:

```
CLSIDFromProgID(L"Spaceship", &clsid);
```

You'll see the MFC library's Unicode string conversion capabilities starting in Chapter 24.

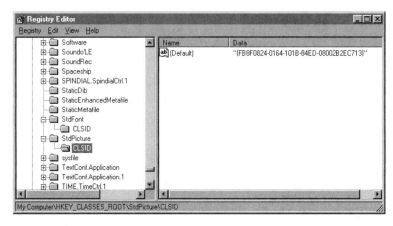

Figure 23-6.
Human-readable program IDs in the registry.

How does the registration information get into the registry? In two ways. First, Regedit has an ASCII file import facility that accepts data in a REG file like this one:

```
REGEDIT4

[HKEY_CLASSES_ROOT\StdPicture]
@="Standard Picture"

[HKEY_CLASSES_ROOT\StdPicture\CLSID]
@="{FB8F0824-0164-101B-84ED-08002B2EC713}"
```

Regedit can load a REG file in batch mode, or you can load such a file through the Regedit Registry menu.

Second, instead of using Regedit, you can program your server application to call OLE functions that update the registry directly. The MFC library conveniently wraps these functions with the function *COleObjectFactory::UpdateRegistryAll*, which finds all your program's global class factory objects and registers their names and class IDs.

Runtime Object Registration

You've just seen how the Windows registry registers OLE classes on disk. Class factory <u>objects</u> also must be registered, and it's a shame that the same word, "register," is used in both contexts. Objects in EXE servers are registered at runtime with a call to the OLE *CoRegisterClassObject* function, and the registration information is maintained in memory by the OLE DLLs. If the factory is registered in a mode that permits a single instance of the server to create multiple COM objects, OLE can use an existing server instance when a client calls *CoGetClassObject*.

How a COM Client Calls a DLL Server

We're beginning with a DLL server instead of an EXE server because the program interactions are simpler. I'll show pseudocode here because you're going to be using the MFC library classes, which hide much of the detail. Different levels of indentation show code for the client, COM, and the DLL server.

Client	COM	DLL Server

```
CLSID clsid;
IClassFactory* pClf;
IUnknown* pUnk;
CoInitialize(NULL); // initialize COM
CLSIDFromProgID("servername", &clsid);
            COM uses the registry to look up the class ID from "servername"
CoGetClassObject(clsid, IID_IClassFactory, (void**) &pClf );
                COM uses the class ID to look for a server in memory
            if (server DLL is not loaded already) {
                COM gets DLL filename from the registry
                Loads the server DLL into process memory
            }
```

Client	COM	DLL Server
		if (server just loaded) {
		Global factory objects are constructed
		DLL's InitInstance called (MFC only)
		}
	COM calls DLL's global exported DllGetClassObject with the	
	CLSID value that was passed to CoGetClassObject	
		DllGetClassObject returns IClassFactory*
	COM returns IClassFactory* to client	
pClf->CreateInstance(IID_IUnknown, (void**) &pUnk);		
		Class factory's CreateInstance function called
		(called directly—through the server's vtable)
		Constructs object of "servername" class
		Returns requested interface pointer
pClf->Release();		
pUnk->Release();		
		"servername" Release is called through vtable
		if (refcount == 0) {
		Object destroys itself
		}
CoFreeUnusedLibraries();		
	COM calls DLL's global exported DllCanUnloadNow	
		DllCanUnloadNow called
		if (all DLL's objects destroyed) {
		return TRUE
		}
CoUninitialize(); //COM frees the DLL if DllCanUnloadNow returns		
	TRUE just prior to exit	
	COM releases resources	
Client exits		
		Windows unloads the DLL if it is still loaded and no
		other programs are using it

Some important points are worth noting. First, the DLL's exported *DllGetClassObject* function is called in response to the client's *CoGetClassObject* call. Second, the class factory interface address returned is the actual physical address of the class factory vtable pointer in the DLL. And third, when the client calls *CreateInstance*, or any other interface function, the call is direct (through the server's vtable).

The COM linkage between a client EXE and a server DLL is quite efficient. It's just as efficient as the linkage to any C++ virtual function in the same process, plus there's full C++ parameter and return type checking at compile time. The only penalty for using ordinary DLL linkage is the extra step of looking up the class ID in the registry when the DLL is first loaded.

How a COM Client Calls an EXE Server

The COM linkage to a separate EXE file is more complicated than the linkage to a DLL server. The EXE server is in a different process, and a 16-bit/32-bit mismatch is possible. In the future, the server might be on a different computer. Don't worry, though. Write your programs as if a direct connection exists. COM takes care of the details through a process called marshaling.

With marshaling, the client makes calls to a DLL called a proxy. The proxy sends a stream of data via a remote procedure call (RPC) to a stub, which is DLL code in the server. If you use standard interfaces such as *IUnknown* and *IClassFactory*, the proxy and stub code is provided by the OLE DLLs. If you invent your own interfaces, such as *IMotion* and *IVisual*, you're stuck with the tedious job of writing the marshaling code yourself. That's why few software firms develop their own interfaces but instead rely on existing COM interfaces, such as *IDispatch* (which you'll see in Chapter 24).

Here's the pseudocode interaction between an EXE client and an EXE server. Compare it to the DLL version on pages 564 and 565. Notice that the client-side calls are exactly the same.

Client	COM	EXE Server

```
CLSID clsid;
IClassFactory* pClf;
IUnknown* pUnk;
CoInitialize(NULL);  // initialize COM
CLSIDFromProgID("servername", &clsid);
            COM uses the registry to look up the class ID from "servername"
CoGetClassObject(clsid, IID_IClassFactory, (void**) &pClf );
            COM uses the class ID to look for a server in memory
            if (server EXE is not loaded already, or if we need another instance) {
```

Client	COM	EXE Server

COM gets EXE filename from the registry

Loads the server EXE into memory

}

      if (just loaded) {

        Global factory objects are constructed

        InitInstance called (MFC only)

         CoInitialize(NULL);

        for each factory object {

          CoRegisterClassObject(...);

          Returns IClassFactory* to COM

        }

      }

COM returns the requested interface pointer to the client

    (client's pointer is not the same as the server's interface pointer)

pClf->CreateInstance(IID_IUnknown, (void**) &pUnk);

      Class factory's CreateInstance function called

       (called indirectly through marshaling)

       Constructs object of "servername" class

       Returns requested interface pointer indirectly

pClf->Release();

pUnk->Release();

      "servername" Release is called indirectly

      if (refcount == 0) {

       Object destroys itself

      }

      if (all objects released) {

       Server exits gracefully

      }

CoUninitialize(); // just prior to exit

    COM calls Release for any objects this client has failed to release

      Server exits if this causes all objects to be released

    COM releases resources

Client exits

As you can see, COM plays an important role in the communication between the client and the server. COM keeps an in-memory list of class factories that are in active EXE servers but does not keep track of individual COM objects such as the *CSpaceship* object. Those objects are responsible for destroying themselves through the *AddRef/Release* mechanism. COM does step in when a client exits. If that client is using an EXE server, COM "listens in" on the communication and keeps track of the reference count on each object. COM disconnects from server objects when the client exits, and, under certain circumstances, this causes those objects to be released. Don't depend on this behavior, however. Be sure that your client program releases all its interface pointers prior to exit.

The MFC Interface Macros

In EX23A, you saw the use of nested classes for interface implementation. The MFC library has a set of macros that automate this process. For the *CSpaceship* class, derived from the real MFC *CCmdTarget* class, you use the following macros inside the declaration:

```
BEGIN_INTERFACE_PART(Motion, IMotion)
    STDMETHOD_(void, Fly) ();
    STDMETHOD_(int&, GetPosition) ();
END_INTERFACE_PART(Motion)

BEGIN_INTERFACE_PART(Visual, IVisual)
    STDMETHOD_(void, Display) ();
END_INTERFACE_PART(Visual)

DECLARE_INTERFACE_MAP()
```

The *INTERFACE_PART* macros generate the nested classes, adding *X* to the first parameter to form the class name and adding *m_x* to form the embedded object name. The macros generate prototypes for the specified interface functions plus prototypes for *QueryInterface*, *AddRef*, and *Release*.

The *DECLARE_INTERFACE_MAP* macro generates the declarations for a table that holds the IDs of all the class's interfaces. The *CCmdTarget::ExternalQueryInterface* function uses the table to retrieve the interface pointers.

In the *CSpaceship* implementation file, use the following macros:

```
BEGIN_INTERFACE_MAP(CSpaceship, CCmdTarget)
    INTERFACE_PART(CSpaceship, IID_IMotion, Motion)
    INTERFACE_PART(CSpaceship, IID_IVisual, Visual)
END_INTERFACE_MAP()
```

These macros build the interface table used by *CCmdTarget::ExternalQuery-Interface*. A typical interface member function looks like this:

```
STDMETHODIMP_(void) CSpaceship::XMotion::Fly()
{
    METHOD_PROLOGUE(CSpaceship, Motion)
    pThis->m_nPosition += 10;
    return;
}
```

Don't forget that you must implement all the functions for each interface, including *QueryInterface*, *AddRef*, and *Release*. Those three functions can delegate to functions in *CCmdTarget*.

> **NOTE:** The *STDMETHOD_* and *STDMETHODIMP_* macros declare and implement functions with the _ _*stdcall* parameter passing convention, as required by COM. These macros allow you to specify the return value as the first parameter. Another set of macros, *STDMETHOD* and *STDMETHODIMP*, assume an *HRESULT* return value.

The MFC *COleObjectFactory* Class

In the simulated COM example, you saw a *CSpaceshipFactory* class that was hard-coded to generate *CSpaceship* objects. The MFC library applies its dynamic creation technology to the problem. Thus, a single class, aptly named *COleObjectFactory*, can create objects of any class specified at runtime. All you need to do is use macros like these in the class declaration:

```
DECLARE_DYNCREATE(CSpaceship)
DECLARE_OLECREATE(CSpaceship)
```

and macros like these in the implementation file:

```
IMPLEMENT_DYNCREATE(CSpaceship, CCmdTarget)
// {692D03A3-C689-11CE-B337-88EA36DE9E4E}
IMPLEMENT_OLECREATE(CSpaceship, "Spaceship", 0x692d03a3, 0xc689, 0x11ce,
        0xb3, 0x37, 0x88, 0xea, 0x36, 0xde, 0x9e, 0x4e)
```

The *DYNCREATE* macros set up the standard dynamic creation mechanism as described in Appendix C. The *OLECREATE* macros declare and define a global object of class *COleObjectFactory* with the specified unique CLSID. In a DLL server, the exported *DllGetClassObject* function finds the specified class factory object and returns a pointer to it, based on global variables set by the *OLECREATE* macros. In an EXE server, initialization code calls the static *COleObjectFactory::RegisterAll*, which finds all factory objects and registers each one by calling *CoRegisterClassObject*. The *RegisterAll* function is called also when a DLL is initialized. In that case, it merely sets a flag in the factory object(s).

AppWizard/ClassWizard Support for COM DLL Servers

AppWizard isn't optimized for creating COM DLL servers, but you can fool it by requesting a regular DLL with OLE Automation support. The following functions in the project's main source file are of interest:

```
BOOL CEx23bApp::InitInstance()
{
    COleObjectFactory::RegisterAll();
    return TRUE;
}

STDAPI DllGetClassObject(REFCLSID rclsid, REFIID riid, LPVOID* ppv)
{
    AFX_MANAGE_STATE(AfxGetStaticModule_State());
    return AfxDllGetClassObject(rclsid, riid, ppv);
}

STDAPI DllCanUnloadNow(void)
{
    AFX_MANAGE_STATE(AfxGetStaticModule_State());
    return AfxDllCanUnloadNow();
}

STDAPI DllRegisterServer(void)
{
    AFX_MANAGE_STATE(AfxGetStaticModule_State());
    COleObjectFactory::UpdateRegistryAll();
    return S_OK;
}
```

The three global functions are exported in the project's DEF file. By calling MFC functions, the global functions do everything you need in a COM DLL. The *DllRegisterServer* function can be called by a utility program to update the system registry.

Once you've created the skeleton project, your next step is to use ClassWizard to add one or more OLE-creatable classes to the project. Just fill in the Create New Class dialog, as shown here:

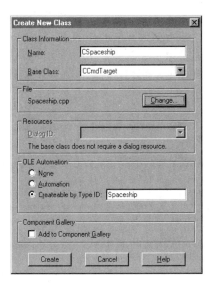

In your generated class, you end up with some OLE Automation elements such as dispatch maps, but you can safely remove those. You can also remove the following two lines from StdAfx.h:

```
#include <afxodlgs.h>
#include <afxdisp.h>
```

MFC COM Client Programs

Writing an MFC COM client program is a no-brainer. You just use AppWizard to generate a normal application. Add the following line in StdAfx.h:

```
#include <afxole.h>
```

and then add the following line in the application class *InitInstance* member function:

```
AfxOleInit();
```

You're now ready to add code that calls *CoGetClassObject*.

The EX23B Example—An MFC COM DLL Server

The EX23B example is an MFC regular DLL that incorporates a true COM version of the *CSpaceship* class you saw in EX23A. The ex23b.cpp and ex23b.h files were generated by AppWizard as described above. Figure 23-7 on the following page shows the Interface.h file, which declares the *IMotion* and

IUnknown interfaces. Figures 23-8 and 23-9 show the code for the *CSpaceship* class. Compare the code to the code in EX23A. Do you see how the use of the MFC macros reduces code size? Note that the MFC *CCmdTarget* class takes care of the reference counting and *QueryInterface* logic.

INTERFACE.H

```
struct IMotion : public IUnknown
{
    STDMETHOD_(void, Fly) () = 0;
    STDMETHOD_(int&, GetPosition) () = 0;
};

struct IVisual : public IUnknown

{
    STDMETHOD_(void, Display) () = 0;
};
```

Figure 23-7.
The Interface.h file.

SPACESHIP.H

```
void ITrace(REFIID iid, const char* str);


/////////////////////////////////////////////////////////////////////////
// CSpaceship command target

class CSpaceship : public CCmdTarget
{
    DECLARE_DYNCREATE(CSpaceship)
private:
    int m_nPosition; // we can access this from all the interfaces
    int m_nAcceleration;
    int m_nColor;
protected:
    CSpaceship();    // protected constructor used by dynamic creation

// Attributes
public:

// Operations
public:
```

Figure 23-8.
The Spaceship.h file.

(continued)

Figure 23-8. *continued*

```
// Overrides
    // ClassWizard generated virtual function overrides
    //{{AFX_VIRTUAL(CSpaceship)
    public:
    virtual void OnFinalRelease();
    //}}AFX_VIRTUAL

// Implementation
protected:
    virtual ~CSpaceship();

    // Generated message map functions
    //{{AFX_MSG(CSpaceship)
    // NOTE - the ClassWizard will add and remove member functions here.
    //}}AFX_MSG

    DECLARE_MESSAGE_MAP()
    DECLARE_OLECREATE(CSpaceship)

    BEGIN_INTERFACE_PART(Motion, IMotion)
        STDMETHOD_(void, Fly) ();
        STDMETHOD_(int&, GetPosition) ();
    END_INTERFACE_PART(Motion)

    BEGIN_INTERFACE_PART(Visual, IVisual)
        STDMETHOD_(void, Display) ();
    END_INTERFACE_PART(Visual)

    DECLARE_INTERFACE_MAP()
};


////////////////////////////////////////////////////////////////////
```

SPACESHIP.CPP

```
#include "StdAfx.h"
#include "ex23b.h"
#include "Interface.h"
#include "Spaceship.h"

#ifdef _DEBUG
#undef THIS_FILE
static char THIS_FILE[] = __FILE__;
#endif
```

Figure 23-9. *(continued)*

The Spaceship.cpp file.

Figure 23-9. *continued*

```
/////////////////////////////////////////////////////////////////////
// CSpaceship

// {692D03A4-C689-11CE-B337-88EA36DE9E4E}
static const IID IID_IMotion =
{ 0x692d03a4, 0xc689, 0x11ce,
    { 0xb3, 0x37, 0x88, 0xea, 0x36, 0xde, 0x9e, 0x4e } };

// {692D03A5-C689-11CE-B337-88EA36DE9E4E}
static const IID IID_IVisual =
{ 0x692d03a5, 0xc689, 0x11ce,
    { 0xb3, 0x37, 0x88, 0xea, 0x36, 0xde, 0x9e, 0x4e } };

IMPLEMENT_DYNCREATE(CSpaceship, CCmdTarget)

CSpaceship::CSpaceship()
{
    TRACE("CSpaceship ctor\n");
    m_nPosition = 100;
    m_nAcceleration = 101;
    m_nColor = 102;
    // To keep the application running as long as an OLE automation
    //   object is active, the constructor calls AfxOleLockApp.

    AfxOleLockApp();
}

CSpaceship::~CSpaceship()
{
    TRACE("CSpaceship dtor\n");
    // To terminate the application when all objects created with
    //   OLE automation, the destructor calls AfxOleUnlockApp.

    AfxOleUnlockApp();
}


void CSpaceship::OnFinalRelease()
{
    // When the last reference for an automation object is released
    //   OnFinalRelease is called. This implementation deletes the
    //   object. Add additional cleanup required for your object before
    //   deleting it from memory.

    delete this;
}
```

(continued)

Figure 23-9. *continued*

```
BEGIN_MESSAGE_MAP(CSpaceship, CCmdTarget)
    //{{AFX_MSG_MAP(CSpaceship)
    // NOTE - the ClassWizard will add and remove mapping macros here.
    //}}AFX_MSG_MAP
END_MESSAGE_MAP()

BEGIN_INTERFACE_MAP(CSpaceship, CCmdTarget)
    INTERFACE_PART(CSpaceship, IID_IMotion, Motion)
    INTERFACE_PART(CSpaceship, IID_IVisual, Visual)
END_INTERFACE_MAP()

// {692D03A3-C689-11CE-B337-88EA36DE9E4E}
IMPLEMENT_OLECREATE(CSpaceship, "Spaceship", 0x692d03a3, 0xc689,
                    0x11ce, 0xb3, 0x37, 0x88, 0xea, 0x36, 0xde,
                    0x9e, 0x4e)

STDMETHODIMP_(ULONG) CSpaceship::XMotion::AddRef()
{
    TRACE("CSpaceship::XMotion::AddRef\n");
    METHOD_PROLOGUE(CSpaceship, Motion)
    return pThis->ExternalAddRef();
}

STDMETHODIMP_(ULONG) CSpaceship::XMotion::Release()
{
    TRACE("CSpaceship::XMotion::Release\n");
    METHOD_PROLOGUE(CSpaceship, Motion)
    return pThis->ExternalRelease();
}

STDMETHODIMP CSpaceship::XMotion::QueryInterface(
    REFIID iid, LPVOID* ppvObj)
{
    ITrace(iid, "CSpaceship::XMotion::QueryInterface");
    METHOD_PROLOGUE(CSpaceship, Motion)
    return pThis->ExternalQueryInterface(&iid, ppvObj);
}


STDMETHODIMP_(void) CSpaceship::XMotion::Fly()
{
    TRACE("CSpaceship::XMotion::Fly\n");
    METHOD_PROLOGUE(CSpaceship, Motion)
    TRACE("m_nPosition = %d\n", pThis->m_nPosition);
    TRACE("m_nAcceleration = %d\n", pThis->m_nAcceleration);
    return;
}
```

(continued)

Figure 23-9. *continued*

```
STDMETHODIMP_(int&)  CSpaceship::XMotion::GetPosition()
{
    TRACE("CSpaceship::XMotion::GetPosition\n");
    METHOD_PROLOGUE(CSpaceship, Motion)
    TRACE("m_nPosition = %d\n", pThis->m_nPosition);
    TRACE("m_nAcceleration = %d\n", pThis->m_nAcceleration);
    return pThis->m_nPosition;
}


/////////////////////////////////////////////////////////////////////
STDMETHODIMP_(ULONG)  CSpaceship::XVisual::AddRef()
{
    TRACE("CSpaceship::XVisual::AddRef\n");
    METHOD_PROLOGUE(CSpaceship, Visual)
    return pThis->ExternalAddRef();
}


STDMETHODIMP_(ULONG)  CSpaceship::XVisual::Release()
{
    TRACE("CSpaceship::XVisual::Release\n");
    METHOD_PROLOGUE(CSpaceship, Visual)
    return pThis->ExternalRelease();
}


STDMETHODIMP  CSpaceship::XVisual::QueryInterface(
    REFIID iid, LPVOID* ppvObj)
{
    ITrace(iid, "CSpaceship::XVisual::QueryInterface");
    METHOD_PROLOGUE(CSpaceship, Visual)
    return pThis->ExternalQueryInterface(&iid, ppvObj);
}


STDMETHODIMP_(void)  CSpaceship::XVisual::Display()
{
    TRACE("CSpaceship::XVisual::Display\n");
    METHOD_PROLOGUE(CSpaceship, Visual)
    TRACE("m_nPosition = %d\n", pThis->m_nPosition);
    TRACE("m_nColor = %d\n", pThis->m_nColor);
}


/////////////////////////////////////////////////////////////////////
void ITrace(REFIID iid, const char* str)
{
    OLECHAR* lpszIID;
    ::StringFromIID(iid, &lpszIID);
    CString strTemp = (LPCWSTR) lpszIID;
```

(continued)

Figure 23-9. *continued*

```
        TRACE("%s - %s\n", (const char*) strTemp, (const char*) str);
        AfxFreeTaskMem(lpszIID);
    }


    /////////////////////////////////////////////////////////////////////////
    // CSpaceship message handlers
```

The EX23C Example—An MFC COM Client

The EX23C example is an MFC program that incorporates a true COM version of the client code you saw in EX23A. This is a generic AppWizard MFC Single Document Interface (SDI) EXE program with an added *#include* statement for the MFC OLE headers and a call to *AfxOleInit*. A Spaceship option on an added Test menu is mapped to the view class handler function shown in Figure 23-10. The project also contains a copy of the server's Interface.h file, shown in Figure 23-7 on page 572. There is a *#include* statement for this file at the top of ex23cView.cpp.

```
void CEx23cView::OnTestSpaceship()
{
    CLSID clsid;
    LPCLASSFACTORY pClf;
    LPUNKNOWN pUnk;
    IMotion* pMot;
    IVisual* pVis;
    HRESULT hr;

    if ((hr = ::CLSIDFromProgID(L"Spaceship", &clsid)) != NOERROR) {
      TRACE("unable to find Program ID -- error = %x\n", hr);
      return;
    }
    if ((hr = ::CoGetClassObject(clsid, CLSCTX_INPROC_SERVER,
        NULL, IID_IClassFactory, (void **) &pClf)) != NOERROR) {;
      TRACE("unable to find CLSID -- error = %x\n", hr);
      return;
    }

    pClf->CreateInstance(NULL, IID_IUnknown, (void**) &pUnk);
    pUnk->QueryInterface(IID_IMotion, (void**) &pMot); // all three
    pMot->QueryInterface(IID_IVisual, (void**) &pVis); //   pointers
                                                       //   should work
    TRACE("main: pUnk = %p, pMot = %p, pDis = %p\n", pUnk, pMot, pVis);
```

Figure 23-10. *(continued)*

The client's command handler that loads and tests the CSpaceship *server.*

Figure 23-10. *continued*

```
// test all the interface virtual functions
pMot->Fly();
int nPos = pMot->GetPosition();
TRACE("nPos = %d\n", nPos);
pVis->Display();

pClf->Release();

pUnk->Release();
pMot->Release();
pVis->Release();
AfxMessageBox("Test succeeded. See Debug window for output.");
}
```

To test the client and the server, you must first run the server to update the registry. There are several utilities that do this, but you might want to try the Regserv.exe program in the \vcpp32\Regserv project on the companion CD-ROM. This program prompts you to select a DLL or an OCX file, and then it calls the exported *DllRegisterServer* function.

Both client and server show their progress through *TRACE* calls, so you need the debugger. You can run either the client or the server from the debugger. If you try to run the server, you'll be prompted for the client pathname. In either case, you don't have to copy the DLL because Windows finds it through the registry.

Containment and Aggregation vs. Inheritance

In normal C++ programming, you frequently use inheritance to factor out common behavior into a reusable base class. The *CPersistentFrame* class (discussed in Chapter 14) and the *Orbiter* base class (discussed in Appendix A) are examples of reusability through inheritance.

COM uses containment and aggregation instead of inheritance. Let's start with containment. If the planetary-motion simulation example from Appendix A were to be translated to OLE, there would be "outer" *CSpaceship* and *CPlanet* classes plus an "inner" *COrbiter* class. The outer classes would implement the *IVisual* interface directly, but those outer classes would "delegate" their *IMotion* interfaces to the inner class. The result would look something like this:

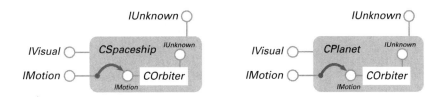

Note that the *COrbiter* object doesn't know that it's inside a *CSpaceship* or *CPlanet* object, but the outer object certainly knows that it has a *COrbiter* object embedded inside. The outer class needs to implement all its interface functions, but in the *IMotion* functions, including *QueryInterface*, simply call the same *IMotion* functions of the inner class.

A more complex alternative to containment is aggregation. With aggregation, the client can have direct access to the inner object's interfaces. Shown here is the aggregation version of the space simulation:

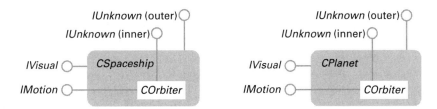

The orbiter is embedded in the spaceship and planet, just as it was in the containment case. Suppose the client obtains an *IVisual* pointer for a spaceship and then calls *QueryInterface* for an *IMotion* pointer. Use of the outer *IUnknown* pointer will draw a blank because the *CSpaceship* class doesn't support *IMotion*. The *CSpaceship* class keeps track of the inner *IUnknown* pointer (of its embedded *COrbiter* object), so it uses that to obtain the *IMotion* pointer for the *COrbiter* object.

Now suppose the client obtains an *IMotion* pointer and then calls *QueryInterface* for *IVisual*. The inner object must be able to navigate to the outer object, but how does it do this? Take a close look at the *CreateInstance* call in Figure 23-10 beginning on page 577. The first parameter is set to *NULL* in that case. If you are creating an aggregated (inner) object, you use that parameter to pass an *IUnknown* pointer for the outer object that you have already created. This pointer is called the <u>controlling</u> <u>unknown</u>. The *COrbiter* class saves this pointer in a data member and then uses it to call *QueryInterface* for interfaces the class itself doesn't support.

The MFC library supports aggregation. The *CCmdTarget* class has a public data member *m_pOuterUnknown* that holds the outer object's *IUnknown* pointer (if the object is aggregated). The *CCmdTarget* member functions *ExternalQueryInterface, ExternalAddRef,* and *ExternalRelease* delegate to the outer *IUnknown* if it exists. Another set of member functions, *InternalQueryInterface, InternalAddRef,* and *InternalRelease* do not delegate. See Technical Note #38 for a description of the MFC macros that support aggregation.

CHAPTER TWENTY-FOUR

OLE Automation

After Chapter 23, you know what an interface is, and you've already seen two standard OLE interfaces, *IUnknown* and *IClassFactory*. Now you're ready for "applied" OLE, or at least one aspect of it, OLE Automation. You'll be learning about the OLE *IDispatch* interface, which enables C++ programs to communicate with Visual Basic for Applications (VBA) programs and with programs written in other languages. You'll be using the MFC library implementation of *IDispatch* to write C++ OLE Automation server and controller programs. Both EXE servers and DLL servers are covered.

But before you jump into C++ OLE Automation programming, you need to know how the rest of the world writes programs. In this chapter, you'll get some exposure to VBA as implemented in Microsoft Excel. You'll be running your C++ servers from Excel, and you'll be controlling Excel from a C++ controller.

Connecting C++ with Visual Basic for Applications (VBA)

Not all Windows programmers are going to be C++ programmers, especially if they have to learn the intricacies of OLE. There's talk of a programming "division of labor," in which C++ programmers will produce reusable modules and Visual Basic for Applications (VBA) programmers will consume those modules by integrating them into applications. You can prepare for this eventuality now by learning how to make your software "VBA-friendly." OLE Automation is one tool that's available now and supported by the MFC library. The OCX is another tool for C++/VBA integration and is very much a superset of OLE Automation because both use the *IDispatch* interface. An OCX might be overkill in many situations. Some applications, such as Microsoft Excel version 7.0, support VBA but do not yet support OCXs. All that you learn about OLE Automation you can apply to the writing and using of OCXs.

Two factors are working on behalf of OLE Automation's success. First, VBA is now the programming standard in most Microsoft applications, including Word, Excel, and Access, not to mention Visual Basic itself. All these applications support OLE Automation, which means they can be linked to other OLE Automation–compatible components, including those written in C++ and VBA. For example, you can write a C++ program that uses the text processing capability of Word, or you can write a C++ matrix inversion program that can be called from a VBA macro in an Excel worksheet. Second, dozens of software companies are providing OLE Automation interfaces for their applications, mostly for the benefit of VBA programmers. With a little extra effort, you can use these interfaces from C++. You can, for example, write an MFC program that controls Shapeware's Visio drawing program.

OLE Automation isn't just for C++ and VBA. Software-tools companies are already announcing OLE-compatible Basic-like languages that you can license for your own programmable applications. There's even a version of Smalltalk that supports OLE Automation!

Automation Controllers and Automation Servers

A clearly defined master–slave relationship is always present in an OLE Automation communication dialog. The master is the automation controller (or client), and the slave is the automation server. The controller initiates the interaction by constructing a server object (it might have to load the server program) or by attaching to an existing object in a server program that is already running. The controller then calls interface functions in the server and releases those interfaces when it's finished. Here are some interaction scenarios:

■ A C++ automation controller uses a Microsoft or third-party application as a server. The interaction could trigger the execution of VBA code in the server.

■ A C++ automation server is used from inside a Microsoft application (or a Visual Basic application), which acts as the automation controller. Thus, VBA code can construct and use C++ objects.

■ A C++ automation server is used by a C++ automation controller.

■ A Visual Basic program uses an Automation-aware application such as Excel. In this case, Visual Basic is the controller, and Excel is the server.

Microsoft Excel—
A Better Visual Basic than Visual Basic

When I wrote the previous edition of this book, Visual Basic worked as an automation controller, but you couldn't use it to create an automation server. Now Visual Basic 4.0 lets you write servers too. I used Microsoft Excel originally instead of VB because it was the first Microsoft application to support VBA syntax, and it could serve as both a controller and a server. I decided to stick with Excel because C++ programmers who look down their noses at Visual Basic might be inclined to buy Excel if only to track their software royalties.

I strongly recommend that you get a copy of Excel 7.0 (or later). This is a true 32-bit application and a part of the Microsoft Office 95 suite. With this version of Excel, you can write VBA code in a separate module that accesses worksheet cells in an object-oriented manner. It's easy to add visual programming elements such as pushbuttons. Forget all you ever knew about the old spreadsheet programs that made you wedge macro code inside cells.

This chapter isn't meant to be an Excel tutorial, but I have included a simple Excel workbook. (A workbook is a file that can contain multiple worksheets plus separate VBA code.) This workbook demonstrates a VBA macro that executes from a pushbutton. You can use Excel to load demo.xls from the \VCPP32\EX24A subdirectory, or you can key in the example from scratch. Figure 24-1 shows the actual spreadsheet with the button and sample data. You highlight cell A4 and click the Process Col button. A VBA program

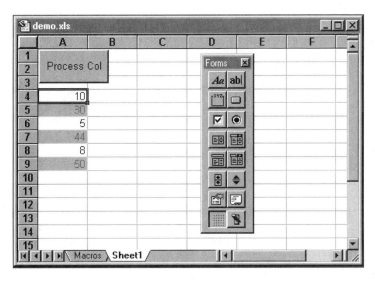

Figure 24-1.
An Excel spreadsheet that uses VBA code.

iterates down the column and draws a hatched pattern on cells that have numeric values greater than 10. Figure 24-2 shows the macro code itself, which is stored in a separate section of the workbook—in this example, named Macros.

```
demo.xls                                          _ □ ×

Sub ProcessColumn()
    Do Until ActiveCell.Value = ""
        If ActiveCell.Value > 10 Then
            Selection.Interior.Pattern = xlCrissCross
        Else
            Selection.Interior.Pattern = xlNone
        End If
        Selection.Offset(1, 0).Range("A1").Select
    Loop
End Sub

|◄|◄|►|►| Macros / Sheet1 /        |◄|
```

Figure 24-2.
The VBA code for the Excel spreadsheet.

If you want to create the example yourself, follow these steps:

1. Start Excel with a new workbook, choose Macro from the Insert menu, and choose Module.

2. Type in the macro code shown in Figure 24-2.

3. Double-click on Module1 at the bottom of the screen, and change the name to Macros.

4. Click on the Sheet1 tab, and choose Toolbars from the View menu. Check the Forms check box to display the Forms toolbar. Click OK. (You can also access the list of toolbars by right-clicking on any existing toolbar.)

5. Click the Create Button control, and drag in the upper left corner of the worksheet to create a pushbutton. Assign the button to the ProcessColumn macro.

6. Size the pushbutton, and type the caption shown in Figure 24-1.

7. Type some numbers in the column starting at cell A4. Then select A4, and click the button to test the program.

Pretty easy, isn't it?

Let's look at one Excel VBA statement from the macro above and analyze it:

```
Selection.Offset(1, 0).Range("A1").Select
```

The first element, Selection, is a <u>property</u> of an implied <u>object</u>, the Excel application. The Selection property in this case is assumed to be a *Range* object that represents a rectangular array of cells. The second element, *Offset*, is a <u>method</u> of the *Range* object that returns another *Range* object based on the two parameters. In this case, the returned *Range* object is the one-cell range that begins one row down from the original range. The third element, *Range*, is a method of the *Range* object that returns yet another range. This time it's the upper left cell in the second range. Finally, the *Select* method causes Excel to highlight the selected cell and makes it the new Selection property of the application.

As the program iterates through the loop, the preceding statement moves the selected cell down the worksheet one row at a time. This style of programming takes some getting used to, but you can't afford to ignore it. The real value here is that you now have all the capabilities of the Excel spreadsheet and graphics engine available to you in a seamless programming environment.

Properties, Methods, and Collections

The distinction between a property and a method is somewhat artificial. Basically, a property is a value that can be both set and retrieved. You can, for example, set and get the Selection property for an Excel application. Another example is Excel's Width property, which applies to many object types. Some Excel properties are read-only; most are read/write. Properties don't officially have parameters, but some properties are <u>indexed</u>. The property index acts a lot like a parameter. It doesn't have to be an integer, and it can have more than one element (row and column, for example). You won't find indexed properties in Excel's object model, but Excel VBA can handle indexed properties in OLE Automation servers.

Methods are more flexible than properties. They can have zero or many parameters, they can either set or retrieve object data, or they can perform some action, such as showing a window. Excel's Select method is an example of an action method. The Offset method returns an object based on two parameters.

Excel supports collection objects. An example is the Worksheets object, which is returned by the Worksheets method of the Workbook object. The Worksheets method has an index parameter that specifies the individual Worksheets object you want. What's the difference between a collection and an indexed property? With an indexed property, the controller can't delete or insert elements; with a collection, it can.

The Problem That OLE Automation Solves

You've already learned that an OLE interface is the ideal way for Windows programs to communicate with one another, but you've learned that it's mostly impractical to design your own OLE interfaces. OLE Automation provides a general-purpose interface, *IDispatch*, that serves the needs of both C++ and VBA programmers. As you might guess from your glimpse of Excel VBA, this interface involves objects, methods, and properties.

You can write OLE interfaces that have functions with any parameter types and return values you specify. *IMotion* and *IVisual* are examples. If you're going to let VBA programmers in, however, you can't be fast and loose anymore. You can solve the communication problem with one interface that has only a single member function that's smart enough to accommodate methods and properties as defined by VBA. Needless to say, *IDispatch* has such a function, and it's named *Invoke*. You use *IDispatch::Invoke* for COM objects that can be constructed and used in either C++ or VBA programs.

Now you're beginning to see what OLE Automation does. It funnels all intermodule communication through the *IDispatch::Invoke* function. How does a controller first connect to its server? Because *IDispatch* is merely another OLE interface, all the registration logic supported by COM comes into play. Automation servers can be DLLs or EXEs, and they can be accessed over a network as soon as OLE supports that feature.

The *IDispatch* Interface

IDispatch is the heart of OLE Automation. It's fully supported by OLE marshaling, as are *IUnknown* and *IClassFactory*, and it's very well supported by the MFC library. At the server end, you need a COM class with an *IDispatch* interface (plus the prerequisite class factory, of course). At the controller end, you use standard OLE techniques to obtain an *IDispatch* pointer. (As you'll see, the MFC library and the wizards take care of a lot of these details for you.)

Remember that *Invoke* is the principal member function of *IDispatch*. If you looked up *IDispatch::Invoke* in Books Online, you'd see a really ugly set of parameters. Don't worry about those now. The MFC library steps in on both sides of the *Invoke* call, using a data-driven scheme to call server functions based on dispatch map parameters you define with macros.

Invoke isn't the only *IDispatch* member function. Another function your controller might call is *GetIDsOfNames*. From the VBA programmer's point of view, properties and methods have symbolic names, but C++ programmers prefer more efficient integer indexes. *Invoke* uses integers to specify properties and methods, so *GetIDsOfNames* is useful at the start of a program to convert each name to a number if you don't know the index numbers at compile time. You've already seen that *IDispatch* supports symbolic names for methods. In addition, the interface supports symbolic names for a method's parameters. The *GetIDsOfNames* function returns those parameter names along with the method name. Unfortunately, the MFC *IDispatch* implementation doesn't support named parameters.

OLE Automation Programming Choices

Suppose you're writing an automation server in C++. You've got some choices to make. Do you want a DLL server or an EXE server? What kind of user interface do you want? Does the server need a user interface at all? Can users run your EXE server as a stand-alone application? If the server is an EXE, will it be SDI or MDI? Can the user shut down the server directly?

If your server is a DLL, OLE linkage will be more efficient than with an EXE server because no marshaling is required. With a DLL, however, your user interface options are limited. A modal dialog is about your only option—no frame window. (If you need your server to run in a client's child window, consider using an OCX.) Be aware that DLL automation servers can connect quite happily to VBA controllers. As with any 32-bit DLL, an OLE Automation DLL is mapped into the client's process memory. If two controllers happen to request the same DLL, OLE loads and links the DLL twice. Each controller is unaware that the other is using the same server.

With an EXE server, however, you must be careful to distinguish between a server program and a server object. When a controller calls *IClassFactory::CreateInstance* to construct a server object, the server's class factory constructs the object, but OLE might or might not need to start the server program. Here are some scenarios:

■ The server class is programmed to require a new instance of the program for each object constructed. Assuming the server program is able to run in multi-instance mode, OLE will start a new instance in response to the second and following *CreateInstance* calls, each of which returns an *IDispatch* pointer.

■ A special case of the scenario above, specific to MFC applications: The server class is an MFC document class in an SDI application. Each time a controller calls *CreateInstance*, a new instance of the server application starts, complete with a document object, a view object, and an SDI main frame window.

587

■ The server class is programmed to allow multiple objects in a single program instance. Each time a controller calls *CreateInstance*, a new server object is constructed. There is only one instance of the server program, however.

■ A special case of the scenario above, specific to MFC applications: The server class is an MFC document class in an MDI application. There is a single instance of the server application with one MDI main frame window. Each time a controller calls *CreateInstance*, a new document object is constructed, along with a view object and an MDI child frame window.

There's one more interesting case. Suppose a server EXE is running before the controller needs it, and then the controller decides to access a server object that already exists. You'll see this case with Excel. The user might have Excel running but minimized on the desktop, and the controller needs access to Excel's one and only application object. Here the controller calls the OLE function *GetActiveObject*, which provides an interface pointer for an existing server object. If the call fails, the controller can create the object with *CoCreateInstance*.

For server object deletion, normal COM rules apply. Automation objects have reference counts, and they delete themselves when the controller calls *Release* and the reference count goes to 0. In an MDI server, if the automation object is an MFC document, its destruction causes the corresponding MDI child window to close. In an SDI server, the destruction of the document object causes the server to exit. The controller is responsible for calling *Release* for each *IDispatch* interface before exit. For EXE servers, OLE will intervene if the controller exits without releasing an interface, thus allowing the server to exit. You can't always depend on this intervention, however, so be sure that your controller cleans up its interfaces!

With generic OLE, a client application often obtains multiple interface pointers for a single server object. Look back at the spaceship example in Chapter 23, in which the simulated OLE server class had both an *IMotion* pointer and an *IVisual* pointer. With OLE Automation, however, there's usually only a single (*IDispatch*) pointer per object. As in all OLE programming, you must be careful to release all your interface pointers. In Excel, for example, many methods return an *IDispatch* pointer to new or existing objects. If you fail to release a pointer, the Debug version of the MFC library alerts you with a memory leak dump when the controller program exits.

The MFC *IDispatch* Implementation

If you read the *OLE 2 Programmer's Reference Library,* 2d ed., Volume 2 (Microsoft Press, 1995), you'll notice that OLE provides an implementation for the *IDispatch* interface, which you can activate by calling the function *Create-StandardDispatch.* This built-in implementation uses an OLE Automation feature called a type library. A type library is a table, locatable through the registry, that allows a controller to query the server for the symbolic names of objects, methods, and properties. A controller could, for example, contain a browser that allows the user to explore the server's capabilities.

The MFC library supports type libraries, but it doesn't use them in its implementation of *IDispatch,* which is instead driven by a dispatch map. MFC programs don't call *CreateStandardDispatch* at all, nor do they use a type library to implement *IDispatch::GetIDsOfNames.* This means that you can't use the MFC library if you implement a multilingual automation server—one that supports English and German property and method names, for example. (*CreateStandardDispatch* doesn't support multilingual servers either.)

Later in this chapter, you'll learn how a controller can use a type library, and you'll see how AppWizard and ClassWizard create and maintain type libraries for you. Once your server has a type library, a controller can use it for browsing, independently of the *IDispatch* implementation.

An MFC OLE Automation Server

Let's look at what happens in an MFC automation server—in this case, a simplified version of the EX24C alarm clock program that is discussed later in this chapter. In the MFC library, the *IDispatch* implementation is part of the *CCmdTarget* base class, so you don't need *INTERFACE_MAP* macros. You write an automation server class, *CClockServ,* for example, that is derived from *CCmd-Target,* and this class's CPP file contains *DISPATCH_MAP* macros:

```
BEGIN_DISPATCH_MAP(CClockServ, CCmdTarget)
    DISP_PROPERTY(CClockServ, "Time", m_time, VT_DATE)
    DISP_PROPERTY_PARAM(CClockServ, "Figure", GetFigure,
                        SetFigure, VT_VARIANT, VTS_I2)
    DISP_FUNCTION(CClockServ, "RefreshWin", Refresh, VT_EMPTY, VTS_NONE)
    DISP_FUNCTION(CClockServ, "ShowWin", ShowWin, VT_BOOL, VTS_I2)
END_DISPATCH_MAP()
```

Looks a little like an MFC message map, doesn't it? The *CClockServ* class header file contains related code, shown on the following page:

```
public:
    DATE m_time;
    afx_msg VARIANT GetFigure(short n);
    afx_msg void SetFigure(short n, const VARIANT& vaNew);
    afx_msg void Refresh();
    afx_msg BOOL ShowWin(short n);
    DECLARE_DISPATCH_MAP()
```

What's all this stuff mean? It means that the *CClockServ* class has the following properties and methods:

Name	Type	Description
Time	Property	Linked directly to class data member *m_time*.
Figure	Property	Indexed property, accessed through member functions *GetFigure* and *SetFigure*: first parameter is the index; second (for *SetFigure*) is the string value. (The figures are the "XII," "III," "VI," and "IX" that appear on the clock face.)
RefreshWin	Method	Linked to class member function *Refresh*—no parameters or return value.
ShowWin	Method	Linked to class member function *ShowWin*— short integer parameter, Boolean return value.

How does the MFC dispatch map relate to *IDispatch* and the *Invoke* member function? The dispatch map macros generate static data tables that the MFC library's *Invoke* implementation can read. A controller gets an *IDispatch* pointer for *CClockServ* (connected through the *CCmdTarget* base class), and it calls *Invoke* with an array of pointers as a parameter. The MFC library's implementation of *Invoke*, buried somewhere inside *CCmdTarget*, uses the *CClockServ* dispatch map to decode the supplied pointers and either calls one of your member functions or accesses *m_time* directly.

As you'll see when you get to the examples, ClassWizard can generate the automation server class for you, and it can help you code the dispatch map.

An MFC OLE Automation Controller

Let's move on to the controller's end of the automation dialog. How does an MFC automation controller program call *Invoke*? The MFC library provides a base class *COleDispatchDriver* for this purpose. To shield you from the complexities of the OLE *Invoke* parameter sequence, *COleDispatchDriver* has three member functions—*InvokeHelper, GetProperty,* and *SetProperty.* Each of these functions calls *Invoke* for an *IDispatch* pointer that links to the server. The *COleDispatchDriver* object incorporates the *IDispatch* pointer.

Let's suppose our controller program has a class *CClockControl,* derived from *COleDispatchDriver,* that controls *CClockServ* objects in an automation server. Here are the functions that get and set the Time property:

```
DATE CClockControl::GetTime()
{
    DATE result;
    GetProperty(1, VT_DATE, (void*)&result);
    return result;
}

void CClockControl::SetTime(DATE propVal)
{
    SetProperty(1, VT_DATE, propVal);
}
```

Here are the functions for the indexed Figure property:

```
VARIANT CClockControl::GetFigure(short i)
{
    VARIANT result;
    static BYTE parms[] = VTS_I2;
    InvokeHelper(2, DISPATCH_PROPERTYGET, VT_VARIANT,
              (void*)&result, parms, i);
    return result;
}

void CClockControl::SetFigure(short i, const VARIANT& propVal)
{
    static BYTE parms[] = VTS_I2 VTS_VARIANT;
    InvokeHelper(2, DISPATCH_PROPERTYPUT, VT_EMPTY, NULL,
              parms, i, &propVal);
}
```

And finally, here are the functions that access the server's methods:

```
void CClockControl::RefreshWin()
{
    InvokeHelper(3, DISPATCH_METHOD, VT_EMPTY, NULL, NULL);
}

BOOL CClockControl::ShowWin(short i)
{
```

(continued)

```
      BOOL result;
      static BYTE parms[] = VTS_I2;
      InvokeHelper(4, DISPATCH_METHOD, VT_BOOL,
                   (void*)&result, parms, i);
      return result;
}
```

The function parameters identify the property or method, its return value, and its parameters. You'll learn more about dispatch function parameters later, but for now take special note of the first parameter for the *InvokeHelper*, *GetProperty*, and *SetProperty* functions. This is the unique integer index, or dispatch ID (DISPID), for the property or method. Because you're using compiled C++, you can establish these IDs at compile time. If you're using an MFC automation server with a dispatch map, the indexes are determined by the map sequence, beginning with 1. If you don't know a server's dispatch indexes, you can call the *IDispatch* member function *GetIDsOfNames* to convert the symbolic property or method names to integers.

The following illustration shows the interactions between the controller and the server:

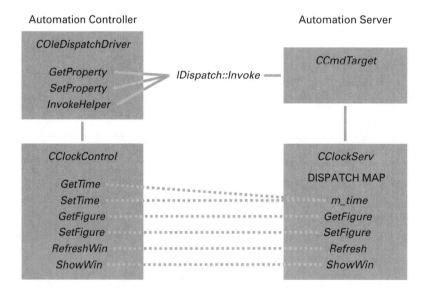

The solid lines show the actual connections through the MFC base classes and the *Invoke* function. The dotted lines represent the resulting logical connections between controller class members and server class members.

Most automation servers, including Excel, have a type library. Excel's type library is in a separate binary file with an OLB extension. ClassWizard can access this type library file to generate a class derived from *COleDispatch-Driver*. This generated controller class contains member functions for all the server's methods and properties with hard-coded dispatch IDs. Sometimes you need to do some surgery on this generated code, but that's better than writing the functions from scratch.

The *VARIANT* Type

No doubt you've noticed the *VARIANT* type used in both automation controller and server functions in the previous example. *VARIANT* is an all-purpose data type that *IDispatch::Invoke* uses to transmit parameters and return values. The *VARIANT* type is the natural type to use when exchanging data with VBA. Let's look at a <u>simplified</u> version of the *VARIANT* definition in the Win32 OLE header files:

```
struct tagVARIANT {
    VARTYPE vt; // unsigned short integer type code
    WORD wReserved1;
    WORD wReserved2;
    WORD wReserved3;
    union {
        short       iVal;                    // VT_I2   short integer
        long        lVal;                    // VT_I4   long integer
        float       fltVal;                  // VT_R4   4-byte float
        double      dblVal;                  // VT_R8   8-byte IEEE float
        DATE        date;                    // VT_DATE stored as dbl
                                             //   date.time
        BSTR        bstrVal;                 // VT_BSTR
        IUnknown    FAR* punkVal;            // VT_UNKNOWN
        IDispatch   FAR* pdispVal;           // VT_DISPATCH
        short       FAR* piVal;              // VT_BYREF¦VT_I2
        long        FAR* plVal;              // VT_BYREF¦VT_I4
        float       FAR* pfltVal;            // VT_BYREF¦VT_R4
        double      FAR* pdblVal;            // VT_BYREF¦VT_R8
        DATE        FAR* pdate;              // VT_BYREF¦VT_DATE
        BSTR        FAR* pbstrVal;           // VT_BYREF¦VT_BSTR
        IUnknown    FAR* FAR* ppunkVal;      // VT_BYREF¦VT_UNKNOWN
        IDispatch   FAR* FAR* ppdispVal      // VT_BYREF¦VT_DISPATCH
    }
};

typedef struct tagVARIANT VARIANT;
```

As you can see, the *VARIANT* type is a C structure that contains a type code *vt*, some filler bytes, and a big *union* of types that you already know about. If *vt* is VT_I2, for example, you can read the *VARIANT*'s value from *iVal*. If *vt* is VT_R8, you want *dblVal*.

A *VARIANT* object can contain actual data or a pointer to data. If *vt* has the VT_BYREF bit set, you must access a pointer in *piVal*, *plVal*, and so on. Note that a *VARIANT* object can contain an *IUnknown* pointer or an *IDispatch* pointer. This means that you can pass a complete COM object via an OLE Automation call, but if you want VBA to process that object, its class should have an *IDispatch* interface.

Strings are special. The *BSTR* type is yet another way to represent character strings. A *BSTR* variable is a pointer to a zero-terminated character array with a character count in front. A *BSTR* variable could, therefore, contain binary characters, including 0s. If you had a *VARIANT* object with *vt* = VT_BSTR, memory would look like this:

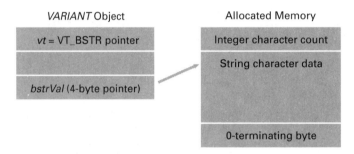

Because the string has a terminating 0, you can use *bstrVal* as though it were an ordinary *char* pointer, but you have to be very, very careful about memory cleanup. You can't simply delete the string pointer, because the allocated memory begins with the character count. OLE provides the *SysAllocString* and *SysFreeString* functions for allocating and deleting *BSTR* objects.

> NOTE: The *SysAllocString* function is another OLE function that takes a wide string pointer as a parameter. This means that all *BSTR*s contain wide characters, even if you haven't defined *_UNICODE*. Be careful.

OLE supplies some useful functions for *VARIANT*s, including *VariantInit*, *VariantClear*, *VariantCopy*, *VariantCopyInd*, and *VariantChangeType*. If a *VARIANT* contains a *BSTR*, these functions ensure that memory is allocated and cleared properly. The *VariantInit* and *VariantClear* functions set *vt* to VT_EMPTY. All the variant functions are global functions and take a *VARIANT** parameter.

The *COleVariant* Class

It makes a lot of sense to write a C++ class to wrap the *VARIANT* structure. Constructors can call *VariantInit,* and the destructor can call *VariantClear.* The class can have a constructor for each standard type, and it can have copy constructors and assignment operators that call *VariantCopy.* When a variant object goes out of scope, its destructor is called, and memory is cleaned up automatically.

Well, the MFC team went and created just such a class, mostly for use in the Data Access Objects (DAO) subsystem, described in Chapter 29. It works well with ordinary OLE Automation, however. Here's a simplified declaration:

```
class COleVariant : public tagVARIANT
{
// Constructors
public:
    COleVariant();

    COleVariant(const VARIANT& varSrc);
    COleVariant(const COleVariant& varSrc);

    COleVariant(LPCTSTR lpszSrc);
    COleVariant(CString& strSrc);

    COleVariant(BYTE nSrc);
    COleVariant(short nSrc, VARTYPE vtSrc = VT_I2);
    COleVariant(long lSrc, VARTYPE vtSrc = VT_I4);

    COleVariant(float fltSrc);
    COleVariant(double dblSrc);
    COleVariant(const COleDateTime& timeSrc);
// destructor
    ~COleVariant(); // deallocates BSTR
// Operations
public:
    void Clear(); // deallocates BSTR
    VARIANT Detach(); // more later
    void ChangeType(VARTYPE vartype, LPVARIANT pSrc = NULL);
};
```

In addition, there are comparison operators, assignment operators, conversion operators, and friend insertion/extraction operators for the *CArchive* and *CDumpContext* classes. See Books Online for a complete description of this useful MFC class.

Now let's see how the *COleVariant* class helps us write the server's *GetFigure* function that you saw referenced previously in the sample dispatch map. Assume that the server stores strings for four figures in a class data member, like this:

```
private:
    CString m_strFigure[4];
```

Here's what we'd have to do if we used the *VARIANT* structure directly:

```
VARIANT CClockServ::GetFigure(short n)
{
    VARIANT vaResult;
    ::VariantInit(&vaResult);
    vaResult.vt = VT_BSTR;
    // CString::AllocSysString creates a BSTR
    vaResult.bstrVal = m_strFigure[n].AllocSysString();
    return vaResult; // copies vaResult without copying BSTR
                     // BSTR still must be freed later
}
```

Here's the equivalent, with a *COleVariant* return value:

```
VARIANT CClockServ::GetFigure(short n)
{
    return COleVariant(m_strFigure[n]).Detach();
}
```

Calling the *COleVariant::Detach* function is critical here. The *GetFigure* function is constructing a temporary object that contains a pointer to a *BSTR*. That object gets bitwise-copied to the return value. If you didn't call *Detach*, the *COleVariant* destructor would free the *BSTR* memory, and the calling program would get a *VARIANT* that contained a pointer to nothing.

A server's variant dispatch function parameters are declared as *const VARIANT&*. You can always cast a *VARIANT* pointer to a *COleVariant* pointer inside the function. Here's the *SetFigure* function:

```
void CClockServ::SetFigure(short n, const VARIANT& vaNew)
{
    COleVariant vaTemp;
    vaTemp.ChangeType(VT_BSTR, (COleVariant*) &vaNew);
    m_strFigure[n] = vaTemp.bstrVal;
}
```

> **NOTE:** Remember that all *BSTR*s contain wide characters. The *CString* class has a constructor and an assignment operator for the *LPCWSTR* (wide-character pointer) type. Thus, the *m_strFigure* string will contain single-byte characters, even though *bstrVal* points to a wide-character array.

<u>Controller</u> dispatch function variant parameters are also typed as *const VARIANT&*. You can call those functions with either a *VARIANT* or a *COleVariant* object. Here's an example of a call to the *CClockServ::SetFigure* function shown on the previous page:

```
pClockControl->SetFigure(0, COleVariant("XII"));
```

Parameter and Return Type Conversions for *Invoke*

All *IDispatch::Invoke* parameters and return values are processed internally as *VARIANT*s. Remember that. The MFC library implementation of *Invoke* is smart enough to convert between a *VARIANT* and whatever type you supply (where possible), so you have some flexibility in declaring parameter and return types. Suppose, for example, that your controller's *GetFigure* function specifies the return type *BSTR*. If a server returns an *int* or a *long*, all is OK: OLE and the MFC library convert the number to a string. Suppose your server declares a *long* parameter and the controller supplies an *int*. Again, no problem. Even though OLE and the MFC library can handle *BSTR* parameters and return values, your life will be easier if you use *VARIANT* parameters and return values instead.

> NOTE: An MFC library automation controller specifies the expected return type as a *VT_* parameter to the *COleDispatchDriver* functions *GetProperty*, *SetProperty*, and *InvokeHelper*. An MFC library automation server specifies the expected parameter types as *VTS_* parameters in the *DISP_PROPERTY* and *DISP_FUNCTION* macros.

Unlike C++, VBA is not a strongly typed language. VBA variables are often stored internally as *VARIANT*s. Take an Excel spreadsheet cell value, for example. A spreadsheet user can type a text string, an integer, a floating-point number, or a date/time into the cell. VBA treats the cell value as a *VARIANT* and returns a *VARIANT* object to an automation controller. If your controller function declares a *VARIANT* return value, it can test *vt* and process the data accordingly.

VBA uses yet another date/time format. Variables of type *DATE* hold both the date and the time in one *double* value. The fractional part represents time (.25 is 6:00 AM), and the whole part represents the date (number of days since December 30, 1899). The MFC library provides a *COleDateTime* class that makes dates easy to deal with. You could construct a date this way:

```
COleDateTime date(1995, 10, 1, 18, 0, 0);
```

The *COleVariant* class has an assignment operator for *COleDateTime*, and the *COleDateTime* class has member functions for extracting date/time components. Here's how you print the time:

```
TRACE("time = %d:%d:%d\n",
    date.GetHour(),date.GetMinute(),date.GetSecond());
```

If you have a variant that contains a *DATE*, you can use the *COleVariant-::ChangeType* function to convert a date to a string, as shown here:

```
COleVariant vaTimeDate = date;
COleVariant vaTemp;
vaTemp.ChangeType(VT_BSTR, &vaTimeDate);
CString str = vaTemp.bstrVal;
TRACE("date = %s\n", (const char*) str);
```

One last item concerning *Invoke* parameters: a dispatch function can have <u>optional</u> <u>parameters</u>. If the server declares trailing parameters as *VARIANT*s, the controller doesn't have to supply them. If the controller calls the function without supplying an optional parameter, the *VARIANT* object's *vt* value on the server end is VT_ERROR.

NOTE: Some dispatch functions pass a legitimate OLE error code in a *VARIANT* parameter. If you don't know whether a parameter is omitted or represents a real error, test the value of the *scode* union member for *DISP_E_PARAMNOTFOUND*.

OLE Automation Examples

The remainder of this chapter presents four sample programs. The first three programs are OLE Automation servers—an EXE server with no user interface, a DLL server, and a multi-instance SDI EXE server. Each of these programs comes with a Microsoft Excel driver workbook. The last sample program is an MFC OLE Automation controller program that drives the three servers and also runs Excel.

The EX24A Automation Server EXE Example—No User Interface

The Autoclik example is a good demonstration of an MDI framework application with the document object as the automation server. (To find the Autoclik example, look for "Creating an OLE Automation Server" in Books Online.) The EX24A example is different because it has no user interface. There is one automation-aware class, and in the first version of the program a single instance of the server supports the construction of multiple automation objects. In the second version, a new instance starts up each time an automation controller creates an object.

The EX24A example represents a typical use of OLE Automation. A C++ server implements financial transactions. VBA programmers can write UI-intensive applications that rely on the audit rules imposed by the server. A production server would probably use a database, but EX24A is simpler. It implements a bank account with two methods, Deposit and Withdrawal, and one read-only property, Balance. Obviously, the Withdrawal method can't permit withdrawals that make the balance negative. You can use Excel to control the server, as shown in Figure 24-3.

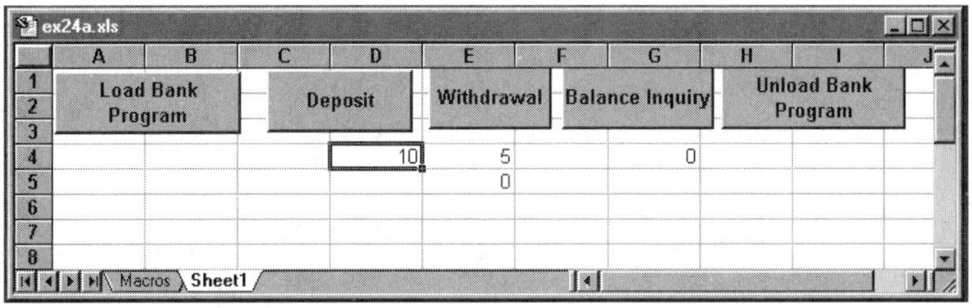

Figure 24-3.
This Excel workbook is controlling the EX24A server.

Here are the steps for creating the program from scratch:

1. **Run AppWizard to create the EX24A project in the \VCPP32\EX24A directory.** Select the Dialog-Based option. Deselect the About Box option, but select OLE Automation. This is the simplest OLE application that AppWizard can generate.

2. **Eliminate the dialog class from the project.** From Explorer or the command-line prompt, delete the files ex24aDlg.cpp and ex24aDlg.h. Remove ex24aDlg.cpp from the project by deleting it from the project's Workspace window. Edit ex24a.cpp. Remove the dialog #include, and remove all dialog-related code from the *InitInstance* function. Also delete the *IDD_EX24A_DIALOG* dialog resource template. The *InitInstance* function should now look like this (after the addition of some diagnostic statements):

```
BOOL CEx24aApp::InitInstance()
{
    // Initialize OLE libraries
    if (!AfxOleInit())
    {
        AfxMessageBox(IDP_OLE_INIT_FAILED);
        return FALSE;
    }

    // Standard initialization
    // If you are not using these features and wish to reduce the size
    //  of your final executable, you should remove from the following
    //  the specific initialization routines you do not need.

#ifdef _AFXDLL
    Enable3dControls();         // Call this when using MFC in a shared DLL
#else
    Enable3dControlsStatic(); // Call this when linking to MFC statically
#endif

    // Parse the command line to see if launched as OLE server
    if (RunEmbedded() || RunAutomated())
    {
        // Register all OLE server factories as running. This enables
        //  the OLE libraries to create objects from other applications.
        COleTemplateServer::RegisterAll();

        // Application was run with /Embedding or /Automation. Don't
        //  show the main window in this case.
        return TRUE;
    }

    // When a server application is launched stand-alone, it is a good
    //  idea to update the system registry in case it has been damaged.
    COleObjectFactory::UpdateRegistryAll();
    AfxMessageBox("Bank server is registered"); // add this line
    return FALSE;
}
```

3. Use ClassWizard to add a new class, *CBank*, as shown here:

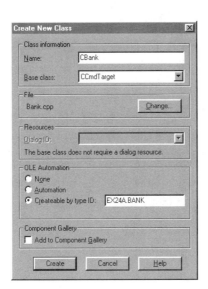

Be sure to select the Createable By Type ID option.

4. Use ClassWizard to add two methods and a property. Click on the OLE Automation tab, and then add a Withdrawal method, as shown here:

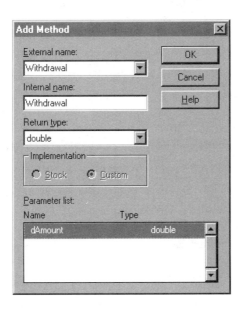

The *dAmount* parameter is the amount to be withdrawn, and the return value is the actual amount withdrawn. If you try to withdraw $100 from an account that contains $60, the amount withdrawn is $60.

Add a similar Deposit method that returns *void*, and then add the Balance property, as shown here:

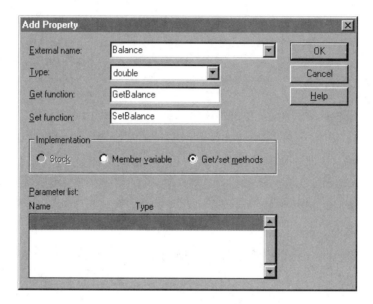

We could have chosen direct access to a server data member, but then we wouldn't have read-only access. We choose Get/Set Methods so that we can code the *SetBalance* function to do nothing.

5. **Add a public *m_dBalance* data member of type *double* to the *CBank* class.** Because we've chosen the Get/Set Methods option for the Balance property, ClassWizard doesn't generate a data member for us. You should initialize *m_dBalance* to 0.0 in the *CBank* constructor.

6. **Edit the generated method and property functions.** Add the following shaded code:

```
double CBank::Withdrawal(double dAmount)
{
    if (dAmount < 0.0) {
        return 0.0;
    }
    if (dAmount <= m_dBalance) {
        m_dBalance -= dAmount;
        return dAmount;
    }
```

```
    double dTemp = m_dBalance;
    m_dBalance = 0.0;
    return dTemp;
}

void CBank::Deposit(double dAmount)
{
    if (dAmount < 0.0) {
      return;
    }
    m_dBalance += dAmount;
}

double CBank::GetBalance()
{
    return m_dBalance;
}

void CBank::SetBalance(double newValue)
{
    TRACE("Sorry, Dave, I can't do that!\n");
}
```

7. **Build the EX24A program, and run it once to register the server.**

8. **Set up five Excel macros in a new workbook file, ex24a.xls.** Add the following code:

```
Dim Bank As Object
Sub LoadBank()
    Set Bank = CreateObject("Ex24a.Bank")
End Sub

Sub UnloadBank()
    Set Bank = Nothing
End Sub

Sub DoDeposit()
    Range("D4").Select
    Bank.Deposit (ActiveCell.Value)
End Sub

Sub DoWithdrawal()
    Range("E4").Select
    Amt = Bank.Withdrawal(ActiveCell.Value)
    Range("E5").Select
```

(continued)

```
      ActiveCell.Value = Amt
End Sub

Sub DoInquiry()
    Amt = Bank.Balance()
    Range("G4").Select
    ActiveCell.Value = Amt
End Sub
```

9. Arrange an Excel worksheet as shown in Figure 24-3 on page 599.
Attach the macros to the pushbuttons (using the right mouse button).

10. Test the EX24A bank server. Click the Load Bank Program button,
and then enter a deposit value in cell D4 and click the Deposit button.
Click the Balance Inquiry button, and watch the balance appear in cell
G4. Enter a withdrawal value in cell E5, and click the Withdrawal button.

> NOTE: Sometimes you need to click the buttons twice. The first
> click switches the focus to the worksheet, and the second click runs
> the macro. The hourglass cursor tells you the macro is working.

What's happening in this program? Look closely at the *CEx24aApp::Init-
Instance* function. When you run the program directly from Windows, it displays a message box and then quits, but not before it updates the registry. The
COleObjectFactory::UpdateRegistryAll function hunts for global class factory
objects, and the *CBank* class's *IMPLEMENT_OLECREATE* macro invocation
defines such an object. (The *IMPLEMENT_OLECREATE* line was generated
because you checked ClassWizard's Ole Creatable check box for *CBank*.)
The unique class ID and the program ID, EX24A.BANK, are added to the
registry.

When Excel now calls *CreateObject*, OLE loads the EX24A program,
which contains the global factory for *CBank* objects; OLE then calls the factory
object's *CreateInstance* function to construct the *CBank* object and return an
IDispatch pointer. Here's the *CBank* class that ClassWizard generated, with
unnecessary detail (and the method and property functions you've already
seen) omitted:

```
class CBank : public CCmdTarget
{
    DECLARE_DYNCREATE(CBank)
public:
    double m_dBalance;
    CBank();   // protected constructor used by dynamic creation
```

```
// Attributes
public:

// Operations
public:

// Overrides
    // ClassWizard generated virtual function overrides
    //{{AFX_VIRTUAL(CBank)
    public:
    virtual void OnFinalRelease();
    //}}AFX_VIRTUAL

// Implementation
protected:
    virtual ~CBank();

    // Generated message map functions
    //{{AFX_MSG(CBank)
    // NOTE - the ClassWizard will add and remove member functions here.
    //}}AFX_MSG

    DECLARE_MESSAGE_MAP()
    DECLARE_OLECREATE(CBank)

    // Generated OLE dispatch map functions
    //{{AFX_DISPATCH(CBank)
    afx_msg double GetBalance();
    afx_msg void SetBalance(double newValue);
    afx_msg double Withdrawal(double dAmount);
    afx_msg void Deposit(double dAmount);
    //}}AFX_DISPATCH
    DECLARE_DISPATCH_MAP()
    DECLARE_INTERFACE_MAP()
};
IMPLEMENT_DYNCREATE(CBank, CCmdTarget)

CBank::CBank()
{
    EnableAutomation();

    // To keep the application running as long as an OLE automation
    //  object is active, the constructor calls AfxOleLockApp.

    AfxOleLockApp();
}
```

(continued)

```
CBank::~CBank()
{
    // To terminate the application when all objects created with
    //  OLE automation, the destructor calls AfxOleUnlockApp.

    AfxOleUnlockApp();
}

void CBank::OnFinalRelease()
{
    // When the last reference for an automation object is released
    //  OnFinalRelease is called. This implementation deletes the
    //  object. Add additional cleanup required for your object before
    //  deleting it from memory.

    delete this;
}

BEGIN_MESSAGE_MAP(CBank, CCmdTarget)
    //{{AFX_MSG_MAP(CBank)
    // NOTE - the ClassWizard will add and remove mapping macros here.
    //}}AFX_MSG_MAP
END_MESSAGE_MAP()

BEGIN_DISPATCH_MAP(CBank, CCmdTarget)
    //{{AFX_DISPATCH_MAP(CBank)
    DISP_PROPERTY_EX(CBank, "Balance", GetBalance, SetBalance, VT_R8)
    DISP_FUNCTION(CBank, "Withdrawal", Withdrawal, VT_R8, VTS_R8)
    DISP_FUNCTION(CBank, "Deposit", Deposit, VT_EMPTY, VTS_R8)
    //}}AFX_DISPATCH_MAP
END_DISPATCH_MAP()

// Note: we add support for IID_IBank to support typesafe binding
//  from VBA.  This IID must match the GUID that is attached to the
//  dispinterface in the .ODL file.

// {632B1E4B-F287-11CE-B5E3-00AA005B1574}
static const IID IID_IBank =
{ 0x632b1e4b, 0xf287, 0x11ce, { 0xb5, 0xe3, 0x0, 0xaa, 0x0, 0x5b,
    0x15, 0x74 } };

BEGIN_INTERFACE_MAP(CBank, CCmdTarget)
    INTERFACE_PART(CBank, IID_IBank, Dispatch)
END_INTERFACE_MAP()

// {632B1E4C-F287-11CE-B5E3-00AA005B1574}
IMPLEMENT_OLECREATE2(CBank, "EX24A.BANK", 0x632b1e4c, 0xf287, 0x11ce,
    0xb5, 0xe3, 0x0, 0xaa, 0x0, 0x5b, 0x15, 0x74)
```

606

Debugging an EXE Server

When an automation controller launches an EXE server, it sets the
/Embedding command-line parameter. If you want to debug your
server, you must do the same. Choose Settings from the Developer
Studio Build menu, and then enter */Embedding* in the Program Arguments box on the Debug page, as shown here:

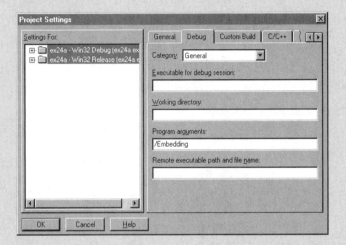

When you click the Debug Go toolbar button, your program will
start and then wait for a controller to activate it. At this point, you
should start the controller program from Windows (if it is not already
running) and then use it to create a server object. Your server program in the debugger should then construct its server object. It
might be a good idea to include a *TRACE* statement in the server
object's constructor.

Don't forget that your server program must be registered before
the controller can find it. That means you have to run it once <u>without</u>
the */Embedding* flag. Many controllers don't synchronize with registry
changes. If your controller is running when you register the server,
you may have to restart the controller.

This first version of the program runs in single-instance mode, as does
the Autoclik program. If a second automation controller asks for a new
CBank object, OLE calls the class factory *CreateInstance* function again, and
the existing instance constructs another *CBank* object on the heap. You can

verify this by making a copy of the ex24a.xls workbook (under a different name) and loading both the original and the copy. Click the Load Bank Program button in each workbook, and watch the Debug window. *InitInstance* should be called only once.

Parameters Passed by Reference

So far, you've seen VBA parameters passed by <u>value</u>. VBA has pretty strange rules for calling methods. If the method has one parameter, you can use parentheses; if it has more than one, you can't (unless you're using the function's return value, in which case you <u>must</u> use parentheses). Here is some sample VBA code that passes the string parameter by value:

```
Object.Method1 parm1, "text"
Object.Method2("text")
Dim s as String
s = "text"
Object.Method2(s)
```

Sometimes, though, VBA passes the address of a parameter (a reference). In this example, the string is passed by reference:

```
Dim s as String
s = "text"
Object.Method1 parm1, s
```

You can override VBA's default behavior by prefixing a parameter with ByVal or ByRef. As you can see, your server can never know in advance whether it's getting a value or a reference, so it must be prepared for both. The trick is to test *vt* to see whether its *VT_BYREF* bit is set. Here's a sample method implementation that accepts a string (in a *VARIANT*) passed either by reference or by value:

```
void CMyServer::Method(long nParm1, const VARIANT& vaParm2)
{
    CString str;
    if ((vaParm2.vt & 0x7f) == VT_BSTR) {
      if ((vaParm2.vt & VT_BYREF) != 0)
        str = *(vaParm2.pbstrVal); // byref
      else
        str = vaParm2.bstrVal; // byval
    }
    AfxMessageBox(str);
}
```

A small change in the EX24A program makes it behave differently. To have a new instance of EX24A start up each time a new server object is requested, follow these steps:

1. Add the following macro in bank.h:

```
#define IMPLEMENT_OLECREATE2(class_name, external_name, \
  l, w1, w2, b1, b2, b3, b4, b5, b6, b7, b8) \
  AFX_DATADEF COleObjectFactory class_name::factory(class_name::guid, \
  RUNTIME_CLASS(class_name), TRUE, _T(external_name)); \
  const AFX_DATADEF GUID class_name::guid = \
  { l, w1, w2, { b1, b2, b3, b4, b5, b6, b7, b8 } };
```

This macro is the same as the standard MFC *IMPLEMENT_OLECREATE* macro except that the original *FALSE* parameter (after the *RUNTIME-_CLASS* parameter) has been changed to *TRUE*.

2. In bank.cpp, change the *IMPLEMENT_OLECREATE* macro invocation to *IMPLEMENT_OLECREATE2*.

3. Build the program, and test it using Excel. Use the same two workbooks, and notice that *InitInstance* gets called each time you click the Load Bank Program button.

NOTE: The EX24A program on the companion CD-ROM uses the *IMPLEMENT_OLECREATE2* macro.

The EX24B Automation Server DLL Example

You could easily convert EX24A from an EXE to a DLL. The *CBank* class would be exactly the same, and the Excel driver would be similar. It's more interesting, though, to write a new application—this time with a minimal user interface (UI). We'll use a modal dialog because it's about the most complex UI we can easily use in an automation server DLL.

The EX24B program is fairly simple. An automation server class, identified by the registered name *Ex24b.Auto*, has the following properties and method:

LongData	Long integer property
TextData	*VARIANT* property
DisplayDialog	Method—no parameters, *BOOL* return

DisplayDialog displays the EX24B OLE Data Gathering dialog shown in Figure 24-4. An Excel macro passes two cell values to the DLL and then updates the same cells with the updated values.

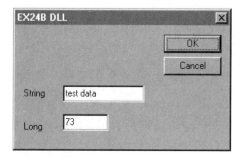

Figure 24-4.
The EX24B DLL dialog in action.

The example was first generated as an MFC AppWizard DLL with the Regular DLL Using Shared MFC DLL option and the OLE Automation option. Here are the steps for building and testing the EX24B server DLL from the code installed from the companion CD-ROM:

1. **From the Developer Studio, open the project \vcpp32\ex24b-\ex24b.mdp.** Build the project.

2. **Register the DLL with the Regsrv32 utility.** You can also use the Regserv program in the \VCPP32\REGSERV directory on the companion CD-ROM; it has a file dialog that makes it easy to select the DLL file.

3. **Start Excel, and then load the workbook file \vcpp32\ex24b-\ex24b.xls.** Type an integer in cell C3, and type some text in cell D3, as shown here:

	A	B	C	D	E	F	G
1	Load DLL		Gather Data			Unload DLL	
2							
3			73	test data			
4							
5							
6							

Click the Load DLL button, and then click the Gather Data button. Edit the data, click OK, and watch the new values appear in the spreadsheet.

4. Click the Unload DLL button. If you've started the DLL (and Excel) from the debugger, you can watch the Debug window to be sure the DLL's *ExitInstance* function is called.

Debugging a DLL Server

To debug a DLL, you must tell the debugger which EXE file to load. Choose Settings from the Developer Studio's Build menu, and then enter the controller's full pathname (including the EXE extension) in the Executable For Debug Session box on the Debug page, as shown here:

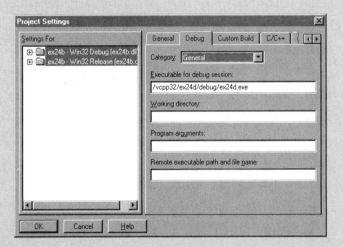

When you click the Debug Go toolbar button, your controller will start (loading the DLL as part of its process) and then wait for you to activate the server.

When you activate the server, your server DLL in the debugger should then construct its server object. It might be a good idea to include a *TRACE* statement in the server object's constructor. Don't forget that your server DLL must be registered before the controller can load it.

Now let's look at the EX24B code. Like an MFC EXE, an MFC regular DLL has an application class (derived from *CWinApp*) and a global application object. The overridden *InitInstance* member function in ex24b.cpp looks like this:

```
BOOL CEx24bApp::InitInstance()
{
    TRACE("Entering CEx24bApp::InitInstance\n");
    COleObjectFactory::RegisterAll();
    return TRUE;
}
```

There's also an *ExitInstance* function for diagnostic purposes only, as well as the following code for the three standard COM DLL exported functions:

```
STDAPI DllGetClassObject(REFCLSID rclsid, REFIID riid, LPVOID* ppv)
{
    AFX_MANAGE_STATE(AfxGetStaticModuleState());
    return AfxDllGetClassObject(rclsid, riid, ppv);
}

STDAPI DllCanUnloadNow(void)
{
    AFX_MANAGE_STATE(AfxGetStaticModuleState());
    return AfxDllCanUnloadNow();
}

STDAPI DllRegisterServer(void)
{
    AFX_MANAGE_STATE(AfxGetStaticModuleState());
    COleObjectFactory::UpdateRegistryAll();
    return S_OK;
}
```

The PromptDl.cpp file contains code for the *CPromptDlg* class, but that class is a standard class derived from *CDialog*. The file PromptDl.h contains the *CPromptDlg* class header.

The *CEx24bAuto* class, the automation server class initially generated by ClassWizard (with the OLE Createable option), is more interesting. This class is exposed to OLE under the program ID Ex24b.Auto. Figure 24-5 shows the header file ex24bAut.h.

EX24BAUT.H

```
class CEx24bAuto : public CCmdTarget
{
    DECLARE_DYNCREATE(CEx24bAuto)

    CEx24bAuto(); // protected constructor used by dynamic creation

// Attributes
public:

// Operations
public:

// Overrides
    // ClassWizard generated virtual function overrides
    //{{AFX_VIRTUAL(CEx24bAuto)
    public:
    virtual void OnFinalRelease();
    //}}AFX_VIRTUAL

// Implementation
protected:
    virtual ~CEx24bAuto();

    // Generated message map functions
    //{{AFX_MSG(CEx24bAuto)
    // NOTE: the ClassWizard will add and remove member functions here.
    //}}AFX_MSG

    DECLARE_MESSAGE_MAP()
    DECLARE_OLECREATE(CEx24bAuto)

    // Generated OLE dispatch map functions
    //{{AFX_DISPATCH(CEx24bAuto)
    VARIANT m_vaTextData;
    long m_lData;
    afx_msg void OnLongDataChanged();
    afx_msg BOOL DisplayDialog();
    //}}AFX_DISPATCH
    DECLARE_DISPATCH_MAP()
    DECLARE_INTERFACE_MAP()
};
```

Figure 24-5.
The ex24bAut.h header file.

Figure 24-6 shows the implementation file ex24bAut.cpp.

EX24BAUT.CPP

```
#include "StdAfx.h"
#include "ex24b.h"
#include "Ex24bAut.h"
#include "PromptDl.h"

#ifdef _DEBUG
#undef THIS_FILE
static char THIS_FILE[] = __FILE__;
#endif

/////////////////////////////////////////////////////////////////////////////
// CEx24bAuto

IMPLEMENT_DYNCREATE(CEx24bAuto, CCmdTarget)

CEx24bAuto::CEx24bAuto()
{
    TRACE("CEx24bAuto constructor\n");
    EnableAutomation();
    ::VariantInit(&m_vaTextData); // necessary initialization
    m_lData = 0;
    // To keep the application running as long as an OLE automation
    //  object is active, the constructor calls AfxOleLockApp.

    AfxOleLockApp();
}

CEx24bAuto::~CEx24bAuto()
{
    // To terminate the application when all objects created with
    //  OLE automation, the destructor calls AfxOleUnlockApp.

    AfxOleUnlockApp();
}

void CEx24bAuto::OnFinalRelease()
{
    // When the last reference for an automation object is released
    //  OnFinalRelease is called. This implementation deletes the
    //  object. Add additional cleanup required for your object before
    //  deleting it from memory.

    delete this;
}
```

Figure 24-6.   *(continued)*

The ex24bAut.cpp implementation file.

Figure 24-6. *continued*

```
BEGIN_MESSAGE_MAP(CEx24bAuto, CCmdTarget)
    //{{AFX_MSG_MAP(CEx24bAuto)
    // NOTE: the ClassWizard will add and remove mapping macros here.
    //}}AFX_MSG_MAP
END_MESSAGE_MAP()

BEGIN_DISPATCH_MAP(CEx24bAuto, CCmdTarget)
    //{{AFX_DISPATCH_MAP(CEx24bAuto)
    DISP_PROPERTY_NOTIFY(CEx24bAuto, "LongData", m_lData,
                         OnLongDataChanged, VT_I4)
    DISP_PROPERTY(CEx24bAuto, "TextData", m_vaTextData, VT_VARIANT)
    DISP_FUNCTION(CEx24bAuto, "DisplayDialog", DisplayDialog, VT_BOOL,
                  VTS_NONE)
    //}}AFX_DISPATCH_MAP
END_DISPATCH_MAP()

// Note: we add support for IID_IEx24bAuto to support typesafe binding
//   from VBA. This IID must match the GUID that is attached to the
//   dispinterface in the .ODL file.

// {923011EA-CBEB-11CE-B337-88EA36DE9E4E}
static const IID IID_IEx24bAuto = { 0x923011ea, 0xcbeb, 0x11ce,
    { 0xb3, 0x37, 0x88, 0xea, 0x36, 0xde, 0x9e, 0x4e } };

BEGIN_INTERFACE_MAP(CEx24bAuto, CCmdTarget)
    INTERFACE_PART(CEx24bAuto, IID_IEx24bAuto, Dispatch)
END_INTERFACE_MAP()

// {923011EB-CBEB-11CE-B337-88EA36DE9E4E}
IMPLEMENT_OLECREATE(CEx24bAuto, "Ex24b.Auto", 0x923011eb, 0xcbeb,
    0x11ce, 0xb3, 0x37, 0x88, 0xea, 0x36, 0xde, 0x9e, 0x4e)

/////////////////////////////////////////////////////////////////////
// CEx24bAuto message handlers

BOOL CEx24bAuto::DisplayDialog()
{
    TRACE("Entering CEx24bAuto::DisplayDialog %p\n", this);
    BOOL bRet = TRUE;
    AfxLockTempMaps();  // see MFC Tech Note #3
//  CWnd* pTopWnd = CWnd::GetForegroundWindow();
    CWnd* pTopWnd = CWnd::FromHandle(::GetTopWindow(NULL)); // problem?
    TRY {
        CPromptDlg dlg(pTopWnd);
        if (m_vaTextData.vt == VT_BSTR){
```

(continued)

Figure 24-6. *continued*

```
            dlg.m_strData = m_vaTextData.bstrVal; // converts double-byte
                                                  //  character to
                                                  //  single-byte character
        }
        dlg.m_lData = m_lData;
        if (dlg.DoModal() == IDOK) {
          m_vaTextData = COleVariant(dlg.m_strData).Detach();
          m_lData = dlg.m_lData;
          bRet = TRUE;
        }
        else {
          bRet = FALSE;
        }
    }
    CATCH_ALL(e) {
        TRACE("Exception: failure to display dialog\n");
        bRet = FALSE;
    }
    END_CATCH_ALL
    AfxUnlockTempMaps();
    return bRet;
}

void CEx24bAuto::OnLongDataChanged()
{
    TRACE("CEx24bAuto::OnLongDataChanged\n");
}
```

The two properties, LongData and TextData, are represented by class data members *m_lData* and *m_vaTextData*, both initialized in the constructor. When the LongData property was added in ClassWizard, a notification function, *OnLongDataChanged*, was specified. This function is called whenever the controller changes the property value. Notification functions apply only to properties that are represented by data members. Don't confuse this notification with the notifications that OCXs give their container when a bound property changes.

The *DisplayDialog* member function, which is the *DisplayDialog* method, is ordinary except for two things: First, the dialog's parent window must be set to the client application's top-level window. The Win32 *GetTopWindow* function provides this window to the dialog's constructor. Second, the *AfxLockTempMaps* and *AfxUnlockTempMaps* functions are necessary for cleaning up temporary object pointers that would normally be deleted in an EXE program's idle loop.

NOTE: If you use the Win32 *GetTopWindow* function as your dialog's parent, things get a little strange when another program sets its main window to be "always on top." If you call the static *CWnd::GetForegroundWindow* function instead, things get strange when you try to edit VBA code in Excel. Take your pick, or think of something better.

What about the Excel VBA code? Here are the three macros and the global declarations:

```
Dim Dllserv As Object
Declare Sub CoFreeUnusedLibraries Lib "OLE32" ()

Sub LoadDllServ()
    Set Dllserv = CreateObject("Ex24b.Auto")
    Range("C3").Select
    Dllserv.LongData = Selection.Value
    Range("D3").Select
    Dllserv.TextData = Selection.Value
End Sub

Sub RefreshDllServ() 'Gather Data button
    Range("C3").Select
    Dllserv.LongData = Selection.Value
    Range("D3").Select
    Dllserv.TextData = Selection.Value
    Dllserv.DisplayDialog
    Range("C3").Select
    Selection.Value = Dllserv.LongData
    Range("D3").Select
    Selection.Value = Dllserv.TextData
End Sub

Sub UnloadDllServ()
    Set Dllserv = Nothing
    Call CoFreeUnusedLibraries
End Sub
```

The first line in *LoadDllServ* creates a server object as identified by the registered name *Ex24b.Auto*. The *RefreshDllServ* macro accesses the server object's LongData and TextData properties. The first time you run *LoadDllServ*, it loads the DLL and constructs an *Ex24b.Auto* object. The second time you run *LoadDllServ*, something curious happens: a second object is constructed, and the original object is destroyed. If you run *LoadDllServ* from another copy of the workbook, you get two separate *Ex24b.Auto* objects. Of course, there's only one mapping of ex24b.dll in memory at any time unless you're running more than one instance of Excel.

Look closely at the *UnloadDllServ* macro. When the "Set Dllserv = Nothing" statement is executed, the DLL is disconnected, but it's not unmapped from Excel's address space, and that means the server's *ExitInstance* function is not called. The OLE *CoFreeUnusedLibraries* function calls the exported *DllCanUnloadNow* function for each server DLL, and, if that function returns *TRUE*, frees the DLL. MFC programs call *CoFreeUnusedLibraries* in the idle loop, but Excel doesn't. That's why *UnloadDllServ* must call *CoFreeUnusedLibraries* after disconnecting the server.

> NOTE: The *CoFreeUnusedLibraries* function doesn't do anything in Windows NT 3.51 unless you have Service Pack 2 (SP2) installed.

The EX24C SDI Automation Server EXE Example— With User Interface

This last OLE server example illustrates the use of a document server class in a multi-instance SDI application. This server demonstrates an indexed property plus a method that constructs a new OLE object.

The first automation server you saw, EX24A, didn't have a user interface. The global class factory constructed a *CBank* object that did the server's work. What if you want your EXE server to have a window? If you've bought into the MFC document–view architecture, you'll want the document, view, and frame with all the benefits they provide.

Suppose you created a regular MFC application and then added an OLE creatable class such as *CBank*. How do you attach the *CBank* object to the document and view? From a *CBank* class member function, you could navigate through the application object and main frame to the current document or view, but you'd have a tough time in an MDI application if you encountered several server objects and several documents. There is a better way. You make the document class itself the OLE creatable class, and you have the full support of AppWizard for this task—and that's true for both MDI and SDI applications.

The MDI Autoclik example demonstrates how OLE triggers the construction of new document, view, and child frame objects each time an automation controller creates a new server object. Because the EX24C example is an SDI program, OLE starts a new instance each time the controller creates an object. Immediately after it starts the program, OLE constructs not only the automation-aware document but also the view and the main frame window.

Now's a good time to experiment with the EX24C application, which was first generated by AppWizard with the OLE Automation Support option checked. It's a Windows-based alarm-clock program that's designed to be manipulated from an automation controller such as Excel. EX24C has the following properties and methods:

Time	*DATE* property that holds an OLE *DATE* (*m_vaTime*)
Figure	Indexed *VARIANT* property for the four figures on the clock face (*m_strFigure[]*)
RefreshWin	Method that invalidates the view window and brings the main frame window to the top (*Refresh*)
ShowWin	Method that displays the application's main window (*ShowWin*)
CreateAlarm	Method that creates a *CAlarm* object and returns its *IDispatch* pointer (*CreateAlarm*)

Here are the steps for building and running EX24C from the companion CD-ROM:

1. **From the Developer Studio, open the project \vcpp32\ex24c-\ex24c.mdp.** Build the project to produce the ex24c.exe file in the project's Debug subdirectory.

2. **Run the program once to register it.** The program is designed to be executed either as a stand-alone application or as an OLE Automation server. When you run it from Windows or from the Developer Studio, it updates the registry and displays the face of a clock with the characters XII, III, VI, and IX at the 12, 3, 6, and 9 o'clock positions. Exit the program.

3. **Load the Excel workbook file \vcpp32\ex24c\ex24c.xls.** The worksheet should look like the one shown here:

Click the Load Clock button, and then click the Set Alarm button. (There is a long delay after you click the Load Clock button.) The clock should appear as shown on the following page, with the letter *A* indicating the alarm setting:

If you've started the server from the debugger, you can watch the Debug window to see when *InitInstance* is called and when the document object is constructed.

4. Click the Unload Clock button. If you've started the server from the debugger, you can watch the Debug window for a message box that indicates that the *ExitInstance* function is called.

AppWizard did most of the work of setting up the document as an automation server. In the derived application class *CEx24cApp*, it generated a data member for the server, as shown here:

```
public:
    COleTemplateServer m_server;
```

The MFC *COleTemplateServer* class is derived from *COleObjectFactory*. It is designed to create a COM document object when a client calls *IClassFactory::CreateInstance*. The class ID comes from the global *clsid* variable defined in ex24c.cpp. The human-readable program ID (Ex24c.Document) comes from the *IDR_MAINFRAME* string resource.

In the *InitInstance* function (in ex24c.cpp), AppWizard generated the following code, which connects the server object (the document) to the application's document template:

```
CSingleDocTemplate* pDocTemplate;
pDocTemplate = new CSingleDocTemplate(
    IDR_MAINFRAME,
    RUNTIME_CLASS(CEx24cDoc),
    RUNTIME_CLASS(CMainFrame),      // main SDI frame window
    RUNTIME_CLASS(CEx24cView));
AddDocTemplate(pDocTemplate);
m_server.ConnectTemplate(clsid, pDocTemplate, TRUE);
```

Now all the plumbing is in place for OLE to construct the document, together with the view and frame. When the objects are constructed, however, the main window is not made visible. That's your job. You must write a method that shows the window.

The following *UpdateRegistry* call updates the Windows registry with the contents of the project's *IDR_MAINFRAME* string resource:

```
m_server.UpdateRegistry(OAT_DISPATCH_OBJECT);
```

The following dispatch map shows the properties and methods for the *CEx24cDoc* class. Note that the Figure property is an indexed property, which ClassWizard can generate if you specify a parameter. Later you'll see the code that you have to write for the *GetFigure* and *SetFigure* functions.

```
BEGIN_DISPATCH_MAP(CEx24cDoc, CDocument)
    //{{AFX_DISPATCH_MAP(CEx24cDoc)
    DISP_PROPERTY(CEx24cDoc, "Time", m_time, VT_DATE)
    DISP_FUNCTION(CEx24cDoc, "ShowWin", ShowWin, VT_EMPTY, VTS_NONE)
    DISP_FUNCTION(CEx24cDoc, "CreateAlarm", CreateAlarm, VT_DISPATCH,
        VTS_DATE)
    DISP_FUNCTION(CEx24cDoc, "RefreshWin", Refresh, VT_EMPTY, VTS_NONE)
    DISP_PROPERTY_PARAM(CEx24cDoc, "Figure", GetFigure, SetFigure,
        VT_VARIANT, VTS_I2)
    //}}AFX_DISPATCH_MAP
END_DISPATCH_MAP()
```

The RefreshWin and ShowWin methods aren't very interesting, but the CreateAlarm method is worth a close look. Here's the corresponding *CreateAlarm* member function:

```
LPDISPATCH CEx24cDoc::CreateAlarm(DATE time)
{
    m_pAlarm = new CAlarm(time);
    return m_pAlarm->GetIDispatch(FALSE);   // no AddRef here
}
```

We've chosen to have the server create an alarm object when a controller calls *CreateAlarm*. *CAlarm* is an automation server class that we've generated with ClassWizard. It is <u>not</u> OLE creatable, and that means there's no *IMPLEMENT_OLECREATE* macro and no class factory. The *CreateAlarm* function constructs a *CAlarm* object and returns an *IDispatch* pointer. (The *FALSE* parameter for *CCmdTarget::GetIDispatch* means that the reference count is not incremented; the *CAlarm* object already has a reference count of 1 when it is constructed.)

The *CAlarm* class is declared in alarm.h as follows:

```
class CAlarm : public CCmdTarget
{
// DECLARE_DYNCREATE(CAlarm)

public:
    CAlarm(DATE time);
// Overrides
    // ClassWizard generated virtual function overrides
    //{{AFX_VIRTUAL(CAlarm)
public:
    virtual void OnFinalRelease();
    //}}AFX_VIRTUAL

// Implementation
protected:
    virtual ~CAlarm();

    // Generated message map functions
    //{{AFX_MSG(CAlarm)
    // NOTE - the ClassWizard will add and remove member functions here.
    //}}AFX_MSG

    DECLARE_MESSAGE_MAP()
    // Generated OLE dispatch map functions
public:
    //{{AFX_DISPATCH(CAlarm)
    DATE m_time;
    //}}AFX_DISPATCH
    DECLARE_DISPATCH_MAP()
    DECLARE_INTERFACE_MAP()
};
```

Notice the absence of the *DECLARE_DYNCREATE* macro.
ALARM.CPP contains a dispatch map, as follows:

```
BEGIN_DISPATCH_MAP(CAlarm, CCmdTarget)
    //{{AFX_DISPATCH_MAP(CAlarm)
    DISP_PROPERTY(CAlarm, "Time", m_time, VT_DATE)
    //}}AFX_DISPATCH_MAP
END_DISPATCH_MAP()
```

Why do we have a *CAlarm* class? We could have added an AlarmTime property in the *CEx24cDoc* class instead, but then we would have needed another property or method to turn the alarm on and off. By using the *CAlarm* class, what we're really doing is setting ourselves up to support multiple alarms—a collection of alarms.

To implement an OLE Automation collection, we would write another class, *CAlarms*, which would contain the methods *Add*, *Remove*, and *Item*. *Add* and *Remove* are self-explanatory; *Item* returns an *IDispatch* pointer for a collection element identified by an index, numeric or otherwise. We would also implement a read-only Count property that returned the number of elements. The document class (which owns the collection) would have an *Alarms* method with an optional *VARIANT* parameter. If the parameter were omitted, the method would return the *IDispatch* pointer for the collection. If the parameter specified an index, the method would return an *IDispatch* pointer for the selected alarm.

> NOTE: If we wanted our collection to support the VBA "For Each" syntax, we'd have some more work to do. We'd add an *IEnumVARIANT* interface to the *CAlarms* class and implement the *Next* member function to step through the collection. Then we'd add a *CAlarms* method named *_NewEnum* that returned an *IEnumVARIANT* interface pointer. If we wanted the collection to be general, we'd allow separate enumerator objects (with an *IEnumVARIANT* interface) and we'd implement the other *IEnumVARIANT* functions—*Skip*, *Reset*, and *Clone*.

The Figures property is an indexed property, and that makes it interesting. The Figures property represents the four figures on the clock face—XII, III, VI, and IX. It's a *CString* array, so we can use Roman numerals. Here's the declaration in ex24cDoc.h:

```
public:
    CString m_strFigure[4];
```

and here are the *GetFigure* and *SetFigure* functions in ex24cDoc.cpp:

```
VARIANT CEx24cDoc::GetFigure(short n)
{
    return COleVariant(m_strFigure[n]);
}

void CEx24cDoc::SetFigure(short n, const VARIANT& vaNew)
{
    COleVariant vaTemp;
    vaTemp.ChangeType(VT_BSTR, (COleVariant*) &vaNew);
    m_strFigure[n] = vaTemp.bstrVal;
}
```

These functions tie back to the *DISP_PROPERTY_PARAM* macro in the *CEx24cDoc* dispatch map. The first parameter is the index number, specified as a short integer by the last macro parameter. Property indexes don't have to be integers, and the index can have several components (row and column number, for example). The *ChangeType* call in *SetFigure* is necessary because the controller might otherwise pass numbers instead of strings.

You've just seen collection properties and indexed properties. What's the difference? A controller can't add or delete elements of an indexed property, but it can add elements to a collection, and it can delete elements.

What draws the clock face? As you might expect, it's the *OnDraw* member function of the view class. This function uses *GetDocument* to get a pointer to the document object, and then it accesses the document's property data members and method member functions.

Finally, here's the Excel macro code:

```
Dim Clock As Object
Dim Alarm As Object

Sub LoadClock()
    Set Clock = CreateObject("Ex24c.Document")
    Range("A3").Select
    n = 0
    Do Until n = 4
        Clock.figure(n) = Selection.Value
        Selection.Offset(0, 1).Range("A1").Select
        n = n + 1
    Loop
    RefreshClock
    Clock.ShowWin
End Sub

Sub RefreshClock()
    Clock.Time = Now()
    Clock.RefreshWin
End Sub

Sub CreateAlarm()
    Range("E3").Select
    Set Alarm = Clock.CreateAlarm(Selection.Value)
    RefreshClock
End Sub

Sub UnloadClock()
    Set Clock = Nothing
End Sub
```

Notice the Set Alarm statement in the CreateAlarm macro. It calls the Create-Alarm method to return an *IDispatch* pointer, which is stored in an object variable. If the macro is run a second time, a new alarm is created, but the original one is destroyed because its reference count goes to 0.

WARNING: You've seen a modal dialog in a DLL (EX24B), and you've seen a main frame window in an EXE (EX24C). Be careful with modal dialogs in EXEs. It's OK to have an About dialog that is invoked directly by the server program, but it isn't a good idea to invoke a modal dialog in an EXE server method function. The problem is that once the modal dialog is on the screen, the user can switch back to the controller program. MFC controllers handle this situation with a special "Server Busy" message box, which appears right away. Excel does something similar, but it waits 30 seconds, and this could confuse the user. If you want to see this effect, uncomment the *OnAppAbout* line in *CEx24cDoc::CreateAlarm*.

The EX24D Automation Controller Example

So far, you've seen C++ OLE Automation server programs. Now you'll see a C++ OLE Automation controller program that runs all the previous servers and also controls Microsoft Excel. The EX24D program was originally generated by AppWizard, but without any OLE options. It was easier to add the OLE code than it would have been to rip out the server-specific code. If you do use AppWizard to build such an automation controller, add the following line at the end of StdAfx.h:

```
#include <afxdisp.h>
```

and add the following call in the application's *InitInstance* function:

```
AfxOleInit();
```

To prepare EX24D, open the \VCPP32\EX24D\EX24D project and do the build. Run the application from the debugger, and you'll see a standard SDI application with a menu structure as shown in Figure 24-7.

File	Edit	Bank OLE	DLL OLE	Clock OLE	Excel OLE	View	Help
		Load	Load	Load	Load		
		Test	Get Data	Create Alarm	Execute		
		Unload	Unload	Refresh Time			
				Unload			

Figure 24-7.
A sample menu structure for a standard SDI application.

If you have built and registered all the servers, you can test them from EX24D. Notice that the DLL doesn't have to be in the \WINDOWS\SYSTEM directory because OLE finds it through the registry. For some servers, you'll have to watch the Debug window to verify that the test results are correct. The program is reasonably modular. Menu commands and update command UI events are mapped to the view class. Each server object has its own C++ controller class and an embedded data member in ex24dView.h. We'll look at each part separately after we delve into type libraries.

Type Libraries and ODL Files

I've told you that type libraries aren't necessary for the MFC *IDispatch* implementation, but the Developer Studio has been quietly generating type libraries for all your servers. What good are these type libraries? VBA can use a type library to browse your server's methods and properties, and it can use the type library for improved access to properties and methods, a process called <u>early</u> <u>binding</u> that I'll describe later in this chapter. But we're building a C++ controller here, not a VBA program. It so happens that ClassWizard can read a server's type library and use the information to generate C++ code for the controller to use to access an automation server.

> NOTE: AppWizard initializes a project's ODL (Object Description Language) file when you first create it. ClassWizard edits this file each time you generate a new automation server class or add properties and methods to an existing class. Unlike with the CLW file, ClassWizard can't rebuild an ODL file from the contents of your source files. If you mess up your ODL file, you'll have to re-create it manually.

When you were adding properties and methods to your server classes, ClassWizard was updating the project's ODL file. This file is a text file that describes the server in an Object Description Language. (Your GUID will be different if you used AppWizard to generate this project.) Here's the ODL file for the bank server:

```
// ex24a.odl : type library source for ex24a.exe

// This file will be processed by the Make Type Library (mktyplib) tool
// to produce the type library (ex24a.tlb).

[ uuid(632B1E47-F287-11CE-B5E3-00AA005B1574), version(1.0) ]
library Ex24a
{
```

```
importlib("stdole32.tlb");

//  Primary dispatch interface for CBank

[ uuid(632B1E4B-F287-11CE-B5E3-00AA005B1574) ]
dispinterface IBank
{
    properties:
        // NOTE - ClassWizard will maintain property information
        //    here. Use extreme caution when editing this section.
        //{{AFX_ODL_PROP(CBank)
        [id(1)] double Balance;
        //}}AFX_ODL_PROP

    methods:
        // NOTE - ClassWizard will maintain method information
        //    here. Use extreme caution when editing this section.
        //{{AFX_ODL_METHOD(CBank)
        [id(2)] double Withdrawal(double dAmount);
        [id(3)] void Deposit(double dAmount);
        //}}AFX_ODL_METHOD
};

//  Class information for CBank

[ uuid(632B1E4C-F287-11CE-B5E3-00AA005B1574) ]
coclass CBank
{
    [default] dispinterface IBank;
};

//{{AFX_APPEND_ODL}}
};
```

The ODL file has a unique GUID type library identifier, 632B1E47-F287-11CE-B5E3-00AA005B1574, and it completely describes the bank server's properties and methods under a <u>dispinterface</u> named *IBank*. In addition, it specifies the dispinterface GUID, 632B1E4B-F287-11CE-B5E3-00AA005B1574, which is the same GUID that's in the interface map of the *CBank* class listed on page 606. You'll see the significance of this GUID when you read the "VBA Early Binding" sidebar at the end of this chapter. The CLSID, 632B1E4C-F287-11CE-B5E3-00AA005B1574, is what a VBA browser can use to actually load your server.

Anyway, when you build your <u>server</u> project, the Developer Studio invokes the MKTYPLIB utility, which reads the ODL file and generates a binary TLB file in your project's debug or release subdirectory. Now, when you develop a C++ <u>controller,</u> you can ask ClassWizard to generate a controller class from the server project's TLB file.

> NOTE: The MKTYPLIB utility generates the type library in a stand-alone TLB file, and that's what automation controllers such as Excel look for. OCXs have their type libraries bound into their resources.

To actually do this, you click the ClassWizard Add Class button and then select From An OLE Type Library from the pull-down list. You navigate to the server's TLB file, and then ClassWizard shows you a dialog similar to this:

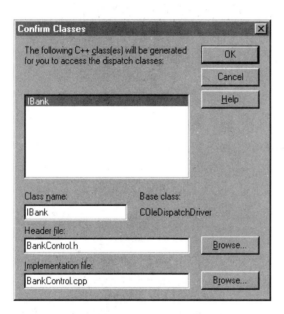

IBank is the name of the dispinterface specified in the ODL file. You can keep this name for the class if you want, and you can specify the H and CPP filenames. If a type library contains several interfaces, you can make multiple selections. You'll see the generated controller classes in the sections that follow.

The Controller Class for ex24a.exe

ClassWizard generated the *IBank* class (derived from *COleDispatchDriver*) listed in Figure 24-8. Look closely at the member function implementations.

Note the first parameters of the *GetProperty*, *SetProperty*, and *InvokeHelper* function calls. These are hard-coded DISPIDs for the server's properties and methods, as determined by the server's dispatch map sequence.

> WARNING: If you use ClassWizard to delete a property and then you add it back, you'll probably change the server's dispatch IDs. That means that you'll have to regenerate or edit the controller class so that the IDs match.

BANKCONTROL.H

```
class IBank : public COleDispatchDriver
{
public:
    IBank() {}
    IBank(LPDISPATCH pDispatch) : COleDispatchDriver(pDispatch) {}
    IBank(const IBank& dispatchSrc) :
        COleDispatchDriver(dispatchSrc) {}

// Attributes
public:
    double GetBalance();
    void SetBalance(double);

// Operations
public:
    double Withdrawal(double dAmount);
    void Deposit(double dAmount);
};
```

BANKCONTROL.CPP

```
#include "StdAfx.h"
#include "bankcontrol.h"

#ifdef _DEBUG
#define new DEBUG_NEW
#undef THIS_FILE
static char THIS_FILE[] = __FILE__;
#endif


/////////////////////////////////////////////////////////////////////
// IBank properties

double IBank::GetBalance()
{
```

Figure 24-8.   *(continued)*
The IBank *class listing.*

Figure 24-8. *continued*

```
        double result;
        GetProperty(0x1, VT_R8, (void*)&result);
        return result;
    }

    void IBank::SetBalance(double propVal)
    {
        SetProperty(0x1, VT_R8, propVal);
    }

    /////////////////////////////////////////////////////////////////////////////
    // IBank operations

    double IBank::Withdrawal(double dAmount)
    {
        double result;
        static BYTE parms[] =
            VTS_R8;
        InvokeHelper(0x2, DISPATCH_METHOD, VT_R8, (void*)&result, parms,
                    dAmount);
        return result;
    }

    void IBank::Deposit(double dAmount)
    {
        static BYTE parms[] =
            VTS_R8;
        InvokeHelper(0x3, DISPATCH_METHOD, VT_EMPTY, NULL, parms,
                    dAmount);
    }
```

The *CEx24dView* class has a data member *m_bank* of class *IBank*. The *CEx24dView* member functions for the Ex24a.Bank server are listed below. They are hooked up to options on the controller's main menu. Of particular interest is the *OnBankoleLoad* function. The *COleDispatchDriver::CreateDispatch* function loads the server program (by calling *CoGetClassObject* and *IClassFactory::CreateInstance*) and calls *QueryInterface* to get an *IDispatch* pointer, which it stores in the object's *m_lpDispatch* data member. The *COleDispatchDriver::ReleaseDispatch* function, called in *OnBankoleUnload*, calls *Release* on the pointer.

```
void CEx24dView::OnBankoleLoad()
{
    BeginWaitCursor();
    VERIFY(m_bank.CreateDispatch("Ex24a.Bank") == TRUE);
    EndWaitCursor();
}
```

```
void CEx24dView::OnUpdateBankoleLoad(CCmdUI* pCmdUI)
{
    pCmdUI->Enable(m_bank.m_lpDispatch == NULL);
}

void CEx24dView::OnBankoleTest()
{
    m_bank.Deposit(20.0);
    m_bank.Withdrawal(15.0);
    TRACE("new balance = %f\n", m_bank.GetBalance());
}

void CEx24dView::OnUpdateBankoleTest(CCmdUI* pCmdUI)
{
    pCmdUI->Enable(m_bank.m_lpDispatch != NULL);
}

void CEx24dView::OnBankoleUnload()
{
    m_bank.ReleaseDispatch();
}

void CEx24dView::OnUpdateBankoleUnload(CCmdUI* pCmdUI)
{
    pCmdUI->Enable(m_bank.m_lpDispatch != NULL);
}
```

The Controller Class for ex24b.dll

Figure 24-9 shows the class header file that ClassWizard generated for the ex24b DLL.

AUTOCONTROL.H

```
class IEx24bAuto : public COleDispatchDriver
{
public:
    IEx24bAuto() {}
    IEx24bAuto(LPDISPATCH pDispatch) : COleDispatchDriver(pDispatch) {}
    IEx24bAuto(const IEx24bAuto& dispatchSrc) :
        COleDispatchDriver(dispatchSrc) {}

// Attributes
public:
    long GetLongData();
    void SetLongData(long);
```

Figure 24-9. *(continued)*
The IEx24bAuto *class header file.*

631

Figure 24-9. *continued*

```
      VARIANT GetTextData();
      void SetTextData(const VARIANT&);

// Operations
public:
      BOOL DisplayDialog();
};
```

Notice that each property requires separate *Get* and *Set* functions in the controller class, even though the property is represented by a data member in the server.

The view class header has a data member *m_auto* of class *IEx24bAuto.* Here are two DLL-related command handler member functions from Ex24dView.cpp:

```
void CEx24dView::OnDlloleGetdata()
{
    m_auto.DisplayDialog();
    COleVariant vaData = m_auto.GetTextData();
    ASSERT(vaData.vt == VT_BSTR);
    CString strTextData = vaData.bstrVal;
    long lData = m_auto.GetLongData();
    TRACE("CEx24dView::OnDlloleGetdata -- long = %ld, text = %s\n",
          lData, strTextData);
}


void CEx24dView::OnUpdateDlloleGetdata(CCmdUI* pCmdUI)
{
    pCmdUI->Enable(m_auto.m_lpDispatch != NULL);
}


void CEx24dView::OnDlloleLoad()
{
    BeginWaitCursor();
    VERIFY(m_auto.CreateDispatch("Ex24b.Auto") == TRUE);
    m_auto.SetTextData(COleVariant("test"));  // testing
    m_auto.SetLongData(79);  // testing
    EndWaitCursor();
}


void CEx24dView::OnUpdateDlloleLoad(CCmdUI* pCmdUI)
{
    pCmdUI->Enable(m_auto.m_lpDispatch == NULL);
}
```

```
void CEx24dView::OnDlloleUnload()
{
    m_auto.ReleaseDispatch();
}

void CEx24dView::OnUpdateDlloleUnload(CCmdUI* pCmdUI)
{
    pCmdUI->Enable(m_auto.m_lpDispatch != NULL);
}
```

The Controller Class for ex24c.exe

Figure 24-10 shows the header for the *IEx24c* class, which controls the EX24C automation server.

CLOCKCONTROL.H

```
class IEx24c : public COleDispatchDriver
{
public:
    IEx24c() {}
    IEx24c(LPDISPATCH pDispatch) : COleDispatchDriver(pDispatch) {}
    IEx24c(const IEx24c& dispatchSrc) :
        COleDispatchDriver(dispatchSrc) {}

// Attributes
public:
    DATE GetTime();
    void SetTime(DATE);

// Operations
public:
    void ShowWin();
    LPDISPATCH CreateAlarm(DATE time);
    void RefreshWin();
    void SetFigure(short n, const VARIANT& newValue);
    VARIANT GetFigure(short n);
};
```

Figure 24-10.
The IEx24c *class header file.*

Of particular interest is the *IEx24c::CreateAlarm* member function in ClockControl.cpp. Notice that the function returns an *IDispatch* pointer to an alarm object that must be released, as shown on the following page:

633

```
LPDISPATCH IEx24c::CreateAlarm(DATE time)
{
    LPDISPATCH result;
    static BYTE parms[] =
        VTS_DATE;
    InvokeHelper(0x3, DISPATCH_METHOD, VT_DISPATCH, (void*)&result,
        parms, time);
    return result;
}
```

Figure 24-11 shows a class for the alarm controller as well, and it's declared in a separate file.

ALARMCONTROL.H

```
class IAlarm : public COleDispatchDriver
{
public:
    IAlarm() {}
    IAlarm(LPDISPATCH pDispatch) : COleDispatchDriver(pDispatch) {}
    IAlarm(const IAlarm& dispatchSrc) :
        COleDispatchDriver(dispatchSrc) {}

// Attributes
public:
    DATE GetTime();
    void SetTime(DATE);

// Operations
public:
};
```

Figure 24-11.
The IAlarm *class header file.*

The view class has the data members *m_clock* and *m_alarm*. Here are the view class command handlers:

```
void CEx24dView::OnClockoleCreatealarm()
{
    CAlarmDialog dlg;
    if (dlg.DoModal() == IDOK) {
      COleDateTime dt(1, 1, 1,
          dlg.m_nHours, dlg.m_nMinutes, dlg.m_nSeconds);
      LPDISPATCH pAlarm = m_clock.CreateAlarm(dt);
      m_alarm.AttachDispatch(pAlarm);  // releases prior object!
      m_clock.RefreshWin();
    }
}
```

```
void CEx24dView::OnUpdateClockoleCreatealarm(CCmdUI* pCmdUI)
{
    pCmdUI->Enable(m_clock.m_lpDispatch != NULL);
}

void CEx24dView::OnClockoleLoad()
{
    BeginWaitCursor();
    VERIFY(m_clock.CreateDispatch("Ex24c.Document") == TRUE);
    m_clock.SetFigure(0, COleVariant("twelve"));
    m_clock.SetFigure(1, COleVariant("three"));
    m_clock.SetFigure(2, COleVariant("six"));
    m_clock.SetFigure(3, COleVariant("nine"));
    OnClockoleRefreshtime();
    m_clock.ShowWin();
    EndWaitCursor();
}

void CEx24dView::OnUpdateClockoleLoad(CCmdUI* pCmdUI)
{
    pCmdUI->Enable(m_clock.m_lpDispatch == NULL);
}

void CEx24dView::OnClockoleRefreshtime()
{
    COleDateTime now = COleDateTime::GetCurrentTime();
    m_clock.SetTime(now);
    m_clock.RefreshWin();
}

void CEx24dView::OnUpdateClockoleRefreshtime(CCmdUI* pCmdUI)
{
    pCmdUI->Enable(m_clock.m_lpDispatch != NULL);
}

void CEx24dView::OnClockoleUnload()
{
    m_clock.ReleaseDispatch();
}

void CEx24dView::OnUpdateClockoleUnload(CCmdUI* pCmdUI)
{
    pCmdUI->Enable(m_clock.m_lpDispatch != NULL);
}
```

The *IEx24c::CreateAlarm* function causes the server to construct a clock object and return an *IDispatch* pointer with a reference count of 1. The *COle-DispatchDriver::AttachDispatch* function connects that pointer to the *m_alarm* object, but if that object already has a dispatch pointer, the old pointer is released. That's why, if you watch the Debug window, you'll see that the old EX24C instance exits immediately after you ask for a new instance. You'll have to test this behavior with the Excel driver because EX24D disables the Load menu option when the clock is running.

Controlling Microsoft Excel

The EX24D program contains code that loads Excel, creates a workbook, and reads and writes cells from the active worksheet. Controlling Excel is exactly like controlling an MFC automation server, but you need to know about a few Excel peculiarities.

If you study Excel VBA, you'll notice that there are over 100 "objects" you can use in your programs. All of these objects are accessible through OLE Automation, but if you write an MFC automation controller program, you'll need to know about the objects' properties and methods. Ideally, you'd like a C++ class for each object, complete with member functions coded to the proper dispatch IDs.

Excel has its own type library, found in the file xl5en32.olb in the Excel directory. ClassWizard can read this file, exactly as it reads TLB files, to create C++ controller classes for individual Excel objects. It makes sense to select the objects you need and then combine the classes into a single set of files. Figure 24-12 shows the process:

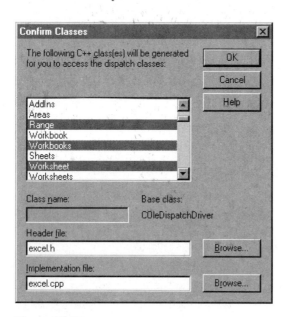

Figure 24-12.
ClassWizard can create C++ classes for the Excel objects listed in xl5en32.olb.

You might need to edit the generated code to suit your needs. Let's look at an example. If you use ClassWizard to generate a controller class for the Worksheet object, you get a *Range* member function, as shown here:

```
VARIANT Worksheet::Range(const VARIANT& Cell1,
                         const VARIANT& Cell2)
{
    VARIANT result;
    static BYTE BASED_CODE parms[] = VTS_VARIANT VTS_VARIANT;
    InvokeHelper(0xc5, DISPATCH_METHOD, VT_VARIANT,
             (void*)&result, parms, &Cell1, &Cell2);
    return result;
}
```

The trouble is that you know (from the Excel documentation) that the Range method returns a dispatch pointer, not a *VARIANT*, and that you can call the method with either a single cell (one parameter) or a rectangular area specified by two cells (two parameters). Remember: you can omit optional parameters in a call to *InvokeHelper*. Now it makes sense to replace the generated *Range* function with two overloaded functions:

```
LPDISPATCH Worksheet::Range(const VARIANT& Cell1,
                            const VARIANT& Cell2)
{
    LPDISPATCH result;
    static BYTE BASED_CODE parms[] = VTS_VARIANT VTS_VARIANT;
    InvokeHelper(0xc5, DISPATCH_METHOD, VT_DISPATCH,
             (void*)&result, parms, &Cell1, &Cell2);
    return result;
}

LPDISPATCH Worksheet::Range(const VARIANT& Cell1)
{
    LPDISPATCH result;
    static BYTE BASED_CODE parms[] = VTS_VARIANT;
    InvokeHelper(0xc5, DISPATCH_METHOD, VT_DISPATCH,
             (void*)&result, parms, &Cell1);
    return result;
}
```

How do you know which functions to fix up? They're the functions you decide to use in your program. You'll have to read the Excel VBA reference manual to figure out the required parameters and return values. Perhaps someday soon someone will write a set of Excel controller classes.

The EX24D program uses the following Excel objects and contains the corresponding classes, as shown in the table on the following page. All the code is contained in the files excel.h and excel.cpp.

Object/Class	View Class Data Member
Application	*m_app*
Range	*m_range[5]*
Worksheet	*m_worksheet*
Workbooks	*m_workbooks*

The following view member function, *OnExceloleLoad*, handles the Excel OLE Load menu command. This function must work if the user already has Excel running on the desktop. The OLE *GetActiveObject* function tries to return an *IUnknown* pointer for Excel. *GetActiveObject* requires a class ID, so we must first call *CLSIDFromProgID*. If *GetActiveObject* is successful, we call *QueryInterface* to get an *IDispatch* pointer, and we attach it to the view's *m_excel* controller object of class *Application*. If *GetActiveObject* is unsuccessful, we call *COleDispatchDriver::CreateDispatch*, as we did for the other servers.

```
void CEx24dView::OnExceloleLoad()
{   // if Excel is already running, attach to it, otherwise start it
    LPDISPATCH pDisp;
    LPUNKNOWN pUnk;
    CLSID clsid;
    BeginWaitCursor();
    ::CLSIDFromProgID(L"Excel.Application.5", &clsid); // from registry
    if (::GetActiveObject(clsid, NULL, &pUnk) == S_OK) {
      TRACE("attaching\n");
      VERIFY(pUnk->QueryInterface(IID_IDispatch,
          (void**) &pDisp) == S_OK);
      m_app.AttachDispatch(pDisp);
      pUnk->Release();
    }
    else {
      TRACE("creating\n");
      VERIFY(m_app.CreateDispatch("Excel.Application.5") == TRUE);
    }
    EndWaitCursor();
}
```

OnExceloleExecute is the command handler for Excel OLE Execute. Its first task is to find the Excel main window and bring it to the top. We must write some Windows code here because the Excel developers weren't kind enough to supply a method for this purpose. We must also create a workbook if no workbook is currently open.

We have to watch our method return values closely. The Workbooks Add method, for example, returns an *IDispatch* pointer for a Workbook object and, of course, increments the reference count. If we generated a class for Workbook, we could call *AttachDispatch* so that *Release* would be called when the Workbook object was destroyed. Because we don't need a Workbook class, we'll simply release the pointer ourselves at the end of the function. If we don't clean up our pointers properly, we'll get memory leak messages from the Debug version of MFC.

The rest of the *OnExceloleExecute* function accesses the cells in the worksheet. You can see how easy it is to get and set numbers, dates, strings, and formulas. The C++ code is similar to the VBA code you would write to do the same job.

```
void CEx24dView::OnExceloleExecute()
{
    LPDISPATCH pRange, pWorkbooks;

    CWnd* pWnd = CWnd::FindWindow("XLMAIN", NULL);
    if (pWnd != NULL) {
      TRACE("Excel window found\n");
      pWnd->ShowWindow(SW_SHOWNORMAL);
      pWnd->UpdateWindow();
      pWnd->BringWindowToTop();
    }

    m_app.SetSheetsInNewWorkbook(1);

    ASSERT(pWorkbooks = m_app.Workbooks());
    m_workbooks.AttachDispatch(pWorkbooks);

    LPDISPATCH pWorkbook = NULL;
    if (m_workbooks.GetCount() == 0) {
      // Add returns a Workbook pointer, but we
      //   don't have a Workbook class
      pWorkbook = m_workbooks.Add(); // save the pointer for
                                     //   later release
    }
    LPDISPATCH pWorksheet = m_app.Worksheets(COleVariant((short) 1));
    ASSERT(pWorksheet != NULL);

    m_worksheet.AttachDispatch(pWorksheet);
    m_worksheet.Select();

    ASSERT(pRange = m_worksheet.Range(COleVariant("A1")));
    m_range[0].AttachDispatch(pRange);
```

(continued)

```
ASSERT(pRange = m_worksheet.Range(COleVariant("A2")));
m_range[1].AttachDispatch(pRange);

ASSERT(pRange = m_worksheet.Range(COleVariant("A3")));
m_range[2].AttachDispatch(pRange);

ASSERT(pRange = m_worksheet.Range(COleVariant("A3"),
    COleVariant("C5")));
m_range[3].AttachDispatch(pRange);

ASSERT(pRange = m_worksheet.Range(COleVariant("A6")));
m_range[4].AttachDispatch(pRange);

m_range[4].SetValue(COleVariant(COleDateTime(1994, 4,
    24, 15, 47, 8)));
// retrieve the stored date and print it as a string
COleVariant vaTimeDate = m_range[4].GetValue();
TRACE("returned date type = %d\n", vaTimeDate.vt);
COleVariant vaTemp;
vaTemp.ChangeType(VT_BSTR, &vaTimeDate);
CString str = vaTemp.bstrVal;
TRACE("date = %s\n", (const char*) str);

m_range[0].SetValue(COleVariant("test string"));

COleVariant vaResult0 = m_range[0].GetValue();
if (vaResult0.vt == VT_BSTR) {
  CString str = vaResult0.bstrVal;
  TRACE("vaResult0 = %s\n", (const char*) str);
}

m_range[1].SetValue(COleVariant(3.14159));

COlcVariant vaResult1 = m_range[1].GetValue();
if (vaResult1.vt == VT_R8) {
  TRACE("vaResult1 = %f\n", vaResult1.dblVal);
}

m_range[2].SetFormula(COleVariant("=$A2*2.0"));

COleVariant vaResult2 = m_range[2].GetValue();
if (vaResult2.vt == VT_R8) {
  TRACE("vaResult2 = %f\n", vaResult2.dblVal);
}

COleVariant vaResult2a = m_range[2].GetFormula();
if (vaResult2a.vt == VT_BSTR) {
  CString str = vaResult2a.bstrVal;
  TRACE("vaResult2a = %s\n", (const char*) str);
}
```

```
    m_range[3].FillRight();
    m_range[3].FillDown();

// cleanup
    if (pWorkbook != NULL) {
      pWorkbook->Release();
    }
}
```

VBA Early Binding

When you ran the EX24A, EX24B, and EX24C servers from Excel VBA, you were using something called <u>late</u> binding. Normally, each time VBA accesses a property or a method, it calls *IDispatch::GetIDsOfNames* to look up the dispatch ID from the symbolic name. This isn't very efficient, but what is more significant is that VBA can't do type checking until it actually accesses a property or a method. Suppose, for example, that a VBA program tried to get a property value that it assumed was a number, but the server provided a string instead. VBA would give you a runtime error when it executed the Property Get statement.

With <u>early</u> binding, VBA can preprocess the Basic code, converting property and method symbols to DISPIDs before it runs the server. In so doing, it can check property types, method return types, and method parameters, giving you compile-time error messages. How can VBA get the advance information it needs? From the server's type library, of course. It can use that same type library to allow the VBA programmer to browse the server's properties and methods. VBA reads the type library before it even loads the server, but this process is "interesting," to say the least. If you can think of a way to make it more complex, write to Microsoft. I'm sure they'll appreciate your suggestions.

Registering a Type Library

You've already seen that the Developer Studio generates a TLB file for each server. For VBA to locate that type library, its location must be specified in the Windows registry. The simplest way of doing this is to write a text REG file that the Windows Regedit program can import. Here's the ex24b.reg file for the EX24B DLL server:

```
REGEDIT4

[HKEY_CLASSES_ROOT\TypeLib\
    {923011E1-CBEB-11CE-B337-88EA36DE9E4E}]
```

(continued)

```
[HKEY_CLASSES_ROOT\TypeLib\
     {923011E1-CBEB-11CE-B337-88EA36DE9E4E}\1.0]
@="Ex24b Type Library"
[HKEY_CLASSES_ROOT\TypeLib\
     {923011E1-CBEB-11CE-B337-88EA36DE9E4E}\1.0\0\win32]
@= "c:\\vcpp32\\ex24b\\debug\\ex24b.tlb"
[HKEY_CLASSES_ROOT\TypeLib\
     {923011E1-CBEB-11CE-B337-88EA36DE9E4E}\1.0\HELPDIR]
@=""

[HKEY_CLASSES_ROOT\Interface\{923011EA-CBEB-11CE-B337-88EA36DE9E4E}]
@="IEx24bAuto"
[HKEY_CLASSES_ROOT\Interface\
     {923011EA-CBEB-11CE-B337-88EA36DE9E4E}\ProxyStubClsid]
@="{00020420-0000-0000-C000-000000000046}"
[HKEY_CLASSES_ROOT\Interface\
     {923011EA-CBEB-11CE-B337-88EA36DE9E4E}\ProxyStubClsid32]
@="{00020420-0000-0000-C000-000000000046}"
[HKEY_CLASSES_ROOT\Interface\
     {923011EA-CBEB-11CE-B337-88EA36DE9E4E}\TypeLib]
@="{923011E6-CBEB-11CE-B337-88EA36DE9E4E}"
```

Notice that this file generates subtrees under the registry's TypeLib and Interface keys. The third entry specifies the path for the version 1.0 TLB file. The 0 subkey stands for "neutral language." If you had a multilingual application, you would have separate entries for English, French, and so forth. The TypeLib entries are used by browsers, and the Interface entries are used for runtime type checking and, for an EXE server, marshaling the dispinterface.

How a Server Can Register Its Own Type Library

When an EXE server is run stand-alone, it can call the MFC *AfxRegisterTypeLib* function to make the necessary registry entries, as shown here:

```
VERIFY(AfxOleRegisterTypeLib(AfxGetInstanceHandle(), theTypeLibGUID,
     "ex24b.tlb"));
```

theTypeLibGUID is a static variable of type *GUID*, as shown here:

```
static const GUID theTypeLibGUID =
{ 0x923011e6, 0xcbeb, 0x11ce, { 0xb3, 0x37, 0x88, 0xea, 0x36,
  0xde, 0x9e, 0x4e } };
```

The *AfxRegisterTypeLib* function is declared in the afxctl.h header, which requires _AFXDLL to be defined. That means you can't use it in a regular DLL unless you copy the code from the MFC source files.

The ODL File

Now is a good time to look at the ODL file for the same project.

```
[ uuid(923011E6-CB0EB-11CE-B337-88EA36DE9E4E),
```

*GUID for the type library—matches TypeLib registry key and
AfxOleRegisterTypeLib parameter*

```
helpstring("Ex24B LIB"),
```

String for Excel's References list—must add manually

```
version(1.0) ]
```

```
library Ex24b
```

Library name for Excel's object browser

```
{
    importlib("stdole32.tlb");

    //  Primary dispatch interface for CEx24bAuto

    [ uuid(923011EA-CBEB-11CE-B337-88EA36DE9E4E) ]
```

GUID from server's interface map—matches registry Interface entry

```
    dispinterface IEx24bAuto
```

Name used in VBA Dim statement and Object list

```
    {
      properties:
      // NOTE - ClassWizard will maintain property information here.
      //    Use extreme caution when editing this section.
      //{{AFX_ODL_PROP(CEx24bAuto)
      [id(1)] long LongData;
      [id(2)] VARIANT TextData;
      //}}AFX_ODL_PROP

      methods:
      // NOTE - ClassWizard will maintain method information here.
      //    Use extreme caution when editing this section.
      //{{AFX_ODL_METHOD(CEx24bAuto)
      [id(3)] boolean DisplayDialog();
```

(continued)

```
        //}}AFX_ODL_METHOD

    };

    //  Class information for CEx24bAuto

    [ uuid(923011EB-CBEB-11CE-B337-88EA36DE9E4E) ]
        Server's CLSID

    coclass CEx24bAuto
    {
      [default] dispinterface IEx24bAuto;
    };

    //{{AFX_APPEND_ODL}}
};
```

As you can see, there are numerous connections between the registry, the
type library, the server, and the VBA client.

How Excel Uses a Type Library

Now is a good time to examine the sequence of steps Excel uses to utilize your
type library:

1. When Excel starts up, it reads the TypeLib section of the registry to
   compile a list of all type libraries. It loads the type libraries for VBA
   and for the Excel object library.

2. After starting Excel, loading a workbook, and opening a macro
   module, the user (or workbook author) chooses References from
   the Tools menu and checks the EX24B LIB line, as shown here:

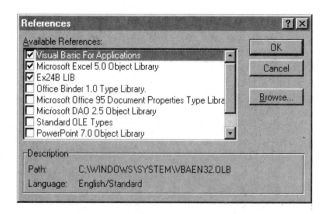

For this Reference line to be nonblank, you must have manually added the helpstring line in the ODL file as shown in the previous ODL file listing. When the workbook is saved, this reference information is saved with it.

3. After that, the Excel user will be able to browse through the EX24B properties and methods by selecting Object Browser from the View menu, as shown here:

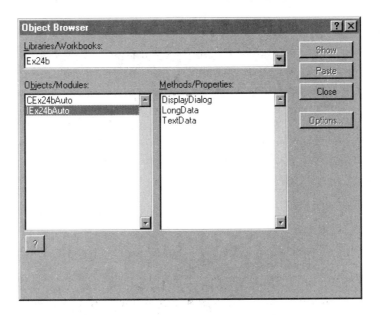

If you added help text in the ODL file, the user could access that information here.

4. To make use of the type library in your VBA program, you simply replace the line

```
Dim DllServ as Object
```

with

```
Dim DllServ as IEx24bAuto
```

The VBA program will exit immediately if it can't find *IEx24bAuto* in its list of references.

5. After VBA executes the CreateObject statement and loads the server, the first thing it does is call *QueryInterface* for *IID_IEx24bAuto*, which is defined in the registry, the type library, and the server class's interface map. (*IEx24bAuto* is really an *IDispatch* interface.) This is a sort of security check. If the server can't deliver this interface, the VBA program exits. Theoretically, Excel could use the CLSID in the type library to load the server, but it uses the CLSID from the registry instead, just as it did in late binding mode.

Why Use Early Binding?

You might think that early binding would make your automation server run faster. You probably won't notice any speed increase, though, because the *IDispatch::Invoke* calls are the limiting factor. A typical MFC *Invoke* call from a compiled C++ controller to a compiled C++ server requires about 0.5 millisecond, which is pretty gross.

The browse capability that the type library provides is probably more valuable than the compiled linkage. If you are writing a C++ controller, you can load the type library through various OLE functions, including *LoadTypeLib*, and then you can access it via the *ITypeLib* and *ITypeInfo* interfaces. Plan to spend some time on that project, however, because the type library interfaces are tricky.

Faster Controller–Server Connections

Microsoft has recognized the limitations of the *IDispatch* interface. It's naturally slow because all data must be funneled through *VARIANT*s and possibly converted on both ends. There's a new variation called a <u>dual</u> <u>interface</u>. (Dual interfaces are beyond the scope of this book. See Kraig Brockschmidt's *Inside OLE*, 2d edition [Microsoft Press, 1995], for more information.) In a dual interface, you define your own custom interface, derived from *IDispatch*. The *Invoke* and *GetIDsOfNames* functions are included, but so are other functions. If the controller is smart enough, it can bypass the inefficient *Invoke* calls and use the specialized functions instead. Dual interfaces can support only standard automation types, or they can support arbitrary types.

There is no MFC support for dual interfaces in Visual C++ 4.0, but future releases might support it. In the meantime, you could implement dual interfaces in straight OLE.

OLE Uniform Data Transfer— Clipboard Transfer and Drag and Drop

OLE includes a powerful mechanism for transferring data within and among Windows applications. The *IDataObject* interface is the key element of what is known as OLE Uniform Data Transfer. As you'll see, Uniform Data Transfer gives you all sorts of options for the formatting and storage of your transferred data, going well beyond standard clipboard transfers.

There's MFC support for Uniform Data Transfer, but it's not so pervasive as to obscure what's going on at the OLE interface level. One of the useful applications of Uniform Data Transfer is drag and drop. Many developers want to put drag and drop in their applications, and OLE drag-and-drop support means that programs now have a standard for information interchange. The MFC library supports drag and drop, and that, together with clipboard transfer, is the main focus of this chapter.

What you learn about the *IDataObject* interface in this chapter will carry forward to your study of compound documents.

The *IDataObject* Interface

The OLE *IDataObject* interface is used for clipboard transfers and drag and drop, but it's also used in compound documents, OLE Controls (OCXs), and custom OLE features. Brockschmidt (*Inside OLE*, 2d ed., Microsoft Press, 1995) says, "Think of objects as little piles of stuff." The *IDataObject* interface helps you move those piles around, no matter what kind of stuff they contain.

If you were programming at the Win32 level, you would write a C++ class that supported the *IDataObject* interface. Your program would then construct <u>data objects</u> of this class, and you would manipulate those objects with the *IDataObject* member functions.

How *IDataObject* Improves on Standard Clipboard Support

There has never been much MFC support for the Windows clipboard. If you've programmed the clipboard already, you've used Win32 clipboard functions such as *OpenClipboard*, *CloseClipboard*, *GetClipboardData*, and *SetClipboardData*. One program copies a single data element of a specified format to the clipboard, and another program selects the data by format code and pastes it. Standard clipboard formats include global memory (specified by an *HGLOBAL* variable) and various GDI objects, such as bitmaps and metafiles (specified by their handles). Global memory can contain text as well as custom formats.

The *IDataObject* interface picks up where the Windows clipboard leaves off. To make a long story short, you transfer a single *IDataObject* pointer to or from the clipboard instead of a series of discrete formats. The underlying data object can contain a whole array of formats. Those formats can carry information about target devices, such as printer characteristics, and they can specify the data's <u>aspect</u>. The standard aspect is content. Other aspects include an icon for the data and a thumbnail picture.

It's important to note that the *IDataObject* interface specifies the <u>storage medium</u> of a data object format. Conventional clipboard transfer relies exclusively on global memory. The *IDataObject* interface permits the transmission of a disk filename or a structured storage pointer instead. Thus, if you have a very large block of data to transfer that's in a disk file already, you don't have to waste time copying it to and from a memory block.

In case you were wondering, *IDataObject* pointers are compatible with programs that use existing clipboard transfer methods. The format codes are the same. Windows takes care of the conversion to and from the data object. Of course, if an OLE-aware program put an *IStorage* pointer in a data object and put the object on the clipboard, older programs would be unable to read that format.

The *FORMATETC* Structure

Before you're ready for the *IDataObject* member functions, you need to examine two important OLE structures that are used as parameter types. The *FORMATETC* structure is one of them. Here are the members:

Type	Name	Description
CLIPFORMAT	*cfFormat*	*CF_TEXT*, *CF_DIB*, and so on and custom formats such as rich text
DVTARGETDEVICE*	*ptd*	Structure that contains information about the target device, including the device driver name (can be NULL)
DWORD	*dwAspect*	*DVASPECT_CONTENT, DVASPECT-_THUMBNAIL*, and so on
LONG	*lindex*	−1 for aspect = content
DWORD	*tymed*	Specifies type of media *(TYMED-_HGLOBAL, TYMED_FILE, TYMED_ISTORAGE*, and so on)

An individual data object accommodates a collection of *FORMATETC* elements, and the *IDataObject* interface provides a way to enumerate them. Here's a useful macro for filling in a *FORMATETC* structure:

```
#define SETFORMATETC(fe, cf, asp, td, med, li)   \
  ((fe).cfFormat=cf, \
   (fe).dwAspect=asp, \
   (fe).ptd=td, \
   (fe).tymed=med, \
   (fe).lindex=li)
```

The *STGMEDIUM* Structure

The other important structure for *IDataObject* members is the *STGMEDIUM* structure. Here are the members:

Type	Name	Description
DWORD	*tymed*	Format code as for *FORMATETC*
HBITMAP	*hBitmap*	Bitmap handle[†]
HMETAFILEPICT	*hMetaFilePict*	Metafile handle[†]
HENHMETAFILE	*hEnhMetaFile*	Enhanced metafile handle[†]
HGLOBAL	*hGlobal*	Global memory handle[†]
LPOLESTR	*lpszFileName*	Disk filename (double-byte)[†]
ISTREAM*	*pstm*	*IStream* interface pointer[†]
ISTORAGE*	*pstg*	*IStorage* interface pointer[†]
IUNKNOWN*	*pUnkForRelease*	Used by clients to call *Release* for formats with interface pointers[†]

[†] This member is part of a union, along with the other similarly denoted members.

As you can see, the *STGMEDIUM* structure specifies where data is stored. The *tymed* code determines which union member is valid.

The *IDataObject* Interface Member Functions

There are nine member functions in this interface. Brockschmidt's *Inside OLE*, 2d edition, and Books Online do a good job of describing all these functions. Here are the ones that are important for this chapter.

HRESULT EnumFormatEtc(DWORD *dwDirection*, IEnumFORMATETC** *ppEnum*);

If you have an *IDataObject* pointer for a data object, you can use *Enum-FormatEtc* to enumerate all the formats that it supports. This is an ugly API that the MFC library insulates you from. You'll learn how when you examine the *COleDataObject* class.

HRESULT GetData(FORMATETC* *pFEIn*, STGMEDIUM* *pSTM*);

GetData is the most important function in the interface. Somewhere up in the sky there's a data object, and you have an *IDataObject* pointer to it. You specify, in a *FORMATETC* variable, the exact format you want, and you prepare an empty *STGMEDIUM* variable to accept the results. If the data object has the format you want, *GetData* fills in the *STGMEDIUM* structure. Otherwise, you get an error return value.

HRESULT QueryGetData(FORMATETC* *pFE*);

You call *QueryGetData* if you're not sure whether the data object can deliver your format. The return code says, "Yes, I can" (*S_OK*) or "No, I can't" (*S_FALSE*). Calling this function is definitely more efficient than allocating a *STGMEDIUM* variable and calling *GetData*.

HRESULT SetData(FORMATETC* *pFEIn*, STGMEDIUM* *pSTM*, BOOL *fRelease*);

SetData is rarely supported by data objects. Data objects are normally loaded with formats in their own server module; clients retrieve data by calling *GetData*. With *SetData*, you'd be transferring data in the other direction—like pumping water from your house back to the water company.

Other *IDataObject* Member Functions—Advisory Connections

The interface contains other important functions that let you implement an advisory connection. When the program using a data object needs to be notified if the object's data changes, the program can pass an *IAdviseSink* pointer to the object by calling the *IDataObject::DAdvise* function. The object then calls various *IAdviseSink* member functions, which the client program implements. You won't need advisory connections for drag and drop, but you will when you get to embedding in Chapter 27.

MFC Uniform Data Transfer Support

The MFC library does a lot to make data object programming easier. As you study the MFC data object classes, you'll start to see a pattern in MFC OLE support. At the server end, the MFC library provides a base class that implements one or more OLE interfaces. The interface member functions call virtual functions that you override in your derived class. At the client end, the MFC library provides a class that wraps an interface pointer. You call simple member functions that use the interface pointer to make OLE calls.

The terminology needs some clarification here. The data object I've been describing is the actual C++ object that you construct, and that's the way Brockschmidt uses the term. In the MFC documentation, a data object is what the client program sees through an *IDataObject* pointer. A <u>data</u> <u>source</u> is the object you construct in a server program.

The *COleDataSource* Class

When you want a data source, you construct an object of class *COleDataSource*, which implements the *IDataObject* interface (without advisory connection support). This class builds and manages a <u>collection</u> of data formats called a <u>cache</u>. A data source is a regular COM object that keeps a reference count. Usually, you construct and fill a data source, and then you pass it to the clipboard or to drag and drop, never to worry about it again. If you decide not to pass off a data source, you can invoke the destructor, which cleans up all its formats.

Here are some of the more useful member functions of the *COleData-Source* class:

void CacheData(CLIPFORMAT *cfFormat*, STGMEDIUM∗ *lpStgMedium*, FORMATETC∗ *lpFormatEtc* = NULL);

This function inserts an element in the data object's cache. The *lpStgMedium* parameter specifies where the data is now, and the *lpFormatEtc* parameter describes the data. If, for example, the *STGMEDIUM* structure specifies a disk filename, that filename gets stored inside the data object. If you omit the *lpFormatEtc* parameter, the function fills in a *FORMATETC* structure with default values. It's safer, though, if you create your *FORMATETC* variable with the *tymed* member set.

void CacheGlobalData(CLIPFORMAT *cfFormat*,
HGLOBAL *hGlobal*, FORMATETC∗ *lpFormatEtc* = NULL);

This is a specialized version of *CacheData*. You call it only if your data is contained in global memory (identified by an *HGLOBAL* variable). The data source object is considered the owner of that global memory block, so you'd better not free it after you cache it. You can usually omit the *lpFormatEtc* parameter. The *CacheGlobalData* function does <u>not</u> make a copy of the data.

DROPEFFECT DoDragDrop(DWORD *dwEffects* =
DROPEFFECT_COPY ¦ DROPEFFECT_MOVE ¦
DROPEFFECT_LINK, LPCRECT *lpRectStartDrag* = NULL,
COleDropSource∗ *pDropSource* = NULL);

This is the function to call for drag and drop. You'll see it used in the EX25B example.

void SetClipboard();

The *SetClipboard* function, which you'll see in the EX25A example, calls the *OleSetClipboard* function to put a data source on the Windows clipboard. The clipboard is responsible for deleting the data source and thus freeing the global memory associated with the formats in the cache. When you construct a *COleDataSource* object and call *SetClipboard*, OLE calls *AddRef* on the object.

The *COleDataObject* Class

This is the class on the destination side of a data object transfer. Its base class is *CCmdTarget*, and it has a public member *m_lpDataObject* that holds an *IDataObject* pointer. That member must be set before you can effectively use the object. The class destructor only calls *Release* on the *IDataObject* pointer.

Here are a few of the more useful *COleDataObject* member functions:

BOOL AttachClipboard();

As Brockschmidt points out, OLE clipboard processing is internally complex. From your point of view, however, it's straightforward as long as you use the *COleDataObject* member functions. You first construct an "empty" *COleDataObject* object, and then you call *AttachClipboard*, which calls the global *OleGetClipboard* function. Now the *m_lpDataObject* data member points back to the source data object (or so it appears), and you can access its formats.

If you call the *GetData* member function to get a format, you must remember that the clipboard owns the format, and you cannot alter its contents. If the format consists of an *HGLOBAL* pointer, you must not free that memory, and you cannot hang on to the pointer. Consider calling *GetGlobal-Data* instead if you need to have long-term access to the data in global memory.

If a non-OLE-aware program copies data onto the clipboard, the *Attach-Clipboard* function still works because OLE invents a data object that contains formats corresponding to the regular Windows data on the clipboard.

void BeginEnumFormats();
BOOL GetNextFormat(FORMATETC* *lpFormatEtc*);

These two functions allow you to iterate through the formats that the data object contains. You call *BeginEnumFormats* first, and then you call *GetNext-Format* in a loop until it returns *FALSE*.

BOOL GetData(CLIPFORMAT *cfFormat*,
STGMEDIUM* *lpStgMedium*,
FORMATETC* *lpFormatEtc* = NULL);

This function calls *IDataObject::GetData* and not much more. The function returns *TRUE* if the data source contains the format you asked for. You generally need to supply the *lpFormatEtc* parameter.

HGLOBAL GetGlobalData(CLIPFORMAT *cfFormat*,
FORMATETC* *lpFormatEtc* = NULL);

Use the *GetGlobalData* function if you know your requested format is compatible with global memory. This function makes a copy of the selected format's memory block, and it gives you an *HGLOBAL* handle that you must free later. You can often omit the *lpFormatEtc* parameter.

BOOL IsDataAvailable(CLIPFORMAT *cfFormat*,
FORMATETC* *lpFormatEtc* = NULL);

The *IsDataAvailable* function tests whether the data object contains a given format.

MFC Data Object Clipboard Transfer

Now that you've seen the *COleDataObject* and *COleDataSource* classes, you'll have an easy time doing clipboard data object transfers. But why not just do clipboard transfers the old way with *GetClipboardData* and *SetClipboardData?* You could for most common formats, but if you write functions that process data objects, you can use those same functions for drag and drop.

Figure 25-1 shows the relationship between the clipboard and the *COle-DataSource* and *COleDataObject* classes. You construct a *COleDataSource* object on the copy side, and then you fill its cache with formats. When you call *SetClipboard*, the formats are copied to the clipboard. On the paste side, you call *AttachClipboard* to attach an *IDataObject* pointer to a *COleDataObject* object, after which you can retrieve individual formats.

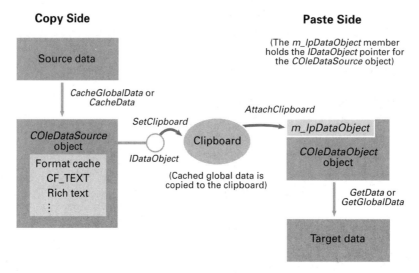

Figure 25-1.
MFC OLE clipboard processing.

Suppose you have a document–view application whose document has a *CString* data member *m_strText*. You want view class command handler functions that copy to and paste from the clipboard. Before you write those functions, you should write two helper functions. The first, *SaveText*, creates a data source object from the contents of *m_strText*. The function constructs a *COleDataSource* object, and then it copies the string contents to global memory. Last it calls *CacheGlobalData* to store the *HGLOBAL* handle in the data source object. Here is the *SaveText* code:

```
COleDataSource* CMyView::SaveText()
{
    CEx25fDoc* pDoc = GetDocument();
      if (!pDoc->m_strtext.IsEmpty()) {
        COleDataSource* pSource = new COleDataSource();
        int nTextSize = GetDocument()->m_strText.GetLength() + 1;
        HGLOBAL hText = ::GlobalAlloc(GMEM_SHARE, nTextSize);
        LPSTR pText = (LPSTR) ::GlobalLock(hText);
        ASSERT(pText);
```

```
        strcpy(pText, GetDocument()->m_strText);
        ::GlobalUnlock(hText);
        pSource->CacheGlobalData(CF_TEXT, hText);
        return pSource;
    }
    return NULL;
}
```

The second helper function, *DoPasteText*, fills in *m_strText* from a data object specified as a parameter. We're using *COleDataObject::GetData* here instead of *GetGlobalData* because *GetGlobalData* makes a copy of the global memory block. That extra copy operation is unnecessary because we're copying the text to the *CString* object. We don't free the original memory block because the data object owns it. Here is the *DoPasteText* code:

```
BOOL CMyView::DoPasteText(COleDataObject* pDataObject)
{
    STGMEDIUM stg;
    FORMATETC fmt;
    // update command UI should keep us out of here if not CF_TEXT
    if (!pDataObject->IsDataAvailable(CF_TEXT)) {
      TRACE("CF_TEXT format is unavailable\n");
      return FALSE;
    }
    // memory is MOVEABLE, so we must use GlobalLock!
    SETFORMATETC(fmt, CF_TEXT, DVASPECT_CONTENT, NULL, TYMED_HGLOBAL, -1);
    VERIFY(pDataObject->GetData(CF_TEXT, &stg, &fmt));
    HGLOBAL hText = stg.hGlobal;
    GetDocument()->m_strText = (LPSTR) ::GlobalLock(hText);
    ::GlobalUnlock(hText);
    return TRUE;
}
```

Here are the two command handler functions:

```
void CMyView::OnEditCopy()
{
    COleDataSource* pSource = SaveText();
    if (pSource) {
      pSource->SetClipboard();
    }
}
void CMyView::OnEditPaste()
{
    COleDataObject dataObject;
    VERIFY(dataObject.AttachClipboard());
    DoPasteText(&dataObject);
    // dataObject released
}
```

The MFC *CRectTracker* Class

The *CRectTracker* class is useful in both OLE and non-OLE programs. It allows the user to move and resize a rectangular object in a view window. There are two important data members: the *m_nStyle* member determines the border, resize handle, and other characteristics; and the *m_rect* member holds the <u>device</u> coordinates for the rectangle.

The important member functions are as follows:

void Draw(CDC∗ *pDC*) const;

The *Draw* function draws the tracker, including border and resize handles, but it does not draw anything inside the rectangle. That's your job.

BOOL Track(CWnd∗ *pWnd*, CPoint *point*,
BOOL *bAllowInvert* = FALSE, CWnd∗ *pWndClipTo* = NULL);

You call this function in a WM_LBUTTONDOWN handler. If the cursor is on the rectangle border, the user can resize the tracker by holding down the mouse button, and if the cursor is inside the rectangle, the user can move the tracker. If the cursor is outside the rectangle, *Track* returns *FALSE* immediately, but otherwise, *Track* returns *TRUE* only when the user releases the mouse button. That means *Track* works a little like *CDialog::DoModal*. It contains its own message dispatch logic.

int HitTest(CPoint *point*) const;

Call *HitTest* if you need to distinguish between mouse button hits inside and on the tracker rectangle. The function returns immediately with the hit status in the return value.

BOOL SetCursor(CWnd∗ *pWnd*, UINT *nHitTest*) const;

Call this function in your view's WM_SETCURSOR handler to ensure that the cursor changes during tracking. If *SetCursor* returns *FALSE*, call the base class *OnSetCursor* function; if *SetCursor* returns *TRUE*, you then return *TRUE*.

CRectTracker Rectangle Coordinate Conversion

You must deal with the fact that the *CRectTracker::m_rect* member stores device coordinates. If you are using a scrolling view or have otherwise changed the mapping mode or viewport origin, you must do coordinate conversion. Here's a strategy:

1. Define a *CRectTracker* data member in your view class. Use the name *m_tracker*.

2. Define a separate data member in your view class to hold the rectangle in logical coordinates. Use the name *m_rectTracker*.

3. In your view's *OnDraw* function, set *m_rect* to the updated device coordinates, and then draw the tracker. This adjusts for any scrolling since the last *OnDraw*. Here's some sample code:

```
m_tracker.m_rect = m_rectTracker;
pDC->LPtoDP(m_tracker.m_rect);  // tracker wants device coordinates
m_tracker.Draw(pDC);
```

4. In your mouse button down message handler, call *Track*, set *m_rectTracker* to the updated logical coordinates, and call *Invalidate*, as shown here:

```
if (m_tracker.Track(this, point, FALSE, NULL)) {
  CClientDC dc(this);
  OnPrepareDC(&dc);
  m_rectTracker = m_tracker.m_rect;
  dc.DPtoLP(m_rectTracker);
  Invalidate();
}
```

The EX25A Example—A Data Object Clipboard

This example uses the *CDib* class from EX10C. Here you'll be able to move and resize the DIB image with a tracker rectangle, and you'll be able to copy and paste the DIB to and from the clipboard using an OLE data object. There are also functions for reading DIBs from and writing DIBs to BMP files.

If you create such an example from scratch, use AppWizard without any OLE options, and then add the following line in your StdAfx.h file:

```
#include <afxole.h>
```

and add the following call in the application's *InitInstance* function:

```
AfxOleInit();
```

To prepare EX25A, open the \vcpp32\ex25a\ex25a.mdp project, and build the project. Run the application, and you'll see an MDI application, as shown in Figure 25-2 on the following page.

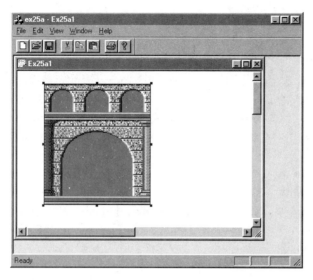

Figure 25-2.
The EX25A program in operation.

The *CEx25aDoc* Class

This class is pretty straightforward. It contains an embedded *CDib* object, *m_dib*, plus a Clear All command handler. The overridden *DeleteContents* member function calls the *CDib::Empty* function.

The *CEx25aView* Class

This class contains the clipboard function command handlers, the tracking code, and the DIB drawing code. Figure 25-3 shows the header and implementation files with manually entered code shaded.

EX25AVIEW.H

```
class CEx25aView : public CScrollView
{
// for tracking
    CRectTracker m_tracker;
    CRect m_rectTracker; // logical coordinates
    CSize m_sizeTotal;   // document size
protected: // create from serialization only
    CEx25aView();
    DECLARE_DYNCREATE(CEx25aView)
```

Figure 25-3.
The CEx25aView *class listing.*

(continued)

Figure 25-3. *continued*

```
// Attributes
public:
    CEx25aDoc* GetDocument();

// Operations
public:

// Overrides
    // ClassWizard generated virtual function overrides
    //{{AFX_VIRTUAL(CEx25aView)
    public:
    virtual void OnDraw(CDC* pDC);  // overridden to draw this view
    virtual BOOL PreCreateWindow(CREATESTRUCT& cs);
    virtual void OnPrepareDC(CDC* pDC, CPrintInfo* pInfo = NULL);
    virtual void OnInitialUpdate();
    protected:
    virtual BOOL OnPreparePrinting(CPrintInfo* pInfo);
    virtual void OnBeginPrinting(CDC* pDC, CPrintInfo* pInfo);
    virtual void OnEndPrinting(CDC* pDC, CPrintInfo* pInfo);
    //}}AFX_VIRTUAL

// Implementation
public:
    virtual ~CEx25aView();
#ifdef _DEBUG
    virtual void AssertValid() const;
    virtual void Dump(CDumpContext& dc) const;
#endif

protected:

// Generated message map functions
protected:
    //{{AFX_MSG(CEx25aView)
    afx_msg void OnEditCopy();
    afx_msg void OnUpdateEditCopy(CCmdUI* pCmdUI);
    afx_msg void OnEditCopyto();
    afx_msg void OnEditCut();
    afx_msg void OnEditPaste();
    afx_msg void OnUpdateEditPaste(CCmdUI* pCmdUI);
    afx_msg void OnEditPastefrom();
    afx_msg void OnLButtonDown(UINT nFlags, CPoint point);
    afx_msg BOOL OnSetCursor(CWnd* pWnd, UINT nHitTest, UINT message);
    //}}AFX_MSG
    DECLARE_MESSAGE_MAP()
```

(continued)

Figure 25-3. *continued*

```
private:
    BOOL DoPasteDib(COleDataObject* pDataObject);
    COleDataSource* SaveDib();
};


#ifndef _DEBUG  // debug version in ex25aView.cpp
inline CEx25aDoc* CEx25aView::GetDocument()
    { return (CEx25aDoc*)m_pDocument; }
#endif
```

EX25AVIEW.CPP

```
// ex25aView.cpp : implementation of the CEx25aView class
//

#include "StdAfx.h"
#include "ex25a.h"

#include "cdib.h"
#include "ex25aDoc.h"
#include "ex25aView.h"

#ifdef _DEBUG
#define new DEBUG_NEW
#undef THIS_FILE
static char THIS_FILE[] = __FILE__;
#endif


/////////////////////////////////////////////////////////////////////////
// CEx25aView

IMPLEMENT_DYNCREATE(CEx25aView, CScrollView)

BEGIN_MESSAGE_MAP(CEx25aView, CScrollView)
    //{{AFX_MSG_MAP(CEx25aView)
    ON_COMMAND(ID_EDIT_COPY, OnEditCopy)
    ON_UPDATE_COMMAND_UI(ID_EDIT_COPY, OnUpdateEditCopy)
    ON_COMMAND(ID_EDIT_COPYTO, OnEditCopyto)
    ON_COMMAND(ID_EDIT_CUT, OnEditCut)
    ON_COMMAND(ID_EDIT_PASTE, OnEditPaste)
    ON_UPDATE_COMMAND_UI(ID_EDIT_PASTE, OnUpdateEditPaste)
    ON_COMMAND(ID_EDIT_PASTEFROM, OnEditPastefrom)
    ON_WM_LBUTTONDOWN()
    ON_UPDATE_COMMAND_UI(ID_EDIT_COPYTO, OnUpdateEditCopy)
    ON_UPDATE_COMMAND_UI(ID_EDIT_CUT, OnUpdateEditCopy)
```

(continued)

Figure 25-3. *continued*

```
        ON_WM_SETCURSOR()
        //}}AFX_MSG_MAP
        // Standard printing commands
        ON_COMMAND(ID_FILE_PRINT, CScrollView::OnFilePrint)
        ON_COMMAND(ID_FILE_PRINT_DIRECT, CScrollView::OnFilePrint)
        ON_COMMAND(ID_FILE_PRINT_PREVIEW, CScrollView::OnFilePrintPreview)
END_MESSAGE_MAP()


/////////////////////////////////////////////////////////////////////
// CEx25aView construction/destruction


CEx25aView::CEx25aView() : m_sizeTotal(800, 1050), // 8 by 10.5 inches
                                                   //  when printed
    m_rectTracker(50, 50, 250, 250)
{
}


CEx25aView::~CEx25aView()
{
}


BOOL CEx25aView::PreCreateWindow(CREATESTRUCT& cs)
{
    // TODO: Modify the Window class or styles here by modifying
    //  the CREATESTRUCT cs

    return CScrollView::PreCreateWindow(cs);
}


/////////////////////////////////////////////////////////////////////
// CEx25aView drawing

void CEx25aView::OnDraw(CDC* pDC)
{
    CDib& dib = GetDocument()->m_dib;
    m_tracker.m_rect = m_rectTracker;
    pDC->LPtoDP(m_tracker.m_rect); // tracker wants device coordinates
    m_tracker.Draw(pDC);
    dib.UsePalette(pDC);
    dib.Draw(pDC, m_rectTracker.TopLeft(), m_rectTracker.Size());
}


/////////////////////////////////////////////////////////////////////
// CEx25aView printing
```

(continued)

Figure 25-3. *continued*

```
BOOL CEx25aView::OnPreparePrinting(CPrintInfo* pInfo)
{
    pInfo->SetMaxPage(1);
    return DoPreparePrinting(pInfo);
}

void CEx25aView::OnBeginPrinting(CDC* /*pDC*/, CPrintInfo* /*pInfo*/)
{
    // TODO: add extra initialization before printing
}

void CEx25aView::OnEndPrinting(CDC* /*pDC*/, CPrintInfo* /*pInfo*/)
{
    // TODO: add cleanup after printing
}


/////////////////////////////////////////////////////////////////////////
// CEx25aView diagnostics

#ifdef _DEBUG
void CEx25aView::AssertValid() const
{
    CScrollView::AssertValid();
}

void CEx25aView::Dump(CDumpContext& dc) const
{
    CScrollView::Dump(dc);
}

CEx25aDoc* CEx25aView::GetDocument() // non-debug version is inline
{
    ASSERT(m_pDocument->IsKindOf(RUNTIME_CLASS(CEx25aDoc)));
    return (CEx25aDoc*)m_pDocument;
}
#endif //_DEBUG


/////////////////////////////////////////////////////////////////////
// helper functions used for clipboard and drag and drop
BOOL CEx25aView::DoPasteDib(COleDataObject* pDataObject)
{
    // update command UI should keep us out of here if not CF_DIB
    if (!pDataObject->IsDataAvailable(CF_DIB)) {
      TRACE("CF_DIB format is unavailable\n");
      return FALSE;
    }
```

(continued)

Figure 25-3. *continued*

```
    CEx25aDoc* pDoc = GetDocument();
    // seems to be MOVEABLE memory, so we must use GlobalLock!
    //  (hDib != lpDib) GetGlobalData copies the memory, so we can
    //  hang on to it until we delete the CDib
    HGLOBAL hDib = pDataObject->GetGlobalData(CF_DIB);
    ASSERT(hDib != NULL);
    LPVOID lpDib = ::GlobalLock(hDib);
    ASSERT(lpDib != NULL);
    pDoc->m_dib.AttachMemory(lpDib, TRUE, hDib);
    pDoc->SetModifiedFlag();
    pDoc->UpdateAllViews(NULL);
    return TRUE;
}


COleDataSource* CEx25aView::SaveDib()
{
    CDib& dib = GetDocument()->m_dib;
    if (dib.GetSizeImage() > 0) {
      COleDataSource* pSource = new COleDataSource();
      int nHeaderSize =  dib.GetSizeHeader();
      int nImageSize = dib.GetSizeImage();
      HGLOBAL hHeader = ::GlobalAlloc(GMEM_SHARE,
          nHeaderSize + nImageSize);
      LPVOID pHeader = ::GlobalLock(hHeader);
      ASSERT(pHeader != NULL);
      LPVOID pImage = (LPBYTE) pHeader + nHeaderSize;
      memcpy(pHeader, dib.m_lpBMIH, nHeaderSize);
      memcpy(pImage, dib.m_lpImage, nImageSize);
      // receiver is supposed to free the global memory
      ::GlobalUnlock(hHeader);
      pSource->CacheGlobalData(CF_DIB, hHeader);
      return pSource;
    }
    return NULL;
}

/////////////////////////////////////////////////////////////////
// CEx25aView message handlers

void CEx25aView::OnEditCopy()
{
    COleDataSource* pSource = SaveDib();
    if (pSource) {
      pSource->SetClipboard(); // OLE deletes data source
    }
}
```

(continued)

Figure 25-3. *continued*

```
void CEx25aView::OnUpdateEditCopy(CCmdUI* pCmdUI)
{
    // serves Copy, Cut, and Copy To
    CDib& dib = GetDocument()->m_dib;
    pCmdUI->Enable(dib.GetSizeImage() > 0L);
}

void CEx25aView::OnEditCopyto()
{
    CDib& dib = GetDocument()->m_dib;
    CFileDialog dlg(FALSE, "bmp", "*.bmp");
    if (dlg.DoModal() != IDOK) return;

    BeginWaitCursor();
    dib.CopyToMapFile(dlg.GetPathName());
    EndWaitCursor();
}

void CEx25aView::OnEditCut()
{
    OnEditCopy();
    GetDocument()->OnEditClearAll();
}

void CEx25aView::OnEditPaste()
{
    CEx25aDoc* pDoc = GetDocument();
    COleDataObject dataObject;
    VERIFY(dataObject.AttachClipboard());
    DoPasteDib(&dataObject);
    pDoc->SetModifiedFlag();
    pDoc->UpdateAllViews(NULL);
}

void CEx25aView::OnUpdateEditPaste(CCmdUI* pCmdUI)
{
    COleDataObject dataObject;
    BOOL bAvail = dataObject.AttachClipboard() &&
        dataObject.IsDataAvailable(CF_DIB);
    pCmdUI->Enable(bAvail);
}

void CEx25aView::OnEditPastefrom()
{
```

(continued)

Figure 25-3. *continued*

```
    CEx25aDoc* pDoc = GetDocument();
    CFileDialog dlg(TRUE, "bmp", "*.bmp");
    if (dlg.DoModal() != IDOK) return;
    if (pDoc->m_dib.AttachMapFile(dlg.GetPathName(), TRUE)) { // share
      pDoc->SetModifiedFlag();
      pDoc->UpdateAllViews(NULL);
    }
}

void CEx25aView::OnPrepareDC(CDC* pDC, CPrintInfo* pInfo)
{
    // custom MM_LOENGLISH; positive y is down
    if (pDC->IsPrinting()) {
      int nHsize = pDC->GetDeviceCaps(HORZSIZE) * 1000 / 254;
      int nVsize = pDC->GetDeviceCaps(VERTSIZE) * 1000 / 254;
      pDC->SetMapMode(MM_ANISOTROPIC);
      pDC->SetWindowExt(nHsize, nVsize);
      pDC->SetViewportExt(pDC->GetDeviceCaps(HORZRES),
                          pDC->GetDeviceCaps(VERTRES));
    }
    else {
      CScrollView::OnPrepareDC(pDC, pInfo);
    }
}

void CEx25aView::OnInitialUpdate()
{
    SetScrollSizes(MM_TEXT, m_sizeTotal);
    m_tracker.m_nStyle = CRectTracker::solidLine |
        CRectTracker::resizeOutside;
    CScrollView::OnInitialUpdate();
}

void CEx25aView::OnLButtonDown(UINT nFlags, CPoint point)
{
    if (m_tracker.Track(this, point, FALSE, NULL)) {
      CClientDC dc(this);
      OnPrepareDC(&dc);
      m_rectTracker = m_tracker.m_rect;
      dc.DPtoLP(m_rectTracker); // update logical coordinates
      Invalidate();
    }
}
```

(continued)

Figure 25-3. *continued*

```
BOOL CEx25aView::OnSetCursor(CWnd* pWnd, UINT nHitTest, UINT message)
{
    if (m_tracker.SetCursor(pWnd, nHitTest)) {
        return TRUE;
    }
    else {
        return CScrollView::OnSetCursor(pWnd, nHitTest, message);
    }
}
```

A few interesting things are happening in the view class. In the *DoPaste-Dib* helper, we can call *GetGlobalData* because we can attach the returned *HGLOBAL* variable to the document's *CDib* object. If we called *GetData*, we would have to copy the memory block ourselves. The Paste From and Copy To command handlers rely on the memory-mapped file support in the *CDib* class. The *OnPrepareDC* function creates a special printer mapping mode that is just like MM_LOENGLISH except that positive *y* is down. One pixel on the display corresponds to 0.01 inch on the printer.

MFC Drag and Drop

Drag and drop was the ultimate justification for the data object code you've been looking at. OLE supports this feature with its *IDropSource* and *IDrop-Target* interfaces, plus some library code that manages the drag-and-drop process. The MFC library offers good drag-and-drop support at the view level, so we'll use it. Be aware that drag-and-drop transfers are immediate and independent of the clipboard. If the user cancels the operation, there's no "memory" of the object being dragged.

Drag-and-drop transfers should work consistently between applications, between windows of the same application, and within a window. When the user starts the operation, the cursor should change to an arrow–rectangle combination. If the user holds down the Ctrl key, a plus sign (+) in the cursor indicates that the object is being copied rather than moved.

MFC also supports drag and drop for items in compound documents. This is the next level up in MFC OLE support, and it's not covered in this chapter. See the OCLIENT example in the MFC OLE samples directory.

The Source Side of the Transfer

When your source program starts a drag-and-drop operation for a data object, it calls *COleDataSource::DoDragDrop*. This function internally creates an object of MFC class *COleDropSource*, which implements the *IOleDropSource* interface. *DoDragDrop* is another one of those functions that don't return for a while. It returns only when the user drops the object or cancels the operation.

If you're programming drag and drop to work with a *CRectTracker* object, you should call *DoDragDrop* only when the user clicks <u>inside</u> the tracking rectangle, not on the border. *CRectTracker::HitTest* gives you that information. When you call *DoDragDrop*, you need to set a flag that tells you whether the user is dropping the object into the same view (or document) that it was dragged from.

The Destination Side of the Transfer

If you want to use the MFC library's view class drag-and-drop support, you must add a data member of class *COleDropTarget* to your derived view class. This class implements the *IDropTarget* interface, and it holds an *IDropSource* pointer that links back to the *COleDropSource* object. In your view's *OnInitial-Update* function, you call the *Register* member function for the embedded *COleDropTarget* object.

After you have made your view a drop target, you must override four *CView* virtual functions, which the framework calls during the drag-and-drop operation. Here's a summary of what they should do, assuming you're using a tracker:

OnDragEnter	Adjusts the focus rectangle and then calls *OnDragOver*
OnDragOver	Moves the dotted focus rectangle and sets the drop effect (determines cursor shape)
OnDragLeave	Cancels operation; returns the rectangle to its original position and size
OnDrop	Adjusts the focus rectangle and then calls the *DoPaste* helper function to get formats from the data object

The Drag-and-Drop Sequence

Figure 25-4 illustrates the MFC drag-and-drop process. Here's a summary of what's going on:

1. User presses the left mouse button in the source view window.

2. Mouse button handler calls *CRectTracker::HitTest* and finds out that the cursor was inside the tracker rectangle.

3. Handler stores formats in a *COleDataSource* object.

4. Handler calls *COleDataSource::DoDragDrop* for the data source.

5. User moves the cursor to the view window of the target application.

6. OLE calls *IDropTarget::OnDragEnter* and *OnDragOver* for the *COleDropTarget* object, which calls the corresponding virtual functions in the target's view. The *OnDragOver* function is passed a *COleDataObject* pointer for the source object, which the target tests for a format it can understand.

7. *OnDragOver* returns a drop effect code, which OLE uses to set the cursor.

8. OLE calls *IDataSource::QueryContinueDrag* on the source side to find out whether the drag operation is still in progress. The MFC *COleDataSource* class responds appropriately.

9. User lifts the mouse button to drop the object in the target view window.

10. OLE calls *IDropTarget::OnDrop*, which calls *OnDrop* for the target's view. Because *OnDrop* is passed a *COleDataObject* pointer, it can retrieve the desired format from that object.

11. When *OnDrop* returns in the target program, *DoDragDrop* can return in the source program.

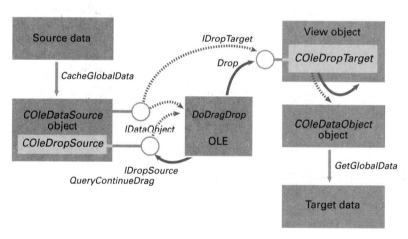

Figure 25-4.
MFC OLE drag-and-drop processing.

The EX25B Example—Drag and Drop

This example picks up where the EX25A example leaves off. It adds drag-and-drop support, using the existing *SaveDib* and *DoPasteDib* helper functions. All of the clipboard code is the same. You should be able to adapt EX25B to other applications that require drag and drop for data objects.

To prepare EX25B, open the \vcpp32\ex25b\ex25b.mdp project and build the project. Run the application, and test drag and drop between child windows and between instances of the program.

The *CEx25bDoc* Class

This class is just like the EX25A version except for an added flag data member, *m_bDragHere*. This flag is *TRUE* when a drag-and-drop operation is in progress for this document. The flag is in the document and not in the view because it's possible to have multiple views attached to the same document. It doesn't make sense to drag a DIB from one view to another when both views reflect the document's *m_dib* member.

The *CEx25bView* Class

To start with, this class has three additional data members and a constructor that initializes all the data members, as shown here:

```
CRect m_rectTrackerEnter; // original logical coordinates
COleDropTarget m_dropTarget;
CSize m_dragOffset; // device coordinates

CEx25bView::CEx25bView() : m_sizeTotal(800, 1050), // 8 by 10.5 inches
                                                   // when printed
    m_rectTracker(50, 50, 250, 250),
    m_dragOffset(0, 0),
    m_rectTrackerEnter(50, 50, 250, 250)
{
}
```

The *OnInitialUpdate* function needs one additional line to register the drop target:

```
m_dropTarget.Register(this);
```

On the following page are the drag-and-drop virtual override functions. Note that *OnDrop* replaces the DIB only if the document's *m_bDragHere* flag is *TRUE*, so if the user drops the DIB in the same window or in another window that's connected to the same document, nothing happens.

```
DROPEFFECT CEx25bView::OnDragEnter(COleDataObject* pDataObject,
    DWORD dwKeyState, CPoint point)
{
    m_rectTrackerEnter = m_rectTracker; // save original coordinates
                                        //   for cursor leaving
                                        //   rectangle
    CClientDC dc(this);
    OnPrepareDC(&dc);
    dc.DrawFocusRect(m_rectTracker); // will be erased in OnDragOver
    return OnDragOver(pDataObject, dwKeyState, point);
}

DROPEFFECT CEx25bView::OnDragOver(COleDataObject* pDataObject,
    DWORD dwKeyState, CPoint point)
{
    if (!pDataObject->IsDataAvailable(CF_DIB)) {
      return DROPEFFECT_NONE;
    }
    MoveTrackRect(point);
    if ((dwKeyState & MK_CONTROL) == MK_CONTROL) {
      return DROPEFFECT_COPY;
    }
    // check for force move
    if ((dwKeyState & MK_ALT) == MK_ALT) {
      return DROPEFFECT_MOVE;
    }
    // default -- recommended action is move
    return DROPEFFECT_MOVE;
}

void CEx25bView::OnDragLeave()
{
    TRACE("Entering CEx25bView::OnDragLeave\n");
    CClientDC dc(this);
    OnPrepareDC(&dc);
    dc.DrawFocusRect(m_rectTracker);
    m_rectTracker = m_rectTrackerEnter; // forget it ever happened
}

BOOL CEx25bView::OnDrop(COleDataObject* pDataObject,
    DROPEFFECT dropEffect, CPoint point)
{
    TRACE("Entering CEx25bView::OnDrop -- dropEffect = %d\n", dropEffect);
    BOOL bRet;
    CEx25bDoc* pDoc = GetDocument();
    MoveTrackRect(point);
    if (pDoc->m_bDragHere) {
      pDoc->m_bDragHere = FALSE;
```

```
      bRet = TRUE;
    }
    else {
      bRet = DoPasteDib(pDataObject);
    }
    return bRet;
}
```

The handler for the WM_LBUTTONDOWN message needs substantial overhaul. It must call *DoDragDrop* if the cursor is inside the rectangle and *Track* if it is on the rectangle border. The revised code is shown here:

```
void CEx25bView::OnLButtonDown(UINT nFlags, CPoint point)
{
    CEx25bDoc* pDoc = GetDocument();
    if (m_tracker.HitTest(point) == CRectTracker::hitMiddle) {
      COleDataSource* pSource = SaveDib();
        if (pSource) {
          // DoDragDrop returns only after drop is complete
          CClientDC dc(this);
          OnPrepareDC(&dc);
          CPoint topleft = m_rectTracker.TopLeft();
          dc.LPtoDP(&topleft);
          // 'point' here is not the same as the point parameter in
          //  OnDragEnter, so we use this one to compute the offset
          m_dragOffset = point - topleft;  // device coordinates
          pDoc->m_bDragHere = TRUE;
          DROPEFFECT dropEffect = pSource->DoDragDrop(
              DROPEFFECT_MOVE | DROPEFFECT_COPY, CRect(0, 0, 0, 0));
          if (dropEffect == DROPEFFECT_MOVE && pDoc->m_bDragHere) {
            pDoc->OnEditClearAll();
          }
          pDoc->m_bDragHere = FALSE;
          delete pSource;
        }
    }
    else {
      if (m_tracker.Track(this, point, FALSE, NULL)) {
        CClientDC dc(this);
        OnPrepareDC(&dc);
        // should have some way to prevent it going out of bounds
        m_rectTracker = m_tracker.m_rect;
        dc.DPtoLP(m_rectTracker); // update logical coordinates
        }
    }
    Invalidate();
}
```

Finally, the new *MoveTrackRect* helper function, shown below, moves the tracker's focus rectangle each time the *OnDragOver* function is called. This job was done by *CRectTracker::Track* in the EX25A example.

```
void CEx25bView::MoveTrackRect(CPoint point)
{
    CClientDC dc(this);
    OnPrepareDC(&dc);
    dc.DrawFocusRect(m_rectTracker);
    dc.LPtoDP(m_rectTracker);
    CSize sizeTrack = m_rectTracker.Size();
    CPoint newTopleft = point - m_dragOffset;  // still device
    m_rectTracker = CRect(newTopleft, sizeTrack);
    m_tracker.m_rect = m_rectTracker;
    dc.DPtoLP(m_rectTracker);
    dc.DrawFocusRect(m_rectTracker);
}
```

Windows 95 Applications and Drag and Drop—Dobjview

I tested EX25B with the Microsoft Office suite. I tried both drag-and-drop and clipboard transfers, with the results shown in the following table:

EX25B	Word	Excel	PowerPoint
Sends clipboard data to	√	√	√
Accepts clipboard data from	√		
Sends drag-drop data to	√		√
Accepts drag-drop data from	√		

When I started to investigate why Excel and PowerPoint were so uncooperative, I discovered a useful OLE utility called Dobjview (*IDataObject* viewer). I could use Dobjview to examine a data object on the clipboard, and I could drag objects to the Dobjview window. Here's what I got when I dragged a picture from Excel:

There is no *CF_DIB* format present. If you want pictures from Excel, you must enhance EX25B to process metafiles. Another alternative is to rewrite the program with compound document support as described in Chapter 27. The OLE libraries contain code to display bitmaps and metafiles.

OLE Structured Storage

Like OLE Automation and Uniform Data Transfer, Structured Storage is one of those OLE features that you can use effectively by itself. Of course, it's also the foundation of other parts of OLE, particularly compound documents.

In this chapter, you'll learn to write and read compound files with the OLE *IStorage* and *IStream* interfaces. These interfaces, like all OLE interfaces, are simply virtual function declarations. Compound files, on the other hand, are implemented by code in the Windows OLE32 DLL. Compound files represent a new Microsoft file I/O standard that you can think of as "a file system inside a file."

After you're familiar with *IStorage* and *IStream*, you'll move on to the *IPersistStorage* and *IPersistStream* interfaces. With these two interfaces, you can program a class to save and load objects to and from a compound file. You say to an object, "Save yourself," and it knows how.

OLE Compound Files

Up to now, you've had three options for file I/O: you could read and write whole sequential files, like the MFC archive files you saw first in Chapter 16; you could use a database management system, as described in Chapters 28 and 29; or you could write your own code for random file access. Now you have a fourth option—OLE compound files.

Think of a compound file as a whole file system within a file. Figure 26-1 shows a traditional disk directory as supported by early MS-DOS systems and by Microsoft Windows. It's composed of files and subdirectories, with a root directory at the top. Now imagine the same structure inside a single disk file. The files are called <u>streams</u>, and the directories are called <u>storages</u>. A stream is a logically sequential array of bytes, and a storage is a collection of streams and substorages. (A storage can contain other storages, just as a directory can contain subdirectories.) In a disk file, the bytes aren't necessarily stored in contiguous clusters. Similarly, the bytes in a stream aren't necessarily contiguous in their compound file. They just appear that way.

NOTE: Storage and stream names cannot contain the characters / \ : or !. If the first character is less than ASCII 32, the element is marked as managed by OLE or some agent other than the owner.

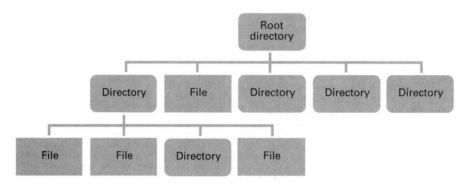

Figure 26-1.
A disk directory with files and subdirectories.

You can probably think of many applications for a compound file. The classic example is a large document composed of chapters and paragraphs within chapters. The document is large enough that you don't want to read the whole thing into memory when your program starts, and you want to be able to insert and delete portions of the document. You could design a compound file with a root storage that contained substorages for chapters. The chapter substorages would contain streams for the paragraphs. There could be other streams for index information.

One very useful feature of compound files is <u>transactioning</u>. When you start a transaction for a compound file, all changes are written to a temporary file. Only when you commit the transaction are the changes made to your file.

Storages and the *IStorage* Interface

If you have a storage object, you can manipulate it through the *IStorage* interface. Pay attention to these functions because there's no MFC support for storage access. Here are some of the important member functions and their significant parameters:

HRESULT Commit(...);
Commits all the changes to this storage and to all elements below it.

HRESULT CopyTo(...IStorage∗∗ *pStgDest*);
Copies a storage, together with its name and all its substorages and streams (recursively), to another existing storage. Elements are merged into the target storage, replacing elements with matching names.

HRESULT CreateStorage(const OLECHAR∗ *pName*, ...
DWORD *mode*, ... IStorage∗∗ *ppStg*);
Creates a new substorage under this storage.

HRESULT CreateStream(const OLECHAR∗ *pName*, ...
DWORD *mode*, ... IStream∗∗ *ppStream*);
Creates a new stream under this storage.

HRESULT DestroyElement(const OLECHAR∗ *pName*);
Destroys the named storage or stream that is under this storage. A storage cannot destroy itself.

HRESULT EnumElements(...IEnumSTATSTG∗∗ *ppEnumStatstg*);
Iterates through all the storages and streams under this storage. The *IEnumSTATSTG* interface has *Next, Skip,* and *Clone* member functions, as do other OLE enumerator interfaces.

HRESULT MoveElementTo(const OLECHAR∗ *pName*,
IStorage∗ *pStgDest*, const OLECHAR∗ *pNewName*,
DWORD *flags*);
Moves an element from this storage to another storage.

HRESULT OpenStream(const OLECHAR∗ *pName*, ...
DWORD *mode*, ... IStorage∗∗ *ppStg*);
Opens an existing stream, designated by name, under this storage.

HRESULT OpenStorage(const OLECHAR∗ *pName*, ...
DWORD *mode*, ... IStorage∗∗ *ppStg*);
Opens an existing substorage, designated by name, under this storage.

DWORD Release( );
If the storage is a root storage, representing a disk file, *Release* closes the file when the reference count goes to 0.

HRESULT RenameElement(const OLECHAR* *pOldName*,
const OLECHAR* *pNewName*);

Assigns a new name to an existing storage or stream under this storage.

HRESULT Revert( );

Abandons a transaction, leaving the compound file unchanged.

HRESULT SetClass(CLSID& *clsid*);

Inserts a 128-bit class identifier into this storage. This ID can then be re-trieved with the *Stat* function.

HRESULT Stat(STATSTG* *pStatstg*, DWORD *flag*);

Fills in a structure with useful information about the storage, including its name and class ID.

Getting an *IStorage* Pointer

But where do you get the first *IStorage* pointer? OLE gives you the global func-tion *StgCreateDocfile* to create a new structured storage file on disk and the function *StgOpenStorage* to open an existing file. Both of these set a pointer to the file's <u>root</u> storage. Here's some code that opens an existing storage file named MyStore.stg and then creates a new substorage:

```
IStorage* pStgRoot;
IStorage* pSubStg;

if (::StgCreateDocfile(L"MyStore.stg",
    STGM_READWRITE | STGM_SHARE_EXCLUSIVE | STGM_CREATE,
    0, &pStgRoot) == S_OK) {
  if (pStgRoot->CreateStorage(L"MySubstorageName",
      STGM_READWRITE | STGM_SHARE_EXCLUSIVE | STGM_CREATE,
      0, 0, &pSubStg) == S_OK) {
    // do something with pSubStg
    pSubStg->Release();
  }
  pStgRoot->Release();
}
```

Freeing STATSTG Memory

When you call *IStorage::Stat* with a 0 flag parameter, OLE allocates memory for the element name. You must free this memory in a manner compatible with its allocation. OLE has its own allocation system that uses an <u>allocator</u>

object with an *IMalloc* interface. You must get an *IMalloc* pointer from OLE, then call *IMalloc::Free* for the string, and then release the allocator. The code in the next section illustrates this.

If you want just the element size and type and not the name, you can call *Stat* with the *STATFLAG_NONAME* flag. In that case, no memory is allocated, and you don't have to free it. This seems like an irritating detail, but if you don't follow the recipe, you'll have a memory leak.

Enumerating the Elements in a Storage

Here is some code that iterates through all the elements under a storage, differentiating between substorages and streams. The elements are retrieved in a seemingly random sequence, independent of the sequence in which they were created; however, I've found that streams are always retrieved first. The *IEnumSTATSTG::Next* element fills in a *STATSTG* structure that tells you whether the element is a stream or a storage.

```
IEnumSTATSTG* pEnum;
IMalloc* pMalloc;
STATSTG statstg;
extern IStorage* pStg;  // maybe from OpenStorage
::CoGetMalloc(MEMCTX_TASK, &pMalloc); // Assumes AfxOleInit called
VERIFY(pStg->EnumElements(0, NULL, 0, &pEnum) == S_OK)
while (pEnum->Next(1, &statstg, NULL) == NOERROR) {
   if (statstg.type == STGTY_STORAGE) {
      if (pStg->OpenStorage(statstg.pwcsName, NULL,
         STGM_READ | STGM_SHARE_EXCLUSIVE,
         NULL, 0, &pSubStg) == S_OK) {
      // do something with the substorage
      }
      else if (statstg.type == STGTY_STREAM) {
      // process the stream
      }
      pMalloc->Free(statstg.pwcsName); // avoids memory leaks
}
pMalloc->Release();
```

Sharing Storages Among Processes

If you pass an *IStorage* pointer to another process, the OLE marshaling code ensures that the other process can access the corresponding storage element and everything below it. This is a very convenient way of sharing part of a file. One of the standard data object media types is *TYMED_ISTORAGE*, and this means you can pass an *IStorage* pointer on the clipboard or through drag and drop.

Streams and the *IStream* Interface

If you have a stream object, you can manipulate it through the *IStream* interface. Streams are always located under a root storage or a substorage. Streams grow automatically (in 512-byte increments) as you write to them. There is an MFC class for streams, *COleStreamFile*, that makes a stream look like a *CFile* object. That class won't be of much use to us in this chapter.

HRESULT CopyTo(IStream** *pStm*, ULARGE_INTEGER *cb*, ...);

Copies *cb* bytes from this stream to the named stream. *ULARGE_INTEGER* is a structure with two 32-bit members—*HighPart* and *LowPart*.

HRESULT Clone(IStream** *ppStm*);

Creates a new stream object with its own seek pointer that references the bytes in this stream. The bytes are not copied, so changes in one stream are visible in the other.

HRESULT Commit(...);

Not currently implemented for streams.

HRESULT Read(void const* *pv*, ULONG *cb*, ULONG* *pcbRead*);

Tries to read *cb* bytes from this stream into the buffer pointed to by *pv*. The variable *pcbRead* indicates how many bytes were actually read.

DWORD Release( );

Closes this stream.

HRESULT Revert( );

Not currently implemented for streams.

HRESULT Seek(LARGE_INTEGER *dlibMove*, DWORD *mode*, ...);

Seeks to the specified position in this stream. The *mode* parameter specifies various absolute/relative options.

HRESULT SetSize(ULARGE_INTEGER *libNewSize*);

Extends or truncates a stream. Streams grow automatically as they are written, but calling *SetSize* can optimize performance.

HRESULT Stat(STATSTG* *pStatstg*, DWORD *flag*);

Fills in a structure with useful information about the stream, including its name and size. The size is useful if you need to allocate memory for a read.

HRESULT Write(void* *pv*, ULONG *cb*, ULONG* *pcbWritten*);

Tries to write *cb* bytes to this stream from the buffer pointed to by *pv*. The variable *pcbWritten* indicates how many bytes were actually written.

IStream Programming

Here is some sample code that creates a stream under a given storage and writes some bytes from *m_buffer* to the stream:

```
extern IStorage* pStg;
IStream* pStream;
ULONG nBytesWritten;

if (pStg->CreateStream(L"MyStreamName",
    STGM_CREATE | STGM_READWRITE | STGM_SHARE_EXCLUSIVE,
    0, 0, &pStream) == S_OK) {
  ASSERT(pStream != NULL);
  pStream->Write(m_buffer, m_nLength, &nBytesWritten);
  pStream->Release();
}
```

The *ILockBytes* Interface

As already mentioned, the compound file system you've been looking at is implemented in the OLE32 DLL. The structured storage interfaces are flexible enough, however, to permit you to change the underlying implementation. The key to this flexibility is the *ILockBytes* interface. The *StgCreateDocfile* and *StgOpenStorage* global functions use the default Windows file system. You can write your own file access code that implements the *ILockBytes* interface and then call *StgCreateDocfileOnILockBytes* or *StgOpenStorageOnILockBytes* instead of the other global functions.

Rather than implementing your own *ILockBytes* interface, you can call *CreateLockBytesOnHGlobal* to create a compound file in RAM. If you wanted to put compound files inside a database, you would implement an *ILockBytes* interface that used the database's <u>blobs</u> (binary large objects).

The EX26A Example—Structured Storage

When you choose the EX26A Storage Write option, the program walks through your entire disk directory looking for TXT files. As it goes, it writes a compound file (\direct.stg) with storages that match your subdirectories. For each TXT file it finds in a subdirectory, it copies the text to a stream in the corresponding storage.

When you choose the Storage Read option, the program reads the compound file and prints the contents in the Debug window.

If you create such an example from scratch, use AppWizard without any OLE options and then add the following lines in your StdAfx.h file:

```
#include <afxole.h>
#include <afxpriv.h> // for wide-character conversion
```

and delete the following line:

```
#define VC_EXTRALEAN
```

Add the following call in the application's *InitInstance* function:

```
AfxOleInit();
```

To prepare EX26A, open the \vcpp32\ex26a\ex26a.mdp project, and build the project. Run the program from the debugger. First choose Write from the Storage menu and wait for a "Write complete" message box. Then choose Read. Observe the output in the Debug window.

The Menu

The EX26A example has an added top-level Storage menu with Write and Read options.

The *CEx26aView* Class

This class maps the new menu commands listed above to start worker threads. The handlers are shown here:

```
void CEx26aView::OnStorageRead()
{
    CWinThread* pThread = AfxBeginThread(ReadThreadProc, GetSafeHwnd());
}

void CEx26aView::OnStorageWrite()
{
    CWinThread* pThread = AfxBeginThread(WriteThreadProc, GetSafeHwnd());
}
```

The Worker Threads

Figure 26-2 lists the code for the Storage Write and Storage Read worker threads.

THREAD.H

```
extern int g_nIndent;
extern const char* g_szBlanks;
extern const char* g_szRootStorageName;

UINT WriteThreadProc(LPVOID pParam);
UINT ReadThreadProc(LPVOID pParam);
void ReadDirectory(const char* szPath, LPSTORAGE pStg);
void ReadStorage(LPSTORAGE pStg);
```

WRITETHREAD.CPP

```
#include "StdAfx.h"
#include "Thread.h"

int g_nIndent = 0;
const char* g_szBlanks = "                              ";
const char* g_szRootStorageName = "\\direct.stg";


UINT WriteThreadProc(LPVOID pParam)
{
    USES_CONVERSION;
    LPSTORAGE pStgRoot = NULL;
    g_nIndent = 0;
    VERIFY(::StgCreateDocfile(T2COLE(g_szRootStorageName),
        STGM_READWRITE | STGM_SHARE_EXCLUSIVE | STGM_CREATE,
        0, &pStgRoot) == S_OK);
    ReadDirectory("\\", pStgRoot);
    pStgRoot->Release();
    AfxMessageBox("Write complete");
    return 0;
}

void ReadDirectory(const char* szPath, LPSTORAGE pStg)
{
    // recursive function
    USES_CONVERSION;
    WIN32_FIND_DATA fData;
    HANDLE h;
    char szNewPath[MAX_PATH];
    char szStorageName[100];
    char* pch;
    int nFileSize;
```

Figure 26-2.
The code listing for the two worker threads in EX26A.

(continued)

Figure 26-2. *continued*

```
LPSTORAGE pSubStg = NULL;
LPSTREAM pStream = NULL;

g_nIndent++;
strcpy(szNewPath, szPath);
strcat(szNewPath, "*.*");
h = ::FindFirstFile(szNewPath, &fData);
if (h == (HANDLE) 0xFFFFFFFF) return;  // can't find directory
do {
  if (!strcmp(fData.cFileName, "..") ||
      !strcmp(fData.cFileName, ".") ) continue;
  if (fData.dwFileAttributes & FILE_ATTRIBUTE_DIRECTORY ) {
    strcpy(szNewPath, szPath);
    strcat(szNewPath,fData.cFileName);
    strcat(szNewPath, "\\");

    strcpy(szStorageName, fData.cFileName);
    szStorageName[31] = '\0';    // limit imposed by OLE
    TRACE("%0.*sStorage = %s\n", (g_nIndent - 1) * 4,
        g_szBlanks, szStorageName);
    VERIFY(pStg->CreateStorage(T2COLE(szStorageName),
        STGM_CREATE | STGM_READWRITE | STGM_SHARE_EXCLUSIVE,
        0, 0, &pSubStg) == S_OK);
    ASSERT(pSubStg != NULL);
    ReadDirectory(szNewPath, pSubStg);
    pSubStg->Release();
  }
  else {
    if ((pch = strrchr(fData.cFileName, '.')) != NULL) {
      if (!stricmp(pch, ".TXT")) {
        strcpy(szNewPath, szPath);
        strcat(szNewPath, fData.cFileName);
        TRACE("%0.*sStream = %s\n", (g_nIndent - 1) * 4,
            g_szBlanks, szNewPath);
        HANDLE hFile = ::CreateFile(szNewPath, GENERIC_READ,
            FILE_SHARE_READ, NULL, OPEN_EXISTING,
            FILE_ATTRIBUTE_NORMAL, NULL);
        ASSERT(hFile != NULL);
        // check for zero-length file
        if ((nFileSize = ::GetFileSize(hFile, NULL)) > 0) {
```

(continued)

Figure 26-2. *continued*

```
                HANDLE hMap = ::CreateFileMapping(hFile, NULL,
                    PAGE_READONLY, 0, 0, NULL);
                ASSERT(hMap != NULL);
                LPVOID lpvFile = ::MapViewOfFile(hMap,
                    FILE_MAP_READ, 0, 0, 0); // whole file
                TRACE("%80.80s\n", lpvFile);
                VERIFY(pStg->CreateStream(T2COLE(fData.cFileName),
                    STGM_CREATE | STGM_READWRITE | STGM_SHARE_EXCLUSIVE,
                    0, 0, &pStream) == S_OK);
                ASSERT(pStream != NULL);
                pStream->Write(lpvFile, nFileSize, NULL);
                pStream->Release();
                ::UnmapViewOfFile(lpvFile); // don't forget this
                ::CloseHandle(hMap);
            }
            ::CloseHandle(hFile);
        }
      }
    }
    } while (::FindNextFile(h, &fData));
    g_nIndent--;
}
```

READTHREAD.CPP

```
#include "StdAfx.h"
#include "Thread.h"

UINT ReadThreadProc(LPVOID pParam)
{
    USES_CONVERSION;
    LPSTORAGE pStgRoot = NULL;
    // doesn't work without STGM_SHARE_EXCLUSIVE
    g_nIndent = 0;
    if (::StgOpenStorage(T2COLE(g_szRootStorageName), NULL,
        STGM_READ | STGM_SHARE_EXCLUSIVE,
        NULL, 0, &pStgRoot) == S_OK) {
      ASSERT(pStgRoot!= NULL);
      ReadStorage(pStgRoot);
      pStgRoot->Release();
    }
```

(continued)

Figure 26-2. *continued*

```
    else {
      AfxMessageBox("Storage file not available or not readable");
    }
    AfxMessageBox("Read complete");
    return 0;
}

void ReadStorage(LPSTORAGE pStg)
// reads one storage -- recursive calls for substorages
{
    USES_CONVERSION;
    LPSTORAGE pSubStg = NULL;
    LPSTREAM pStream = NULL;
    LPENUMSTATSTG pEnum = NULL;
    LPMALLOC pMalloc = NULL; // for freeing statstg
    STATSTG statstg;
    ULONG nLength;
    BYTE buffer[101];

    g_nIndent++;
    ::CoGetMalloc(MEMCTX_TASK, &pMalloc); // Assumes AfxOleInit
                                          //   was called
    VERIFY(pStg->EnumElements(0, NULL, 0, &pEnum) == S_OK);
    while (pEnum->Next(1, &statstg, NULL) == S_OK) {
      if (statstg.type == STGTY_STORAGE) {
        VERIFY(pStg->OpenStorage(statstg.pwcsName, NULL,
            STGM_READ | STGM_SHARE_EXCLUSIVE,
            NULL, 0, &pSubStg) == S_OK);
        ASSERT(pSubStg != NULL);
        TRACE("%0.*sStorage = %s\n", (g_nIndent - 1) * 4,
            g_szBlanks, OLE2CT(statstg.pwcsName));
        ReadStorage(pSubStg);
        pSubStg->Release();
      }
      else if (statstg.type == STGTY_STREAM) {
        VERIFY(pStg->OpenStream(statstg.pwcsName, NULL,
            STGM_READ | STGM_SHARE_EXCLUSIVE,
            0, &pStream) == S_OK);
        ASSERT(pStream != NULL);
        TRACE("%0.*sStream = %s\n", (g_nIndent - 1) * 4,
            g_szBlanks, OLE2CT(statstg.pwcsName));
        pStream->Read(buffer, 100, &nLength);
        buffer[nLength] = '\0';
        TRACE("%s\n", buffer);
        pStream->Release();
      }
```

(continued)

Figure 26-2. *continued*

```
    else {
       ASSERT(FALSE);   // LockBytes?
    }
    pMalloc->Free(statstg.pwcsName); // avoids memory leaks
  }
  pMalloc->Release();
  pEnum->Release();
  g_nIndent--;
}
```

To keep the program simple, there's no coordination between the main thread and the two worker threads. If the user quits the program before a thread is finished, Windows unceremoniously terminates the thread, closing the storage file but not necessarily flushing its buffer. You could run both threads at the same time if you used two separate compound files.

Both threads use recursive functions. The *ReadStorage* function reads a storage and calls itself to read the substorages. The *ReadDirectory* function reads a directory and calls itself to read the subdirectories. This function calls the Win32 functions *FindFirstFile* and *FindNextFile* to iterate through the elements in a directory. The *dwFileAttributes* member of the *WIN32_FIND_DATA* structure indicates whether the element is a file or a subdirectory. *ReadDirectory* opens files as memory-mapped and then writes to a stream directly from mapped memory.

The *USES_CONVERSION* macro is necessary to support the wide-character conversion macros *OLE2CT* and *T2COLE*. These macros are used here because the example doesn't use the *CString* class, which has built-in conversion logic.

Structured Storage and Persistent COM Objects

The EX26A program explicitly called member functions of *IStorage* and *IStream* to write and read a compound file. In the object-oriented world, objects should know how to save and load themselves to and from a compound file. That's what the *IPersistStorage* and *IPersistStream* interfaces are for. If a COM class implements these interfaces, a container program can "connect" the object to a compound file by passing the file's *IStorage* pointer as a parameter to the *IPersistStorage Save* and *Load* member functions. Such objects are said to be <u>persistent</u>. Figure 26-3 shows the process of calling the *IPersistStorage::Save* function.

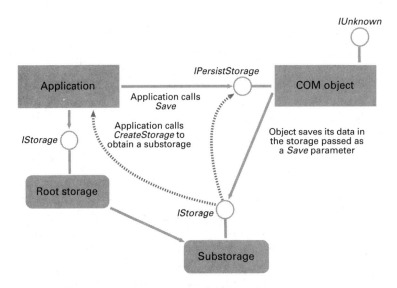

Figure 26-3.
Calling IPersistStorage::Save.

A COM class is more likely to implement an *IStorage* interface than an *IStream* interface. If the COM object is associated with a particular storage, the COM class can manage substorages and streams under that storage once it gets the *IStorage* pointer. A COM class implements the *IStream* interface only if it stores all its data in a stream. OCXs implement the *IStream* interface for storing and loading property values.

The *IPersistStorage* Interface

Both the *IPersistStorage* and *IPersistStream* interfaces are derived from *IPersist*, which contributes the *GetClassID* member function. Here's a summary of the *IPersistStorage* member functions:

HRESULT GetClassID(CLSID* *pClsid*);
Returns the COM object's 128-bit class identifier.

HRESULT InitNew(IStorage* *pStg*);
Initializes a newly created object. The server might need to use the storage for temporary data, so the container must provide an *IStorage* pointer valid for the life of the object. The server should call *AddRef* if it intends to use the storage. The server should not use this *IStorage* pointer for saving and loading; it should wait for *Save* and *Load* calls and then use the passed-in *IStorage* pointer to call *IStorage::Write* and *Read*.

HRESULT IsDirty();

Returns *S_OK* if the object has changed since it was last saved; otherwise, returns *S_FALSE*.

HRESULT Load(IStorage* *pStg*);

Loads the COM object's data from the designated storage.

HRESULT Save(IStorage* *pStg*, BOOL *fSameAsLoad*);

Saves the COM object's data in the designated storage.

The *IPersistStream* Interface

Here's a summary of the *IPersistStream* member functions:

HRESULT GetClassID(CLSID* *pClsid*);

Returns the COM object's 128-bit class identifier.

HRESULT GetMaxSize(ULARGE_INTEGER* *pcbSize*);

Returns the number of bytes needed to save the object.

HRESULT IsDirty( );

Returns *S_OK* if the object has changed since it was last saved; otherwise, returns *S_FALSE*.

HRESULT Load(IStream* *pStm*);

Loads the COM object's data from the designated stream.

HRESULT Save(IStream* *pStm*, BOOL *fClearDirty*);

Saves the COM object's data to the designated stream. If the *fClearDirty* parameter is *TRUE, Save* clears the object's dirty flag.

IPersistStream Programming

The following container program code fragment creates a stream and saves a COM object's data in it. Both the *IPersistStream* pointer for the COM object and the *IStorage* pointer are set elsewhere.

```
extern IStorage* pStg;
extern IPersistStream* pPersistStream;
IStream* pStream;
```

(continued)

```
if (pStg->CreateStream(L"MyStreamName",
    STGM_CREATE | STGM_READWRITE | STGM_SHARE_EXCLUSIVE,
    0, 0, &pStream) == S_OK) {
  ASSERT(pStream != NULL);
  pPersistStream->Save(pStream, TRUE);
  pStream->Release();
}
```

If you program your own COM class for use in a container, you'll need to use the MFC interface macros to add the *IPersistStream* interface. Too bad there's not an "interface wizard" to do the job.

The EX26B Example—A Persistent Object

This program is similar to EX26A in function. Internally, however, both worker threads use a persistent COM class *CText* for the TXT files. The read thread builds a list of *CText* objects as it reads streams from the storage. Each *CText* object stores the entire associated TXT file along with a copy of the first line. Some crude synchronization logic prevents the user from closing the main window if a worker thread is running.

To prepare EX26B, open the \vcpp32\ex26b\ex26b.mdp project, and build the project. Run the program from the debugger, and observe the output in the Debug window. The stored list of first lines appears after you clear the "Read complete" message box.

The menu, the view class, and the application class are the same as the EX26A versions. Only the thread code and the frame window class are different. The Thread.h file has the following three additional lines:

```
extern CTextList g_list;
extern BOOL g_bWriteThreadActive;
extern BOOL g_bReadThreadActive;
```

The *CMainFrame* class has a handler for the WM_CLOSE message that checks the status of the worker threads, as shown here:

```
void CMainFrame::OnClose()
{
    if (g_bWriteThreadActive) return;
    if (g_bReadThreadActive) return;
    CFrameWnd::OnClose();
}
```

Figure 26-4 lists the code for both the WriteThread.cpp and the Read-Thread.cpp file.

WRITETHREAD.CPP

```
#include "StdAfx.h"
#include "text.h"
#include "Thread.h"

int g_nIndent = 0;
BOOL g_bWriteThreadActive = FALSE;
const char* g_szBlanks = "                                    ";
const char* g_szRootStorageName = "\\direct.stg";


UINT WriteThreadProc(LPVOID pParam)
{
    USES_CONVERSION;
    g_bWriteThreadActive = TRUE;
    LPSTORAGE pStgRoot = NULL;
    // doesn't work without STGM_SHARE_EXCLUSIVE
    g_nIndent = 0;
    if (::StgCreateDocfile(T2COLE(g_szRootStorageName),
        STGM_READWRITE | STGM_SHARE_EXCLUSIVE | STGM_CREATE,
        0, &pStgRoot) == S_OK) {
      ASSERT(pStgRoot!= NULL);
      ReadDirectory("\\", pStgRoot);
      pStgRoot->Release();
    }
    AfxMessageBox("Write complete");
    g_bWriteThreadActive = FALSE;
    return 0;
}

void ReadDirectory(const char* szPath, LPSTORAGE pStg)
{
    USES_CONVERSION;
    WIN32_FIND_DATA fData;
    HANDLE h;
    char szNewPath[MAX_PATH];
    char szStorageName[100];
    char* pch;

    LPSTORAGE pSubStg = NULL;
    LPSTREAM pStream = NULL;
    LPPERSISTSTREAM pPersistStream = NULL;
```

Figure 26-4.   *(continued)*

The code listing for the two worker threads in EX26B.

691

Figure 26-4. *continued*

```
g_nIndent++;
strcpy(szNewPath, szPath);
strcat(szNewPath, "*.*");
h = ::FindFirstFile(szNewPath, &fData);
if (h == (HANDLE) 0xFFFFFFFF) return;  // empty disk drive only
do {
  if (!strcmp(fData.cFileName, "..") ||
      !strcmp(fData.cFileName, ".")) continue;
  if (fData.dwFileAttributes & FILE_ATTRIBUTE_DIRECTORY ) {
    strcpy(szNewPath, szPath);
    strcat(szNewPath,fData.cFileName);
    strcat(szNewPath, "\\");

    strcpy(szStorageName, fData.cFileName);
    szStorageName[31] = '\0';     // limit imposed by OLE
    TRACE("%0.*sStorage = %s\n", (g_nIndent - 1) * 4,
        g_szBlanks, szStorageName);
    VERIFY(pStg->CreateStorage(T2COLE(szStorageName),
        STGM_CREATE | STGM_READWRITE | STGM_SHARE_EXCLUSIVE,
        0, 0, &pSubStg) == S_OK);
    ASSERT(pSubStg != NULL);
    ReadDirectory(szNewPath, pSubStg);
    pSubStg->Release();
  }
  else {
    if ((pch = strrchr(fData.cFileName, '.')) != NULL) {
      if (!stricmp(pch, ".TXT")) {
        strcpy(szNewPath, szPath);
        strcat(szNewPath, fData.cFileName);
        TRACE("%0.*sStream path = %s\n", (g_nIndent - 1) * 4,
            g_szBlanks, szNewPath);
        CText* pText = new CText;
        VERIFY(pText->LoadFromFile(szNewPath));
        VERIFY(pStg->CreateStream(T2COLE(fData.cFileName),
            STGM_CREATE | STGM_READWRITE | STGM_SHARE_EXCLUSIVE,
            0, 0, &pStream) == S_OK);
        ASSERT(pStream != NULL);
        pText->ExternalQueryInterface(&IID_IPersistStream,
            (void**) &pPersistStream);
        ASSERT(pPersistStream != NULL);
        pPersistStream->Save(pStream, FALSE);
        pText->ExternalRelease(); //  because ExternalQI added 1
        pStream->Release();
        pText->ExternalRelease(); // delete it
      }
```

(continued)

Figure 26-4. *continued*

```
        }
     }

  } while ( ::FindNextFile(h, &fData) );
  g_nIndent--;
}
```

READTHREAD.CPP

```
#include "StdAfx.h"
#include "text.h"
#include "Thread.h"

CTextList g_list;
BOOL g_bReadThreadActive = FALSE;

UINT ReadThreadProc(LPVOID pParam)
{
    USES_CONVERSION;
    g_bReadThreadActive = TRUE;
    LPSTORAGE pStgRoot = NULL;
    CText* pText;
    g_nIndent = 0;
    if (::StgOpenStorage(T2COLE(g_szRootStorageName), NULL,
        STGM_READ | STGM_SHARE_EXCLUSIVE,
        NULL, 0, &pStgRoot) == S_OK) {
      ASSERT(pStgRoot!= NULL);
      ReadStorage(pStgRoot);
      pStgRoot->Release();
    }
    else {
      AfxMessageBox("Storage file not available or not readable");
    }
    TRACE("\n");
    AfxMessageBox("Read complete - ready to dump text list");
    // print text strings and empty the list
    while (!g_list.IsEmpty()) {
      pText = g_list.RemoveHead();
      TRACE("%s\n", pText->m_szFirstLine);
      pText->ExternalRelease(); //  because ctor made refcnt = 1
    }
    g_bReadThreadActive = FALSE;
    return 0;
}
```

(continued)

Figure 26-4. *continued*

```
void ReadStorage(LPSTORAGE pStg)
// reads one storage -- recursive calls for substorages
{
    USES_CONVERSION;
    LPSTORAGE pSubStg = NULL;
    LPSTREAM pStream = NULL;
    LPENUMSTATSTG pEnum = NULL;
    LPMALLOC pMalloc = NULL; // for freeing statstg
    STATSTG statstg;
    LPPERSISTSTREAM pPersistStream = NULL;

    g_nIndent++;
    ::CoGetMalloc(MEMCTX_TASK, &pMalloc); // Assumes AfxOleInit
                                          //   was called
    if (pStg->EnumElements(0, NULL, 0, &pEnum) != NOERROR) {
      ASSERT(FALSE);
      return;
    }
    while (pEnum->Next(1, &statstg, NULL) == NOERROR) {
      if (statstg.type == STGTY_STORAGE) {
        VERIFY(pStg->OpenStorage(statstg.pwcsName, NULL,
            STGM_READ | STGM_SHARE_EXCLUSIVE,
            NULL, 0, &pSubStg) == S_OK);
        ASSERT(pSubStg != NULL);
        ReadStorage(pSubStg);
        pSubStg->Release();
      }
      else if (statstg.type == STGTY_STREAM) {
        TRACE(".");
        VERIFY(pStg->OpenStream(statstg.pwcsName, NULL,
            STGM_READ | STGM_SHARE_EXCLUSIVE,
            0, &pStream) == S_OK);
        ASSERT(pStream != NULL);
        CText* pText = new CText;
        pText->ExternalQueryInterface(&IID_IPersistStream,
            (void**) &pPersistStream);
        ASSERT(pPersistStream != NULL);
        // if we store the object ptr instead of the interface
        //   pointer, we'll be able to access the object's data
        //   later in this program
        pPersistStream->Load(pStream);
        pText->ExternalRelease(); //  because ExternalQI added 1
        g_list.AddTail(pText);

        pStream->Release();
      }
```

(continued)

Figure 26-4. *continued*

```
        else {
          ASSERT(FALSE);  // LockBytes?
        }
        pMalloc->Free(statstg.pwcsName); // avoids memory leaks
      }
      pMalloc->Release();
      pEnum->Release();
      g_nIndent--;
  }
```

Figure 26-5 lists the code for the *CText* class in Text.h and Text.cpp.

TEXT.H

```
//////////////////////////////////////////////////////////////////////
// CText command target
class CText : public CCmdTarget
{
private:
    LPVOID m_lpvFile;
    int m_nFileSize;
    HANDLE m_hFile;
    HANDLE m_hMap;
    static const CLSID BASED_CODE s_clsid;
    void CleanupMemory();
    void GetFirstLine();
    DECLARE_DYNAMIC(CText)
protected:
    DECLARE_INTERFACE_MAP()
    BEGIN_INTERFACE_PART(PersistStream, IPersistStream)
        STDMETHOD(GetClassID)(LPCLSID);
        STDMETHOD(IsDirty)();
        STDMETHOD(Load)(LPSTREAM);
        STDMETHOD(Save)(LPSTREAM, BOOL);
        STDMETHOD(GetSizeMax)(ULARGE_INTEGER FAR*);
    END_INTERFACE_PART(PersistStream)
public:
    CText();
    virtual ~CText();
    BOOL LoadFromFile(const char* szPathname);
    char m_szFirstLine[81];
};


//////////////////////////////////////////////////////////////////////
typedef CTypedPtrList<CObList, CText*> CTextList; // template
                                                  //  collection
```

Figure 26-5.   *(continued)*

The CText *class listing.*

Figure 26-5. *continued*

TEXT.CPP

```
#include "StdAfx.h"
#include "ex26b.h"
#include "text.h"

#ifdef _DEBUG
#undef THIS_FILE
static char BASED_CODE THIS_FILE[] = __FILE__;
#endif

const CLSID BASED_CODE CText::s_clsid =
    {0x77720841, 0x0000, 0x0000, {0xc0, 0x00, 0, 0, 0, 0, 0, 0x46 } };

///////////////////////////////////////////////////////////////////
// CText
IMPLEMENT_DYNAMIC(CText, CCmdTarget)

BEGIN_INTERFACE_MAP(CText, CCmdTarget)
    INTERFACE_PART(CText, IID_IPersistStream, PersistStream)
END_INTERFACE_MAP()

CText::CText()
{
    m_lpvFile = NULL;
    m_hMap = NULL;
    m_hFile = NULL;
    m_nFileSize = 0;
}

CText::~CText()
{
    CleanupMemory();
}

BOOL CText::LoadFromFile(const char* szPathname)
{
    CleanupMemory();
    m_hFile = ::CreateFile(szPathname, GENERIC_READ, FILE_SHARE_READ,
        NULL, OPEN_EXISTING, FILE_ATTRIBUTE_NORMAL, NULL);
    if (m_hFile == NULL) return FALSE;
    // check for zero-length file
```

(continued)

Figure 26-5. *continued*

```
        if ((m_nFileSize = ::GetFileSize(m_hFile, NULL)) > 0) {
          m_hMap = ::CreateFileMapping(m_hFile, NULL, PAGE_READONLY,
              0, 0, NULL);
          if (m_hMap == NULL) return FALSE;
          m_lpvFile = ::MapViewOfFile(m_hMap, FILE_MAP_READ,
              0, 0, 0); // whole file
          GetFirstLine();
          return TRUE;
        }
        // empty file
        m_lpvFile = NULL;
        m_szFirstLine[0] = '\0';
        return TRUE;
    }


    void CText::GetFirstLine()
    {
        int nLength = min(80, m_nFileSize);
        strncpy(m_szFirstLine, (char*) m_lpvFile, nLength);
        m_szFirstLine[nLength] = '\0';
        char* pnl = strchr(m_szFirstLine, '\n');
        if (pnl != NULL) *pnl = '\0'; // truncate at first nl
    }


    void CText::CleanupMemory()
    {
        if (m_hMap != NULL) {
          ::UnmapViewOfFile(m_lpvFile);
          ::CloseHandle(m_hMap);
          ::CloseHandle(m_hFile);
        }
        else if (m_lpvFile != NULL) {
          delete [] m_lpvFile;
        }
        m_lpvFile = NULL;
        m_hMap = NULL;
        m_hFile = NULL;
    }
    /////////////////////////////////////////////////////////////////////

    STDMETHODIMP_(ULONG) CText::XPersistStream::AddRef()
    {
        METHOD_PROLOGUE(CText, PersistStream)
        return (ULONG) pThis->ExternalAddRef();
    }
```

(continued)

697

Figure 26-5. *continued*

```
STDMETHODIMP_(ULONG) CText::XPersistStream::Release()
{
    METHOD_PROLOGUE(CText, PersistStream)
    return (ULONG) pThis->ExternalRelease();
}


STDMETHODIMP CText::XPersistStream::QueryInterface(REFIID iid,
                                    void FAR* FAR* ppvObj)
{
    METHOD_PROLOGUE(CText, PersistStream)
    // ExternalQueryInterface looks up iid
    //   in the macro-generated tables
    return (HRESULT) pThis->ExternalQueryInterface(&iid, ppvObj);
}
/////////////////////////////////////////////////////////////////////


STDMETHODIMP CText::XPersistStream::GetClassID(LPCLSID lpClassID)
{
    TRACE("Entering CText::XPersistStream::GetClassID\n");
    METHOD_PROLOGUE(CText, PersistStream)
    ASSERT_VALID(pThis);

    *lpClassID = CText::s_clsid;
    return NOERROR;
}


STDMETHODIMP CText::XPersistStream::IsDirty()
{
    TRACE("Entering CText::XPersistStream::IsDirty\n");
    METHOD_PROLOGUE(CText, PersistStream)
    ASSERT_VALID(pThis);

    return NOERROR;
}


STDMETHODIMP CText::XPersistStream::Load(LPSTREAM pStm)
{
    ULONG nLength;
    STATSTG statstg;

    METHOD_PROLOGUE(CText, PersistStream)
    ASSERT_VALID(pThis);
    ASSERT(pThis->m_lpvFile == NULL);
    // don't need to free statstg.pwcsName because of NONAME flag
    VERIFY(pStm->Stat(&statstg, STATFLAG_NONAME) == NOERROR);
```

(continued)

Figure 26-5. *continued*

```
        pThis->m_nFileSize = statstg.cbSize.LowPart; // assume < 4 GB
        if (pThis->m_nFileSize > 0) {
          pThis->m_lpvFile = new BYTE[pThis->m_nFileSize];
          pStm->Read(pThis->m_lpvFile, pThis->m_nFileSize, &nLength);
          pThis->GetFirstLine();
        }
        return NOERROR;
    }


    STDMETHODIMP CText::XPersistStream::Save(LPSTREAM pStm,
                                             BOOL fClearDirty)
    {
        METHOD_PROLOGUE(CText, PersistStream)
        ASSERT_VALID(pThis);
        pStm->Write(pThis->m_lpvFile, pThis->m_nFileSize, NULL);
        TRACE("FIRST LINE = %s\n", pThis->m_szFirstLine);
        return NOERROR;
    }


    STDMETHODIMP  CText::XPersistStream::GetSizeMax(ULARGE_INTEGER
                                                    FAR* pcbSize)
    {
        TRACE("Entering CText::XPersistStream::GetSizeMax\n");
        METHOD_PROLOGUE(CText, PersistStream)
        ASSERT_VALID(pThis);
        pcbSize->LowPart = pThis->m_nFileSize;
        pcbSize->HighPart = 0; // assume < 4 GB
        return NOERROR;
    }
```

Look first at the *CText* class. It's a COM class because it supports an OLE interface, *IPersistStream*. It's not OLE-creatable, though, and thus doesn't live in its own DLL. Its *IPersistStream::Load* function allocates heap memory and then calls *IStream::Read* to load the contents of the stream. The *Save* function copies the object's data to the stream by calling *IStream::Write*. A public member function, *LoadFromFile*, solves the problem of "how do we get data into the object if we don't load it from a stream?" It uses memory-mapped file logic to load text from a TXT file.

Now look at the second half of the *ReadDirectory* function in the Write-Thread.cpp file in Figure 26-4 beginning on page 691. For each stream, the program constructs a *CText* object and then calls the *LoadFromFile* member function to load the object from the TXT file. After that, it calls *IPersistStream::Save* to write the object to the compound file. Then it deletes the *CText* object. Clearly, *ReadDirectory* needs direct access to *CText* objects in order to put text in them. It can't do that with the *IPersistStream* interface alone.

The second half of the *ReadStorage* function in the ReadThread.cpp file is more interesting. It constructs *CText* objects and stores their pointers in a collection. For each object, it calls *IPersistStream::Load* to read text from the stream. Theoretically, *ReadStorage* could manipulate *CText* objects solely with interface pointers and OLE functions. Of course, the *CText* class would need a class factory, and you'd have to store *IPersistStream* pointers in the list instead of *CText* pointers. You would also have to call the real *Release* and *QueryInterface* functions instead of the *CCmdTarget* versions.

But look at the end of *ReadThreadProc* in ReadThread.cpp. The *while* loop executes after the *CText* pointer list has been filled. It prints the first text line from each object and then releases the object. You couldn't do that if all you had was an *IPersistStream* pointer.

As you're starting to see, the EX26B example is rather contrived. Sure, we're using *CText* objects, but they're not very well connected to the streams, which hold only plain text. Use of the *CText* class hasn't bought us much over EX26A. But what if *CText* had more interfaces, and what if the container program had its own interesting interfaces besides *IStorage* and *IStream*? Maybe there could be a more meaningful dialog between the container and the COM object. The container would then not need direct access to the COM class's constructor and member functions.

As you've learned already, a COM class usually implements *IPersistStorage*, not *IPersistStream*. The *CText* class could have worked this way, but then the compound file would have been more complex because each TXT file would have needed both a storage element (to support the interface) and a subsidiary stream element (to hold the text).

Now get ready to take a giant leap. Suppose you have a true OLE-creatable COM class that supports the *IPersistStorage* interface. Recall the *IStorage* functions for class IDs. If a storage element contains a class ID, together with all the data an object needs, OLE can load the server, use the class factory to construct the object, get an *IPersistStorage* pointer, and call *Load* to load the data from a compound file. This is a preview of OLE Compound Documents, which you'll see in Chapter 27.

Compound File Fragmentation

Structured storage has a dark side. Like the disk drive itself, compound files can become fragmented with frequent use. If a disk drive becomes fragmented, however, you still have the same amount of free space. With a compound file, the space from deleted elements isn't always recovered. This means that compound files can keep growing even if you delete data.

Fortunately, there is a way to recover unused space in a compound file. You just create a new file and copy the contents. The *IStorage::CopyTo* function can do the whole job in one call if you use it to copy the root storage. You can either write a stand-alone utility or build a file regeneration capability into your application.

Other Compound File Advantages

You've seen how compound files add a kind of random access capability to your programs, and you can appreciate the value of transactioning. Now consider the brave new world in which every program can read every other program's documents. We're not there yet, but we have a start. Compound files from Microsoft applications have a stream under the root storage named \005SummaryInformation. This stream is formatted as a property set, as defined for OLE Controls. If you can decode the format for this stream, you can open any conforming file and read the summary.

Visual C++ comes with a compound file viewing utility named Dfview, which uses a tree view to display the file's storages and streams. Here is the Dfview output for the structured storage file generated by EX26A:

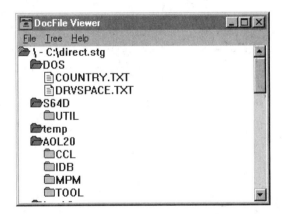

As a matter of fact, you can use EX26A to view the structure of any compound file. Are you starting to see the potential of this "universal file format"?

OLE Embedded Servers and Containers

Now you'll start to see the interesting part of OLE. In this chapter, you'll learn how an embedded server talks to its container. This is the knowledge base you need for OLE Controls (OCXs), in-place activation (Visual Editing), and linking, which are described in Adam Denning's *OLE Controls Inside Out* (Microsoft Press, 1995), Kraig Brockschmidt's *Inside OLE,* 2d ed. (Microsoft Press, 1995), and other books.

You'll get started with an MFC miniserver that supports in-place activation. Running this server will give you a good idea of what OLE looks like to the user, in case you didn't know already. You'll also see the extensive MFC support for this kind of application. If you work at only the top MFC level, however, you won't appreciate or understand the underlying OLE mechanisms. For that, you'll have to dig deeper.

Next you'll build a container program that uses the familiar parts of the MFC library but that supports embedded OLE objects that can be edited in their own windows. This container can, of course, run your MFC miniserver, but you'll really start to learn OLE when you build a miniserver from scratch and watch the interactions between it and the container.

Embedding vs. In-Place Activation (Visual Editing)

Visual Editing is Microsoft's trademarked name for in-place activation. A server that supports in-place activation also supports embedding. Both store their data in a container's document, and both can be activated by the container. An in-place–capable server can run inside the container application's main window, taking over the container's menu and toolbar, and it can run in its own top-level window if necessary. An embedded server can run only in its own window, and that window has a special menu that does not include file commands. Figure 27-1 shows a Microsoft Excel spreadsheet in-place activated inside a Microsoft Word document. Notice the Excel menus and toolbars.

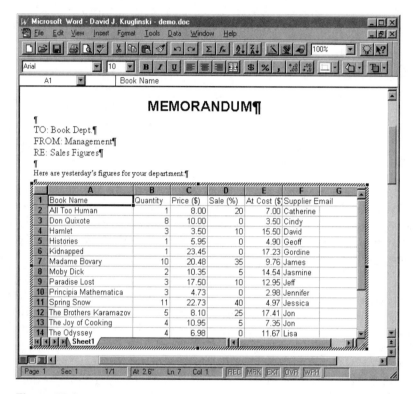

Figure 27-1.
An Excel spreadsheet activated inside a Word document.

Some container applications support only embedded servers; others support both in-place and embedded servers. Usually, an in-place–capable container program allows the user to activate in-place–capable servers either in-place or in their own windows. You should be getting the idea that embedding is a subset of in-place activation. This is true not only at the user level but also at the OLE implementation level. Embedding relies on two key interfaces, *IOleObject* and *IOleClientSite*, which are used for in-place activation as well.

Miniservers vs. Full Servers—Linking

A miniserver can't be run as a stand-alone program; it depends on a container application to launch it. It can't do its own file I/O but depends on the container's files. A full server, on the other hand, can be run both as a stand-alone program and from a container. When it's running as a stand-alone program, it can read and write its own files, which means it supports OLE linking. With embedding, the container document contains all the data that the server needs; with linking, the container contains only the name of a file that the server must open.

The Dark Side of Visual Editing

I'm really enthusiastic about the OLE COM architecture, and I truly believe that OCXs will take over the world. I'm not so sure about Visual Editing, though, and I'm not alone. From my teaching experience, I've learned that few developers are writing applications that fit the "objects embedded in a document" model. From my programming experience, I've learned that it is tricky for containers and servers to coordinate the size and scale of embedded objects. From my "user" experience, I've learned that in-place activation can be slow and awkward, even in the 32-bit world with a fast computer.

If you don't believe me, try embedding an Excel worksheet in a Word document, as shown in Figure 27-1. Resize the worksheet in both the active mode and the nonactive mode. Notice that the two sizes don't track and that processing is slow.

Consider the need for drawing graphics. Older versions of Microsoft PowerPoint used an in-place server named Microsoft Draw. The idea was that other applications could use this server for all their graphics needs. Well, it didn't work out that way, and PowerPoint now has its own built-in drawing code. If you have old PowerPoint files with Microsoft Draw objects, you'll have a problem converting them.

Now consider printing. You receive a Word document over the net from Singapore, and that document contains the metafiles for some embedded objects. You don't have the objects' servers, however. You print the document on your trusty 1200-dpi color laser printer, and the metafiles print with it. Embedded object metafiles can be rendered for a specific printer, but it's doubtful that the person in Singapore used your printer driver when creating the document. The result is less than optimal output with incorrect line breaks.

I do believe, however, that the OLE embedding technology has a lot of potential. Playing sounds and movies is cool, and storing objects in a database is interesting. What you learn in this chapter will help you think of new uses for this part of OLE.

Windows Metafiles and Embedded Objects

You're going to need a little more Windows theory before you can understand how in-place and embedded servers draw in their clients' windows. We've avoided metafiles up to this point because we haven't needed them, but they've always been an integral part of Windows. Think of a metafile as a cassette tape for GDI instructions. To use a cassette, you'll need a player/recorder, and that's what the metafile device context is. If you specify a filename when you create the metafile DC, your metafile will be saved on disk; otherwise, it's saved in memory and you get a handle.

In the world of OLE embedding, servers create metafiles and containers play them. Here's some server code that creates a metafile that contains some text and a rectangle:

```
CMetaFileDC dcm; // MFC class for metafile DC
VERIFY(dcm.Create());
dcm.SetMapMode(MM_ANISOTROPIC);
dcm.SetWindowOrg(0,0);
dcm.SetWindowExt(5000, -5000);
// drawing code
dcm.Rectangle(CRect(500, -1000, 1500, -2000));
dcm.TextOut(0, 0, m_strText);
HMETAFILE hMF = dcm.Close();
ASSERT(hMF != NULL);
```

It's possible to create a metafile that uses a fixed mapping mode such as *MM_LOENGLISH*, but with OLE we'll always use the *MM_ANISOTROPIC* mode. The metafile contains a *SetWindowExt* call, and the program that plays the metafile calls *SetViewportExt*. Here's some code that you might put inside your container view's *OnDraw* function:

```
pDC->SetMapMode(MM_HIMETRIC);
pDC->SetViewportExt(5000, 5000);
pDC->PlayMetafile(hMF);
```

Now what's supposed to show up on the screen is a rectangle 1 by 1 cm square because the server assumes the *MM_HIMETRIC* mapping mode. It will be 1 by 1 cm as long as the viewport extent matches the window extent. If the container sets the viewport extent to (5000, 10000) instead, the rectangle

TWENTY-SEVEN: OLE Embedded Servers and Containers

will be stretched vertically, but the text will be the same size because it's drawn with the nonscalable system font. If the container decided to use a mapping mode other than *MM_HIMETRIC*, it could adjust the viewport extent to retain the 1-by-1-cm size.

To reiterate, the <u>server</u> sets the window extent to the assumed size of the viewable area and draws inside that box. If the server uses a negative *y* extent, the drawing code works just as it does in *MM_HIMETRIC* mapping mode. The <u>container</u> somehow gets the server's extent size and attempts to draw the metafile in an area with those HIMETRIC dimensions.

Why are we bothering with metafiles anyway? Because the container needs to draw something in the server's rectangle, even if the server program isn't running. The server creates the metafile and hands it off in a data object to the OLE handler module on the container side of the Remote Procedure Call (RPC) link. The handler then caches the metafile and plays it on demand and also transfers it to and from the container's storage. When a server is in-place active, however, its view code is drawing directly in a window that's managed by the container.

The MFC OLE Server Architecture

We're not going into too many details here—just enough to allow you to understand the new files in the next example. There are three new MFC base classes you need to know about—*COleIPFrameWnd*, *COleServerDoc*, and *COleServerItem*. When you use AppWizard to generate an OLE server, it generates a class derived from each, in addition to an application class, a main frame class, and a view class. The *COleIPFrameWnd* class is rather like *CFrameWnd*. It's your application's main frame window, which contains the view. It has a menu associated with it, *IDR_SRVR_INPLACE*, which will be merged into the container program's menu. When your server is running in place, it's using the in-place frame, and when it's running stand-alone or embedded, it's using the regular frame, which is an object of a class derived from *CFrameWnd*. The embedded menu is *IDR_SRVR_EMBEDDED*, and the stand-alone menu is *IDR_MAINFRAME*.

The *COleServerDoc* class is a replacement for *CDocument*. It contains added features that support OLE connections to the container. The *COleServerItem* class works with the *COleServerDoc* class. If servers never supported OLE linking, the functionality of the two classes could be combined into one class. Because stand-alone servers do support linking, the MFC architecture dictates that both classes be present in all servers. You'll see in the EX27C example that we can make our own simple miniserver without this division.

Together, the *COleServerItem* class and the *COleServerDoc* class implement a whole series of OLE interfaces, including *IOleObject*, *IDataObject*, *IPersistStorage*, and *IOleInPlaceActiveObject*. These classes make calls to the container, using interface pointers that the container passes to them. The important things to know, however, are that your derived *CView* class draws in the server's in-place–active window and that the derived *COleServerItem* class draws in the metafile on command from the container.

The EX27A Example—
An MFC In-Place–Activated Miniserver

You don't need much OLE theory to build an MFC miniserver. This example is a good place to start, though, because you'll get an idea of how containers and servers interact. This server isn't too sophisticated. It just draws some text and graphics in a window. The text is stored in the document, and there's a dialog for updating it.

Here are the steps for creating the program from scratch:

1. **Run AppWizard to create the EX27A project in the \VCPP32\EX27A directory.** Select Single Document Interface, and then check the Miniserver option in the AppWizard Step 3 dialog, as shown here:

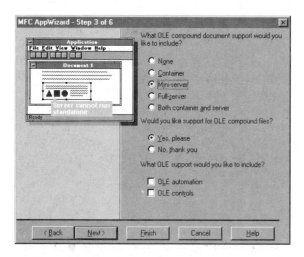

2. **Examine the generated files.** You've got the familiar application, document, main frame, and view files, but you've got a few new files too.

Header	Implementation	Class	MFC Base Class
SrvrItem.h	SrvrItem.cpp	*CEx27aSrvrItem*	*COleServerItem*
IpFrame.h	IpFrame.cpp	*CInPlaceFrame*	*COleIPFrameWnd*

3. **Add a text member to the document class.**   Add the following public data member in the class declaration in ex27aDoc.h:

```
CString m_strText;
```

Set the string's initial value to "Initial default text" in the document's *OnNewDocument* member function.

4. **Add a dialog to modify the text.**   Insert a new dialog template with an edit control, then use ClassWizard to generate a *CTextDialog* class derived from *CDialog*. Don't forget to include the dialog class header on ex27aDoc.cpp. Also, use ClassWizard to add a *CString* member variable named *m_strText* for the edit control.

5. **Add a new menu choice in both the embedded and in-place menus.** Add a Modify menu choice in both the *IDR_SRVR_EMBEDDED* and *IDR_SRVR_INPLACE* menus, and then use ClassWizard to map that choice to one function, *OnModify*, in the document class. Code the Modify command handler as follows:

```
void CEx27aDoc::OnModify()
{
    CTextDialog dlg;
    dlg.m_strText = m_strText;
    if (dlg.DoModal() == IDOK) {
        m_strText = dlg.m_strText;
        UpdateAllViews(NULL); // trigger CEx27aView::OnDraw
        UpdateAllItems(NULL); // trigger CEx27aSrvrItem::OnDraw
        SetModifiedFlag();
    }
}
```

6. **Override the view's *OnPrepareDC* function.**   Use ClassWizard to generate the function, and then insert the following line:

```
pDC->SetMapMode(MM_HIMETRIC);
```

7. Edit the view's *OnDraw* function.   The following code in
ex27aView.cpp draws a 2-cm circle centered in the client rectangle,
along with the text wordwrapped in the window:

```
void CEx27aView::OnDraw(CDC* pDC)
{
    CEx27aDoc* pDoc = GetDocument();
    ASSERT_VALID(pDoc);
    CFont font;
    font.CreateFont(-500, 0, 0, 0, 400, FALSE, FALSE, 0,
                    ANSI_CHARSET, OUT_DEFAULT_PRECIS,
                    CLIP_DEFAULT_PRECIS, DEFAULT_QUALITY,
                    DEFAULT_PITCH | FF_SWISS, "Arial");
    CFont* pFont = pDC->SelectObject(&font);
    CRect rectClient;
    GetClientRect(rectClient);
    CSize sizeClient = rectClient.Size();
    pDC->DPtoHIMETRIC(&sizeClient);
    CRect rectEllipse(sizeClient.cx / 2 - 1000,
                     -sizeClient.cy / 2 + 1000,
                      sizeClient.cx / 2 + 1000,
                     -sizeClient.cy / 2 - 1000);
    pDC->Ellipse(rectEllipse);
    pDC->DrawText(pDoc->m_strText, -1,
        CRect(0, 0, sizeClient.cx, -sizeClient.cy),
        DT_LEFT | DT_WORDBREAK);
        pDC->SelectObject(pFont);
}
```

8. Edit the server item's *OnDraw* function.   The following code in
SrvrItem.cpp tries to draw the same thing as the view's *OnDraw* function.
You'll learn what a server item is shortly.

```
BOOL CEx27aSrvrItem::OnDraw(CDC* pDC, CSize& rSize)
{
    // rSize is zero
    CEx27aDoc* pDoc = GetDocument();
    ASSERT_VALID(pDoc);

    pDC->SetMapMode(MM_ANISOTROPIC);
    pDC->SetWindowOrg(0, 0);
    pDC->SetWindowExt(3000, -3000);
    CFont font;
    font.CreateFont(-500, 0, 0, 0, 400, FALSE, FALSE, 0,
                    ANSI_CHARSET, OUT_DEFAULT_PRECIS,
                    CLIP_DEFAULT_PRECIS, DEFAULT_QUALITY,
                    DEFAULT_PITCH | FF_SWISS, "Arial");
```

```
CFont* pFont = pDC->SelectObject(&font);
CRect rectEllipse(CRect(500, -500, 2500, -2500));
pDC->Ellipse(rectEllipse);
pDC->DrawText(pDoc->m_strText, -1, CRect(0, 0, 3000, -3000),
              DT_LEFT | DT_WORDBREAK);
pDC->SelectObject(pFont);
return TRUE;
}
```

9. **Edit the document's *Serialize* function.** The framework takes care of loading and saving the document's data from and to an OLE stream named Contents, attached to the object's main storage. All you have to do is write normal serialization code, as shown here:

```
void CEx27aDoc::Serialize(CArchive& ar)
{
    if (ar.IsStoring())
    {
      ar << m_strText;
    }
    else
    {
      ar >> m_strText;
    }
}
```

There is a *CEx27aSrvrItem::Serialize* function too. It simply delegates to the document *Serialize* function.

10. **Build and register the EX27A application.** You must run the application directly once to update the registry.

11. **Test the EX27A application.** You need a container program that supports in-place activation. Use Microsoft Excel Version 7 if you have it, or build the project in the SAMPLES\MFC\OLE\DRAWCLI directory. Choose the container's Insert Object menu item. This option might be on the Edit menu, or it might be on the Insert menu. Then select Ex27a Document from the list.

> NOTE: You debug an embedded server the same way you debug an automation EXE server. See the sidebar on page 607.

When you first insert the EX27A object, you'll see a hatched border, which indicates that the object is in-place active. The bounding rectangle is 3 by 3 cm square, and there's a 2-cm circle in the center, as shown at the top of the following page:

Now, if you click elsewhere in the container's window, the object be-comes inactive, and it's shown like this:

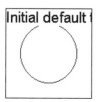

In the first case, you saw the output of the <u>view's</u> *OnDraw* function; in the sec-ond case, you saw the output of the <u>server</u> <u>item's</u> *OnDraw* function. The circles are the same, but the text is formatted differently. The server item code is drawing on a metafile device context, which can't handle the *DrawText* function the way a display device context can.

Now, if you use the resize handles to extend the height of the object (click once on the object to get the resize handles; don't double-click), you'll see the circle stretch and the font get bigger, as shown here:

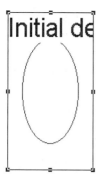

If you reactivate the object by double-clicking on it, it's reformatted as shown at the top of the facing page:

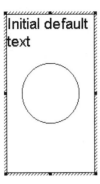

Click elsewhere in the container's window, single-click on the object, and then choose Ex27a Object from the bottom of the Edit menu. Choose Open from the submenu. This starts the server in embedded mode rather than in-place mode, as shown here:

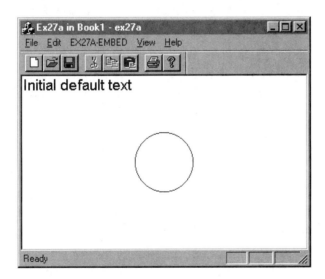

Notice that the server's *IDR_SRVR_EMBEDDED* menu is now visible.

An MDI Embedded Server?

The EX27A example is an SDI miniserver. Each time a controller creates an EX27A object, a new EX27A process is started. You might expect an MDI miniserver process to support multiple server objects, each with its own document. This is not the case. When you ask AppWizard to generate an MDI miniserver, it generates an SDI program, as in EX27A. It's theoretically possible to have a single process support multiple embedded objects in different windows, but you can't easily create such a program with the MFC library.

In-Place Server Sizing Strategy

If you look at the EX27A output above, you'll observe that the metafile image does not always match the image in the in-place frame window. I was hoping to create another example in which the two images matched. I was unsuccessful, however, when I tried to use the Microsoft Office 95 applications as containers. Each one did something a little different and unpredictable. A complicating factor is the containers' ability to zoom.

When AppWizard generates a server, it gives you an overridden *OnGetExtent* function in your server item class. This function returns a hard-coded size of (3000, 3000). You can certainly change this value to suit your needs, but be careful if you change it dynamically. I tried maintaining my own document data member for the server's extent, but that messed me up when the container's zoom factor changed. I thought containers would make more use of another server item virtual function, *OnSetExtent*, but they didn't.

You'll be safest if you simply make your server extents fixed and assume that the container will do the right thing. Keep in mind that when the container application prints its document, it prints the server metafiles. The metafiles are really more important than the in-place views.

If you have control over both container programs and server programs, however, you have more flexibility. You can build up a modular document processing system with its own sizing protocol. You can even use other OLE interfaces if you want.

Container–Server Interactions

Analyzing the server and the container separately won't work. You must watch them working together to understand the interactions. We can reveal the complexity one step at a time, however. Consider first that you have a container EXE and a server EXE, and that the container must manage the server by means of OLE interfaces. Look back to the space simulation example in Chapter 23. The client program called *CoGetClassObject* and *IClassFactory-::CreateInstance* to load the spaceship server and create a spaceship object, and then it called *QueryInterface* to get *IMotion* and *IVisual* pointers.

Well, an embedding container program works the same way as the space simulation client does. It starts the server program based on the server's class

ID, and the server constructs an object. Only the interfaces are different. Figure 27-2 shows a container program looking at a server. You've already seen all the interfaces except one—*IOleObject*.

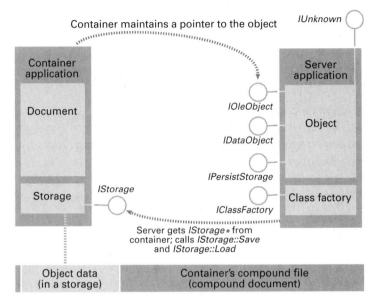

Figure 27-2.
A container program's view of the server.

Using the Server's *IOleObject* Interface

Loading a server is not the same as activating it. Loading merely starts a process, which then sits there waiting for further instructions. If the container gets an *IOleObject* pointer to the server object, it can call the *DoVerb* member function with a verb parameter such as *OLEIVERB_SHOW*. The server should then show its main window and act like a Windows-based program. If you look at the *IOleObject::DoVerb* description on page 721, you'll see an *IOleClientSite** parameter. We'll talk about client sites shortly, but for now you can simply set the parameter to *NULL*, and most servers will work OK.

Another important *IOleObject* function is useful at this stage—*Close*. As you might expect, the container calls *Close* when it wants to terminate the server. If the server process is currently servicing one embedded object (as is the case with MFC servers), the process exits.

Loading and Saving the Server's Native Data— Compound Documents

Figure 27-2 demonstrates that the container manages a storage through an *IStorage* pointer and that the server implements *IPersistStorage*. That means that the server can load and save its native data when the container calls *IPersistStorage::Load* and *Save*. You've seen these interfaces used in Chapter 26, but this time the container is going to save the server's class ID in the storage. Now the container can read the class ID from the storage and use it to start the server prior to calling *IPersistStorage::Load*.

Actually, the storage is very important to the embedded object. Just as a virus needs to live in a cell, an embedded object needs to live in a storage. The storage needs to be available always, because the object is constantly loading and saving itself and reading and writing temporary data.

What you have at the bottom of Figure 27-2 is a <u>compound</u> <u>document</u>. The container manages the whole file, but the embedded servers are responsible for the storages inside it. There's one main storage for each embedded object, and the container doesn't know or care what's inside those storages.

Clipboard Data Transfers

If you've run any OLE container program, including Microsoft Excel, you've noticed that you can copy and paste whole embedded objects. There's a special data object format *CF_EMBEDDEDOBJECT* for embedded objects. If you put an *IDataObject* pointer on the clipboard and that data object contains the *CF_EMBEDDEDOBJECT* format (and the companion *CF_OBJECTDESCRIPTOR* format), another program can reconstruct the object and load the proper server program.

There's actually less here than meets the eye. The only thing inside the *CF_EMBEDDEDOBJECT* format is an *IStorage* pointer. The clipboard copy program verifies that *IPersistStorage::Save* has been called to save the embedded object's data in the storage, and then it passes off the *IStorage* pointer in a data object. The clipboard paste program first gets the class ID from the source storage, then loads the server, and then calls *IPersistStorage::Load* to load the data from the source storage.

The data objects for the clipboard are generated as needed by the container program. The server's *IDataObject* interface isn't used for transferring the object's native data.

Getting the Server's Metafile

You already know that a server is supposed to draw in a metafile and that a container is supposed to play it. But how does the server deliver the metafile?

That's what the *IDataObject* interface, shown in Figure 27-2 on page 715, is for. The container simply calls *IDataObject::GetData*, asking for a *CF_META-FILEPICT* format. But wait a minute. The container is supposed to get the metafile even if the server isn't running. So now you're ready for the next complexity level.

The Role of the In-Process Handler

If the server program is running, it's in a separate process. Sometimes it's not running at all. In either case, the OLE32 DLL is linked into the container's process. This DLL is known as the <u>object</u> <u>handler</u>.

> **N O T E :** It's possible for an EXE server to have its own custom handler DLL, but most servers use the "default" OLE32 DLL instead.

Figure 27-3 shows the new picture. The handler communicates with the server over the RPC link, marshaling all interface function calls. But the handler does more than act as the server's proxy for marshaling; it maintains a <u>cache</u> that contains the server object's metafile. The handler saves and loads the cache to and from storage, and it can fill the cache by calling the server's *IDataObject::GetData* function.

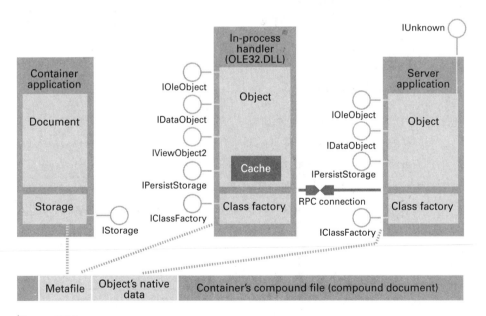

Figure 27-3.
The in-process handler and the server.

When the container wants to draw the metafile, it doesn't do the drawing itself; instead, it asks the handler to draw the metafile by calling the handler's *IViewObject2::Draw* function. The handler tries to satisfy as many container requests as it can without bothering the server, but if it needs to call a server function, it takes care of loading the server program if it is not already loaded.

> **NOTE:** The *IViewObject2* interface is an example of OLE's design evolution. Someone decided to add a new function—in this case, *GetExtent*—to the *IViewObject* interface. *IViewObject2* is derived from *IViewObject* and contains the new function. All new servers should implement the new interface and should return an *IViewObject2* pointer when *QueryInterface* is called for either *IID_IViewObject* or *IID_IViewObject2*. This is easy with the MFC library because you write two interface map entries that link to the same nested class.

Figure 27-3 shows both object data and metafile data in the object's storage. When the container calls the handler's *IPersistStorage::Save* function, the handler first writes the cache (containing the metafile) to the storage, and then it calls the server's *IPersistStorage::Save* function, which writes the object's native data to the same storage. The reverse happens when the object is loaded.

Server States

Now that you know what a handler is, you're ready for a description of the four states that an embedded object can assume:

State	Description
Passive	Object exists only in a storage.
Loaded	Object handler is running and has a metafile in its cache, but EXE server is not running.
Running	EXE server is loaded and running, but server's window is not visible to the user.
Active	EXE server's window is visible to the user.

The Container Interfaces

Now for the container side of the conversation… Look at Figure 27-4. The container consists of a document and one or more <u>sites</u>. The *IOleContainer* interface has functions for iterating over the sites, but we won't worry about it here. The important interface is *IOleClientSite*. Each site is an object that the server accesses through an *IOleClientSite* pointer. When the container creates an embedded object, it calls *IOleObject::SetClientSite* to establish one of the two connections from server to container. The site maintains an *IOleObject* pointer to its server object.

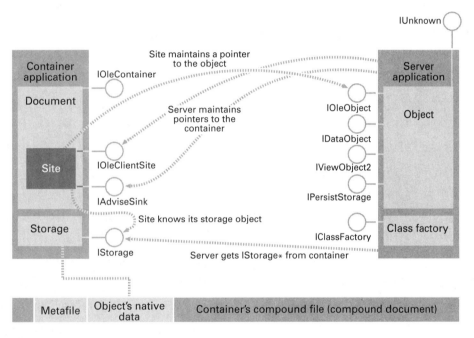

Figure 27-4.
The interaction between the container and the server.

One important *IOleClientSite* function is *SaveObject*. When the server decides it's time to save itself to its storage, it doesn't do so directly; instead, it asks the site to do the job by calling *IOleClientSite::SaveObject*. "Why the indirection?" you ask. The handler needs to save the metafile to the storage, that's why. The *SaveObject* function calls *IPersistStorage::Save* at the handler level, so the handler can do its job before calling the server's *Save* function.

Another important *IOleClientSite* function is *OnShowWindow*. The server calls this function when the server program starts running and when it stops running. The client is supposed to display a hatched pattern in the embedded object's rectangle when the server program is running or active.

The Advisory Connection

Figure 27-4 shows another interface attached to the site, *IAdviseSink*. This is the container's end of the second server connection. Why have another connection? The *IOleClientSite* connection goes directly from the server to the container, but the *IAdviseSink* connection is routed through the handler. After the site has created the embedded object, it calls *IViewObject2::SetAdvise*, passing its *IAdviseSink* pointer. Meanwhile, the handler has gone ahead and established <u>two</u> advisory connections to the server. When the embedded object is created, the handler calls *IOleObject::Advise* and then calls *IDataObject::DAdvise*. When the server's data changes, it notifies the handler through the *IDataObject* advisory connection. When the user saves the server's data or closes the server, the server notifies the handler through the *IOleObject* advisory connection. Figure 27-5 shows these connections.

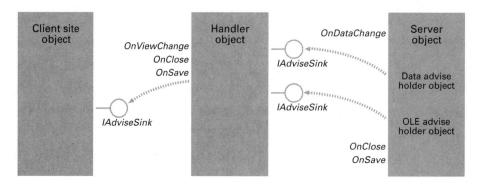

Figure 27-5.
Advisory connection details.

Now, when the handler gets the notification that the server's data has changed (server calls *IAdviseSink::OnDataChange*), it can notify the container by calling *IAdviseSink::OnViewChange*. The container responds by calling *IViewObject2::Draw* in the handler. If the server is not running, the handler draws its metafile from the cache. If the server is running, the handler calls the server's *IDataObject::GetData* function to get the latest metafile, which it draws. The *OnClose* and *OnSave* notifications are passed in a similar manner.

A Metafile for the Clipboard

As you've just learned, the container doesn't deal with the metafile directly when it wants to draw the embedded object; instead, it calls *IViewObject2::Draw*. There is a case, however, in which the container needs direct access to the metafile. When the container copies an embedded object to the clipboard, it must copy a metafile in addition to the embedded object and the object descriptor. That's what the handler's *IDataObject* interface is for. The container calls *IDataObject::GetData*, requesting a metafile format, and it copies that format into the clipboard's data object.

An Interface Summary

Shown here is a summary of the important OLE interfaces we'll be using in the following examples. The function lists are by no means complete, nor are the parameter lists. See Books Online or Brockschmidt's book for the complete specifications.

The *IOleObject* Interface

Embedded servers implement this interface. The client site maintains an *IOleObject* pointer to an embedded object.

HRESULT Advise(IAdviseSink* *pAdvSink*, DWORD* *dwConnection*);

The handler calls this function to establish one of the two advisory connections from the server to the handler. The server usually implements *Advise* with an OLE advise holder object, which can manage multiple advisory connections.

HRESULT Close(DWORD *dwSaveOption*);

The container calls *Close* to terminate the server application but to leave the object in the loaded state. Containers call this function when the user clicks outside an in-place–active server's window. Servers that support in-place activation should clean up and terminate.

HRESULT DoVerb(LONG *iVerb*, …IOleClientSite* *pActiveSite*, …);

Servers support numeric <u>verbs</u> as defined in the registry. A sound server might support a "Play" verb, for example. Embedded servers should support the *OLEIVERB_SHOW* verb, which instructs the object to show itself for editing or viewing. If the server supports in-place activation, this verb starts the visual editing process; otherwise, it starts the server in a separate window. The *OLEIVERB_OPEN* verb causes an in-place-activation–capable server to start in a separate window.

HRESULT GetExtent(DWORD *dwDrawAspect*, SIZEL* *pSizel*);

The server returns the object extent in HIMETRIC dimensions. The container uses these dimensions to size the rectangle for the server's metafile. Sometimes the container uses the extents that are included in the server's metafile picture.

HRESULT SetClientSite(IOleClientSite* *pClientSite*);

The container calls *SetClientSite* to enable the server to store a pointer back to the site in the container.

HRESULT SetExtent(DWORD *dwDrawAspect*, SIZEL* *pSizel*);

Some containers call this function to impose extents on the server.

HRESULT SetHostNames(const OLECHAR* *szContainerApp*, const OLECHAR* *szContainerObj*);

The container calls *SetHostNames* so that the server can display the container program's name in its window caption.

HRESULT Unadvise(DWORD* *dwConnection*);

This function terminates the advisory connection set up by *Advise*.

The *IViewObject2* Interface

Embedded server <u>handlers</u> implement this interface. The container calls its functions, but the server itself doesn't implement them. An *IViewObject2* interface cannot be marshaled across a process boundary because it's associated with a device context.

HRESULT Draw(DWORD *dwAspect*, ... const LPRECTL *lprcBounds*, ...);

The container calls this function to draw the server's metafile in a specified rectangle.

HRESULT SetAdvise(DWORD *dwAspect*, ..., IAdviseSink* *pAdvSink*);

The container calls *SetAdvise* to set up the advisory connection to the handler, which in turn sets up the advisory connection to the server.

The *IOleClientSite* Interface

Containers implement this interface. There is one client site object per server object.

HRESULT GetContainer(IOleContainer** *ppContainer*);

The *GetContainer* function retrieves a pointer to the container object (document), which can be used to enumerate the container's sites.

HRESULT OnShowWindow(BOOL *fShow*);

The server calls this function when it switches between the running and the loaded (or active) state. When the object is in the loaded or active state, the container should display a hatched pattern on the embedded object's rectangle.

HRESULT SaveObject();

The server calls *SaveObject* when it wants to be saved to its storage. The container calls *IPersistStorage::Save*.

The *IAdviseSink* Interface

Containers implement this interface. Embedded object handlers call its functions in response to server notifications.

void OnClose();

Servers call this function when they are being terminated.

void OnViewChange(BOOL dwAspect, ...);

The handler calls *OnViewChange* when the metafile has changed. Because the server must have been running for this notification to have been sent, the handler can call the server's *IDataObject::GetData* function to get the latest metafile for its cache. The container can then draw this metafile by calling *IViewObject2::Draw*.

OLE Helper Functions

A number of global OLE functions encapsulate a sequence of OLE interface calls. Here are some that we'll use in the EX27B example:

HRESULT OleCreate(REFCLSID *rclsid*, REFIID *riid*, ..., IOleClientSite* *pClientSite*, IStorage* *pStg*, void** *ppvObj*);

The *OleCreate* function first executes the COM creation sequence using the specified class ID. This loads the server program. Then the function calls

QueryInterface for an *IPersistStorage* pointer, which it uses to call *InitNew*, passing the *pStg* parameter. It also calls *QueryInterface* to get an *IOleObject* pointer, which it uses to call *SetClientSite* using the *pClientSite* parameter. Finally, it calls *QueryInterface* for the interface specified by *riid*, which is usually *IID_IOleObject*.

HRESULT OleCreateFromData(IDataObject* *pSrcDataObj*, REFIID *riid*, ..., IOleClientSite* *pClientSite*, IStorage* *pStg*, void** *ppvObj*);

The *OleCreateFromData* function creates an embedded object from a data object. In the EX27B example, the incoming data object has the *CF_EMBEDDEDOBJECT* format with an *IStorage* pointer. The function then loads the server program based on the class ID in the storage, and then it calls *IPersistStorage::Load* to make the server load the object's native data. Along the way, it calls *IOleObject::SetClientSite*.

HRESULT OleDraw(IUnknown* *pUnk*, DWORD *dwAspect*, HDC *hdcDraw*, LPCRECT *lprcBounds*);

This function calls *QueryInterface* on *pUnk* to get an *IViewObject* pointer, and then it calls *IViewObject::Draw*, passing the *lprcBounds* parameter.

HRESULT OleLoad(IStorage* *pStg*, REFIID *riid*, IOleClientSite* *pClientSite*, void** *ppvObj*);

The *OleLoad* function first executes the COM creation sequence using the class ID in the specified storage. Then it calls *IOleObject::SetClientSite* and *IPersistStorage::Load*. Finally, it calls *QueryInterface* for the interface specified by *riid*, which is usually *IID_IOleObject*.

HRESULT OleSave(IPersistStorage* *pPS*, IStorage* *pStg*, ...);

This function calls *IPersistStorage::GetClassID* to get the object's class ID, and then it writes that class ID in the storage specified by *pStg*. Finally, it calls *IPersistStorage::Save*.

An OLE Embedding Container Application

Now that we've got a working miniserver that supports embedding (EX27A), we'll write a container program to run it. We're not going to use the MFC container support, however, because you need to see what's happening at the OLE interface level. We will use the MFC document–view architecture and the MFC interface maps, and we'll also use the MFC data object classes.

MFC Support for OLE Containers

If you did use AppWizard to build an MFC OLE container application, you'd get a class derived from *COleDocument* and a class derived from *COleClientItem*. These MFC base classes implement a number of important OLE container interfaces for embedding and in-place activation. The idea is that you have one *COleClientItem* object for each embedded object in a single container document. Each *COleClientItem* object defines a site, which is where the server's object lives in the window.

The *COleDocument* class maintains a list of client items, but it's up to you to specify how to select an item and how to synchronize the metafile's position with the in-place frame position. AppWizard generates a basic container application with no support for linking, clipboard processing, or drag and drop. If you want those features, you might be better off looking at the MFC DRAWCLI and OCLIENT samples.

There is one MFC OLE class that we will use in the container—*COleInsertDialog*. This class wraps the *OleUIInsertObject* function. This Insert Object dialog enables the user to select from a list of registered server programs.

Some Container Limitations

Because our container application is designed for learning, we'll make some simplifications to reduce the bulk of the code. First of all, this container won't support in-place activation—it allows the user to edit embedded objects only in a separate window. Also, the container supports only one embedded item per document, and that means there's no linking support. The container uses a structured storage file to hold the document's embedded item, but it handles the storage directly, bypassing the framework's serialization system. There's clipboard support but not drag-and-drop support. Outside of these limitations, however, it's a pretty good container!

Container Features

OK, what does the container actually do? Here's a list of features:

- As an MFC MDI application, handles multiple documents.
- Displays the server's metafile in a sizable, moveable tracker rectangle in the view window.
- Maintains a temporary storage for each embedded object.

■ Implements the Insert Object menu option, which allows the user to select a registered server. The selected server program starts in its own window.

■ Allows embedded objects to be copied (and cut) to the clipboard and pasted. These objects can be transferred to and from other containers such as Microsoft Word and Microsoft Excel.

■ Allows an embedded object to be deleted.

■ Tracks the server's loaded–running transitions and hatches the tracker rectangle when the server is running or active.

■ Redraws the embedded object's metafile on receipt of server change notifications.

■ Saves the object in its temporary storage when the server updates the object or exits.

■ Copies the embedded object's temporary storage to and from named storage files in response to Copy To and Paste From commands on the Edit menu.

The EX27B Example—An Embedding Container

Now for the working program. It's a good time to open and build the EX27B project. If you choose Insert Object from the Edit menu and select Ex27a Document, the EX27A server will start. If you change the server's data and switch back to the container, the container will look like this:

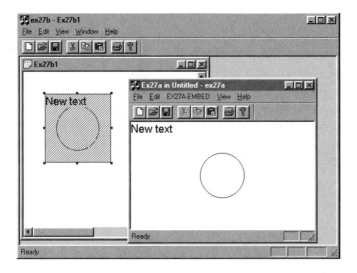

The *CEx27bView* Class

You can best understand the program by first concentrating on the view class. Look at the code in Figure 27-6, but ignore all *IOleClientSite* pointers. The container program will actually work if you pass *NULL* in every *IOleClientSite* pointer parameter. It just won't get notifications when the metafile or the native data changes. Also, servers will appear displaying their stand-alone menus instead of the special embedded menus.

EX27BVIEW.H

```
#define CF_OBJECTDESCRIPTOR  "Object Descriptor"
#define CF_EMBEDDEDOBJECT    "Embedded Object"
#define SETFORMATETC(fe, cf, asp, td, med, li)   \
    ((fe).cfFormat=cf, \
     (fe).dwAspect=asp, \
     (fe).ptd=td, \
     (fe).tymed=med, \
     (fe).lindex=li)


///////////////////////////////////////////////////////////////////
class CEx27bView : public CScrollView
{
public:
    CLIPFORMAT m_cfObjDesc;
    CLIPFORMAT m_cfEmbedded;
    CSize m_sizeTotal;  // document size
    CRectTracker m_tracker;
    CRect m_rectTracker; // logical coordinates
protected: // create from serialization only
    CEx27bView();
    DECLARE_DYNCREATE(CEx27bView)

// Attributes
public:
    CEx27bDoc* GetDocument();

private:
    void GetSize();
    void SetNames();
    void SetViewAdvise();
    BOOL MakeMetafilePict(COleDataSource* pSource);
    COleDataSource* SaveObject();
    BOOL DoPasteObject(COleDataObject* pDataObject);
    BOOL DoPasteObjectDescriptor(COleDataObject* pDataObject);
```

Figure 27-6.   *(continued)*

The container's CEx27bView *class listing.*

Figure 27-6. *continued*

```
// Overrides
    // ClassWizard generated virtual function overrides
    //{{AFX_VIRTUAL(CEx27bView)
    public:
    virtual void OnDraw(CDC* pDC);  // overridden to draw this view
    virtual BOOL PreCreateWindow(CREATESTRUCT& cs);
    virtual void OnInitialUpdate();
    protected:
    virtual BOOL OnPreparePrinting(CPrintInfo* pInfo);
    virtual void OnBeginPrinting(CDC* pDC, CPrintInfo* pInfo);
    virtual void OnEndPrinting(CDC* pDC, CPrintInfo* pInfo);
    //}}AFX_VIRTUAL

// Implementation
public:
    virtual ~CEx27bView();
#ifdef _DEBUG
    virtual void AssertValid() const;
    virtual void Dump(CDumpContext& dc) const;
#endif

protected:

// Generated message map functions
protected:
    //{{AFX_MSG(CEx27bView)
    afx_msg void OnEditCopy();
    afx_msg void OnUpdateEditCopy(CCmdUI* pCmdUI);
    afx_msg void OnEditCopyto();
    afx_msg void OnEditCut();
    afx_msg void OnEditPaste();
    afx_msg void OnUpdateEditPaste(CCmdUI* pCmdUI);
    afx_msg void OnEditPastefrom();
    afx_msg void OnEditInsertobject();
    afx_msg void OnUpdateEditInsertobject(CCmdUI* pCmdUI);
    afx_msg void OnLButtonDown(UINT nFlags, CPoint point);
    afx_msg void OnLButtonDblClk(UINT nFlags, CPoint point);
    afx_msg BOOL OnSetCursor(CWnd* pWnd, UINT nHitTest, UINT message);
    //}}AFX_MSG
    DECLARE_MESSAGE_MAP()
};

#ifndef _DEBUG  // debug version in ex27bView.cpp
inline CEx27bDoc* CEx27bView::GetDocument()
    { return (CEx27bDoc*)m_pDocument; }
#endif
```

(continued)

Figure 27-6. *continued*

EX27BVIEW.CPP

```cpp
#include "StdAfx.h"
#include "ex27b.h"
#include "ex27bDoc.h"
#include "ex27bView.h"

#ifdef _DEBUG
#define new DEBUG_NEW
#undef THIS_FILE
static char THIS_FILE[] = __FILE__;
#endif

/////////////////////////////////////////////////////////////////////
// CEx27bView

IMPLEMENT_DYNCREATE(CEx27bView, CScrollView)

BEGIN_MESSAGE_MAP(CEx27bView, CScrollView)
    //{{AFX_MSG_MAP(CEx27bView)
    ON_COMMAND(ID_EDIT_COPY, OnEditCopy)
    ON_UPDATE_COMMAND_UI(ID_EDIT_COPY, OnUpdateEditCopy)
    ON_COMMAND(ID_EDIT_COPYTO, OnEditCopyto)
    ON_UPDATE_COMMAND_UI(ID_EDIT_COPYTO, OnUpdateEditCopy)
    ON_COMMAND(ID_EDIT_CUT, OnEditCut)
    ON_UPDATE_COMMAND_UI(ID_EDIT_CUT, OnUpdateEditCopy)
    ON_COMMAND(ID_EDIT_PASTE, OnEditPaste)
    ON_UPDATE_COMMAND_UI(ID_EDIT_PASTE, OnUpdateEditPaste)
    ON_COMMAND(ID_EDIT_PASTEFROM, OnEditPastefrom)
    ON_COMMAND(ID_EDIT_INSERTOBJECT, OnEditInsertobject)
    ON_UPDATE_COMMAND_UI(ID_EDIT_INSERTOBJECT,
        OnUpdateEditInsertobject)
    ON_WM_LBUTTONDOWN()
    ON_WM_LBUTTONDBLCLK()
    ON_WM_SETCURSOR()
    //}}AFX_MSG_MAP
    // Standard printing commands
    ON_COMMAND(ID_FILE_PRINT, CScrollView::OnFilePrint)
    ON_COMMAND(ID_FILE_PRINT_DIRECT, CScrollView::OnFilePrint)
    ON_COMMAND(ID_FILE_PRINT_PREVIEW, CScrollView::OnFilePrintPreview)
END_MESSAGE_MAP()

/////////////////////////////////////////////////////////////////////
// CEx27bView construction/destruction
```

(continued)

Figure 27-6. *continued*

```
CEx27bView::CEx27bView() : m_sizeTotal(20000, 25000),
    m_rectTracker(0, 0, 0, 0) // 20 by 25 cm when printed
{
    m_cfObjDesc = ::RegisterClipboardFormat(CF_OBJECTDESCRIPTOR);
    m_cfEmbedded = ::RegisterClipboardFormat(CF_EMBEDDEDOBJECT);
}


CEx27bView::~CEx27bView()
{
}


BOOL CEx27bView::PreCreateWindow(CREATESTRUCT& cs)
{
    // TODO: Modify the Window class or styles here by modifying
    //   the CREATESTRUCT cs

    return CScrollView::PreCreateWindow(cs);
}


/////////////////////////////////////////////////////////////////////
// CEx27bView drawing

void CEx27bView::OnDraw(CDC* pDC)
{
    CEx27bDoc* pDoc = GetDocument();

    if (pDoc->m_lpOleObj != NULL) {
      VERIFY(::OleDraw(pDoc->m_lpOleObj, DVASPECT_CONTENT,
            pDC->GetSafeHdc(), m_rectTracker) == S_OK);
    }

    m_tracker.m_rect = m_rectTracker;
    pDC->LPtoDP(m_tracker.m_rect);   // device
    if (pDoc->m_bHatch) {
      m_tracker.m_nStyle |= CRectTracker::hatchInside;
    }
    else {
      m_tracker.m_nStyle &= ~CRectTracker::hatchInside;
    }
    m_tracker.Draw(pDC);
}


/////////////////////////////////////////////////////////////////////
// CEx27bView printing
```

(continued)

Figure 27-6. *continued*

```
BOOL CEx27bView::OnPreparePrinting(CPrintInfo* pInfo)
{
    pInfo->SetMaxPage(1);
    return DoPreparePrinting(pInfo);
}


void CEx27bView::OnBeginPrinting(CDC* /*pDC*/, CPrintInfo* /*pInfo*/)
{
    // TODO: add extra initialization before printing
}


void CEx27bView::OnEndPrinting(CDC* /*pDC*/, CPrintInfo* /*pInfo*/)
{
    // TODO: add cleanup after printing
}


/////////////////////////////////////////////////////////////////////////
// CEx27bView diagnostics

#ifdef _DEBUG
void CEx27bView::AssertValid() const
{
    CScrollView::AssertValid();
}


void CEx27bView::Dump(CDumpContext& dc) const
{
    CScrollView::Dump(dc);
}


CEx27bDoc* CEx27bView::GetDocument() // non-debug version is inline
{

    ASSERT(m_pDocument->IsKindOf(RUNTIME_CLASS(CEx27bDoc)));
    return (CEx27bDoc*)m_pDocument;
}
#endif //_DEBUG


/////////////////////////////////////////////////////////////////////////
// CEx27bView message handlers

void CEx27bView::OnInitialUpdate()
{
    TRACE("CEx27bView::OnInitialUpdate\n");
    m_rectTracker = CRect(1000, -1000, 5000, -5000);
```

(continued)

Figure 27-6. *continued*

```
    m_tracker.m_nStyle = CRectTracker::solidLine |
                         CRectTracker::resizeOutside;
    SetScrollSizes(MM_HIMETRIC, m_sizeTotal);
    CScrollView::OnInitialUpdate();
}

void CEx27bView::OnEditCopy()
{
    COleDataSource* pSource = SaveObject();
    if (pSource) {
      pSource->SetClipboard(); // OLE deletes data source
    }
}

void CEx27bView::OnUpdateEditCopy(CCmdUI* pCmdUI)
{
    // serves Copy, Cut, and Copy To
    pCmdUI->Enable(GetDocument()->m_lpOleObj != NULL);
}

void CEx27bView::OnEditCopyto()
{
    // copy text to a .STG file (nothing special about STG ext)
    CFileDialog dlg(FALSE, "stg", "*.stg");
    if (dlg.DoModal() != IDOK) {
        return;
    }
    CEx27bDoc* pDoc = GetDocument();
// create a structured storage home for the object (m_pStgSub)
// create a root storage file, then a substorage named "sub"
    LPSTORAGE pStgRoot;
    VERIFY(::StgCreateDocfile(dlg.GetPathName().AllocSysString(),
           STGM_READWRITE | STGM_SHARE_EXCLUSIVE | STGM_CREATE,
           0, &pStgRoot) == S_OK);
    ASSERT(pStgRoot!= NULL);

    LPSTORAGE pStgSub;
    VERIFY(pStgRoot->CreateStorage(CEx27bDoc::s_szSub,
           STGM_CREATE | STGM_READWRITE | STGM_SHARE_EXCLUSIVE,
           0, 0, &pStgSub) == S_OK);
    ASSERT(pStgSub!= NULL);

// get the IPersistStorage* for the object
    LPPERSISTSTORAGE pPS = NULL;
    VERIFY(pDoc->m_lpOleObj->QueryInterface(IID_IPersistStorage,
           (void**) &pPS) == S_OK);
```

(continued)

Figure 27-6. *continued*

```
// finally, save the object in its new home in the user's file
    VERIFY(::OleSave(pPS, pStgSub, FALSE) == S_OK); // FALSE means
                                                    //  different stg

    pPS->SaveCompleted(NULL);
    pPS->Release();

    pStgSub->Release();
    pStgRoot->Release();
}


void CEx27bView::OnEditCut()
{
    OnEditCopy();
    GetDocument()->OnEditClearAll();
}


void CEx27bView::OnEditPaste()
{
    CEx27bDoc* pDoc = GetDocument();
    COleDataObject dataObject;
    VERIFY(dataObject.AttachClipboard());
    pDoc->DeleteContents();
    DoPasteObjectDescriptor(&dataObject);
    DoPasteObject(&dataObject);
    SetViewAdvise();
    GetSize();
    pDoc->SetModifiedFlag();
    pDoc->UpdateAllViews(NULL);
}


void CEx27bView::OnUpdateEditPaste(CCmdUI* pCmdUI)
{
    // Ensure that object data is available
    COleDataObject dataObject;
    if (dataObject.AttachClipboard() &&
      dataObject.IsDataAvailable(m_cfEmbedded)) {
      pCmdUI->Enable(TRUE);
    }
    else {
      pCmdUI->Enable(FALSE);
    }
}


void CEx27bView::OnEditPastefrom()
{
```

(continued)

733

Figure 27-6. *continued*

```
    CEx27bDoc* pDoc = GetDocument();
    // paste from a .STG file
    CFileDialog dlg(TRUE, "stg", "*.stg");
    if (dlg.DoModal() != IDOK) {
      return;
    }
// open the storage and substorage
    LPSTORAGE pStgRoot;
    VERIFY(::StgOpenStorage(dlg.GetPathName().AllocSysString(), NULL,
          STGM_READ | STGM_SHARE_EXCLUSIVE,
          NULL, 0, &pStgRoot) == S_OK);
    ASSERT(pStgRoot!= NULL);

    LPSTORAGE pStgSub;
    VERIFY(pStgRoot->OpenStorage(CEx27bDoc::s_szSub, NULL,
          STGM_READ | STGM_SHARE_EXCLUSIVE,
          NULL, 0, &pStgSub) == S_OK);
    ASSERT(pStgSub!= NULL);

// copy the object data from the user storage to the temporary storage
    VERIFY(pStgSub->CopyTo(NULL, NULL, NULL,
                           pDoc->m_pTempStgSub) == S_OK);
// finally, load the object--pClientSite not necessary
    LPOLECLIENTSITE pClientSite =
        (LPOLECLIENTSITE) pDoc->GetInterface(&IID_IOleClientSite);
    ASSERT(pClientSite != NULL);
    pDoc->DeleteContents();
    VERIFY(::OleLoad(pDoc->m_pTempStgSub, IID_IOleObject, pClientSite,
        (void**) &pDoc->m_lpOleObj) == S_OK);
    SetViewAdvise();
    pStgSub->Release();
    pStgRoot->Release();
    GetSize();
    pDoc->SetModifiedFlag();
    pDoc->UpdateAllViews(NULL);
}


void CEx27bView::OnEditInsertobject()
{
    CEx27bDoc* pDoc = GetDocument();
    COleInsertDialog dlg;
    if (dlg.DoModal() == IDCANCEL) return;
    // no addrefs done for GetInterface
    LPOLECLIENTSITE pClientSite =
        (LPOLECLIENTSITE) pDoc->GetInterface(&IID_IOleClientSite);
    ASSERT(pClientSite != NULL);
```

(continued)

Figure 27-6. *continued*

```
    pDoc->DeleteContents();
    VERIFY(::OleCreate(dlg.GetClassID(), IID_IOleObject,
            OLERENDER_DRAW, NULL, pClientSite, pDoc->m_pTempStgSub,
            (void**) &pDoc->m_lpOleObj) == S_OK);
    SetViewAdvise();

    pDoc->m_lpOleObj->DoVerb(OLEIVERB_SHOW, NULL, pClientSite,
                            0, NULL, NULL);
    SetNames();
    GetDocument()->SetModifiedFlag();
    GetSize();
    pDoc->UpdateAllViews(NULL);
}


void CEx27bView::OnUpdateEditInsertobject(CCmdUI* pCmdUI)
{
    pCmdUI->Enable(GetDocument()->m_lpOleObj == NULL);
}


void CEx27bView::OnLButtonDown(UINT nFlags, CPoint point)
{
    TRACE("**Entering CEx27bView::OnLButtonDown--point = (%d, %d)\n",
            point.x, point.y);
    if (m_tracker.Track(this, point, FALSE, NULL)) {
      CClientDC dc(this);
      OnPrepareDC(&dc);
      m_rectTracker = m_tracker.m_rect;
      dc.DPtoLP(m_rectTracker); // update logical coordinates
      GetDocument()->UpdateAllViews(NULL);
    }
    TRACE("**Leaving CEx27bView::OnLButtonDown\n");
}


void CEx27bView::OnLButtonDblClk(UINT nFlags, CPoint point)
{
    if (m_tracker.HitTest(point) == CRectTracker::hitNothing) return;
    // activate the object
    CEx27bDoc* pDoc = GetDocument();
    if (pDoc->m_lpOleObj != NULL) {
      LPOLECLIENTSITE pClientSite =
          (LPOLECLIENTSITE) pDoc->GetInterface(&IID_IOleClientSite);
      ASSERT(pClientSite != NULL);
      VERIFY(pDoc->m_lpOleObj->DoVerb(OLEIVERB_OPEN, NULL,
            pClientSite, 0, GetSafeHwnd(),
            CRect(0, 0, 0, 0)) == S_OK);
```

(continued)

735

Figure 27-6. *continued*

```
        SetNames();
        GetDocument()->SetModifiedFlag();
    }
}

BOOL CEx27bView::OnSetCursor(CWnd* pWnd, UINT nHitTest, UINT message)
{
    if (m_tracker.SetCursor(pWnd, nHitTest)) {
      return TRUE;
    }
    else {
      return CScrollView::OnSetCursor(pWnd, nHitTest, message);
    }
}

////////////////////////////////////////////////////////////////////////

void CEx27bView::SetViewAdvise()
{
    CEx27bDoc* pDoc = GetDocument();
    if (pDoc->m_lpOleObj != NULL) {
      LPVIEWOBJECT2 pViewObj;
        pDoc->m_lpOleObj->QueryInterface(IID_IViewObject2,
                                         (void**) &pViewObj);
      LPADVISESINK pAdviseSink =
          (LPADVISESINK) pDoc->GetInterface(&IID_IAdviseSink);
      VERIFY(pViewObj->SetAdvise(DVASPECT_CONTENT, 0,
            pAdviseSink) == S_OK);
      pViewObj->Release();
    }
}

void CEx27bView::SetNames() // sets host names
{
    CEx27bDoc* pDoc = GetDocument();
    CString strApp = AfxGetApp()->m_pszAppName;
    if (pDoc->m_lpOleObj != NULL) {
      pDoc->m_lpOleObj->SetHostNames(strApp.AllocSysString(), NULL);
    }
}

void CEx27bView::GetSize()
{
    CEx27bDoc* pDoc = GetDocument();
    if (pDoc->m_lpOleObj != NULL) {
```

(continued)

Figure 27-6. *continued*

```
    SIZEL size;  // ask the server for its size
    pDoc->m_lpOleObj->GetExtent(DVASPECT_CONTENT, &size);
    m_rectTracker.right = m_rectTracker.left + size.cx;
    m_rectTracker.bottom = m_rectTracker.top - size.cy;
  }
}


BOOL CEx27bView::DoPasteObject(COleDataObject* pDataObject)
{
    TRACE("Entering CEx27bView::DoPasteObject\n");
    // update command UI should keep us out of here
    //   if not CF_EMBEDDEDOBJECT
    if (!pDataObject->IsDataAvailable(m_cfEmbedded)) {
      TRACE("CF_EMBEDDEDOBJECT format is unavailable\n");
      return FALSE;
    }
    CEx27bDoc* pDoc = GetDocument();
// now create the object from the IDataObject*
// OleCreateFromData will use CF_EMBEDDEDOBJECT format if available
    LPOLECLIENTSITE pClientSite =
        (LPOLECLIENTSITE) pDoc->GetInterface(&IID_IOleClientSite);
    ASSERT(pClientSite != NULL);
    VERIFY(::OleCreateFromData(pDataObject->m_lpDataObject,
          IID_IOleObject, OLERENDER_DRAW, NULL, pClientSite,
          pDoc->m_pTempStgSub,
          (void**) &pDoc->m_lpOleObj) == S_OK);
    return TRUE;
}


BOOL CEx27bView::DoPasteObjectDescriptor(COleDataObject* pDataObject)
{
    TRACE("Entering CEx27bView::DoPasteObjectDescriptor\n");
    STGMEDIUM stg;
    FORMATETC fmt;
    CEx27bDoc* pDoc = GetDocument();
    if (!pDataObject->IsDataAvailable(m_cfObjDesc)) {
      TRACE("OBJECTDESCRIPTOR format is unavailable\n");
      return FALSE;
    }
    SETFORMATETC(fmt, m_cfObjDesc, DVASPECT_CONTENT, NULL,
                TYMED_HGLOBAL, -1);
    VERIFY(pDataObject->GetData(m_cfObjDesc, &stg, &fmt));

    return TRUE;
}
```

(continued)

Figure 27-6. *continued*

```
// helper function used for clipboard and drag and drop
COleDataSource* CEx27bView::SaveObject()
{
    TRACE("Entering CEx27bView::SaveObject\n");
    CEx27bDoc* pDoc = GetDocument();
    if (pDoc->m_lpOleObj != NULL) {
      COleDataSource* pSource = new COleDataSource();

      // CODE FOR OBJECT DATA
      FORMATETC fmte;
      SETFORMATETC(fmte, m_cfEmbedded, DVASPECT_CONTENT, NULL,
                   TYMED_ISTORAGE, -1);
      STGMEDIUM stgm;
      stgm.tymed = TYMED_ISTORAGE;
      stgm.pstg = pDoc->m_pTempStgSub;
      stgm.pUnkForRelease = NULL;
      pDoc->m_pTempStgSub->AddRef();    // don't forget this!
      pSource->CacheData(m_cfEmbedded, &stgm, &fmte);

      // metafile needed too
      MakeMetafilePict(pSource);
      // CODE FOR OBJECT DESCRIPTION DATA

      HGLOBAL hObjDesc = ::GlobalAlloc(GMEM_SHARE,
                          sizeof(OBJECTDESCRIPTOR));
      LPOBJECTDESCRIPTOR pObjDesc =
          (LPOBJECTDESCRIPTOR) ::GlobalLock(hObjDesc);
      pObjDesc->cbSize = sizeof(OBJECTDESCRIPTOR);
      pObjDesc->clsid = CLSID_NULL;
      pObjDesc->dwDrawAspect = 0;
      pObjDesc->dwStatus = 0;
      pObjDesc->dwFullUserTypeName = 0;
      pObjDesc->dwSrcOfCopy = 0;
      pObjDesc->sizel.cx = 0;
      pObjDesc->sizel.cy = 0;
      pObjDesc->pointl.x = 0;
      pObjDesc->pointl.y = 0;
      ::GlobalUnlock(hObjDesc);
      pSource->CacheGlobalData(m_cfObjDesc, hObjDesc);
      return pSource;
    }
    return NULL;
}
```

(continued)

Figure 27-6. *continued*

```
BOOL CEx27bView::MakeMetafilePict(COleDataSource* pSource)
{
    CEx27bDoc* pDoc = GetDocument();
    COleDataObject dataObject;
    LPDATAOBJECT pDataObj; // OLE object's IDataObject interface
    VERIFY(pDoc->m_lpOleObj->QueryInterface(IID_IDataObject,
            (void**) &pDataObj) == S_OK);
    dataObject.Attach(pDataObj);
    FORMATETC fmtem;
    SETFORMATETC(fmtem, CF_METAFILEPICT, DVASPECT_CONTENT, NULL,
                 TYMED_MFPICT, -1);
    if (!dataObject.IsDataAvailable(CF_METAFILEPICT, &fmtem)) {
      TRACE("CF_METAFILEPICT format is unavailable\n");
      return FALSE;
    }
    // just copy the metafile handle from the ole object
    //  to the clipboard data object
    STGMEDIUM stgmm;
    VERIFY(dataObject.GetData(CF_METAFILEPICT, &stgmm, &fmtem));
    pSource->CacheData(CF_METAFILEPICT, &stgmm, &fmtem);
    return TRUE;
}
```

Study the message map and the associated command handlers. They're all relatively short, and they mostly call the OLE functions described earlier. There are a few private helper functions that need some explanation, however:

NOTE: You'll see many calls to a *GetInterface* function. This is a member of class *CCmdTarget* and returns the specified OLE interface pointer for a class in your project. It's used mostly to get the *IOleClientSite* interface pointer for your document. It's more efficient than calling *ExternalQueryInterface*, but it doesn't increment the object's reference count.

GetSize

This function calls *IOleObject::GetSize* to get the embedded object's extents, which it converts to a rectangle for storage in the tracker.

SetNames

The *SetNames* function calls *IOleObject::SetHostNames* to send the container application's name to the server.

SetViewAdvise

This function calls the embedded object's *IViewObject2::SetAdvise* to set up the advisory connection from server object to container document.

MakeMetafilePict

The *MakeMetafilePict* function calls the embedded object's *IDataObject::GetData* function to get a metafile picture to copy to the clipboard data object. A metafile picture, by the way, is a Windows *METAFILEPICT* structure instance, which contains a pointer to the metafile plus extent information.

SaveObject

This function acts like the *SaveDib* function in the EX25A example. It creates a *COleDataSource* object with three formats: embedded object, metafile, and object descriptor.

DoPasteObjectDescriptor

The *DoPasteObjectDescriptor* function pastes an object descriptor from the clipboard but doesn't do anything with it. It is necessary to call this function prior to calling *DoPasteObject*.

DoPasteObject

This function calls *OleCreateFromData* to create an embedded object from an embedded object format on the clipboard.

The *CEx27bDoc* Class

This class implements the *IOleClientSite* and *IAdviseSink* interfaces. Because of our one-embedded-item-per-document simplification, we don't need to track separate site objects. The document is the site. We're using the standard MFC interface macros, and, as always, we must provide at least a skeleton function for all interface members.

Look carefully at the functions *XOleClientSite::SaveObject*, *XOleClientSite::OnShowWindow*, and *XAdviseSink::OnViewChange* in Figure 27-7. They're the important ones. All other functions have at least a *TRACE* statement so that you can see what functions the server or handler is trying to call. Look also at the *OnNewDocument*, *OnCloseDocument*, and *DeleteContents* functions. Notice how the document is managing a temporary storage. The document's *m_pTempStgSub* data member holds the storage pointer for the embedded object, and the *m_lpOleObj* data member holds the embedded object's *IOleObject* pointer.

EX27BDOC.H

```
void ITrace(REFIID iid, const char* str);

class CEx27bDoc : public CDocument
{
protected: // create from serialization only
    CEx27bDoc();
    DECLARE_DYNCREATE(CEx27bDoc)

    BEGIN_INTERFACE_PART(OleClientSite, IOleClientSite)
        STDMETHOD(SaveObject)();
        STDMETHOD(GetMoniker)(DWORD, DWORD, LPMONIKER*);
        STDMETHOD(GetContainer)(LPOLECONTAINER*);
        STDMETHOD(ShowObject)();
        STDMETHOD(OnShowWindow)(BOOL);
        STDMETHOD(RequestNewObjectLayout)();
    END_INTERFACE_PART(OleClientSite)

    BEGIN_INTERFACE_PART(AdviseSink, IAdviseSink)
        STDMETHOD_(void,OnDataChange)(LPFORMATETC, LPSTGMEDIUM);
        STDMETHOD_(void,OnViewChange)(DWORD, LONG);
        STDMETHOD_(void,OnRename)(LPMONIKER);
        STDMETHOD_(void,OnSave)();
        STDMETHOD_(void,OnClose)();
    END_INTERFACE_PART(AdviseSink)

    DECLARE_INTERFACE_MAP()

friend class CEx27bView;
private:
    LPOLEOBJECT m_lpOleObj;
    LPSTORAGE m_pTempStgRoot;
    LPSTORAGE m_pTempStgSub;
    BOOL m_bHatch;
    static const OLECHAR* s_szSub;
// Overrides
    // ClassWizard generated virtual function overrides
    //{{AFX_VIRTUAL(CEx27bDoc)
    public:
    virtual BOOL OnNewDocument();
    virtual void Serialize(CArchive& ar);
    virtual void OnCloseDocument();
    virtual void DeleteContents();
    //}}AFX_VIRTUAL
```

Figure 27-7.　　　　　　　　　　　　　　　　　　　　*(continued)*

The container's CEx27bDoc *class listing.*

Figure 27-7. *continued*

```
// Implementation
public:
    virtual ~CEx27bDoc();
#ifdef _DEBUG
    virtual void AssertValid() const;
    virtual void Dump(CDumpContext& dc) const;
#endif

protected:

// Generated message map functions
protected:
    //{{AFX_MSG(CEx27bDoc)
    afx_msg void OnEditClearAll();
    //}}AFX_MSG
    DECLARE_MESSAGE_MAP()
};
```

EX27BDOC.CPP

```
#include "StdAfx.h"
#include "ex27b.h"
#include "ex27bDoc.h"

#ifdef _DEBUG
#define new DEBUG_NEW
#undef THIS_FILE
static char THIS_FILE[] = __FILE__;
#endif
const OLECHAR* CEx27bDoc::s_szSub = L"sub";    // static

//////////////////////////////////////////////////////////////////////
// CEx27bDoc

IMPLEMENT_DYNCREATE(CEx27bDoc, CDocument)

BEGIN_MESSAGE_MAP(CEx27bDoc, CDocument)
    //{{AFX_MSG_MAP(CEx27bDoc)
    ON_COMMAND(ID_EDIT_CLEAR_ALL, OnEditClearAll)
    //}}AFX_MSG_MAP
END_MESSAGE_MAP()

BEGIN_INTERFACE_MAP(CEx27bDoc, CDocument)
  ·  INTERFACE_PART(CEx27bDoc, IID_IOleClientSite, OleClientSite)
     INTERFACE_PART(CEx27bDoc, IID_IAdviseSink, AdviseSink)
END_INTERFACE_MAP()
```

(continued)

Figure 27-7. *continued*

```
///////////////////////////////////////////////////////////////////
// Implementation of IOleClientSite

STDMETHODIMP_(ULONG) CEx27bDoc::XOleClientSite::AddRef()
{
    TRACE("CEx27bDoc::XOleClientSite::AddRef\n");
    METHOD_PROLOGUE(CEx27bDoc, OleClientSite)
    return pThis->InternalAddRef();
}


STDMETHODIMP_(ULONG) CEx27bDoc::XOleClientSite::Release()
{
    TRACE("CEx27bDoc::XOleClientSite::Release\n");
    METHOD_PROLOGUE(CEx27bDoc, OleClientSite)
    return pThis->InternalRelease();
}


STDMETHODIMP CEx27bDoc::XOleClientSite::QueryInterface(
                        REFIID iid, LPVOID* ppvObj)
{
    ITrace(iid, "CEx27bDoc::XOleClientSite::QueryInterface");
    METHOD_PROLOGUE(CEx27bDoc, OleClientSite)
    return pThis->InternalQueryInterface(&iid, ppvObj);
}


STDMETHODIMP CEx27bDoc::XOleClientSite::SaveObject()
{
    TRACE("CEx27bDoc::XOleClientSite::SaveObject\n");
    METHOD_PROLOGUE(CEx27bDoc, OleClientSite)
    ASSERT_VALID(pThis);

    LPPERSISTSTORAGE lpPersistStorage;
    pThis->m_lpOleObj->QueryInterface(IID_IPersistStorage,
                                (void**) &lpPersistStorage);
    ASSERT(lpPersistStorage != NULL);
    HRESULT hr = NOERROR;
    if (lpPersistStorage->IsDirty() == NOERROR) {
      // NOERROR == S_OK != S_FALSE, therefore object is dirty!
      hr = ::OleSave(lpPersistStorage, pThis->m_pTempStgSub, TRUE);
      if (hr != NOERROR)
        hr = lpPersistStorage->SaveCompleted(NULL);

      // mark the document as dirty, if save successful.
      pThis->SetModifiedFlag();
    }
    lpPersistStorage->Release();
```

(continued)

743

Figure 27-7. *continued*

```
    pThis->UpdateAllViews(NULL);
    return hr;
}


STDMETHODIMP CEx27bDoc::XOleClientSite::GetMoniker(
    DWORD dwAssign, DWORD dwWhichMoniker, LPMONIKER* ppMoniker)
{
    TRACE("CEx27bDoc::XOleClientSite::GetMoniker\n");
    return E_NOTIMPL;
}


STDMETHODIMP CEx27bDoc::XOleClientSite::GetContainer(
    LPOLECONTAINER* ppContainer)
{
    TRACE("CEx27bDoc::XOleClientSite::GetContainer\n");
    return E_NOTIMPL;
}


STDMETHODIMP CEx27bDoc::XOleClientSite::ShowObject()
{
    TRACE("CEx27bDoc::XOleClientSite::ShowObject\n");
    METHOD_PROLOGUE(CEx27bDoc, OleClientSite)
    ASSERT_VALID(pThis);
    pThis->UpdateAllViews(NULL);
    return NOERROR;
}


STDMETHODIMP CEx27bDoc::XOleClientSite::OnShowWindow(BOOL fShow)
{
    TRACE("CEx27bDoc::XOleClientSite::OnShowWindow\n");
    METHOD_PROLOGUE(CEx27bDoc, OleClientSite)
    ASSERT_VALID(pThis);
    pThis->m_bHatch = fShow;
    pThis->UpdateAllViews(NULL);
    return NOERROR;
}


STDMETHODIMP CEx27bDoc::XOleClientSite::RequestNewObjectLayout()
{
    TRACE("CEx27bDoc::XOleClientSite::RequestNewObjectLayout\n");
    return E_NOTIMPL;
}


/////////////////////////////////////////////////////////////////////
// Implementation of IAdviseSink
```

(continued)

Figure 27-7. *continued*

```
STDMETHODIMP_(ULONG) CEx27bDoc::XAdviseSink::AddRef()
{
    TRACE("CEx27bDoc::XAdviseSink::AddRef\n");
    METHOD_PROLOGUE(CEx27bDoc, AdviseSink)
    return pThis->InternalAddRef();
}


STDMETHODIMP_(ULONG) CEx27bDoc::XAdviseSink::Release()
{
    TRACE("CEx27bDoc::XAdviseSink::Release\n");
    METHOD_PROLOGUE(CEx27bDoc, AdviseSink)
    return pThis->InternalRelease();
}


STDMETHODIMP CEx27bDoc::XAdviseSink::QueryInterface(
                        REFIID iid, LPVOID* ppvObj)
{
    ITrace(iid, "CEx27bDoc::XAdviseSink::QueryInterface");
    METHOD_PROLOGUE(CEx27bDoc, AdviseSink)
    return pThis->InternalQueryInterface(&iid, ppvObj);
}


STDMETHODIMP_(void) CEx27bDoc::XAdviseSink::OnDataChange(
    LPFORMATETC lpFormatEtc, LPSTGMEDIUM lpStgMedium)
{
    TRACE("CEx27bDoc::XAdviseSink::OnDataChange\n");
    METHOD_PROLOGUE(CEx27bDoc, AdviseSink)
    ASSERT_VALID(pThis);

    // Only interesting for advanced containers. Forward it such that
    // containers do not have to implement the entire interface.
}


STDMETHODIMP_(void) CEx27bDoc::XAdviseSink::OnViewChange(
    DWORD aspects, LONG /*lindex*/)
{
    TRACE("CEx27bDoc::XAdviseSink::OnViewChange\n");
    METHOD_PROLOGUE(CEx27bDoc, AdviseSink)
    ASSERT_VALID(pThis);

    pThis->UpdateAllViews(NULL);    // the really important one
}


STDMETHODIMP_(void) CEx27bDoc::XAdviseSink::OnRename(
    LPMONIKER /*lpMoniker*/)
```

(continued)

745

Figure 27-7. *continued*

```
{
    TRACE("CEx27bDoc::XAdviseSink::OnRename\n");
    // only interesting to the OLE link object.
    // containers ignore this.
}


STDMETHODIMP_(void) CEx27bDoc::XAdviseSink::OnSave()
{
    TRACE("CEx27bDoc::XAdviseSink::OnSave\n");
    METHOD_PROLOGUE(CEx27bDoc, AdviseSink)
    ASSERT_VALID(pThis);
    pThis->UpdateAllViews(NULL);
}


STDMETHODIMP_(void) CEx27bDoc::XAdviseSink::OnClose()
{
    TRACE("CEx27bDoc::XAdviseSink::OnClose\n");
    METHOD_PROLOGUE(CEx27bDoc, AdviseSink)
    ASSERT_VALID(pThis);

    pThis->UpdateAllViews(NULL);
}


/////////////////////////////////////////////////////////////////////
// CEx27bDoc construction/destruction

CEx27bDoc::CEx27bDoc()
{
    m_lpOleObj = NULL;
    m_pTempStgRoot = NULL;
    m_pTempStgSub = NULL;
    m_bHatch = FALSE;
}


CEx27bDoc::~CEx27bDoc()
{
}


BOOL CEx27bDoc::OnNewDocument()
{
    TRACE("Entering CEx27bDoc::OnNewDocument\n");
// create a structured storage home for the object (m_pTempStgSub)
// this is a temporary file -- random name supplied by OLE
    VERIFY(::StgCreateDocfile(NULL,
            STGM_READWRITE | STGM_SHARE_EXCLUSIVE |
            STGM_CREATE | STGM_DELETEONRELEASE,
```

(continued)

Figure 27-7. *continued*

```
            0, &m_pTempStgRoot) == S_OK);
    ASSERT(m_pTempStgRoot!= NULL);

    VERIFY(m_pTempStgRoot->CreateStorage(OLESTR("sub"),
            STGM_CREATE | STGM_READWRITE | STGM_SHARE_EXCLUSIVE,
            0, 0, &m_pTempStgSub) == S_OK);
    ASSERT(m_pTempStgSub!= NULL);
    return CDocument::OnNewDocument();
}


/////////////////////////////////////////////////////////////////////
// CEx27bDoc serialization

void CEx27bDoc::Serialize(CArchive& ar)
{
    // no hookup to MFC serialization
    if (ar.IsStoring())
    {
        // TODO: add storing code here
    }
    else
    {
        // TODO: add loading code here
    }
}


/////////////////////////////////////////////////////////////////////
// CEx27bDoc diagnostics

#ifdef _DEBUG
void CEx27bDoc::AssertValid() const
{
    CDocument::AssertValid();
}

void CEx27bDoc::Dump(CDumpContext& dc) const
{
    CDocument::Dump(dc);
}
#endif //_DEBUG


/////////////////////////////////////////////////////////////////////
// CEx27bDoc commands

void CEx27bDoc::OnCloseDocument()
```

(continued)

Figure 27-7. *continued*

```
{
    m_pTempStgSub->Release(); // must release BEFORE calling
                              //  base class
    m_pTempStgRoot->Release();
    CDocument::OnCloseDocument();
}


void CEx27bDoc::DeleteContents()
{
    if (m_lpOleObj != NULL) {
      // if object is running, close it, which
      //  releases our IOleClientSite
      m_lpOleObj->Close(OLECLOSE_NOSAVE);
      m_lpOleObj->Release(); // should be final release (or else...)
      m_lpOleObj = NULL;
    }
}


void CEx27bDoc::OnEditClearAll()
{
    DeleteContents();
    UpdateAllViews(NULL);
    SetModifiedFlag();
    m_bHatch = FALSE;
}


void ITrace(REFIID iid, const char* str)
{
    OLECHAR* lpszIID;
    ::StringFromIID(iid, &lpszIID);
    CString strIID = lpszIID;
    TRACE("%s - %s\n", (const char*) strIID, (const char*) str);
    AfxFreeTaskMem(lpszIID);
}
```

The EX27C Example—An OLE Embedded Server

You've already seen an MFC embedded server with in-place–activation capability (EX27A). Now you'll see a bare-bones server program that activates an embedded object in a separate window. It doesn't do much except display text and graphics in the window, but you'll learn a lot if you study the code. The application started as an SDI AppWizard OLE Automation server with the document as the OLE-creatable object. The document's *IDispatch* interface was ripped out and replaced with *IOleObject*, *IDataObject*, and *IPersist-*

Storage interfaces. All the template server code carries through, so the document, view, and main frame objects get created when the container starts the server.

Open and build the EX27C project now. Run the application once to register it, and then try it with the EX27B container or any other container program.

The *CEx27cView* Class

This class is straightforward. The only member functions of interest are the *OnDraw* function and the *OnPrepareDC* function, as shown here:

```
void CEx27cView::OnDraw(CDC* pDC)
{
    CEx27cDoc* pDoc = GetDocument();
    ASSERT_VALID(pDoc);
    pDC->Rectangle(CRect(500, -1000, 1500, -2000));
    pDC->TextOut(0, 0, pDoc->m_strText);
}
void CEx27cView::OnPrepareDC(CDC* pDC, CPrintInfo* pInfo)
{
    pDC->SetMapMode(MM_HIMETRIC);
}
```

The *CEx27cDoc* Class

This class does most of the server's work and is too big to list here. Figure 27-8 lists the header file, but you'll have to go to the companion CD-ROM for the implementation code. A few of the important functions are listed here, however.

EX27CDOC.H

```
extern const CLSID clsid; // defined in ex27c.cpp
void ITrace(REFIID iid, const char* str);

#define SETFORMATETC(fe, cf, asp, td, med, li)  \
    ((fe).cfFormat=cf, \
     (fe).dwAspect=asp, \
     (fe).ptd=td, \
     (fe).tymed=med, \
     (fe).lindex=li)

class CEx27cDoc : public CDocument
{
friend class CEx27cView;
```

Figure 27-8. *(continued)*

The server's CEx27cDoc *class header file listing.*

Figure 27-8. *continued*

```
private:
    CString m_strText;
    LPOLECLIENTSITE m_lpClientSite;
    LPOLEADVISEHOLDER m_lpOleAdviseHolder;
    LPDATAADVISEHOLDER m_lpDataAdviseHolder;
    CString m_strContainerApp;
    CString m_strContainerObj;
    HGLOBAL MakeMetaFile();

    BEGIN_INTERFACE_PART(OleObject, IOleObject)
        STDMETHOD(SetClientSite)(LPOLECLIENTSITE);
        STDMETHOD(GetClientSite)(LPOLECLIENTSITE*);
        STDMETHOD(SetHostNames)(LPCOLESTR, LPCOLESTR);
        STDMETHOD(Close)(DWORD);
        STDMETHOD(SetMoniker)(DWORD, LPMONIKER);
        STDMETHOD(GetMoniker)(DWORD, DWORD, LPMONIKER*);
        STDMETHOD(InitFromData)(LPDATAOBJECT, BOOL, DWORD);
        STDMETHOD(GetClipboardData)(DWORD, LPDATAOBJECT*);
        STDMETHOD(DoVerb)(LONG, LPMSG, LPOLECLIENTSITE,
                          LONG, HWND, LPCRECT);
        STDMETHOD(EnumVerbs)(LPENUMOLEVERB*);
        STDMETHOD(Update)();
        STDMETHOD(IsUpToDate)();
        STDMETHOD(GetUserClassID)(LPCLSID);
        STDMETHOD(GetUserType)(DWORD, LPOLESTR*);
        STDMETHOD(SetExtent)(DWORD, LPSIZEL);
        STDMETHOD(GetExtent)(DWORD, LPSIZEL);
        STDMETHOD(Advise)(LPADVISESINK, LPDWORD);
        STDMETHOD(Unadvise)(DWORD);
        STDMETHOD(EnumAdvise)(LPENUMSTATDATA*);
        STDMETHOD(GetMiscStatus)(DWORD, LPDWORD);
        STDMETHOD(SetColorScheme)(LPLOGPALETTE);
    END_INTERFACE_PART(OleObject)

    BEGIN_INTERFACE_PART(DataObject, IDataObject)
        STDMETHOD(GetData)(LPFORMATETC, LPSTGMEDIUM);
        STDMETHOD(GetDataHere)(LPFORMATETC, LPSTGMEDIUM);
        STDMETHOD(QueryGetData)(LPFORMATETC);
        STDMETHOD(GetCanonicalFormatEtc)(LPFORMATETC, LPFORMATETC);
        STDMETHOD(SetData)(LPFORMATETC, LPSTGMEDIUM, BOOL);
        STDMETHOD(EnumFormatEtc)(DWORD, LPENUMFORMATETC*);
        STDMETHOD(DAdvise)(LPFORMATETC, DWORD, LPADVISESINK, LPDWORD);
        STDMETHOD(DUnadvise)(DWORD);
        STDMETHOD(EnumDAdvise)(LPENUMSTATDATA*);
    END_INTERFACE_PART(DataObject)
```

(continued)

Figure 27-8. *continued*

```
    BEGIN_INTERFACE_PART(PersistStorage, IPersistStorage)
        STDMETHOD(GetClassID)(LPCLSID);
        STDMETHOD(IsDirty)();
        STDMETHOD(InitNew)(LPSTORAGE);
        STDMETHOD(Load)(LPSTORAGE);
        STDMETHOD(Save)(LPSTORAGE, BOOL);
        STDMETHOD(SaveCompleted)(LPSTORAGE);
        STDMETHOD(HandsOffStorage)();
    END_INTERFACE_PART(PersistStorage)

    DECLARE_INTERFACE_MAP()

protected: // create from serialization only
    CEx27cDoc();
    DECLARE_DYNCREATE(CEx27cDoc)

// Overrides
    // ClassWizard generated virtual function overrides
    //{{AFX_VIRTUAL(CEx27cDoc)
    public:
    virtual BOOL OnNewDocument();
    virtual void Serialize(CArchive& ar);
    virtual void OnFinalRelease();
    virtual void OnCloseDocument();
    //}}AFX_VIRTUAL

// Implementation
public:
    virtual ~CEx27cDoc();
#ifdef _DEBUG
    virtual void AssertValid() const;
    virtual void Dump(CDumpContext& dc) const;
#endif

// Generated message map functions
protected:
    //{{AFX_MSG(CEx27cDoc)
    afx_msg void OnModify();
    afx_msg void OnFileUpdate();
    afx_msg void OnUpdateFileUpdate(CCmdUI* pCmdUI);
    afx_msg void OnAppExit();
    //}}AFX_MSG
    DECLARE_MESSAGE_MAP()
};
```

Here's a list of the important interface functions in ex27cDoc.cpp:

XOleObject::SetClientSite

XOleObject::DoVerb

XOleObject::Advise

XDataObject::GetData

XDataObject::QueryGetData

XDataObject::DAdvise

XPersistStorage::GetClassID

XPersistStorage::InitNew

XPersistStorage::Load

XPersistStorage::Save

You've seen the container code that draws a metafile. Now here's the server code that creates it. The object handler calls the server's *IDataObject- ::GetData* when it needs a metafile. This *GetData* implementation calls a helper function *MakeMetaFile*, which creates the metafile picture. Compare the drawing code with the drawing code in *CEx27cView::OnDraw*.

```
STDMETHODIMP CEx27cDoc::XDataObject::GetData(
    LPFORMATETC lpFormatEtc, LPSTGMEDIUM lpStgMedium)
{
    TRACE("CEx27cDoc::XDataObject::GetData -- %d\n",
        lpFormatEtc->cfFormat);
    METHOD_PROLOGUE(CEx27cDoc, DataObject)
    ASSERT_VALID(pThis);

    if (lpFormatEtc->cfFormat != CF_METAFILEPICT) {
      return S_FALSE;
    }
    HGLOBAL hPict = pThis->MakeMetaFile();
    lpStgMedium->tymed = TYMED_MFPICT;
    lpStgMedium->hMetaFilePict = hPict;
    lpStgMedium->pUnkForRelease = NULL;
    return S_OK;
}

HGLOBAL CEx27cDoc::MakeMetaFile()
{
    HGLOBAL hPict;
    CMetaFileDC dcm;
    VERIFY(dcm.Create());
    CSize size(5000, 5000); // initial size of object in Excel & Word
```

```
dcm.SetMapMode(MM_ANISOTROPIC);
dcm.SetWindowOrg(0,0);
dcm.SetWindowExt(size.cx, -size.cy);
// drawing code
dcm.Rectangle(CRect(500, -1000, 1500, -2000));
dcm.TextOut(0, 0, m_strText);
//
HMETAFILE hMF = dcm.Close();
ASSERT(hMF != NULL);
hPict = ::GlobalAlloc(GMEM_SHARE | GMEM_MOVEABLE,
                      sizeof(METAFILEPICT));
ASSERT(hPict != NULL);
LPMETAFILEPICT lpPict;
lpPict = (LPMETAFILEPICT) ::GlobalLock(hPict);
ASSERT(lpPict != NULL);
lpPict->mm = MM_ANISOTROPIC;
lpPict->hMF = hMF;
lpPict->xExt = size.cx;
lpPict->yExt = size.cy;   // HIMETRIC height
::GlobalUnlock(hPict);
return hPict;
}
```

The *XOleObject::Advise* and *XDataObject::DAdvise* functions are similar. Both call global OLE functions to set up OLE advise holder objects that can manage multiple advise sinks. (In this program, there's only one advise sink per OLE advise holder object.) The *XOleObject::Advise* function, listed below, establishes an OLE advise holder object with the *IOleAdviseHolder* interface. Other document functions call *IOleAdviseHolder::SendOnClose* and *SendOn-Save*, which in turn call *IAdviseSink::OnClose* and *OnSave* for each attached sink.

```
STDMETHODIMP CEx27cDoc::XOleObject::Advise(
    IAdviseSink* pAdvSink, DWORD* pdwConnection)
{
    TRACE("CEx27cDoc::XOleObject::Advise\n");
    METHOD_PROLOGUE(CEx27cDoc, OleObject)
    ASSERT_VALID(pThis);
    *pdwConnection = 0;
    if (pThis->m_lpOleAdviseHolder == NULL &&
      ::CreateOleAdviseHolder(&pThis->m_lpOleAdviseHolder) != NOERROR) {
      return E_OUTOFMEMORY;
    }
    ASSERT(pThis->m_lpOleAdviseHolder != NULL);
    return pThis->m_lpOleAdviseHolder->Advise(pAdvSink, pdwConnection);
}
```

The framework calls the *OnModify* function when the user chooses Modify from the EX27C-MAIN menu. The user enters a string through a dialog, and the function sends the *OnDataChange* notification to the object handler's data advise sink. (Figure 27-5 on page 720 illustrates the advisory connections.) Here is the *OnModify* function code:

```
void CEx27cDoc::OnModify()
{
    CTextDialog dlg;
    dlg.m_strText = m_strText;
    if (dlg.DoModal() == IDOK) {
      m_strText = dlg.m_strText;
      UpdateAllViews(NULL); // redraw view
      // notify the client the metafile has changed
      // client must call IViewObject::SetAdvise
      LPDATAOBJECT lpDataObject = (LPDATAOBJECT)
          GetInterface(&IID_IDataObject);
      HRESULT hr =
          m_lpDataAdviseHolder->SendOnDataChange(lpDataObject, 0, NULL);
      ASSERT(hr == NOERROR);
      SetModifiedFlag(); // won't update without this
    }
}
```

The framework calls the *OnFileUpdate* function when the user chooses Update from the File menu. The function calls *IOleClientSite::SaveObject*, which in turn causes the container to save the metafile and the object's native data in the storage. The function also sends the *OnSave* notification back to the client's advise sink. Here is the *OnFileUpdate* function code:

```
void CEx27cDoc::OnFileUpdate()
{
    if (m_lpClientSite == NULL) return;
    VERIFY(m_lpClientSite->SaveObject() == NOERROR);
    if (m_lpOleAdviseHolder != NULL)
      m_lpOleAdviseHolder->SendOnSave();
    SetModifiedFlag(FALSE);
}
```

DATABASE
MANAGEMENT

Database Management with Microsoft ODBC

Microcomputers became popular, in part, because businesspeople saw them as a low-cost means of tracking inventory, processing orders, printing payroll checks, and so forth. These applications required fast access to individual records in a large database. One of the first microcomputer database tools was dBASE II, a single-user product with its own programming language and file format. Today Microsoft Windows programmers have a wide choice of programmable database management systems (DBMS's), including Powersoft PowerBuilder, Borland Paradox, Microsoft Access, and Microsoft FoxPro. Most of these products can access both local data and remote data on a central computer. The latter case requires the addition of database server software such as ORACLE or Microsoft SQL Server.

How do you, as an MFC programmer, fit into the picture? Visual C++ contains all the components you'll need to write C++ database applications for Windows. Indeed, the product contains two separate database access systems: ODBC (Open Database Connectivity) and DAO (Data Access Objects). This chapter covers the ODBC standard, which consists of an extensible set of dynamic link libraries (DLLs) that provide a standard database application programming interface. ODBC is based on a standardized version of SQL (Structured Query Language). With ODBC and SQL, you can write database access code that is independent of any database product.

Visual C++ includes tools and MFC classes for ODBC, and that's the subject of this chapter. You'll learn the basics of ODBC, and you'll see three sample programs—one that uses the ODBC rowset with support from the MFC *CRecordset* class, one that uses the MFC *CRecordView* class, and one that uses multiple recordsets.

The Advantages of Database Management

The serialization process, introduced in Chapters 16 and 17, ties a document object to a disk file. All the document's data must be read into memory when the document is opened, and all the data must be written back to disk when an updated document is closed. Obviously, you can't serialize a document that's bigger than the available virtual memory. Even if the document is small enough to fit in memory, you might not need to read and write all the data every time the program runs.

You could, of course, program your own random access disk file, thus inventing your own DBMS, but you probably have enough other work to do. Besides, using a real DBMS gives you many advantages, including the following:

- **Use of standard file formats**—Many people think of dBASE/Xbase DBF files when they think of database formats. This is only one database file format, but it's a popular one. A lot of data is distributed in DBF files, and many programs can read and write in this format. Lately the Microsoft Access MDB format has become popular too. With the MDB format, all of a database's tables and indexes can be contained in a single disk file.

- **Indexed file access**—If you need quick access to records by key (a customer name, for example), you need indexed file access. You could always write your own B-tree file access routines, but that's a tedious job that's been done already. All DBMS's contain efficient indexed access routines.

- **Data integrity safeguards**—Many professional DBMS products have procedures for protecting their data. One example is transaction processing. A transaction encompasses a series of related changes. If the entire transaction can't be processed, it is rolled back so that the database reverts to its original state before the transaction.

- **Multiuser access control**—If your application doesn't need multiuser access now, it might in the future. Most DBMS's provide record locking to prevent interference among simultaneous users. Some multiuser DBMS's use the client–server model, which means that most processing is handled on a single database server computer; the workstations handle the user interface. Other multiuser DBMS's handle database processing on the workstations, and they control each workstation's access to shared files.

SQL

You could not have worked in the software field without at least hearing about SQL, a standard database access language with its own grammar. In the SQL world, a database is a collection of tables that consist of rows and columns. Many DBMS products support SQL, and many programmers know SQL. The SQL standard is continually evolving, and SQL grammar varies among products. SQL extensions, such as <u>blob</u> (binary large object) capability, allow storage of pictures, sound, and complex data structures.

The ODBC Standard

The Microsoft Open Database Connectivity (ODBC) standard defines not only the rules of SQL grammar but also the C-language programming interface to an SQL database. It's now possible for a single compiled C or C++ program to access any DBMS that has an ODBC driver. The ODBC Software Development Kit (SDK), included with Visual C++, contains 32-bit drivers for DBF files, Microsoft Access MDB databases, Microsoft Excel XLS files, Microsoft FoxPro files, ASCII text files, and Microsoft SQL Server databases.

Other database companies, including Oracle, Informix, Progress, Ingres, and Gupta, provide ODBC drivers for their own DBMS's. If you develop an MFC program with the dBASE/Xbase driver, for example, you can run the same program with an Access database driver. No recompilation is necessary—the program simply loads a different DLL.

Not only can C++ programs use ODBC, but other DBMS programming environments can also take advantage of this new standard. You could write a C++ program to update an SQL Server database, and then you could use an off-the-shelf ODBC-compatible report writer to format and print the data. ODBC thus separates the user interface from the actual database management process. You no longer have to buy your interface tools from the same company that supplies the database engine.

Some people have criticized ODBC because it doesn't let programmers take advantage of the special features of some particular DBMS. Well, that's the whole point! Programmers need learn only one application programming interface (API), and they can choose their software components based on price, performance, and support. No longer will developers be locked into buying all their tools from their database supplier.

What's the future of ODBC? That's a difficult question. Microsoft is driving the standard, but it isn't actually "selling" ODBC; it's giving ODBC away for the purpose of promoting other products. Another company, Q+E Software, is supporting ODBC along with its own proprietary multi-DBMS access library. Q+E sells ODBC drivers, which it claims have a performance advantage over Microsoft's "free" drivers. Meanwhile, Microsoft has introduced OLE-based Data Access Objects (DAO), which relies on the Jet database engine from Microsoft Access. Chapter 29 describes DAO and compares its features with the features of ODBC.

The ODBC Architecture

ODBC has a unique DLL-based architecture that makes the system fully modular. A small top-level DLL, ODBC32.DLL, defines the API. ODBC32.DLL calls database-specific DLLs, known as <u>drivers</u>, during program execution. With the help of the Windows registry (maintained by the ODBC Administrator module in the Windows Control Panel), ODBC32.DLL tracks which database-specific DLLs are available and thus allows a single program to access data in several DBMS's simultaneously. A program could, for example, keep some local tables in DBF format and use other tables controlled by a database server. Figure 28-1 shows the 32-bit ODBC DLL hierarchy.

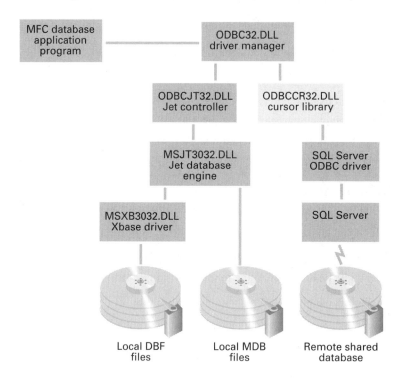

Figure 28-1.
32-bit ODBC architecture.

Note from Figure 28-1 that many standard database formats can be accessed through the Microsoft Access Jet database engine, which is a redistributable module packaged with Visual C++. If, for example, you access a DBF file through the Jet engine, you're using the same code that Microsoft Access uses.

ODBC SDK Programming

If you program directly at the ODBC C-language API level, you must know about three important ODBC elements: the environment, the connection, and the statement. All three are accessed through handles. First you need an environment, which establishes the link between your program and the ODBC system. An application usually has only one environment handle.

Next you need one or more connections. The connection references a specific driver and data source combination. You might have several connections to subdirectories that contain DBF files, and you might have connections to several SQL Servers on the same network. A specific ODBC connection can be hardwired into a program, or the user can be allowed to choose from a list of available drivers and data sources.

ODBC32.DLL has a built-in Windows dialog that lists the connections that are defined in the registry (under HKEY_USERS\Software\ODBC). Once you have a connection, you need an SQL statement to execute. The statement might be a query, such as this:

```
SELECT FNAME, LNAME, CITY FROM AUTHORS
WHERE STATE = 'UT' ORDER BY LNAME
```

Or the statement could be an update statement, such as this:

```
UPDATE AUTHORS SET PHONE = '801 232-5780'
WHERE ID = '357-86-4343'
```

Because query statements need a program loop to process the returned rows, your program might need several statements active at the same time. Many ODBC drivers allow multiple active statement handles per connection.

Look again at the SQL statement above. Suppose there were 10 authors in Utah. ODBC lets you define the query result as a block of data called a <u>rowset</u>, which is associated with an SQL statement. Through the ODBC SDK function *SQLExtendedFetch*, your program can move through the 10 selected records, forward and backward, by means of an ODBC cursor. This cursor is a programmable pointer into the rowset.

What if, in a multiuser situation, another program modified (or deleted) a Utah author record while your program was stepping through the rowset? With an ODBC Level 2 driver, the rowset would probably be dynamic, and ODBC could update the rowset whenever the database changed. A dynamic rowset is called a <u>dynaset</u>. The Jet engine supports ODBC Level 2, and thus it supports dynasets.

> NOTE: If another user <u>adds</u> a record to a table that underlies your dynaset, the new record will not appear in your dynaset. Deleted records remain in the dynaset but are flagged as deleted.

Visual C++ includes the ODBC cursor library module ODBCCR32.DLL, which supports static rowsets (called <u>snapshots</u>) for Level 1 drivers. With a snapshot, a *SELECT* statement causes ODBC to make what amounts to a local copy of the 10 author records and build an in-memory list of pointers to those records. These records are guaranteed not to change once you've scrolled into them, so in a multiuser situation you might need to requery the database periodically to rebuild the snapshot.

The MFC ODBC Classes— *CRecordset* and *CDatabase*

With the MFC classes for Windows, you use C++ objects instead of window handles and device context handles; with the MFC ODBC classes, you use objects instead of connection handles and statement handles. The environment handle is stored in a global variable and is not represented by a C++ object. The two principal ODBC classes are *CDatabase* and *CRecordset*. Objects of class *CDatabase* represent ODBC connections to data sources, and objects of class *CRecordset* represent scrollable rowsets (usually snapshots). The Visual C++ documentation uses the term "recordset" instead of "rowset" to be consistent with Microsoft Visual Basic and Microsoft Access. You seldom derive classes from *CDatabase*, but you always derive classes from *CRecordset* to match the columns in your database tables.

For the author query on page 761, you would derive (with the help of ClassWizard) a *CAuthorSet* class from *CRecordset* that had data members for first name, last name, city, state, and zip code. Your program would construct a *CAuthorSet* object (typically embedded in the document) and call its inherited *Open* member function. Using the values of parameters and data members, *CRecordset::Open* constructs and opens a *CDatabase* object; it issues an SQL *SELECT* statement and then moves to the first record. Your program would then call other *CRecordset* member functions to position the ODBC cursor and exchange data between the database fields and the *CAuthorSet* data members. When the *CAuthorSet* object is deleted, the recordset is closed, and, under certain conditions, the database is closed and deleted. Figure 28-2 shows the relationships between the C++ objects and ODBC components.

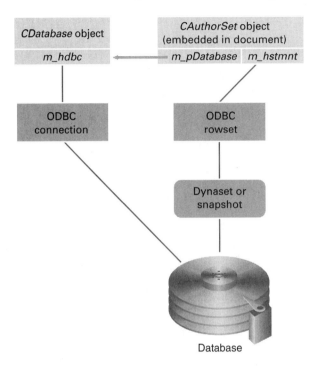

Figure 28-2.
MFC ODBC class database relationships.

It's important to recognize that the *CAuthorSet* object contains data members that represent only one row in a table, the so-called "current record." The *CRecordset* class, together with the underlying ODBC rowset code, manages the database dynaset or snapshot.

NOTE: It's possible to have several active dynasets or snapshots per data source, and you can use multiple data sources within the same program.

The Student Registration Database

The Visual C++ ODBC Tutorial uses a ready-made sample Access database (STDREG32.MDB) that tracks students, classes, and instructors. Figure 28-3 on the following page shows the five database tables and the relationships among them. The boldfaced fields are indexed fields, and the 1–∞ relationships represent <u>referential</u> <u>integrity</u> constraints. If there's at least one section for course MATH101, for example, Access prevents the user from deleting the MATH101 course record.

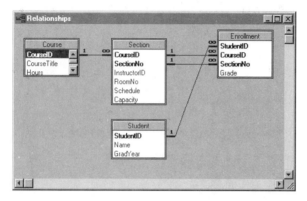

Figure 28-3.
The Student registration database schema.

The EX28A Recordset Example

You can use AppWizard to generate a complete forms-oriented database application, and that's what the Books Online ODBC Tutorial is all about. If customers or users wanted a straightforward business database application like that, however, they probably wouldn't call in a Visual C++ programmer; instead, they might use a less technical tool, such as Microsoft Access. Visual C++ and the MFC ODBC classes are more appropriate for a complex application that might have an incidental need for database access. You can also use the classes to make your own general-purpose database query tool.

The EX28A program isolates the database access code from user interface code so that you can see how to add ODBC database capability to any MFC application. You'll be using ClassWizard to generate a *CRecordset* class, but you won't be using the *CRecordView* class that AppWizard generates when you ask for a database view application.

The application is fairly simple. It displays the rows from the student database table in a scrolling view, as shown in the screen on page 770. The student table is part of the Student Registration (Microsoft Access version 7.0) sample database that's included with Visual C++.

Here are the steps for building the EX28A example:

1. Copy the Student Registration database to your hard disk. You can find the file stdreg32.mdb in the \MSDEV\SAMPLES\MFC\DATA-BASE\STDREG directory on the Visual C++ CD-ROM. Copy it to a new \STDREG directory on your hard disk.

2. Run the ODBC Administrator to install the Student Registration data source. Click the 32-bit ODBC icon in the Windows Control Panel. The Visual C++ Setup program should have already installed the required ODBC drivers on your hard disk. Click the Drivers button to see whether the Microsoft Access driver is available. (If not, rerun Visual C++ Setup.) Click the Add button, choose Microsoft Access Driver in the Add Data Source dialog, and fill in the ODBC Microsoft Access 7.0 Setup dialog as shown here:

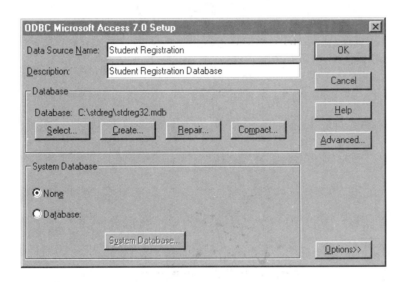

NOTE: If you're using Visual C++ under Windows NT version 3.51, look for the ODBC icon (not 32-bit ODBC) in the Control Panel.

3. Run AppWizard to produce \VCPP32\EX28A\EX28A. Specify an SDI application with *CScrollView* as the view's class type. Select the Header Files Only option from the AppWizard Step 2 dialog, as shown at the top of the following page:

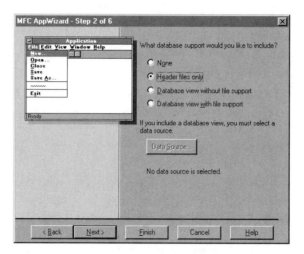

4. Use ClassWizard to create the *CEx28aSet* recordset class. Click the Add Class button, and then fill in the Create New Class dialog as shown here:

5. Select the Student Registration database's Student table for the *CEx28aSet* class. When you click the Create button in the Create New Class dialog, ClassWizard displays the Database Options dialog. Select the Student Registration data source and check the Dynaset option, as shown here:

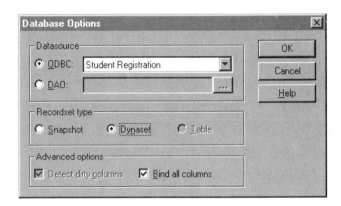

After you select the data source, ClassWizard prompts you to select a table. Select Student, as shown here:

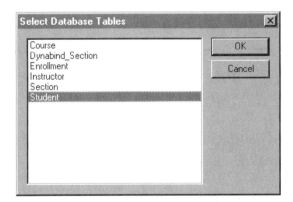

6. Examine the data members that ClassWizard generates. Click on the Member Variables tab for the newly generated *CEx28aSet* class. ClassWizard should have generated data members based on student column names, as shown on the following page:

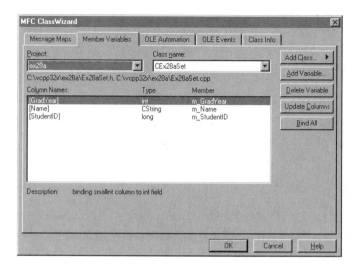

7. Declare an embedded recordset object in ex28aDoc.h. Add the following public data member in the *CEx28aDoc* class declaration:

```
CEx28aSet m_ex28aSet;
```

8. Edit the ex28aDoc.cpp file. Add the line

```
#include "ex28aSet.h"
```

just before the line

```
#include "ex28aDoc.h"
```

9. Declare a recordset pointer in ex28aView.h. Add the following private data member in the *CEx28aView* class declaration:

```
CEx28aSet* m_pSet;
```

10. Edit the *OnDraw* and *OnInitialUpdate* functions in ex28aView.cpp. Add the following shaded code:

```
void CEx28aView::OnDraw(CDC* pDC)
{
    int  y = 0;
    CString str;
```

```
    if (m_pSet->IsEOF()) { // detects empty recordset
      return;
    }
    m_pSet->MoveFirst();   // fails if recordset is empty
    while (!m_pSet->IsEOF()) {
      str.Format("%ld", m_pSet->m_StudentID);
      pDC->TextOut(0, y, str);
      pDC->TextOut(500, y, m_pSet->m_Name);
      str.Format("%d", m_pSet->m_GradYear);
      pDC->TextOut(2500, y, str);
      m_pSet->MoveNext();
      y -= 200;  // 0.2 inch down
    }
}
```

```
void CEx28aView::OnInitialUpdate()
{
    CScrollView::OnInitialUpdate();
    CSize sizeTotal(8000, 10500);

    SetScrollSizes(MM_HIENGLISH, sizeTotal);

    m_pSet = &GetDocument()->m_ex28aSet;
    // remember that documents/views are reused in SDI applications!
    if (m_pSet->IsOpen()) {
    m_pSet->Close();
    }
    m_pSet->Open();
}
```

Also in ex28aView.cpp, add the line

```
#include "ex28aSet.h"
```

just before the line

```
#include "ex28aDoc.h"
```

11. Edit the ex28a.cpp file.   Add the line

```
#include "ex28aSet.h"
```

just before the line

```
#include "ex28aDoc.h"
```

12. Build and test the EX28A application. Does the resulting screen look like the one shown here?

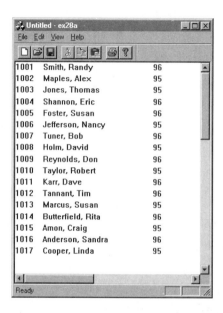

Adding ODBC Capability to an MFC Application

If you need to add ODBC capability to an existing MFC application, make the following changes to the project:

1. Add the following line at the end of StdAfx.h:

   ```
   #include <afxdb.h>
   ```

2. Edit the RC file in text mode. (Use Notepad or some other program.) After the line

   ```
   "#include ""afxprint.rc""" // printing/print preview\
   resources\r\n"
   ```

   add the line

   ```
   "#include ""afxdb.rc""    // database resources\r\n"
   ```

   And after the line

   ```
   #include "afxprint.rc"    // printing/print preview resources
   ```

   add the line

   ```
   #include "afxdb.rc"       // database resources
   ```

The EX28A Program Elements

The following is a discussion of the major elements in the EX28A program.

Connecting the Recordset Class to the Application

When ClassWizard generates the *CEx28aSet* class, it adds the CPP file to the project—and that's all it does. It's up to you to link the recordset to your view and to your document. By embedding a *CEx28aSet* object inside the *CEx28a-Doc* class, you ensure that the recordset object will be constructed when the application starts.

The view could always get the recordset via the document, but it's more efficient if the view keeps its own recordset pointer. Notice how the view's *OnInitialUpdate* function sets the *m_pSet* data member.

> NOTE: If you run AppWizard with either of the Database View options, AppWizard generates a class derived from *CRecordset*, a class derived from *CRecordView*, and all the necessary linkage as just described. We're not using AppWizard in this mode because we don't want a form-based application.

The *CEx28aView* Class's *OnInitialUpdate* Member Function

The job of the *OnInitialUpdate* function is to open the recordset that's associated with the view. The recordset constructor was called with a NULL database pointer parameter, so the *CRecordset::Open* function knows it must construct a *CDatabase* object and link that database one to one with the recordset. But how does *Open* know what data source and table to use? It calls two *CRecordset* virtual functions, *GetDefaultConnect* and *GetDefaultSQL*. Class-Wizard generates implementations of these functions in your derived recordset class, as shown here:

```
CString CEx28aSet::GetDefaultConnect()
{
    return _T("ODBC;DSN=Student Registration");
}

CString CEx28aSet::GetDefaultSQL()
{
    return _T("[Student]");
}
```

> NOTE: ClassWizard and AppWizard place brackets around all column and table [names]. These brackets are necessary only if the names contain embedded blanks.

GetDefaultSQL is a pure virtual function, so the derived class must implement it. *GetDefaultConnect,* on the other hand, has a base class implementation that opens an ODBC dialog, which in turn prompts the user for the data source name.

Because documents are reused in SDI applications, the *OnInitialUpdate* function must close any open recordset before it opens a new recordset. The *IsOpen* member function makes the test.

The *CEx28aView* Class's *OnDraw* Member Function

As in any document–view application, the *OnDraw* function is called every time the view is invalidated and once for every printed page. Here *OnDraw* inefficiently slogs through every row in the recordset and paints its column values with the *CDC::TextOut* function. The principal *CRecordset* member functions it calls are *MoveFirst* and *MoveNext. MoveFirst* will fail if the recordset is empty, so the initial call to *IsBOF* is necessary to detect the beginning-of-file condition. The *IsEOF* call detects the end-of-file condition for the recordset and terminates the row loop.

Remember that ClassWizard generated *CEx28aSet* class data members for the recordset's columns. This means that the recordset class, and now the view class, are both hard-coded for the student record. The *CRecordset* member functions call a pure virtual function, *DoFieldExchange,* that ClassWizard generates based on the data members *m_StudentID, m_Name,* and *m_GradYear.* Here is the code for this example's derived recordset class:

```
void CEx28aSet::DoFieldExchange(CFieldExchange* pFX)
{
    //{{AFX_FIELD_MAP(CEx28aSet)
    pFX->SetFieldType(CFieldExchange::outputColumn);
    RFX_Long(pFX, _T("[StudentID]"), m_StudentID);
    RFX_Text(pFX, _T("[Name]"), m_Name);
    RFX_Int(pFX, _T("[GradYear]"), m_GradYear);
    //}}AFX_FIELD_MAP
}
```

Each SQL data type has a record field exchange (*RFX*) function. These functions are quite complex and are called many times during database processing. You might first think, as I did, that the *RFX* functions are like the *CDialog DDX* functions and thus actually transfer data between the database and the data members. This is not the case. The primary purpose of the *RFX* functions is to "bind" the database columns to the data members so that the underlying ODBC functions, such as *SQLExtendedFetch,* can transfer the column data. To this end, the *DoFieldExchange* function is called from *CRecordSet::Open*. *DoFieldExchange* is also called by the *Move* functions for the purpose of reallocating strings and clearing status bits.

Because the *DoFieldExchange* function is so tightly integrated with MFC database processing, you are advised not to call this function directly in your programs.

Filter and Sort Strings

SQL query statements can have an ORDER BY clause and a WHERE clause. The *CRecordset* class has a public data member *m_strSort* that holds the text of the ORDER BY clause (excluding the words "ORDER BY"). Another public data member, *m_strFilter*, holds the text of the WHERE clause (excluding the word "WHERE"). You can set the values of these strings prior to opening the recordset.

Joining Two Database Tables

Most database programmers know that a join is one big logical table composed of fields from two or more related tables. In the Student Registration database, you could join the Student table with the Enrollment table to get a list of students and the classes they were enrolled in.

Joins are easy to do with Visual C++ because ClassWizard lets you add tables to an existing recordset. There are a few additional programming tasks, though. Here are the steps for joining the Enrollment table to the Student table in EX28A.

1. Use ClassWizard to access the *CEx28aSet* class. Click the Update Columns button, and then select the Enrollment table from the Student Registration database. Click the Bind All button to add the data members for the Enrollment fields.

2. Edit the *CEx28aSet::GetDefaultSQL* function to access two tables:

```
CString CEx28aSet::GetDefaultSQL()
{
    return _T("[Student],[Enrollment]");
}
```

3. There are now two StudentID fields in the joined table. In the *CEx28aSet::DoFieldExchange* function, edit the StudentID line to qualify the field with a table name:

```
RFX_Long(pFX, _T("[Student].[StudentID]"), m_StudentID);
```

773

4. In the *CEx28aView::OnInitialUpdate* function, set the recordset's *m_strFilter* string as follows:

```
m_pSet->m_strFilter = "[Student].[StudentID] ==
    [Enrollment].[StudentID]";
```

5. In the *CEx28aView::OnDraw* function, add code to display the new Enrollment fields. Here is a sample:

```
pDC->TextOut(4000, y, m_pSet->m_CourseID);
```

The MFC *CRecordView* Class

The *CRecordView* class is a form view class that's attached to a recordset. Figure 28-4 illustrates an MFC record view application. The toolbar buttons enable the user to step forward and backward through a database table.

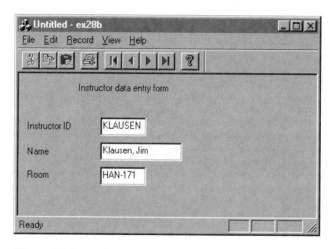

Figure 28-4.
An MFC application based on the CRecordView *class.*

Like the *CFormView* class, the *CRecordView* class depends on a dialog template. The *CFormView* class has data members that correspond to the controls in the dialog, but the *CRecordView* class accesses data members in a <u>foreign object</u>, namely the attached *CRecordset* object. When the user enters data in the controls, the record view's DDX (Dialog Data Exchange) code moves the data into the recordset's data members, which are bound to database columns by the recordset's RFX (Record Field Exchange) code.

When you specify a database view application, AppWizard generates a class derived from *CRecordView* together with an empty dialog template. App-Wizard also generates a class derived from *CRecordset*, so it must ask you for a database table name. At runtime, the record view object and the recordset object are connected. Your job is to add controls to the dialog template and match the controls to recordset data members—no C++ programming is required to create a working form-based database application.

AppWizard generates a "read-only" view-based database application. If you want to modify, add, and delete records, you must do some coding. The default behavior of the resulting application matches the behavior of Visual Basic and Access, which is a little weird. A record is added or modified only when the user moves out of it. If that's what you want, you can pattern your applications after the ENROLL sample program in the\MSDEV\SAMPLES\ MFC\TUTORIAL\ENROLL directory on the Visual C++ CD-ROM.

The EX28B Record View Example

The EX28B example is an "add-change-delete" application that's different from the Access standard. The user must explicitly add, update, and delete records. Even if you prefer the Access-style behavior, you can learn a lot about the *CRecordView* class by going through the steps in the EX28B example.

Here are the steps for building the EX28B example:

1. Run AppWizard to produce \VCPP32\EX28B\EX28B. Select Single Document Interface, and deselect Printing And Print Preview. Select the Database View Without File Support option from the AppWizard Step 2 dialog, and then click the Data Source button to select the Instructor table from the Student Registration database. Choose the Dynaset option. The options and the default class names are shown here:

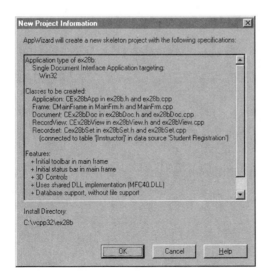

2. **Add edit controls to the *IDD_EX28B_FORM* template.** Use the IDs *IDC_ID*, *IDC_NAME*, and *IDC_ROOM*, and position the controls as shown here:

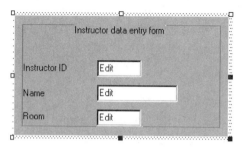

3. **Use ClassWizard to link the edit controls to the recordset data members.** If you click the arrow in the member variable name combo box, you'll get a list of all the *CEx28bSet* data members. Just select the appropriate one, as shown here:

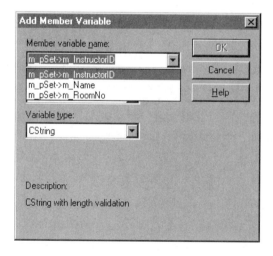

When you're finished, you'll see a screen like the one shown on the facing page:

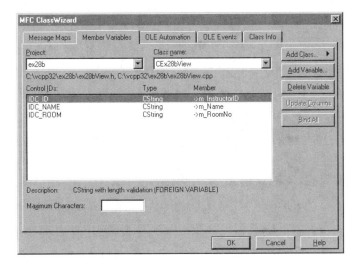

4. **Build and test the EX28B application.** You should have a working read-only database application that looks like Figure 28-4 on page 774. Use the toolbar buttons to sequence through the instructor records.

5. **Back up your database.** Now you're going to include the logic to add, change, and delete records. It would be a good idea to make a copy of the STDREG32.MDB file first. That way you have something to go back to after you delete all the records.

6. **Add menu commands.** Add the following items to the Record pop-up menu in the *IDR_MAINFRAME* menu. Also, use ClassWizard to map the commands to the specified *CEx28bView* class members.

Menu Command	Command ID	Command Handler	Update Command UI Handler
Add Record	*ID_RECORD_ADD*	*OnRecordAdd*	
Clear Fields	*ID_RECORD _CLEARFIELDS*	*OnRecordClearfields*	
Delete Record	*ID_RECORD_DELETE*	*OnRecordDelete*	*OnUpdate-RecordDelete*
Update Record	*ID_RECORD_UPDATE*	*OnRecordUpdate*	*OnUpdate-RecordUpdate*

7. Override the *OnMove* function in the *CEx28bView* class. The *CRecordView::OnMove* function does the work of updating the database when the user moves out of a record. Because we don't want this behavior, we must override the function as follows:

```
BOOL CEx28bView::OnMove(UINT nIDMoveCommand)
{
    if (CDatabase::InWaitForDataSource())
    {
#ifdef _DEBUG
    if (afxTraceFlags & traceDatabase)
      TRACE0("Warning: ignored move request.\n");
#endif
      return TRUE;
    }

    switch (nIDMoveCommand)
    {
      case ID_RECORD_PREV:
          m_pSet->MovePrev();
          if (!m_pSet->IsBOF())
            break;

      case ID_RECORD_FIRST:
          m_pSet->MoveFirst();
          break;

      case ID_RECORD_NEXT:
          m_pSet->MoveNext();
          if (!m_pSet->IsEOF())
            break;
          if (!m_pSet->CanScroll())
          {
            // clear out screen since we're sitting on EOF
            m_pSet->SetFieldNull(NULL);
            break;
          }

      case ID_RECORD_LAST:
          m_pSet->MoveLast();
          break;

      default:
          // unexpected case value
          ASSERT(FALSE);
    }
```

```
// show results of move operation
UpdateData(FALSE);
return TRUE;
}
```

8. **Edit the menu command handlers.**   The following functions call various *CRecordset* member functions to edit the database. To add a record, you must call *CRecordset::AddNew,* followed by *Update.* To modify a record, you must call *CRecordset::Edit,* followed by *Update.* Note that when you add a new record to the database, you must call *CRecordset::Requery* to completely regenerate the recordset. There's no convenient way to position the cursor on the newly added record, and that's a basic problem with SQL. Add the following shaded code:

```
void CEx28bView::OnRecordAdd()
{
    m_pSet->AddNew();
    UpdateData(TRUE);
    if (m_pSet->CanUpdate())
    {
        m_pSet->Update();
    }
    m_pSet->Requery();
    UpdateData(FALSE);
}

void CEx28bView::OnRecordClearfields()
{
    m_pSet->m_InstructorID = _T("");
    m_pSet->m_Name = _T("");
    m_pSet->m_RoomNo = _T("");
    UpdateData(FALSE);
}

void CEx28bView::OnRecordDelete()
{
    m_pSet->Delete();
    m_pSet->MoveNext();
    // back to last if we moved off the end
    if (m_pSet->IsEOF()) {
        m_pSet->MoveLast();
    }
    // is the set now empty?
    if (m_pSet->IsEOF()) {
        m_pSet->SetFieldNull(NULL);
```

(continued)

```
    }
    UpdateData(FALSE);
}


void CEx28bView::OnUpdateRecordDelete(CCmdUI* pCmdUI)
{
    pCmdUI->Enable(!m_pSet->IsEOF());
}


void CEx28bView::OnRecordUpdate()
{
    m_pSet->Edit();
    UpdateData(TRUE);
    if (m_pSet->CanUpdate())
    {

        m_pSet->Update();
    }
// should requery if key field changed
}


void CEx28bView::OnUpdateRecordUpdate(CCmdUI* pCmdUI)
{
    pCmdUI->Enable(!m_pSet->IsEOF());
}
```

9. **Build and test the EX28B application again.**   Now you can add,
   change, and delete records. Observe what happens if you try to add a
   record with a duplicate key. You get an error message that comes from
   an exception handler inside the framework. You can add try/catch logic
   in *OnRecordAdd* to customize the error processing.

Multiple Recordsets

Both the EX28A and EX28B examples relied on a single recordset. In many
cases, you'll need simultaneous access to multiple recordsets. Suppose you're
writing a program that lets the user add Section records, but you want the

user to select a valid CourseID and InstructorID. You'll need auxiliary Course and Instructor recordsets in addition to the primary Section recordset.

In the previous examples, the view object contained an embedded recordset that was created with the *CRecordset* default constructor, which caused the creation of a *CDatabase* object. The view's *OnInitialUpdate* function called *CRecordset::Open*, which called the virtual *GetDefaultConnect* function, opened the database, and then called the virtual *GetDefaultSQL* function. The problem with this scenario is that there can be only one recordset per database because the database is <u>embedded</u> in the recordset.

To get multiple recordsets, you have to do things a different way—you must create the *CDatabase* object first. Once you've done that, you can construct as many recordsets as you want, passing a *CDatabase* pointer as a parameter to the *CRecordset* constructor. You start by embedding a *CDatabase* object in the document in place of the *CRecordset* object. You also include a pointer to the primary recordset. Here are the document data members:

```
CEx28bSet* m_pEx28bSet;
CDatabase m_database;
```

In your overridden *CDocument::OnNewDocument* function, you construct the primary recordset on the heap, passing the address of the *CDatabase* object to the recordset constructor. Here's the code you insert:

```
if (m_pEx28bSet == NULL) {
  m_pEx28bSet = new CEx28bSet(&m_database);
  CString strConnect = m_pEx28bSet->GetDefaultConnect();
  m_database.Open(NULL, FALSE, FALSE, strConnect, FALSE);
}
```

The *CRecordView::OnInitialUpdate* function still opens the recordset, but this time *CRecordset::Open* does not open the database. (It's already open.) Now the code for setting the view's *m_pSet* data member is a little different:

```
m_pSet = GetDocument()->m_pEx28bSet;
```

Figure 28-5 on the following page shows the new relationship between the document, the view, and the primary recordset. Also shown are possible auxiliary recordsets.

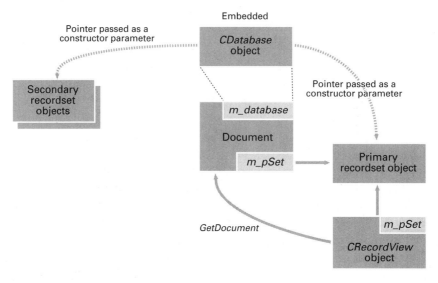

Embedded

CDatabase object

Pointer passed as a constructor parameter

Secondary recordset objects

m_database

Pointer passed as a constructor parameter

Document

m_pSet

Primary recordset object

GetDocument

m_pSet

CRecordView object

Figure 28-5.
Object relationships for multiple recordsets.

The EX28C Multiple Recordset Example

The EX28C program is similar to EX28B except that the new database–recordset relationships are implemented and an auxiliary recordset allows listing of the sections an instructor teaches. The EX28C window looks like this:

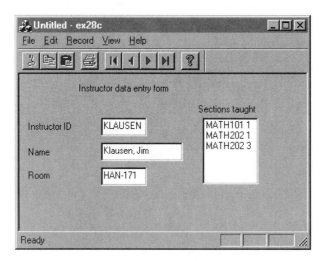

Build the \wcpp32\ex28c\ex28c.mdp project, and test the application. Sequence through the instructor records, and watch the Sections Taught list change.

As you can see, there's a new list-box control in the form dialog. Also, there's one short helper function in the view class, *LoadListbox*, that loads the list box with the rows in the Section recordset, as shown here:

```
void CEx28cView::LoadListbox()
{
    CEx28cDoc* pDoc = GetDocument();
    CListBox* pLB = (CListBox*) GetDlgItem(IDC_SECTIONS);
    CSectionSet sect(&pDoc->m_database);   // db passed via constructor

    sect.m_strFilter.Format("InstructorID = '%s'",
        (LPCSTR) m_pSet->m_InstructorID);

    sect.Open();
    pLB->ResetContent();
    while (!sect.IsEOF()) {
    pLB->AddString(sect.m_CourseID + " " + sect.m_SectionNo);
    sect.MoveNext();
    }
    // sect closed by CRecordset destructor
}
```

Notice that this function sets up a filter string based on the value of the *InstructorID* field in the primary recordset. *LoadListbox* is called from the *OnInitDialog*, *OnMove*, *OnRecordAdd*, and *OnRecordDelete* member functions.

Database Management with Microsoft Data Access Objects (DAO)

In Chapter 28, you saw database management programming with the Microsoft Foundation Class (MFC) library and Microsoft ODBC. In this chapter, you'll see a completely different database programming approach— the MFC Data Access Objects (DAO) classes and the underlying DAO software. Actually, the approach is not so different. Instead of the ODBC classes *CDatabase* and *CRecordset*, you'll be using *CDaoDatabase* and *CDaoRecordset*. The ODBC and DAO classes are so similar (many member function names are the same) that you can convert ODBC applications, such as the examples in Chapter 28, to DAO applications simply by changing class names and not much else. Thus, you can look at DAO as a sort of replacement for ODBC. But as you'll see, DAO goes far beyond ODBC.

This chapter merely scratches the surface of DAO, highlighting its features and outlining the differences between DAO and ODBC. Along the way, it explains the relationships between DAO, OLE, the Jet database engine, Visual Basic for Applications (VBA), and the MFC library. Finally, it presents a dynamic database example that would be difficult to program in ODBC.

DAO, OLE, and the Microsoft Jet Database Engine

One feature of DAO is a set of OLE interfaces, which, like all OLE interfaces, are nothing more than a specification—sets of pure virtual function declarations. These interfaces have names such as *DAOWorkspace*, *DAODatabase*, and *DAORecordset*. (Note: These interface names don't begin with the letter *I* as do most other OLE interface names.)

The other feature of DAO is the implementation of those interfaces. Microsoft supplies the COM module DAO3032.DLL, which connects to the same Jet database engine DLL that serves the Microsoft Access database product. As a Visual C++ developer, you have royalty-free redistribution rights to these DLLs. At the moment, the only DAO implementation available with Jet is DAO3032.DLL, but nothing prevents other database software companies from providing their own DAO implementations.

DAO and VBA

In Chapter 24, you learned about OLE Automation. A VBA automation controller (such as Microsoft Excel or Visual Basic 4.0) can load any automation server and then use it to create objects. Once the objects are created, the server can get and set properties and call methods. The servers you created in Chapter 24 all communicated through the OLE *IDispatch* interface. But VBA can use interfaces other than *IDispatch* to communicate with a server.

If you look in the Windows registry under HKEY_CLASSES_ROOT\ TypeLib, you'll find the class ID {00025E01-0000-0000-C000-000000000046} and the pathname for DAO3032.DLL, which contains the DAO type library. If you select this item as a VBA reference (by choosing References from the Excel Tools menu, for example), your VBA programs can use the DAO objects, and you can browse the DAO library, as shown here:

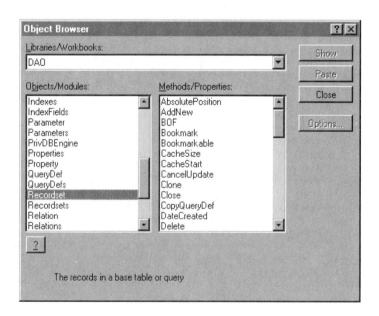

Like *IDispatch* servers, the Microsoft DAO server implements objects that have properties and methods.

DAO and MFC

The MFC library has the following five DAO database classes:

CDaoWorkspace
CDaoDatabase
CDaoRecordset
CDaoTableDef
CDaoQueryDef

These classes more or less wrap the OLE interfaces with corresponding names. (*CDaoRecordset* wraps *DAORecordset*, for example.) The *CDaoWorkspace* class actually wraps two interfaces, *DAOWorkspace* and *DAODBEngine*. The MFC wrapping is fairly complete, so you need to make direct OLE DAO calls only when you need access to certain database security features. If you use the MFC library, all reference counting is taken care of; if you call DAO directly, you must be sure to call *Release* on your interfaces.

Both AppWizard and ClassWizard fully support DAO. You can use AppWizard to generate a complete form-based application that works like EX28B in the previous chapter, and you can use ClassWizard to generate a table-specific class that is derived from *CDaoRecordset*.

What Databases Can You Open with DAO?

Four database options are supported by DAO:

■ **Opening an Access database (MDB file)**—An MDB file is a self-contained database that includes query definitions, security information, indexes, relationships, and of course the actual data tables. You simply specify the MDB file's pathname.

■ **Opening an ODBC data source directly**—There's a significant limitation here. You can't open an ODBC data source that uses the Jet engine as a driver; you can use only data sources that have their own ODBC driver DLLs.

■ **Opening an ISAM-type (indexed-sequential access method) data source (a group of dBASE, FoxPro, Paradox, Btrieve, Excel, or text files) through the Jet engine**—Even if you've set up an ODBC data source that uses the Jet engine to access one of these file types, you must open the files as an ISAM-type data source, not as an ODBC data source.

■ **Attaching external tables to an Access database**—This is actually the preferred way of using DAO to access ODBC data. First you use Access to attach the ODBC tables to an MDB file, and then you use DAO to open the MDB file as in the first option. You can also use Access to attach ISAM files to an MDB file.

Using DAO in ODBC Mode— Snapshots and Dynasets

I've already said that DAO goes far beyond ODBC, but let's take things one step at a time. We'll start with DAO snapshots and dynasets, which behave pretty much the same way in DAO as they do in ODBC. You can use snapshots and dynasets with ODBC data sources, ISAM-type files, and Access tables. You write programs using the MFC library classes *CDaoDatabase* and *CDaoRecordset*, which are very similar to the ODBC classes *CDatabase* and *CRecordset*. There are a few notable differences, however:

■ The *CDaoDatabase::GetCurrentRecord* function works differently from the *CDatabase::GetCurrentRecord* function. For attached tables and ODBC data sources, it always returns −1. For Access tables and ISAM-type files, it returns the number of records actually read, which is the final count for the recordset only if you have moved to the last record. Unfortunately, DAO has no equivalent for the ODBC *CRecordset::GetStatus* function, so you can't test a DAO recordset to find out whether the record count is indeed final.

■ With DAO, you can set and get the absolute position of the current record in a dynaset or snapshot, you can get and set a percent position, you can find a record containing a matching string, and you can use <u>bookmarks</u> to mark records for later retrieval.

■ DAO makes it easy to get and set column values without binding. Because values are passed as *VARIANT*s, you can build dynamic applications that adjust to the database schema at runtime.

788

One important thing to remember about snapshot recordsets is that the record count <u>never</u> <u>changes</u>. With dynasets, the record count changes only if you delete or add records in the dynaset. If another user deletes a record, that record is marked as deleted in your dynaset; if another user adds a record, you don't see that record in your dynaset. If you add a record to a dynaset, that record is added at the end of the dynaset, regardless of the sort order.

DAO Table-Type Recordsets

DAO introduces a new type of recordset unknown in the ODBC universe. A <u>table-type</u> <u>recordset</u> (supported by the *CDaoRecordset* class) is a direct view of an entire database table. You can use a table-type recordset <u>only</u> with a table in an Access database. Table-type recordsets have the following characteristics that distinguish them from snapshots and dynasets:

- The *CDaoRecordset::GetCurrentRecord* function returns an approximate record count that reflects records added or deleted by other users.

- You <u>can't</u> use the *CDaoRecordset* functions that access a record's absolute position or percent position.

- The *CDaoRecordset::Seek* function lets you position to a record by key value. You first call the *SetCurrentIndex* function to select the index.

- If you add a record to a table-type recordset, the record is added in its proper place in the sort order as determined by the current index.

The table-type recordset is a significant departure from ODBC and SQL. You can now select an individual record without first issuing a query. You can find a record with one index and then move sequentially using a different index. It's like dBASE or FoxPro programming!

DAO *QueryDefs* and *TableDefs*

If you're working with an Access database, you can store parameterized queries in the database, using the MFC *CDaoQueryDef* class. Also, you can use the *CDaoTableDef* class to define tables at runtime, which is more convenient than using an SQL CREATE statement.

Displaying Database Rows in a Scrolling Window

You've seen all the general DAO theory you're going to get here. Now you're ready for a practical example. Before you dig into the code for EX29A, however, you need to study the general problem of displaying database rows in a scrolling window. If this were an easy problem to solve, there would probably be an MFC *CScrollDatabaseView* class. But there isn't, so we'll write our own class. Actually, it's not that difficult if we make some simplifying assumptions about the database. First, our scrolling row–view class will be based on a dynaset, and that means that it can accommodate <u>any</u> table, including those in ODBC data sources and ISAM-type files. Second, we'll specify read-only access, which means that the number of rows in the dynaset can't change.

Scrolling Alternatives

There are lots of ways to implement scrolling with Visual C++. If you look at the DAOVIEW MFC sample database program on the Visual C++ CD-ROM, you'll see the use of the MFC *CListView* class, which encapsulates the Windows 95 list view common control. The trouble with this approach is that you must copy all the selected rows into the control, which can be slow, and, more significantly, you can't see updates that other programs are making in the same table. The list view is a de facto snapshot of a database table.

We'll base our scrolling view on the MFC *CScrollView* class, and our code will be smart enough to retrieve only those records that are needed for the client area of the window. The only limitation here is the logical size of the scrolling window. In Windows 95, the limits are ±32,767, and that limits the rows we can display. If the distance between rows is 14 units, we're limited to 2340 rows.

A Row–View Class

If you've read other books about programming for Windows, you know that authors spend lots of time on the problem of scrolling lists. This is a tricky programming exercise that must be repeated over and over. Why not encapsulate a scrolling list in a base class? All the ugly details would be hidden, and you could get on with the business of writing your application.

The *CRowView* class, adapted from the class of the identical name in the CHKBOOK MFC sample program on the Visual C++ CD-ROM, does the job. Through its use of virtual callback functions, it serves as a model for other derivable base classes. *CRowView* has some limitations, and it's not built to industrial-strength specifications, but it works well in the DAO example. Figure 29-1 shows the header file listing.

ROWVIEW.H

```
// rowview.h : interface of the CRowView class
//
// This class implements the behavior of a scrolling view that
//   presents multiple rows of fixed-height data.  A row view is
//   similar to an owner-draw list box in its visual behavior; but
//   unlike a list box, a row view has all the benefits of a
//   view (as well as a scroll view), including--perhaps most
//   important--printing and print preview.
///////////////////////////////////////////////////////////////////

class CRowView : public CScrollView   // abstract base class
{
DECLARE_DYNAMIC(CRowView)

// Construction/destruction
protected:
    CRowView();
    virtual ~CRowView();

// Attributes
protected:
    int m_nRowWidth;              // width of row in
                                  //   logical units
    int m_nRowHeight;             // height of row in
                                  //   logical units
    int m_nCharWidth;             // avg character width in
                                  //   logical units
    int m_nPrevSelectedRow;       // index of most recently
                                  //   selected row
    int m_nPrevRowCount;          // most recent row count,
                                  //   before update
    int m_nRowsPerPrintedPage;    // how many rows fit on a
                                  //   printed page
// Operations-Attributes
protected:
    virtual void UpdateRow(int nInvalidRow); // called by derived
                                             //   class OnUpdate
    virtual void CalculateRowMetrics(CDC* pDC)
            { GetRowWidthHeight(pDC, m_nRowWidth, m_nRowHeight,
                            m_nCharWidth); }
    virtual void UpdateScrollSizes();
    virtual CRect RowToWndRect(CDC* pDC, int nRow);
    virtual int RowToYPos(int nRow);
```

Figure 29-1. *(continued)*

The CRowView *header file listing.*

Figure 29-1. *continued*

```
      virtual void RectLPtoRowRange(const CRect& rectLP,
                                    int& nFirstRow, int& nLastRow,
                                    BOOL bIncludePartiallyShownRows);
      virtual int LastViewableRow();

// Overridables
protected:
      virtual void GetRowWidthHeight(CDC* pDC, int& nRowWidth,
                                     int& nRowHeight,
                                     int& nCharWidth) = 0;
      virtual int GetActiveRow() = 0;
      virtual int GetRowCount() = 0;
      virtual void OnDrawRow(CDC* pDC, int nRow, int y,
                             BOOL bSelected) = 0;
      virtual void ChangeSelectionNextRow(BOOL bNext) = 0;
      virtual void ChangeSelectionToRow(int nRow) = 0;

// Implementation
protected:
      // standard overrides of MFC classes
      virtual void OnInitialUpdate();
      virtual void OnDraw(CDC* pDC);  // overridden to draw
                                      //   this view
      virtual void OnPrepareDC(CDC* pDC,
                               CPrintInfo* pInfo = NULL);
      virtual BOOL OnPreparePrinting(CPrintInfo* pInfo);
      virtual void OnBeginPrinting(CDC* pDC, CPrintInfo* pInfo);
      virtual void OnPrint(CDC* pDC, CPrintInfo* pInfo);

// Generated message map functions
protected:
      //{{AFX_MSG(CRowView)
      afx_msg void OnKeyDown(UINT nChar, UINT nRepCnt,
                             UINT nFlags);
      afx_msg void OnSize(UINT nType, int cx, int cy);
      afx_msg void OnLButtonDown(UINT nFlags, CPoint point);
      //}}AFX_MSG
      DECLARE_MESSAGE_MAP()
};
```

Dividing the Work Between Base and Derived Classes

Because the *CRowView* class (itself derived from *CScrollView*) is designed to be a base class, it is as general as possible. *CRowView* relies on its derived class to access and paint the row's data. The EX29A example's document class obtains its row data from a scrollable DAO database, but the CHKBOOK example uses a random access disk file. The *CRowView* class serves both examples effectively. It supports the concept of a selected row that is highlighted in the view. Through the *CRowView* virtual member functions, the derived class is alerted when the user changes the selected row.

The *CRowView* Pure Virtual Member Functions

Classes derived from *CRowView* must implement the following pure virtual member functions:

- *GetRowWidthHeight*—This function returns the character width and height of the currently selected font and the width of the row, based on average character widths. As the device context switches between printer and display, the returned font metric values change accordingly.

- *GetActiveRow*—The base class calls this function frequently, so if another view changes the selected row, this view can track it.

- *ChangeSelectionNextRow, ChangeSelectionToRow*—These two functions serve to alert the derived class that the user has changed the selected row. The derived class can then update the document (and other views) if necessary.

- *OnDrawRow*—The *OnDrawRow* function is called by the *CRow-View::OnDraw* function to draw a specific row.

Other *CRowView* Functions

Three other *CRowView* functions are available to be called by derived classes and the application framework:

- *UpdateRow*—This public function triggers a view update when the row selection changes. Normally, only the newly selected row and the deselected row are invalidated, and this means that the final invalid rectangle spans both rows. If the total number of rows has changed, *UpdateRow* calls *UpdateScrollSizes*.

- *UpdateScrollSizes*—This is a virtual function, so you can override it if necessary. The *CRowView* implementation updates the size of the view, which invalidates the visible portion. *UpdateScrollSizes* is called by *OnSize* and by *OnUpdate* (after the user executes a new query).

■ *OnPrint*—The *CRowView* class overrides this function to cleverly adjust the viewport origin and clipping rectangle so that *OnDraw* can paint on the printed page exactly as it does in the visible portion of a window.

Programming a Dynamic Recordset

If you use AppWizard to create a DAO database application, AppWizard generates a class derived from *CDaoRecordset* with a *DoFieldExchange* function that binds data members to the columns in a specific database table. For a dynamic recordset class, however, you need to determine the column names and data types at runtime. With ODBC, this is a difficult job. The previous edition of this book presented an example that used a class derived from *CRecordset* to bind a table's columns to allocated storage. This example has been updated for Visual C++ 4.0 and is included on the companion CD-ROM as EX28D.

With DAO, you don't need a derived recordset class—you simply construct a *CDaoRecordset* object and call the *GetFieldValue* member function, which returns a *VARIANT* representing the column value. Other member functions tell you the number of columns in the table and the name, type, and width of each column.

NOTE: If a field *VARIANT* contains a *BSTR*, assume the string contains 8-bit characters. This is an exception to the rule that all OLE *BSTR*s contain wide characters.

The EX29A Example

Now we'll put everything together and build another working program—an MDI application that connects to any DAO data source. The application dynamically displays tables in scrolling view windows, and it allows the user to type in the SQL QUERY statement, which is stored in the document along with data source and table information. AppWizard generates the usual MDI main frame, document, application, and view classes, and we change the view class base to *CRowView* and add the DAO-specific code. Figure 29-2 on page 796 shows the EX29A program in operation.

The MFC Dialog Bar

You haven't seen the *CDialogBar* class yet because it didn't make sense to use it. (A dialog bar is a child of the frame window that is arranged according to a dialog template resource and that routes commands in a manner similar to that of a toolbar.) It fits well in the DAO example, however. Look at Figure 29-2 on page 796, which shows the EX29A example in operation. The dialog bar contains an edit control for the SQL query string, and it has a pushbutton to reexecute the query. The button sends a command message that can be handled in the view, and it can be disabled by an update command UI handler. Most dialog bars reside at the top of the frame window, immediately under the toolbar.

It's surprisingly easy to add a dialog bar to an application. You don't even need a new derived class. Here are the steps:

1. Use the graphic editor to lay out the dialog. Apply the following styles:

   Style = Child

   Border = None

   Visible = unchecked

   You can choose a horizontally oriented bar for the top or bottom of the frame, or you can choose a vertically oriented bar for the left or right side of the frame. Add any controls you need, including buttons and edit controls.

2. Declare an embedded *CDialogBar* object in your derived main frame class declaration, as shown here:

   ```
   CDialogBar m_wndMyBar;
   ```

3. Add dialog bar object creation code in your main frame class *OnCreate* member function, as shown here:

   ```
   if (!m_wndMyBar.Create(this, IDD_MY_BAR, CBRS_TOP,
       ID_MY_BAR)) {
     TRACE("Failed to create dialog bar\n");
     return -1;
   }
   ```

   IDD_MY_BAR is the dialog resource ID assigned in the graphic editor. The *CBRS_TOP* style tells the application framework to place the dialog bar at the top of the frame window. *ID_MY-_BAR* is the dialog bar's control window ID, which should be within the range 0xE800 through 0xE820 to ensure that the Print Preview window preempts the dialog bar.

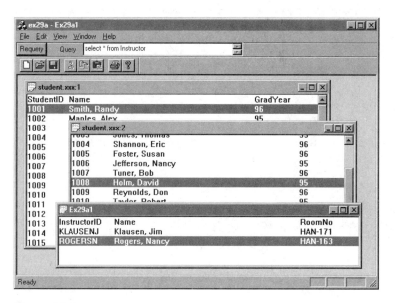

Figure 29-2.
The EX29A program in operation.

The document's File menu includes the following commands:

DAO Open MDB
DAO Open ISAM
DAO Open ODBC

The user must choose one of these commands after opening a document. As you will see, the code for opening the database is different depending on the data source type.

You can learn a lot about this application by looking at the three-view window in Figure 29-2. The two view windows at the top are tied to the same document, and the bottom view is tied to another document. The dialog bar shows the SQL statement that's associated with the active view window.

The EX29A example includes source code listings and resource requirements. Here is a table of the files and classes:

Header File	Source Code File	Class	Description
ex29a.h	ex29a.cpp	*CEx29aApp*	Main application
MainFrm.h	MainFrm.cpp	*CMainFrame*	MDI main frame
ChildFrm.h	ChildFrm.cpp	*CChildFrame*	MDI child frame
ex29aDoc.h	ex29aDoc.cpp	*CEx29aDoc*	EX29A document
ex29aView.h	ex29aView.cpp	*CEx29aView*	Scrolling database view class
RowView.h	RowView.cpp	*CRowView*	Row view base class
Tablesel.h	Tablesel.cpp	*CTableSelect*	Table selection dialog class
IsamSelect.h	IsamSelect.cpp		ISAM-type data source selection dialog class
StdAfx.h	StdAfx.cpp		Precompiled headers

Now we'll go through the application's classes one at a time, excluding *CRowView*. You'll see the important data members and the principal member functions.

CEx29aApp

The application class is the unmodified output from AppWizard. Nothing special here.

CMainFrame and CChildFrame

These classes are the standard output from AppWizard except for the addition of the dialog bar, which is created in the *CMainFrame::OnCreate* member function.

CEx29aDoc

The document class manages the database connections and recordsets. Each document object can support one main recordset attached to one data source. A document object can have several views attached. Data sources (represented by *CDaoDatabase* objects) are not shared among document objects; each document has its own.

Data Members

The important *CEx29aDoc* data members are as follows:

m_pRecordset	Pointer to the document's recordset object
m_database	Document's embedded *CDaoDatabase* object
m_strDatabase	Database pathname (MDB file)
m_strConnect	ODBC connection string or ISAM connection string
m_strQuery	Entire SQL SELECT statement
m_bConnected	Flag that is *TRUE* when the document is connected to a recordset
m_nFields	Number of fields (columns) in the recordset
m_nRowCount	Number of records (rows) in the recordset

OnCloseDocument

This overridden *CDocument* function closes the database if one is connected:

```
void CEx29aDoc::OnCloseDocument()
{
    m_strQuery.Empty();
    PutQuery();
    if (m_bConnected) {
      delete m_pRecordset; // destructor calls Close
      m_database.Close();
      m_bConnected = FALSE;
      m_pRecordset = NULL;
    }
    CDocument::OnCloseDocument();
}
```

OnFileDaoOpenOdbc

This function is called in response to the DAO Open ODBC command on the File menu. It calls *CDaoDatabase::Open* with the connect parameter string. The string "ODBC;" causes the ODBC data source selection dialog to be displayed. Notice the use of the *try/catch* block to detect SQL processing errors.

```
void CEx29aDoc::OnFileDaoOpenOdbc()
{
    // can't open ODBC via Access driver
    BeginWaitCursor();
    if (m_strConnect.IsEmpty()) {
      m_strConnect = "ODBC;";
    }
```

```
    try {
      // non-exclusive, read-only
      m_database.Open("", FALSE, TRUE, m_strConnect);
    }
    catch (CDaoException* e) {
      ::DaoErrorMsg(e);
      EndWaitCursor();
      e->Delete();
      return;
    }
    m_strConnect = m_database.GetConnect();
    TRACE("database name = %s, connect = %s\n",
        (const char*) m_strDatabase,
        (const char*) m_strConnect);
    OpenRecordset();
    EndWaitCursor();
}
```

OnFileDaoOpenIsam

This function is called in response to the DAO Open ISAM command on the
File menu. It gets a directory name from the user (through the *CIsamSelect*
class) and then calls *CDaoDatabase::Open* with the connect parameter string.
The *CIsamSelect::m_strIsam* string specifies the type of file. Example strings are
"dBASE III", "FoxPro 2.6", and "Excel 7.0".

```
void CEx29aDoc::OnFileDaoopenIsam()
{
    BeginWaitCursor();
    if (m_strConnect.IsEmpty()) {
      CIsamSelect isamDlg;
      if (isamDlg.DoModal() != IDOK) {
        return;
      }
      m_strConnect = isamDlg.m_strIsam + ";DATABASE=" +
          isamDlg.m_strDirectory;
      TRACE("m_strConnect = %s\n", (const char*) m_strConnect);
    }
    try {
      // non-exclusive, read-only
      m_database.Open("", FALSE, TRUE, m_strConnect);
    }
    catch(CDaoException* e) {
      ::DaoErrorMsg(e);
      EndWaitCursor();
      e->Delete();
      return;
```

(continued)

```
    }
    m_strConnect = m_database.GetConnect();
    TRACE("database name = %s, connect = %s\n",
        (const char*) m_strDatabase, (const char*) m_strConnect);
    OpenRecordset();
    EndWaitCursor();
}
```

OnFileDaoOpenMdb

This function is called in response to the DAO Open MDB command on the File menu. It uses the MFC *CFileDialog* class to get an MDB file pathname from the user. Compare the *CDaoDatabase::Open* call with the calls in the two preceding functions. Notice that the MDB pathname is passed as the first parameter.

```
void CEx29aDoc::OnFileDaoOpenMdb()
{
    if (m_strDatabase.IsEmpty()) {
      CFileDialog dlg(TRUE, ".mdb", "*.mdb");
      if (dlg.DoModal() == IDCANCEL) return;
      m_strDatabase = dlg.GetPathName();
    }
    BeginWaitCursor();
    try {
      // non-exclusive, read-only
      m_database.Open(m_strDatabase, FALSE, TRUE);
    }
    catch (CDaoException* e) {
      ::DaoErrorMsg(e);
      EndWaitCursor();
      e->Delete();
      return;
    }
    m_strDatabase = m_database.GetName();
    TRACE("database name = %s, connect = %s\n",
        (const char*) m_strDatabase, (const char*) m_strConnect);
    OpenRecordset();
    EndWaitCursor();
}
```

OnOpenRecordset

This helper function is called by *OnFileDaoOpenOdbc, OnFileDaoOpenIsam,* and *OnFileDaoOpenMdb.* The *CTableSelect* class allows the user to select a table name, which is used to construct a SELECT statement. Calls to *CDaoRecordset::Move-Last* and *GetAbsolutePosition* set the record count for ODBC, ISAM, and MDB data sources.

```
void CEx29aDoc::OpenRecordset()
{
    GetQuery();
    if (m_strQuery.IsEmpty()) {
      CTableSelect tableDlg(&m_database);
      if (tableDlg.DoModal() != IDOK) {
        m_database.Close();  // escape route
        return;
      }
      m_strQuery.Format("select * from %s", tableDlg.m_strSelection);
      PutQuery();
    }

    m_pRecordset = new CDaoRecordset(&m_database);
    try {
      m_pRecordset->Open(dbOpenDynaset, m_strQuery, dbReadOnly);
    }
    catch (CDaoException* e) {
      ::DaoErrorMsg(e);
      UpdateAllViews(NULL);
      m_bConnected = FALSE;
      e->Delete();
      return;
    }
    if (!m_pRecordset->IsBOF()) {
      m_pRecordset->MoveLast(); // to validate record count
    }
    m_nRowCount = m_pRecordset->GetAbsolutePosition() + 1;
    TRACE("m_nRowCount = %d\n", m_nRowCount);
    GetFieldSpecs();
    UpdateAllViews(NULL);
    m_bConnected = TRUE;
}
```

NOTE: The MFC *CDaoRecordset* class has *m_strFilter* and *m_strSort* data members as does the ODBC *CRecordset* class. You can't use these strings, however, if your recordset doesn't have bound fields; you must construct the entire SELECT statement as shown above.

OnQueryRequery

This message handler is called in response to the Requery button on the dialog bar. It reads the query string value and regenerates the recordset. Note that the *CDaoRecordset::Requery* function doesn't handle an updated SELECT statement, so we close and reopen the recordset instead.

```
void CEx29aDoc::OnRequery()
{
    BeginWaitCursor();
    GetQuery();
    // Requery won't work because we're changing the query string
    m_pRecordset->Close();
    try {
      m_pRecordset->Open(dbOpenDynaset, m_strQuery, dbReadOnly);
    }
    catch (CDaoException* e) {
      ::DaoErrorMsg(e);
      UpdateAllViews(NULL);
      m_bConnected = FALSE;
      e->Delete();
      EndWaitCursor();
      return;
    }
    GetFieldSpecs();
    if (!m_pRecordset->IsBOF()) {
      m_pRecordset->MoveLast(); // to validate record count
    }
    UpdateAllViews(NULL);
    EndWaitCursor();
}
```

PutQuery and GetQuery

These utility functions move the document's query string to and from the edit control on the dialog bar.

Serialize

The *Serialize* function reads and writes the data members *m_strConnect*, *m_strDatabase*, and *m_strQuery*.

CEx29aView

This class is derived from *CRowView* and implements the virtual functions.

Data Members

The *CEx29aView* class uses the integer variable *m_nSelectedRow* to track the currently selected row. The recordset pointer is held in *m_pSet*.

OnUpdate

This virtual *CView* function is called through the application framework when the view is created and when the document's contents change in response to a database open or requery event. If several views are active for a given document, all views reflect the current query, but each can maintain its own current row and scroll position. *OnUpdate* also sets the value of the *m_pSet* data member. This can't be done in *OnInitialUpdate* because the recordset is not open at that point.

GetRowWidthHeight, GetActiveRow, ChangeSelectionNextRow, and ChangeSelectionToRow

These functions are implementations of the *CRowView* class pure virtual functions. They take care of drawing a specified query result row, and they track the current selection.

GetRowCount

This virtual function, which is called from *CRowView*, simply returns the record count value stored in the document.

OnDrawRow and DrawDataRow

The *OnDrawRow* virtual function is called from *CRowView* member functions to perform the actual work of drawing a designated row. *OnDrawRow* reads the recordset's current row and then calls the *CDaoRecordset::Move* function to position the cursor and read the data. The *try/catch* block detects catastrophic errors resulting from unreadable data. The *DrawDataRow* helper function steps through the columns and prints the values. Notice that *OnDrawRow* displays "**RECORD DELETED**" when it encounters a record that has been deleted by another user since the dynaset was first created. *OnDrawRow* and *DrawDataRow* are shown here:

```
void CEx29aView::OnDrawRow(CDC* pDC, int nRow, int y, BOOL bSelected)
{
    int x = 0;
    int i;
    CEx29aDoc* pDoc = GetDocument();
    if (m_pSet == NULL) return;

    if (nRow == 0) {      // title row
      for (i = 0; i < pDoc->m_nFields; i++) {
        pDC->TextOut(x, y, pDoc->m_arrayFieldName[i]);
        x += pDoc->m_arrayFieldSize[i] * m_nCharWidth;
```

(continued)

803

```
        }
      }
    else {
      try {
        m_pSet->SetAbsolutePosition(nRow - 1); // adjust for title row
        if (m_pSet->IsEOF()) {
          TRACE("MoveLast\n");
          m_pSet->MoveLast();
        }
        else {
          DrawDataRow(pDC, y);
        }
      }
      catch (CDaoException* e) {
        if (e->m_pErrorInfo->m_lErrorCode == 3167) {
          pDC->TextOut(0, y, "**RECORD DELETED**");
        }
        else {
          ::DaoErrorMsg(e);
        }
        e->Delete();
        // figure out some way to escape from here
      }
    }
}

void CEx29aView::DrawDataRow(CDC* pDC, int y)
{
    int x = 0;
    CString strTime;

    COleVariant var;
    CString str;
    CEx29aDoc* pDoc = GetDocument();
    for (int i = 0; i < pDoc->m_nFields; i++) {
      var = m_pSet->GetFieldValue(i);
      switch (var.vt) {
      case VT_BSTR:
        str = (LPCSTR) var.bstrVal; // narrow characters in DAO
        break;
      case VT_I2:
        str.Format("%d", (int) var.iVal);
        break;
      case VT_I4:
        str.Format("%d", var.lVal);
        break;
```

```
        case VT_R4:
          str.Format("%10.2f", (double) var.fltVal);
          break;
        case VT_R8:
          str.Format("%10.2f", var.dblVal);
          break;
        case VT_DATE:
          str = COleDateTime(var).Format();
          break;
        case VT_BOOL:
          str = (var.bool == 0) ? "FALSE" : "TRUE";
          break;
        case VT_NULL:
          str = "----";
          break;
        default:
          str.Format("Unk type %d\n", var.vt);
          TRACE("Unknown type %d\n", var.vt);
        }
        pDC->TextOut(x, y, str);
        x += pDoc->m_arrayFieldSize[i] * m_nCharWidth;
    }
}
```

OnInitialUpdate and *OnTimer*

Because we're working with a dynaset, we want to show database changes made by other programs. The timer handler calls *CWnd::Invalidate,* which causes all records in the client area to be refreshed, as shown here:

```
void CEx29aView::OnInitialUpdate()
{
    SetTimer(1, 5000, NULL); // every 5 seconds
    CRowView::OnInitialUpdate();
}

void CEx29aView::OnTimer(UINT nIDEvent)
{
    Invalidate(); // update view from database
}
```

CTableSelect

This is a ClassWizard-generated dialog class that contains a list box used for selecting the table. For the student registration database, the dialog looks like the one on the following page:

Data Members

The *CTableSelect* data members are as follows:

m_pDatabase	Pointer to the recordset's *CDaoDatabase* object
m_strSelection	ClassWizard-generated variable that corresponds to the list-box selection

Constructor

The constructor takes a database pointer parameter, which it uses to set the *m_pDatabase* data member, as shown here:

```
CTableSelect::CTableSelect(CDaoDatabase* pDatabase,
    CWnd* pParent /*=NULL*/)
    : CDialog(CTableSelect::IDD, pParent)
{
    //{{AFX_DATA_INIT(CTableSelect)
    m_strSelection = "";
    //}}AFX_DATA_INIT
    m_pDatabase = pDatabase;
}
```

OnInitDialog

This self-contained function creates, opens, and reads the data source's list of tables, and it puts the table name strings in the dialog's list box, as shown here:

```
BOOL CTableSelect::OnInitDialog()
{
    CListBox* pLB = (CListBox*) GetDlgItem(IDC_LIST1);
    int nTables = m_pDatabase->GetTableDefCount();
    TRACE("CTableSelect::OnInitDialog, nTables = %d\n", nTables);
    CDaoTableDefInfo tdi;
```

```
        for (int n = 0; n < nTables; n++) {
          m_pDatabase->GetTableDefInfo(n, tdi);
          TRACE("table name = %s\n", (const char*) tdi.m_strName);
          if (tdi.m_strName.Left(4) != "MSys") {
            pLB->AddString(tdi.m_strName);
          }
        }
        return CDialog::OnInitDialog();
    }
```

OnDblclkList1

It's handy for the user to choose a list-box entry with a double click. This function is mapped to the appropriate list-box notification message, as shown here:

```
void CTableSelect::OnDblclkList1()
{
    OnOK();  // double-click on list-box item exits dialog
}
```

CIsamSelect

This is a ClassWizard-generated dialog class that contains a list box and an edit control used for selecting the ISAM-type data source. The user must type the directory for the files, as shown here:

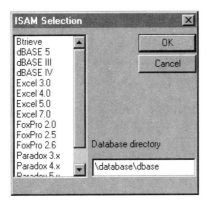

Data Members

The *CIsamSelect* class data members are as follows:

m_strIsam   ClassWizard-generated variable that corresponds
to the list-box selection

m_strDirectory   ClassWizard-generated variable that corresponds
to the edit control contents

OnInitDialog

This function sets the initial values of the list box, which are the options from
the Connect Property topic in Books Online, as shown here:

```
BOOL CIsamSelect::OnInitDialog()
{
    CListBox* pLB = (CListBox*) GetDlgItem(IDC_LIST1);
    pLB->AddString("dBASE III");
    pLB->AddString("dBASE IV");
    pLB->AddString("dBASE 5");
    pLB->AddString("Paradox 3.x");
    pLB->AddString("Paradox 4.x");
    pLB->AddString("Paradox 5.x");
    pLB->AddString("Btrieve");
    pLB->AddString("FoxPro 2.0");
    pLB->AddString("FoxPro 2.5");
    pLB->AddString("FoxPro 2.6");
    pLB->AddString("Excel 3.0");
    pLB->AddString("Excel 4.0");
    pLB->AddString("Excel 5.0");
    pLB->AddString("Excel 7.0");
    pLB->AddString("Text");
    CDialog::OnInitDialog();

    return TRUE;  // return TRUE unless you set the focus to a control
                  // EXCEPTION: OCX Property Pages should return FALSE
}
```

The EX29A Resource File

This application uses a dialog bar, so you'll need a dialog resource for it. Figure 29-2 on page 796 shows the dialog bar. The dialog resource ID is *IDD-
_QUERY_BAR*. The controls are listed here:

Control	ID
Button	*IDC_REQUERY*
Edit	*IDC_QUERY*

The dialog resource ID is *IDD_QUERY_BAR*, and the following styles are set:

Style = Child
Border = None
Visible = unchecked

There's also a table selection dialog template, *IDD_TABLE_SELECT*, which has a list-box control with ID *IDC_LIST1*, and there's an ISAM selection dialog template, *IDD_ISAM_SELECT*. The File menu has the following three added items:

Menu Item	Command ID
DAO Open MDB	*ID_FILE_DAOOPEN_MDB*
DAO Open ISAM	*ID_FILE_DAOOPEN_ISAM*
DAO Open ODBC	*ID_FILE_DAOOPEN_ODBC*

Running the EX29A Program

You can run the EX29A program with any DAO data source, but try the student registration database (STDREG32.MDB) first. To test the multiuser capabilities of the program, run it simultaneously with EX28B. Use EX28B to change and delete instructor records while displaying the instructor table in EX29A.

PART VI

APPENDIXES

A Crash Course
in the C++ Language

Have you ever started reading a C++ textbook and given up because there was too much detail and you weren't motivated? If so, this appendix is for you. It's based on an example that I used when I taught myself C++, but it's flavored by my experience learning the classes of the Microsoft Foundation Class (MFC) Library. It's not meant to be comprehensive, and each C++ expert will find something to complain about, but I think it serves well as a C++ crash course.

As you read this appendix, you'll be hit straightaway by the essence of C++—classes and objects—and then you'll learn how to "wire" objects together to build an application. Important details are introduced as you need them, but I recommend that you keep a C++ textbook close at hand. The more you already know about C programming, the better.

An Introduction to Classes and Objects

The <u>class</u> is the language element that C++ programmers use to write modular, maintainable programs. This section teaches you how the class encapsulates code and data. Later sections introduce two other C++ features you might have heard about: <u>inheritance</u> and <u>polymorphism</u>.

Because classes and objects are such important C++ concepts, you must understand them thoroughly before proceeding. Understanding C's *struct* and *typedef* syntax will help you get started.

User-Defined Types in C

A C++ class declaration is an outgrowth of the C structure declaration. In C, the following code declares a structure with the name *xy*, but the compiler allocates no storage:

```
struct xy {
    double dX;
    double dY;
};
```

After you declare the structure, you can use *xy* instances in your C code this way:

```
struct xy topLeft = { 0.0, 0.0 };
struct xy bottomRight = { 1.0, 1.0 };
printf("topLeft = (%f, %f)\n", topLeft.dX, topLeft.dY);
printf("bottomRight = (%f, %f)\n", bottomRight.dX, bottomRight.dY);
```

If you use the C *typedef* syntax, the code becomes a little cleaner, as shown here:

```
typedef struct xy {
    double dX;
    double dY;
} XY;
```

The type definition *XY* now substitutes for the more awkward *struct xy*, as shown here:

```
XY topLeft = { 0.0, 0.0 };
XY bottomRight = { 1.0, 1.0 };
printf("topLeft = (%f, %f)\n", topLeft.dX, topLeft.dY);
printf("bottomRight = (%f, %f)\n", bottomRight.dX, bottomRight.dY);
```

Instances of *XY*, such as *topLeft* and *bottomRight*, correspond to C++ objects. Each occupies storage on the stack, and you can get away with writing simple assignment statements such as

```
bottomRight = topLeft;
```

However, the C compiler doesn't understand statements such as

```
bottomRight = topLeft + 1;
```

Moving to C++

Now let's recode the previous example in C++, using real classes and objects. Here's the simplest form of the class declaration:

```
class XY {
public:
    double m_dX;
    double m_dY;
};
```

The *public* keyword allows direct access to *m_dX* and *m_dY*, as though these data members were structure members.

> NOTE: By convention, the MFC group and most other Microsoft developers use *m_* to begin the names of data members in C++ classes. I'll start using this convention now so that you'll get used to it. Also, I'll use Hungarian notation, in which the first letter identifies the type of a variable.

Here's the code to make an *XY* object:

```
XY bottomRight; // an uninitialized object
bottomRight.m_dX = 1.0;
bottomRight.m_dY = 1.0;
printf("bottomRight = (%f, %f)\n", bottomRight.m_dX, bottomRight.m_dY);
```

The class elements *x* and *y* were individually assigned values because, for most classes, the C++ compiler won't accept a statement such as

```
XY bottomRight = { 1.0, 1.0 };
```

> NOTE: The compiler does indeed accept the statement above for the simple *XY* class, but it won't accept it after you add the class's constructor, described in the following section.

C++ has structures too, but I was well into my C++ career before I realized that C++ structures were different from C structures. Instead of declaring an *XY* class, you could declare a C++ *XY* structure like this:

```
struct XY {
    double m_dX;
    double m_dY;
};
```

In C++, the only difference between a class and a structure is that structure members are, by default, publicly accessible. C++ structures can have member functions (which you'll see later), and they can participate in C++ inheritance (which you'll also see later).

Constructors

You've seen how awkward it is to initialize the data members of an *XY* object with assignment statements. As you'll see later, C++ classes, unlike C structures, can contain member functions as well as data members. Member functions have full access to all data members of the class. All C++ classes have one or more special member functions, called constructors, that are called to initialize objects. If you don't specify a constructor function in your class definition, the compiler generates a <u>default</u> <u>constructor</u> with no arguments. This default constructor calls the constructors for any C++ objects that are data members of the class. When the compiler generates a call to the default constructor, the compiler assigns storage for an object of the class <u>but</u> <u>does</u> <u>not</u> initialize <u>values</u> of <u>built-in</u> <u>types</u>. Indeed, in the previous example, the *XY* default constructor is called in the function shown here:

```
void func()
{
    XY bottomRight;   // XY object bottomRight constructed on the stack
                      // m_dX and m_dY values are uninitialized
}
```

> **NOTE:** Many beginning C++ programmers try to call default constructors by writing code in this way:
>
> ```
> XY bottomRight(); // don't do this!
> ```
>
> The compiler interprets the statement as a forward declaration of a function named *bottomRight* that returns an object of type *XY*—clearly not the intended result.

A reasonable "explicit" constructor for the *XY* class would take two double-precision arguments. Here is a new *XY* class declaration with this constructor added:

```
class XY {
public:
    double m_dX, m_dY;
    XY(double dX, double dY)   { m_dX = dX; m_dY = dY; }
};
```

The constructor function name is always the same as the class name, and the constructor always returns nothing. In this example, the constructor is defined as <u>in line</u>, which means that the compiler directly substitutes the two assignment statements wherever the constructor is called. Now the previous example code becomes

```
XY bottomRight(1.0, 1.0);  // object named bottomRight of class XY
printf("bottomRight = (%f, %f)\n", bottomRight.m_dX, bottomRight.m_dY);
```

Yes, it's a little weird to write a function named *XY* and then to call it by the name *bottomRight*, but that's just the way C++ works. It makes sense if you consider that, for the default constructor, the statement

```
XY topLeft;
```

is analogous to

```
double dX;
```

Both result in the creation of an entity on the stack—a C++ object of class *XY* or standard type *double*. Now, with the two-argument constructor, the statement

```
XY bottomRight(1.0, 1.0);
```

is a logical extension of

```
XY bottomRight;
```

Because you have written your own constructor, the compiler does not generate a default constructor. The compiler now rejects the statement

```
XY bottomRight;
```

If you write your own default (empty argument list) constructor that sets the data members to 0, the class declaration, with two constructors, looks like this:

```
class XY {
public:
    double m_dX, m_dY;
    XY() { m_dX = 0.0; m_dY = 0.0; }
    XY(double dX, double dY)     {m_dX = dX; m_dY = dY;}
};
```

Now two functions are named *XY*, a situation clearly not allowed in C. The C++ compiler does permit multiple declarations and, furthermore, can tell from the function call statement which version of *XY( )* you want. Therefore, both of the following statements are legal in the same program:

```
XY topLeft;
XY bottomRight(1.0, 1.0);
```

Destructors

No discussion of constructors would be complete without a companion discussion of <u>destructors</u>. A destructor is another special C++ member function; its name consists of the class name preceded by a tilde (~). Each class has one and only one destructor function, and that function takes no arguments and returns nothing. The destructor is automatically called for any stack or global object when that object goes out of scope.

We have no need for an explicit *XY* destructor, but we'll write one anyway. This time, neither the constructors nor the destructor will be in line, so we can show off some new C++ notation. The destructor code is shown on the following page:

```
class XY {
public:
    double m_dX, m_dY;
    XY();   // default constructor
    XY(double dX, double dY);
    ~XY(); // destructor
};

XY::XY()
{
    printf("XY default constructor called\n");
    m_dX = m_dY = 0.0;
}

XY::XY(double dX, double dY)
{
    printf("XY explicit constructor called\n");
    m_dX = dX;
    m_dY = dY;
}

XY::~XY()
{
    printf("XY destructor called\n");
}
```

Now for an explanation of the new notation: The tilde character preceding the class name identifies the destructor and is part of the function name. The *XY::* prefix, used for both the constructor and the destructor definitions, tells the compiler that a function is a member function of the *XY* class.

If you made the following function call

```
void func() {
    XY bottomRight(1.0, 1.0);
    printf("the x coordinate is: %5.1f\n", bottomRight.m_dX);
}
```

the output would be

```
XY explicit constructor called
the x coordinate is: 1.0
XY destructor called
```

Notice that the destructor is called automatically when the *bottomRight* object goes out of scope at the end of *func*'s execution.

If you don't write a destructor, the compiler generates a default destructor for you. For data members that are C++ objects, the default constructor calls those objects' destructors. When the compiler generates a call to a destructor for an object, the compiler generates code that releases storage occupied by that object.

Other Member Functions

You've seen the constructor and destructor member functions, and you know that they're always present, even if the compiler has to generate them for you. You can also write your own special-purpose class member functions.

Suppose you need member functions that retrieve the *m_dX* and *m_dY* values of an *XY* object. Here is the class declaration that includes the inline member functions *Getx* and *Gety*:

```
class XY {
public:
    double m_dX, m_dY;
    XY();
    XY(double dX, double dY);
    double Getx() const { return m_dX; }
    double Gety() const { return m_dY; }
};
```

Getx and *Gety* can directly access all data members of their class functions, as can other member functions (including constructors and destructors).

> **NOTE:** The *const* modifier used with *Getx* and *Gety* indicates that these functions do not modify class data members. This means that the compiler rejects any statements inside these functions that write to data members.

In the application code, *assert* is a C/C++ diagnostic macro that tests the given condition:

```
XY bottomRight(1.0, 1.0);
assert(bottomRight.Getx() == 1.0);
```

The notation *bottomRight.Getx( )* means "Call the *Getx* member function for the object *bottomRight*." That's all there is to it.

> **NOTE:** In Microsoft Foundation Class (MFC) Library version 4.0 code, you'll see the MFC library *ASSERT* macro used instead of the C/C++ *assert* macro.

Private vs. Public Class Members

Up to now, the *m_dX* and *m_dY* data members in our *XY* class have been <u>public</u> and thus accessible throughout the program, as they are in a C structure. C++ allows a class's data to be hidden. If you designate a data member as

<u>private</u>, it is inaccessible outside the class; only class member functions can get at it.

Now that the *XY* class has member functions that return the coordinate values, we can write a useful program that doesn't require direct access to any data members. Here is the new class declaration:

```
class XY {
private:
    double m_dX, m_dY;
public:
    XY();
    XY(double dX, double dY);
    double Getx() const;
    double Gety() const;
};
```

Class members are private by default, so technically we could eliminate the *private* keyword. The program is easier to read, however, if we leave it in.

Now the same application code still works, as shown here:

```
XY bottomRight(1.0, 1.0);
assert(bottomRight.Getx() == 1.0);
```

But outside the class, the compiler no longer accepts statements such as

```
bottomRight.m_dX = 1.0;
```

The *m_dX* data member is now private and accessible only through the *Getx* member function. This clearly illustrates C++'s encapsulation feature. Encapsulation is particularly useful in more complex classes, in which a need exists for tight control over internal data access.

Member functions can also be private. A private member function, sometimes called a <u>helper</u> function, isn't callable outside the class, but it is accessible to other member functions of the same class. As with any member function, a private member function can be named anything you want, even something like *sqrt*, because you know it won't conflict with other like-named functions, even global ones.

Global Functions

Sometimes you need to write new class-related functions without changing the class declaration or writing a derived class. If, for example, you need a function *Show* that displays the values of the *XY* data members, you could write a global function such as this:

```
void Show(XY xy)
{
    printf("x = %f, y = %f\n", xy.Getx(), xy.Gety());
}
```

This technique works only when the existing class member functions provide all the necessary access to the data members (or if the data members are public). An alternative method is the friend function, described later, which does require a change to the *XY* class declaration.

Even though *Show* is global, it won't conflict with other *Show* functions because the compiler matches the calls according to parameter types.

C++ Encapsulation—A Recap

You've just learned about one of the three big C++ features: <u>encapsulation</u>. The data members in the *XY* class example, *m_dX* and *m_dY*, are encapsulated with a set of useful functions that operate on them. The resulting *XY* class is a modular programming unit that, as you will see, you can use as a building block in an application.

Inheritance and Polymorphism—An Example

You're probably bored with the *XY* class by now, so let's move on to something out of this world. We'll create a two-dimensional simulation of the solar system, adaptable to both video games and Star Wars defense projects. This exercise in object-oriented design lets you relate C++ objects to physical entities.

We want a computer program containing objects that represent heavenly bodies (such as planets and moons) and spaceships, that move in the sun's gravitational field. Ultimately, we'd like to display the moving planets and spaceships on the screen, but we'll leave that as an exercise for the reader.

The *Orbiter* Base Class and Virtual Functions

An important step in object-oriented design, after initially identifying classes, is arranging the classes into a hierarchy with common functionality factored out to a <u>base class</u>. In the solar system example, we define a base class *Orbiter* that has functionality common to both planets and spaceships. An orbiter is aware of Kepler's laws and thus knows how to move in the sun's gravitational field.

Here's the first try at an *Orbiter* class declaration:

```
class Orbiter {
private:          // data members
    double m_dMass;
    XY      m_xyCurrent, m_xyPrior, m_xyThrust;
public:           // member functions
    Orbiter(XY xyCurrent, XY xyPrior, double dMass); // constructor
    XY GetPosition() const;
    void Fly();
};
```

Notice your old friend the *XY* class. Objects of class *XY* represent sun-based position coordinates that are "embedded" within an *Orbiter* object, as is the standard type *m_dMass*.

The *GetPosition* member function returns an object of class *XY* that corresponds to the orbiter's current position. (Later you'll learn how references make this process more efficient.) The *Fly* member function (not shown) applies a formula to the current and prior coordinate values, thus moving the orbiter through space. On the next iteration, the new prior coordinates are set to this iteration's current coordinates.

The *m_xyThrust* data member is included in the *Orbiter* class, even though planets don't have thrust, because the *Fly* member function needs thrust for its calculations, and we want a single general *Fly* function. For planets, *m_xyThrust* is always (0, 0).

Before we can "derive" the planet and spaceship classes from *Orbiter*, we must fix a few things. First, if the *Orbiter* data members are all private, they will be totally inaccessible to the derived classes. The C++ *protected* keyword allows a derived class to access base-class data members.

Next we need a member function that displays an orbiter. This *Display* function must be implemented differently for each derived *Orbiter* class because, for example, spaceships look different from planets. The C++ keyword *virtual* in the base-class declaration identifies *Display* as a function of this special category. Here is the new class declaration:

```
class Orbiter {
protected:
    double m_dMass;
    XY      m_xyCurrent, m_xyPrior, m_xyThrust;
public:
    Orbiter(XY xyCurrent, XY xyPrior, double dMass) {
        m_xyCurrent = xyCurrent;
        m_xyPrior = xyPrior;
        m_dMass = dMass;
    }
```

```
    XY GetPosition() const;
    void Fly();
    virtual void Display() const;
};
```

Now, if you have an array of orbiters, including planets, spaceships, and other space junk, you call the *Fly* function to update positions, and you call *Display* to show the objects on the screen. You call the same *Fly* function for each object, but which *Display* function you call depends on the object's class. The use of the virtual *Display* function illustrates the C++ polymorphism feature.

The following example assumes that *orbiterArray* contains pointers to a mixture of objects of classes derived from *Orbiter*.

```
extern Orbiter* orbiterArray[];
for (int i = 0; i < MAX; i++) {
    orbiterArray[i]->Fly();
    orbiterArray[i]->Display();
}
```

> **NOTE:** This example uses pointers to *Orbiter* objects rather than the objects themselves. You'll see more object pointer usage later.

Observe that, in the *Display* call above, the object's class is determined at <u>runtime</u>, not at compile time. That means there must be something inside <u>each object</u> that identifies its class. That "something" is a 32-bit pointer to a <u>vtable</u> (virtual function table), inserted by the *Spaceship* and *Planet* class constructors. The compiler thus generates two separate vtables, one for *Spaceship* and one for *Planet*, each consisting of a table of virtual function addresses (in this case, just one address each). The *Spaceship* vtable contains a pointer to *Spaceship::Display*, and the *Planet* vtable contains a pointer to *Planet::Display*. If the compiler has enough information to make a direct call to a *Display* function, it does, but in the case above, the compiler generates a <u>polymorphic</u> (indirect) call through the object's vtable pointer.

Pure Virtual Functions

In the example above, a program could construct objects of class *Orbiter*, but that doesn't make sense because an orbiter is an abstract concept. You can prevent construction of *Orbiter* base-class objects by declaring one or more functions as <u>pure virtual</u> with this syntax:

```
virtual void Display() const = 0; // '= 0' means pure virtual
```

Now *Orbiter* is officially an <u>abstract base class</u>, and the compiler forces all derived classes (which are used for constructing objects) to provide implementations of the *Display* member function. As a side benefit, the linker doesn't make you actually write the *Orbiter::Display* function.

Derived Classes

We'll be writing two classes derived from *Orbiter*: *Planet* and *Spaceship*. The *Planet* derived class isn't very interesting. Perhaps all it needs is its own *Display* function and, of course, a constructor. Here's the declaration:

```
class Planet : public Orbiter {
public:
    Planet(XY xyCurrent, XY xyPrior, double dMass) :
        Orbiter(xyCurrent, xyPrior, dMass) {}
    void Display() const;
};
```

The first line states that the *Planet* class is publicly derived from the *Orbiter* class. Any derived class inherits all the data members and member functions (except constructors and destructors) of its base class. For a publicly derived class, inherited public base-class members are public, and inherited protected base-class members are protected. All the derived classes in this book are publicly derived.

The colon (:) notation in the *Planet* class constructor declaration means that the base-class (*Orbiter*) constructor is called first to create the *Orbiter* component of the *Planet* object. Any *Planet*-specific code (nothing, in this case) is then executed. Actually, all the memory for both the base-class and the derived-class data members is allocated prior to execution of any constructor code.

> N O T E: If you had not included the *Orbiter* constructor as part of the *Planet* constructor, the compiler would have rejected the statement. Why? The compiler would have tried to use a default *Orbiter* constructor, but, because you had declared only an explicit three-argument *Orbiter* constructor, the compiler would have given up.

The *Spaceship* class is more complex than the *Planet* class because it has its own data members and a new member function:

```
class Spaceship : public Orbiter {
private:
    double m_Fuel;
    XY      m_xyOrientation;
public:
    Spaceship(XY xyCurrent, XY xyPrior, XY xyThrust, double dMass,
            double dFuel, XY xyOrientation) :
        Orbiter(xyCurrent, xyPrior, dMass) {
            m_dFuel = dFuel;
            m_xyOrientation = xyOrientation;
            m_xyThrust = xyThrust; // m_xyThrust is an Orbiter data member
        }
```

```
    void Display() const;
    void FireThrusters();
};
```

Now you must provide constructor code to initialize the spaceship-specific data members.

Virtual Functions Called in Base Classes

You've seen the virtual *Display* function called for elements of an *Orbiter* object array. Virtual functions can be called polymorphically in a base class as well as from outside the class. Suppose that the *Orbiter::Fly* function needs to compute angular momentum and that this computation is specific to the derived class. If the *Orbiter* class contains the following declaration, derived classes are obliged to provide override functions:

```
protected:
    virtual XY GetAngularMomentum() const = 0;
```

Embedded Objects

What about the *XY* objects embedded in the *Planet* and *Spaceship* objects? When are they constructed? Here things get complicated, but you must understand the process to prepare yourself for the more complex C++ class interrelationships you'll see in MFC library programming. Before you go any further, however, you need to know about copy constructors and assignment operators.

Copy Constructors

Like the default constructor, the copy constructor is a class member function that the compiler often generates. Indeed, the compiler frequently generates invisible calls to the copy constructor, sometimes where you least expect them.

The purpose of the copy constructor is to make a new object of the same class from an existing object that is passed as an argument. An inline copy constructor for the *XY* class looks like this:

```
XY(const XY& xy) {
    m_dX = xy.m_dX;
    m_dY = xy.m_dY;
}
```

NOTE: The *const* modifier indicates that the function does not modify the values referenced by the *xy* parameter. The absence of *const* would alert you to the possibility that the function might indeed modify the values.

If you don't define a copy constructor for a class, the compiler generates one for you that simply does a memberwise copy of all the object's data. (The compiler can safely optimize this to a bitwise copy when appropriate.) Because the *XY* class is so simple, the default copy constructor is sufficient. For more complex classes, such as those that require memory allocation or other special processing, the default copy constructor isn't sufficient. It's good practice to write copy constructors for all but the most trivial classes.

NOTE: When the compiler generates a copy constructor, that function invokes the base class copy constructor. If you write your own copy constructor, you can decide which base class constructor to call.

The notation *const XY&* that you saw earlier in the *Orbiter* class declaration is a C++ <u>reference</u>, and its use is required in copy constructors. The compiler passes the address of the *XY* object as an argument to the *XY* copy constructor rather than passing a copy of the object itself. It's like passing a pointer, but the notation is cleaner. You'll see references again, and you'll learn why they're more than a pointer substitute.

An obvious use for a compiler-generated copy constructor call is in code such as the following:

```
XY alpha(1.0, 2.0);
XY beta = alpha;
XY gamma(alpha); // same result as preceding statement
```

Here two new *XY* objects, *beta* and *gamma*, are constructed from the existing object *alpha*.

Less obvious is the copy constructor call in the following sequence:

```
void func(XY xy);
XY alpha(2.0, 3.0);
func(alpha);
```

Here the *alpha* object is constructed on the calling program's stack using the explicit constructor, and then the copy constructor is called to copy the *alpha* object to the argument list for *func*.

Assignment Operators

The <u>assignment</u> <u>operator</u> is a lot like a copy constructor except that it operates on an existing object rather than creating a new object. The compiler generates default assignment operators, and it generates calls to them. The assignment operator is an example of a C++ overloaded operator, which you'll learn more about later in this appendix. You need to understand the use of assignment operators now, however.

If you were to write your own inline assignment operator for the *XY* class, it would look like this:

```
const XY& operator=(const XY& xy) { // uses references
    m_dX = xy.m_dX;                  // copies the values
    m_dY = xy.m_dY;
    return *this;
}
```

> NOTE: The returned *XY* reference permits assignment operators to be "chained," as in the statement
>
> ```
> xy1 = xy2 = XY(0.0, 0.0);
> ```
>
> The first *const* modifier indicates that the result of the assignment can be used only where a *const* parameter is specified. If *ClearContents* is declared as a non-*const XY* member function, the compiler rejects this statement:
>
> ```
> (xy1 = xy2).ClearContents();
> ```
>
> but the compiler accepts the statement
>
> ```
> (xy1 = xy2).Getx();
> ```
>
> because *Getx* is declared a *const* function. (See the section titled "Use of the *this* Pointer" later in this appendix.)

This code illustrates an obvious use of the assignment operator:

```
XY alpha(1.0, 2.0);
XY beta(3.0, 4.0);
beta = alpha;
```

Here the contents of *alpha* are copied to *beta*, overwriting the latter's previous contents.

Here's another example:

```
class Container {
private:
    XY m_xyPoint;
```

(continued)

827

```
public:
    Container(XY xyPoint) { m_xyPoint = xyPoint; }
};
```

When an object of class *Container* is constructed, the *XY* default constructor is called to make an *m_xyPoint* object before the body of the *Container* constructor is executed. The assignment statement

```
m_xyPoint = xyPoint;
```

triggers a call to the *XY* assignment operator.

The compiler-generated default assignment operator does a memberwise copy of all the object's data, and that's sufficient for the *XY* class. Plan to write your own assignment operators for more complex classes.

Reference Parameters: *const* vs. non-*const*

Remember that <u>reference</u> <u>parameters</u> are just disguised pointer parameters. If you see a reference parameter in a function declaration, you can assume the programmer used it for one of two reasons. Perhaps the function uses the parameter to change a variable in the calling program, or possibly the programmer wanted to avoid copying a large object onto the function's call stack. Fortunately, there's an easy way to determine the real reason. In the first case, the reference will be non-*const*, and in the second case, the reference will be *const*.

Consider the following global function:

```
void TimesTwo(XY& xy) { xy.m_dX *= 2.0; xy.m_dY *= 2.0; }
```

and its usage:

```
XY pos(1.0, 2.0);
TimesTwo(pos);
assert(pos.m_dX == 2.0 && pos.m_dY == 4.0);
```

Here the function *TimesTwo* definitely changes the value of its non-*const* parameter. Some would argue that this parameter usage violates C++ encapsulation—a member function would be more correct. Naturally, the *m_dX* and *m_dY* data members must be public, or *TimesTwo* must be a friend of the class.

Now let's see the usage of a *const* reference parameter. We'll revisit the global *Show* function and make it more efficient:

```
void Show(const XY& xy)  {
    printf("x = %f, y = %f\n", xy.Getx(), xy.Gety());
}
```

Show now cannot change the value of the *XY* object in the calling program. Not only does a statement (inside *Show*) such as

```
xy.m_dX = 5.0;
```

generate a compile error, the statement also causes any calls to non-*const XY* member functions to generate errors. Calling *Getx* and *Gety* would be illegal unless we had the foresight to declare *Getx* and *Gety* as *const* functions (which we did). *Getx* and *Gety* promise not to change the object, so it's OK to call them for a *const XY* reference.

C++ References at Work

The following application code constructs our home planet:

```
XY xyCurrent(100.0, 200.0); // constructs current XY coordinate pair
XY xyPrior(100.1, 200.1);   // constructs prior XY coordinate pair
Planet earth(xyCurrent, xyPrior, 1.0E+10); // constructs Earth object
```

If you use the following versions of the class declarations that you've already seen:

```
class XY {
public:
    double m_dX, m_dY;
    XY() { m_dX = 0.0; m_dY = 0.0; }    // default constructor
    XY(double dXarg, double dYarg)      // explicit constructor
        { m_dX = dXarg; m_dY = dYarg; }
    XY(const XY& xy) {                  // copy constructor
        m_dX = xy.m_dX;
        m_dY = xy.m_dY;
    }
    const XY& operator=(const XY& xy) { // assignment operator
        m_dX = xy.m_dX;
        m_dY = xy.m_dY;
        return *this;
    }
};

class Orbiter {
protected:
    double m_dMass;
    XY      m_xyCurrent, m_xyPrior, m_xyThrust;
public:
    Orbiter(XY xyCurrent, XY xyPrior, double dMass) {
        m_xyCurrent = xyCurrent;
        m_xyPrior = xyPrior;
        m_dMass = dMass;
    }
    XY GetPosition() const;
```

(continued)

```
        void Fly();
        virtual void Display() = 0;
};

class Planet : public Orbiter {
public:
    Planet(XY xyCurrent, XY xyPrior, double dMass)
        : Orbiter(xyCurrent, xyPrior, dMass) { }
    void Display();
};
```

the following sequence of *XY* constructor calls is necessary to create an object named *Earth*:

1. The explicit *XY* constructor creates *xyCurrent* and *xyPrior* objects on the stack.

2. The *XY* copy constructor copies the *xyCurrent* and *xyPrior* objects to the *Planet* constructor's argument list.

3. The *XY* copy constructor copies the *xyCurrent* and *xyPrior* objects from the *Planet* constructor's argument list to the *Orbiter* constructor's argument list.

4. The *XY* default constructor (required) creates *m_xyCurrent* and *m_xyPrior* members and initializes them to (0, 0).

5. The *XY* assignment operator copies the *xyCurrent* and *xyPrior* objects from the *Orbiter* constructor's argument list to the corresponding data members.

Wow! That's a lot of construction! For efficiency's sake, we'll rearrange the *Orbiter* and *Planet* code, particularly that of the constructors:

```
class Orbiter {
protected:
    double m_dMass;
    XY      m_xyCurrent, m_xyPrior, m_xyThrust;
public:
    Orbiter(const XY& xyCurrent, const XY& xyPrior, double dMass)
        : m_xyCurrent(xyCurrent), m_xyPrior(xyPrior), m_dMass(dMass) { }
    const XY& GetPosition() const;
    void Fly();
    virtual void Display() = 0;
};

class Planet : public Orbiter {
public:
```

```
    // copy constructor and assignment operator not shown
    Planet(const XY& xyCurrent, const XY& xyPrior, double dMass)
        : Orbiter(xyCurrent, xyPrior, dMass) { }
    void Display();
};
```

You'll notice that the *Orbiter* and *Planet* constructors use *XY* references now. Also, the *Orbiter* constructor is quite different. We've dropped the statements

```
m_xyCurrent = xyCurrent;
m_xyPrior = xyPrior;
m_dMass = dMass;
```

and substituted the clause

```
: m_xyCurrent(xyCurrent), m_xyPrior(xyPrior), m_dMass(dMass) { }
```

> NOTE: C++ allows the function syntax *m_dMass(dMass)*, even though *m_dMass* is a data member of a built-in data type (*double*). If *m_dMass* were declared a *const* data member, this would be the only way you could initialize it.

Now, instead of generating two calls to the *XY* default constructor and two calls to the assignment operator, the compiler simply generates two calls to the *XY* copy constructor ahead of the mass assignment (in the *Orbiter* constructor body). This should give you some insight into the real meaning of the constructor colon syntax: the statements after the colon, including (but not limited to) calls to the base class and contained object constructors, are executed before the constructor body.

For variety's sake, we'll rewrite the "create Earth" code as follows:

```
Planet earth(XY(100.00, 200.00), XY(100.01, 200.01), 1.0E+10);
```

Here you see another variation of constructor call syntax for the two *XY* objects. Now the *XY* constructor calls for planet Earth are as follows:

1. Temporary current and prior objects are constructed in the constructor's argument list with the explicit *XY* constructor.

2. The *m_xyCurrent* and *m_xyPrior* objects are constructed, with the *XY* copy constructor, from the objects from step 1. Those objects were passed all the way down to the *Orbiter* constructor as references, thereby avoiding extra copy operations.

In both planet construction scenarios, the *m_xyThrust* embedded object is constructed with the default *XY* constructor, which sets both the *m_dX* and *m_dY* components to 0.

Returning References

A function can return a reference, which is equivalent to returning a pointer, and these references can be *const* or non-*const*. Here's a new version of *Getx* that returns a *const* reference to an *XY* object:

```
const double& XY::GetConstRefx() const { return m_dX; }
```

The *GetConstRefx* function can be used on the right side of an assignment statement but, because the reference is *const*, not on the left side. Thus, the statement

```
topLeft.GetConstRefx() = 3.0;   // topLeft is an object of class XY
```

causes a compiler error. If you removed the *const* keyword from the reference, the statement would be allowed, and you could use the function to modify the state of the *topLeft* object.

> NOTE: If you write a C++ function that returns a reference, you could end up making the same mistake that beginning C programmers often make. Here's the classic C example:
>
> ```
> double *GetNumber()
> {
>     double dResult = (double) rand() / (double) RAND_MAX;
>     return &dResult; /* don't do this */
> }
> ```
>
> The function returns a pointer to stack memory that will be used for something else after the function returns.
>
> Here's the C++ equivalent with a reference:
>
> ```
> double& GetNumber()
> {
>     double dResult = (double) rand() / (double) RAND_MAX;
>     return dResult; // don't do this either
> }
> ```

It's just as wrong as the C example because the compiler is still returning a pointer to a temporary variable.

References vs. Pointers—Null Values

If the compiler generates pointer code for a reference, how do you know when to use a reference and when to use a pointer? The two elements are interchangeable—you can cast a reference exactly as you can cast a pointer, for example. But there's one important difference: a pointer can have a null value. If your function declares a pointer parameter, the caller can pass in

NULL, and the function can test for it; with a reference parameter, the caller must specify an object. If a function returns a pointer, it can return *NULL*, and the caller can test for it; with a reference return, the function must return an object.

Construction of Embedded Objects—A Summary

You've seen the construction sequence for a *Planet* object. The *Spaceship* class is more interesting because both the *Orbiter* class and the *Spaceship* class have their own embedded objects. Here's the construction sequence for a *Spaceship* object:

1. The compiler already knows how much total memory a *Spaceship* object (including all embedded objects) requires, so that amount of memory is allocated.

2. The *m_xyCurrent, m_xyPrior,* and *m_xyThrust* embedded objects are constructed.

3. The *Orbiter* constructor function is called.

4. The *m_xyOrientation* embedded object is constructed.

5. The *Spaceship* constructor function is called.

The class design and initial *Spaceship* constructor call determine exactly which constructors (default, explicit, or copy) are called, but the list above is an accurate summary.

Destruction of Embedded Objects

Consider what happens when an object of class *Spaceship* is destroyed. The *Spaceship* class is interesting because it's a derived class with embedded objects defined both in the base class and in the derived class. Here's the sequence of events:

1. The compiler-generated *Spaceship* destructor is called.

2. The *m_xyOrientation* embedded object is destroyed.

3. The compiler-generated *Orbiter* destructor is called.

4. The *m_xyCurrent, m_xyPrior,* and *m_xyThrust* embedded objects are destroyed.

5. The memory allocated for the *Spaceship* object is freed.

Notice that this destruction sequence is the exact opposite of the construction sequence.

Allocation of Objects on the Heap

So far, all objects have been allocated on the stack, and except for the virtual *Display* function, the objects have been referenced directly. You'll recall that stack objects are destroyed when they go out of scope. As you do in C with the help of the runtime library, when you program in C++, you allocate objects on the heap so that their memory remains in use until you specifically free it. You keep track of heap objects with pointers.

The C++ *new* and *delete* Operators

The operators *new* and *delete* are roughly equivalent to the C *malloc* and *free* functions. You can use *new* to allocate raw storage this way:

```
char* pCommBuffer = new char[4096];
```

More often, however, you'll use *new* to construct objects on the heap this way:

```
Planet* pEarth = new Planet(XY(100.0, 200.0),
    XY(100.1, 200.1), 1.0E+10);
```

The variable *pEarth* contains the address of an object of class *Planet* and is thus a pointer. Here the compiler first calculates the total size of a *Planet* object, then it allocates the required memory on the heap, and then it calls the constructor function. Note that the constructor syntax for heap allocation is different from the syntax for stack allocation.

To free the memory pointer to *pCommBuffer*, use the <u>delete</u> operator this way:

```
delete [] pCommBuffer;
```

To get rid of *pEarth*, simply call the *Planet* destructor this way:

```
delete pEarth;
```

All the contained objects are destroyed, as they are when a stack-allocated *Planet* object goes out of scope.

Referring to Objects Through Pointers

You can see that pointers go hand in hand with heap-allocated objects. You could use pointers to stack objects, but then you'd be vulnerable to a common programming error—the use of a pointer to an object that has gone out of scope.

Pointer Declarations—A C++ Coding Convention

The following pointer examples illustrate a C++ coding convention that is used both in this book and in the Microsoft Foundation Class Library documentation. In pointer declarations, the asterisk always appears next to the type name rather than next to the variable name; this is different from the usual C convention. For example:

```
char *szLastName; /* C-style pointer declaration */
char* szLastname; // C++/MFC library-style pointer declaration
```

This convention has two advantages:

■ It differentiates between pointer declarations and dereference operators.

  The following statement, at first glance, appears to assign the first characters of the *szLastName* string the value of the *szDefault* pointer:

```
char *szLastName = szDefault;
```

  With the C++ notation, however, the statement clearly declares a new pointer and assigns it the value of *szDefault*:

```
char* szLastName = szDefault;
```

■ It's compatible with the C++ reference notation.

  References are always indicated by an ampersand (&) following the type name to distinguish them from the "address of" operator. References to pointers, then, are shown this way:

```
XY*& pxy;
```

The disadvantage of the convention shows up in multiple declarations in a single statement. With the familiar C notation, the following statement declares three character pointers:

```
char *a, *b, *c;
```

With the new convention, the following statement declares one pointer and two individual character variables:

```
char* a, b, c;  // perhaps not what you wanted
```

If you consistently use the new convention, you must use separate statements for each declaration, like this:

```
char* a; char* b; char* c;
```

Once you have a pointer to an object, you can call its class member functions using this convenient notation:

```
pEarth->Fly();
```

Pointers are necessary if you want to reference objects polymorphically. For example, you could construct an object of class *Planet*, but you would store its pointer as an *Orbiter* pointer this way:

```
Orbiter* pAny = new Planet(XY(100.0, 200.0),
    XY(100.1, 200.1), 1.0E+10);
```

C++ allows this conversion because the *Planet* class is derived from *Orbiter*. You could not convert an *Orbiter* pointer to a *Planet* pointer without a specific (and dangerous) cast operator.

Now you can call *Orbiter* virtual functions this way:

```
pAny->Display();
```

At runtime, the *Display* function of the *Planet* class is called because *Display* is declared as a virtual function in the *Orbiter* class.

Virtual Destructors

Be aware that destructors are not inherited, that the compiler generates a default destructor for each class if you do not explicitly write one, and that a derived-class destructor <u>always</u> calls its base-class destructor. What if you had a pointer to an object of an unknown class derived from *Orbiter* and you wanted to destroy that object? If you called the *Orbiter* default destructor, it would destroy only those object elements specified by the *Orbiter* class itself. Suppose you constructed a *Spaceship* object on the heap, assigned its address to an *Orbiter* pointer, and then deleted the pointer like this:

```
Orbiter* pAny = new Spaceship(xyCurrent, xyPrior, xyThrust, dMass,
                             dFuel, xyOrientation);
delete pAny;
```

Even though the correct quantity of heap memory will be freed, the *Spaceship* object's deletion would be incomplete. In particular, the destructor for the *XY* object *m_xyOrientation* would not be called.

How do you solve this problem? You declare a <u>virtual</u> <u>destructor</u> for the *Orbiter* class, which adds an entry to both the *Spaceship* and the *Planet* class vtables:

```
virtual ~Orbiter() { }
```

You don't need any code or declarations for derived-class destructors unless you're not satisfied with the compiler-generated defaults.

If you repeat the previous example now, the statement

```
delete pAny;
```

calls the proper derived-class destructor—in this case, the destructor for class *Spaceship*, which first destroys all elements particular to spaceships, including *m_orientation*, and then calls the *Orbiter* destructor.

Allocation of Global Objects

You've seen stack objects, heap objects, and objects contained in other objects. <u>Global objects</u> are constructed before your main program is called, and they are destroyed after the main program exits. Like global variables, global objects are accessible to all functions in your program.

Suppose you have encapsulated all the Microsoft non-Windows graphics functions (declared in graph.h) in a C++ class named *GraphScreen*. The program skeleton would look like this:

```
class GraphScreen {
private:
    // miscellaneous data members
public:
    GraphScreen();  // constructor that initializes the display for
                    //  graphics
    ~GraphScreen(); // destructor that resets the screen back to
                    //  text mode
    void MoveTo(int nX, int nY);
    void LineTo(int nX, int nY);
    // more member functions
};

GraphScreen screen; // a single global screen object

void main() {
    screen.MoveTo(100, 200);
    screen.LineTo(200, 200);  // draws a line from (100, 200) to
                              //  (200, 200)
}
```

Because the *GraphScreen* constructor is called before *main*, it can do any necessary video mode initialization. Because the destructor is called automatically after *main* exits, it can reset the video.

Object Interrelationships—Pointer Data Members

You'll recall that the *Planet* class provided for several embedded *XY* objects. Because an *XY* object is only 16 bytes long, and because *XY* objects are not shared among *Planet* objects, it's reasonable to make them embedded objects. A benefit of this arrangement is the automatic destruction of all *XY* objects when the *Planet* object is destroyed. A restriction is that the compiler must see the *XY* class declaration before the *Planet* class declaration.

What if you want to establish a relationship between two existing objects? Suppose your universe contains moons, in addition to planets and spaceships, and you want to associate each moon with its planet. Our moon has little effect on the motion of the Earth around the sun, but the Earth profoundly affects the moon's motion. The Earth has only one moon, but other planets have several moons. It makes sense, then, for the *Moon* class to have a *Planet* pointer data member, as shown here:

```
class Planet;

class Moon : public Orbiter {
private:
    Planet* m_pPlanet; // pointer to associated Planet object
public:
    Moon(XY& xyCurrent, XY& xyPrior, double dMass, Planet* pPlanet)
        : Orbiter(xyCurrent, xyPrior, dMass), m_pPlanet(pPlanet) { }
    void Display() const { } // necessary because Display is pure virtual
    Planet* GetPlanet() const { return m_pPlanet; }
    void SetPlanet(const Planet* pPlanet) { m_pPlanet = pPlanet; }
};
```

The *Moon* constructor takes a *Planet* pointer as an argument. The *GetPlanet* and *SetPlanet* member functions allow access to the pointer. Notice that the compiler doesn't have to see the complete *Planet* class declaration prior to the *Moon* declaration. The forward declaration

```
class Planet;
```

is sufficient because the compiler merely has to reserve space for a pointer, and all object pointers are the same size. The size of the *Moon* object itself is of no consequence.

Now, when you construct a *Moon* object, you must include a *Planet* object pointer in the constructor call:

```
Planet* pEarth = new Planet(XY(100.00, 200.00),
                            XY(100.01, 200.01), 1.0E+10);
Moon* pMoon = new Moon(XY(100.10, 200.10),
                       XY(100.11, 200.11), 1.0E+10, pEarth);
```

Please be careful when deleting interrelated objects. If, in this example, you deleted the *Earth* object, your program would crash if it continued to use the dependent *Moon* object.

NOTE: The addition of moons to the solar system seriously complicates the *Orbiter::Fly* function. Now an *Orbiter* object's state is no longer solely dependent on current and prior sun-based coordinates. We must make *Fly* a virtual function with a special version for moons, or we must rewrite *Fly* to process gravitational interactions among all heavenly bodies.

Use of the *this* Pointer

The C++ language provides a self-reference syntax that allows a program to obtain a pointer to the current object. This pointer, denoted by the keyword *this*, can be used as a function call parameter, and it can be returned by a member function or an overloaded operator. In the following example, a *Planet* class member function connects to a specified *Moon* object:

```
void Planet::ConnectToMoon(Moon* pMoon) {
    pMoon->SetPlanet(this); // this planet object
}
```

References to Pointers

Most C++ textbooks explain references and illustrate pointer usage. Few, however, give good examples of references to pointers, a feature used in some MFC library classes. You've already seen the separate *Moon* class member functions *SetPlanet* and *GetPlanet*. You can combine these two functions into one easy-to-use function like this:

```
Planet*& Moon::GetPlanet() { return m_pPlanet; }
```

The returned reference to a pointer is, in effect, a double pointer; therefore, you can place *GetPlanet* on either the right or the left of an assignment statement, as shown here:

```
XY      xy11, xy12, xy21, xy22, xy31, xy32;
double dMass1, dMass2, dMass3;

Planet* pEarth = new Planet(xy11, xy12, dMass1);
Planet* pMars = new Planet(xy21, xy22, dMass2);
Moon*   pMoon = new Moon(xy31, xy32, dMass3, pEarth);
assert(pMoon->GetPlanet() == pEarth); // rvalue
```

(continued)

```
pMoon->GetPlanet() = pMars;              // lvalue
assert(pMoon->GetPlanet() == pMars);     // rvalue
```

If you're confused, consider the more C-like equivalent notation:

```
Planet** Moon::GetPlanet() { return &m_pPlanet; }
```

```
*(pMoon->GetPlanet()) = pMars;
```

Does that make it any better?

In the MFC library classes, the declaration

```
Planet*& Moon::GetPlanet();
```

is often paired with the declaration

```
Planet* Moon::GetPlanet() const;
```

This second overloaded variation allows *GetPlanet* to be used (on the right side of an assignment statement) with *const* pointers to *Planet* objects. The following example shows use of the *const* variation of *GetPlanet*:

```
const Moon* cpMoon = new Moon(xy1, xy2, dMass, pEarth);
Planet* pPlanet = cpMoon->GetPlanet();
```

The compiler will not accept the second statement unless the second *Get-Planet* declaration is present. For more information about *const* pointers, refer to a C++ textbook.

Friend Classes and Friend Functions

Sometimes two classes are closely related, and the C++ <u>friendship</u> feature can formalize this relationship. Class friendship is similar to human friendship. For example, you are free to declare yourself a friend to the president of the United States, but that doesn't give you the right to show up at the White House for dinner. If, on the other hand, the president declares you a friend, chances are you can drop by any time as long as you've remembered to bring a campaign contribution.

Friend Classes

As we move from Washington, D.C., out to space for a minute, it would be handy if *Moon* objects could directly access *Planet* data members, particularly the planet's mass and current position. This is possible only if the *Planet* class is declared a friend to class *Moon*, as shown here:

```
class Planet : public Orbiter {
    friend class Moon;  // no prior declaration required
```

```
public:
    // constructors and other member functions
};
```

Now the following code is allowed in <u>all</u> *Moon* class member functions:

```
double Moon::MassProduct() {
    return GetPlanet()->m_dMass * m_dMass; // planet's mass * moon's mass
}
```

You could restrict friendship to the *MassProduct* member function in the following way:

```
class Planet : public Orbiter {
    friend double Moon::MassProduct();
public:
    // constructors and other member functions
};
```

Global Friend Functions

Suppose, in a particular application, that the *XY* class represents a vector and that you need the tangent of the vector's angle. You could write an ordinary *tan* member function as follows:

```
double XY::tan() {
    if (y != 0.0) {
        return m_dX / m_dY;
    }
    else {
        return 0.0;
    }
}
```

You could then call *tan* as you would any class member function:

```
XY      vector(1.0, 1.0);
double result = vector.tan();
```

If you want a more familiar calling syntax, however, you can declare *tan* as a global friend function to class *XY* as follows:

```
class XY {
    friend double tan(const XY& xy);
private:
    double m_dX, m_dY;
public:
    // constructors, etc.
};
```

(continued)

```
double tan(const XY& xy) {
    if (xy.m_dY != 0.0) {
        return xy.m_dX / xy.m_dY;
    }
    else {
        return 0.0;
    }
}
```

You now call the new *tan* function like this:

```
XY      vector(1.0, 1.0);
double result = tan(vector);
```

There won't be a conflict with the standard library *tan* functions because the compiler selects the proper function by looking at the parameter types.

Static Class Members

What if you needed a count of all currently active space orbiters? You could define a global variable, but that would compromise encapsulation. C++ provides <u>static</u> data members and member functions that are associated with a class rather than with any specific object.

Static Data Members

Here's the *Orbiter* class declaration with a static integer data member, *s_nCount*:

```
class Orbiter {
protected:
    double m_dMass;
    XY      m_xyCurrent, m_xyPrior, m_xyThrust;
public:
    static int s_nCount;
    Orbiter(XY& xyCurrent, XY& xyPrior, double dMass);
    const XY& GetPosition() const;
    void Fly();
    virtual void Display() const = 0;
};
```

There will be only one copy of *s_nCount*, no matter how many orbiter objects there are. The class declaration above declares the class, but it doesn't reserve memory for *s_nCount*. You must write your own global definition code, to appear only once in the link, similar to the following:

```
int Orbiter::s_nCount = 0; // initialization is optional
```

Because the variable is declared public, you can use it in your program like this:

```
Orbiter::s_nCount++;
```

Of course, if you access *s_nCount* inside an *Orbiter* member function, such as a constructor, you can omit *Orbiter::*.

If you declare a constant static data member like this:

```
static const int s_nMaxCount;
```

you can still initialize it globally like this:

```
const int Orbiter::s_nMaxCount = 256;
```

Enumerated Types—A Static Data Member Shortcut

If your class needs a constant static integer, you can use a shortcut that avoids a separate initialization statement. You simply place an *enum* statement in your class declaration, as shown here:

```
enum { nMaxCount = 256 };
```

The compiler generates a "load immediate" instruction when you use *nMax-Count*, exactly as it would if you used a *#define* instead of an *enum*. For a static data member such as *s_nCount*, the compiler generates a "load from memory" instruction.

Static Member Functions

If the static *Orbiter* data member *s_nCount* were private, you would need a static member function to access it. If you define a public function *Count* that returns a reference to an integer, you can use it on either side of an assignment statement:

```
public:
    static int& Count() { return s_nCount; }
```

Here's some code that uses the new *Count* function:

```
int nOldCount = Orbiter::Count()++;
int nNewCount = Orbiter::Count();
assert(nNewCount == nOldCount + 1);
```

A more interesting use of static class member functions is the construction of objects. Suppose you need to construct a new orbiting object but you don't know until runtime which derived *Orbiter* class you want. Here's a static construction function that uses a *switch* statement to choose the object class:

843

```
static Orbiter* Orbiter::MakeNew(int nSelection, XY& xyCurrent, XY&
xyPrior,
                                  double dMass, XY& xyThrust, double dFuel,
                                  XY& xyOrientation, Planet* pPlanet)
{
    switch (nSelection) {
    case 0:
        return new Planet(xyCurrent, xyPrior, dMass);
    case 1:
        return new Spaceship(xyCurrent, xyPrior, xyThrust, dMass, dFuel,
                             xyOrientation);
    case 2:
        return new Moon(xyCurrent, xyPrior, dMass, pPlanet);
    default:
        return NULL;
    }
}
```

Now you can fill up an array of *Orbiter* pointers:

```
Orbiter* pOrbiterArray[MAX]
XY       xyCurrent, xyPrior, xyThrust, xyOrientation;
double   dMass, dFuel;
Planet*  pPlanet;

for (int i = 0; i < MAX; i++) {
    pOrbiterArray[i] = Orbiter::MakeNew(i % 3, xyCurrent, xyPrior, dMass,
                          xyThrust, dFuel, xyOrientation, pPlanet);
}
```

Once you stuff the *Planet, Spaceship,* and *Moon* pointers into the *Orbiter* pointer array, how do you ever sort out which is which? Of course, you don't need to know the class if you simply call *Fly* and *Display* and then destroy the objects. If you do need to know the class, C++ doesn't help much. You could, of course, add an *Orbiter* data member and associated access functions that indicate the class. As you'll see in Appendix C, the MFC library's runtime class mechanism lets you determine an object's class at runtime.

Overloaded Operators

You might not write many overloaded operators in the early stages of MFC library programming, but you will certainly use the ones that the MFC library provides. The more you know about writing overloaded operators, though, the easier it will be to use them.

Overloaded operators are useful because they can make C++ application code easier to write and to read, but some programmers get carried away. Use overloaded operators only when their meanings are intuitive and natural. After all, they are nothing but substitutes for member function calls, and sometimes member function calls make more sense.

Member Function Operators

Many overloaded operators are implemented as class member functions. In this appendix's examples, *XY* objects are mostly *xy*-coordinate pairs, and the obvious thing to do with coordinate pairs is to add and subtract them. Here is the code for the add and subtract operators:

```
XY XY::operator +(const XY& xy) const { // add
    return XY(m_dX + xy.m_dX, y + xy.y);
}

XY XY::operator -(const XY& xy) const { // subtract
    return XY(m_dX - xy.m_dX, m_dY - xy.m_dY);
}
```

(The declarations are shown in the section titled "Separating Class Declarations from Code" later in this appendix.)

Notice the use of references. For the *XY* class, with its small-size objects, you could get away without the references, but you've already seen how references make the code more efficient, and you've seen that they're required for assignment operators.

Now you use the add operator like this:

```
XY xy1(1.0, 2.0), xy2(3.0, 4.0);
XY xy3 = xy1 + xy2; // should be (4.0, 6.0)
```

That was easy. What about some more operators? The unary minus is another useful one. Notice that it doesn't have an argument.

```
XY XY::operator -() const { // unary minus
    return XY(-m_dX, -m_dY);
}
```

What about the multiply operator? It doesn't make sense to multiply one coordinate pair by another, but you can multiply a coordinate pair by a scalar. Here's the code for the * and *= operators:

```
XY operator *(double dMult) { // scalar multiply
    return XY(m_dX * dMult, m_dY * dMult);
}

const XY& operator *=(const double dMult) {
    m_dX *= dMult;
```

(continued)

```
        m_dY *= dMult;
        return *this;
    }
```

And here's the application code:

```
XY xy1(1.0, 2.0);
XY xy2 = xy1 * 3.0; // should be (3.0, 6.0)
xy2 *= 2.0;         // should be (6.0, 12.0)
```

And now for something a little more difficult. In the *Spaceship* class, you might have noticed an *XY* data member named *m_xyOrientation*. This isn't really a coordinate pair but a representation of an angle. (There's a possible case for a derived *XY* class here.) You could, of course, represent an angle by a scalar radian or a degree value, but subsequent math is easier if you store the angle as a cosine/sine pair. We'll now expropriate the C++ right-shift and left-shift operators and make them rotation operators for *XY* objects:

```
XY operator >>(const XY& xy) const { // rotate cos/sin pair plus
    return XY(m_dX * xy.m_dX - m_dY * xy.m_dY,
        m_dY * xy.m_dX + m_dX * xy.m_dY);
}

XY operator <<(const XY& xy) const { // rotate cos/sin pair minus
    return XY(m_dX * xy.m_dX + m_dY * xy.m_dY,
        m_dY * xy.m_dX - m_dX * xy.m_dY);
}
```

The formulas are standard trigonometric identities that require no use of the *sin* or *cos* function.

Here are the new rotation operators in use:

```
XY xyAngle1(0.707, 0.707);        // 45 degrees
XY xyRot(0.0, 1.0);               // 90 degrees
XY xyAngle2 = xyAngle1 >> xyRot; // should be (-.707, .070), 135 degrees
```

In a video game application I designed, the player controlled the spaceship's master rotation angle from the keyboard. The spaceship outline points were stored in an array of polar coordinates consisting of an *XY* angle and a scalar distance from the center of the ship. For each point, the *XY* value was rotated by the current angle and then multiplied by the scalar value, yielding a new *xy*-coordinate pair for the display.

Conversion Operators

Both C and C++ allow extensive automatic conversion among built-in types. Consider these statements:

```
int    nRadians = 2;
double dResult = atan(nRadians);
```

The function *atan* expects a *double* argument, so the compiler converts the integer *nRadians* to a *double* before passing it to the function.

What about conversions for your own classes? You must write them yourself, of course. Suppose you have a *String* class that contains a character array *m_pch*. The following operator function returns a constant pointer to an object's internal array:

```
String::operator const char*() const
{
    return (const char*) m_pch;
}
```

You can now use a *String* argument anywhere the compiler expects a *const char*** argument, as shown here:

```
String s1("test");      // construct S1 from character array
String s2;
char   c1[20];
int    n = strlen(s1); // OK
strcpy(s2, s1);         // won't compile because first parameter is not
                        //  const
strcpy(c1, s1);         // OK
```

We purposely didn't declare a (non-*const*) *char*** operator because getting data into a *String* object isn't as easy as extracting it. (You could easily overwrite the array boundary.)

The MFC library provides a useful string class named *CString* that has this same overloaded *const char*** conversion operator. You'll use this operator quite frequently when you write MFC library programs.

Global Operators

The operators you've seen so far are class member functions. Suppose you need a new operator but you don't want to derive a new class. If your class has public data members and member functions sufficient to access the required data, you can write stand-alone global operators for your class.

Because we "forgot" to write a divide member function operator for the *XY* class, we'll write one now, but the code is a little different from the overloaded multiply operator you've seen already:

```
XY operator / (const XY& xy, const double dDiv) // scalar divide
{
    return XY(xy.m_dX / dDiv, yx.m_dY / dDiv);
}
```

Notice that the data members *m_dX* and *m_dY* must be public, or if they are not, you must write *XY* member functions that access them.

Global operators can enhance the arithmetic capabilities of a class. The *XY* multiply member function operator that you've already seen is called by this expression:

```
XY xy2 = xy1 * 3.0;
```

But it won't work for this expression:

```
XY xy2 = 3.0 * xy1;
```

For the second case, you need a multiply helper operator such as this one:

```
XY operator *(const double dMult, const XY& xy)  // scalar multiply
{
    return XY(xy.m_dX * dMult, xy.m_dY * dMult);
}
```

Separating Class Declarations from Code

In the previous examples, class declarations have been mixed with code. The modularity of C++ depends, however, on the separation of the class implementation code from the class declaration. Class "users" need only the declarations; class "authors" write the code and might choose to deliver it in compiled, linkable form only.

Often, as in the case of the MFC library, all the class declarations are combined into one or several H files, and the code, broken into small, independently linkable modules, is stored in a LIB file. Application programmers include the H file in their C++ source code, and then they link with the corresponding library.

Below is a view of what the solar system header might look like (minus the moon):

```
// Solar.h class declaration file

class XY { // all member functions are inline
private:
    double m_dX, m_dY;
public:
    XY();
    XY(double dX, double dY);
    XY(const XY& xy);
    const XY& operator =(const XY& xy);
    XY operator +(const XY& xy) const;
    XY operator -(const XY& xy) const;
```

```
    XY operator *(const double dMult) const;
    XY operator /(const double dDiv) const;
    XY operator -() const;
};

class Orbiter {

protected:
    double m_dMass;
    XY      m_xyCurrent, m_xyPrior, m_xyThrust;
public:
    static int s_nCount;
    Orbiter(XY& xyCurrent, XY& xyPrior, double dMass); // inline
    const XY& GetPosition() const;
    void Fly();
    virtual void Display() const = 0;
};

class Planet : public Orbiter {
public:
    // copy constructor and assignment operator not shown
    Planet(XY& xyCurrent, XY& xyPrior, double dMass) :
        Orbiter(xyCurrent, xyPrior, dMass) { }
    void Display();
};

class Spaceship : public Orbiter {
private:
    double m_dFuel;
    XY      m_xyOrientation;
public:
    // copy constructor and assignment operator not shown
    Spaceship(XY& xyCurrent, XY& xyPrior, XY& xyThrust,
            double dMass, double dFuel, XY& xyOrientation);
    void Display();
    void FireThrusters();
};
// **** all XY class inline functions here ****
```

Some programmers choose to nest *#include* files, but this requires that code not be inadvertently included more than once, and it complicates make file dependencies. MFC library programs, by convention, don't generally nest their *#include* files. Your MFC library CPP files will always show you exactly which header files are included.

Notice that all the inline functions are grouped at the bottom of the header. This isn't necessary for the solar system example, but it makes the declaration more readable, and it allows the inline functions to be moved to a separate *#include* file. Some applications require the separation because in-line code might depend on prior declarations.

The non-inline functions—*Orbiter::Fly*, *Orbiter::GetPosition*, *Planet::Display*, *Spaceship::Display*, and *Spaceship::FireThrusters*—are kept in CPP files. You choose how to split them up. If you put them all in one file, they are all linked, even if only one is used (unless you set the compiler's function-level linking option). Often you'll separate member functions by class. A class code file is a good place for static data member definitions.

Message Map Functions in the Microsoft Foundation Class Library

HANDLERS FOR WM_COMMAND MESSAGES

Map Entry	Function Prototype
ON_COMMAND(<id>, <memberFxn>)	afx_msg void memberFxn( );
ON_COMMAND_EX(<id>, <memberFxn>)	afx_msg BOOL memberFxn(UINT);
ON_COMMAND_EX_RANGE(<id>, <idLast>, <memberFxn>)	afx_msg void memberFxn(UINT);
ON_COMMAND_RANGE(<id>, <idLast>, <memberFxn>)	afx_msg void memberFxn( );
ON_UPDATE_COMMAND_UI(<id>, <memberFxn>)	afx_msg void memberFxn(CCmdTarget*);
ON_UPDATE_COMMAND_UI_RANGE(<id>, <idLast>, <memberFxn>)	afx_msg void memberFxn(CCmdTarget*);

HANDLERS FOR CHILD WINDOW NOTIFICATION MESSAGES

Map Entry	Function Prototype
Generic Control Notification Codes	
ON_CONTROL(<wNotifyCode>, <id>, <memberFxn>)	afx_msg void memberFxn( );
ON_CONTROL_RANGE(<wNotifyCode>, <id>, <idLast>, <memberFxn>)	afx_msg void memberFxn(UINT);
ON_NOTIFY(<wNotifyCode>, <id>, <memberFxn>)	afx_msg void memberFxn(NMHDR*, LRESULT*);
ON_NOTIFY_EX(<wNotifyCode>, <id>, <memberFxn>)	afx_msg BOOL memberFxn(UINT, NMHDR*, LRESULT*);
ON_NOTIFY_EX_RANGE(<wNotifyCode>, <id>, <idLast>, <memberFxn>)	afx_msg void memberFxn(UINT, NMHDR*, LRESULT*);
ON_NOTIFY_RANGE(<wNotifyCode>, <id>, <idLast>, <memberFxn>)	afx_msg void memberFxn(NMHDR*, LRESULT*);
User Button Notification Codes	
ON_BN_CLICKED(<id>, <memberFxn>)	afx_msg void memberFxn( );
ON_BN_DOUBLECLICKED(<id>, <memberFxn>)	afx_msg void memberFxn( );
ON_BN_KILLFOCUS(<id>, <memberFxn>)	afx_msg void memberFxn( );
ON_BN_SETFOCUS(<id>, <memberFxn>)	afx_msg void memberFxn( );
Combo Box Notification Codes	
ON_CBN_CLOSEUP(<id>, <memberFxn>)	afx_msg void memberFxn( );
ON_CBN_DBLCLK(<id>, <memberFxn>)	afx_msg void memberFxn( );
ON_CBN_DROPDOWN(<id>, <memberFxn>)	afx_msg void memberFxn( );
ON_CBN_EDITCHANGE(<id>, <memberFxn>)	afx_msg void memberFxn( );
ON_CBN_EDITUPDATE(<id>, <memberFxn>)	afx_msg void memberFxn( );
ON_CBN_ERRSPACE(<id>, <memberFxn>)	afx_msg void memberFxn( );
ON_CBN_KILLFOCUS(<id>, <memberFxn>)	afx_msg void memberFxn( );
ON_CBN_SELCHANGE(<id>, <memberFxn>)	afx_msg void memberFxn( );
ON_CBN_SELENDCANCEL(<id>, <memberFxn>)	afx_msg void memberFxn( );
ON_CBN_SELENDOK(<id>, <memberFxn>)	afx_msg void memberFxn( );
ON_CBN_SETFOCUS(<id>, <memberFxn>)	afx_msg void memberFxn( );

(continued)

HANDLERS FOR CHILD WINDOW NOTIFICATION MESSAGES *continued*

Map Entry	Function Prototype
Check List Box Notification Codes	
ON_CLBN_CHKCHANGE(<id>, <memberFxn>)	afx_msg void memberFxn( );
Edit Control Notification Codes	
ON_EN_CHANGE(<id>, <memberFxn>)	afx_msg void memberFxn( );
ON_EN_ERRSPACE(<id>, <memberFxn>)	afx_msg void memberFxn( );
ON_EN_HSCROLL(<id>, <memberFxn>)	afx_msg void memberFxn( );
ON_EN_KILLFOCUS(<id>, <memberFxn>)	afx_msg void memberFxn( );
ON_EN_MAXTEXT(<id>, <memberFxn>)	afx_msg void memberFxn( );
ON_EN_SETFOCUS(<id>, <memberFxn>)	afx_msg void memberFxn( );
ON_EN_UPDATE(<id>, <memberFxn>)	afx_msg void memberFxn( );
ON_EN_VSCROLL(<id>, <memberFxn>)	afx_msg void memberFxn( );
List Box Notification Codes	
ON_LBN_DBLCLK(<id>, <memberFxn>)	afx_msg void memberFxn( );
ON_LBN_ERRSPACE(<id>, <memberFxn>)	afx_msg void memberFxn( );
ON_LBN_KILLFOCUS(<id>, <memberFxn>)	afx_msg void memberFxn( );
ON_LBN_SELCANCEL(<id>, <memberFxn>)	afx_msg void memberFxn( );
ON_LBN_SELCHANGE(<id>, <memberFxn>)	afx_msg void memberFxn( );
ON_LBN_SETFOCUS(<id>, <memberFxn>)	afx_msg void memberFxn( );
Static Control Notification Codes	
ON_STN_CLICKED(<id>, <memberFxn>)	afx_msg void memberFxn( );
ON_STN_DBLCLK(<id>, <memberFxn>)	afx_msg void memberFxn( );
ON_STN_DISABLE(<id>, <memberFxn>)	afx_msg void memberFxn( );
ON_STN_ENABLE(<id>, <memberFxn>)	afx_msg void memberFxn( );

HANDLERS FOR WINDOW NOTIFICATION MESSAGES

Map Entry	Function Prototype
ON_WM_ACTIVATE( )	afx_msg void OnActivate(UINT, CWnd*, BOOL);
ON_WM_ACTIVATEAPP( )	afx_msg void OnActivateApp(BOOL, HANDLE);
ON_WM_ASKCBFORMATNAME( )	afx_msg void OnAskCbFormatName(UINT, LPSTR);
ON_WM_CANCELMODE( )	afx_msg void OnCancelMode( );
ON_WM_CAPTURECHANGED( )	afx_msg void OnCaptureChanged(CWnd*);
ON_WM_CHANGECBCHAIN( )	afx_msg void OnChangeCbChain(HWND, HWND);
ON_WM_CHAR( )	afx_msg void OnChar(UINT, UINT, UINT);
ON_WM_CHARTOITEM( )	afx_msg int OnCharToItem(UINT, CWnd*, UINT);
ON_WM_CHILDACTIVATE( )	afx_msg void OnChildActivate( );
ON_WM_CLOSE( )	afx_msg void OnClose( );
ON_WM_COMPACTING( )	afx_msg void OnCompacting(UINT);
ON_WM_COMPAREITEM( )	afx_msg int OnCompareItem(LPCOMPAREITEM-STRUCT);
ON_WM_CONTEXTMENU( )	afx_msg void OnContextMenu(CWnd*, CPoint);
ON_WM_CREATE( )	afx_msg int OnCreate(LPCREATESTRUCT);
ON_WM_CTLCOLOR( )	afx_msg HBRUSH OnCtlColor(CDC*, CWnd*, UINT);
ON_WM_DEADCHAR( )	afx_msg void OnDeadChar(UINT, UINT, UINT);
ON_WM_DELETEITEM( )	afx_msg void OnDeleteItem(LPDELETEITEM-STRUCT);
ON_WM_DESTROY( )	afx_msg void OnDestroy( );
ON_WM_DESTROYCLIPBOARD( )	afx_msg void OnDestroyClipboard( );
ON_WM_DEVICECHANGE( )	afx_msg void OnDeviceChange(UINT, DWORD);
ON_WM_DEVMODECHANGE( )	afx_msg void OnDevModeChange(LPSTR);
ON_WM_DRAWCLIPBOARD( )	afx_msg void OnDrawClipboard( );
ON_WM_DRAWITEM( )	afx_msg void OnDrawItem(LPDRAWITEMSTRUCT);
ON_WM_DROPFILES()	afx_msg void OnDropFiles(HANDLE);
ON_WM_ENABLE( )	afx_msg void OnEnable(BOOL);
ON_WM_ENDSESSION( )	afx_msg void OnEndSession(BOOL);
ON_WM_ENTERIDLE( )	afx_msg void OnEnterIdle(UINT, CWnd*);
ON_WM_ENTERMENULOOP( )	afx_msg void OnEnterMenuLoop(BOOL);
ON_WM_ERASEBKGND( )	afx_msg BOOL OnEraseBkgnd(CDC*);
ON_WM_EXITMENULOOP( )	afx_msg void OnExitMenuLoop(BOOL);
ON_WM_FONTCHANGE( )	afx_msg void OnFontChange( );

(continued)

HANDLERS FOR WINDOW NOTIFICATION MESSAGES *continued*

Map Entry	Function Prototype
ON_WM_GETDLGCODE( )	afx_msg UINT OnGetDlgCode( );
ON_WM_GETMINMAXINFO( )	afx_msg void OnGetMinMaxInfo(LPPOINT);
ON_WM_HELPINFO( )	afx_msg void OnHelpInfo(HELPINFO*);
ON_WM_HSCROLL( )	afx_msg void OnHScroll(UINT, UINT, CWnd*);
ON_WM_HSCROLLCLIPBOARD( )	afx_msg void OnHScrollClipboard(CWnd*, UINT, UINT);
ON_WM_ICONERASEBKGND( )	afx_msg void OnIconEraseBkgnd(CDC*);
ON_WM_INITMENU( )	afx_msg void OnInitMenu(CMenu*);
ON_WM_INITMENUPOPUP( )	afx_msg void OnInitMenuPopup(CMenu*, UINT, BOOL);
ON_WM_KEYDOWN( )	afx_msg void OnKeyDown(UINT, UINT, UINT);
ON_WM_KEYUP( )	afx_msg void OnKeyUp(UINT, UINT, UINT);
ON_WM_KILLFOCUS( )	afx_msg void OnKillFocus(CWnd*);
ON_WM_LBUTTONDBLCLK( )	afx_msg void OnLButtonDblClk(UINT, CPoint);
ON_WM_LBUTTONDOWN( )	afx_msg void OnLButtonDown(UINT, CPoint);
ON_WM_LBUTTONUP( )	afx_msg void OnLButtonUp(UINT, CPoint);
ON_WM_MBUTTONDBLCLK( )	afx_msg void OnMButtonDblClk(UINT, CPoint);
ON_WM_MBUTTONDOWN( )	afx_msg void OnMButtonDown(UINT, CPoint);
ON_WM_MBUTTONUP( )	afx_msg void OnMButtonUp(UINT, CPoint);
ON_WM_MDIACTIVATE( )	afx_msg void OnMDIActivate(BOOL, CWnd*, CWnd*);
ON_WM_MEASUREITEM( )	afx_msg void OnMeasureItem(LPMEASUREITEM-STRUCT);
ON_WM_MENUCHAR( )	afx_msg LONG OnMenuChar(UINT, UINT, CMenu*);
ON_WM_MENUSELECT( )	afx_msg void OnMenuSelect(UINT, UINT, HMENU);
ON_WM_MOUSEACTIVATE( )	afx_msg int OnMouseActivate(CWnd*, UINT, UINT);
ON_WM_MOUSEMOVE( )	afx_msg void OnMouseMove(UINT, CPoint);
ON_WM_MOVE( )	afx_msg void OnMove(int, int);
ON_WM_MOVING( )	afx_msg void OnMoving(UINT, LPRECT);
ON_WM_NCACTIVATE( )	afx_msg BOOL OnNcActivate(BOOL);
ON_WM_NCCALCSIZE( )	afx_msg void OnNcCalcSize(LPRECT);
ON_WM_NCCREATE( )	afx_msg BOOL OnNcCreate(LPCREATESTRUCT);

(continued)

HANDLERS FOR WINDOW NOTIFICATION MESSAGES *continued*

Map Entry	Function Prototype
ON_WM_NCDESTROY( )	afx_msg void OnNcDestroy( );
ON_WM_NCHITTEST( )	afx_msg UINT OnNcHitTest(CPoint);
ON_WM_NCLBUTTONDBLCLK( )	afx_msg void OnNcLButtonDblClk(UINT, CPoint);
ON_WM_NCLBUTTONDOWN( )	afx_msg void OnNcLButtonDown(UINT, CPoint);
ON_WM_NCLBUTTONUP( )	afx_msg void OnNcLButtonUp(UINT, CPoint);
ON_WM_NCMBUTTONDBLCLK( )	afx_msg void OnNcMButtonDblClk(UINT, CPoint);
ON_WM_NCMBUTTONDOWN( )	afx_msg void OnNcMButtonDown(UINT, CPoint);
ON_WM_NCMBUTTONUP( )	afx_msg void OnNcMButtonUp(UINT, CPoint);
ON_WM_NCMOUSEMOVE( )	afx_msg void OnNcMouseMove(UINT, CPoint);
ON_WM_NCPAINT( )	afx_msg void OnNcPaint();
ON_WM_NCRBUTTONDBLCLK( )	afx_msg void OnNcRButtonDblClk(UINT, CPoint);
ON_WM_NCRBUTTONDOWN( )	afx_msg void OnNcRButtonDown(UINT, CPoint);
ON_WM_NCRBUTTONUP( )	afx_msg void OnNcRButtonUp(UINT, CPoint);
ON_WM_PAINT( )	afx_msg void OnPaint( );
ON_WM_PAINTCLIPBOARD( )	afx_msg void OnPaintClipboard(CWnd*, HANDLE);
ON_WM_PALETTECHANGED( )	afx_msg void OnPaletteChanged(CWnd*);
ON_WM_PALETTEISCHANGING( )	afx_msg void OnPaletteIsChanging(CWnd*);
ON_WM_PARENTNOTIFY( )	afx_msg void OnParentNotify(UINT, LONG);
ON_WM_QUERYDRAGICON( )	afx_msg HCURSOR OnQueryDragIcon( );
ON_WM_QUERYENDSESSION( )	afx_msg BOOL OnQueryEndSession( );
ON_WM_QUERYNEWPALETTE( )	afx_msg BOOL OnQueryNewPalette( );
ON_WM_QUERYOPEN( )	afx_msg BOOL OnQueryOpen( );
ON_WM_RBUTTONDBLCLK( )	afx_msg void OnRButtonDblClk(UINT, CPoint);
ON_WM_RBUTTONDOWN( )	afx_msg void OnRButtonDown(UINT, CPoint);
ON_WM_RBUTTONUP( )	afx_msg void OnRButtonUp(UINT, CPoint);
ON_WM_RENDERALLFORMATS( )	afx_msg void OnRenderAllFormats( );
ON_WM_RENDERFORMAT( )	afx_msg void OnRenderFormat(UINT);
ON_WM_SETCURSOR( )	afx_msg BOOL OnSetCursor(CWnd*, UINT, UINT);
ON_WM_SETFOCUS( )	afx_msg void OnSetFocus(CWnd*);
ON_WM_SHOWWINDOW( )	afx_msg void OnShowWindow(BOOL, UINT);
ON_WM_SIZE( )	afx_msg void OnSize(UINT, int, int);
ON_WM_SIZING( )	afx_msg void OnSizing(UINT, LPRECT);
ON_WM_SIZECLIPBOARD( )	afx_msg void OnSizeClipboard(CWnd*, HANDLE);

(continued)

HANDLERS FOR WINDOW NOTIFICATION MESSAGES *continued*

Map Entry	Function Prototype
ON_WM_SPOOLERSTATUS( )	afx_msg void OnSpoolerStatus(UINT, UINT);
ON_WM_STYLECHANGED( )	afx_msg void OnStyleChanged(int, LPSTYLESTRUCT);
ON_WM_STYLECHANGING( )	afx_msg void OnStyleChanging(int, LPSTYLESTRUCT);
ON_WM_SYSCHAR( )	afx_msg void OnSysChar(UINT, UINT, UINT);
ON_WM_SYSCOLORCHANGE( )	afx_msg void OnSysColorChange( );
ON_WM_SYSCOMMAND( )	afx_msg void OnSysCommand(UINT, LONG);
ON_WM_SYSDEADCHAR( )	afx_msg void OnSysDeadChar(UINT, UINT, UINT);
ON_WM_SYSKEYDOWN( )	afx_msg void OnSysKeyDown(UINT, UINT, UINT);
ON_WM_SYSKEYUP( )	afx_msg void OnSysKeyUp(UINT, UINT, UINT);
ON_WM_TCARD( )	afx_msg void OnTCard(UINT, DWORD);
ON_WM_TIMECHANGE( )	afx_msg void OnTimeChange( );
ON_WM_TIMER( )	afx_msg void OnTimer(UINT);
ON_WM_VKEYTOITEM( )	afx_msg int OnVKeyToItem(UINT, CWnd*, UINT);
ON_WM_VSCROLL( )	afx_msg void OnVScroll(UINT, UINT, CWnd*);
ON_WM_VSCROLLCLIPBOARD( )	afx_msg void OnVScrollClipboard(CWnd*, UINT, UINT);
ON_WM_WINDOWPOSCHANGED( )	afx_msg void OnWindowPosChanged(WINDOWPOS FAR*);
ON_WM_WINDOWPOSCHANGING( )	afx_msg void OnWindowPosChanging(WINDOWPOS FAR*);
ON_WM_WININICHANGE( )	afx_msg void OnWinIniChange(LPSTR);

USER-DEFINED MESSAGE CODES

Map Entry	Function Prototype
ON_MESSAGE(<message>, <memberFxn>)	afx_msg LONGmemberFxn(UINT, LONG);
ON_REGISTERED_MESSAGE (<nMessageVariable>, <memberFxn>)	afx_msg LONG memberFxn(UINT, LONG);

MFC Library Runtime Class Identification and Dynamic Object Creation

$\mathbf{L}$ong before runtime type information (RTTI) was added to the C++ language specification, the MFC library designers realized that they needed runtime access to an object's class name and position of the class in the hierarchy. Also, the document–view architecture (and, later, OLE class factories) demanded that objects be constructed from a class specified at runtime. So the MFC team created an integrated macro-based class identification and dynamic creation system that depends on the universal *CObject* base class. And in spite of the fact that the Visual C++ version 4.0 compiler supports the ANSI RTTI syntax, the MFC library continues to use the original system, which actually has more features.

This appendix explains how the MFC library implements the class identification and dynamic creation features. You'll see how the *DECLARE_DYNAMIC*, *DECLARE_DYNCREATE*, and associated macros work, and you'll learn about the *RUNTIME_CLASS* macro and the *CRuntimeClass* structure.

Getting an Object's Class Name at Runtime

If all you wanted was an object's class name, you'd have an easy time—assuming all your classes were derived from a common base class, *CObject*. Here's how you'd get the class name:

```
class CObject
{
public:
```

(continued)

```
        virtual char* GetClassName() const { return NULL; }
};

class CMyClass : public CObject
{
public:
    static char s_lpszClassName[];
    virtual char* GetClassName() const { return s_lpszClassName; }
};
char CMyClass::s_szClassName[] = "CMyClass";
```

Each derived class overrides the virtual *GetClassName* function, which returns a static string. This works even if you use a *CObject* pointer to call *Get-ClassName*. If you needed the class-name feature in many classes, you could save yourself some work by writing macros. A *DECLARE_CLASSNAME* macro might insert the static data member and the *GetClassName* function in the class declaration, and an *IMPLEMENT_CLASSNAME* macro might define the class name string in the implementation file.

The MFC *CRuntimeClass* Structure and the *RUNTIME_CLASS* Macro

In a real MFC program, an instance of the *CRuntimeClass* structure replaces the static *s_szClassName* data member shown above. This structure has data members for the class name and the object size; it also contains a pointer to a special static function, *CreateObject*, that's supposed to be implemented in the target class. Here's a simplified version of *CRuntimeClass*:

```
struct CRuntimeClass
{
    char m_lpszClassName[21];
    int m_nObjectSize; // used for memory validation
    CObject* (*m_pfnCreateObject)();
    CObject* CreateObject();
};
```

> **NOTE:** The real MFC *CRuntimeClass* structure has additional data members and functions that navigate through the class's hierarchy. This navigation feature is not supported by the official C++ RTTI implementation.

This structure supports not only class name retrieval but also dynamic creation. Each class you derive from *CObject* has a <u>static</u> *CRuntimeClass* data member provided you use the MFC *DECLARE_DYNAMIC*, *DECLARE_DYN-CREATE*, or *DECLARE_SERIAL* macro in the declaration and the corresponding *IMPLEMENT* macros in the implementation file. The name of the static data member is, by convention, *class<class_name>*. If your class were named *CMyClass*, the *CRuntimeClass* data member would be named *classCMyClass*.

If you want a pointer to a <u>class's</u> static *CRuntimeClass* object, you use the MFC *RUNTIME_CLASS* macro, defined as follows:

```
#define RUNTIME_CLASS(class_name) (&class_name::class##class_name)
```

Here's how you use the macro to get the name string from a class name:

```
ASSERT(RUNTIME_CLASS(CMyClass)->m_lpszClassName == "CMyClass");
```

If you want the class name string from an <u>object</u>, you call the virtual *CObject::GetRuntimeClass* function. The function simply returns a pointer to the class's static *CRuntimeClass* object, just as earlier the *GetClassName* function returned the name string. Here's the function you'd write for *CMyClass*:

```
virtual CRuntimeClass* GetRuntimeClass() const {return &classCMyClass;}
```

And here's how you'd call it:

```
ASSERT(pMyObject->GetRuntimeClass()->m_lpszClassName == "CMyClass");
```

Dynamic Creation

You've already learned that the *DECLARE* and *IMPLEMENT* macros add a static *CRuntimeClass* object to a class. If you use the *DECLARE_DYNCREATE* or *DECLARE_SERIAL* macro (and the corresponding *IMPLEMENT* macros), you get an additional static member function *CreateObject* (distinct from *CRuntimeClass::CreateObject*) in your class. Here's an example:

```
CObject* CMyClass::CreateObject()
{
    return new CMyClass;
}
```

Obviously, *CMyClass* needs a default constructor. This constructor is declared protected in wizard-generated classes that support dynamic creation.

Now look at the code for the *CRuntimeClass::CreateObject* function:

```
CObject* CRuntimeClass::CreateObject()
{
    return (*m_pfnCreateObject)();
}
```

This function makes an indirect call to the *CreateObject* function in the target class. Here's how you would dynamically construct an object of class *CMyClass*:

```
CRuntimeClass* pRTC = RUNTIME_CLASS(CMyObject);
CMyClass* pMyObject = (CMyClass*)pRTC->CreateObject();
```

Now you know how document templates work. A document template object has three *CRuntimeClass** data members initialized at construction to point to the static *CRuntimeClass* data members for the document, frame, and view classes. When *CWinApp::OnFileNew* is called, the framework calls the *CreateObject* functions for the three stored pointers.

A Sample Program

Here is the code for a command-line program that dynamically constructs objects of two classes. Note that this isn't real MFC code—the *CObject* class is a simplified version of the MFC library *CObject* class. You can find this code in the dyncreat.cpp file in the \vcpp32\appendc project.

```
#include <stdio.h>

#define RUNTIME_CLASS(class_name) (&class_name::class##class_name)

class CObject;

struct CRuntimeClass
{
    char m_lpszClassName[21];
    int m_nObjectSize;
    CObject* (* m_pfnCreateObject)();
    CObject* CreateObject();
};
// not a true abstract class because there are not pure
// virtual functions, but user can't create CObject objects
// because of the protected constructor
class CObject
{
public:
    // not pure because derived classes don't necessarily implement it
    virtual CRuntimeClass* GetRuntimeClass()
        const {return NULL;}

    // we never construct objects of class CObject, but in MFC we use
    // this to get class hierarchy information
    static CRuntimeClass classCObject;          // DYNAMIC
    virtual ~CObject() {};  // gotta have it
protected:
    CObject() {printf("CObject ctor\n");}
};
```

```
CRuntimeClass CObject::classCObject = {"CObject",
    sizeof(CObject), NULL };

CObject* CRuntimeClass::CreateObject()
{
    return (*m_pfnCreateObject)(); // indirect function call
}

class CAlpha : public CObject
{
public:
    virtual CRuntimeClass* GetRuntimeClass()
        const {return &classCAlpha;}
    static CRuntimeClass classCAlpha;        // DYNAMIC
    static CObject* CreateObject();          // DYNCREATE
protected:
    CAlpha() {printf("CAlpha ctor\n");}
};

CRuntimeClass CAlpha::classCAlpha = { "CAlpha", sizeof(CAlpha),
    CAlpha::CreateObject };

CObject* CAlpha::CreateObject() // static function
{
    return new CAlpha;
}

class CBeta : public CObject
{
public:
    virtual CRuntimeClass* GetRuntimeClass()
        const {return &classCBeta;}
    static CRuntimeClass classCBeta;         // DYNAMIC
    static CObject* CreateObject();          // DYNCREATE
protected:
    CBeta() {printf("CBeta ctor\n");}
};

CRuntimeClass CBeta::classCBeta = { "CBeta", sizeof(CBeta),
    CBeta::CreateObject };

CObject* CBeta::CreateObject() // static function
{
    return new CBeta;
}
```

(continued)

```
int main()
{
    printf("Entering dyncreate main\n");

    CRuntimeClass* pRTCAlpha = RUNTIME_CLASS(CAlpha);
    CObject* pObj1 = pRTCAlpha->CreateObject();
    printf("class of pObj1 = %s\n",
        pObj1->GetRuntimeClass()->m_lpszClassName);

    CRuntimeClass* pRTCBeta = RUNTIME_CLASS(CBeta);
    CObject* pObj2 = pRTCBeta->CreateObject();
    printf("class of pObj2 = %s\n",
        pObj2->GetRuntimeClass()->m_lpszClassName);

    delete pObj1;
    delete pObj2;
    return 0;
}
```

INDEX

David Kruglinski

David Kruglinski considers himself a programmer who writes rather than a writer who programs. He wrote his first program at Purdue University in 1966 ("probably a game of some sort"), and he got started with microcomputers in 1976 after a friend fished an 8080 board out of a garbage bin.

After some accidental periods of gainful employment, David wrote four books on subjects ranging from microcomputer database management systems to PC communications. He also started a successful software tools company.

When David isn't frantically trying to keep up with all the latest software developments, he is a consultant and also teaches Microsoft Visual C++ and OLE training classes. His Internet address is v-davidk@microsoft.com.

The manuscript for this book was prepared and submitted to Microsoft Press in electronic form. Text files were prepared using Microsoft Word 2.0 for Windows. Pages were composed by Microsoft Press using Aldus PageMaker 5.0 for Windows, with text in New Baskerville and display type in Helvetica Bold. Composed pages were delivered to the printer as electronic prepress files.

Cover Graphic Designer
Rebecca Geisler & Greg Hickman

Interior Graphic Designer
Studio MD

Interior Graphic Artist
David Holter

Principal Compositor
Barbara Remmele

Principal Proofreader/Copy Editor
Shawn Peck

Indexer
Shane-Armstrong
Information Services

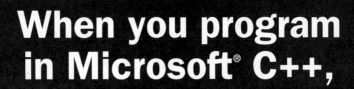

IMPORTANT—READ CAREFULLY BEFORE OPENING SOFTWARE PACKET(S). By opening the sealed packet(s) containing the software, you indicate your acceptance of the following Microsoft License Agreement.

MICROSOFT LICENSE AGREEMENT

(Book Companion Disks)

This is a legal agreement between you (either an individual or an entity) and Microsoft Corporation. By opening the sealed software packet(s) you are agreeing to be bound by the terms of this agreement. If you do not agree to the terms of this agreement, promptly return the unopened software packet(s) and any accompanying written materials to the place you obtained them for a full refund.

MICROSOFT SOFTWARE LICENSE

1. GRANT OF LICENSE. Microsoft grants to you the right to use one copy of the Microsoft software program included with this book (the "SOFTWARE") on a single terminal connected to a single computer. The SOFTWARE is in "use" on a computer when it is loaded into the temporary memory (i.e., RAM) or installed into the permanent memory (e.g., hard disk, CD-ROM, or other storage device) of that computer. You may not network the SOFTWARE or otherwise use it on more than one computer or computer terminal at the same time.

2. COPYRIGHT. The SOFTWARE is owned by Microsoft or its suppliers and is protected by United States copyright laws and international treaty provisions. Therefore, you must treat the SOFTWARE like any other copyrighted material (e.g., a book or musical recording) except that you may either (a) make one copy of the SOFTWARE solely for backup or archival purposes, or (b) transfer the SOFTWARE to a single hard disk provided you keep the original solely for backup or archival purposes. You may not copy the written materials accompanying the SOFTWARE.

3. OTHER RESTRICTIONS. You may not rent or lease the SOFTWARE, but you may transfer the SOFTWARE and accompanying written materials on a permanent basis provided you retain no copies and the recipient agrees to the terms of this Agreement. You may not reverse engineer, decompile, or disassemble the SOFTWARE. If the SOFTWARE is an update or has been updated, any transfer must include the most recent update and all prior versions.

4. DUAL MEDIA SOFTWARE. If the SOFTWARE package contains both 3.5" and 5.25" disks, then you may use only the disks appropriate for your single-user computer. You may not use the other disks on another computer or loan, rent, lease, or transfer them to another user except as part of the permanent transfer (as provided above) of all SOFTWARE and written materials.

5. SAMPLE CODE. If the SOFTWARE includes Sample Code, then Microsoft grants you a royalty-free right to reproduce and distribute the sample code of the SOFTWARE provided that you: (a) distribute the sample code only in conjunction with and as a part of your software product; (b) do not use Microsoft's or its authors' names, logos, or trademarks to market your software product; (c) include the copyright notice that appears on the SOFTWARE on your product label and as a part of the sign-on message for your software product; and (d) agree to indemnify, hold harmless, and defend Microsoft and its authors from and against any claims or lawsuits, including attorneys' fees, that arise or result from the use or distribution of your software product.

DISCLAIMER OF WARRANTY

The SOFTWARE (including instructions for its use) is provided "AS IS" WITHOUT WARRANTY OF ANY KIND. MICROSOFT FURTHER DISCLAIMS ALL IMPLIED WARRANTIES INCLUDING WITHOUT LIMITATION ANY IMPLIED WARRANTIES OF MERCHANTABILITY OR OF FITNESS FOR A PARTICULAR PURPOSE. THE ENTIRE RISK ARISING OUT OF THE USE OR PERFORMANCE OF THE SOFTWARE AND DOCUMENTATION REMAINS WITH YOU.

IN NO EVENT SHALL MICROSOFT, ITS AUTHORS, OR ANYONE ELSE INVOLVED IN THE CREATION, PRODUCTION, OR DELIVERY OF THE SOFTWARE BE LIABLE FOR ANY DAMAGES WHATSOEVER (INCLUDING, WITHOUT LIMITATION, DAMAGES FOR LOSS OF BUSINESS PROFITS, BUSINESS INTERRUPTION, LOSS OF BUSINESS INFORMATION, OR OTHER PECUNIARY LOSS) ARISING OUT OF THE USE OF OR INABILITY TO USE THE SOFTWARE OR DOCUMENTATION, EVEN IF MICROSOFT HAS BEEN ADVISED OF THE POSSIBILITY OF SUCH DAMAGES. BECAUSE SOME STATES/COUNTRIES DO NOT ALLOW THE EXCLUSION OR LIMITATION OF LIABILITY FOR CONSEQUENTIAL OR INCIDENTAL DAMAGES, THE ABOVE LIMITATION MAY NOT APPLY TO YOU.

U.S. GOVERNMENT RESTRICTED RIGHTS

The SOFTWARE and documentation are provided with RESTRICTED RIGHTS. Use, duplication, or disclosure by the Government is subject to restrictions as set forth in subparagraph (c)(1)(ii) of The Rights in Technical Data and Computer Software clause at DFARS 252.227-7013 or subparagraphs (c)(1) and (2) of the Commercial Computer Software — Restricted Rights 48 CFR 52.227-19, as applicable. Manufacturer is Microsoft Corporation, One Microsoft Way, Redmond, WA 98052-6399.

If you acquired this product in the United States, this Agreement is governed by the laws of the State of Washington.

Should you have any questions concerning this Agreement, or if you desire to contact Microsoft Press for any reason, please write: Microsoft Press, One Microsoft Way, Redmond, WA 98052-6399.

097-000-680